MW01620835
BROWNING
ARMS COMPANY

The BROWNING SUPERPOSED

John M. Browning's Last Legacy

Ned Schwing

Published by

700 E. State Street • Iola, WI 54990-0001
Telephone: 715/445-2214

Please call or write for our free catalog.
Our toll-free number to place an order or obtain a free catalog is 800-258-0929
or please use our regular business telephone 715-445-2214
for editorial comment and further information.

Library of Congress Catalog Number: 96-76696
ISBN: 0-87341-350-4

Printed in the United States of America

To

Carolyn

For her patience, understanding, and love,

but most of all for her love.

Other Krause Publications books by Ned Schwing:

The Winchester Model 42

Winchester's Finest: The Model 21

Winchester Slide-Action Rifles, Volume I – The Model 1890 and Model 1906

Winchester Slide-Action Rifles, Volume II – The Model 61 and Model 62

Standard Catalog of Firearms, as Co-editor

Contents

Tables and Charts

Chapter 5

Epilogue

Foreword

The Browning Superposed, certainly an art form among fine firearms, was the final work of our company's founder, John M. Browning. Since John M. Browning is widely recognized as a firearms genius, the Superposed represents consummate design, function and balance, and is, therefore, one of the most desirable firearms among avid hunters and shooters. Owning one is not unlike owning a painting from a recognized master.

Despite this heritage, little research has been done on the Browning Superposed. Ned Schwing has filled this vacuum with the following comprehensive treatise on our flagship gun. The story takes us to the very beginnings of the Superposed. It traces the growth of Superposed sales prior to World War I and gives the reader a never before seen view of the prewar Browning Arms Company and its nascent over and under shotgun.

With the end of the war came a new set of obstacles created by the aftermath of the conflict. Through official Fabrique Nationale photographs showing the destruction of the FN plant in 1945 through its rebirth only a few years later, the author brings to the reader in vivid detail how, through the efforts of Val Browning, FN regained its abilities to produce a quality Superposed only a few short years following the war. Again with the aid of rarely seen FN photographs, Ned Schwing sketches the slow but positive growth of both the Superposed and the company who sold it during the decade of the 1950s. The rest of the story follows in chronological sequence, carefully mapping the ebb and flow of the Browning Company during the 1960s and 1970s along with the modifications in the Superposed designed to reinforce a strong sales history despite rising prices. All of this information is based on official Browning and Fabrique Nationale company records, an essential ingredient for telling an accurate story of the company and its vanguard shotgun, the Superposed.

I did not come on the scene until 1980, when I assumed the presidency from Harm Williams's capable hands. These were difficult times both for the company and the Superposed, but with the help and commitment of capable, loyal management and employees, the company rode the rough seas safely and emerged strong, ready to face global competition with renewed energy and dedication. That part of the story is told here as well with in-depth research and accurately chosen photographs.

It is with great pleasure that I introduce this valuable history of both the Browning Company and its Superposed in this significant edition. I hope the reader will have a lasting impression of the men and women who made the Superposed and the company proud to be the caretaker of John M. Browning's last legacy.

Don Gobel
President, Browning

Prologue

There is no question that John Moses Browning was an authentic genius. His impact on the modern world is felt to this day. That the Superposed was his last invention is a fitting tribute to his love of sporting arms and his devotion to simplicity. But the story of the Superposed is more than just a history of John M. Browning; it is a narrative of the two companies that were directly responsible for its existence: Fabrique Nationale and the Browning Arms Company.

In telling the story of the Superposed, one must move even beyond the companies to the men who devoted their lives to making the Browning Superposed the most popular over and under gun in the world—men such as Val Browning and his son John Val, both of whom directed the course of the Browning Company at critical times; and Harm Williams and Grant Goddard, who formed the essence of the management team that supervised the company in its day-to-day affairs and carried out the decisions of the Browning family faithfully and commendably.

There were, of course, scores of employees who also devoted their working lives to the success of the company and hence the Superposed itself. There is today, embodied in men such as Browning President Don Gobel and Vice President of Sales Rich Bauter, a continuation of the Browning tradition to service and quality that John M. Browning espoused over one hundred years ago. Naturally, the Superposed would not have been possible without the talents of the Belgian gunmakers who practiced their centuries old art with great pride and dedication. Thus, the story of the Superposed is told from the point of view of the gun itself and the companies and men who made it a viable and respected worldwide product.

The information presented in this book is based on official Fabrique Nationale factory records, official Browning Company sales records, and scores of interviews with FN officials, Browning officials, and company employees on both sides of the Atlantic. One of the most satisfying aspects of research is meeting and talking with the people who were actually involved in the events described. Val Browning wrote in great detail concerning the stresses and strains associated with preparing the Superposed for production. John Val Browning recalled his experiences living and working in Belgium, supervising the production of guns his grandfather had designed. Harm Williams enumerated all the difficulties in allocating sales orders for the Superposed when deliveries were uncertain. Grant Goddard recalled his first days as manager in St. Louis and the challenges he faced in bringing Browning sales and service into the modern era. Rich Bauter recollected his early years with Browning as a regional salesman and the importance of the Superposed as a quality leader and flagship of the Browning line. Don Gobel talked about the worldwide challenges that faced Browning when he first became president in 1980. Ray Allen spoke of the formidable task facing him and the company in developing new products in new lands to replace the Superposed.

In Belgium, the experiences and recollections were much the same. Claude Gaier shared his years of knowledge about FN, especially the glory days of the company. Robert Sauvage remembered the difficult times FN faced when ill-timed diversification brought about near collapse. Browning Custom Shop manager Robert Mignon recalled his years of knowledge gained in fighting to obtain a growing high grade sporting gun market share in the UK, Germany, and France. Sitting down with gun designer Joseph Mardaga and product manager Robert Kinon helped to broaden my knowledge and appreciation for the technical details of the Superposed. My hours spent with FN engravers Rene Delcour and Jean Diet listening to their stories and experiences about engraving and engravers during the halcyon days at FN were most enjoyable and beneficial in helping to expand my understanding of Superposed engraving history.

All of these men, and many that are not mentioned here, experienced the rise and decline of a once great gun that will forever be a part of their lives and working experience. But the Superposed lives on, not only in the hearts and minds of the men associated with it, but as a symbol of the quality and reliability that helped build what is today a global company. When taken in its historical context, the Superposed had a long and satisfactory life. Before I began this project, I had never given much thought to the changing influences overseas that affected fine, hand built guns. Being aware of the domestic forces that influenced companies like Winchester, Remington, Parker, L.C. Smith, and others, and how those forces induced them to steer in a new direction, I see that so too did those forces bring about profound changes in the European sporting arms industry. In effect, the slow but inevitable economic and social factors that altered the way people worked, from their environment to their remuneration, also marked the end of hand fitted and hand built guns. It occurred with Winchester's Model 21 and so it did with Browning's Superposed. If change is inevitable, then the inevitable has transpired, and along with it the zenith of fine, hand built sporting firearms. It is fervently hoped that this history will preserve the facts, memories, disappointments, and accomplishments of the men who made this great gun a reality.

Ned Schwing

Acknowledgments

Acknowledgments are often dull passages thanking scores of people who provided assistance on projects such as this one. The thought occurred to me that acknowledgments, while important as a source of appreciation for those individuals who did in fact share their time and knowledge, are also a source of authentication and reference materials. In a sense, these acknowledgments are an annotated bibliography of unpublished information.

No work of this scope and magnitude could be accomplished without the assistance of so many generous people. I use the word generous because all of these individuals not only shared their time and their knowledge, but they contributed part of themselves to seeing that this book contained the most accurate information possible. Simply put, this volume could not have been written without their inestimable assistance.

Collectors are an important source of information because of their long years of experience and keen eye for detail. Dick Spurzem's understanding of prewar and early postwar Superposed is unparalleled. His collection contains some of the finest examples from these eras. Lloyd Crede gladly shared his comprehensive collection of Browning catalogues, pamphlets, and extensive knowledge. Dick DeBruyn has a fine collection of 1950s Browning Superposed and an in-depth knowledge of his subject. Bert O'Neill has an outstanding Presentation Series Superposed collection and his knowledge of this Superposed period was valuable. Over the years, I have leaned heavily on John Diemer's encyclopedic knowledge of the postwar Browning Superposed. His enthusiasm for the gun is unrivaled and his willingness to help proved critical. No one has more Browning catalogues and advertisements than Russ Church. He shared them with me without reservation. Robert Hawkins generously shared his rare and unique Superposed Bicentennial with readers as well as some of his outstanding Exhibition guns from his exquisite collection. The Browning Collector's Association and its president Larry Rodgers made available all of their informative newsletters. This is a superb organization, full of knowledgeable and ardent collectors.

The Browning Company, of course, made this endeavor possible by their willingness to share strategic information, not only on the Superposed but the company history as well. Browning President Don Gobel opened the door and Rich Bauter, vice president of sales, provided critical help and offered sound advice and incisive support that allowed this project to come to fruition. A special thanks to Paul Thompson, Browning public relations, and Chip Hewlett, customer service; Ray Allen, president Browning Arms Company; David Zeigler, advertising manager; Bradley Howard, design engineer; Robert Casey, Browning photographer; Dorothy Maughan, secretary to Mr. Don Gobel; and all of the Browning personnel who made my visit to Mountain Green not only productive, but enjoyable as well. The Browning Company contributed hundreds of photos to this book. That support is greatly appreciated.

Former employees of the Browning Company also shared their time and experience. Val A. Browning—before his death, his mind still keen at the age of 98—gave me precious insight into the development of the Superposed and the history of the company. John Val Browning, Val's son, discussed his years in Liège and those at Browning in a candid and forthright manner. Matt Browning gave me insight into the Browning family as well the Superposed. Harm Williams, former president of the company, shared with me in his straightforward fashion his hardworking thirty years in the company. Grant Goddard, a top executive with Browning and the manager of the St. Louis office for so many years, has retained a wealth of information about the day-to-day operations of the company. Vearl Brown, Jack Callahan, Paul Fuchs, Bob Hawn, Tom McGee, Robert Semonis, Kent Sutton, Larry Thomas, and John Woesthaus—both past and present employees of the service department gave meaningful and perceptive technical assistance based on their years of experience.

In Belgium, my experiences with those associated with the Superposed, Fabrique Nationale and Browning SA, were most informative and delightful. For those fortunate enough to travel to Liège, a visit to the *Musee d'Armes de Liège* is a must. The director, Claude Gaier, understands more about FN than anyone, and his scholarship is expansive and impressive. His help was crucial to this book. Herstal SA communications manager, Robert Sauvage, is a charming and knowledgeable man who went out of his way to provide assistance with securing FN photos. Without his help and his assistant, Daniel Durbut, the reader would not have the opportunity to see these outstanding guns. Mr. Serge Vigier, president of Browning SA, paved the way to make my stay there extremely productive. Joseph Mardaga and Robert Kinon provided important technical information. Robert Mignon shared his twenty-five years of high grade Superposed experience in great detail. Joelle Vandevinne, Mr. Vigier's efficient secretary, provided cheerful assistance. My visits to the Custom Shop were equally fruitful. With invaluable assistance from executive secretary Michele Metayer, I was able to study FN shipping journals and other critical production data. Francis Rollot provided important explanations for FN recordkeeping procedures. Others at the Custom Shop were generous with their time as well. Michel Deborle, Claude David, and Truc N'Go all contributed to my understanding of Custom Shop procedures. Andre Jacquemin, director of the Custom Shop, and Jose Delvenne, foreman of the Custom Shop, arranged to have my questions answered. Former FN engravers Rene Delcour, Angelo Bee, and Jean Diet, with over seventy years at the factory, shared their experiences with me.

There are many others to thank as well. Thomas Henshaw extended encouragement and support during the critical early days of this project. Col. Reid Betz (Ret.) pointed me in the right direction for engraving information. Don Criswell made suggestions regarding the manuscript. Herb Houze listened to my difficulties and made incisive comments. Rod Fuller also made recommendations and offered his support. Richard Freer shared his impressive technical knowledge. Les Freer recounted a fascinating story about his experiences with the Superposed in the early 1950s. Jim Lee obtained a patent for me in record time. Michael McIntosh gave me an expert shooter's perspective of the Superposed. The Browning Museum in Ogden furnished valuable photos. Pat Klug and Krause Publications gave me their confidence and support, which allowed me to pursue this project over a four-year period.

Researching and writing a book requires support and understanding from those most closely associated with the author. My wife Carolyn provided me with that understanding and support. She took notes, did all of the tedious work associated with research, kept me from losing my way when the undertaking kept expanding, and generally put up with the long hours and extended travel. She has my undying gratitude.

Introduction

The Early History of the Brownings and Fabrique Nationale

Genius...is the capacity to see ten things where the ordinary man sees one, and where the man of talent sees two or three, plus the ability to register that multiple perception in the material of his art.

– Ezra Pound

The story of the Browning Superposed is not just a narrative of the gun itself but a history of the men who devoted their corporate lives to the development and promotion of a firearm that became the flagship of the Browning Arms Company for decades. The events surrounding the evolution of the Superposed closely follow the corporate ebb and flow that is part of the inexorable business cycle. This corporate history functions as the backdrop for the story of an over and under shotgun that progressed into one of the most popular double shotguns in America during the last half of the twentieth century.

The chronicle of the Superposed must also include details about Fabrique Nationale d'Armes de Guerre, the Belgian company that had a long and significant connection with many of John M. Browning's firearms and that would play a vital role in the Superposed history. The history of the Browning Superposed cannot be told without Fabrique Nationale. Both companies were dependent on each other in terms of the Superposed, and perhaps that was one of the strengths of the gun. Many Americans appreciated the European workmanship and attention to detail that FN supplied with the Superposed. However, Browning's dependence on FN was also to be one of the great weaknesses in the association between the two companies, and proved to be the principle demise of the Superposed shotgun.

John M. Browning at the age of eighteen. Courtesy Browning Firearms Museum, Union Station, Ogden, Utah.

John M. Browning: An Overview

The story begins, as any does when the name Browning is mentioned, with John Moses Browning. His stature and historical significance place him on the same level as other important members of his generation, such as Woodrow Wilson, Theodore Roosevelt, Thomas Edison, and Alexander Graham Bell. To many, the accomplishments and genius of John M. Browning are well-known, but to some a brief abridgment of his life and accomplishments will set the stage for the prelude to the Browning Superposed and the company that bears his name.

John M. Browning was born in Ogden, Utah, in 1855, one of twenty-two children his father Jonathan, a Mormon, had by three wives. Very early, young John followed his gift for all things mechanical. His father, a talented gunsmith and inventor in his own right, had a lasting and important impact on John. When Jonathan died in 1879 at the age of seventy-three, John took charge of the family business and with his half brothers, Ed and Matthew, continued in the family tradition their father began. All three brothers had ample mechanical mastery, but John was the most original creator. The Browning shop operated with primitive machinery, all of which was hand operated. Under these circumstances, the designs and parts essential for the implementation of those designs were by necessity kept simple. In 1878 the three brothers opened a hardware store in connection with their shop.

These early days occupied John with mostly gunsmith work, and business prospered. It was during this early period that John M. Browning built a model of his single shot rifle. Not feeling comfortable about selling his single shot patent, John resolved to produce and sell the rifle himself. He decided to build a small assembly plant to produce his rifle, and with the help of his brothers, a primitive factory with steam driven machinery was completed. Three months later, twenty-five rifles were in the rack ready for sale. One week later, the rack was empty and John Browning was five hundred dollars richer. John's hard work had paid off and he intended to build on this success. The new factory was named Browning Brothers, and for two years the small plant turned out single shot rifles that were sold in the brothers' hardware store along with other makers' rifles and pistols. Forever searching for new challenges, John's thoughts turned to building other designs and he began work on a .22 caliber tubular magazine lever action rifle, the forerunner of the famous Winchester Model 1886 centerfire rifle.

Matthew Browning, brother of John M. Browning and his most trusted advisor. Courtesy Browning Firearms Museum, Union Station, Ogden, Utah.

In the spring of 1883, John M. Browning's life and career were to take a significant turn. Legend has it that when Mr. T. G. Bennett, president of Winchester Repeating Arms Company, walked into the Brownings's store he was searching for the new single shot rifle he had heard was built in Ogden, Utah. The gun was worth verifying for the possibility of purchase if the design proved worthwhile. The results of that initial meeting brought profound changes to both parties; however, like so many historical episodes, the facts are somewhat different than the fiction. The Brownings's single shot rifle was in fact purchased by a Winchester salesman named Charles Benton, who had made a sales call on the brothers' shop only to discover a patent infringement on a loading tool that the Brownings were manufacturing. When the patent encroachment issue was resolved, T. G. Bennett had Benton purchase, in June of 1883, one of the brothers' single shot rifles that he had heard so much about.[1]

---

1 Herb Houze, *To the Dreams of Youth: Winchester .22 Caliber Single Shot Rifle*, p. 13. Houze goes into great detail on the factual background relating to this first Winchester purchase of a Browning design.

One of the Browning brothers' stores in Ogden shortly after the turn of the century. Courtesy Browning Firearms Museum, Union Station, Ogden, Utah.

In any event, the purchase of this single shot rifle was done when John Browning was only twenty-eight years old. During the nineteen-year relationship between Browning and Winchester, the company bought a total of forty-one inventions from the Brownings. The list of Winchester rifles and shotguns based on John M. Browning patents reads like a Who's Who of the world's great firearms designers. The Winchester Model 1890, the most successful slide action .22 caliber rifle ever produced; the Winchester Model 1886, the centerfire lever action rifle that stayed in the Winchester product line for over forty years; the famous Winchester Model 1894, with over five million sold; and other Winchester models that never outwardly displayed the Browning name, were all part of the fruitful Winchester/Browning partnership.

In 1890, John M. Browning had completed work on a fully automatic machine gun. In 1891, John and his brother Matt went to the Colt factory in Hartford to demonstrate this new design. Colt was the logical choice for John Browning to display his new invention because of Colt's involvement with the Gatling gun since 1866. This was a significant event because it marked a new relationship for Browning that was to establish him as the preeminent designer of military firearms for the first quarter of the twentieth century. The successful demonstration marked the beginning, with the Model 1911 pistol, of Colt-built John M. Browning designs, which are continuing to this day.

The 1890s also marked the first Browning self-loading pistol design. Begun in 1894 and based on a .38 caliber cartridge, John Browning signed an agreement with Colt to manufacture and sell the pistol in the United States. The first of a four-gun agreement was the .38 caliber pistol. It was the first semiautomatic pistol manufactured in the United States, although it was never commercially produced. For over seventy years, every semiautomatic pistol built by Colt was based on a Browning design. John Browning limited his agreement with Colt to the United States because he wanted to establish his own deal in Europe.

During one of his frequent visits to Hartford, John Browning met with Hart O. Berg, an American who lived in Liège, Belgium, where he worked for Fabrique Nationale d'Armes de Guerre. Berg was looking for new business for FN and John gave him a model of his new self-loading pistol in .32 caliber. FN was so impressed with its successful test of the pistol that it gave Browning a contract on July 17, 1897, to manufacture and sell the pistol in Europe with an advance against royalties. First commercially produced in 1899, the Model 1900 was an instant success. In ten years more than five hundred thousand had been manufactured and sold. This initial association with FN was to be an important event in the history of the Browning family and Fabrique Nationale.

The final episode that would bring John M. Browning and Fabrique Nationale to a closer affiliation for the balance of Browning's life would occur early in 1902. In 1899 John Browning had developed a semiautomatic shotgun that would have a profound effect on the sporting arms market for over four generations. As was customary after such a long association with Winchester, John took his self-loading shotgun to T. G. Bennett and explained its intricacies. This shotgun was a totally new concept for Bennett and he needed to think about it. Over two years elapsed before a face-to-face meeting oc-

The Products of John M. Browning's Genius

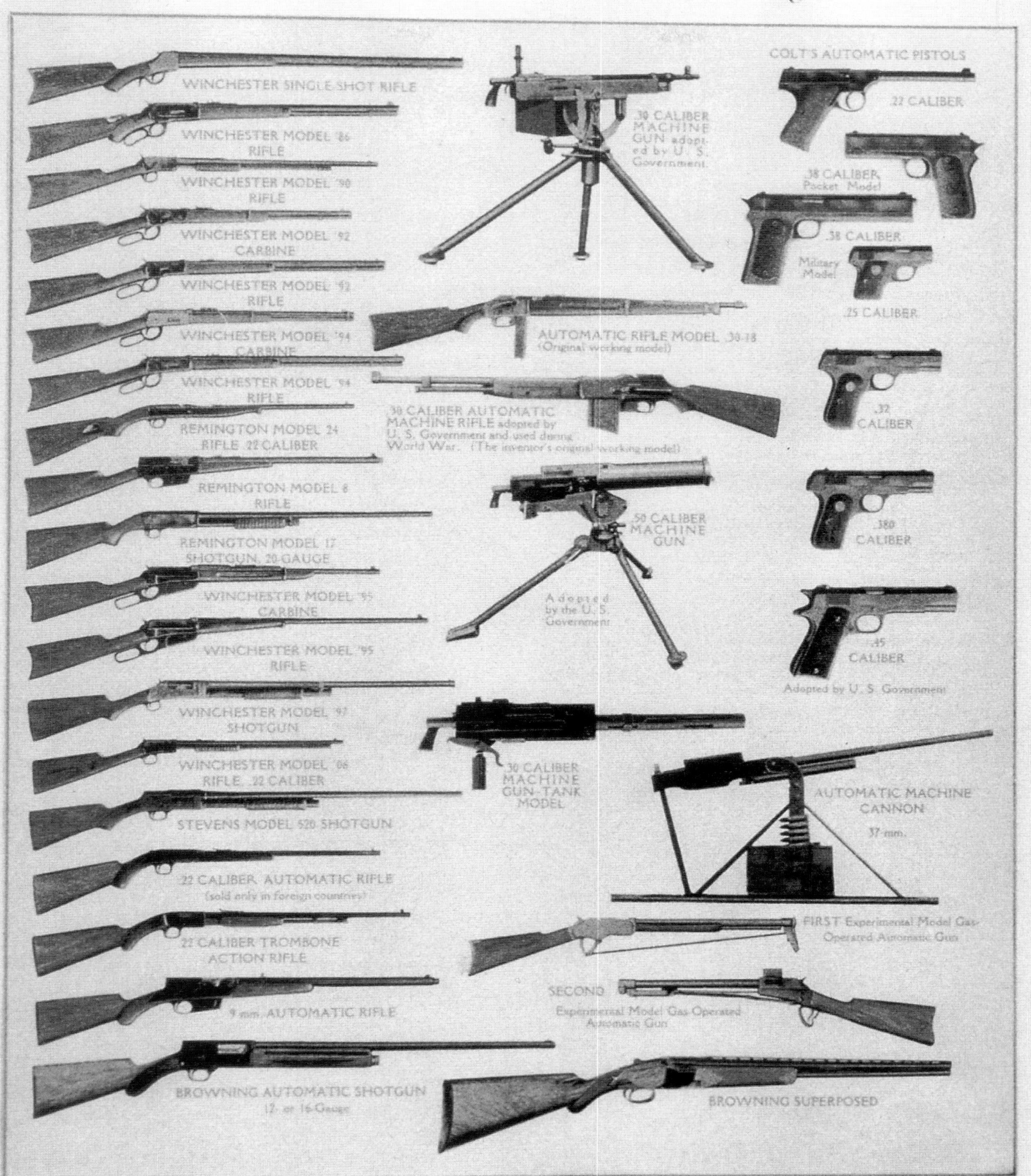

Those who are not familiar with the life and work of John M. Browning will perhaps be surprised to learn that many of their old favorite arms are the results of his inventive genius. His inventions were not confined to the products of his own shop, but were—and in many instances still are—manufactured under royalty contracts by leading American and Foreign factories. The guns shown on this page are all inventions of John M. Browning—quite likely you will find your favorite among them.

{ 3 }

It is difficult to find a firearm in use today that was not in some way influenced by the genius of John M. Browning.

This photo was taken about 1925 and shows a front factory entrance to Fabrique Nationale. This entrance is still standing and looks very much the way it did over seventy years ago. Courtesy Browning Firearms Museum, Union Station, Ogden, Utah.

An overview of the Fabrique Nationale factory in Herstal, Belgium, about the time the Superposed prototype was being developed by John M. Browning. Courtesy Fabrique Nationale Archives.

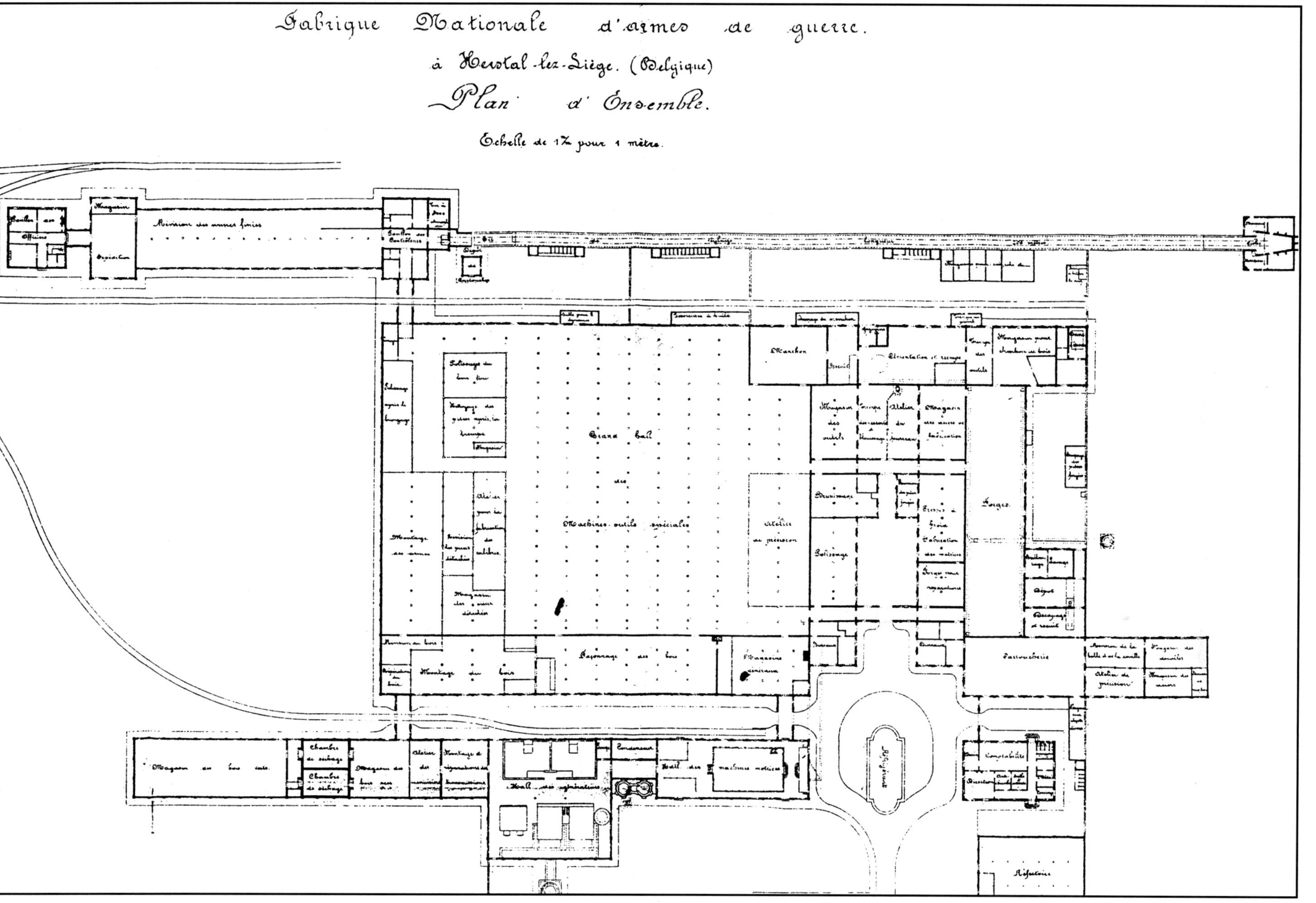

A floor plan of the original FN plant drawn in 1893. Note the 200-meter firing range at the top of the plan. Many of the original structures are still in place. Courtesy Liège Arms Museum.

curred between the two men, and the outcome was predictable. John Browning was angry about the two year delay in the decision and Bennett was upset with Browning's demand for royalty payments, something Winchester had never done before and was not about to start. Perhaps the real conflict lay with the reality that Bennett was uncomfortable about the semiautomatic shotgun and did not want to manufacture it. This episode marked the parting of two giants in the American firearms industry.

This left Browning with two alternatives: try to find another American manufacturer, or take the gun to FN in Belgium. He decided to try Remington. In January of 1902 he made an appointment with Marcellus Hartley, president of Remington Arms. Shortly before the scheduled meeting, Marcellus Hartley died of a heart attack. John M. Browning's options for building one of the most significant shotguns ever designed were down to one: the Belgium firm of Fabrique Nationale.

Fabrique Nationale d'Armes de Guerre: A Synopsis

When John Browning arrived in Liège in February of 1902 with his semiautomatic shotgun, he was on familiar ground despite this being his first trip to Europe. FN had been producing his Model 1900 pistol since 1899 and John had been pleased with the company's high quality, and he was satisfied with the association. The history of FN is interesting and should be understood in order to have a better grasp of the connection between the Browning family and the company that would be so crucial throughout the entire production period of the Superposed shotgun.

From the beginning of the fifteenth century, the city of Liège was at the heart of powder, ammunition, ordnance, and small arms production. Engravers of fine arms also called Liège home. In the revolution of 1830, Belgium separated from the Netherlands and began its existence as an independent country. In the early nineteenth century, factories of various kinds proliferated in the southern part of the country. By the mid-1800s the city of Liège was considered the European center of firearms, and throughout the balance of the nineteenth century the city was to garner an outstanding reputation for developing and building a wide range of firearms.

In March of 1887 the government of Belgium desired to establish a firearms factory to produce military small arms. The Belgian government needed to manufacture 150,000 repeating rifles, and in 1888 a limited liability company was authorized: Fabrique Nationale d'Armes de Guerre. A syndicate was formed consisting of various local arms companies such as Albert Simonis, Dumoulin Bros., Henri Pieper, Auguste Francotte, and Emile and Leon Nagant. A site was purchased for the factory in the Liège urban community of Herstal in 1889. By the end of 1891, the first rifles were produced from the partially completed factory. In December 1894 the company had completed the 150,000 rifles ordered by the Belgian government. The success of the company proved to be a threat to its competitors, several of whom served on the board of directors. After they resigned, legal problems plagued the firm and created questions about its future. A new board was appointed, consisting mainly of representatives of the German Mauser licensee, the Loewe group, and this predominately German influence gave FN the asset of German manufacturing technology, which was to be of great benefit to the company.

The German connection also brought about a noticeable improvement in the company's financial situation, but it also brought a decrease in military firearms orders. Because the German group did not want FN as a competitor, lucrative military contracts were often directed to German subsidiaries. Some military contracts were retained, but excess production capability resulted in idle machines. Management began to look into other manufacturing areas such as bicycles, and hunting and sporting arms. In 1896, FN produced fifty thousand .22 caliber sporting rifles. In 1898 the company developed and built a chainless bicycle. In the same year, a contract with a group of Liège manufacturers was signed to produce sizable quantities of shotgun parts. It was during these early years that FN created for itself a reputation for producing quality products. Despite these efforts to establish additional production, however beneficial, the plant was still underutilized.

The fortuitous meeting between Hart Berg and John Browning at the Colt factory in 1897 was to provide a much needed lift to FN business. But that association was only the start of a long-term relationship between the Browning family and Fabrique Nationale.

The Initial Sporting Arms Link: The Auto-5 Shotgun

John M. Browning's arrival in Liège in February 1902 was enthusiastically greeted by the FN director Henri Frenay. The success of the Browning .32 caliber semiautomatic pistol had proven a timely and important solution for FN's underutilized production

John M. Browning holding his first FN produced automatic shotgun, the Auto-5. Given the huge success this gun enjoyed and FN's outstanding production, it was unfortunate that John Browning would not live to see the full production of his second remarkable FN shotgun, the Superposed. Courtesy Browning Firearms Museum, Union Station, Ogden, Utah.

facilities. No doubt Mr. Frenay hoped John Browning's first visit to the factory would bring additional designs that FN could manufacture, thereby continuing to nurture growth and expansion for the plant.

Browning submitted his new shotgun, now called the Auto-5, for testing and examination and received immediate interest in the gun—a radical departure from the reception given by T. G. Bennett. On March 24, 1902, a contract was signed giving FN exclusive world rights to produce and market the Auto-5 in return for a royalty paid to Browning. John ordered ten thousand of these new shotguns to be sold in the United States through the firm of Schoverling, Daly, and Gates by way of jobbers across the country. The name "BROWNING AUTOMATIC ARMS COMPANY" was stamped on the barrel of the FN built shotgun. After continued testing and refining the design, production began late in 1903. The reader should remember that the American hunter was not even aware of the existence of a semiautomatic shotgun. John M. Browning had faith that the shooting public would embrace the new design. He was not wrong. The initial ten thousand guns were sold within the first year.

The year 1904 marked the beginning for the United States of new restrictive tariffs on foreign products. Facing such punitive rates, John decided to negotiate with FN for the rights to manu-

The Browning brothers' workbench sometime after the introduction of the Auto-5 in 1903. Courtesy Browning Firearms Museum, Union Station, Ogden, Utah.

The Browning Brothers hardware store's last location in Ogden. This photo was taken sometime around the mid-1920s. Courtesy Browning Firearms Museum, Union Station, Ogden, Utah.

An inside view of one of the Browning Brothers hardware stores. It was truly a hardware store, selling a complete line of hardware including bicycles. Sporting firearms were a big part of their business. Not only Browning designs are on the rack, but many other makes of rifles and shotguns as well. Courtesy Browning Firearms Museum, Union Station, Ogden, Utah.

A view of the drafting room at Fabrique Nationale. It was here that John M. Browning brought his designs to production status. Courtesy Browning Firearms Museum, Union Station, Ogden, Utah.

This photo of John M. Browning, standing front and center, was taken in 1914 with Belgian government and Fabrique Nationale officials. Browning was considered an important figure in the European firearms industry, particularly among the Belgians. Courtesy Browning Firearms Museum, Union Station, Ogden, Utah.

Fabrique Nationale produced a wide variety of products during its early years. From bicycles and motorcycles to firearms and automobiles, FN gained a reputation for high quality goods. Courtesy Liège Arms Museum.

The FN factory floor during the 1920s. FN employed a great many women to run its machinery. Here are two women machining Auto-5 receivers. Note the belt-driven machinery powered by a central steam generator. Working conditions were poor, and this would plague FN in the years ahead. Courtesy Browning Firearms Museum, Union Station, Ogden, Utah.

facture and sell the Auto-5 shotgun in the United States in order to avoid the restrictive duties. Remington was conveyed those rights, and production of its version of the Auto-5, the Model 11, began in 1905.

Despite the success of his shotgun and other commercial firearm designs, Browning continued to sell these firearms through his hardware store as he had in the past. Apparently the notion of establishing a sales and distribution outlet of his own either did not occur to him or did not interest him. After all, John Browning thought of himself as an inventor, not a businessman or promoter. In fact, as early as 1907 he granted to Fabrique Nationale the right to use the Browning name as a trademark.

The years leading up to World War I were devoted to advancements in his machine gun design as well as semiautomatic pistols and slide action shotguns. These included the Stevens Model 520 slide action shotgun, a 9mm military semiautomatic pistol for FN, a .25 caliber semiautomatic pistol built by both FN and Colt, a .45 caliber semiautomatic pistol built by Colt, the Remington slide action Model 17 shotgun, a .22 caliber semiautomatic shotgun produced by FN, a .50 caliber water cooled machine gun, the Browning Automatic Rifle, and others. John M. Browning's remaining years were spent designing and perfecting numerous military and sporting arms in concert with Colt and Fabrique Nationale.

FN Revisited

The continued increase in sporting arms production did not distract FN management from seeking additional production sources. The automobile and the motorcycle both found a place in the FN factories. FN's automobile production lasted from 1900 to 1935 and while not of great quantity, the quality was high. The company's

The meeting room at Fabrique Nationale where John M. Browning met with directors and officials of FN to discuss his designs. This room is almost exactly like it was seventy years ago. Courtesy Browning Firearms Museum, Union Station, Ogden, Utah.

motorcycle production was larger and more successful and lasted from 1904 to 1964. Between 1911 and 1914, over nine thousand motorcycles were built and sold. Until the outbreak of the First World War, FN was in a sound financial position and added to its worldwide reputation for building quality products.

With the outbreak of hostilities in 1914, a turning point for the Belgian firm was reached. German occupying forces requisitioned certain machinery for their own war efforts despite the board having a majority of German members. As to the Belgian directors and managers, they refused to work for the enemy. Therefore, the factory was sequestered by the German military. With the surrender of the Germans in 1918, Belgian officials purchased or acquired by decree all of the German shares in the company. The end of the war marked a new Belgian ownership for FN.

The turmoil in Europe following World War I affected FN in several adverse ways. Currency devaluation, high customs duties on its automobiles, increased duties on sporting arms, and the loss of German technical expertise created many serious problems for the company. During the period, duties on sporting arms were constantly increased. For example, the Auto-5 shotgun was taxed at a rate of 82.5 percent of its sales price when it entered the United States.

The management at FN turned its attention to increasing production of military firearms. This manufacturing arena promised large volume production coupled with excellent profit margins, insuring the company of a continuing source of revenue unencumbered by tariff restrictions or capricious consumer demand. During the early half of the 1920s, orders were received for sixty thousand semiautomatic 9mm short pistols FN referred to as the Model 10/22. An order for fifty thousand 7.9mm Mauser rifles was also received. Rifles were also supplied to Brazil and Mexico. This increased demand for military small arms led to improved manufacturing methods, which in turn brought about better quality and even more orders. This

John M. Browning received part of his inspiration for the Superposed from his extensive live bird and trap experience. Here he is pictured with "The Four Bs"; from left to right, Gus Becker, John M. Browning, A. P. Bigelow, and Matt Browning. They are holding Winchester Model 97 pumps and Winchester Model 87 lever actions. Bigelow is holding an unidentified side by side. Courtesy Browning Firearms Museum, Union Station, Ogden, Utah.

growth in business lasted throughout the 1920s and ended only when the Great Depression of 1929 destroyed the world economy.

The Genesis of the Superposed

During the first quarter of the twentieth century, John Browning was occupied with a number of different firearms designs, both military and sporting. Soon after the end of the First World War he turned his thoughts to a sporting shotgun that would fill a niche in the United States that had long been overlooked: the over and under shotgun. The reasons for his interest in selecting the over and under design were twofold.

First, John Browning was searching for a continuing source of income. He was concerned that the rising protests against repeating guns (conservationists called them "game exterminators") would have an adverse effect on the sales of his previous semiautomatic designs. He told his son Val Browning, "I think there is a market for a reasonably priced overunder gun which will be one of the last shotguns to be legislated out of business."[2] Interestingly, at about the same time the same thought occurred to Edwin Pugsley, vice president of engineering at Winchester, ten years before that company designed and marketed its side by side shotgun, the Winchester Model 21.

Secondly, the idea of building an over and under shotgun may have been suggested by John Browning's friend, shooting partner, and Olympic trapshooter, Gus Becker. According to Becker, John discussed with him the idea of building a shotgun with superimposed barrels. Browning felt

[2] Val A. Browning, letter to the author, June 21, 1993.

that the American hunter and target shooter were ready for a quality built, reasonably priced double gun. The over and under design appealed to him because of its single sighting plane. In addition to the single sighting plane, John Browning went further and developed his theory that the sighting plane on a shotgun, "... should not begin close to the eye, but should slope up to an apex, the pitch being pronounced, so that the angle where the slope and the level plane join will be well abrupt enough to be well defined, but not abrupt enough to stop the eye."[3]

John M. Browning standing over two FN draftsmen engrossed in what most likely is a problem solving session. From the looks of the photo it was taken shortly before his death. Perhaps they were working on the Superposed. Courtesy Browning Firearms Museum, Union Station, Ogden, Utah.

John M. Browning was also concerned about quality and price. He was aware that over and under guns were handmade only in Europe and, while of high quality, were expensive to build. Because of this, few were produced in any meaningful quantities. He wanted to design a mechanism that was simple enough to lend itself to copious production. He realized too that it would take a substantial investment of capital to build the facilities to manufacture such a shotgun. Browning also understood that there would be considerably more handwork than that expended on his Auto-5 shotgun. His target price was to be below $150.00. His task was a fairly straightforward one: to design an affordable over and under shotgun that was of high quality, was well balanced, had an efficient single sighting plane, and would lend itself to quantity production. If anyone could rise to the challenge it was John M. Browning, and so he did.

The process for designing and building such a shotgun was not a simple one, and many delays were encountered. Once John Browning completed the prototype sometime in the fall of 1923, it was test fired and deemed an acceptable design. Val Browning took the new gun to attorney Clay Lindsey, who made the patent application on October 15, 1923. This first patent application, serial number 668,575, was granted on March 30, 1926, and was given patent number 1,578,638. In the application, John Browning stipulates that the over and under shotgun has several advantages over the side by side: the single sighting plane, the breech and receiver section are narrower, a comfortable and full forearm encloses both barrels to protect the hand from heat, and the overall appearance of the gun is one of lightness and good balance.

Browning also acknowledged shortcomings with the inherent over and under design, namely, the tendency for the gun to shoot loose because of the distance and angle of the upper barrel in relation to the hinge pin on the forward portion of the bottom of the frame. When the upper barrel is fired there is considerable leverage exerted between the barrel and the receiver sections. Browning claimed to have solved these problems with his new over and under design. Instead of employing a top bolt as Merkel had done on its over and under design, or a doll's head extension of the rib, Browning eliminated this tendency to shoot loose by redefining the relationship between the breech, hinge pin, and upper barrel.

He also gave his Superposed a smoother and less encumbered appearance. He designed an underbolt that was capable of two or three times the bearing as an ordinary lug bolt. The position of the hinge pin cannot be raised beyond a certain point without necessitating the rounding of the barrel ends and

---

[3] "Birth of the Superposed", Reid Betz, Browning Collectors Association Newsletter, May/June, 1987, Volume VIII, No. 6.

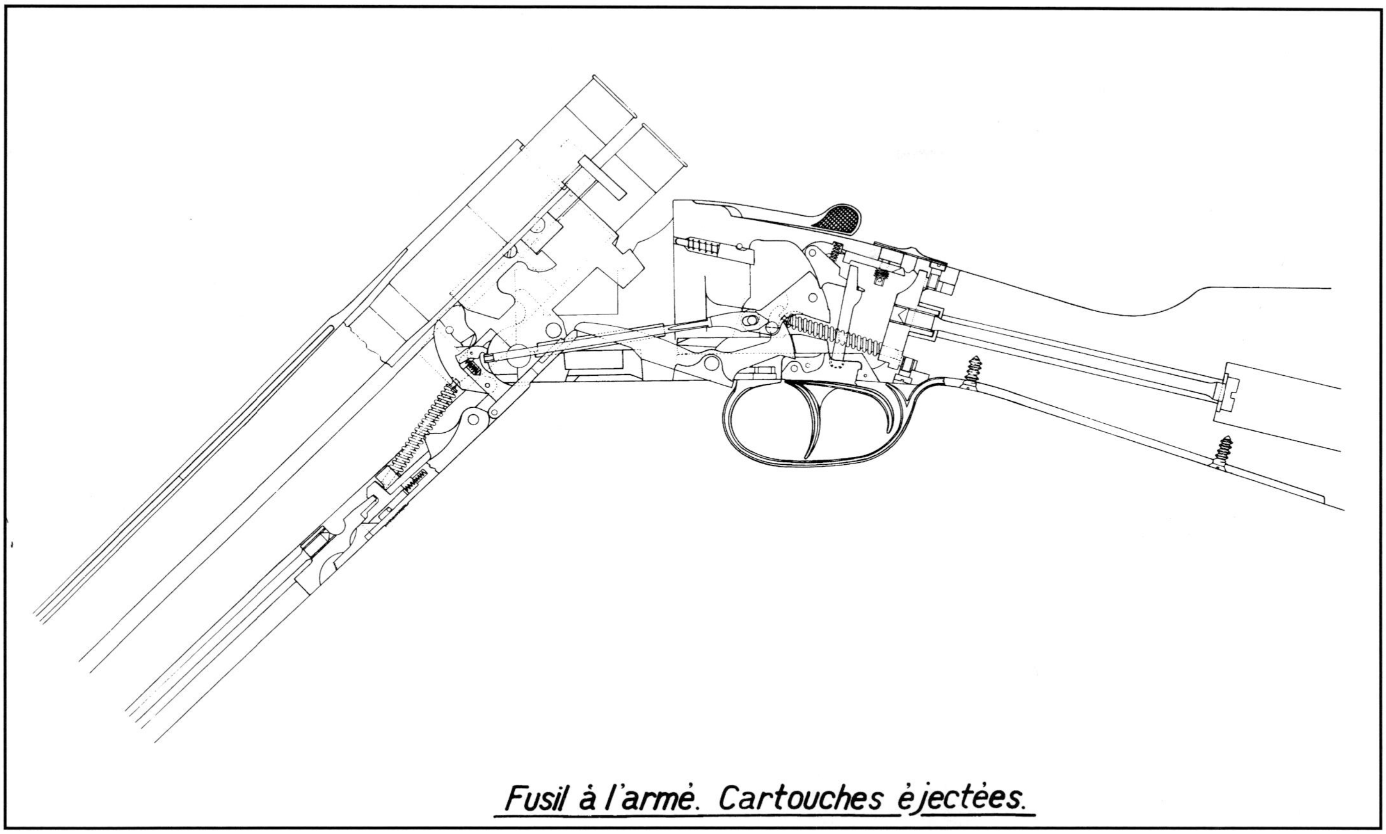

Fusil à l'armè. Cartouches èjectées.

A Fabrique Nationale drawing of the Superposed with the gun broken and the ejectors in operation. This particular drawing was probably one of the first of the pre-production Superposed. Courtesy Fabrique Nationale Archives.

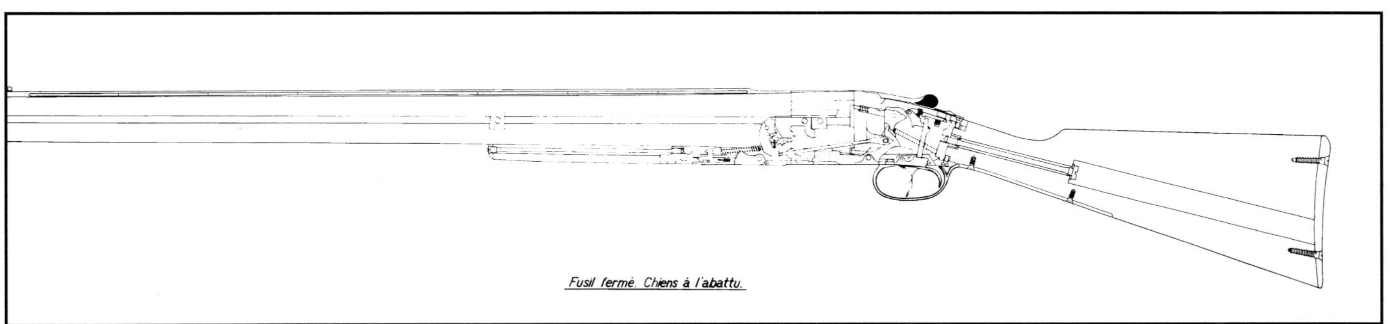

An overall view of the pre-production Browning Superposed. Notice the Non-Crossfire rib. Courtesy Fabrique Nationale Archives.

standing breech to conform to the radius. Some manufacturers have elevated their pin to the extreme limit in order to reduce the strain on the upper barrel during firing. John Browning disproved this practice by firing the Superposed with the locking bolt removed. Browning declared that the greatest wear on the hinge pin was caused not by firing the gun, but by rough opening of the gun. The larger hinge pin gave smoother action and longer wear. Because the Superposed frame did not employ an elevated pin, the trade-off resulted in a greater frame depth. Browning also used a heavy broad lug that engaged the hinge pin so as to provide an unusually large bearing surface and insure a permanent tight fit. The entire frame was built stronger and with more restraints surrounding the breech end of the barrels than other designs.

Also included in this patent was an improved method of taking down the gun without having to remove the forearm from the barrels. While this nondetachable forearm design was a commendable idea, it turned out to be an expensive design feature to produce. In all, there were a total of sixty-eight improvements listed in his first over and

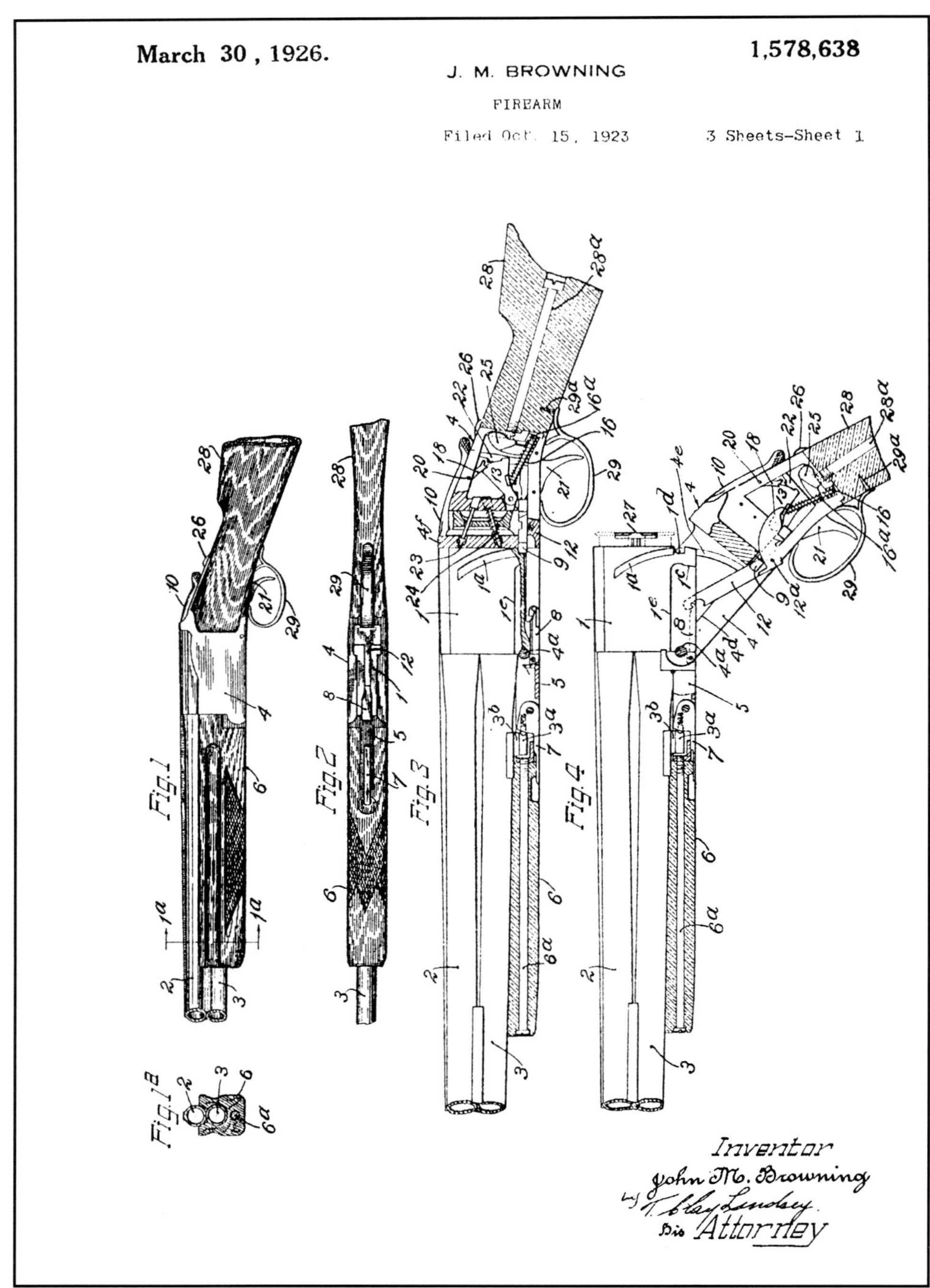

Above and opposite: Patent number 1,578,638 was the first in a series of John M. Browning's over and under designs. Filed on October 15, 1923, and awarded March 30, 1926, this patent stated that the new locking method would eliminate looseness and wear between the receiver and the breech piece. The patent also covered an improved take-down construction between the receiver and the barrel with its most noticeable feature being that the forearm remained with the barrels. Another stated characteristic of the patent was the improved firing mechanism, which was, "simple yet strong and effective." United States Patent Office.

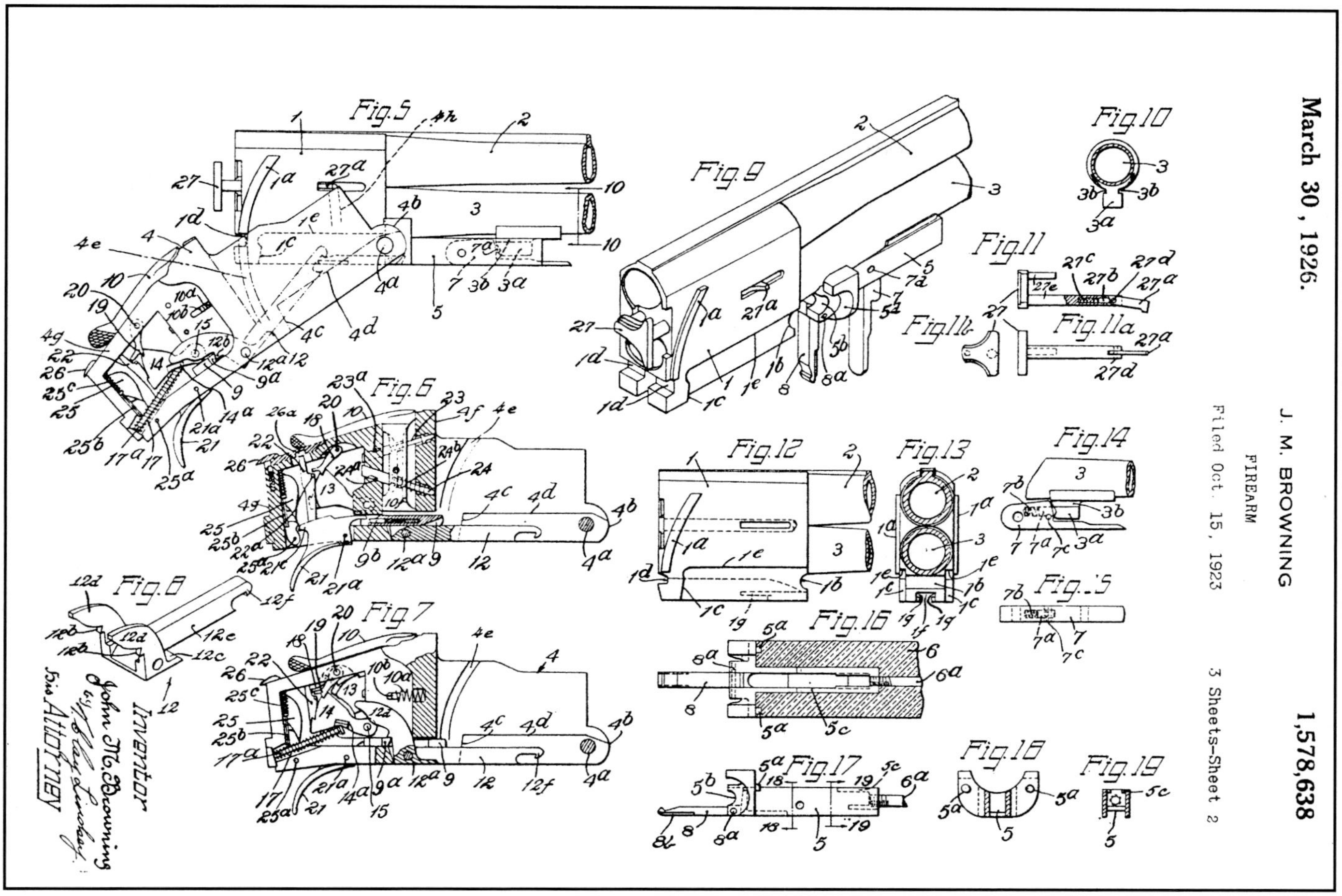

March 30, 1926.

J. M. BROWNING

FIREARM

Filed Oct. 15, 1923

3 Sheets-Sheet 2

1,578,638

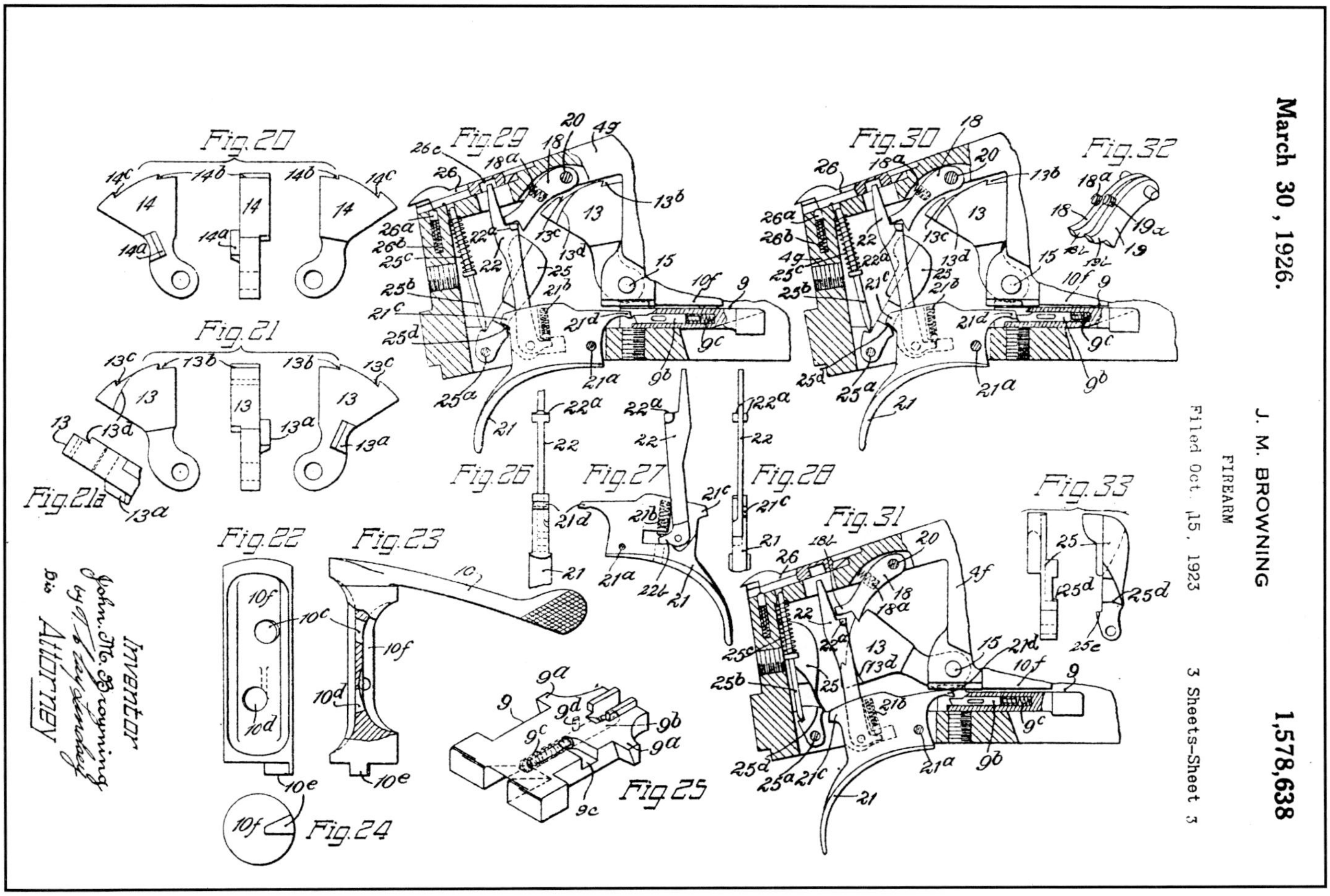

Inventor
John M. Browning
by T. Clay Lindsey
his Attorney

March 30, 1926.

J. M. BROWNING

FIREARM

Filed Oct. 15, 1923

3 Sheets-Sheet 3

1,578,638

Inventor
John M. Browning
by T. Clay Lindsey
his Attorney

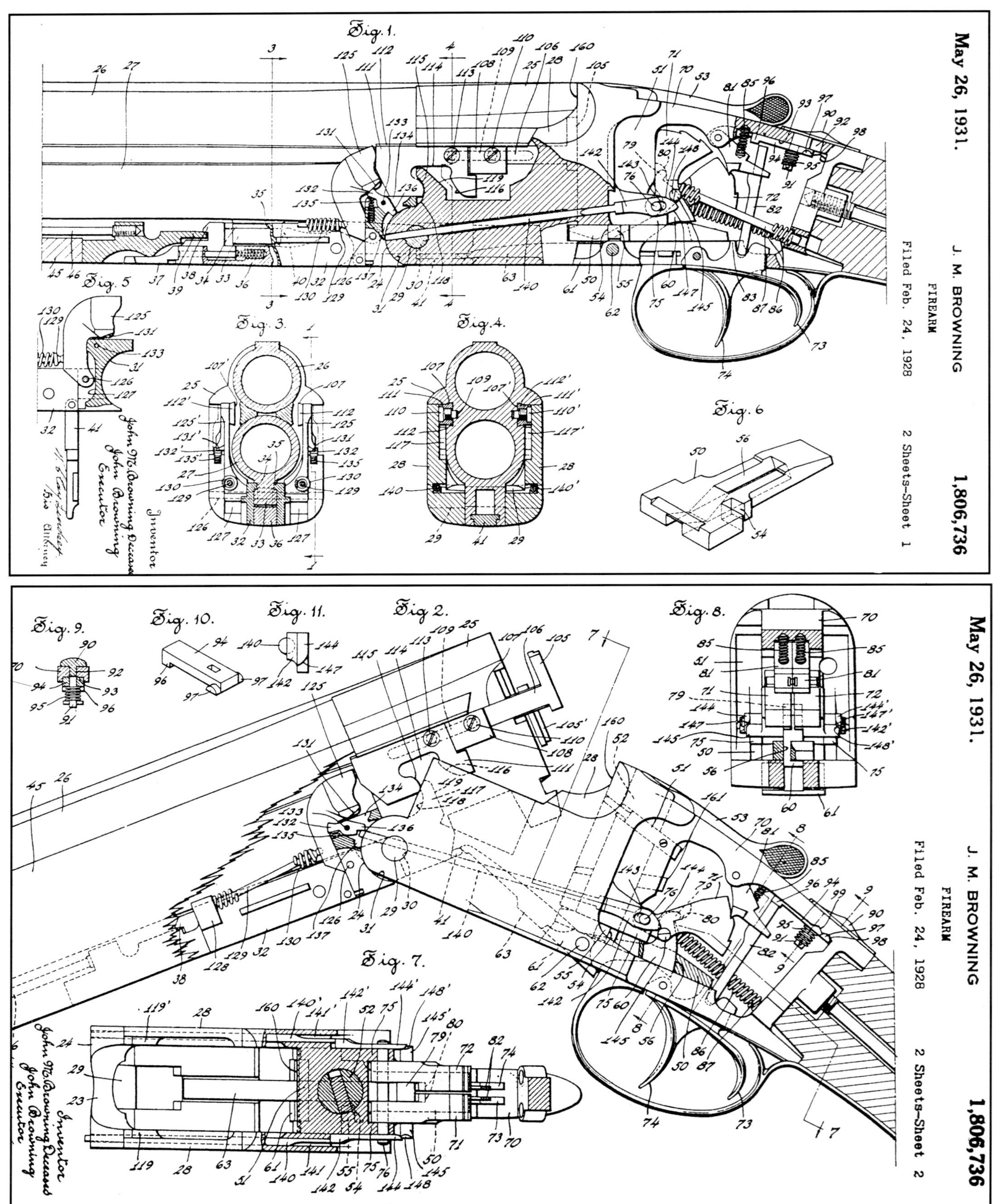

John M. Browning's automatic ejection patent, number 1,806,736. Simply stated, Browning's patent provided for, "... an improved, simplified, and effective arrangement by means of which the extraction of a discharged shell from the barrel in which it has been fired, and the retraction (but not ejection) of an unfired shell are effected when the gun is broken." The patent was not filed until more than a year after John M. Browning's death. United States Patent Office.

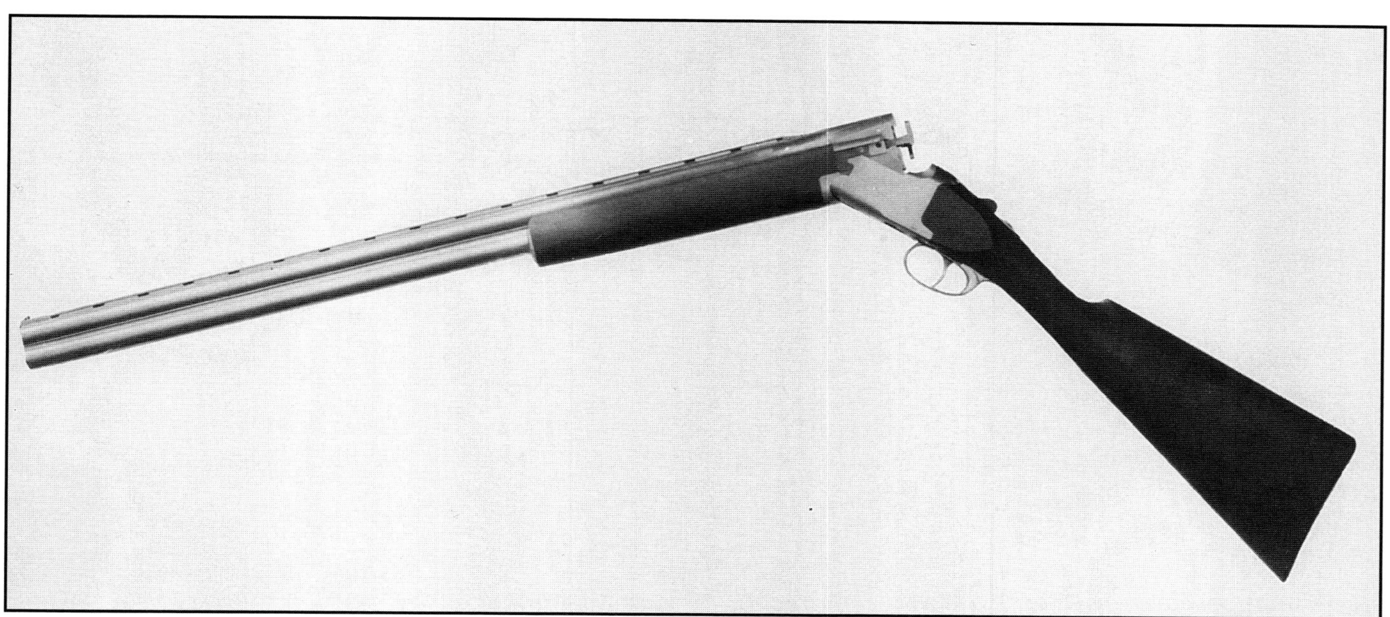

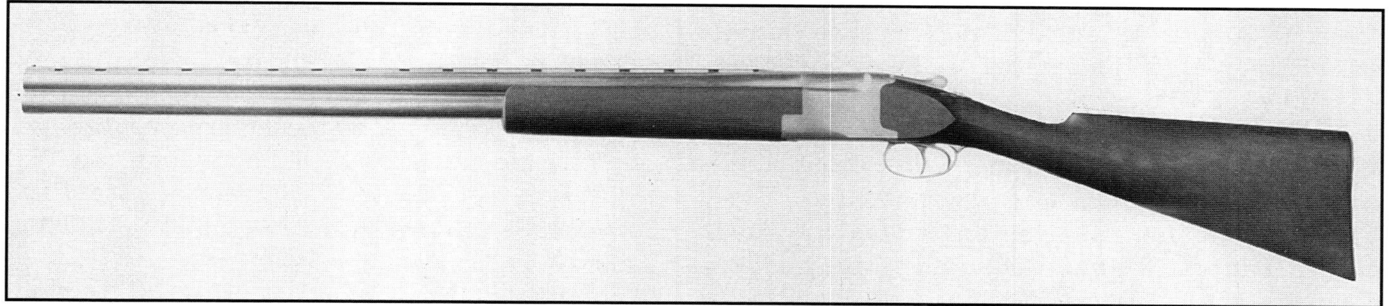

These two photos show a pre-production Superposed with straight grip stock and double triggers in the same configuration as the shop drawings. The photos are in fact based on the shop drawings showing the internal components of the gun. Notice the absence of checkering and metal finish. Courtesy Fabrique Nationale Archives.

under patent that claimed to have been enhancements. But careful reading of the patent reveals that Browning had not yet worked out all the problems he faced with his new design. Although a new single trigger arrangement was included in the application, Browning did not disclose his continuing difficulties with his new single trigger design. John Browning was also having difficulties with his selective ejector mechanism. One day he was to have said to Val Browning, "Son, I'll give you $40,000 for a good auto ejection system design."[4] Soon after, he perfected his own design.[5]

There were still a number of difficulties other than mechanical ones that had to be overcome regarding the over and under. There was some discussion with a few American firearms manufacturers, but none of them indicated any interest in the Superposed. At this juncture, Val Browning, then his father's right-hand man at FN where he supervised quality control and production for his father's designs, took the Superposed to Belgium where he felt FN would surely have an interest in producing the gun.

At that particular time, Fabrique Nationale was running at capacity to fulfill lucrative military orders. The Belgian company had little time or personnel to devote to the necessary cost and testing studies involved in reaching a decision on whether or not to manufacture the new over and under shotgun. Negotiations dragged on with FN for some time, but the main stumbling block seems to have been price. United States import tariffs were high and duties were based on a percentage of the

---

4 Browning Collectors Association Newsletter, September/October, 1989, Volume XI, No. 2.

5 John M. Browning's automatic ejection system was awarded patent number 1,806,736 on May 26, 1931. The patent was not filed until after his death on February 24, 1928, by the administrator of his estate, his oldest son John Browning. This auto ejection system is still in use today, with improvements, on Browning Superposed guns.

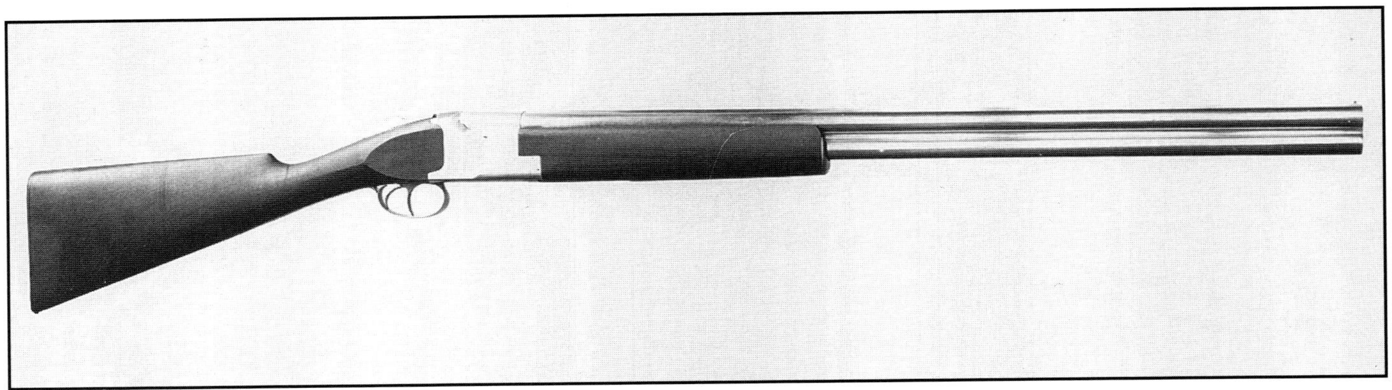

This is the earliest known photograph of a Browning Superposed. The photograph was taken sometime in 1925 at Fabrique Nationale. This may be the prototype of the Superposed as it was envisioned by John Browning. This particular gun has no checkering on the stock, nor is there any finish on the metal. Courtesy Fabrique Nationale Archives.

foreign wholesale price. The Brownings had negotiated a price of $30.00 per gun and a royalty paid for every Superposed sold by FN. They also wanted FN to agree to maintain that price in its European markets. FN refused.

Val then left Belgium and took the Superposed to Suhl, Germany, where he met with a prominent and reputable German arms manufacturer. The German company was eager to produce the gun after it had done some preliminary study. The company agreed to produce the gun at the required price if Browning would contract for a sufficient number of guns to warrant the cost of setting up production facilities. Val wrote to his father in Ogden for advice, and while awaiting his reply, returned to Belgium where he found that FN had decided to match the German proposal. An order for ten thousand Superposed was placed with FN at the agreed upon $30.00 per gun.[6]

Despite overcoming this obstacle with Fabrique Nationale, more difficulties were to come. John Browning's Superposed needed more work before it could be placed into production. On September 29, 1924, Browning filed another patent, serial number 740,454, dealing with improvements in the over and under design, namely his own initial work done less than a year before. This second patent, number 1,578,639, was granted on the same day as his first application, March 30, 1926. This second patent dealt with some of the same inventions as the first, specifically, an improved method of attaching a nonremovable forend to the barrels, as well as a better single selective trigger mechanism. Further work was also done on the ejector system in order for it to precisely eject the fired shell while retracting, but not ejecting, the unfired shell. Work continued on the Superposed throughout 1926 and it was chiefly left up to John's son Val to keep moving forward with the necessary improvements so the gun might go into production soon.

John Browning decided to return to Belgium during the fall of 1926 so he could help move the Superposed closer to production. After reviewing the progress of the Superposed on the plant floor, he climbed the stairs to his office at FN. He mentioned to his son Val that he felt tired. When he reached his office he was experiencing chest pains, and he lay down on a sofa. A company doctor was summoned, but an injection administered by the doctor did not alleviate the pain. He told his son that he was dying and shortly after, John M. Browning passed away. The date was November 26, 1926. He was the holder of 128 patents covering 80 different firearms. He influenced the world of firearms as no other man before or after him had done. His Superposed shotgun was his final masterpiece, but it was left unfinished. There were still obstacles and difficulties to overcome, and the task of completing this shotgun fell to his family, namely his son Val Browning.

---

[6] Val A. Browning, letter to the author, June 21, 1993.

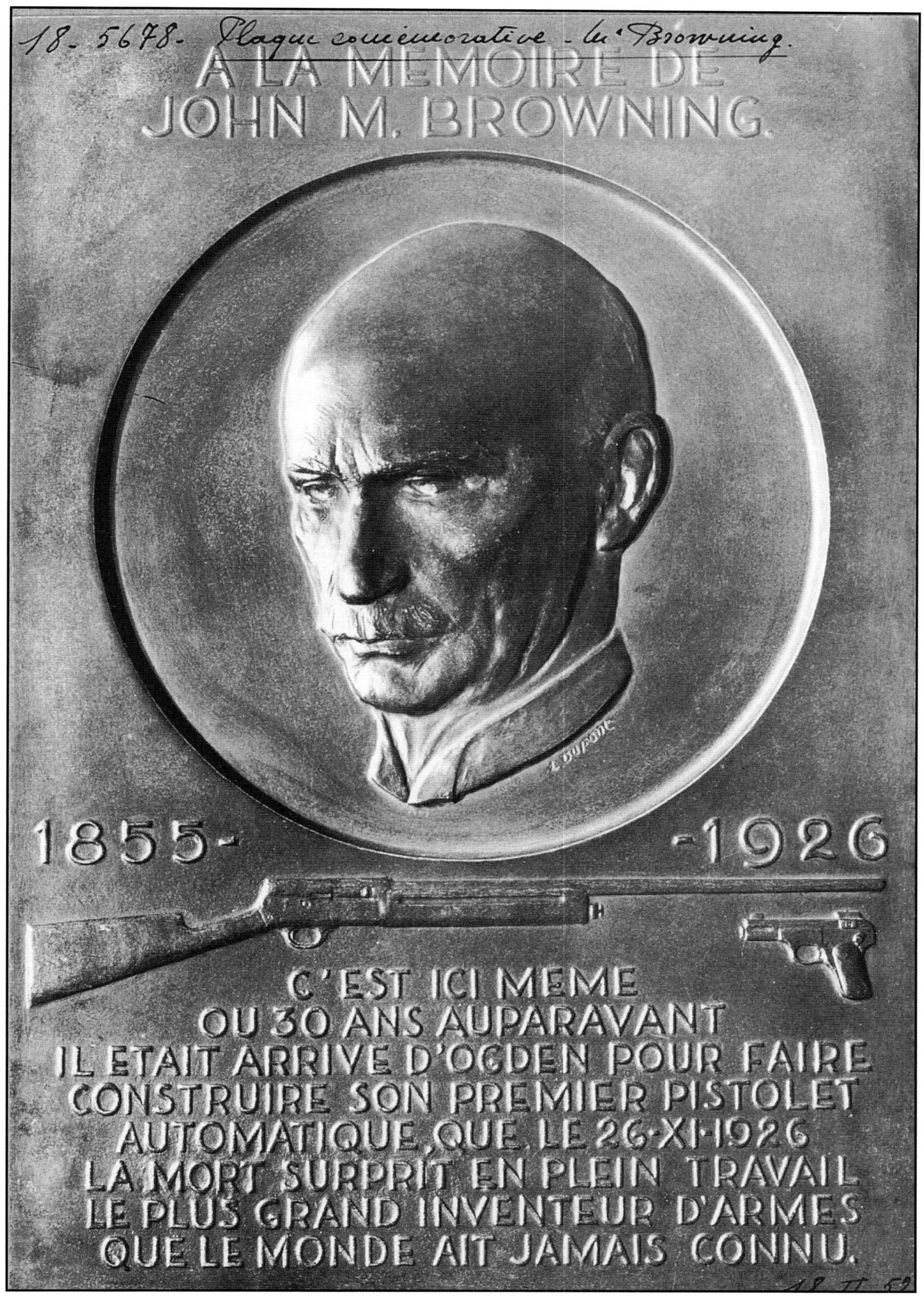

A bronze plaque honoring John M. Browning hangs in the very meeting room at FN where he often presented his designs to Fabrique Nationale executives. The plaque states: "To the Memory of John M. Browning 1855-1926. This is the place where, thirty years previously, he came from Ogden to have his first automatic pistol manufactured and where, on the twenty-sixth of November, 1926, while he was busily engaged at work death overtook the greatest firearms inventor the world has ever known." Courtesy Fabrique Nationale Archives.

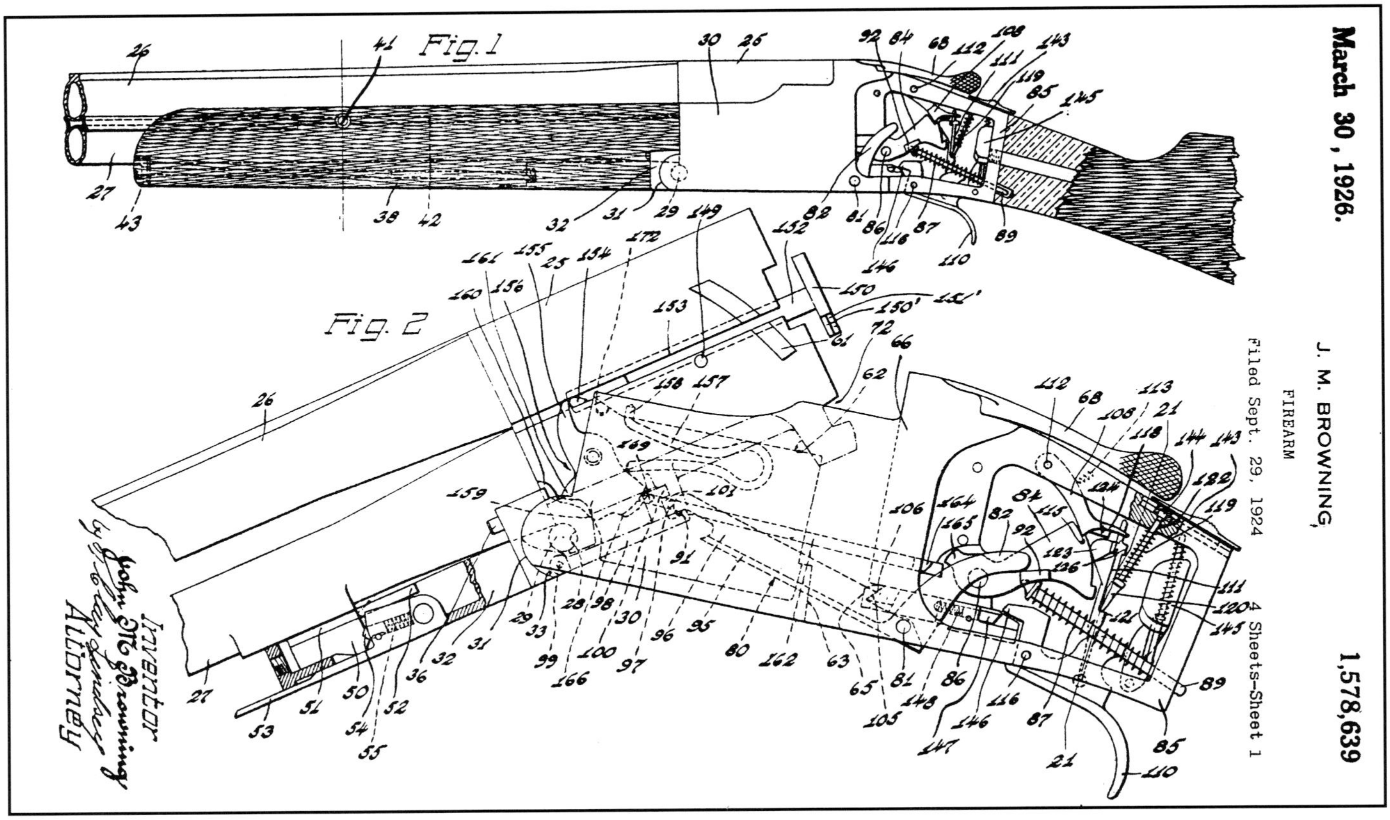

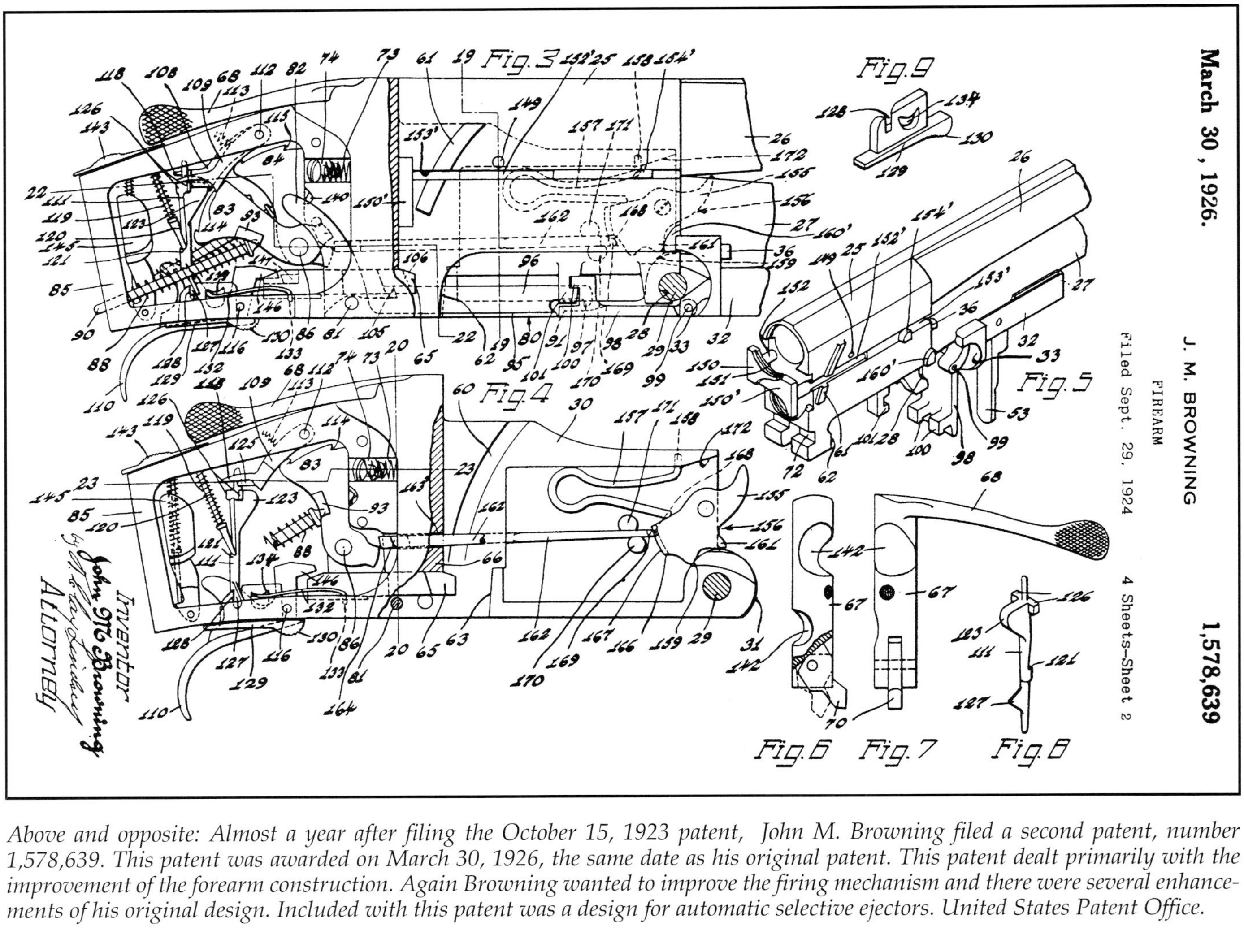

Above and opposite: Almost a year after filing the October 15, 1923 patent, John M. Browning filed a second patent, number 1,578,639. This patent was awarded on March 30, 1926, the same date as his original patent. This patent dealt primarily with the improvement of the forearm construction. Again Browning wanted to improve the firing mechanism and there were several enhancements of his original design. Included with this patent was a design for automatic selective ejectors. United States Patent Office.

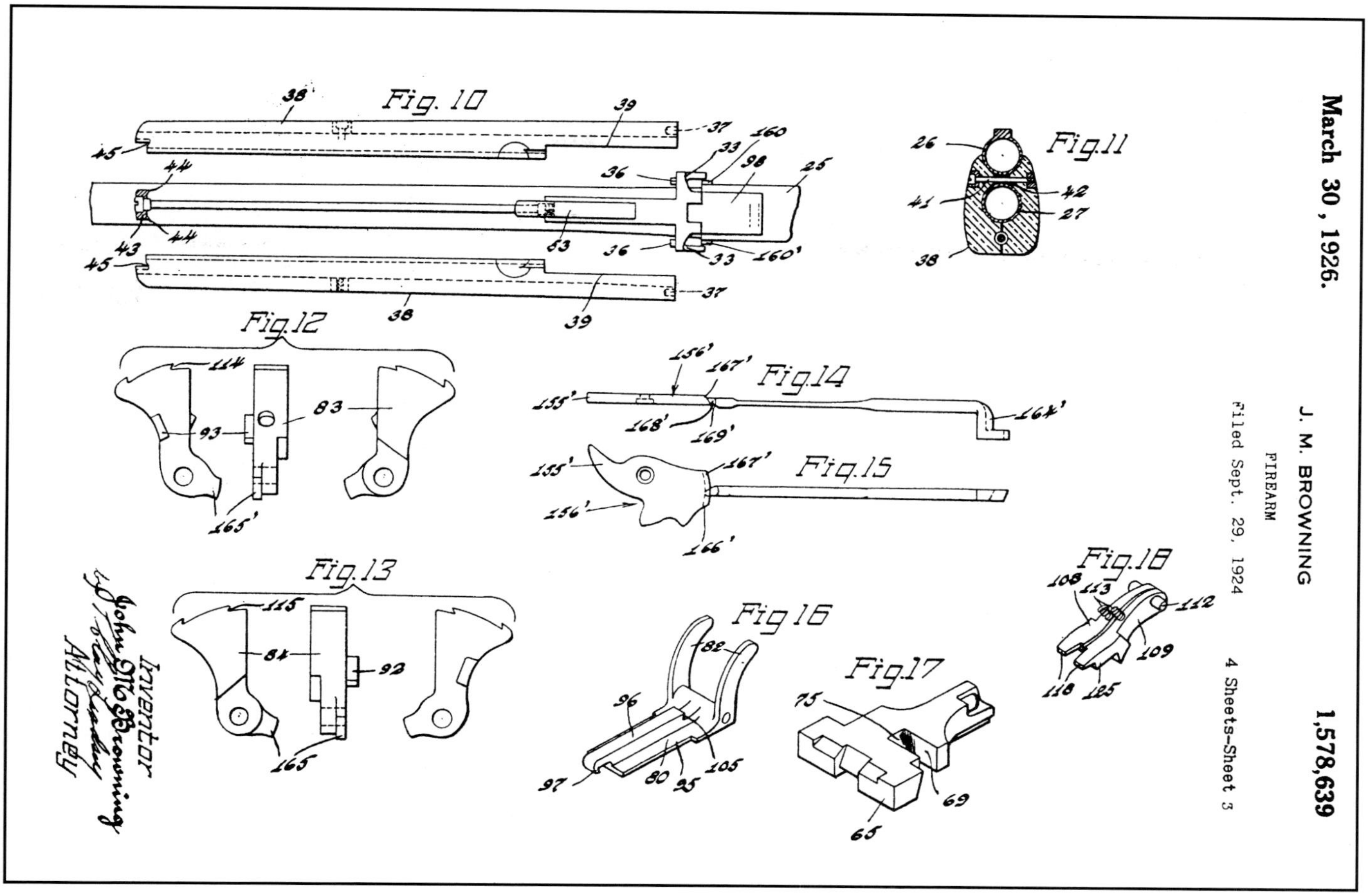

March 30, 1926.

J. M. BROWNING

FIREARM

Filed Sept. 29, 1924

4 Sheets-Sheet 3

1,578,639

Fig. 10 Fig. 11 Fig. 12 Fig. 13 Fig. 14 Fig. 15 Fig. 16 Fig. 17 Fig. 18

Inventor
John M. Browning
By [signature]
Attorney

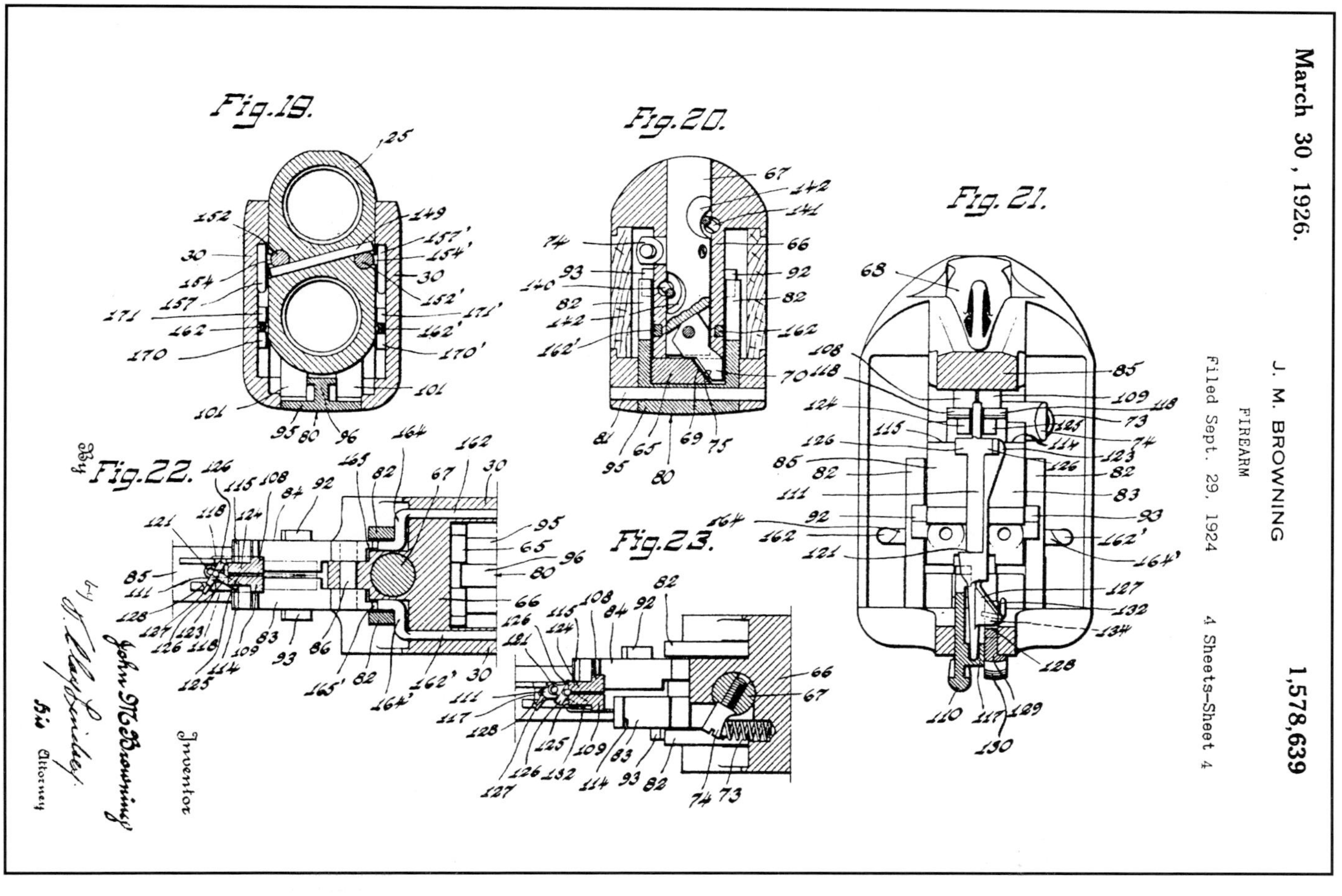

March 30, 1926.

J. M. BROWNING

FIREARM

Filed Sept. 29, 1924

4 Sheets-Sheet 4

1,578,639

Fig. 19. Fig. 20. Fig. 21. Fig. 22. Fig. 23.

Inventor
John M. Browning
By [signature]
his Attorney

Jonathan Browning
Founder of the Browning gun business

John M. Browning
First President Browning Arms Co. and the greatest firearms inventor of history

M. S. Browning
First Vice-President of Browning Arms Co.

Three Generations of Gunmaking

Jonathan Browning, moving westward from Kentucky, where he had learned the trade of gunsmith, set up a shop in Council Bluffs, Iowa, in the thirties. For a few years he repaired and made guns, many of original design, for the pioneers of the Gold Rush. In 1851 he captained a wagon train across the plains, and located permanently in Ogden, Utah.

John M. Browning worked with his father until his death, and thereafter carried on the business with the help of his younger brother, Matthew. An outline of the results of his activities is given in these pages.

V. A. Browning, one of the sons of John M., and for a number of years his technical assistant, has for the past ten years lived in Belgium, in charge of factory interests of the Browning Arms Company. To him has been entrusted the installation of equipment and production is under his active supervision. Browning experience of three generations goes into the manufacture of Browning Superposed and Browning Automatic Shotguns.

M. A. Browning

John Browning

V. A. Browning

Page Two

Three generations of gunmaking are represented here. M. A. Browning, son of Matthew Browning, and John Browning, son of John M. Browning, were in charge of the Ogden office and establishing the new sales office in St. Louis. They both contributed continuing efforts to perfect the Superposed, but the majority of the responsibility fell on Val Allen Browning, who continued to reside in Belgium after his father's death.

Chapter 1

The Prewar Years: 1926-1940

After John M. Browning's death, a number of events occurred that had a profound impact not only on the development of the Superposed, but on the company as well. Until the death of John M. Browning, the company that bore his name was in all reality an empty entity that was not actively engaged in the business of selling Browning designed firearms on a national scale. All of his previous designs were manufactured by other concerns and sold through the Browning Brothers hardware store in Ogden. The family was not involved in the sale and distribution of Browning patented firearms to other dealers. Upon Browning's death, his sons and nephews took the opportunity to create a new company that would import the Auto-5 and the Superposed directly from the FN factory into the United States. Almost a year after the death of John M. Browning, the J. M. & M. S. Browning Company was incorporated in Utah with the Browning Arms Company as a subsidiary. The J. M. & M. S. Browning Company was to act as the importer while the Browning Arms Company was to execute the duties of sales, distribution, parts, and repair on the imported guns. The president of this new company was Marriner Browning, son of the late Matthew Browning, John M. Browning's brother. The corporate headquarters was located in a rented suite of offices in a multistory building in downtown Ogden. However, there was still quite a bit of work to be done on the Superposed, and the bulk of finishing the gun and getting it into production rested with Val Browning.

Val A. Browning: Perfecter of the Superposed

If John M. Browning's Superposed was his last legacy, then enormous credit must be given to his son Val Allen Browning, not only for bringing this unfinished model into production, but also for making subsequent important improvements. Born on August 20, 1895, in Ogden, Utah, Val was imbued with his father's mechanical aptitude. He attended public schools in Ogden and made his first trip to Belgium with his father in 1913. That trip lasted until his return on the steamer *Lusitania* July 4, 1914.[1] The European visit made a lasting impression on then eighteen-year-old Val. He wrote home to his mother of the wonders of Europe and the adulation and respect in which his father was held by the people of Belgium, especially those who worked with him at the Fabrique Nationale plant.[2] During that stay, Val studied FN's production methods and upon his return he enrolled at Cornell University where he studied engineering and law. He graduated from Cornell in 1917.

In 1918 Val was commissioned as an officer in the Army Ordnance Corps where he trained instructors for the U.S. Army machine gun schools in France. Val also had responsibility for reporting to the army on the performance of the Browning machine guns and automatic rifles under actual combat conditions. He was stationed at the front near Verdun with the 79th American Division. When World War I was over, Val went to work with his father on continuing designs, one of which was the

---

1 Val A. Browning, letter to the author, August 15, 1993.

2 Letter from Val A. Browning to his mother, Rachael Browning, 1913. Browning Museum, Ogden, Utah.

Superposed. He moved to Belgium in 1920 where he served as his father's representative at Fabrique Nationale. The establishment of an efficient quality control system at FN was one of his most lasting accomplishments. It was in these circumstances that the relatively young Val Browning found himself upon his father's death in 1926. The responsibility for bringing the Superposed to production rested squarely on his shoulders.

Trials and Tribulations

The first tool room model of the Superposed was finished when Val Browning returned to Belgium after his father's funeral in Ogden. This gun, fitted with the John M. Browning single trigger, was sent to Ogden for field testing. Val's cousin Marriner used it on a duck hunt in the marshes of the Bear River not far from Ogden. He was hunting in a flat bottom duck boat. When a passing duck got within range, Marriner stood up, whirled to his left, and fired. The gun doubled, almost knocking him out of the boat. This was just the kind of malfunction the Brownings could ill afford on the Superposed. It was time to redesign the trigger system. This task again fell to Val, but this time his brother John and cousin Marriner helped. Work proceeded in other areas as well. Early in 1928, a patent having to do with an improved ejector system was filed on behalf of the late John M. Browning by his son John Browning, the administrator of his estate. Patent number 1,806,736 was granted on May 26, 1931.

Numerous other delays were encountered during this period. The first prototype had barrels that were threaded at the rear and screwed into a chambered block or monobloc. The barrels had no side ribs. The selective ejector system was changed to conform to the improvements made in John M. Browning's 1928 patent, and of course work continued on the single selective trigger.

This receiver forging is dated July 28, 1930. This—a solid piece of steel—is what the machine operators had to work with in order to make a Superposed receiver. Courtesy Fabrique Nationale Archives.

In Belgium, the factory was having difficulty meeting quality control standards. One thing John M. Browning insisted upon was absolute top quality in all the firearms that bore his name. His family continued that tradition with equal insistence.

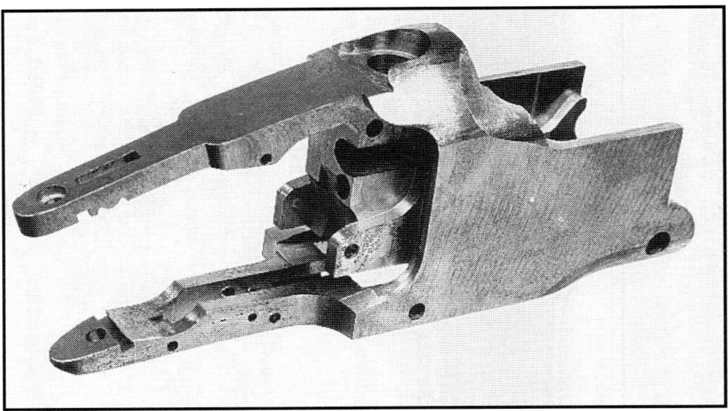

After numerous machine operations performed by skilled FN craftsmen, the result was a nearly completed Superposed receiver with most of its internal cuts finished. The receiver is not yet polished. Courtesy Fabrique Nationale Archives.

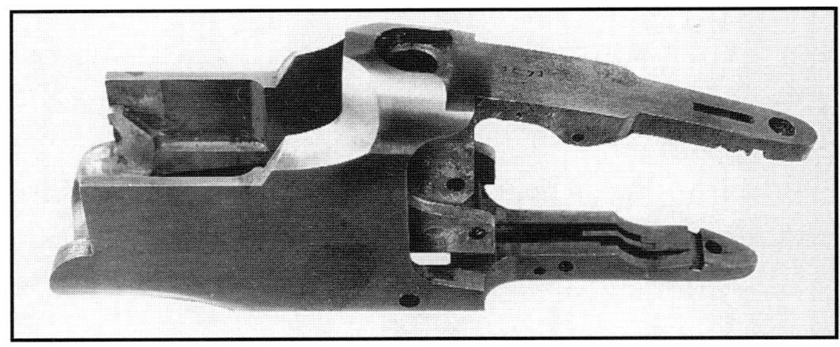

A completed Superposed receiver. It has been polished and inspected. It was then placed in a large bin with other Superposed receivers and FN gunsmiths would use it to assemble a completed gun. Courtesy Fabrique Nationale Archives.

The mechanical workmanship was acceptable on the Superposed, but difficulties were experienced with fit, finish, and wood. The craftsmen at FN were adept at building military firearms and at the assembly of the Auto-5, but they were not as familiar with the construction of a complicated, hand fitted double gun. The Superposed was considerably more difficult to produce than the Auto-5. The finish did not measure up to the high criterion set by Val Browning, and frequent delays resulted from trying to bring the production models up to this high quality. Problems were encountered with the uneven quality of the French walnut used in the stocks, and of the checkering.[3]

It was because of Val Browning's perseverance and hard work that production difficulties were

[3] Val A. Browning, letter to the author, August 15, 1993.

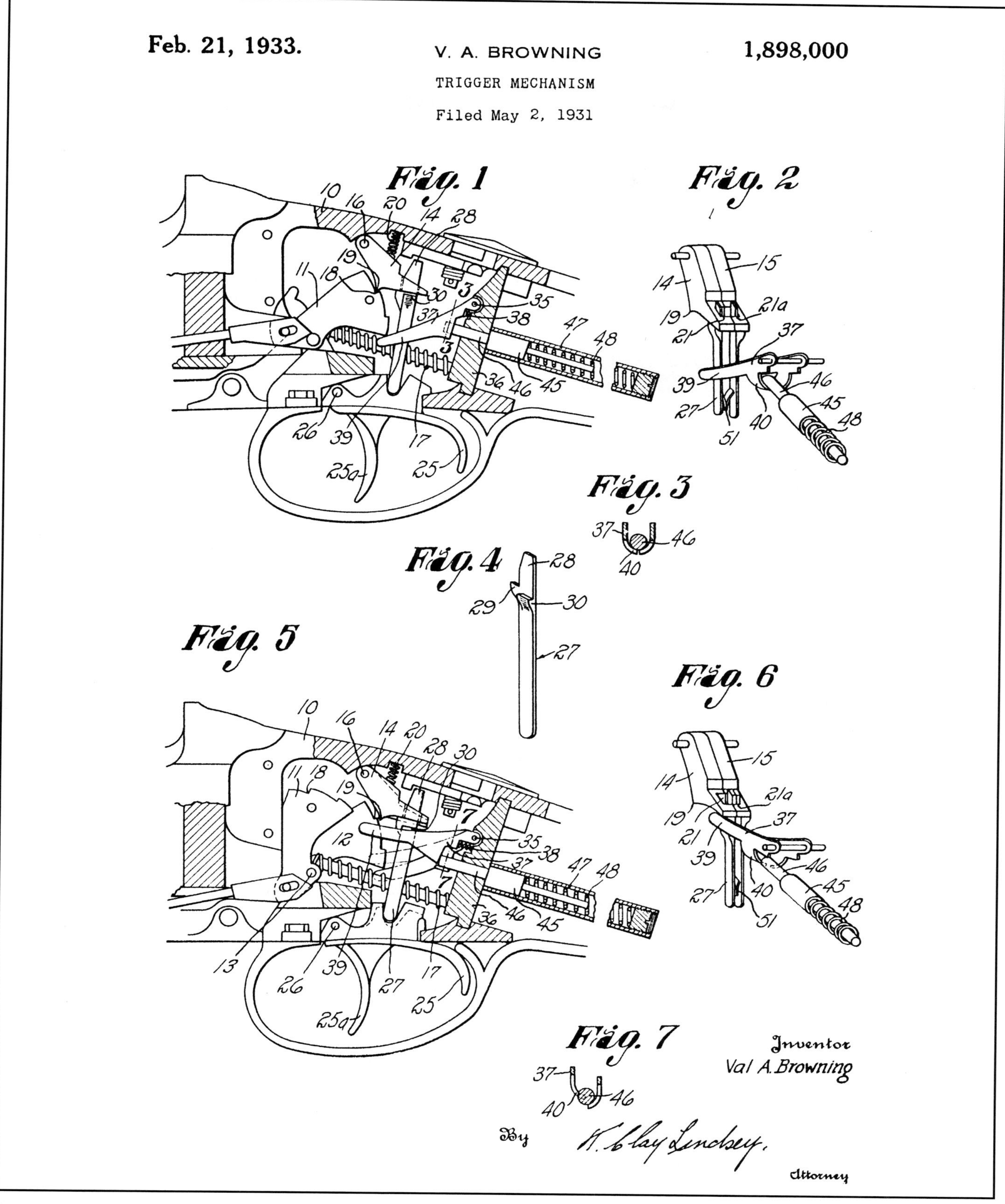

Patent number 1,898,000 was filed by Val Browning on May 2, 1931, and awarded February 21, 1933. The patent was also filed in Belgium on January 7, 1931. Val Browning's patent dealt primarily with improvements in the Superposed trigger mechanism, namely the prevention of doubling. Val solved this problem by designing his Twin-Single triggers. This patent covers that invention. United States Patent Office.

SOMETHING NEW IN SINGLE TRIGGERS

THE BROWNING S$^{\text{TWIN}}_{\text{INGL}}$E TRIGGER

THIS new single trigger is exclusive on the Browning Superposed. It is the most unique and useful advance in two-barrel design in years. The trigger gives you all the advantages of the simplest single trigger ever made, plus two-trigger selectivity.

For years gun designers have struggled to find some means of achieving instant selectivity with a single trigger system. Single triggers have been selective, it is true, but in order for the hunter to select a barrel, it was always necessary for him to shift a latch. Often the time lost was just sufficient to miss a good shot.

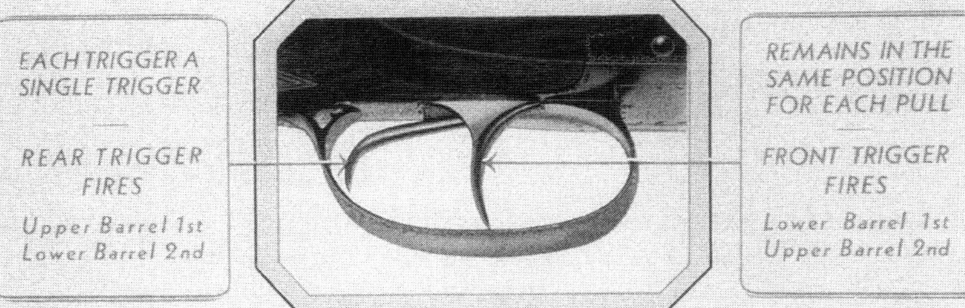

Order of firing may be reversed if desired.

Now with the Browning Twin-Single Trigger, this problem is solved. For this new trigger is just what its name indicates—two triggers mounted exactly as in the ordinary two-trigger double gun, *but each a single trigger*. The result is a trigger system whose selectibility meets every requirement of both trap and field shooting, a thing which cannot be said of any other trigger mechanism. Here's a trigger that combines all the advantages of both the selective single trigger and two triggers. It is in effect both types in versatile combination. In fact, the owner can go beyond this if he wishes, since it is practical, should he develop an exclusive preference for either trigger, to remove the superfluous trigger and have the slot filled with a blank. Such a situation may arise in case the gun is used solely at the traps.

As standard design, the Browning Twin-Single is mounted so that the front trigger fires first the lower barrel then the upper and the rear trigger fires first the upper then the lower barrel. This system, however, is optional and the purchaser may have the trigger mounted to fire in reverse order without additional cost.

Regardless of how these triggers are mounted, the user has at his command either trigger position, front or rear, and may instantly select the barrel best adapted to the occasion—with no latch to shift.

Instant selectibility is particularly advantageous in field shooting. Where a two-barrel is used for upland birds it is the usual practice to have one barrel with a more open choke than the other. Let us suppose with such a gun equipped with the ordinary selective single trigger set for the open barrel that the bird suddenly flushes wild. If the hunter stops to shift the latch he has lost his shot. On the other hand, should he fire the open bore he may merely feather the bird so he might just as well refuse the shot.

Page Fourteen

This Browning 1931 catalogue page illustration clarifies how the Twin-Single trigger operates. Val Browning was justifiably proud of his invention, but the company's sales department did not think highly of the trigger design. In reality it was a provisional trigger option that was used until a more reliable single selective trigger design could be found.

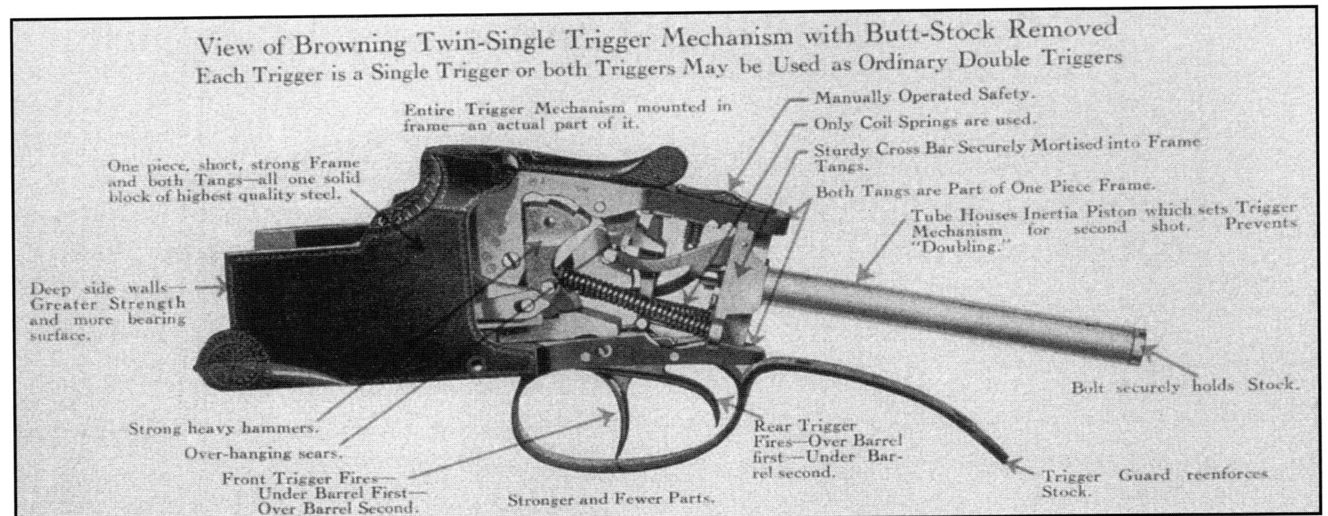

A cutaway view of Val Browning's Twin-Single trigger. It was simple yet effective, but not very popular.

overcome. He was finally able to convince FN that quality and quantity were compatible goals. Val Browning was responsible for instituting independent quality control shortly after he arrived in Herstal after World War I. It was this independent system that played such an important role in solving the Superposed production problems at the factory in the early 1930s.

Meanwhile, work continued on a single trigger design that would function safely and reliably. John Browning, Val's older brother, applied for patent number 1,870,552, on January 11, 1930, for a single selective trigger that would eliminate doubling and provide greater reliability. Although the trigger mechanism worked, it did not provide the reliability that was necessary for a production shotgun. The following year, Val Browning designed a trigger mechanism that was to be a real innovation for American shooters: the Twin-Single trigger. Patent number 1,898,000 was applied for on May 2, 1931, and granted February 21, 1933. This was an interesting resolution to a complex problem, but he had yet to find a reliable solution for a single selective trigger. The Superposed needed to be placed into production and the Twin-Single trigger seemed to be a good interim approach. This Twin-Single design, or "system" as Val liked to call it, was arranged so that each trigger would successively fire each barrel. The front trigger fired the bottom barrel first, then the second pull on the same trigger fired the top barrel. The rear trigger fired the top barrel first, then the under barrel on the next pull. This "system" eliminated doubling, but the sales department did not like the design because American shotgunners favored pistol grip stocks, which made shifting triggers unwieldy.[4] Val continued to work on a single trigger design, but success would not come for several more years.

In the meantime, his cousin Marriner filed an application for a single trigger design based in part on Val's earlier design. Patent number 1,898,291 was filed in September of 1931 with the express purpose of improving a single selective trigger design. In Marriner's patent, the selector switch was located on the bottom of the frame near the root of the trigger and was moved forward and rearward to change the order of barrel firing. This arrangement was used on some of the early single selective Superposed until a more reliable mechanism could be designed. So it was that in spite of its flaws and unfinished condition, John M. Browning's Superposed began to take shape.

Even with the work necessary to get the Superposed into production, there was time for additional study on expanding the newly introduced 12 gauge Superposed. Val Browning seriously thought of widening the Superposed line to include a 16 gauge version as well as a 12 gauge. He even went so far as to build a prototype of the 16 gauge Superposed. That prototype is now on display at the Browning Museum, Union Station in Ogden, Utah. Later in the decade, Val Browning worked on a prototype of a 20 gauge Superposed that he hoped to add to the fledgling Superposed product line.

Preparing for the Superposed

Meanwhile, in Ogden, preparations were being made to market and sell the new Browning shotgun. It was decided that the best way to sell and distribute the new Superposed was directly to dealers. No distributors or jobbers were used, as

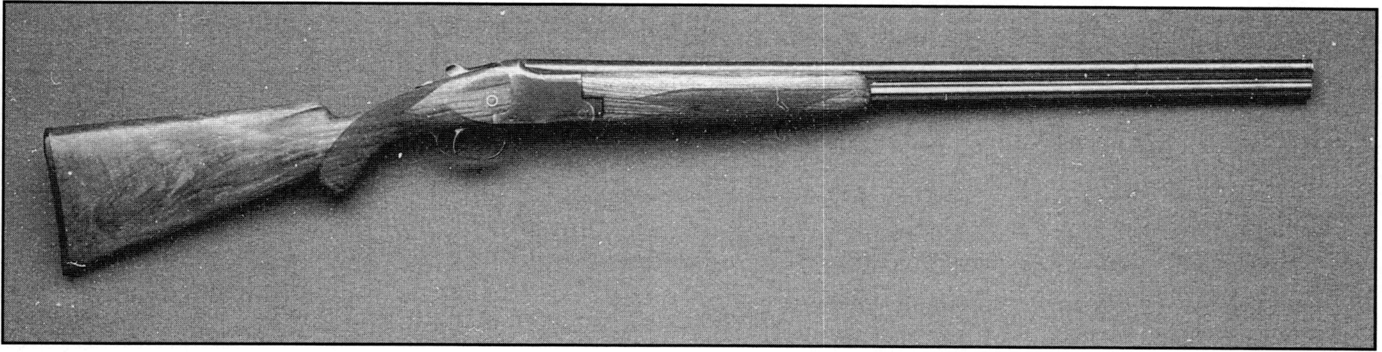

This Browning Superposed is Val Browning's prototype 16 gauge. This is the only known example of a 16 gauge Superposed. It is on display at the Browning Firearms Museum, Union Station, Ogden, Utah.

[4] *Ibid.*

was the common practice of the day. In 1930 the sales, repair, parts, and distribution center was established in St. Louis, Missouri, at 12th and Spruce Street in an old multistory abandoned shoe factory. This facility was under the management of John R. Russell, and he was assisted by Douglas Ellis in supervising sixteen employees. Roy Hoppy was the sole salesman and E. L. Koehrer acted as office manager and order clerk. There were seven gunsmiths employed in the service department with Mitch Heiter as shop foreman. The task of shipping and receiving was left in the highly qualified hands of Harry Altenbernd. It was a small and antiquated beginning to sell and service what would become one of the most popular double shotguns ever sold in the United States.

Val Browning coming off the traps with his engraved Browning Superposed. The photo was taken in 1933. Courtesy Browning Firearms Museum, Union Station, Ogden, Utah.

Anfenger Advertising Agency of St. Louis was retained to prepare the new advertising copy and brochures that were necessary to alert the sporting goods dealers and hardware stores across the country to a new affordable over and under shotgun that promised to be a profitable addition to their firearms line. The new advertising guaranteed that shooters would be pleased with the new Superposed. The company pointed out that eight state championship titles were won with the gun as well as three records, all established in 1931. With his Superposed, Ted Renfro won the World's Live Bird Championship at Monte Carlo with a record two hundred pair. Sam Jenny went 114 straight live pigeons at St. Louis and Kansas City, and in the process set a world record. Val Browning even got in on the act with a win at the Team International Pigeon Shooting Championship in Spain in the early 1930s. Val, Walter Warren, and Ben Galliger took home the trophy, all shooting the Browning Superposed.

Val Browning, Walter Warren, and Ben Galliger won the Team International Pigeon Shooting Championship in Spain in the early 1930s. Val and Walter Warren shot Superposed guns. Galliger is holding an unidentified over and under. Courtesy Browning Firearms Museum, Union Station, Ogden, Utah.

The praise continued with endorsements in which Alec Mermod, editor of *Outdoor America*, claimed to have given up his 20 gauge in favor of the new 12 gauge Superposed because of its light recoil and superb balance. Captain Charles Askins, editor of *Outdoor Life*, liked its light weight, excellent balance, and attractive appearance. Captain Paul A. Curtis, editor of *Field and Stream*, wrote a glowing opinion of the Superposed when he stated, "... I have shot or handled every variety of over and under of any importance produced during the last generation, and I have yet, regardless of price, to open and close a smoother working one than

STRENGTH

JOHN M. BROWNING not only maintained his position for half a century as the greatest of firearms inventors; he also supervised the laying down of many installations for the manufacture of his arms, and guided the process of manufacture through to the completed product. He became, therefore, the master of two arts, designing and manufacturing. In the designing of an arm, he could look forward to factory operations. And his experience in this respect was not limited to one factory, but extended to several, both in this country and in Europe. Thus, in designing an arm, having the parts of the first model made in his own shop (he made his earliest models with his own hands), he was able to project his imagination to the equipment that would be required for the manufacture of each part—the tools, jigs, fixtures, etc., and the number of operations.

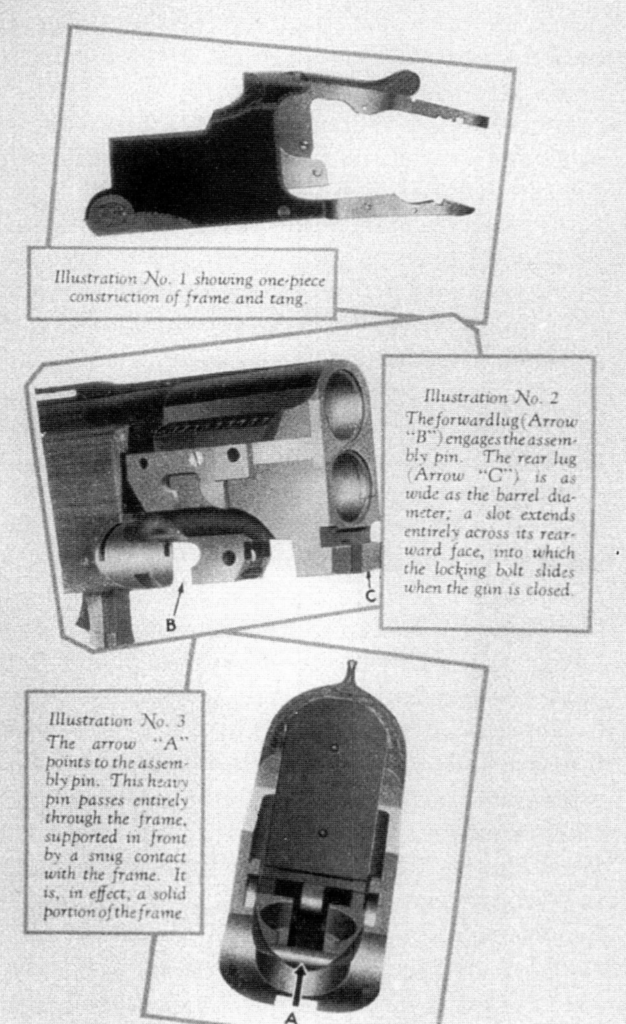

Illustration No. 1 showing one-piece construction of frame and tang.

Illustration No. 2 The forward lug (Arrow "B") engages the assembly pin. The rear lug (Arrow "C") is as wide as the barrel diameter; a slot extends entirely across its rearward face, into which the locking bolt slides when the gun is closed.

Illustration No. 3 The arrow "A" points to the assembly pin. This heavy pin passes entirely through the frame, supported in front by a snug contact with the frame. It is, in effect, a solid portion of the frame.

Many ingenious men lack this dual training, and, bending their attention to devising a mechanism that will work successfully, they fail to foresee the difficult and costly factory operations that will be required. The ingenious mind must have a well developed practical side in order to combine successful functioning with simplicity. Mr. Browning's life was a constant refining of the complex into the simple. In that process, scrutinized by the infinite patience of genius, the intricate and unsightly became simple and beautiful.

The frame of the Browning Superposed is a case in point. It is shown in Illustration No. 1 with the mechanism dismounted. The frame and both tangs are cut from a solid block of steel. The lower tang of other two-barrel guns is a separate piece, screwed to the frame, the ends of the two tangs being held by a screw which passes through the stock. The tangs of the Superposed, in one piece with the frame to begin with, and unusually thick, have a heavy binding post slotted into their ends. The detachable tang construction, which the Superposed avoids, necessitates the cutting of a seat in the bottom of the frame, the fitting of the tang into that seat, and the boring and threading of the two holes for the screws which hold the two pieces together. The Superposed construction eliminates the expense of all those operations, and at the same time achieves an incomparable rigidity.

Both barrel lugs enter deep seats in the frame as the gun closes. The locking bolt is thick (see Illustration No. 3), broad, and hidden from view. With the two-barrel lugs deeply seated in the frame, the assembly pin engaging the forward lug, the fore-end iron bearing against the rounded forward portion of the frame, the heavy locking bolt seated in the slot in the rear lug, the high sides of the frame extending well up the sides of the barrels, and all parts expertly fitted, the Browning Superposed is super-solid.

Page Twenty-two

Using the fine reputation of John M. Browning as a stepping stone to introduce the great inventor's last design was part of the effort to influence likely hunters and shooters as to the inherent safety of the Browning Superposed. In fact, the Superposed was probably overbuilt, and if it had any shortcomings safety was not one of them.

this inexpensive weapon. It is like rubbing velvet together."

Browning also promised to protect its dealers' profits. They were assured a thirty-three percent profit based on a twenty-five percent discount from list price on the Browning Superposed. The company adopted an aggressive price protection plan for its dealers in order to make it attractive for them to carry and sell Browning shotguns. As part of its dealers' price list, Browning stated very plainly its pricing policy, called "Maintenance of Dealer's Profits":

> Arms discounts in the past have been fiction more often than fact. It is the price at which the Dealer sells and not the discount, which determines his actual profit. Price demoralization in arms is a sore spot to which it is not necessary to call any Dealer's attention. By methods which may have appeared devious, but which, nevertheless, have been effectual, we have found a remedy for this condition. As the sole source of supply, we know where every Browning arm goes and Dealers may rest assured that none will go to price cutters. The dealer can therefore realize a full profit on his sale price on every Genuine Browning Automatic and Superposed Shotgun sold.

The initial retail price for the gun was $107.50, which included a level hollow rib, automatic ejectors, and a choice of three standard stock dimensions. A ventilated rib was available for $20.00 extra and there was a choice of three single triggers: selective, nonselective, and the Twin-Single, each for $30.00. Double triggers were offered as standard equipment. The first half of 1931 was spent preparing for the new shotgun. A parts price list was received from FN and converted into retail prices for the trade. A series of authorized service stations was already in place to repair the Browning Automatic and these establishments were given the same discounts on the new Superposed. Most parts, with the exception of stocks and barrels, were sold at a fifty percent discount. A beavertail forearm was offered at these repair facilities for $15.65, a price Browning management felt was equivalent to Parker, Ithaca, and other American gunmakers. A potential problem was solved regarding the duty to be paid on Superposed guns shipped to the U.S. with an extra set of barrels. Negotiations settled on $4.00 per set of barrels rather than $4.00 per barrel. The rate would be the same for Superposed barrels as it was for Browning Automatic barrels.[5]

In a letter to its dealers dated May 27, 1931, Browning management outlined these company pricing policies: St. Louis was to provide a central location for the shipment of parts and guns to any point in the U.S. The West Coast had the longest delivery with seventy-two hour service. The company pointed out that there were about three hundred authorized service stations all over the country to serve the Browning owner, and the shop department was equipped to perform any type of service on Browning shotguns. Browning made it clear that it was the sole source of supply for Browning guns, and dealers buying direct could all count on paying the same price. As the company letter of May 27, 1931, stipulates, "Every transaction is directly between the Dealer and ourselves. And we will not accept further orders from Dealers who sell below our established prices."[6]

Browning Arms Company did not have a sales organization as such. There were no company salesmen on the road assigned to specific territories. In fact, dealers were never called upon by Browning salesmen, and Browning made no effort to actively promote its Superposed directly to the public or through trade shows or other promotional techniques. During these early days, the company even charged its dealers for catalogues and brochures. Beginning the first day of January of each year, the Browning sales department, which was confined to St. Louis, took written orders for its Superposed guns. When that yearly allotment was reached, usually by the end of January, the sales year was over. Any additional orders were not filled, nor were those unfulfilled orders acknowledged. Remarkably, the system seemed to work; at least orders were received and dealers liked the gun and pushed its sales.

There is an additional chapter to the Browning Superposed sales history that is somewhat enigmatic, yet fascinating. In a letter dated August 28, 1931, from John Browning to Mr. E. T. Hyde, Jr. of West Haven, Connecticut, reference was made to Browning's new sales policy called "Direct-from-Browning-to-you." The letter goes on to offer Mr. Hyde the Superposed of his choice for a money back two-day inspection of the gun. He could return it if he was not satisfied with it for any reason. The letter was part of a sales package that included the large format 1931 Browning Super-

---

[5] Letter from JRR (John R. Russell) to M. A Browning, April 16, 1931. Russ Church Collection.

[6] Form letter from Browning Arms Company, St. Louis, MO, to its dealers, May 27, 1931. Russ Church Collection.

posed catalogue. Also included in the catalogue was an additional blue colored printed sheet. The sheet stated in part:

> The new Browning Superposed, our change in selling policy and the popular price of this high quality gun, will be interesting to many of your sportsmen friends....Our new selling policy, "Direct-from-Browning-to-you," has made it possible to sell this new gun at an unusually low price. Won't you help us and do a favor to your friends as well by giving us their names in the spaces provided below?

Gus Becker, John M. Browning's shooting partner and renowned trapshooter, was pictured on the cover of Browning's first Superposed catalogue printed in 1931.

The remainder of the sheet was filled with cut-out coupons. Careful reading of the order form in the back of the 1931 Superposed catalogue also indicates that direct sales was part of the Browning selling strategy. In other company literature, Browning made the distinction that this customer direct program was made available only if the customer's dealer could not or would not supply him with a Browning shotgun. How long this sales policy was utilized is not known for certain, but all indications are that it was short-lived. Browning's dealer network could not be pleased with having to compete with the company for sales. This short-lived direct sales approach was probably an indication of just how difficult it was to break into the American doubles market in the teeth of the Great Depression. The company most likely felt it had to try all sales avenues to capture potential customers.

The Introductory Superposed: 1931-1935

When the Superposed was first introduced in the United States in 1931, it was offered in a limited number of configurations until 1936. From 1931 through 1935, Browning sold the Superposed in 12 gauge only with double triggers standard and a choice of three stock configurations: a Field dimension stock, a Trap configured stock, and a Monte Carlo stock. The Field stock dimensions were listed as follows: length of pull 14-1/2 inches, drop at the heel 2-1/4 inches, and drop at the comb 1-1/2 inches. Browning referred to this particular model as the "Standard Model Long Range." The Trap stock had the same length of pull, 14-1/2 inches, and the same drop at the comb, 1-1/2 inches, while the drop at the heel was 1-1/4 inches. The length of pull and drop at the comb for the Monte Carlo stock was the same as above, but the drop at the heel was 1-1/2 inches by 2-1/4 inches. These Trap guns were referred to as the "Standard Model Trap."

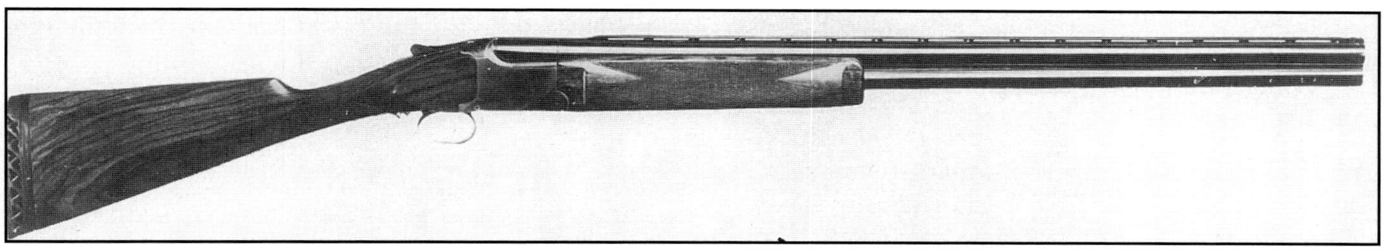

The first production Superposed based on John M. Browning's two patents. This is the shotgun that Val Browning and his family worked so hard to put into production after the death of its designer. Note the single trigger and fancy wood. This Superposed is on display at the Browning Firearms Museum at Union Station in Ogden, Utah. Courtesy Browning.

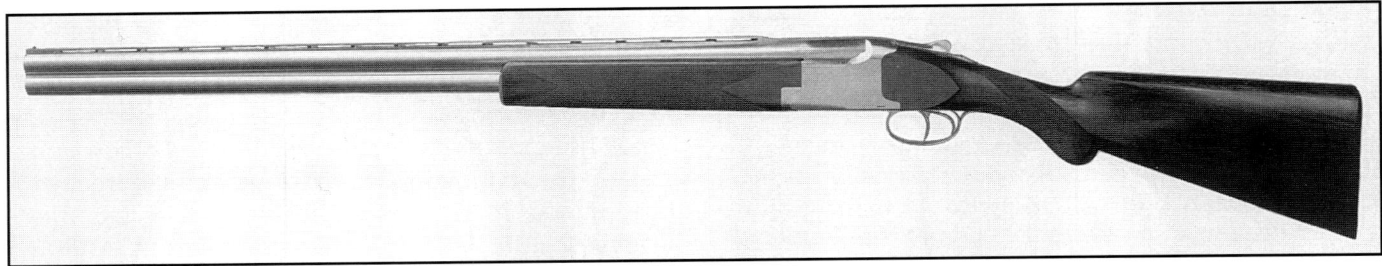

A very early production Superposed with pistol grip, double triggers, and Non-Crossfire ventilated rib. This gun has been checkered and the wood finished, but the metal is still in the white. There is no engraving on the frame nor would there be until 1938. Courtesy Fabrique Nationale Archives.

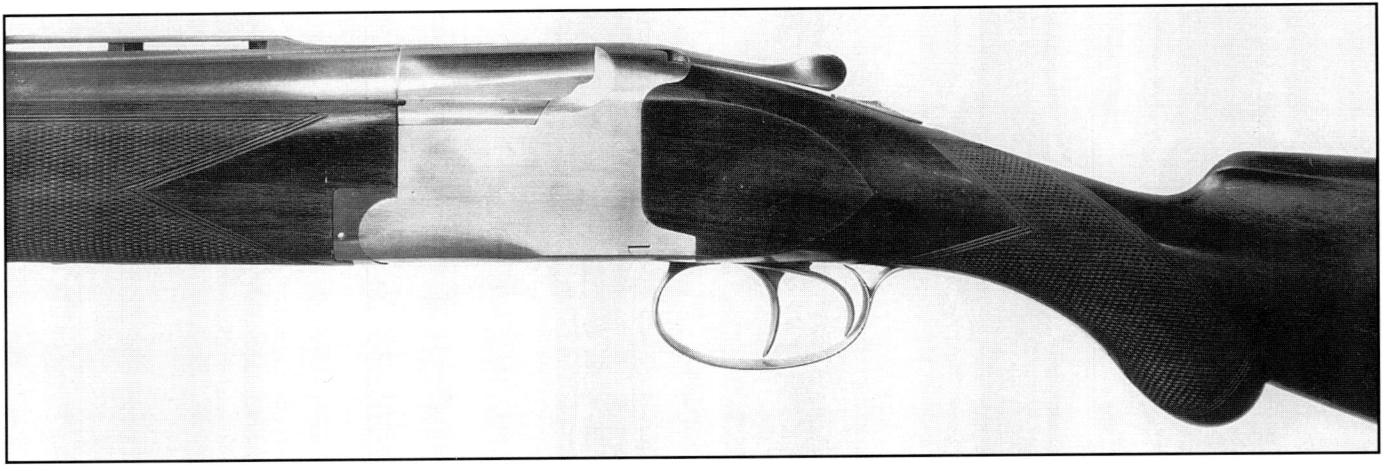

The left side of an early production Superposed receiver. Note how the top barrel is milled to a flat, almost triangular surface to achieve a better barrel to receiver fit. The photo also shows a small step about 2-3/4 inches from the breech end of the top barrel, an almost sure indication of a monobloc barrel construction. Courtesy Fabrique Nationale Archives.

Barrel lengths were available in 28, 30, and 32 inches with a raised matted rib furnished as standard. The customer had the choice of the following chokes in any combination: full, improved modified, modified, improved cylinder, and cylinder. Choke stampings were marked on the left side of the barrel in plain view, either spelled out or by symbols. It has been observed that on very early Superposed, especially those sold by FN, no choke markings of any kind are present. Browning prewar choke symbols are shown in the adjacent box.

Browning Choke Symbols	
Full Choke	*
Improved Modified	*-
Modified	**
Improved Cylinder	**-
Skeet	**$
Cylinder	***

An additional barrel option was offered: a ventilated rib. This particular feature was at the forefront of John M. Browning's mind when he conceptualized the Superposed. A ventilated rib that would guide the eye to the target was at the heart of his design. Browning's "Non-Crossfire" ventilated rib was designed to achieve these results and was offered as a $20.00 option. The Non-Crossfire ventilated rib is sloped downward near the breech end of the barrels so the eye will follow the sight line to the front bead without blurring or obscuring the target. Browning further claimed that the overall lines of the gun, coupled with the distinctiveness of the rib, would keep the eye to the correct plane. Browning Superposed barrels were rust blued because the top and side ribs were soft soldered with tin and could not take the high temperatures associated with hot salt bluing.[7]

[7] Browning Superposed barrels were of the "chopper lump" style. However, very early in production a few "monobloc" barrels were fitted, primarily on FN Superposed in the three digit serial number range. Some speculate that FN contracted outside for these barrels, or the possibility exists that FN and Browning had not yet decided which direction to take in its barrel construction. There was a precedent for this monobloc construction, as the prototype used this method for attaching its barrels together.

SIGHTING

THE speed and ease with which the Browning Non-Crossfire Ventilated Rib picks up its target is due not only to correct balance. The rib is shaped in accordance with a law of optics, which is well known, but which has been disregarded in shotgun designing.

If you will hold the point of a pencil close to the eye, it will blur. If the point is moved away from the eye, it becomes clear. This fact accounts for the position of the rear sight on rifles, which is always some inches in front of the eye. (The peep sight involves a different law of optics and is apart from present discussions.)

The Non-Crossfire Ventilated Rib of the Browning Superposed departs from ordinary methods of construction, in that it is cut from a solid strip of steel. The top and bottom members and the supporting parts are all of one piece.

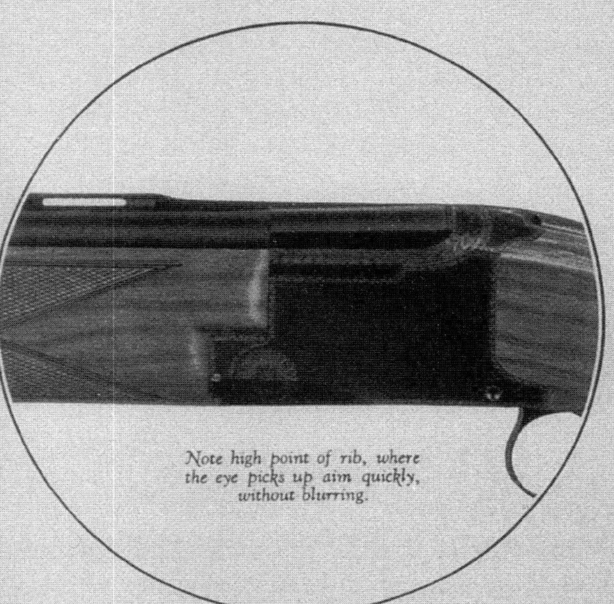

Note high point of rib, where the eye picks up aim quickly, without blurring.

The practice in shotgun designing has been to start the sight line at the rear end of the frame, practically against the eye. This casts a blur through which the eye must follow the line to the front bead, a blur which of necessity somewhat obscures the target itself.

The Superposed Non-Crossfire Ventilated Rib is sloped downward to the rear for some inches, so that the eye picks up the sight line and follows it to the front bead with a perfectly clear vision.

The distinctness of the sight line is still further intensified by the general shape of the gun. The smooth sides and the side depth of both frame and barrels throw the sighting plane of the rib into relief. The eye, instead of wandering to one side or the other of that plane, instinctively clings to it. The distinctness of the line automatically compels a correct positioning of the arm for aiming, *and is an infallible cure for cross-firing.* When one walks along a narrow ledge overhanging a precipice, one instinctively holds the eyes on the trail. The distinct sighting plane of the Superposed rib is like a narrow ledge, and the deep side lines are precipices on either side. Instinctively the eye clings to that plane.

It was the study and correlating of these factors by the master gunmaker which makes the Superposed seem possessed of eyes of its own, with which to pick up and center the flying target.

Numerous trapshooters have been observed when using the Browning Superposed at the traps, and it has been most gratifying to see every user almost invariably equal or surpass his average. This fact becomes all the more remarkable when it is considered that those users, on their own guns, had stocks of various dimensions, and yet, taking up the Superposed for the first time, with standard stock and fore-end, they attained the results noted. Their enthusiasm confirmed Mr. Browning's theories, and that enthusiasm is greeting the Superposed wherever it is exhibited.

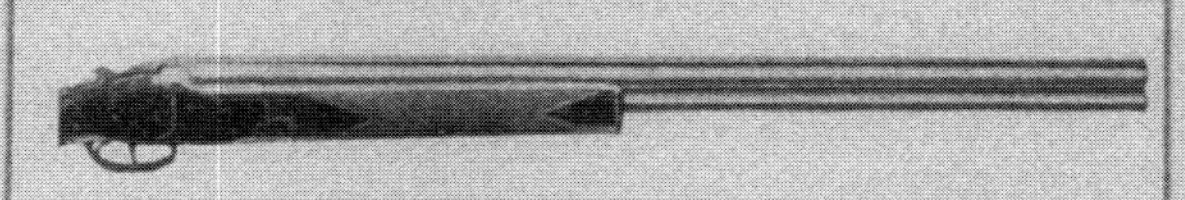

The hollow rib, standard equipment of the Browning Superposed, follows the usual design of level ribs and we refer to it in this book as a Level Hollow Rib.

Page Thirteen

One of John M. Browning's major conceptions for his over and under shotgun was a sighting plane that aided the shooter in sighting the gun. His Non-Crossfire ventilated rib was an integral part of his overall Superposed design. By placing the rib further away from the shooter's eye than was the usual custom, John Browning reasoned that the eye would more easily pick up the sight line.

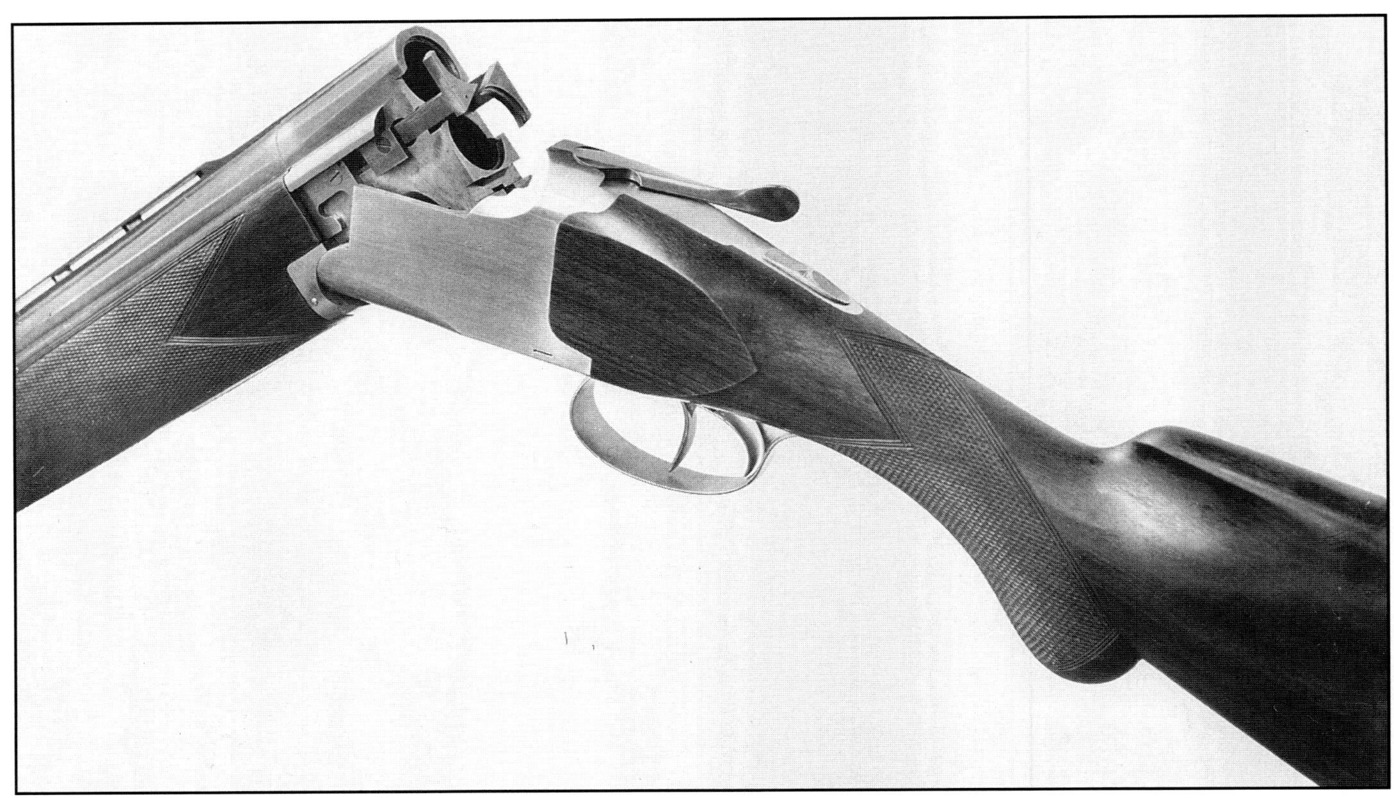

Another view of the left side of this early production Superposed with receiver open and ejectors extended. Courtesy Fabrique Nationale Archives.

Automatic ejectors were standard equipment of all Superposed grades and models. John M. Browning's ejector system was kept as simple as possible. Parts consisted of the ejectors, ejector springs, latches, and latch springs, and a trip rod for each latch. The movement of closing the gun compresses the ejector springs and latches the ejectors. The final action of breaking the gun open trips the latches and allows the ejectors to strike sharply against the ends of the extractors, throwing the shell clear. If only one barrel is fired, then only its respective ejector is released. Browning designed a large area so that nearly one half of the shell head is gripped by the ejectors. This feature prevents the possibility of a sticking shell due to extractors slipping past the shell rim. The entire ejector mechanism is attached to the forearm iron.

Barrel markings can tell a story of their own. The inscriptions, or barrel addresses, stamped on either side of the barrels were applied with a roll die engraved by hand and served to identify the seller and manufacturer. Very early Superposed barrels were stamped on the left side with the inscription:

BROWNING ARMS COMPANY OGDEN, UTAH
12 GA. SPECIAL STEEL

On the right side was the simple inscription:

MADE IN BELGIUM

These early markings indicate that these Superposed barrels were built prior to the decision to place the St. Louis address on them. There are, however, examples of both St. Louis and Ogden appearing in the same barrel address. Notice also that Fabrique Nationale's name is not inscribed on the barrels, another indication of an early address. As production increased, a new barrel marking was seen on the left side. It appears as follows:

BROWNING ARMS COMPANY ST. LOUIS, MO
12 GA. SPECIAL STEEL

This later barrel marking with the St. Louis address will be seen on the balance of prewar Superposed production. The left side of the barrel inscription will be seen in two different variations. The first, showing the two John M. Browning patent numbers, will be as follows:

MADE IN BELGIUM-BROWNING PATENTS
NO 1578638-1578639
FABRIQUE NATIONALE D'ARMES DE GUERRE-HERSTAL

BROWNING SINGLE TRIGGER MECHANISM

IS AVAILABLE IN 3 TYPES

for the

BROWNING SUPERPOSED

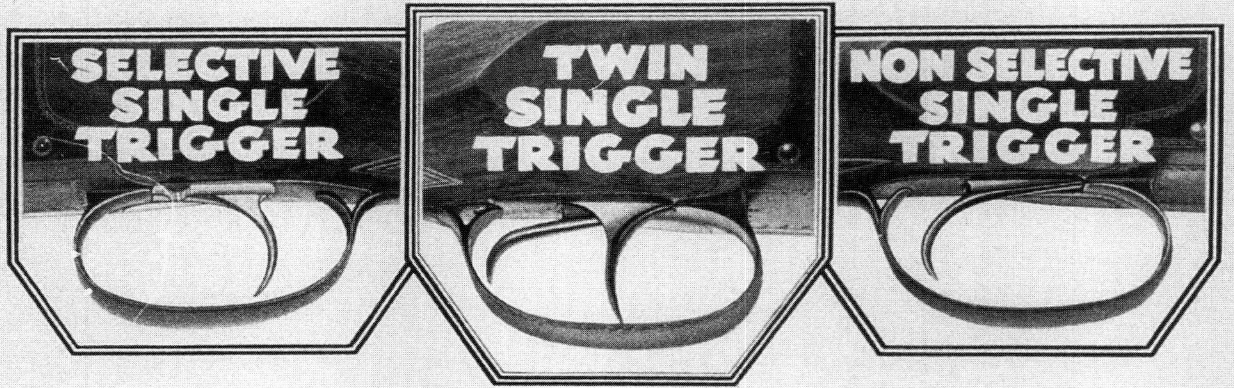

Whatever your choice might be, we can supply you. Every Browning Single Trigger is Perpetually Guaranteed. (See Guarantee on back.)

The Browning Selective Single Trigger

The Browning Selective Single Trigger is smooth and positive. The mechanism and principle of operation are the same as in the Twin-Single and Non-Selective Single. A conveniently located shift latch is provided, as illustrated above.

Unless otherwise specified, this trigger is mounted in midway position, that is, between the front and rear positions of ordinary double triggers.

On the back of this circular, you will find a cutaway view showing the Twin-Single mechanism and also a copy of the Perpetual Guarantee.

The Browning Twin-Single Trigger

The Browning Twin-Single Trigger is the most unique and useful advancement in two-barrel gun construction in years. Each trigger is a single trigger and remains in the same position for each pull. The rear trigger fires first the over barrel and then the under barrel. The front trigger fires first the under, then the over barrel. The triggers can be mounted to fire in reverse order, if desired. If an owner, after using a Browning Twin-Single Trigger, develops an exclusive preference for either trigger, the extra trigger may be removed and the slot filled with a blank.

The Browning Non-Selective Single Trigger

The Browning Non-Selective Single Trigger has the same mechanism as the Twin-Single with one of the triggers removed, and the slot filled with a neat blank especially designed for this purpose. The trigger can be mounted to fire either the over barrel or under barrel first, as desired. The trigger can be placed in midway or center position, if desired. The non-selective single trigger is usually preferred when both barrels are Full Choke.

Browning Single Triggers are positive and certain in action. Smooth, even pull. Cannot double; we learned through many experiments how to produce "doubling" and then found a way to prevent it. The trigger remains in the same position for each pull.

Browning gave its customers a choice of four different trigger mechanisms. Other than the traditional double trigger, Browning offered three single trigger mechanisms: the single selective trigger (note the selector located at the trigger root, which indicates an early pre-1938 design), a single nonselective trigger, and the Twin-Single trigger.

Gus Becker function testing his Superposed inertia trigger against an automobile tire. The gun he is using is the same one that appears on the cover of Browning's 1931 catalogue and appears to be a Pigeon Grade with a beavertail forearm. Courtesy Browning Firearms Museum, Union Station, Ogden, Utah.

The second variation, which will be seen on later Superposed, will appear as follows:

MADE IN BELGIUM-BROWNING PATENTS
NO 1578638-1578639
OTHER PATENTS APPLIED FOR

This second variation indicates that other patents had been applied for, namely Val Browning's two trigger patents which would place this inscription on barrels produced sometime after 1935.

A number of different triggers were offered during this period. The Superposed was sold with double triggers as standard equipment. Three additional trigger options were offered. The first was a single selective trigger with the barrel selection latch located at the root of the trigger. The second trigger option, the Twin-Single trigger, was the big news with its unique design and foolproof doubling feature. In essence, this Val Browning design trigger offered two nonselective single triggers on the same gun. The third option was a single nonselective trigger which was simply the Twin-Single system with one of the triggers removed. This single nonselective trigger could be set to fire either the top or bottom barrel first at the buyer's discretion. The anti-doubling feature of the Superposed triggers was one of Browning's biggest selling features. These early single triggers were set by the inertia of the recoil and were not inclined to double. The Browning Company was so certain of its claims that it offered the following guarantee:

• PERPETUAL GUARANTEE •

Our confidence in the durability of the Browning Twin-Single Trigger, the Browning Non-Selective Single Trigger and the Browning Selective Single Trigger is such, that we offer, without reservation, to furnish without charge any new part that may ever be needed.

BROWNING ARMS COMPANY-St. Louis, Missouri

The tang and frame were one solid piece of drop forged construction. This arrangement allowed the trigger mechanism to be built into the frame so as

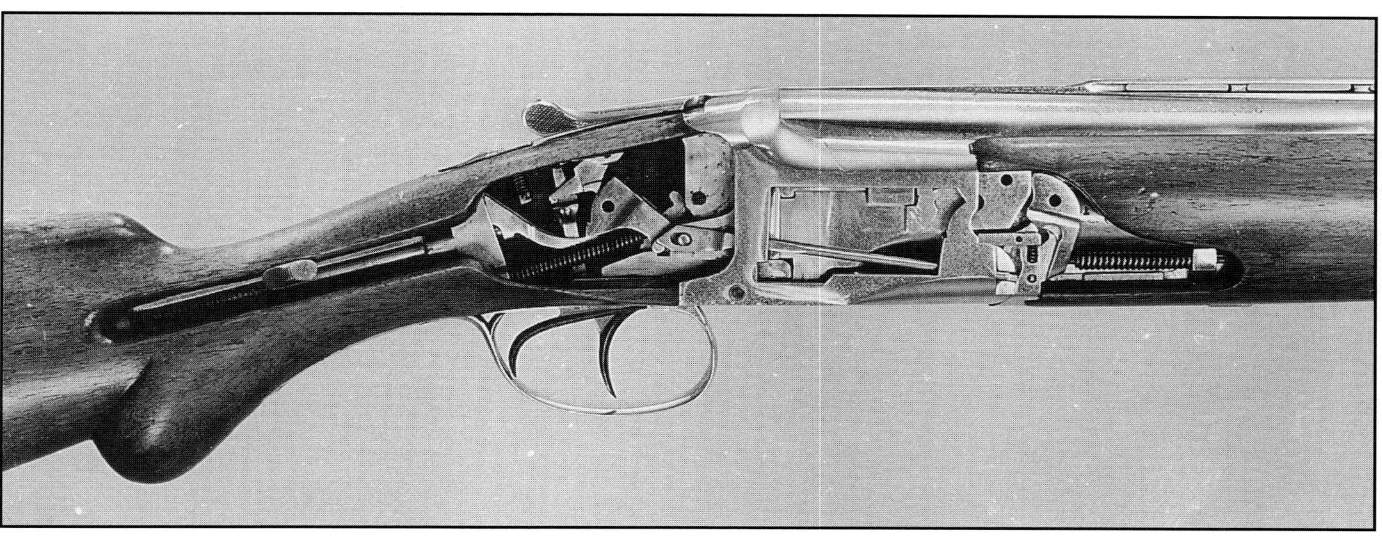

This is an early cutaway of the Superposed used by FN to teach its gunsmiths how to assemble and fit the gun. This particular example, serial number 1468, was a double trigger model with Non-Crossfire ventilated rib. The model is well finished, including full chrome plated parts and barrels. An interesting feature of this Superposed is the length of its barrels—sixteen inches. Courtesy Liège Arms Museum.

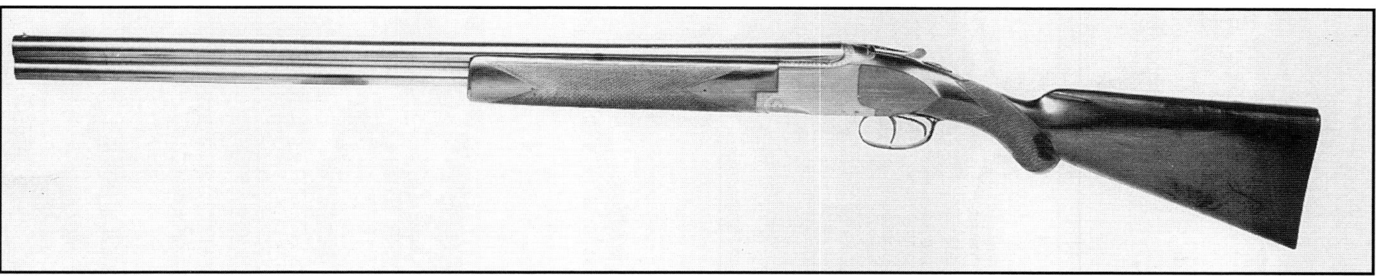

A beautiful example of an early production Grade I Superposed with plain barrel. The majority of prewar Superposed were of this type. Courtesy Fabrique Nationale Archives.

to become integral with it. The frame had deep side walls and large bearing surfaces to provide longer wear and prevent the gun from shooting loose. The forearm had a unique takedown feature that permitted the forearm and barrel to remain together. An oversize hinge pin and locking bolt lug gave considerable strength in anchoring these lugs to the bottom of the frame. The stock was secured to the frame with a bolt fitted with a lock screw. The frame and its component parts were hot water blued. An interesting side note is that FN kept this bluing formula secret throughout the entire production period.

The buttstock and forearm were crafted from European walnut with a French polish finish (a mixture of shellac and oil varnish applied by hand). Checkering on the half pistol grip was done by hand and was about twenty lines to the inch. Customers could special order a stock to their own dimensions for an additional charge of $15.65. When utilizing this option, the customer also had the choice of selecting his special buttstock with a straight grip, half pistol grip, or full pistol grip at no extra charge.

One of the unique features of the Superposed was its forearm. At the time of the Superposed introduction, forearms on over and under guns were often three-piece affairs that required a certain amount of dexterity when mounting or dismounting the gun. The three-piece forearm also required further expert fitting and additional joints. The Superposed forearm could be detached if needed, but at all other times remained attached to the barrels. In mounting or dismounting the gun, only two parts were held. A latch unlocked the forearm, allowing it to slide about three quarters of an inch forward on the barrels, at which point it permitted the barrels to be separated from the frame. The forearm then slipped back in place, the latch was snapped down, and the two parts of the gun were ready for the case. The forearm that was supplied as standard had a squared-off appearance at the end, but had straight, slim sides. It was held in place at the front of the forearm with a horseshoe-looking affair

An early example of a Browning Superposed advertising pamphlet printed by Fabrique Nationale for its English-speaking markets, namely Great Britain and Canada. Note the Art Deco style so popular in the 1930s.

is bringing out a new weapon contrived by **BROWNING** Browning's inventive genius combined with F.N. 's manufacturing possibilities has, in the course of the thirty-five years past, produced firearms of various models, every one of which, has taken the world leadership.

No doubt this supremacy will also be granted to the " Superposed Browning ,, shotgun. In fact, this new gun has all other Browning arms peculiarities, namely Browning's simple and sturdy design and F.N. 's superior workmanship; it will certainly enable expert shooters to improve their score and beginners to gain great skill rapidly.

AN F.N. PRODUCT
CONTRIVED BY BROWNING

SUPERPOSED BROWNING 12 GAUGE WITH EJECTORS

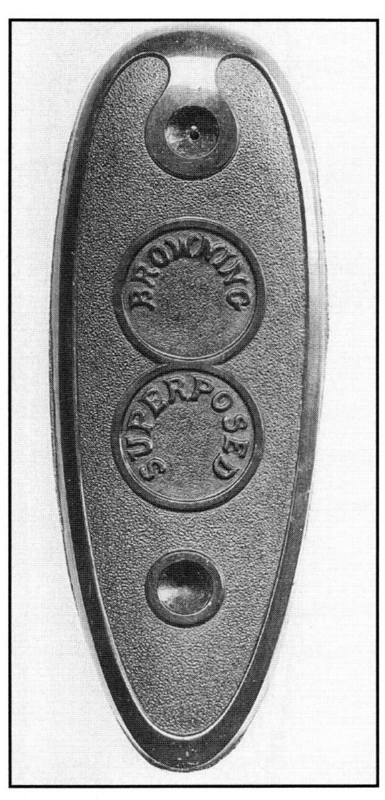

An example of the prewar and early postwar horn buttplate used on the Browning Superposed as standard. Courtesy Fabrique Nationale Archives.

called a forearm cap. The rear was re-enforced by its conjunction with the forearm iron and the frame. A beavertail forearm was available on special order for an additional $20.00 for the Grade I. This early Superposed beavertail was pear shaped with an almost flat bottom. The shape was designed to give a more hand-filling grip, which was preferred by Trap shooters. Another shape of forearm was offered on these early Superposed from 1932 to 1935. This "Light Weight" forearm was the forerunner of the Lightning model and was thinner and shorter than that offered on the basic Trap and Long Range Field guns. This, combined with reducing the heaviness of the buttstock, helped to reduce the weight of the gun to about 6-3/4 pounds.

The buttplate was made from horn and had a double ring design with the name "BROWNING ARMS COMPANY" stamped on the plate. Various brands of recoil pads, such as Noshoc, Hawkins, Jostam, D & W, and Black Diamond, were offered at an additional charge.

Prewar Engraving

From the very beginning, the Superposed was available in four grades: Grade I with no engraving of any kind until 1938, Pigeon Grade, Diana Grade, and Midas Grade. These early guns were engraved at Fabrique Nationale under the direction of master engraver Felix Funken. Funken was instrumental in establishing FN's engraving school and in designing the early engraving patterns used on the Superposed. Born in 1888 in Liège, Felix Funken became a student of engraving at the Fine Arts Academy at the early age of fourteen. He worked in the engraving shop of Mr. Deglain, who required the young Funken to complete pencil sketches of his designs before being allowed to actually work on firearms. After World War I, Funken worked as an independent engraver. In 1926, management at FN decided to bring all aspects of production under one roof. That meant en-

The only known photograph of Felix Funken's first group of students at the newly created Fabrique Nationale engraving school. This photo shows ten or eleven students engraving under the supervision of Felix Funken, shown in the rear left of the picture. The photo is dated September 1, 1927, in Funken's own hand and is from his personal diary. Note the brick floors and antiquated lighting. Courtesy Liège Arms Museum.

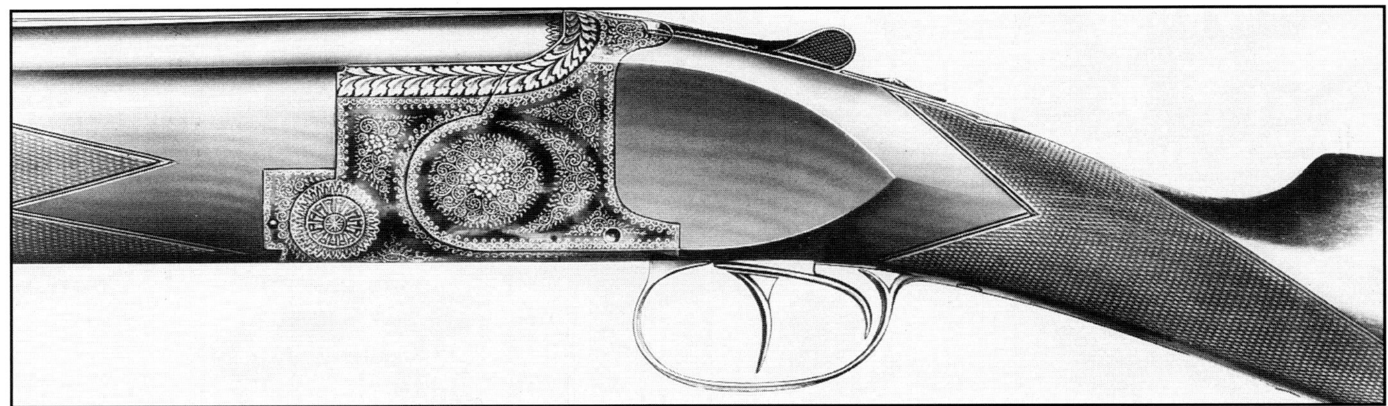

A very early (circa 1931) example of an FN Browning Superposed in either a B1 Grade (if the receiver has a gray finish), or a C1 Grade (if the receiver is case colored). Notice the sculptured frame, a distinctive European characteristic on FN Superposed. Notice, too, the straight grip stock, an uncommon prewar option on American sold Superposed but more common around the rest of the world. Courtesy Fabrique Nationale Archives.

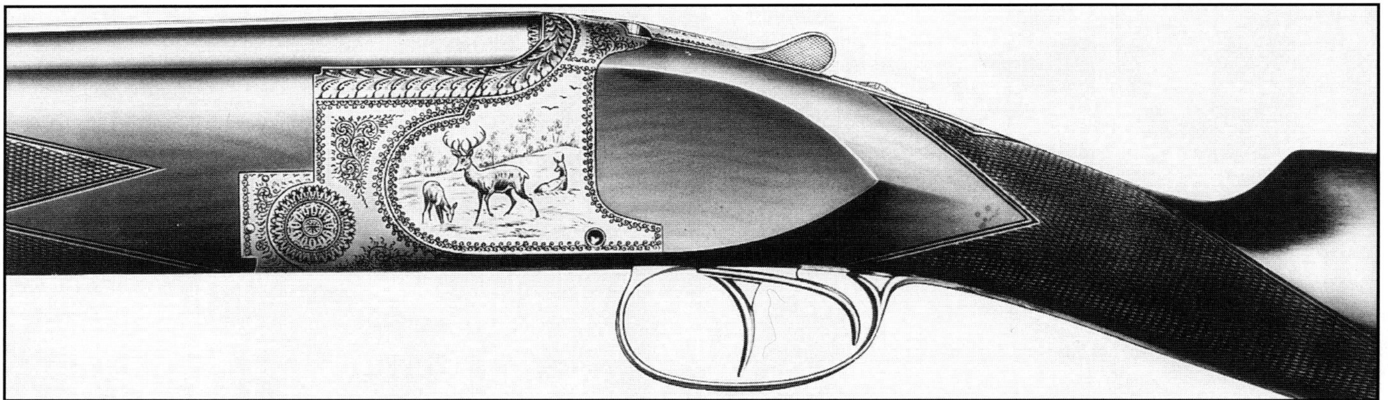

Another very early example of a Browning Superposed intended for Fabrique Nationale's world markets. This grade is similar to FN's C2 Grade and bears some resemblance to the American Diana Grade in terms of subject matter. Notice, also, the sculptured frame and straight grip stock. Courtesy Fabrique Nationale Archives.

graving, which had previously been contracted to engravers outside the factory, was now brought into the plant.[8] Felix Funken was chosen to head Fabrique Nationale's engraving department over the Liège master, Hyppolite Corombelle. The selection of Felix Funken was to prove an important one due to his impact on FN's engraving patterns and the establishment of an apprenticeship program for fledging engravers in the factory. No longer would FN be required to rely on outside contractors for its engraving needs, but, thanks to Felix Funken, would have a highly qualified supply of resident artisans. He started with six engravers from the Liège area—men such as Joseph Gerard and Sylvain Dorval—and at the same time established his factory school.

By 1930 the school had about two dozen students. They were required to have letters of recommendation, and entry was by invitation only. Funken was a perfectionist and demanded the same from his students. He also possessed a mercurial personality and was well-known for his explosive temper, which was sometimes sparked for no apparent reason. As a result of Funken's disposition, the atmosphere in the engraving section was somewhat chaotic, highly charged, and filled with petty politics—all to gain the favor of the master. The school was located in the engraving department of the factory where Funken acted as the primary teacher. Students, also referred to as apprentices, were obligated to draw lines freehand day in and day out until the master was satisfied that his pupil could move on to the next level of difficulty. All of

[8] Col. W. R. Betz, "Felix Funken: Master Engraver of Liège." *American Rifleman*, April 1983, p. 32.

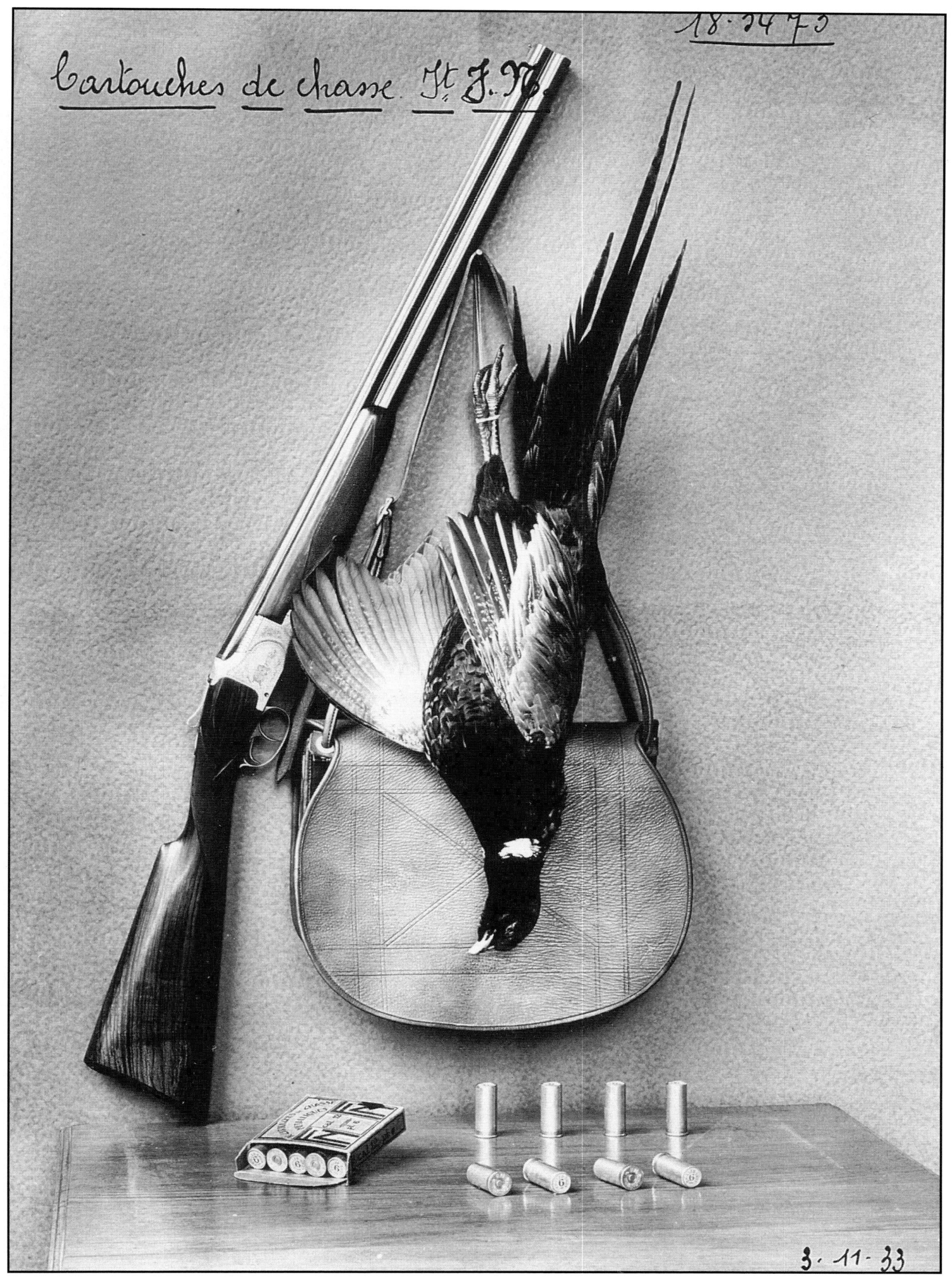

This is one of the first commercial sales photos, dated November 3, 1933, of the Browning Superposed taken at Fabrique Nationale for use in sales campaigns in FN's world markets. The Superposed is an engraved model featuring wild boars on a sculptured receiver, a very European theme. The shotgun shells are FN's Leggia brand in No. 6 shot. Courtesy Fabrique Nationale Archives.

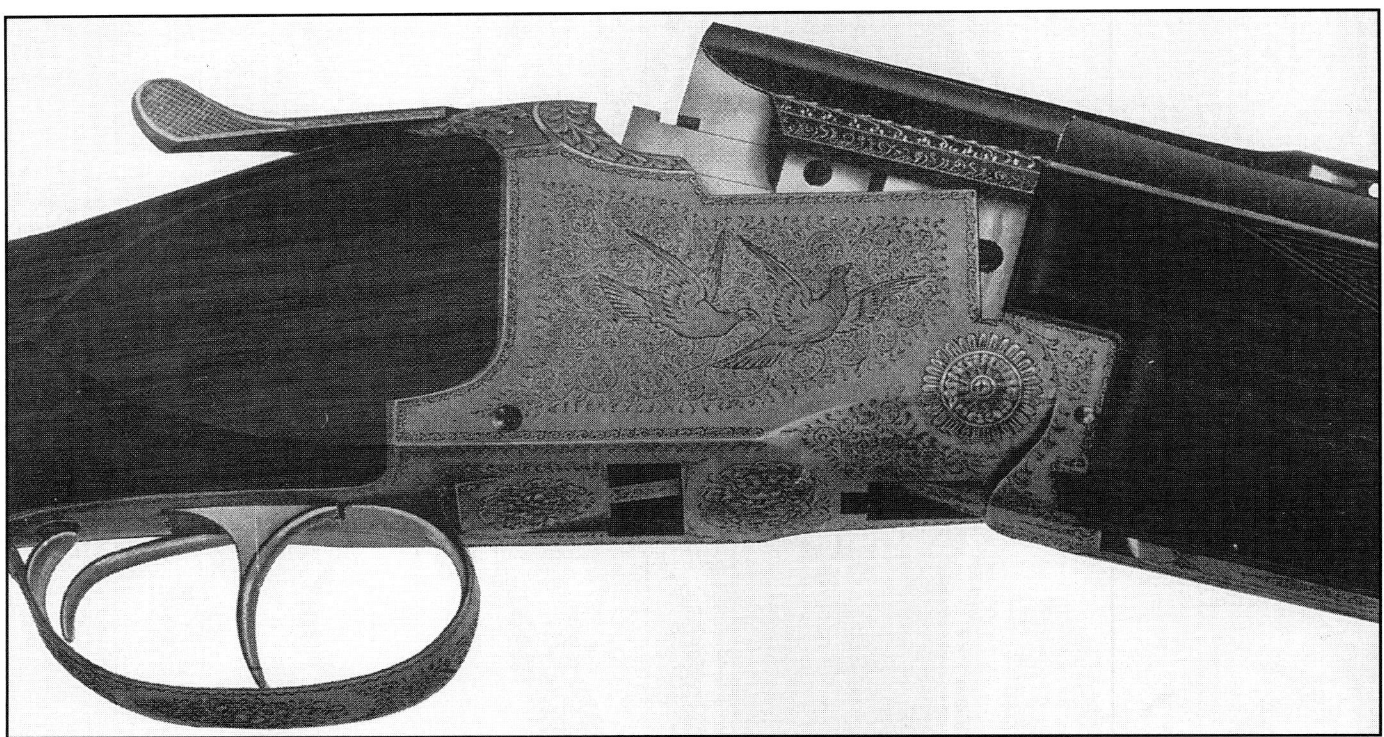

An excellent illustration of a prewar Superposed Pigeon Grade. Courtesy Fabrique Nationale Archives.

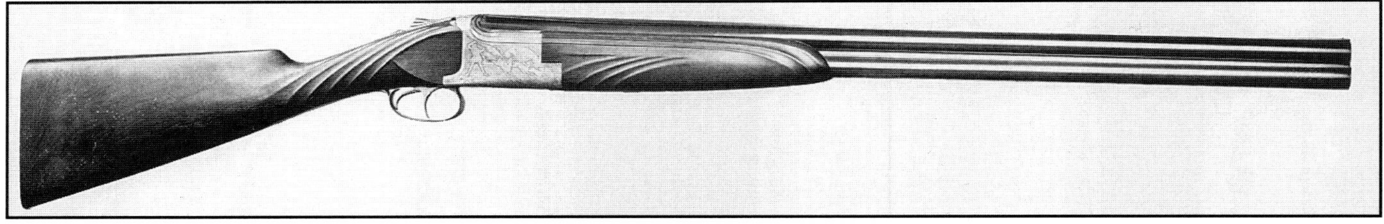

This Superposed was designed and engraved by Felix Funken for the 1937 World's Fair in Paris. It has a uniquely carved stock, most likely executed by Richard Gerard. The gun was awarded an off competition prize by the Belgian government. The Superposed also won a similar prize at the 1939-1940 exhibition in New York, where it remained for many years. This Browning Superposed was another example of Funken's superb skills. It is on display at the Liège Arms Museum. Courtesy Fabrique Nationale Archives.

the drawing was done in pencil. After about one year of intense instruction, students were given steel flats on which to practice their lines and designs. Again Funken would accept nothing less than perfection. Students were also required to attend classes at the Fine Arts Academy. Their courses of study included anatomy, sculpture, perspective, and drawing. The students attended classes at night from 5:30 to 9:00 at FN's expense. These series of lessons, both formal and informal, went on for about three years. At the end of this period, these inexperienced engravers were given parts of guns to engrave, usually trigger guards and small parts that were not considered critical.[9]

New engravers started on the Auto-5 shotgun, which they referred to as the "*mecana.*" They could expect to be engraving scrollwork on the frames and borders of the Grade I Superposed, or "*sarma,*" as that model was called in the engraving shop, after several years of experience.[10] As the years went by and their skills improved, engravers moved on to the more difficult grades, from the Pigeon Grade

---

[9] Personal interview with Angelo Bee, June 30, 1994.

[10] The French word "*sarma*" is derived from a former Liège department store called "*Sarma,*" a store known for its inexpensive goods priced within range of the working man. The Grade I Superposed was referred to in this way to denote its affordability and its status as the lowest priced Superposed.

on through the Midas. All engraving work was done on a piecework basis and engravers were paid only for the work they completed. The rate of pay was determined by the average time it took to perform a specific engraving pattern. This average time was known in the shop as the "taxation," or the officially established time it took to engrave any given grade. Engravers who were slower than average made less money than those who were faster. Frequently, several engravers worked on one Superposed in various stages. For example, one engraver might do only the scrollwork on the sides of the frame while a second engraver would engrave the top of the frame and the trigger guard. A third engraver might only do the birds or animals in a particular scene. In any case, most of these prewar Superposed high grades were stamped with Felix Funken's name, as was the custom in Europe.[11]

Funken was also responsible for designing the patterns that were used on the various grades of the Superposed, including those sold by FN as well as those imported into the United States for sale by Browning. These patterns represent a heavy German influence. When introduced into the American market in 1931, the Grade I had a plain unengraved frame except for chased fillets cut into the top portion of the frame next to the upper barrel. This unadorned version of the Grade I was modified in 1938 to include a sparse but tastefully executed scroll in the center of both sides of the frame.

The Pigeon Grade was done on a rich gray frame, sometimes referred to as a "French gray" finish. This gray background highlighted the fine scrollwork and gave the superficial appearance of relief. The frame, trigger guard, and top lever were engraved with fine line engraving. Oak leaves were carved in relief on the top curve of the frame. Two large pigeons were engraved on both sides of the frame. Traditional designs and borders surrounded the birds, cover joints, screws, and pins. The Pigeon Grade was stocked with a choice French walnut with some grain and was finely hand checkered. All parts were polished by hand. When it was introduced into the U.S. market in 1931, the Pigeon Grade sold for a retail price of $175.00.

The Diana Grade was the next highest Superposed engraving pattern. Its retail price was $277.00 in 1931. This grade was named for Diana, the Roman goddess of the forests and animals, and the game scenes that were engraved were based on that concept. Deer were shown on one side of the frame with wild boars on the other. Hills and forests cut in fine lines provided the background. Oak leaves were cut in relief on the curve of the standing breech. Although this was the standard scene for this grade, the customer could special order the more traditional dog and bird game scenes. Like the Pigeon Grade, the Diana Grade frame was also done in a rich gray finish. Stocks were built from select European walnut with good grain and figure. All parts were hand polished, and the firing pins, ejector hammers, latches, and trip rods were gold plated.

The Midas Grade was Browning's highest production grade Superposed. FN gave the task of designing and executing this pattern to Felix Funken despite the time and expense. On each side of the blued frame a gold pigeon with spreading wings was rendered in relief. The same subject matter was executed on the bottom of the frame as well. Heavy lines of gold work formed a traditional foliage and geometric design around the birds. The trigger guard and top lever were also covered in gold line execution. A small amount of gold line coverage was seen for a short distance on the top barrel. Stocks, checkering patterns, metal polishing, and bluing were of the same high quality as the Diana Grade. Firing pins, ejector hammers, latches, and trip rods were gold plated. The customer could have a special dimension stock built at no additional charge. The retail price for the Midas Grade in 1931 was $374.00.

---

[11] The practice of signing or stamping engraving pieces was done in the tradition of the old German custom of marking work completed under the leading engraving contractor. This was the routine followed during Felix Funken's term as leading contractor. Thus, depending on who the leading contractor was, an engraved Browning may have been signed by the engraver who actually did the work, or marked by the contractor under whom it was done. Because of these circumstances, it is very difficult to determine who engraved a specific Superposed during the prewar era. It appears the fine art world has encountered the same difficulties. At the beginning of the twentieth century, Rembrandt was credited with over 1,000 paintings. By the end of this century he will have painted only 250 canvasses. An ongoing study of the Dutch master has brought to light the practice of his students and apprentices signing Rembrandt's name to their work with the knowledge and consent of the master himself. The result is a number of paintings previously regarded as genuine Rembrandts that are now being disputed by art experts as to the correct attribution. If art experts have this much difficulty with Rembrandt, then one can imagine the complications facing those who wish to authenticate Browning prewar engraving. Peter Plagens, "Real Deal Rembrandt" *Newsweek,* September 30, 1991, pp. 50-52.

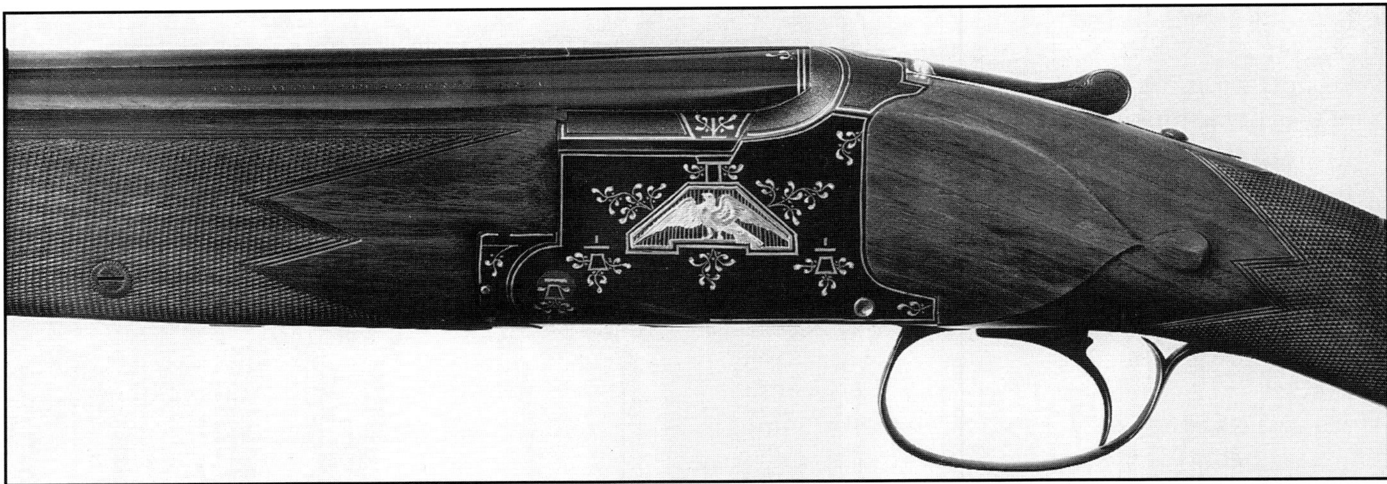

The left side of a Browning Superposed engraved in the Midas Grade pattern. The inlay was done in yellow gold. Courtesy Fabrique Nationale Archives.

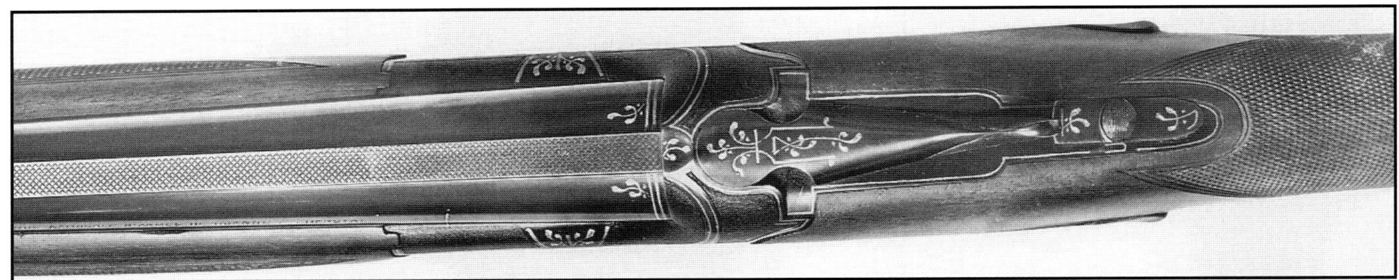

A top view of the Superposed Midas Grade. Note the fine gold wire work on the top lever, the safety/barrel selector switch, and the top barrel breech. Notice, too, that the checkering on the grip folds over the top of the grip, a high grade feature. Courtesy Fabrique Nationale Archives.

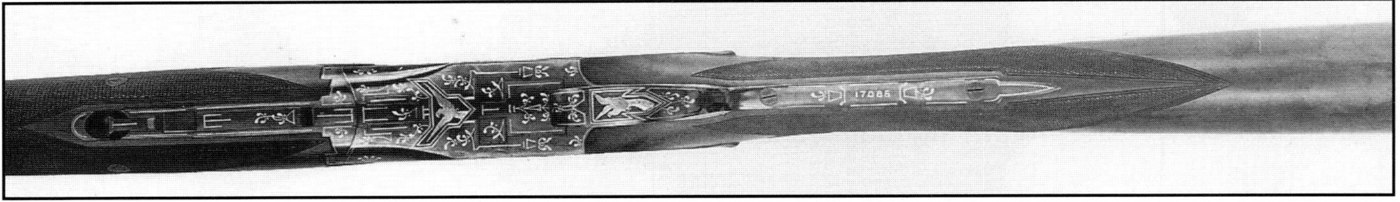

A bottom view of this Midas Grade reveals more fine line gold wire work from forearm release latch to bottom tang. Even the serial number, 17086, is gold inlaid. The view also shows the Midas Grade checkering pattern from underneath. A special order gold initial plate is inlaid near the heal of the buttstock. Courtesy Fabrique Nationale Archives.

An overall view from the left side of the Midas Grade. The gun is fitted with a matte rib and a Lightning style forearm, with single selective trigger and straight grip stock. FN shipping records reveal that this particular Midas Grade was shipped to Ethiopia on June 27, 1947. Perhaps this Superposed was ordered for Emperor Haile Selassie. Courtesy Fabrique Nationale Archives.

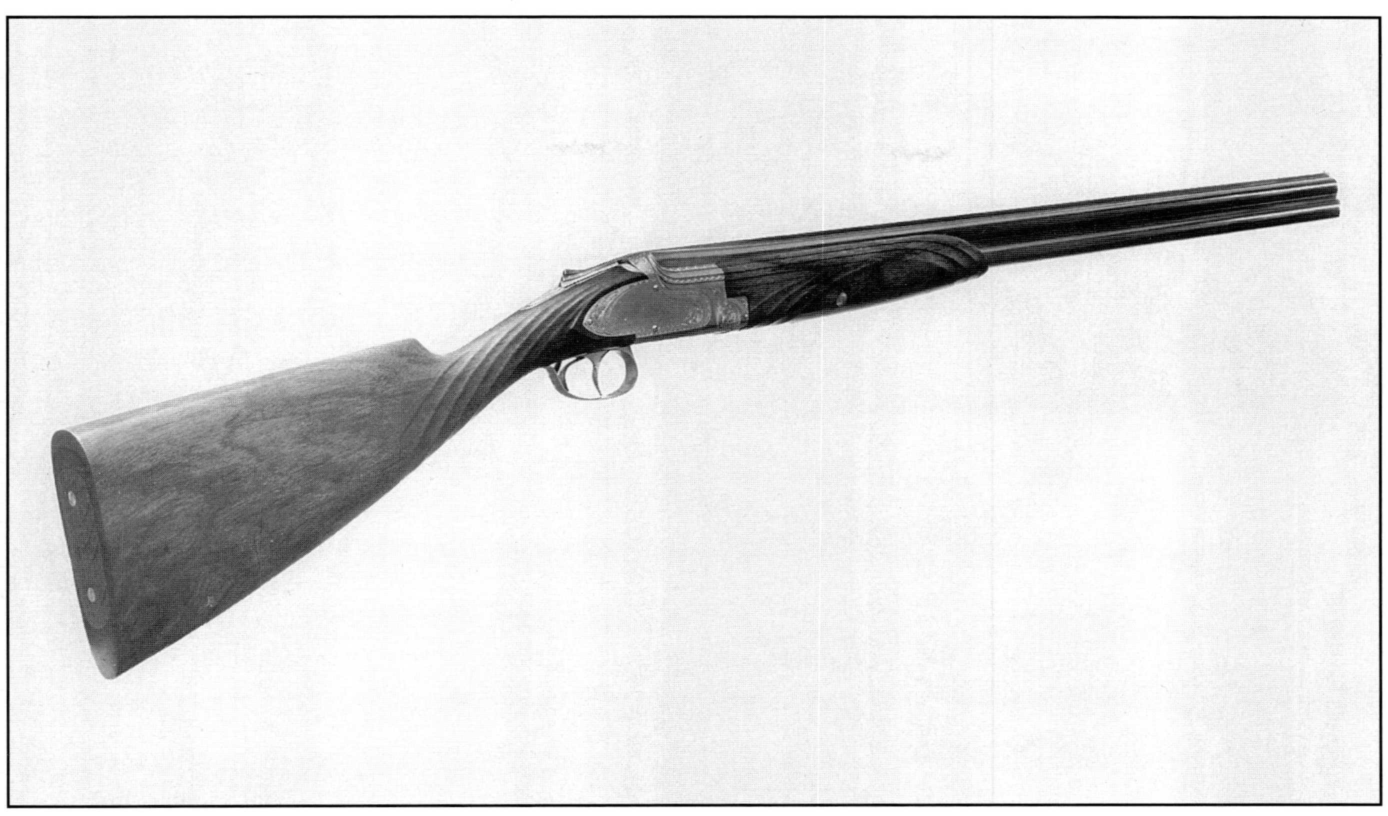

This unique Browning Superposed was engraved by Felix Funken and the stock was carved by Richard Gerard for the Exposition de l'Eau in Liège in 1939. This was a most unusual Superposed, from its sculpted top lever to the unusual stock carving. Funken was a true master of design. The gun is now on display at the Liège Arms Museum. Courtesy Fabrique Nationale Archives.

From the very beginning of production, the Browning Superposed was available with custom engraving patterns. Funken was responsible for engraving several unique Superposed, including one for the Paris World Exhibition in 1937. He also engraved a special Superposed for the *Exposition de l'Eau at Liège* in 1939. Perhaps what set Funken apart from being just an outstanding engraver was his wide range of ability in all engraving styles. Funken's influence on FN engraving patterns, FN engravers, and the whole genre of FN engraving was to be his enduring legacy.

The Superposed: 1935-1940

The last half of the 1930s witnessed some significant changes to Browning's Superposed catalogue offerings. In part this may have been a result of a change in top management. In 1935, after fifteen years in Belgium, Val Browning returned to Ogden to assume the presidency of the company. Times had been difficult for the firearms industry because of the Great Depression, and the economy showed no signs of improvement. In 1934 the price of the Grade I Superposed was reduced from $107.50 to $99.50, but all other grades remained at their initial price levels. In 1935 the Grade I was again reduced in price from $99.50 to $69.75, a thirty percent reduction. The other high grades were lowered in price as well: the Pigeon Grade from $175.00 to $125.00, the Diana Grade from $277.00 to $175.00, and the Midas Grade from $374.00 to $250.00.

These price reductions were undertaken to help sales and attract new customers away from the more established American manufacturers. When Val Browning succeeded to the presidency he wanted to keep sales on an even keel. Not only was the Depression having an adverse effect on sales, but FN was having difficulty keeping pace with its production schedules. In part, the difficulty lay with the stark realities of the worldwide depression. In June of 1929, the FN plant at Herstal employed 9,138 people. In May of 1934, the number of employees had been reduced to 2,580. One single factor was to plague FN throughout the entire Superposed production period—the company almost always had problems fulfilling its orders to Browning. Despite these difficulties, Val Browning was

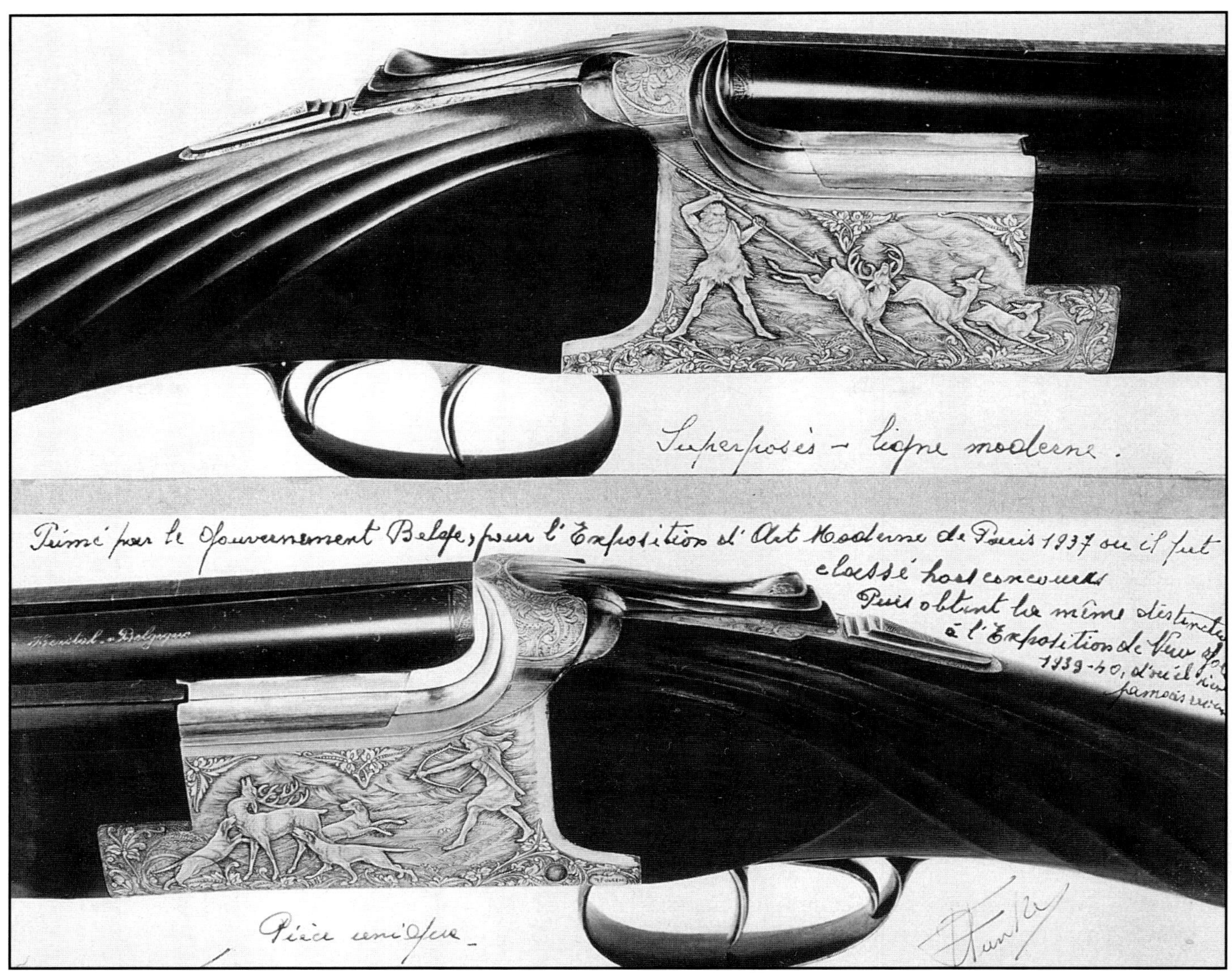

Both the left and right side of the Paris World's Fair Browning Superposed disclose a primeval subject matter that is incorporated into the Art Deco composition that was so popular in that period. The result is a graceful yet powerful effect. The personal comments are in Funken's hand and are part of his personal diary. Courtesy Liège Arms Museum.

pleased with the level of Superposed sales during these early years.[12]

In 1936, with sales apparently stabilized, prices were increased to a level where they remained throughout the balance of the prewar years. The Standard Grade I retailed for $79.80 until 1940 when production ceased, the new Lightning model sold for $75.80 until 1940 when its price was increased to $89.90, the Pigeon Grade was priced at $143.00, the Diana Grade price was increased to $200.00, and the Midas Grade was offered at $285.00.

The catalogue offerings were expanded beginning in 1936 with the addition of the new "Lightning" model. Introduced at $4.00 less than the Standard model, this new model featured a plain concave matted rib which was simply a striped matting on the top of the barrel. Browning placed a stripe down the center of the matting to assist the eye in lining up the barrel with the target. The gun was also equipped with a new thinner "full grip" forearm that had a more rounded nose than that of the Standard forearm. This Lightning forearm had been used before on earlier "Light Weight" models. The new model came standard with Twin-Single triggers and a choice of barrel lengths from 26 inches to 28 inches. The Lightning model weighed

[12] Val A. Browning, letter to the author, August 15, 1993.

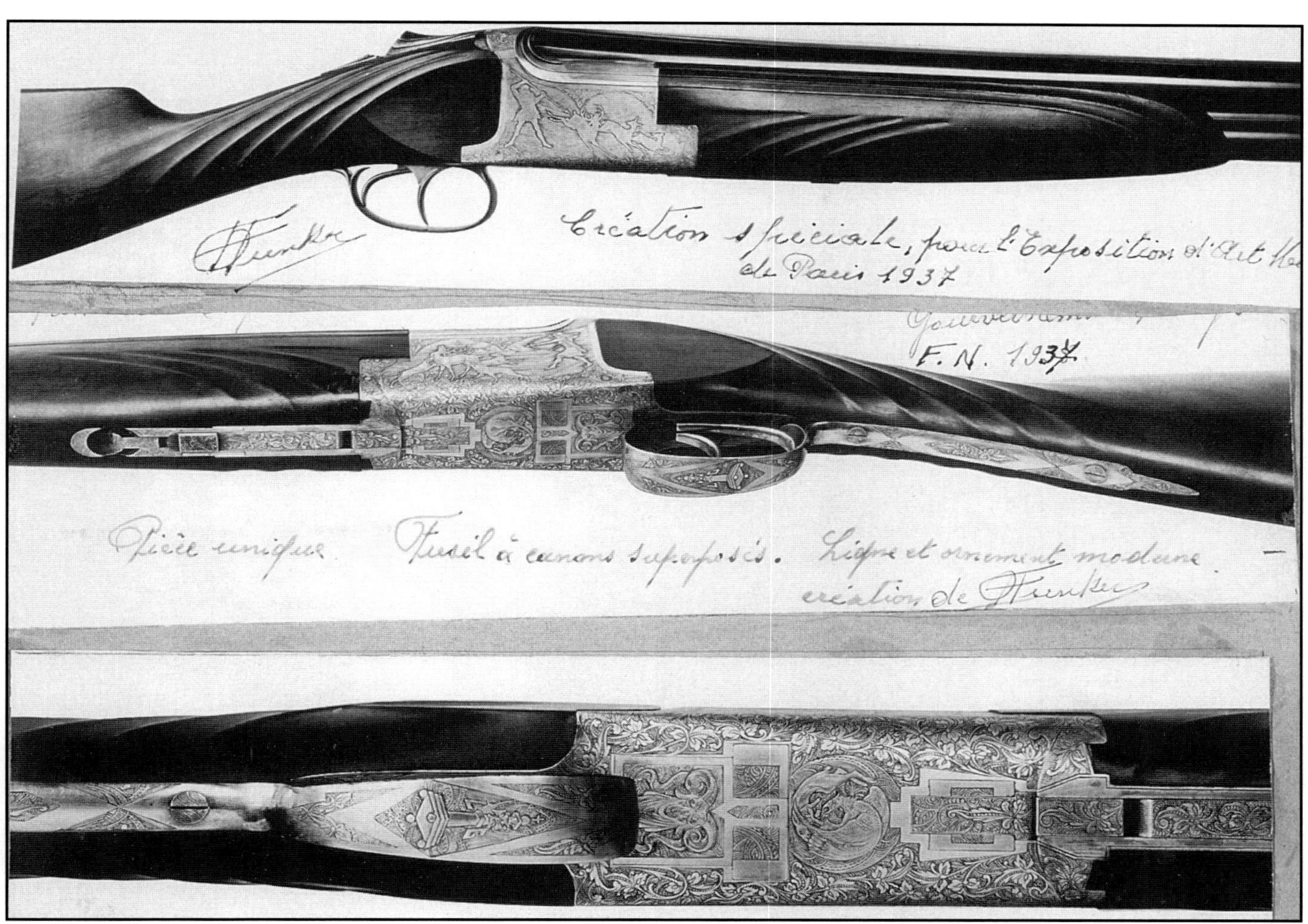

Other views of the Paris Browning Superposed, taken from Funken's personal diary. Courtesy Liège Arms Museum.

BROWNING SUPERPOSED RETAIL PRICES, U.S.A.
1931-1940

Year	Grade I Standard	Grade I Lightning	Pigeon Grade	Diana Grade	Midas Grade
1931	$107.50	N/A	$175.00	$277.00	$374.00
1932	$107.50	N/A	$175.00	$277.00	$374.00
1933	$107.50	N/A	$175.00	$277.00	$374.00
1934	$99.50	N/A	$175.00	$277.00	$374.00
1935	$69.75	N/A	$125.00	$175.00	$250.00
1936	$79.80	$75.80	$143.00	$200.00	$285.00
1937	$79.80	$75.80	$143.00	$200.00	$285.00
1938	$79.80	$75.80	$143.00	$200.00	$285.00
1939	$79.80	$75.80	$143.00	$200.00	$285.00
1940	$79.80	$89.90	$143.00	$200.00	$285.00

Table 1-1

New "Lightning" Model

(Light Weight, about 6¾ pounds)

BROWNING OVERUNDER

The Fastest Handling All-Purpose Two-Barrel Gun

For Field and Skeet Shooting

The new "Lightning" Model Browning Overunder without rib has a single striped matted sighting plane. Because of its light weight and perfect balance it swings, points and shoots with lightning speed and accuracy. It is a counterpart of the well-known Standard Model (see pages 8 and 9), but weighs less.

All hand fitted and all hand finished. It has the same built-in exclusive features of strength, convenience, durability and performance that experience has proven to be so satisfactory in the Standard Model Browning Overunder (see pages 12 and 13) which, within a very few years, has become one of the most popular Shotguns in the World and has earned the title, "The Choice of Champions."

12-Gauge Only

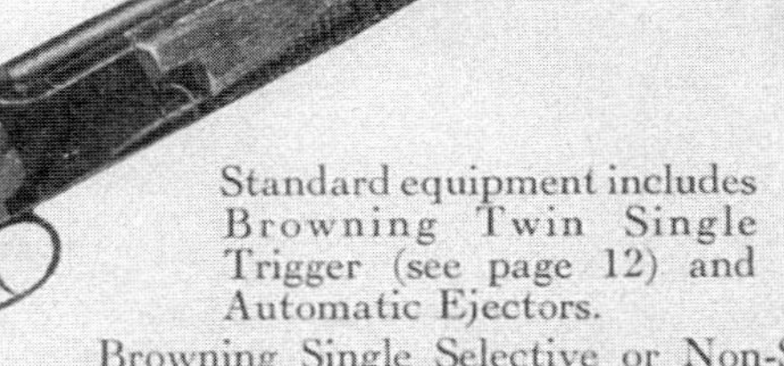

STRIPED MATTED BARREL

Standard equipment includes Browning Twin Single Trigger (see page 12) and Automatic Ejectors.

Browning Single Selective or Non-Selective Trigger available at additional charge.

ILLUSTRATION T

The gun shown in the above illustration is without rib but has striped matting on the barrel. This type of matting has been especially designed for the shooter who does not prefer a ribbed barrel but wants weight reduced to a minimum. Note the new feature of matting the barrel which leaves a stripe through the center of the matting. This new novel feature instantly lines up sight with target.

As in the popular Standard Model Browning Overunder, notwithstanding the lighter weight, the new "Lightning" Model has the center of gravity so placed that the gun is "lightning-fast." A "slow" gun can easily spoil a day in the field. But when the hunter owns a Lightning Model Browning Overunder with its superior pointing and handling qualities he enjoys the satisfaction of knowing that his gun may be depended upon to do its part. Ease of handling, speed in swinging, accurate pointing, automatic ejection, instantaneous selectibility of Browning Twin Single Trigger—features found in this fast handling light weight patented Browning Overunder—all contribute to better shooting and afford advantages and satisfaction obtainable only in the Genuine Browning.

The Browning Overunder combines the advantages claimed for single and double barrel guns—plus additional advantages. Guns designed by Browning have always been famous for strength and simplicity. These same basic principles coupled with ingenious Browning designing have developed this gun which is gaining such widespread popularity. The large number of enthusiastic shooters using the Browning is evidence of its merit and worth. No better gun nor greater gun value can be obtained today.

For complete specifications of the "Lightning" Model see next page—18.

The new Air-Plane Sight, available at an extra charge, aids the shooter to instantly line up sight with target.

See Page 18—For "Lightning" Model With Concave Matted or Ventilated Ribs

17

This page, taken from Browning's No. 53 catalogue, shows the new "Lightning" model. It was fitted with a slightly smaller forearm and lightened buttstock. There was about a half pound difference in weight between the "Standard" Browning Superposed and the new Lightning model.

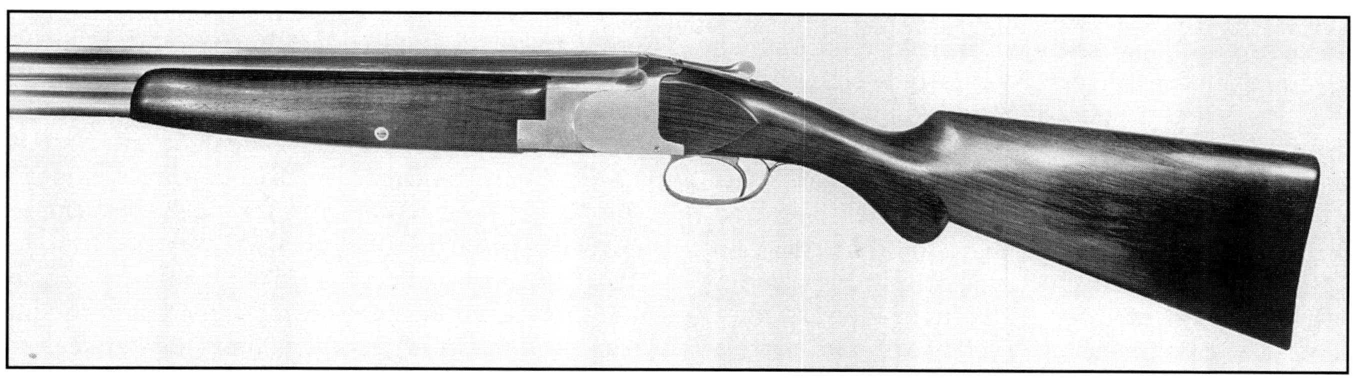

A late prewar Browning Superposed with sculptured frame, pistol grip stock, solid matte rib, Lightning style forearm, and Val Browning's new single selective trigger. This photograph may show the prototype of new single selective trigger, as there is no metal finish, or checkering on the buttstock and forearm. Courtesy Fabrique Nationale Archives.

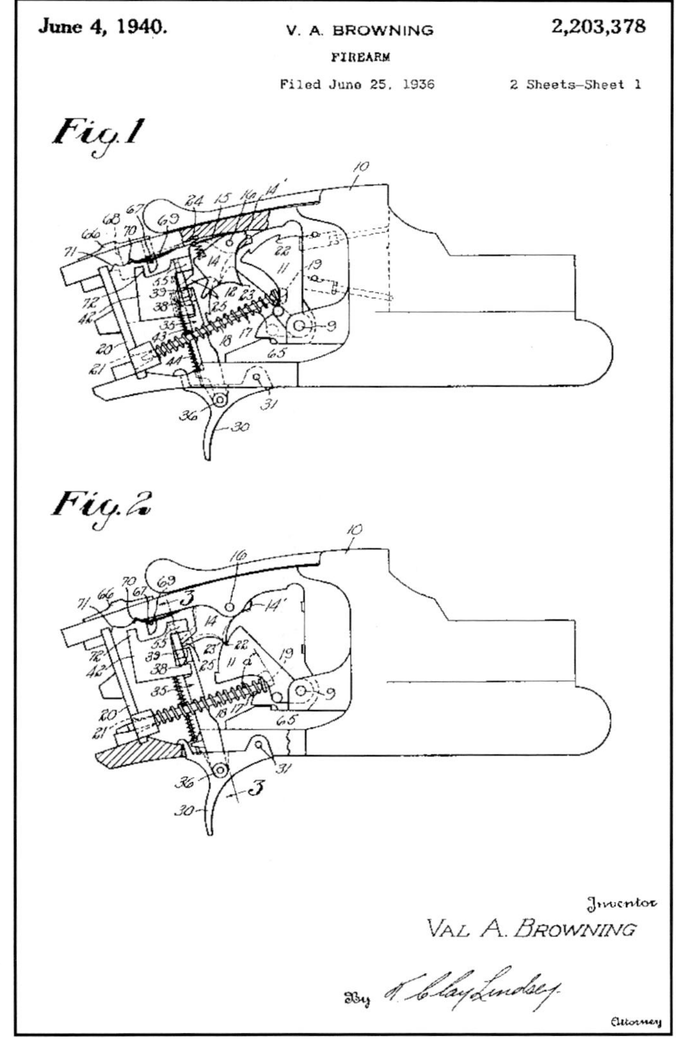

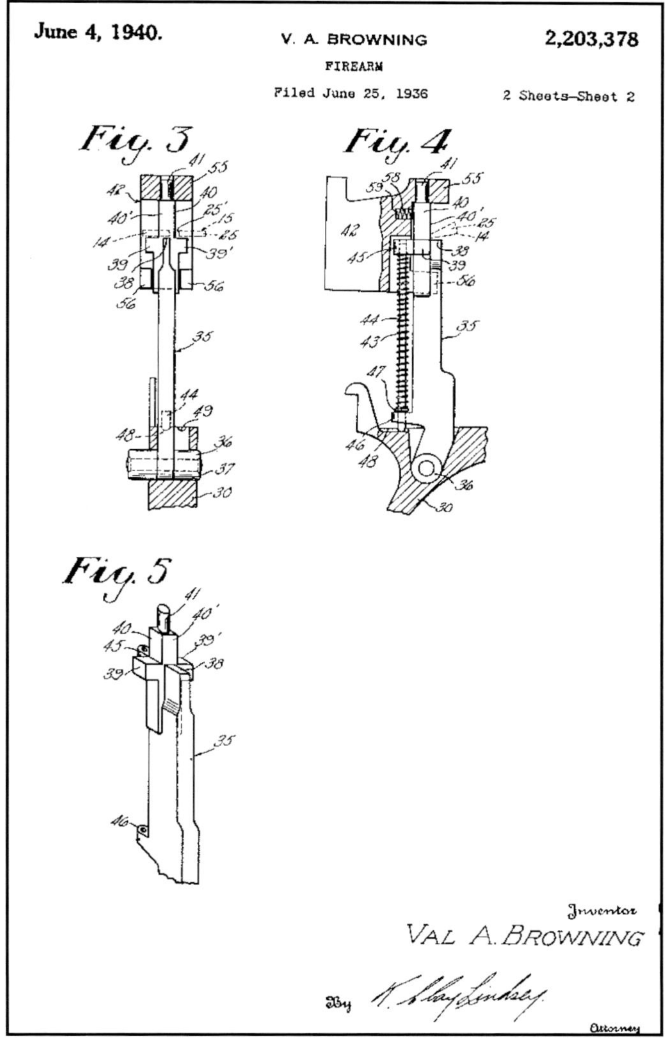

On June 25, 1936, Val Browning filed his patent, number 2,203,378, that improved the reliability of the Superposed system by preventing "doubling." Val's patent stated, "... doubling is absolutely and entirely avoided during the entire period of the jump of the gun upon discharge ...." His patent also improved the lock time of the hammers, or that period where, "the speed and force of the hammer fall is accelerated without increasing the pressure with which the hammer bears against the sear when the hammer is in cocked position." United States Patent Office.

in at about 6-7/8 pounds with the ventilated rib barrel, and 6-3/4 pounds with the striped matted barrel. (Compare this to Standard Weight guns, which weighed in at 7-1/2 pounds with 28-inch barrels, and 7-3/4 pounds with 30-inch barrels.) Because of its weight savings and streamlined forearm, the "Lightning" was so named. The frame still carried no engraving on Grade I models.

Browning offered this new Lightning model with an option of three different choke arrangements. The customer had the choice of both barrels choked skeet; the under barrel choked improved cylinder and the over barrel bored modified; or the under barrel choked modified and the over barrel choked full. All Lightnings were chambered for 2-3/4- inch shells. A ventilated rib was offered at an additional charge of $14.10, as was a raised matted rib for an extra $4.00. Single triggers, either selective or nonselective, were also extra cost options.

The year 1936 saw the continuation of the Standard models from Grade I through Midas Grade in both Long Range configuration or equipped with Trap features. With the introduction of the Lightning model in 1936, Browning began to make a distinction between these different models in its various catalogues. The two Standard Weight models were referred to as "Long Range" and "Trap" models, while the "Lightning" model was referred to as the Skeet/Field model because it was offered with shorter barrel lengths. This was the first example of the Superposed product line being differentiated by weight. An internal improvement was added to the Superposed in 1936 which finally put to rest the problem of "doubling" that Val Browning had been trying to solve since 1926. Patent number 2,203,378 was filed June 25, 1936, and awarded June 4, 1940. Val claimed to have solved the doubling problem that occurred during the recoil of the gun after the first barrel was fired and before the shooter was ready to fire the second barrel. Val also improved the lock time of the hammers without increasing the pressure the hammer bears against the sear when the hammer is in the cocked position. The following year, 1937, catalogue offerings were identical to 1936 except that the Lightning model could be had with 30-inch barrels in addition to 26-inch and 28-inch barrels. Stocks made to special dimensions were now furnished at an additional charge on both the Diana and Midas Grades.

In 1938, the same models were offered with minimal but significant changes. The frame was now engraved with a fine line scroll, and the barrels were fitted as standard with a new slender level matted rib. The Standard model in the Long Range configuration was available in 28-inch, 30-inch, and 32-inch barrel lengths, while the Trap gun was now offered in barrel lengths of 30 inches and 32 inches. The most important difference for 1938 was the addition of Val Browning's single selective trigger design. Having spent a good deal of time on his design, Val was eager to add his improvement to the Superposed. Patent number 2,233,861 was recorded February 8, 1938, and was awarded March 4, 1941. The basic concept of Val's invention had to do with the position of the sears in relation to the sear trips, and the location of the connector between the two. The connector, which would allow the shooter to select which barrel to fire from, was located at the top of the tang integral with the safety. In this way, the shooter could easily see the position of the barrel selector and the safety at the same time. With the addition of the new single trigger, the Browning Lightning model was the first modern example of the Superposed that would remain in production until 1984. Browning advertising described this new feature as follows:

> To select under first, simply move safety from "safe" position slightly to the right and forward. To select over barrel first, move safety from "safe" position slightly left and forward. Movement of the selector resembles the letter U and passes through "SAFE" position when shifted either barrel to the other. The selector is convenient, easy to use and quickly operated.

Browning stressed that this new trigger was recoil operated and was guaranteed to give the shooter satisfaction. Like the original design, the new trigger was set up to prevent doubling by using the inertia of the recoil to set the trigger for the next shot. If the gun had not been fired, it was necessary to move the barrel selector manually. The Superposed catalogue offerings remained the same for the balance of prewar production year 1939 and part of 1940.

Prewar Superposed Options

Perhaps one of the most appealing facets of gun collecting or shooting is the personal stamp that we as owners of a fine shotgun place upon it. It seems this characteristic of human nature has been present for as long as there have been firearms. The Browning Arms Company recognized this and went out of its way to provide its customers with almost any option they might desire. In its 1935 price list, the company stated, "We are prepared to furnish handmade guns to suit individual tastes and require-

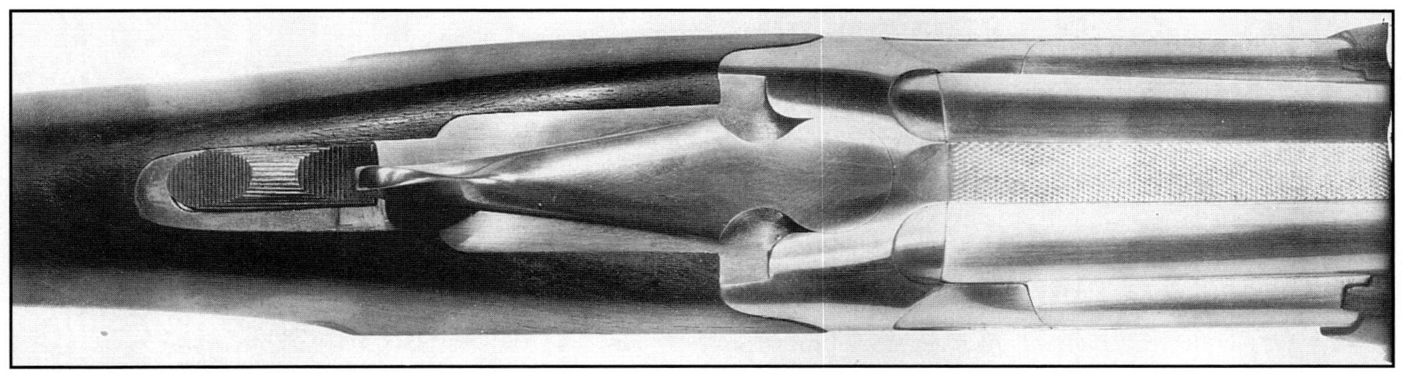

A very early Browning Superposed with Val Browning's new barrel selector switch installed. Notice also the "Y" shaped upper tang that was used throughout the prewar period. Courtesy Fabrique Nationale Archives.

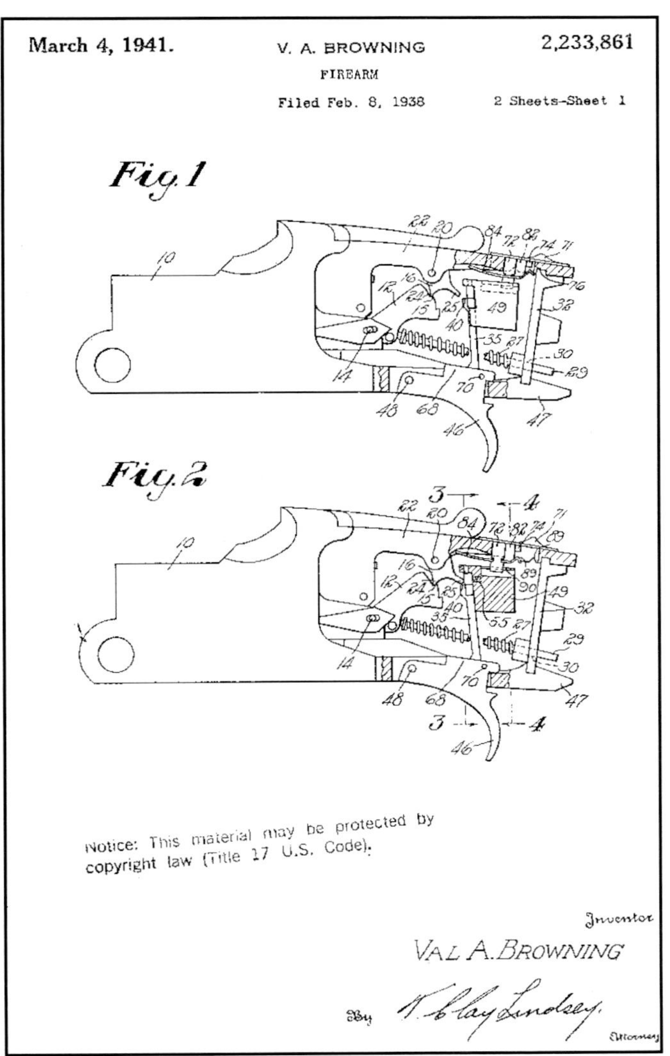

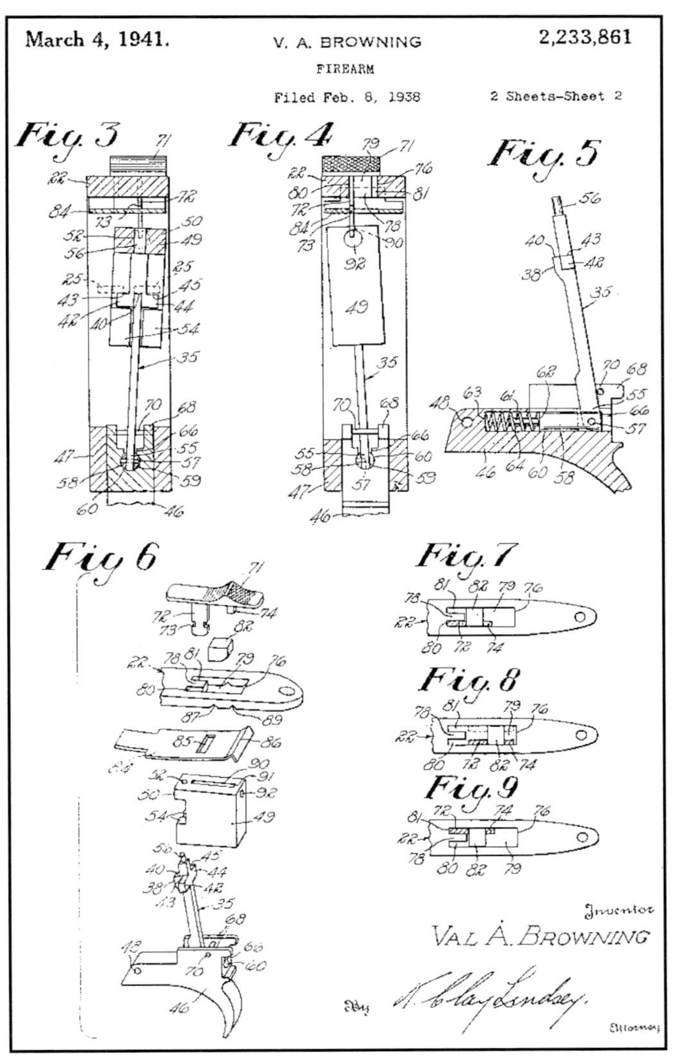

Patent number 2,233,861 covers Val Browning's famous selective fire system. Filed February 8, 1938, and awarded March 4, 1941, this patent provides for a means to combine the safety and barrel selector into one switch on the top tang. This patent marked the final design for the Browning Superposed single selective trigger system and remains in use with small improvements to this day. United States Patent office.

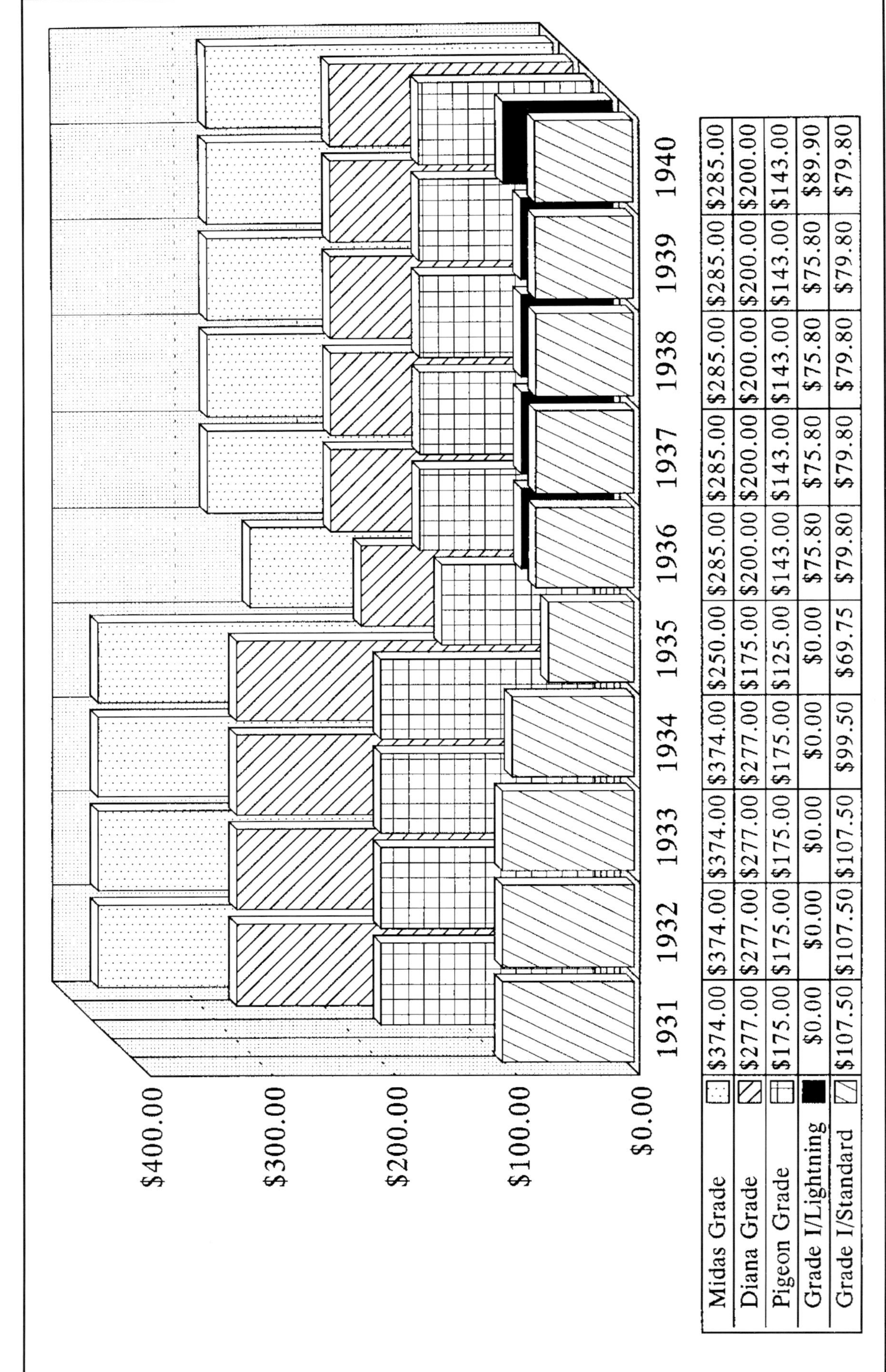

	1931	1932	1933	1934	1935	1936	1937	1938	1939	1940
Midas Grade	$374.00	$374.00	$374.00	$374.00	$250.00	$285.00	$285.00	$285.00	$285.00	$285.00
Diana Grade	$277.00	$277.00	$277.00	$277.00	$175.00	$200.00	$200.00	$200.00	$200.00	$200.00
Pigeon Grade	$175.00	$175.00	$175.00	$175.00	$125.00	$143.00	$143.00	$143.00	$143.00	$143.00
Grade I/Lightning	$0.00	$0.00	$0.00	$0.00	$0.00	$75.80	$75.80	$75.80	$75.80	$89.90
Grade I/Standard	$107.50	$107.50	$107.50	$99.50	$69.75	$79.80	$79.80	$79.80	$79.80	$79.80

Chart 1-1

ments. If you will state your wishes, we shall be glad to quote cost." That statement by the company should leave no doubt as to Browning's willingness to build made-to-order Superposed guns.

As a general rule, the buyer had a choice of a number of extra cost options on his Superposed shotgun during the 1930s. An oil finish was offered, as were special dimension stocks. Stocks could be had with high grade American walnut or high grade Circassian walnut. Any standard type of recoil pad could be supplied by the company and fitted to the gun prior to delivery. The order of firing could be reversed on double triggers as well as Twin-Single triggers. The position of the single trigger types could be fitted in the standard midway position, three-quarter rear, or extreme rear position. Browning also offered a checkered trigger. Triggers could be ordered gold plated, either plain or checkered. The company would rechamber the Superposed for three-inch shells. Any choke combinations could be special ordered. Special ivory sights were offered on the front bead or in pairs (front and middle). Oval name plates in gold, silver, or brass were available in three-quarter-inch or one-inch sizes to be mounted on the buttstock. Monograms would be engraved on one or both sides of the receiver; "... 1/2 dollar size or under." Any name would be engraved on the trigger guard, top tang, or receiver in script, block letters, or signature. Browning also offered gun cases in genuine leather or leatherette in black or brown. A chamois cover for the case was available as well.

Browning also made available to its customers any special custom-built Superposed they might desire. Special engraving and special inlaid gold designs were available on special order. The Superposed was also offered in matched pairs on special order. In other words, Browning was willing to build for its customers whatever they desired, and it is possible to see some very unusual "uncatalogued" prewar Superposed guns. All of these engraved guns were available in either the "Long Range" configuration, the "Trap" model classification, or the "Lightning" model. The end

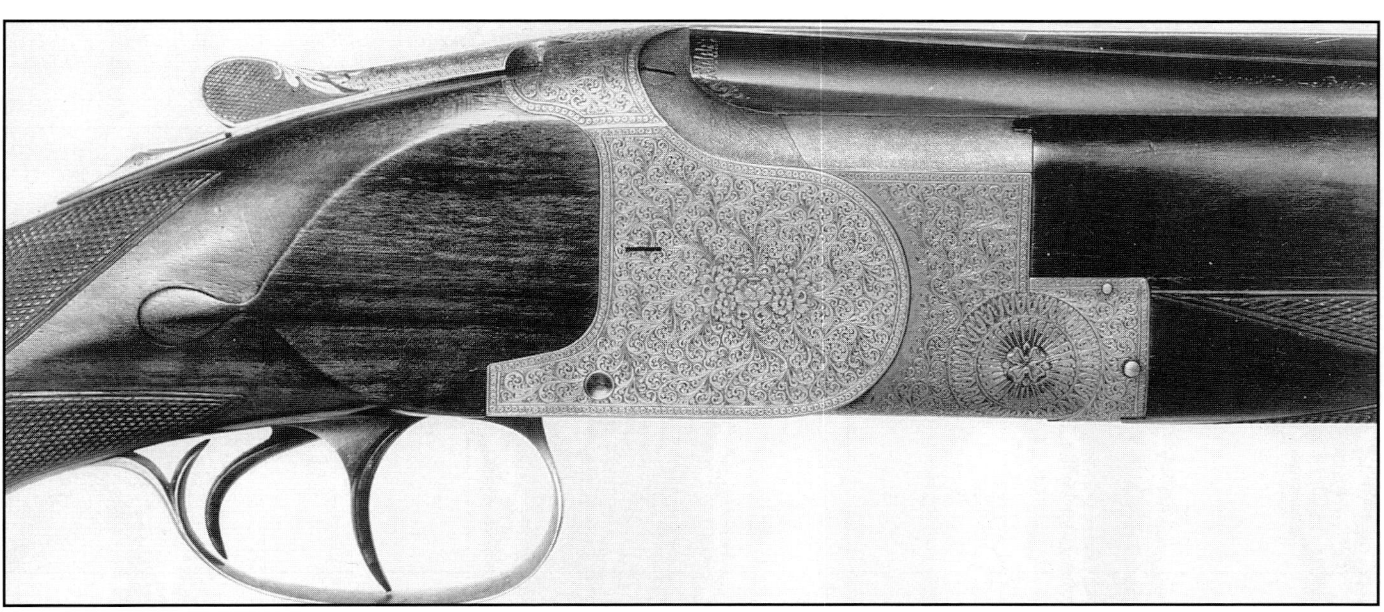

A close-up view of the right side of an FN Superposed double rifle, serial number 5003, in a grade similar to but not exactly like FN's D3 Grade. The screws on the receiver are firing pin retaining screws that also serve as vent screws for rifle barrels. Again, the sculptured frame is a distinctly European trait. This particular rifle was delivered to an Italian agent, Fusi and Co. in Milan, on August 20, 1935. Courtesy Fabrique Nationale Archives.

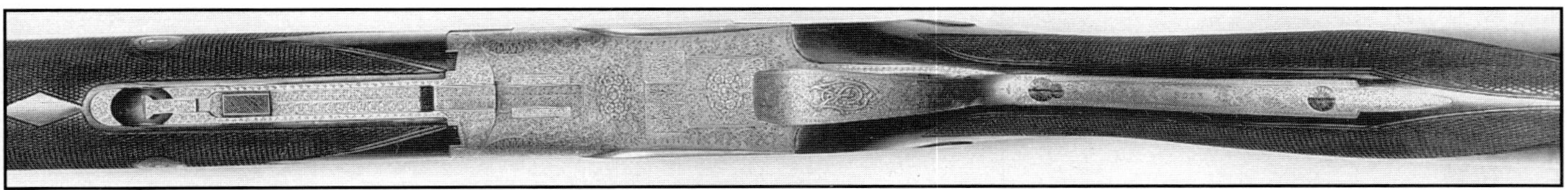

The bottom side of serial number 5003 showing the exquisite engraving details. Notice, also, how the sculptured frame is cut into the receiver. This was an expensive and time consuming operation. Courtesy Fabrique Nationale Archives.

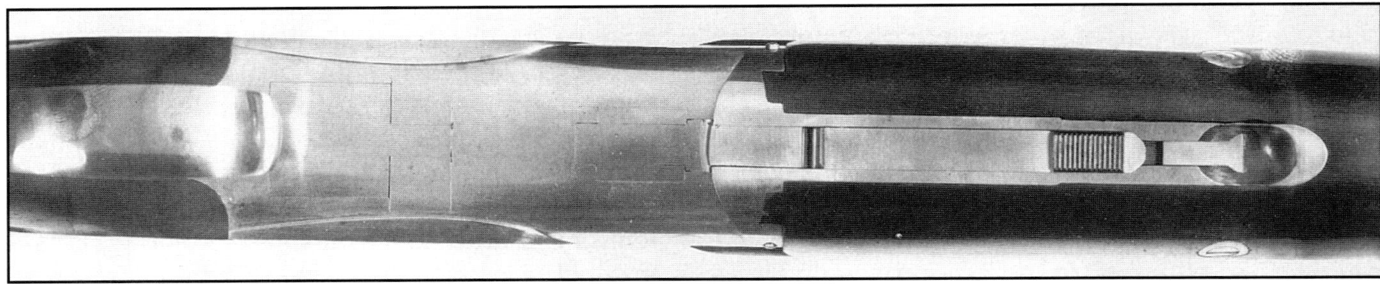

The bottom view of a late prewar Superposed with European style sculptured frame. Note the shape and configuration of the forearm release latch. This arrangement was used throughout the prewar period and early postwar years. Courtesy Fabrique Nationale Archives.

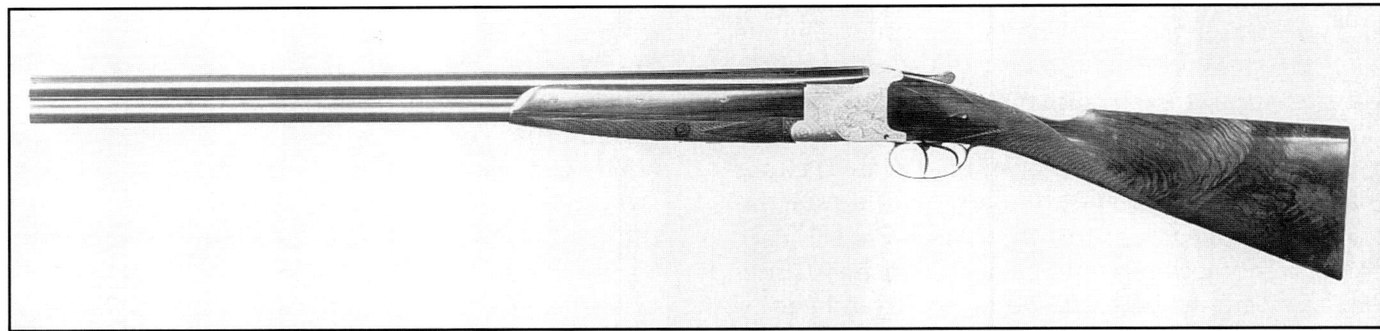

Serial number 6226 is a Fabrique Nationale D3 Grade with double triggers, straight grip stock, and special order three-piece forearm. The French walnut stock has nice figure and the checkering is finely executed. A very elegantly finished European Browning Superposed assembled on July 27, 1934, and delivered to Val Browning at FN on the same date. Courtesy Fabrique Nationale Archives.

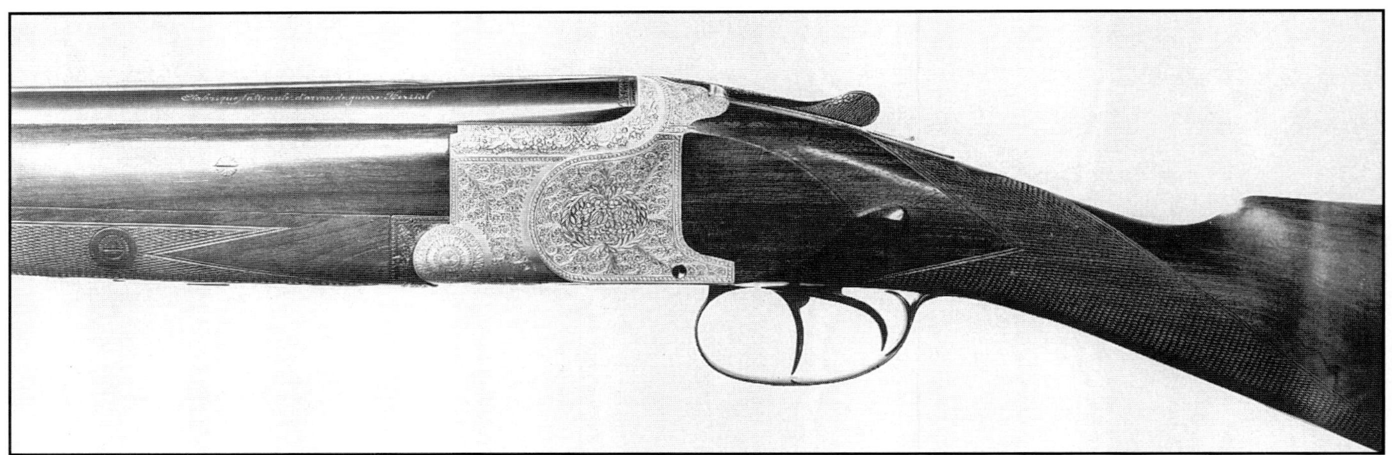

The left side of the D3 Grade clearly showing the Fabrique Nationale barrel address in script, a high grade feature. Notice the delicate flowers engraved into the top lever. Courtesy Fabrique Nationale Archives.

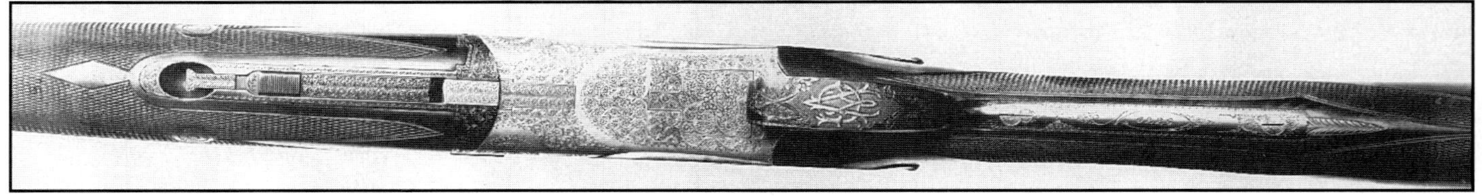

The bottom view of the D3 Grade. Notice the serial number treatment with the "No. 6226" in an ellipse. Courtesy Fabrique Nationale Archives.

result of all of these options was that it became possible for the Superposed to be built to a unique, made-to-order set of specifications far removed from any catalogue offering.

Perhaps the most interesting example of a group of special order Superposed was a series of guns—the exact number is not known—built especially for A. G. Bondi & Sons, one of FN's agents in Cairo, Egypt. These Superposed were furnished with special engraving patterns from Grade II through Grade IV. They were executed in an unrefined manner depicting game scenes of various types unlike the American and European patterns, with the name of the agent engraved in an oval. This same agent had FN's Anson side-by-side shotguns engraved in a similar fashion. These specially engraved Superposed do not appear to be signed by the engraver. The coarse work may have been executed by apprentices or at the very least, inexperienced engravers. There must have been enough demand for these guns in that part of the world during the 1930s to induce a dealer to go to that much effort. It is impossible to say what else FN built for its worldwide customers during this period that differs significantly from its usual offerings, but some unique prewar Superposed are surely scattered throughout the world.

Superposed Prewar Production and Sales

The decade of the 1930s represents a period of formidable and uncertain times for both the Browning Arms Company and Fabrique Nationale. During the first half of the decade, the worldwide depression affected both companies. Trying to introduce a new shotgun in the teeth of the Great Depression was not an easy task for the Brownings, nor was it easy to keep a huge manufacturing facility such as Fabrique Nationale solvent during those difficult economic times. However, during the second half of the decade, the economic situation began to improve slightly in the United States, allowing Browning to solidify its tenuous hold on its fledgling American market. By contrast, FN began a period of strong recovery brought about by the storm clouds of war. European nations, alarmed by Hitler's aggressive posturing, began to re-arm themselves. This response brought about a resurgence in military firearms production as well as increased orders for military trucks, tractors, and motorcycles. This economic ebb and flow affected both production and sales of the Superposed throughout the 1930s.

Chart 1-2 illustrates this situation in a dramatic fashion. The years 1933 and 1934 show a marked decline in sales. The reason for this conspicuous decrease is twofold. First, the worldwide economic circumstance was truly staggering. With an introductory retail price of $107.50 for the Grade I Superposed, the deepening depression in America had affected sales drastically. The American market simply could not support this price level. Browning Arms Company responded by lowering the retail price in 1934 to just under $100.00, and when that reduction had no positive effect, retail prices were reduced further to $69.75 the following year. When increased sales resulted from this lower price, 1936 prices were increased slightly to $79.80. Sales seemed to respond to these prices and they remained at this level for a short time. Sales fell again near the end of the decade, most likely in response to the grave situation in Europe.

The second factor that may have affected sales was quality control. Val Browning fought constantly to maintain high quality, and this sometimes slowed production. He was also involved in attempting to perfect his single trigger mechanism, which presented some difficult production problems. Although the nature of the design was relatively simple, production difficulties tied to quality control problems slowed production. The important fact remains that these problems were overcome successfully and by the end of the decade the Superposed was produced and sold throughout the world with a reputation of high quality and good value.

The information provided to the researcher regarding Superposed production is imperfect and imprecise. Because production records can be based on many factors, such as frame output or assembled gun manufacturing dates, it must be determined what actually constitutes gun production. The Fabrique Nationale records utilized for this research were shipping records that included the date the finished gun was received in the shipping department from the factory after final inspection, and the date the gun was shipped to the dealer or agent. Labeled as, *"REGISTRE DES VENTES D'ARMES DE CHASE ET DE SPORT,"* these journals were numbered from Book No. 1 to Book No. 11, stopping in approximately 1987. Due to the nature of these records, serial numbers of Superposed guns are first recorded as to when the gun was finished, not when the frame was stamped with a serial number on the production line. This is an important distinction, because although FN built its Superposed frames on a consecutive serial numbered system, the guns were not assembled on a

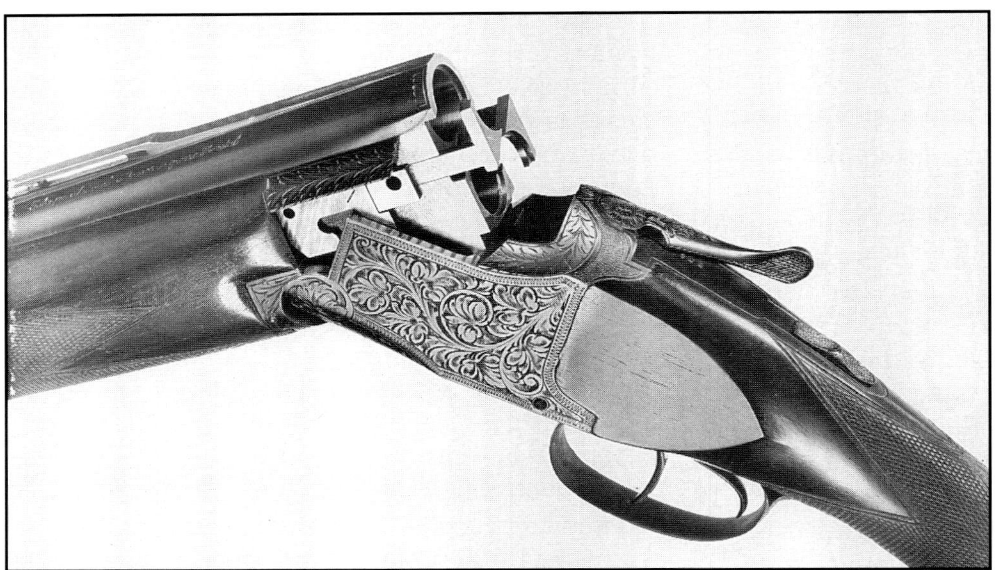

Fabrique Nationale would accommodate its customers with special requests whenever possible. Here is a series of three Browning Superposed guns with special engraving in Grades I, II, and III. These Superposed were made for an agent by the name of Bondi & Sons in Cairo, Egypt. The agent's name was stamped on the top of the rib near the breach end. These three Superposed have three-digit serial numbers in the mid-600 range. Notice that the usual fine engraving details are missing from these guns and a sparse lightly executed pattern is used instead. Courtesy Fabrique Nationale Archives.

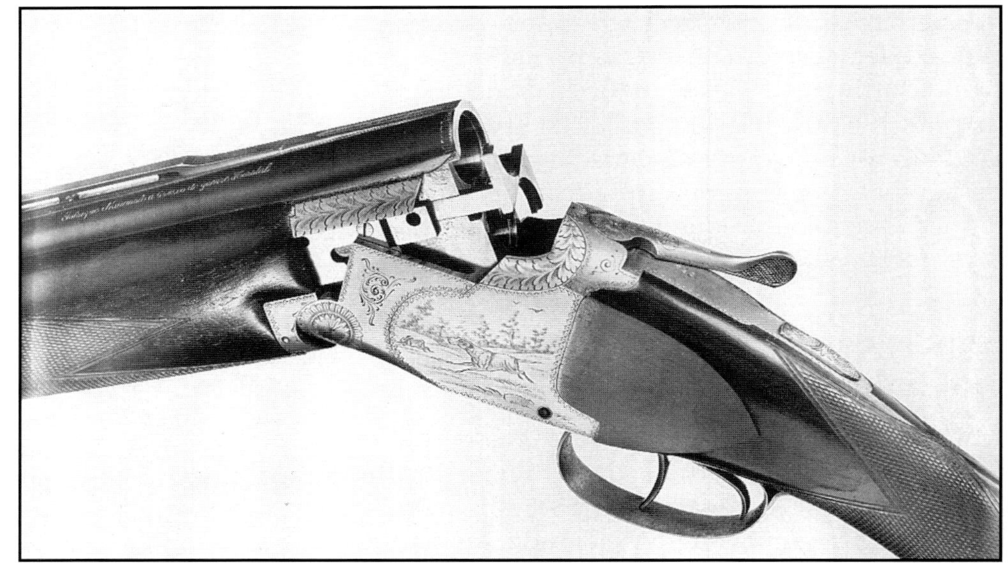

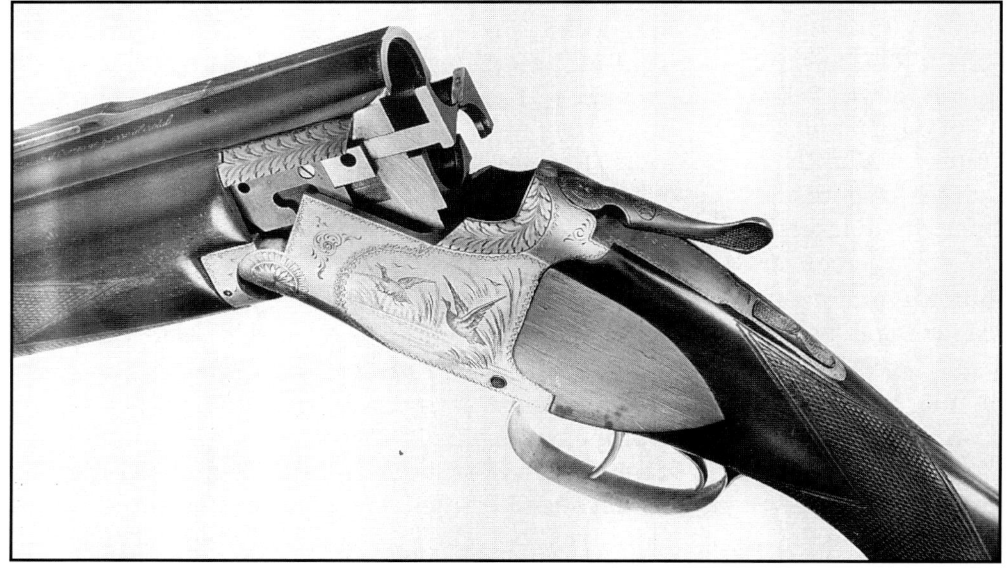

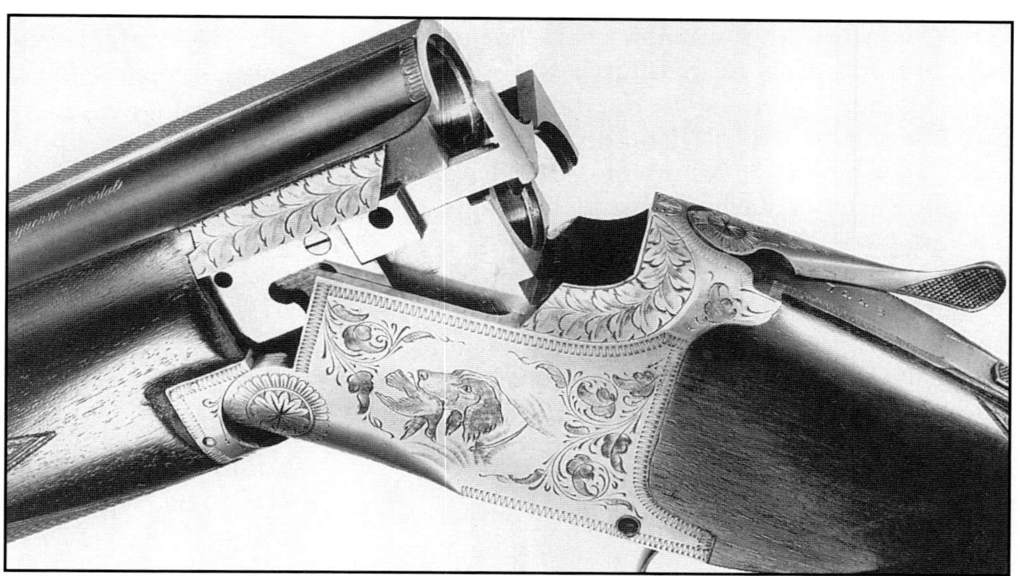

Several years later Bondi & Sons wanted another series of uniquely engraved Superposed. These three guns, serial numbers 7448, 7449, and 7450, were designated Grades I, II, and III. These guns were assembled on February 27, 1936, and sent to Bondi & Sons in Cairo on April 6, 1936. This practice must have been quite unusual because FN documented these guns in its photo archives for a pictorial record. Courtesy Fabrique Nationale Archives.

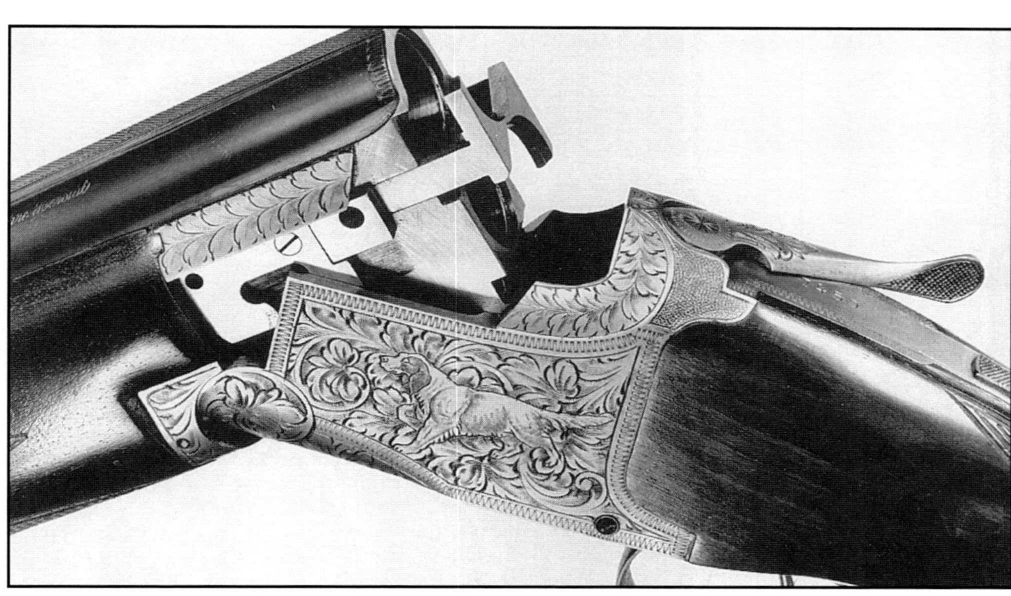

consecutive serial numbered basis. For this reason, the shipping records give the researcher only a general guide as to the date of manufacture of a gun based solely on its serial number.

It should be noted that Superposed sold in the U.S. and those sold elsewhere shared the same serial number pool. That is to say, Superposed sold to Browning in St. Louis had no special or separate serial numbers from those sold in Europe, Africa, or Asia, nor was there any pattern to the serial numbers sold in the United States versus the rest of the world. One or two Superposed with consecutive serial numbers may have been shipped to Browning in St. Louis while the next four or five serial numbers may have been shipped to cities throughout the world.

Detailed analysis of these FN shipping records clearly illustrates the inexactness of equating serial numbers with specific dates of manufacture. Often these records will show that a Superposed assembled in October of 1932 and shipped to a dealer a few days later will have a subsequent serial numbered gun assembled, for example, in April of 1937 and shipped in 1938. Due to this insurmountable dilemma, it is impractical to attempt to formulate a date of manufacture for Superposed guns based on these records. However, these shipping records, used in conjunction with Fabrique Nationale's sales reports, known as the *"Tableaux Comparatifs Facturation,"* can provide the researcher with a general guide to dates of manufacture based imprecisely on serial numbers. This gives us only a rough estimate of the date of assembly of a Superposed gun using its serial number to determine chronology.

The table below represents comparative sales of FN Superposed to both Browning in St. Louis and the rest of the world. These sales figures follow closely the production of the Superposed based on the final date of assembly as seen in the Fabrique Nationale shipping records. It is therefore possible to use Table 1-2 as an authentic but inexact serial number guide to dates of manufacture. One further complication needs to be mentioned: Fabrique Nationale operated on a fiscal year ending June 30. This skews the serial number dates by six months when compared to the calendar year, but the data is still of real value. The reader must be warned that there are many, many exceptions to this guide and it should be used merely as a rough indicator for determining the date a Superposed was assembled.[13]

FABRIQUE NATIONALE SUPERPOSED SALES 1930-1940

Year Ending 6/30	FN Worldwide	Browning St. Louis	Cumulative Totals
1930	408	1015	**1423**
1931	487	1150	**3060**
1932	133	1738	**4931**
1933	149	89	**5169**
1934	199	1	**5369**
1935	352	2130	**7851**
1936	356	2162	**10369**
1937	589	3744	**14702**
1938	419	943	**16064**
1939	154	421	**16639**
1940	0	391	**17030**
Total	**3246**	**13784**	**17030**

Table 1-2

[13] This point can be illustrated with a page taken from the FN shipping records beginning with serial number 4801 and ending with serial number 4900. The first twenty Superposed, serial numbers 4801 to 4820, were received in the shipping department in late 1931 and early 1932; most were shipped in the spring of 1932. Browning Superposed with serial numbers from 4821 to 4843 were assembled in January, February, and March of 1937 and shipped soon after their arrival in the shipping department. Superposed between serial numbers 4844 and 4861 were assembled in October, November, and December of 1931. Some of these were shipped promptly while others were shipped as late as 1934 and some even as late as 1936. Guns from serial numbers 4862 to 4871 were assembled in January, February, and March of 1937 and shipped promptly. From serial numbers 4872 to 4895 most Superposed were assembled in October and November of 1931. Some were shipped promptly while others were not shipped for four or five years. In one case, an October 1931 Superposed, serial number 4890, was not shipped until May of 1937. Guns between serial numbers 4896 and 4900 were assembled in February of 1937 and shipped promptly a few days later. This example clearly illustrates the difficulty of attempting to determine, with any degree of certainty, the date of manufacture of a Superposed based strictly on serial number sequence.

FABRIQUE NATIONALE WORLDWIDE PREWAR SUPERPOSED SALES 1930-1940

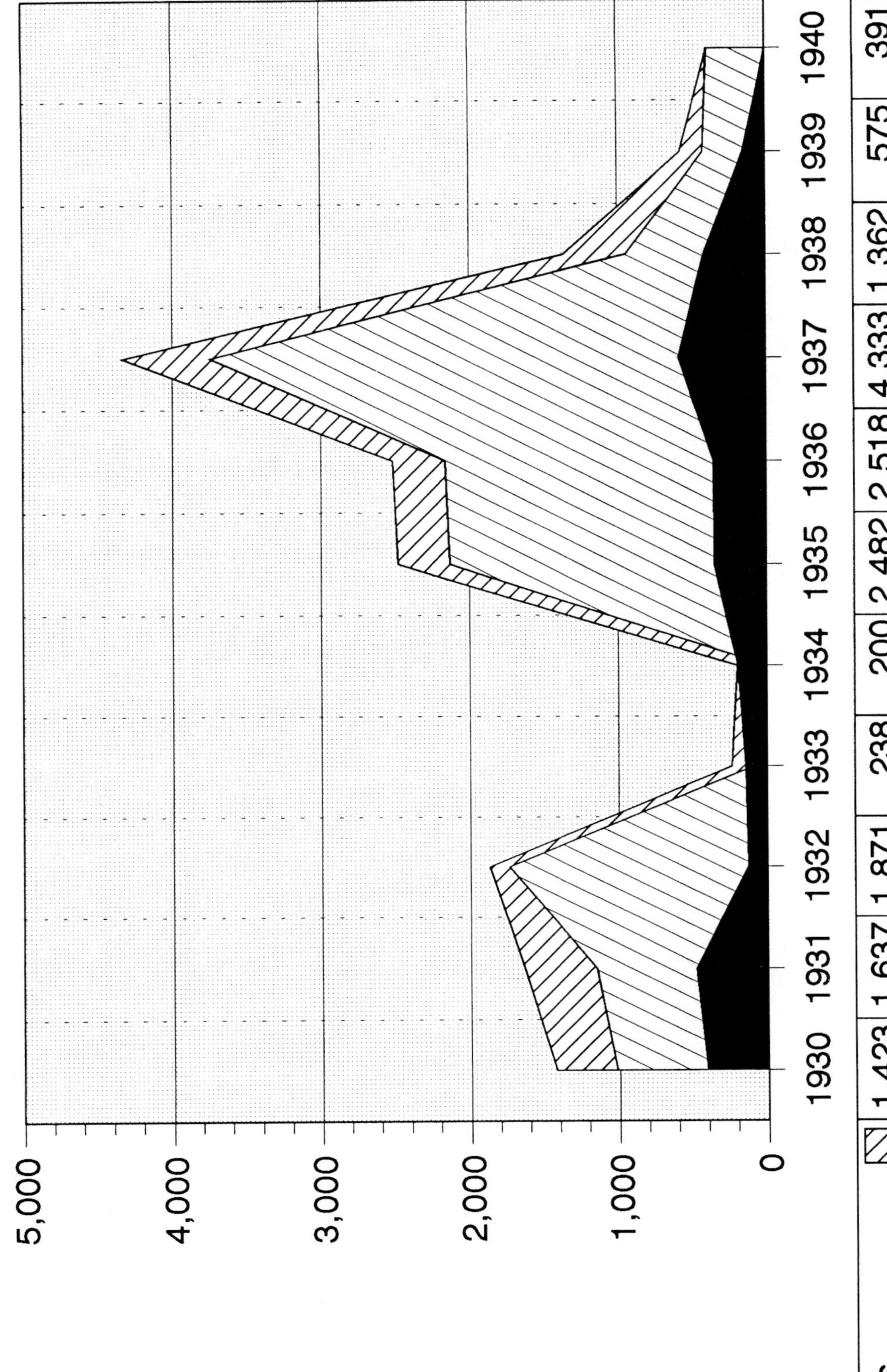

	1930	1931	1932	1933	1934	1935	1936	1937	1938	1939	1940
Total Sales	1,423	1,637	1,871	238	200	2,482	2,518	4,333	1,362	575	391
FN Browning sales	1,015	1,150	1,738	89	1	2,130	2,162	3,744	943	421	391
FN World Wide sales	408	482	133	149	199	352	356	589	419	154	0

Chart 1-2

The first commercial Superposed gun was shipped in August 1930 to Browning's distribution center in St. Louis, beginning with serial number 107. Interestingly enough, most of the first two hundred or three hundred Superposed were shipped to FN's agents throughout Europe instead of the United States. Serial number 1 was sent to FN's St. Leonard ammunition plant located at 615 Rue St. Leonard in Liège on August 6, 1930.[14] Serial number 2 was completed on March 19, 1931, and shipped to an unknown destination in 1935. Mr. Val Browning received serial number 3 on June 30, 1930, at FN. Serial number 4 was completed November 3, 1930, and shipped to Genschow in Vienna, Austria, on April 20, 1931. Serial number 4 was later returned unsold and subsequently shipped to Browning, St. Louis on October 18, 1932. The first regular shipments were sent to Lepersonne of London in July of 1930. Fabrique Nationale did not ship significant numbers of Superposed guns to the Browning Arms Company until the fall of 1930, and it was not until the early months of 1931 that shipments of Superposed began to arrive in St. Louis in large numbers. These first regular shipments of Superposed began with serial number 209, but most serial numbers of these early shipments were in the 400 serial number range. The shipping journal that includes these first Superposed guns has a separate entry written on the front page dated July 10, 1930. The entry reads, "Serial number '0' to Mr. Val Browning, Ogden, Utah, shipped November 7, 1930." Based on this information, it is most likely that the Browning Superposed was not available for sale in the United States until the spring of 1931.

It is important to note that although the number of the Superposed guns sold by Fabrique Nationale to its dealers around the globe was comparatively small in relation to its sales to Browning, FN had an impressive number of agents. Due to its long history of producing and selling military and sporting firearms, FN's dealer network had been well established by the time the Superposed reached production. FN's estimated 150 dealers and agents were represented throughout the world, with its largest agents being Cartoucherie Francaise in Paris; Fusi & Co. in Milan; Lepersonne in London, which also represented British Commonwealth countries, namely Canada; and Schroeder Brothers in Liège, one of its oldest worldwide agents. Fabrique Nationale had agents in such places as Australia, New Zealand, Chile, Indochina, Turkey, the Philippines, Morocco, India, Egypt, Russia, Madagascar and many other countries throughout the world. What is interesting about this network is that the Browning Superposed was sold to these agents, albeit in small numbers, in all of these locations. The Browning Superposed was truly a global shotgun. As far as the Browning Arms Company was concerned, total sales from Browning FN produced firearms amounted to less than a million dollars a year during the decade preceding World War II.

There were approximately 17,030 FN produced Browning Superposed exported and sold throughout the world between 1930 and 1940. These guns are numbered from serial number 1 to approximately 17032. The last Superposed to be assembled before the factory was occupied by the German army was serial number 17026, completed on May 4, 1940. The last serial number completed before the war was serial number 17032, finished April 10, 1940, and shipped to St. Louis on April 30, 1940.

On May 10, 1940, without warning, German armies invaded the Netherlands, Belgium, and Luxembourg. The French and British governments dispatched expeditionary forces into Belgium to cooperate with the Belgian army in its resistance. The Germans captured the key Belgian defensive position at Fort Eben Emael. Brussels fell on May 17 and the remaining British and Belgian forces were forced back to Ostend and Dunkirk. Browning Superposed production ceased on May 10 of 1940. German forces occupied the FN factory and turned its considerable capacity to the benefit of the German war effort.

---

[14] Fabrique Nationale had acquired the cartridge factory just the previous year. Claude Gaier speculates that Superposed serial number 1 was sent to the plant for testing of the Legia shotgun shell. The author speculates that this 12 gauge Superposed was used for function testing. Whichever circumstance is correct (in fact, both may have occurred), Superposed serial number 1 was never intended for commercial sale.

Chapter 2

The Aftermath of War and the Decade of the 1950s

The American 1st Army entered Belgium on September 1, 1944. Six days later, after five years of occupation, Belgian Fabrique Nationale management assumed their rightful place at the head of the company. The effects of war had taken a devastating toll in manpower and equipment. Key personnel had been lost to Nazi collaborators and a substantial portion of the workforce was widely separated or in internment. In addition, twenty-five percent of the machinery had been destroyed or stolen by the Germans. The machinery that remained suffered enormous damage and was in

A portion of the Fabrique Nationale factory after a buzz bomb attack in 1945. A substantial portion of the plant was destroyed by war's end. Courtesy Fabrique Nationale Archives.

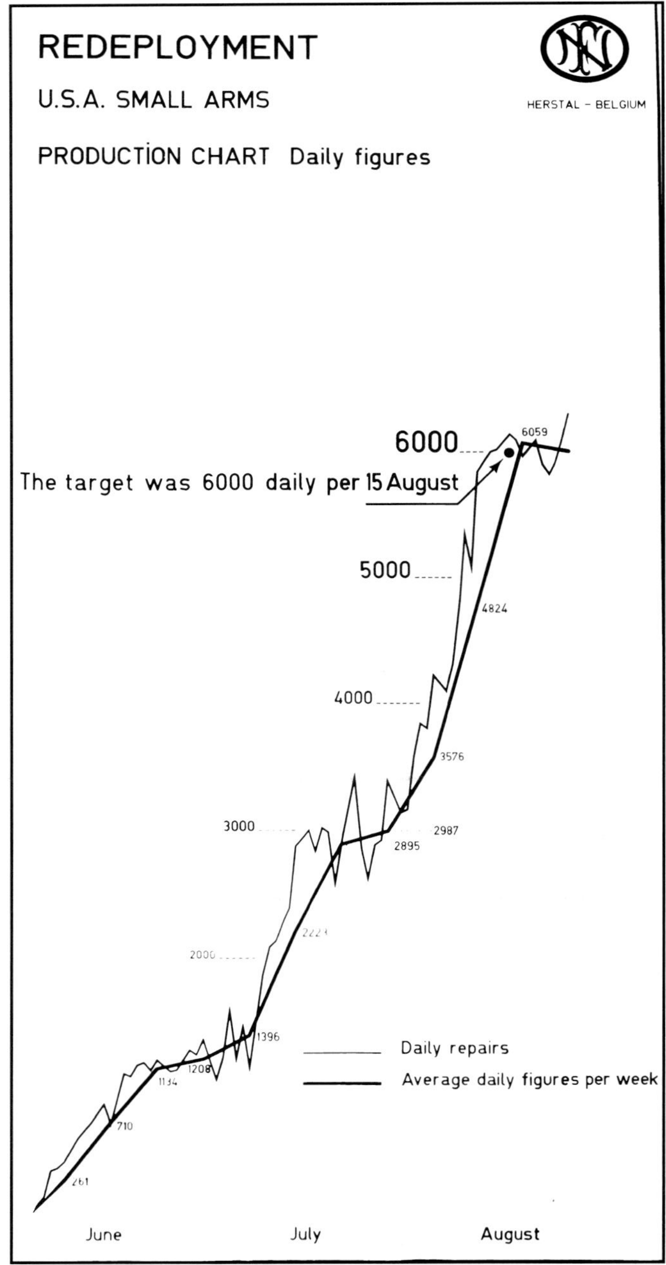

Soon after the allies occupied Liège, they converted what facilities were left standing to their own uses. By the summer of 1945, after the war in Europe was won, the FN plant was dedicated to small arms repair. This chart, which was placed in the factory, shows the successful completion of FN's small arms repair quota for the summer of 1945. Courtesy Fabrique Nationale Archives.

need of extensive repairs. Finally, during the closing phases of hostilities, the factory was hit by German V1 rockets. Such was the legacy of war.

In the fall of 1944, as the factory was struggling to return to operation, the U.S. Army requested that FN build four hundred thousand mud grip tank tracks. Despite the damage and loss of life, this work continued through the Battle of the Bulge when the factory was hit by German rockets. The manufacture of small arms began again with the production of pistols for the American forces and French police. In the spring of 1945, the American army contracted with FN to inspect, clean, repair, and pack all of the small arms American forces had in Western Europe. Over two million firearms were handled between the summer of 1945 and the summer of 1946. Steadily the FN plant returned to normal operating conditions, but not without the sorely required infusion of cash.

The period following the defeat of Germany was one of rebuilding and reorganization for Fabrique Nationale. Some of the stolen machinery was recovered in Belgium and Germany after the end of the war, but machinery in Poland and East Germany was lost to the Russians permanently. FN obtained bank credits in the amount of 320 million francs. The money was needed to reconstruct an enterprise that had been severely ravaged by the war. Many years were to pass before some wartime compensation was paid to Fabrique Nationale for damages and unpaid prewar shipments.[1]

Fabrique Nationale's Decade of Recovery

The year 1950 marked a turning point in the postwar history of the Herstal company. René Laloux succeeded to the directorship of the company after the retirement of Mr. Gustave Joassart. Having completed the rebuilding phase and the re-establishment of profitable product lines, FN was poised to take advantage of a new political climate that would have long-term ramifications for the company: the approach of the cold war.

FN had been involved in the development of a standardized rifle cartridge for NATO that would replace the various infantry cartridges used during the war by the allied forces. Fabrique Nationale subsequently perfected its 7.62mm cartridge, and it was adopted by NATO. FN wanted to capitalize on its cartridge success by building a light infantry rifle chambered for it. In 1951, FN arms designer Dieudonné Saive completed work on his self-loading rifle known as the LAR.[2] It was adopted by

1 Claude Gaier and Auguste Francotte, *FN 100 Years: The Story of the Great Liége Company, 1889-1989*, pp. 77-84.

2 Dieudonné Saive (1888-1970) worked with John M. Browning at FN before his death and subsequently improved the BAR. Saive refined the Hi Power pistol as well as the "Baby" pistols. LAR means Light Automatic Rifle. In French it is called FAL, which stands for *Fusil Automatique Leger*. *Ibid.*, p. 90.

A view from the inside of one of the buildings that was severely damaged at the end of the war. Fabrique Nationale had an enormous rebuilding job to do before production could begin on the Superposed or any other manufactured product built by FN. Courtesy Fabrique Nationale Archives.

NATO in 1954. Three years later, FN designer Ernest Vervier developed the MAG, a gas operated machine gun also chambered for the 7.62mm cartridge.[3] The commercial success of the FN/LAR and FN/MAG designs cannot be exaggerated. Fabrique Nationale sold hundreds of thousands of these weapons during the decade of the 1950s to countries throughout the world. The LAR rifle was to occupy FN's production and manufacturing facilities for a number of decades. In addition, this military production was to have a profound effect on the company's ability to manufacture and produce sporting arms, particularly the Superposed.[4]

Another factor that was to have an impact on the Belgian arms maker was the expansion of Browning's sporting arms product line. Prior to 1950, FN produced for Browning the Auto-5 shotgun and the Superposed. In 1950 the double automatic, designed by Val A. Browning, went into production. Although FN's most important customer, Browning Arms Company, was in the United States, the company began to turn its attention to expanding its hunting arms market in Europe. This expansion put further pressure on its sporting arms manufacturing facilities, which in turn caused deliveries to fall behind to its principal customer, Browning Arms.

Fabrique Nationale continued to expand its production facilities into other areas. Beginning in 1953, the company built the Bofors 57mm antiaircraft gun for the Belgian Army. In 1957 FN manufactured rifle grenades and rockets. During the late 1950s, FN built jet engines for various military aircraft of West Germany, Belgium, the Netherlands, and Italy. Motorcycles, buses, trucks, and automatic milking machines for the dairy industry were

---

[3] The initials MAG in French stand for *Milrailleuse A Gaz,* which means Gas Operated Machine Gun.

[4] C. Gaier and A. Francotte, *FN 100 Years*, pp. 90-93.

A fully rebuilt and expanded FN plant as seen from the air in the mid-1950s. Courtesy Fabrique Nationale Archives.

some of the areas in which FN had developed an interest and a growing market for its products.[5]

Between the end of the war and 1950, internal labor arguments were infrequent. But during the decade of the 1950s, with the return of prosperity, wage demands escalated. Fabrique Nationale management decided to implement an annual bonus for its factory workers as an incentive to keep its highly skilled labor force constant. During the 1950s this bonus was increased on an almost yearly basis. By the end of the decade it amounted to a significant percentage of annual wages. Management felt this reward was necessary in order to remain competitive in a region where skilled labor was in great demand. In addition, FN provided free dental care for its workers, established a scholarship endowment, instituted a pension fund, and set up an unemployment fund for workers laid off or unemployed.[6] These programs instituted by management with the intention of retaining a skilled workforce would provide the necessary labor to produce the products that were in such high demand. These increased wages and benefits forced an upward cost spiral that affected all of FN's pricing. Although it began and escalated in the 1950s, the effects were not felt until the decades of the 1960s and 1970s. Since there was little impact felt during this strong period of recovery and prosperity, little thought was given during the 1950s to the consequences of these generous wage and benefit packages.

By the end of the 1950s, the company's financial position was vastly improved from what it was just ten years before. Fabrique Nationale paid dividends to its shareholders every year of the decade beginning in 1951. By the end of the 1950s, FN was

---

[5] *Ibid.*, pp. 96, 101, 104.

[6] *Ibid.*, pp. 86-88.

composed of three almost equal groups: arms, ammunition, and engines.[7] From this brief description of Fabrique Nationale during the 1950s, the reader may begin to appreciate the complexity of the company and the continually expanding pressures the company was under during this period. It was in this environment that Browning Arms Company had to operate to maximize its production and quality control of all its shotguns, particularly the Superposed.

The Postwar Browning Company

In 1946 Val Browning visited Fabrique Nationale and placed orders for A-5 Browning shotguns. Shipments of the Auto-5 shotgun were soon on their way to Browning's St. Louis facility in the United States, but production was slowed by the war-torn factory. In 1947 a few 12 gauge Superposed were shipped to Browning, but none of the new 20 gauge over and unders were forthcoming. The process of regeneration for the FN plant impeded any semblance of prewar production schedules. In many cases retraining was required, as was hiring additional craftsmen to take the place of those who were no longer employed at FN. This procedure of rebuilding was time-consuming and difficult.

Val Allen Browning, president of Browning Arms Company. This photo was taken shortly after World War II when Val Browning was busy trying to get the FN production facilities back online. After many trips to Belgium he and his son John Val Browning succeeded in getting production back to prewar levels by 1950. Courtesy Browning Firearms Museum, Union Station, Ogden, Utah.

The executive offices of Browning remained in Ogden with Val Browning as president and Marriner Browning as vice president and general manager, a post he held in semiretirement. Marriner's son, M. Bigelow Browning, acted as vice president and was perhaps the most active of the officers in running the day-to-day operations of the company. Bigelow Browning is an interesting, if little known, member of the Browning family. The grandson of Matt Browning, John M. Browning's brother, Bigelow Browning graduated from Stanford Medical School and was practicing medicine as a resident in an Ogden hospital when his father Marriner asked him to come to work in the Browning organization. Leaving his medical career behind, Bigelow became a vice president of Browning and perhaps one of the most knowledgeable men in the company on the Superposed. Many former employees have called him a genius. His attention to detail was legendary, as was his sagacity. Bigelow was once responsible for the return of five thousand Superposed to FN because the barrel concentricity was slightly out of tolerance. He firmly believed that one of the keys to increased sales of the Superposed lay in aggressive marketing of its higher grades.

An interesting fact: There are three known variations of this 1950 "Special Models" catalogue. The photographs of Grades II through V are the same, but the information and length of the catalogues are different. Each of the three may have been printed in the same year (1950) or different years throughout the early 1950s.

In 1950, with the near return to reasonable postwar production levels, Bigelow Browning conceived the idea of creating a Browning catalogue devoted exclusively to higher grade Superposed shotguns. The year 1950 marked the first year of engraved postwar Brownings, and Bigelow used this opportunity to promote these higher grade Superposed. The result was the outstanding catalogue entitled, "Special Models Superposed by Browning," produced in

[7] *Ibid.*, p. 106.

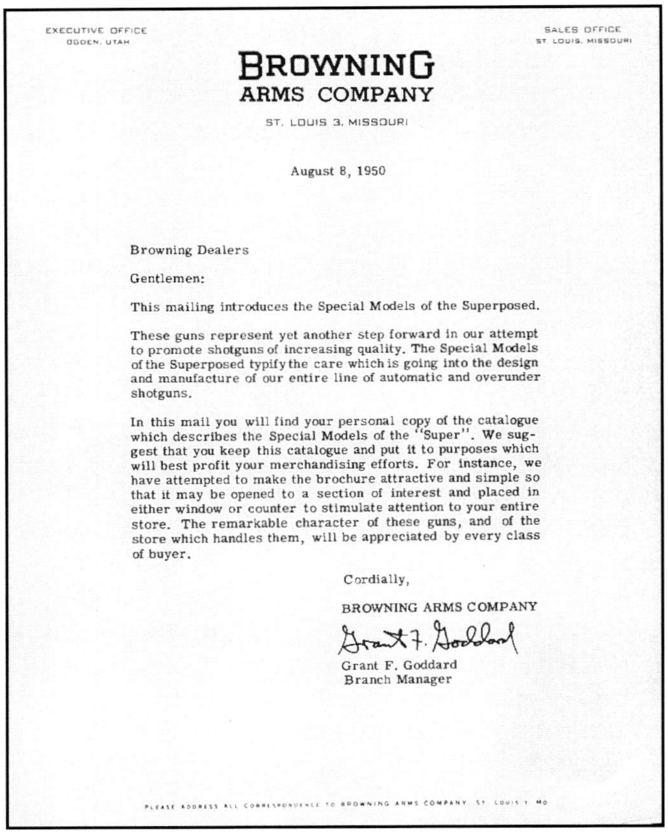

EXECUTIVE OFFICE
OGDEN, UTAH

SALES OFFICE
ST. LOUIS, MISSOURI

BROWNING
ARMS COMPANY

ST. LOUIS 3, MISSOURI

August 8, 1950

Browning Dealers

Gentlemen:

This mailing introduces the Special Models of the Superposed.

These guns represent yet another step forward in our attempt to promote shotguns of increasing quality. The Special Models of the Superposed typify the care which is going into the design and manufacture of our entire line of automatic and overunder shotguns.

In this mail you will find your personal copy of the catalogue which describes the Special Models of the "Super". We suggest that you keep this catalogue and put it to purposes which will best profit your merchandising efforts. For instance, we have attempted to make the brochure attractive and simple so that it may be opened to a section of interest and placed in either window or counter to stimulate attention to your entire store. The remarkable character of these guns, and of the store which handles them, will be appreciated by every class of buyer.

Cordially,

BROWNING ARMS COMPANY

Grant F. Goddard

Grant F. Goddard
Branch Manager

PLEASE ADDRESS ALL CORRESPONDENCE TO BROWNING ARMS COMPANY, ST. LOUIS 3, MO.

SPECIAL MODELS
Superposed
by
BROWNING

This letter, dated August 8, 1950, introduces the famous "Special Models Superposed" Browning catalogue. This was the first time since the end of the war that the company felt confident enough about production to offer engraved Superposed models for sale. The cover of the "Special Models" catalogue was not very dramatic, but the inside pages were boldly graphic. Courtesy Russ Church Collection.

Mr. Harm Williams in his office in Ogden in 1959. Harm Williams was hired as vice president of sales in 1950. He was the company's first sales manager dedicated to marketing and expanding the Browning Arms Company product line. Courtesy Browning Company.

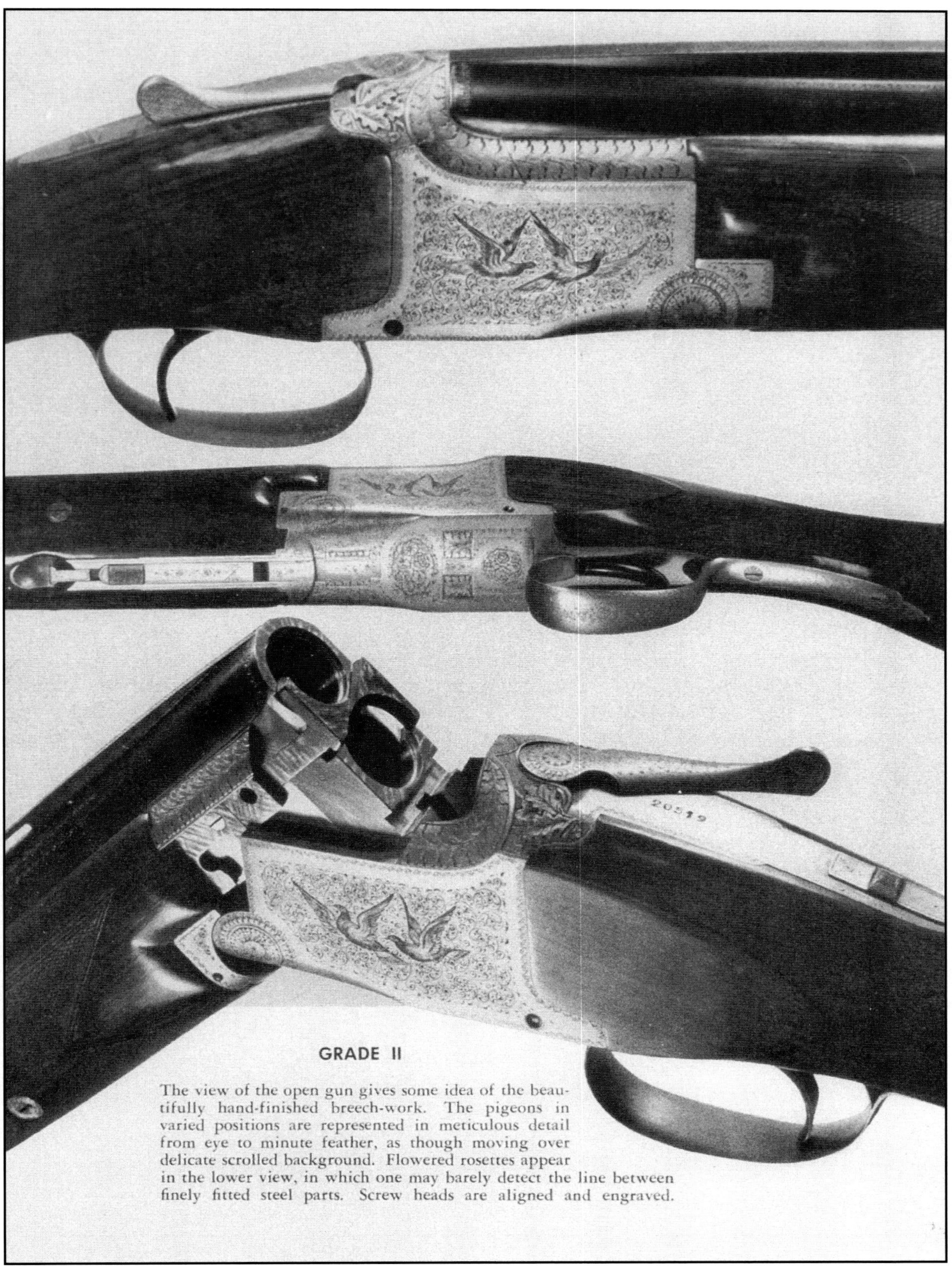

GRADE II

The view of the open gun gives some idea of the beautifully hand-finished breech-work. The pigeons in varied positions are represented in meticulous detail from eye to minute feather, as though moving over delicate scrolled background. Flowered rosettes appear in the lower view, in which one may barely detect the line between finely fitted steel parts. Screw heads are aligned and engraved.

The following sample pages from the "Special Models" catalogue give a wonderful guide to 1950s Browning Superposed engraving patterns, Grades II through V. Courtesy Russ Church Collection.

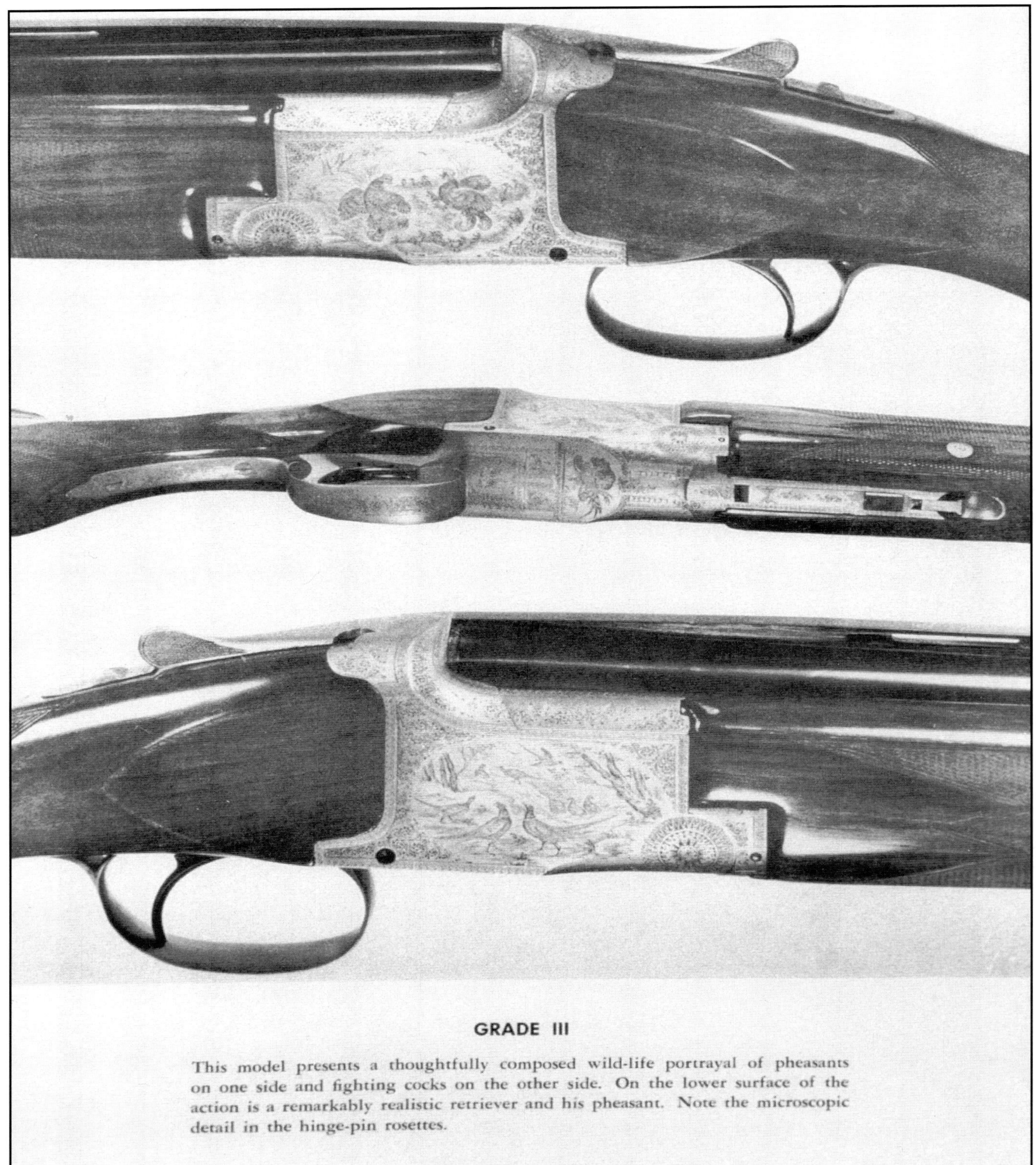

GRADE III

This model presents a thoughtfully composed wild-life portrayal of pheasants on one side and fighting cocks on the other side. On the lower surface of the action is a remarkably realistic retriever and his pheasant. Note the microscopic detail in the hinge-pin rosettes.

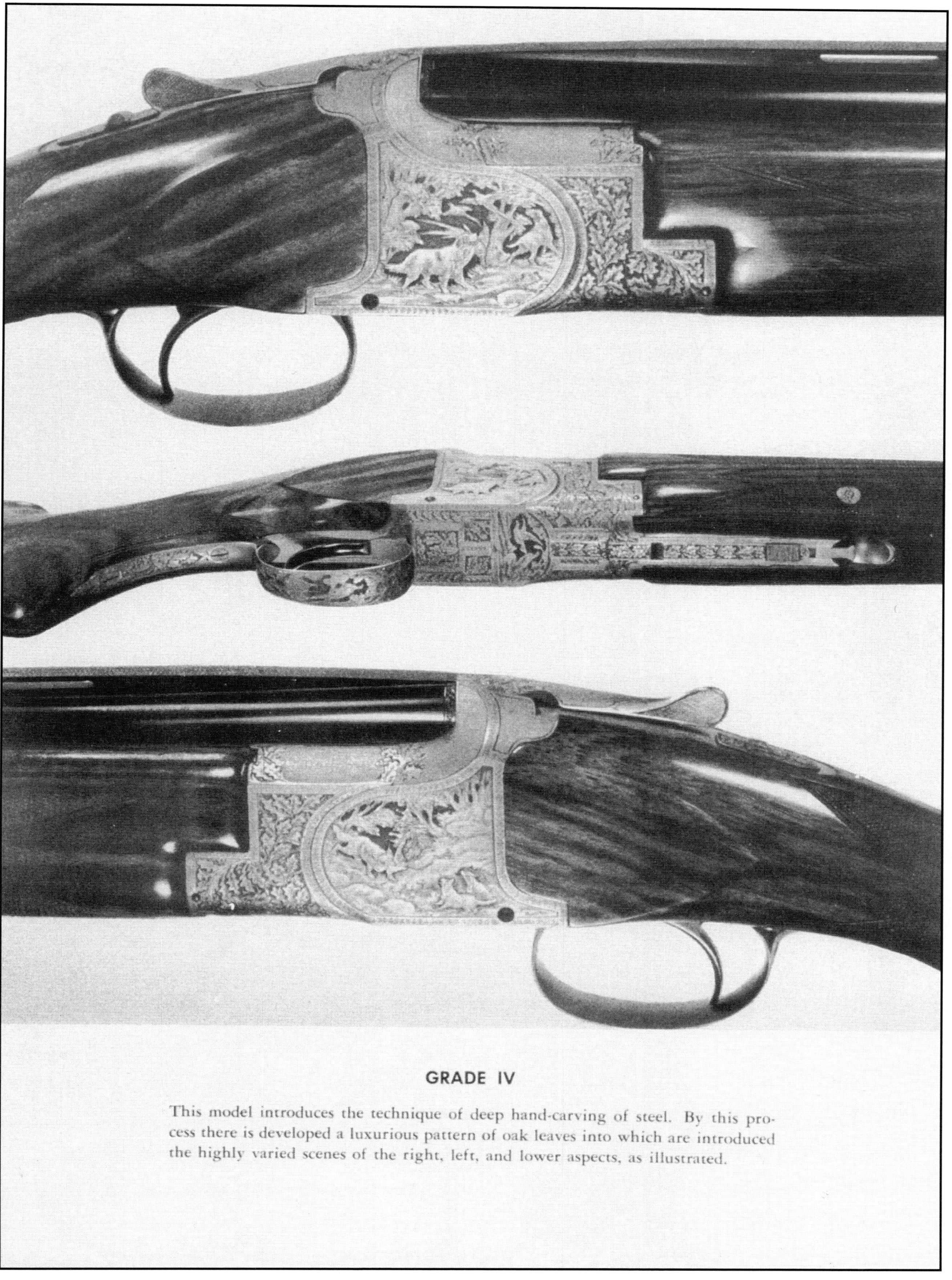

GRADE IV

This model introduces the technique of deep hand-carving of steel. By this process there is developed a luxurious pattern of oak leaves into which are introduced the highly varied scenes of the right, left, and lower aspects, as illustrated.

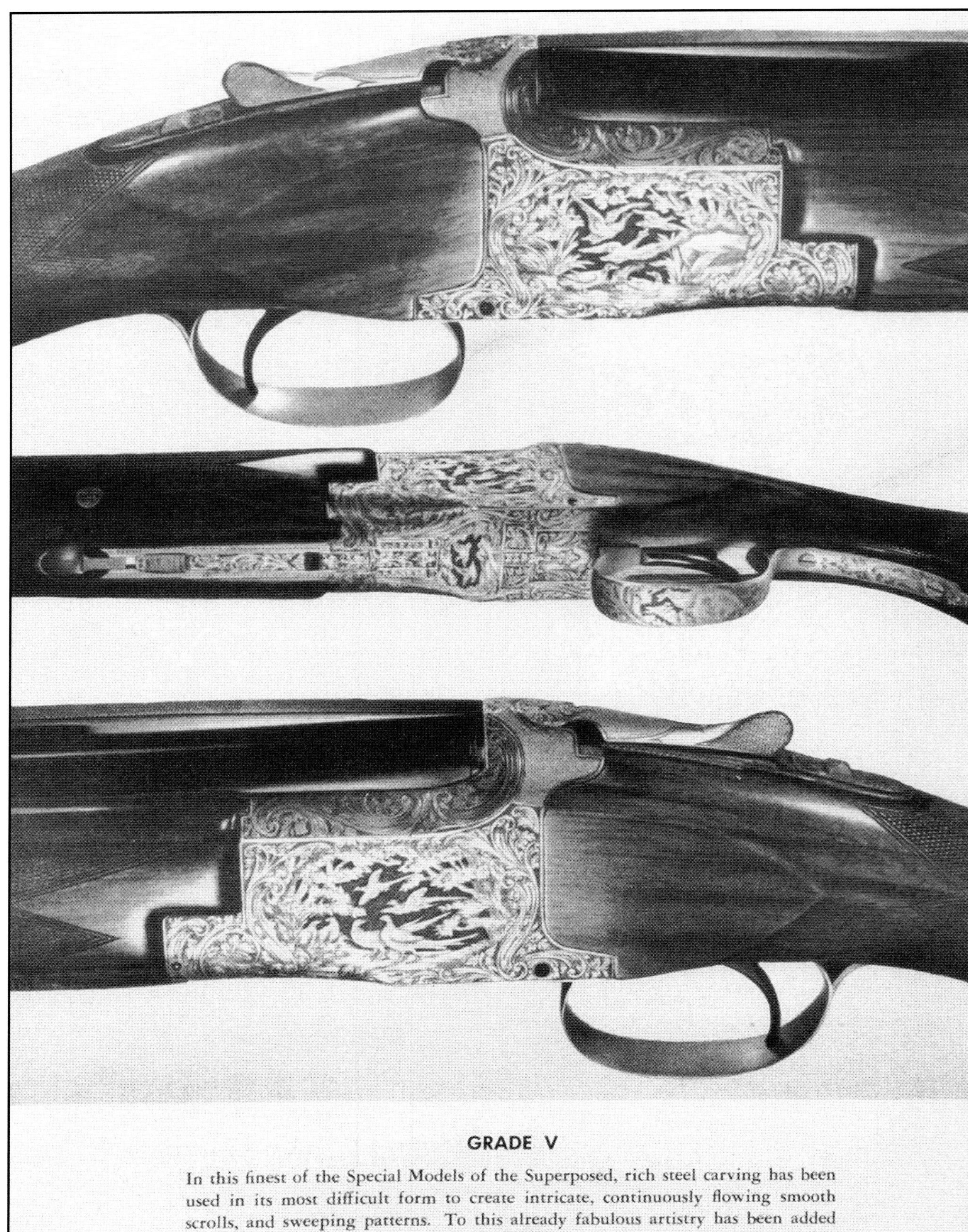

GRADE V

In this finest of the Special Models of the Superposed, rich steel carving has been used in its most difficult form to create intricate, continuously flowing smooth scrolls, and sweeping patterns. To this already fabulous artistry has been added the remarkable gradation and texture visible as illustrated in both background and living figures.

When FN gunsmiths completed their assembly process and each Superposed was function tested, inspected, and passed for shipment, the guns were sent to the shipping department where they were placed in racks awaiting shipment to agents around the world as well as to the Browning Arms Company in North America. Courtesy Fabrique Nationale Archives.

1950. The text copy and photography were done in St. Louis by a local advertising firm and approved by Bigelow Browning. This catalogue marks the first postwar marketing efforts aimed specifically at promoting the more expensive engraved Superposed grades. Bigelow Browning remained vice president at Browning until 1955 when he left the company to pursue other interests.

Another member of the postwar corporate team would soon join the company and complete the last missing piece to the executive puzzle. In 1952 Harmon Williams was hired as the company's first sales manager. His responsibilities included formulating sales policy, establishing price lists, and developing advertising stratagems. Harm worked from the Ogden office and directed all the sales activities through the branch manager in St. Louis. Harm also worked with the dealers directly from Ogden, but used the support of the sales staff in St. Louis. This arrangement was awkward and not the most efficient, but it was a much better attempt to market the Superposed than had been undertaken in the past. After Bigelow Browning left the company in 1955, running the day-to-day operations fell to Harm Williams.

With Val Browning in Ogden as president of Browning Arms Company, formulating the rejuvenation of Browning's shotgun production in

An inside view of the assembly area for Browning Auto-5 shotguns at the FN plant in Herstal. Similar to the way the Superposed was assembled, this process involved the hand fitting that was so time consuming and meticulous. These men were skilled gunsmiths who took great pride in their work. Courtesy Browning Firearms Museum, Union Station, Ogden, Utah.

Herstal fell to Val Browning's son, John Val Browning. John Val Browning, then a recent graduate in engineering from the Massachusetts Institute of Technology, went to Herstal in 1947 to act as Browning's resident engineer at FN. He worked closely with his father to increase production to a point where meaningful quantities of Superposed could be built. In Val Browning's view, the crux of the problem was the lack of a skilled workforce concerned about quality. Browning's definition of quality and FN's definition were sometimes not the same. The basis for believing that "just good enough" was acceptable for FN can be traced to the rise of trade unions in Belgium and the lack of concern for top quality on the part of management. John Val Browning worked with Fabrique Nationale's new director, René Laloux, in order to resolve these problems. With production of the Superposed at a low ten units per day in the late 1940s and no apparent solution to both low production and poor quality, Browning assumed the assembly operation of the Superposed at FN.[8]

The situation was so serious that Val Browning called upon a previous quality control system that he had installed in 1924 after he first moved to Belgium. Val gathered together a number of inspectors from the old defunct Pieper shotgun company in Liège to inspect the Auto-5 shotgun program. He found a bright young Belgian named Louis Nicolaï. Nicolaï was a graduate of the *Ecole d'Armurerie de Liège* and was employed by FN for two years prior to World War II. Val tracked him down coaching a soccer team and persuaded him to work for Browning as head of a special inspection

[8] Val A. Browning, letter to the author, April 25, 1994.

Not only was Val Browning president of Browning Arms Company, he was an active inventor. Here he is shown with his newly finished Double Automatic. Courtesy Browning Company.

team for the Superposed. Nicolaï chose his own group and formed a superb, highly loyal inspection team.[9] Nicolaï worked closely with John Val Browning and proved to be indispensable for his sound ideas and can-do approach to difficult problems. He wielded great power and influence over these procedures and was respected and feared by those who worked for him. Nicolaï and this inspection procedure were so successful that he and it remained in place until FN purchased Browning in 1977.

The excellent results of this inspection process reveal a shotgun that was skillfully hand fitted. The wood to metal fit was exacting, with the gun being taken apart and put together as many as one hundred times to obtain the perfect union between metal and wood. With the successful implementation of the new inspection and assembly procedure, production rose to over thirty units per day by 1952.[10] From this point forward, FN executed the manufacturing functions on the Superposed while Browning was in charge of assembly and finishing operations on Superposed shipped to the U.S. FN had its own separate assembly and final finishing operations apart from the Browning Company.

Perhaps the notion that FN craftsmen were superior to American workers in the art of gunmaking is weakened by the difficult situation Browning faced with Fabrique Nationale concerning quantity and

[9] Val A. Browning, letter to the author, August 15, 1993.

[10] John Val Browning, interview with the author, October 10, 1994.

After World War II the John Inglis Co. Limited was the exclusive distributor of Browning sporting guns in Canada. This arrangement lasted until 1957. In 1958 Browning Arms Company, through negotiations with FN, created Browning Arms of Canada and assumed all sales and marketing for the United States and Canada. This Inglis Catalogue was distributed to its Canadian dealers in 1952. Courtesy Herb Houze.

Browning Gun

PRICE LIST *

TYPE OF GUN	MODEL NO.	PRICE
BROWNING		
OVER AND UNDER SHOTGUN	14120	$295.00
	14123	295.00
	14220	295.00
BROWNING AUTOMATIC SHOTGUN	12000	$169.50
	12010	192.00
	12110	203.00
	12120	207.50
	16000	169.50
BROWNING		
.22 Cal. AUTOMATIC RIFLE	2210	66.50
BROWNING		
.22 Cal. REPEATING RIFLE	2200	84.75
F.N. MAUSER HIGH POWER		
REPEATING RIFLE	2700	199.50
	2570	199.50
	3006	199.50

**Prices slightly higher in Western Canada*

ALL PRICES SUBJECT TO CHANGE WITHOUT NOTICE

distributed by

JOHN INGLIS CO. LIMITED

CONSUMER PRODUCTS DIVISION 14 STRACHAN AVENUE, TORONTO

The Browning Superposed page with price list from the Inglis Company catalogue. The prices listed are in Canadian dollars. Courtesy Herb Houze.

quality. There is an unmistakable difference between building a military firearm and a fine high quality shotgun. The workers were willing to display their skills, but only if Browning showed them precisely what was needed. In spite of the difficulties encountered after the war, Val Browning and his son John Val worked hard to produce a high quality shotgun the company would be proud to sell. With their perseverance and Louis Nicolaï's supervision, Superposed quality and quantity became a reality in the postwar era.

All of the Browning shotguns shipped to the United States were sent to St. Louis, the company's sales, repair, parts, and distribution center. The corporate organization for importing Browning guns was changed in the early 1950s. In 1951 the original J. M. & M. S. Browning Company liquidated, and Browning Arms Company became the importer with wholesale functions. This arrangement remained in place until January 1, 1955, when Browning Industries was created to conduct import functions previously held by the J. M. & M. S. Browning Company. Browning Arms Company became the parent corporation. The reason for this change in corporate structure was due to United States Customs laws. Companies paid duties on goods imported into the United States based on the wholesale price of the products. When Browning Arms Company acted as importer, its wholesale price exacted a high customs duty. By creating a new company whose sole function was to act as importer, Browning saved a considerable sum of money, as the importer paid duties on its guns at a much reduced wholesale price. Thus, Browning Industries imported Belgian firearms and sold them to Browning Arms Company, who acted as the final sales outlet.

In 1958 Browning Arms of Canada was created with seventy percent of the ownership residing with Browning Arms and thirty percent with Fabrique Nationale. This event occurred because when the original agreement to sell the Superposed was signed between Browning and FN, Browning conveyed to the Belgian company the exclusive right to market the over and under in Canada. This Canadian market was serviced after the war by the John Inglis Co. Limited in Toronto, Ontario, who acted as FN's Canadian distributor. By the late 1950s, Browning felt it could do a much better job of selling the Superposed if it controlled the entire North American region. The Canada operation was incorporated on December 15, 1958, in the same fashion as the operation in St. Louis. Canadian sales were conducted from Montreal with the manager, Roland Paquin, assisted by Peter Wilson, reporting directly to Harm Williams in Ogden. Thus, by the beginning of 1959, Browning controlled all sales policies, pricing, advertising, and distribution in both the U.S. and Canada.

Also in 1958, an event occurred that changed the direction the company would take for the next twenty years. The John M. Browning side of the family, led by Val Browning, bought out the Mathew Browning side of the family, led by Marriner Browning. This was a result of a disagreement concerning expansion plans for the company. Val Browning wanted to be more aggressive with the addition of new product lines and desired ever increasing production and sales into other outdoor related ventures. This conflicted with Marriner Browning's philosophy of keeping the company small. From this point until the company was sold to FN in 1977, Browning Arms was controlled by Val A. Browning and his family.[11]

The St. Louis Years: 1948-1959

The Browning Arms Company service facility was located at 1718 Washington Avenue in St. Louis in an old abandoned shoe factory in the wholesale district not far from the Mississippi River. The building was constructed in 1910 as a multistory commercial structure and it was used as a shoe factory for the first twenty years of its existence. In the late 1930s or early 1940s, Browning had moved its service center from the original location at 12th and Spruce Street to the Washington Avenue location. Browning occupied the fifth floor of what was then called the Monogram Building, a twelve-story edifice.

A few years after World War II, Grant Goddard was hired as general manager of the St. Louis facility. He recalled that in 1948 there were about twenty-seven employees working in an atmosphere that was still very much reminiscent of the turn of the century. The offices were open, with all of the accounting and billing people in one large room along with a sales staff of about four people. The walls were brick and old ceiling lights were suspended from horizontal wooden timbers. Furniture and fixtures were antiquated. It was in this environment that the Browning Arms Company

[11] Val A. Browning, letter to the author, April 25, 1994.

Mr. Grant Goddard (left) with Mr. Val Browning in Goddard's St. Louis office. Grant Goddard was the general manager of the St. Louis office from 1948 until its departments were moved to Morgan in 1968. This photo was taken in 1955 on one of Val Browning's visits to the St. Louis office. Courtesy Grant Goddard.

conducted its most important business: sales and collecting money.

Behind this one large principal room was another space that housed the service, repair, parts, and shipping aspects of the business. It was here that spare parts were kept in addition to all gun inventory. In 1948 there were about ten gunsmiths who repaired and serviced Browning shotguns. Their foreman was still Mitch Heiter, who moved over from the original location at 12th and Spruce. These Browning gunsmiths were well trained, having spent a four-year tool and die apprenticeship before being allowed to become journeymen gunsmiths. They were trained on Browning shotguns on the job by the more experienced hands, who themselves had learned through a period of trial and error, the best way to repair and refit a Superposed. There was no direct assistance from FN in the form of working drawings or procedures manuals; only general directives. In spite of these difficulties, repair work was done efficiently and with care.

One of the most serious problems that faced the St. Louis operation was the lack of organization of parts inventory. There were no records of parts and no way of tracking parts sales or low stock. Consequently, parts were always in short supply. Grant Goddard's main task in 1948 was to make

Browning gunsmiths in May of 1948 at the 1718 Washington Avenue location in St. Louis, Missouri. From left to right: Al Sargent, Howard Maas, Red Estes, Marty Ryan, Dick Heiter, Howard Hoker, Bud Worley, Mitch Heiter, Herman Stengel, and Harry Heiter. According to Grant Goddard, Mitch Heiter was the finest gunsmith in America. Courtesy Grant Goddard.

this a more efficient operation. It was time to take an outmoded practice of doing business and transform it into a more modern business administration. The postwar Browning service center directly serviced more than eighteen thousand dealers across the country.

On the back side of the building on Washington Avenue was a loading dock where the Browning guns, both the Auto-5 and the Superposed, were unloaded and brought by elevator to the fifth floor. The guns were logged in by Harry Altenbern and his small but efficient crew of clerks, and then promptly sent out again down the same elevator to the loading dock to be placed on trucks and distributed to dealers across the country. Despite the competency of the staff, this procedure was time-consuming and resulted in needless bottlenecks.

In the early 1950s the old-fashioned St. Louis offices were in dire need of expansion and modernization. The decision was made to move to larger quarters. The Monogram Building had an addition with the address of 1706 Washington. Browning took over the entire second floor as well as the basement. An architect was employed to draw a modern and serviceable floor plan and the entire area, about thirty-two thousand square feet, received a restoration. The basement served as a bonded warehouse where Browning guns could remain until custom duties had been paid. A conveyor belt was installed to allow easy loading from the loading dock to either the warehouse in the basement or the shipping department on the first floor.

The Browning St. Louis sales office remained at this location until it moved to Morgan, Utah, in 1968.

The full St. Louis team as pictured at their annual Christmas party in 1948. Not all of the people in this photograph are employees of Browning; some are guests of the company. At the head of the table in the center is Grant Goddard with shop foreman Mitch Heiter on his left. Courtesy Browning Company.

The shipping, repair, parts, and service facility remained in St. Louis until 1968 when they were relocated to Arnold, Missouri, a small town on the southern outskirts of St. Louis. After Browning moved out of its St. Louis offices, the new owner discovered during renovation that a firing range was located in the basement under the 17th Street sidewalk, and shotgun pattern targets were still in place against the equipment structures located on the roof.[12]

The Browning shotguns that arrived in St. Louis had traveled a long way. They were shipped from Herstal, Belgium, to the Belgian port of Ostend, then to Montreal, Canada, if the water had not yet frozen for winter. During the winter months the port of St. John in New Brunswick received the shipments. The guns went through Canadian Customs, where they were handled more quickly and securely than they might have been along an American East Coast port. From the Canadian port the guns were loaded onto a Canadian Pacific train and shipped to St. Louis. From the train they were again off-loaded to trucks and were delivered to the Browning facility in downtown St. Louis. Although this journey may seem unnecessarily complex and circuitous, it was in fact the safest, most expeditious and efficient route.

Postwar Superposed Catalogue Offerings: 1948-1959

Val Browning was committed to making the Superposed one of the most popular and highly regarded over and under guns in North America for the money. Because of the devastation the war caused on FN's production facilities, Browning was forced to proceed with a conservative sales plan that would reintroduce the Superposed to the American shooter slowly and with a minimum of choices. The company did not want to promise more than it could deliver. From a single gauge offering in one style in 1948, the company expanded its Superposed product line by the end of the decade to include a wide array of Superposed guns in four gauges and numerous styles and barrel lengths. By 1956 the Browning Superposed represented a full product line that was to establish itself as one of the most popular double guns in America.

---

[12] *St. Louis Post-Dispatch*, p. 16 BP, September 18, 1989.

The famous "Rugged as the Rockies" catalogue distributed in the early 1950s. Browning wanted to take advantage of the growing economy of the postwar era by establishing its guns as strong and reliable sporting arms. The Superposed pictured on the front of the brochure is serial number 17119, shipped to Browning in St. Louis on May 31, 1948. The gun was then shipped to Browning's corporate offices in Ogden, Utah, on July 28, 1948. The gun was one of five specially engraved Superposed in that shipment, and was probably the prototype of the Grade V, introduced in 1950. Courtesy Russ Church.

An overall view of the famous "Rugged as the Rockies" Grade V Superposed. Note the field style forearm and the outstanding wood grain on the buttstock. Courtesy Browning Company.

This is the same gun, serial number 17119, used in Browning's advertising campaign and pictured on the front of the company's "Rugged as the Rockies" catalogue. This photo shows in greater detail the outstanding engraving on this distinguished Superposed. Courtesy Browning Company.

The Prewar Superposed

The left side of a prewar special order Browning Superposed in what may be a variation of the Diana Grade. Serial number 7167 is signed by Felix Funken towards the lower front of the receiver. Note also that the receiver is a flat-sided one without the customary European sculptured frame. This is a strong indication that the gun was originally ordered for sale in the United States, where it was delivered to Browning in St. Louis on February 10, 1936. Dick Spurzem Collection.

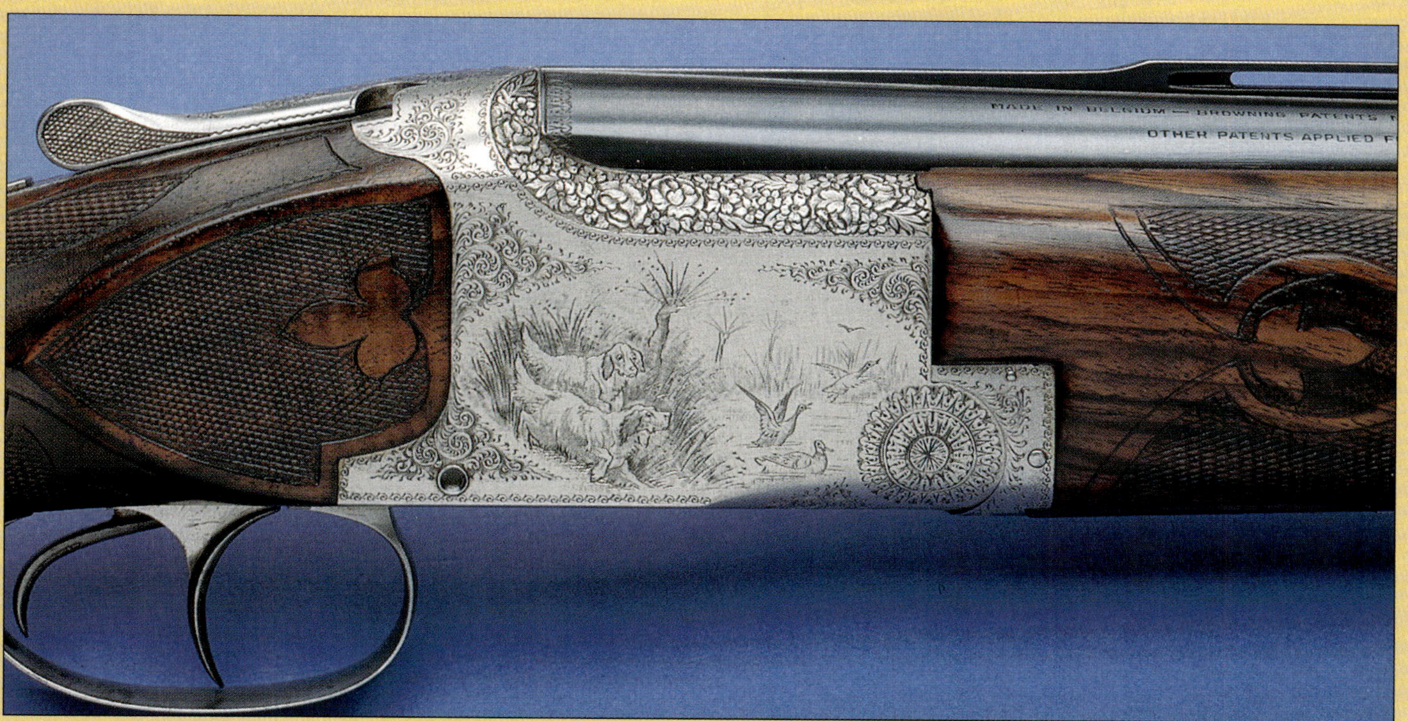

The right side of serial number 7167. Note the flower motif on the barrel ears above the receiver. The bottom of the receiver is scroll engraved, as is the trigger guard. Dick Spurzem Collection.

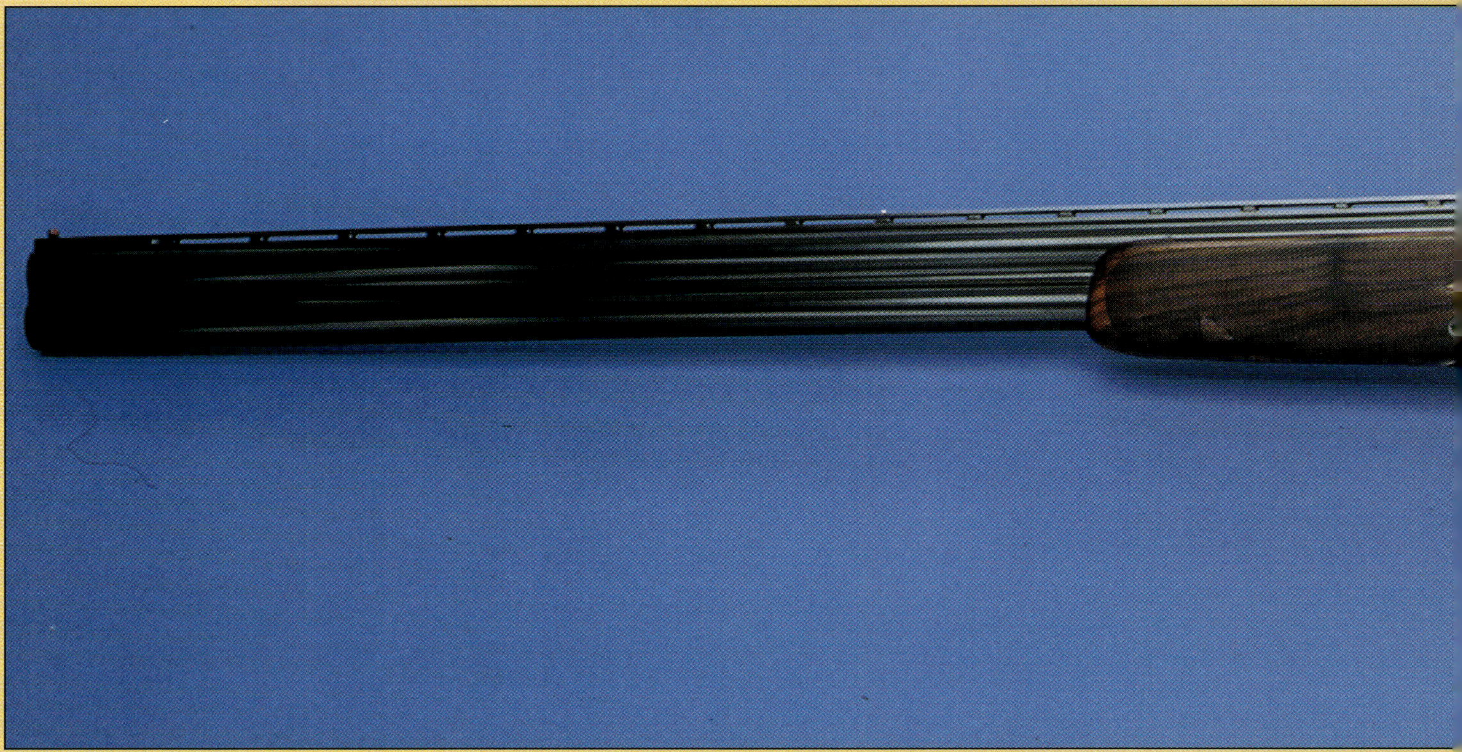

The Superposed of the 1950s

This full-length photograph illustrates the general characteristics found on the Browning Superposed Grade VI. This gun is fitted with a Field style forearm. Notice the checkering pattern on the buttstock and forearm as well as the nicely figured wood. This grade was offered for sale for only two and one-half years. Courtesy Browning Company.

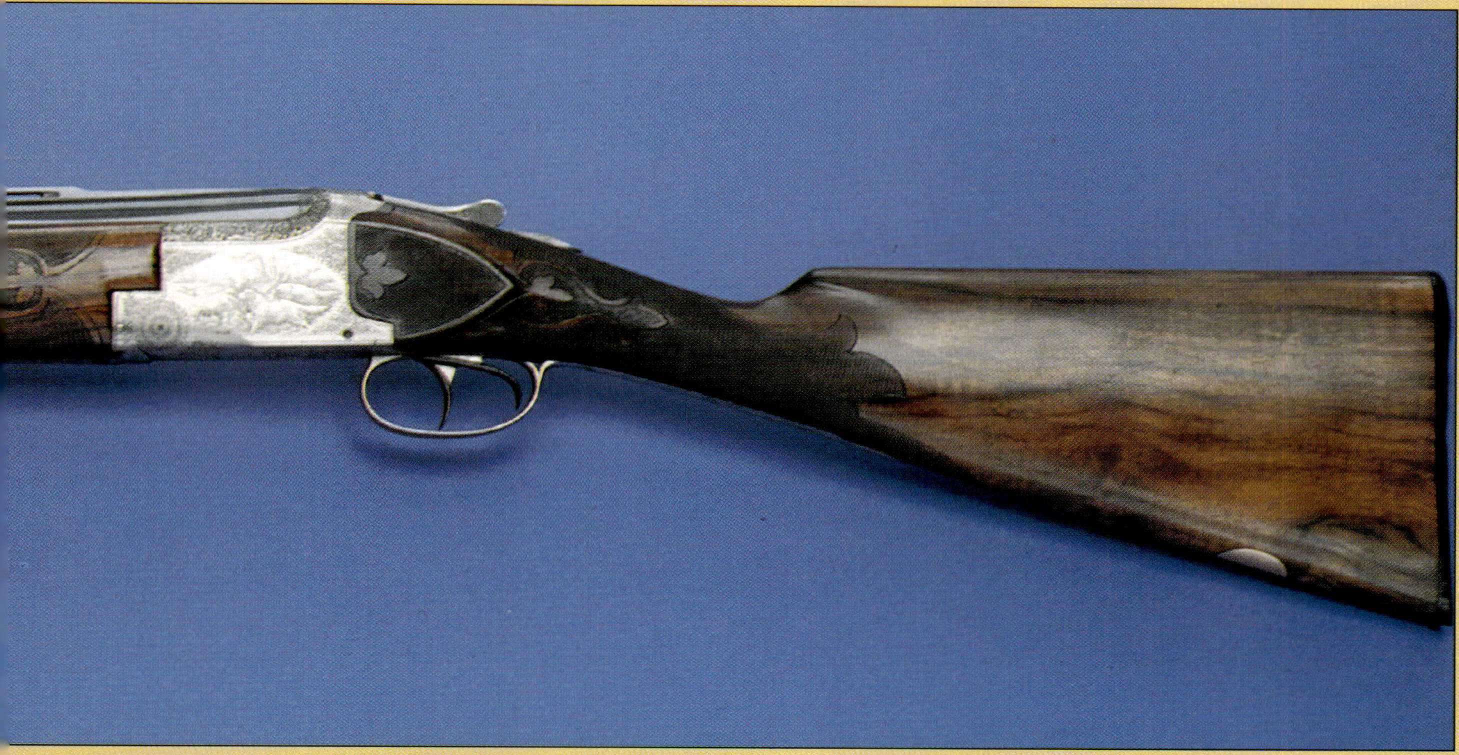

An overall view of the special order Superposed. Not only is the receiver specially engraved, but the buttstock and forearm have distinctive carving, fine line checkering, and fancy wood. This prewar 12 gauge is fitted with double triggers, 28-inch barrels, and a Non-Crossfire ventilated rib. Dick Spurzem Collection.

Browning Superposed Grade VI, serial number 64132, is a 12 gauge fitted with a 30-inch barrel choked full and full with ventilated rib. These photos show in great detail the engraving features of both sides of the receiver on a Grade VI. The gun is signed by Müller and features ducks and pheasants because of its gauge. Compare this Grade VI with the prototype that appears in Chapter 2. All Grade VI Superposed were different in composition even when engraved by the same artisan. Courtesy Dick Spurzem Collection.

It was unusual for an FN engraving pattern to find its way to North America, but this 20 gauge Superposed, serial number 6203, is engraved with the FN C2 pattern. Notice that the trigger has been grayed to match the receiver, a subtle but classic special order feature. Courtesy Dick Spurzem Collection.

This 12 gauge Browning Superposed, serial number 17116, is a two-barrel set with 26-1/2-inch barrels choked improved cylinder and modified, and 28-inch barrels choked improved modified and full. Each barrel is numbered 1 and 2. The engraving pattern on this gun is reminiscent of the FN C2 Grade, but in fact is most likely a special order gun. This Superposed was assembled May 2, 1948, and shipped to Browning in St. Louis, along with four other special order guns, on May 31, 1948. It was then sent to the Browning corporate offices in Ogden, Utah, later in the year. Courtesy Dick Spurzem Collection.

This special order Superposed, serial number 56775, was shipped to Marshall Field in Chicago on November 11, 1959. It is fitted with a 28-inch barrel choked full and full with ventilated rib. The gun is signed by A. Gillet on the underside of the receiver near the trigger guard. The floral engraving pattern is similar to other special order Superposed delivered in Europe. Courtesy Dick Spurzem Collection.

The Superposed of the 1960s

A Browning Superposed Midas Grade in a Trap configuration. Notice the recoil pad and forearm with flat bottom pistol grip. High grade Superposed were very popular with trapshooters. Courtesy Browning Company.

A close-up view of what is most likely a Vrancken engraved Midas Grade executed sometime in the mid-1960s. This is a Trap model, similar to the one pictured above. Courtesy Browning Company.

This Exhibition Grade Superposed, serial number 39400S5, was engraved around 1965 by two of FN's best engravers, André Watrin and Louis Vrancken. This Superposed is fitted with two sets of barrels, one 30 inches choked full and full, and the other 28 inches choked full and full. Watrin signed his name on the left side and Vrancken signed his name on the right side. Both buttstock and forearm are heavily carved, and the wood is extra fancy. Courtesy Dick Spurzem Collection.

This Vrancken and Watrin engraved 20 gauge Superposed Exhibition Grade, serial number 23186, was built in 1962. This gun is signed by both engravers on one side only, the left side. The gun is fitted with two sets of barrels, one 28 inches choked full and full, and the other 26-1/2 inches choked full and full. Both barrels are numbered with Roman numerals. Courtesy Dick Spurzem Collection.

This Midas Grade 12 gauge Superposed BROADway Trap model, serial number 94047, shows a different variation of the usual Midas Grade pattern. Executed by a young engraver, José Baerten, this gun was shipped to a Browning dealer in Alameda, California, in the summer of 1962. This Superposed was a special order gun that not only had a different and more extensive engraving pattern, but a special checkering pattern as well. This Superposed was fitted with two sets of barrels, the first of which was 32 inches choked improved modified and full, and the second was 28 inches choked skeet and improved modified with a Field type forearm. Courtesy Dick Spurzem Collection.

This Funken engraved 12 gauge Superposed, serial number 72384, was one of the first Pointer Grade designs. It is a Trap model fitted with a 30-inch barrel choked full and full. This gun, or one very much like it, was featured in the 1960 Browning catalogue as the Pointer Grade gun. This distinctive Pointer Grade shows a sparse scrollwork border around the game scene. This gun may well have been Funken's last proposed design for the Pointer Grade. This layout was not adopted as the final choice for the Pointer Grade. Courtesy Dick Spurzem Collection.

The Artistry of Felix Funken

The left and right side of serial number 39815 shows the deep relief engraving and incredible attention to detail that each scene exhibits. The vignettes are entirely original and such a particular piece would probably warrant the term Exhibition Grade due to its uniqueness. There are a total of seventeen animals engraved on this Superposed. Both sides of the receiver are signed by Funken. Courtesy Dick Spurzem Collection.

The underside of serial number 39815 shows a profusion of game birds and animals in various vignettes, each telling a different story. Practically every square centimeter is covered with a game scene or scrollwork. Courtesy Dick Spurzem Collection.

A top view of serial number 39815 shows the continuation of profuse coverage on this Superposed. The top lever even has a game scene engraved on it. The serial number is gold inlaid inside of an oval, and the Roman numeral II appears in gold on the barrel rib, which is hand matted. Courtesy Dick Spurzem Collection.

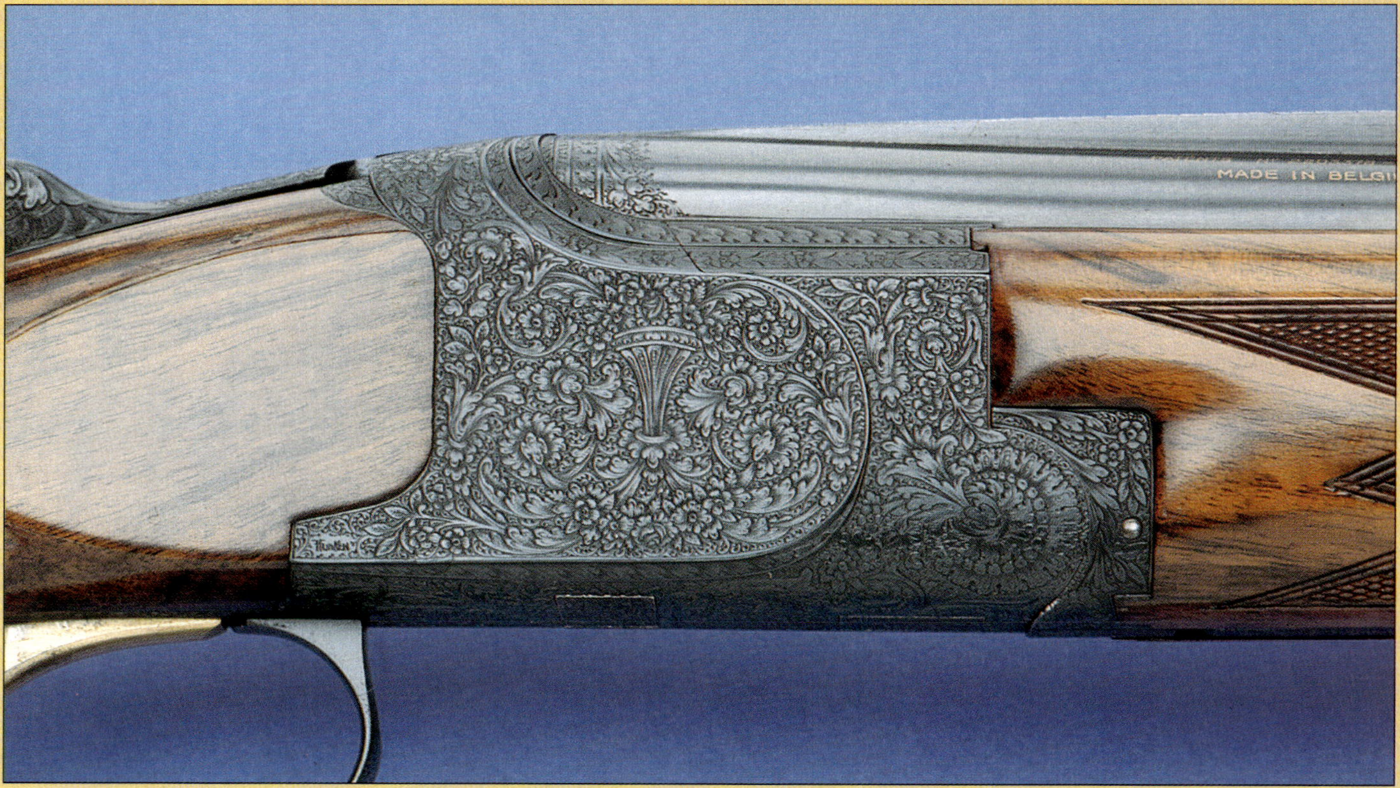

This unique Funken engraved 20 gauge Browning Superposed was fitted with two sets of barrels, hand matted with barrel addresses in gold. Each set of barrels is numbered I and II in gold. The serial number is 8401, which indicates that the gun was probably built sometime around 1956. This is an unusual pattern for an American Browning Superposed with its deeply cut scrollwork and bouquet design. Such a gun would suggest that it was a special order piece designed and executed by Felix Funken. Courtesy Dick Spurzem Collection.

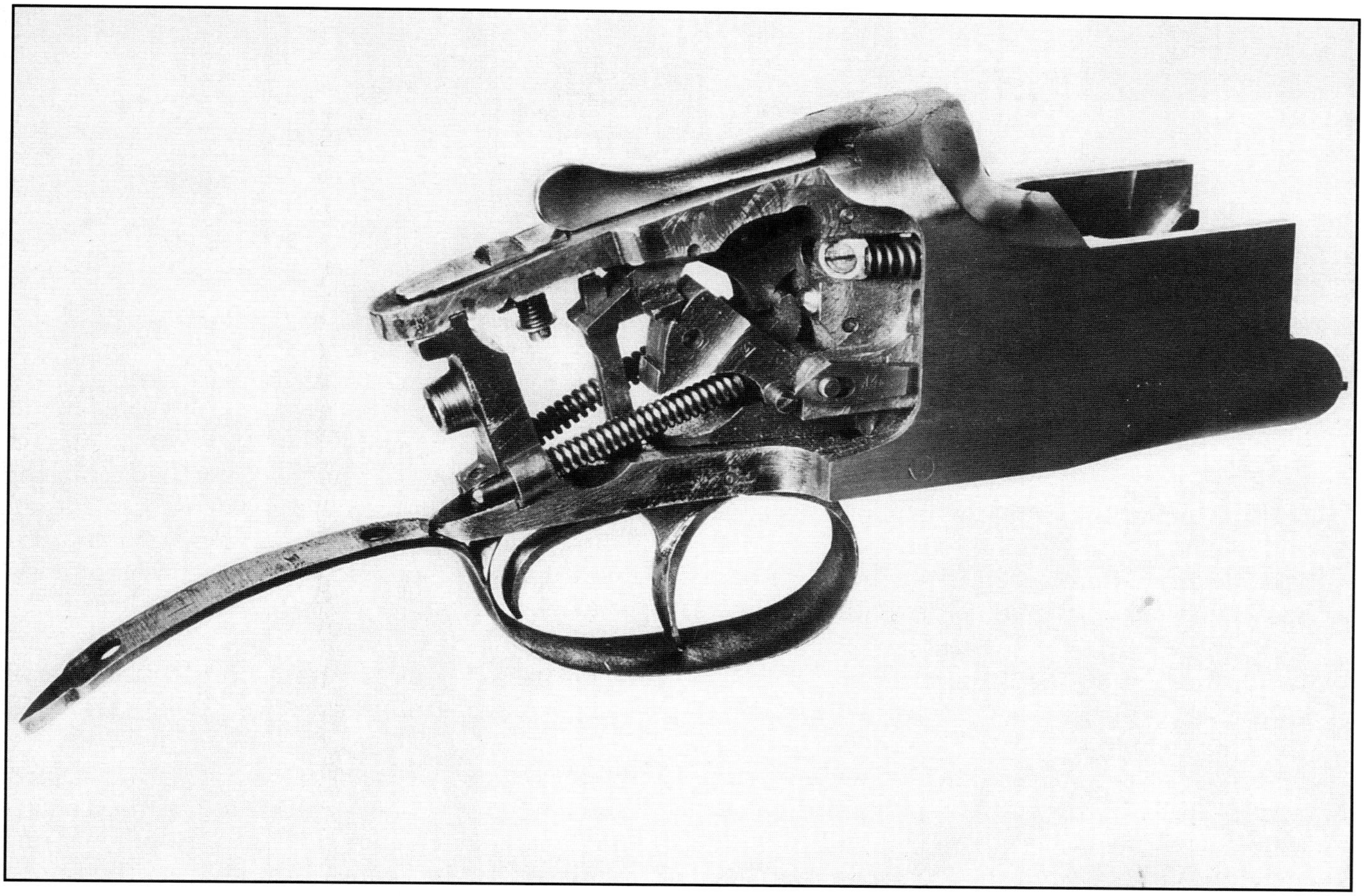

While Val Browning worked very hard to improve the single selective trigger for the Superposed, double triggers were very popular in Europe and around the rest of the world. Fabrique Nationale continued to produce double triggers for its Superposed after World War II. This photograph shows a newly machined double trigger frame built in 1949. Courtesy Fabrique Nationale Archives.

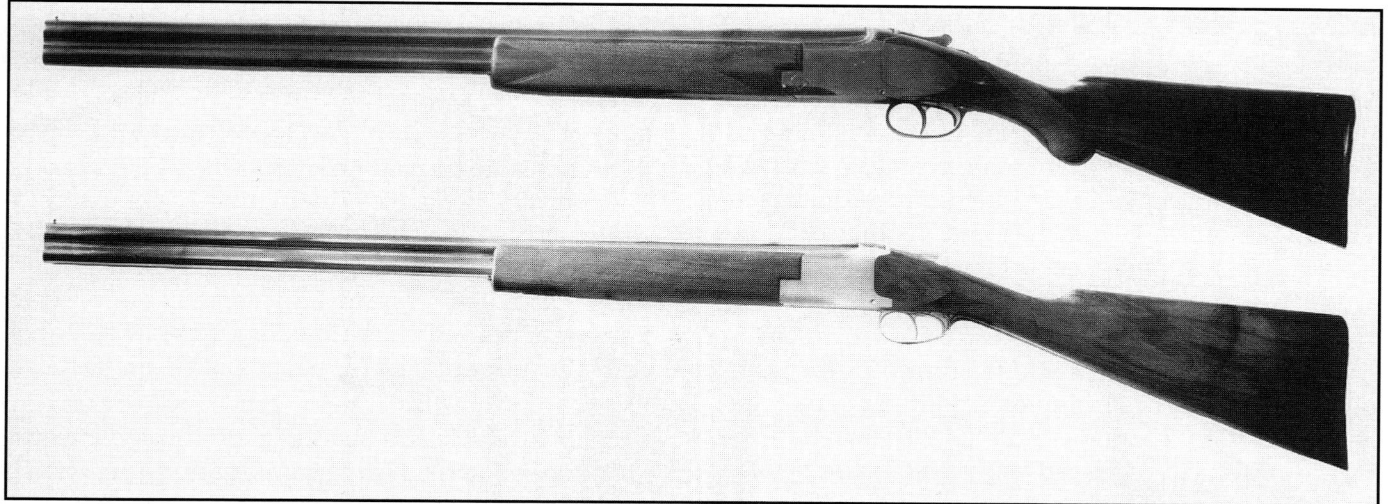

A production 12 gauge Browning Superposed is pictured at the top of this photo for comparison to the 20 gauge prototype shown at the bottom. Val Browning actually worked on this 20 gauge Superposed in the late 1930s and had the downsizing accomplished for production before the outbreak of World War II. But with the beginning of the war and its aftermath, the 20 gauge Superposed was not produced until 1949. Courtesy Fabrique Nationale Archives.

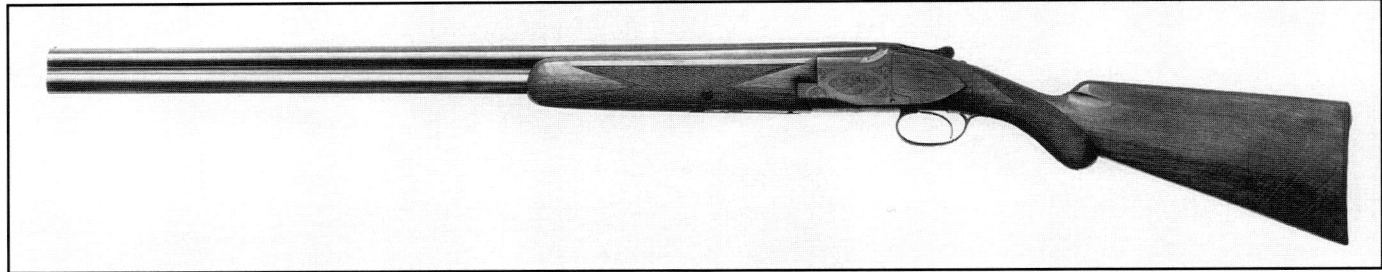

A 1950s Standard Weight Grade I Browning Superposed in a Hunting configuration with solid matted rib and single selective trigger. Courtesy Fabrique Nationale Archives.

1948: When the Superposed was reintroduced in 1948, it was for all practical purposes a continuation of the prewar model. Offered in a basic 12 gauge Hunting configuration with single selective trigger in a Standard Weight, the Grade I was the only grade offered for sale in 1948. The buyer had a choice of either raised matted or ventilated ribs.

1949: The year 1949 witnessed the introduction of the 20 gauge Superposed, but in Grade I only, as was the 12 gauge. The basic model had the same features as offered for sale in the preceding year.

1950: It was not until 1950 that Browning Arms offered the full Superposed line in both 12 gauge and the newly introduced 20 gauge. This was the year engraved models returned to the product line in Grades I through V. In 1950 the Superposed buyer had a choice of raised matted rib or ventilated rib. Superposed with matted ribs were offered in the company's catalogues only in Grade I with single selective trigger. The 12 gauge was available in 26-1/2-inch, 28-inch, and 30-inch barrels with light scroll engraving in Standard Weight only. For Superposed buyers who desired a ventilated rib, both the 12 and 20 gauge guns were available in Grades I through V with single selective triggers and barrel lengths of 26-1/2 inches to 30 inches in 12 gauge and 26-1/2 inches and 28 inches in 20 gauge. Most Superposed offered for sale in 1950 were Standard Weight guns only with Hunting configuration stocks.

The only exception to this is found in the curious fashion that Browning offered its 12 gauge Superposed with 30-inch ventilated rib barrels. This configuration was offered with a Trap dimension buttstock only and a Hunting style forearm—a peculiar combination. Superposed 12 gauge guns with 30-inch raised matted rib barrels were offered with Hunting dimension buttstocks and forearms.

1951: Catalogue offerings were identical to 1950.

1952: Browning Arms continued to offer the usual 12 and 20 gauge Hunting guns that had been available the previous two years. The new offering for 1952 was the 12 gauge Trap model. Featured as a Standard Weight Superposed, the Trap model was available in Grades I through V with 30-inch barrels, single selective trigger, ventilated rib, and semi-beavertail forearm. Regular chokes for the Trap model were full and full; modified and full; and improved modified and full. The Trap model was fitted with a Trap dimension stock featuring a higher comb.

1953: Catalogue offerings were identical to 1952.

1954: Catalogue offerings were identical to 1953.

1955: In 1955 Browning added another new model to its Superposed product line, the 12 gauge 3-inch Magnum. The Magnum buyer had a choice of either a raised matted rib in Grade I only or a ventilated rib in Grades I through V. The Superposed 12 gauge Magnum was offered with 30-inch barrels chambered for 3-inch shells choked full and full, or modified and full. Stock dimensions were the same as the Hunting models except for the addition of a factory installed recoil pad. The weight was approximately 8-1/4 pounds. The retail price was $236.00 with raised matted rib for Grade I, the same as the Hunting models. The balance of Superposed catalogue offerings for 1955 remained the same as the year before.

1956: This year was distinguished by a significant increase in the Superposed catalogue offerings. For the first time since the postwar period, the Lightning was reintroduced into the product line. Available in 12 or 20 gauge with 26-1/2-inch or 28-inch ventilated rib barrels with single selective trigger and half pistol grip stock, the Lightning's buttstock dimensions were the same as the Hunting models. Any combination of chokes could be ordered from full to cylinder on this model. Weight for 12 gauge guns with 26-1/2-inch barrels was 7 pounds, and for the 20 gauge with 26-1/2-inch barrels the weight was 6 pounds. The retail price for the Lightning was $275.00 in Grade I compared to $261.00 for the Standard Weight Grade I model.

A Skeet model was also offered for the first time in 1956. This model was nothing more than a Stan-

One of the first advertisements for the newly introduced 20 gauge Browning Superposed. It was referred to as the "Blue Streak" because of its light weight. This euphemism was used only for a short period of time either because it did not catch on or because the company wanted to standardize model designations. Courtesy Russ Church.

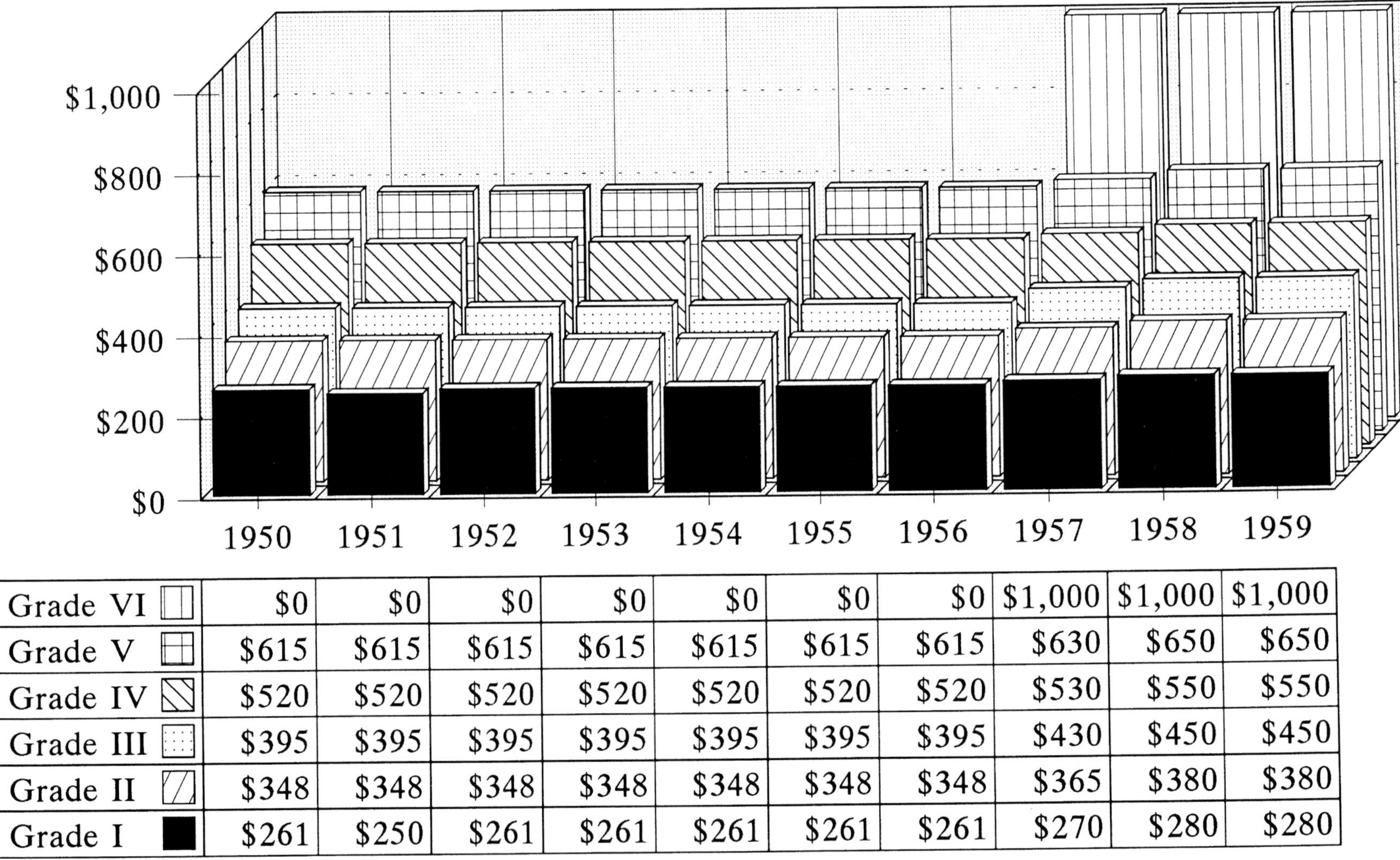

	1950	1951	1952	1953	1954	1955	1956	1957	1958	1959
Grade VI	$0	$0	$0	$0	$0	$0	$0	$1,000	$1,000	$1,000
Grade V	$615	$615	$615	$615	$615	$615	$615	$630	$650	$650
Grade IV	$520	$520	$520	$520	$520	$520	$520	$530	$550	$550
Grade III	$395	$395	$395	$395	$395	$395	$395	$430	$450	$450
Grade II	$348	$348	$348	$348	$348	$348	$348	$365	$380	$380
Grade I	$261	$250	$261	$261	$261	$261	$261	$270	$280	$280

Prices are based on Lightning 12 gauge Hunting model with ventilated rib.
Grade VI added to Superposed line in 1957.

Chart 2-1

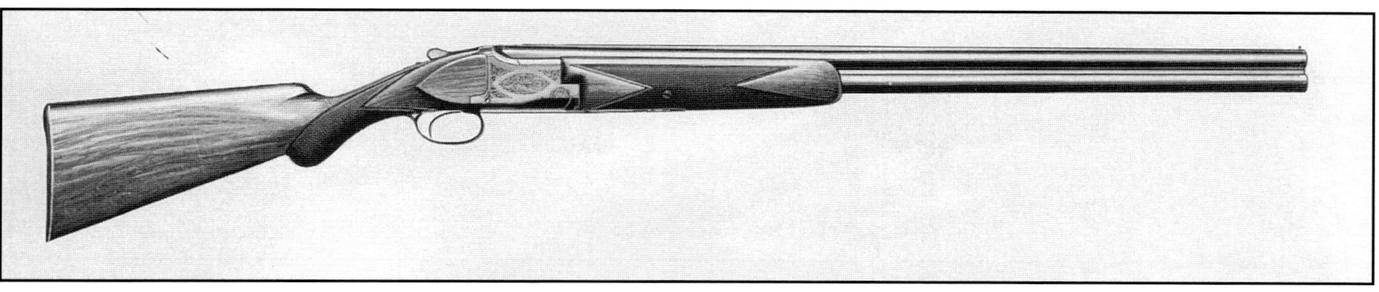

A 1950s Standard Weight Grade I Browning Superposed Skeet model with solid matte rib and single selective trigger. If compared to the Hunting model, strictly by outward appearance there was no difference. Only the chokes, skeet and skeet, made the difference between a Skeet gun and a Hunting model. Courtesy Fabrique Nationale Archives.

dard Weight Hunting model with skeet chokes. The stock dimensions and forearm were identical to the Hunting model, as were weights and barrel lengths. The Skeet model was offered with ventilated rib barrels only.

The Trap and Magnum models continued to be offered with the same features as before, as was the Standard Weight Hunting model.

Browning had offered extra sets of same gauge barrels for its Superposed since the beginning of production, but 1956 was the first year two barrel sets were specifically promoted. The customer could choose any combination of four chokes in two barrel lengths of the same gauge. The price of these two barrel sets included a fitted luggage case. The case used during this time period was built on a solid plywood frame and covered with brown Tolex, a leather-like cloth cover with bronze hardware. The interior was a soft low-pile material. The retail price of a Grade I Lightning with two sets of barrels was $435.00 and increased up to $800.00 for the Grade V. Browning urged its dealers to tell its customers that these extra barrel sets may take at least four months to deliver and that the order could not be canceled. Perhaps the most important point the dealer was required to tell the customer was that these extra barrel sets could only be produced in one gauge (12 or 20) for both sets of barrels. However, one set of barrels could be Standard Weight and the other set Lightning. An extra charge of $15.00 was added for this combination.

1957: This year marked the first time that Browning began to use code numbers in its dealer price list to help simplify ordering guns from the company's expanding product lines. The year began with only a minor change in the Superposed offerings: the addition of 3-inch chambers for its 20 gauge guns was now standard. It was not until July 15, 1957, that a new grade was offered for the Superposed. This grade was designated Grade VI and featured deep relief scroll engraving with gold inlays. The retail price was $1,000.00 in Standard Weight and $1,015.00 in the Lightning weight. The two barrel set was priced to the public for $1,300.00 in Standard Weight and $25 more in the Lightning model. The balance of the Superposed line remained the same except for a modest retail price increase of about three percent.

1958: Catalogue offerings for 1958 were unchanged from the previous year; however, another price increase was implemented of between three and four percent for all grades excluding the Grade VI.

1959: The decade of the 1950s ended with the Superposed product line mostly unchanged for 1959, but greatly expanded from its meager beginnings in 1948. There was however one important change in the Superposed that was to have a significant impact for the next decade: the introduction of the 28 gauge and .410 bore Superposed. Announced to its dealers in May of 1959, these new small bore Superposed were an instant success, but only a few of these guns were delivered very late in 1959. The major impact of these new gauges on the Superposed product line would not be felt until 1960.[13]

The 1950s Browning Superposed

Browning over and under shotguns produced during this period have a special place in the hearts of many collectors and shooters. The years following World War II saw many additions to the Superposed product line. Some consider guns built in this era to have no peer in terms of quality; others find the engraving patterns to be particular-

[13] Browning Arms Company, sales letter to "Authorized Browning Dealers," July 23, 1959, p. 3.

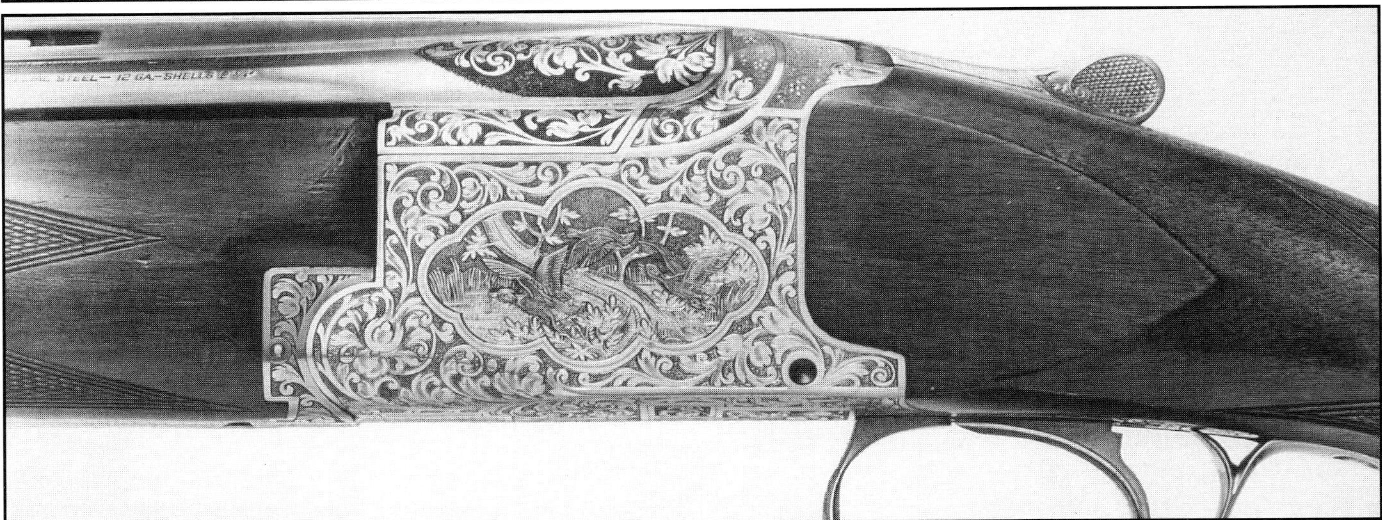

This 12 gauge Browning Superposed is engraved in the Grade VI style with gold inlays. The photograph is dated February 8, 1957, and the receiver is signed by "Müller" on the right side. This Superposed could very well have been the prototype of the Grade VI. Research indicates that Müller was an engraver working in Germany who did contract work for FN. He seems to have specialized in gold inlay work. Introduced in 1957, the Grade VI was the top of the line production grade for the Superposed and each one was different to some small degree. This grade was the forerunner of the Midas Grade. Courtesy Fabrique Nationale Archives.

ly desirable and attractive. All would agree that the decade of the '50s brought forth a new and fascinating variation to the Superposed: the 20 gauge.

The idea to expand the Superposed line with the addition of the popular 20 bore was Val Browning's. His conclusion to proceed with the design was encouraged by the sales department, which indicated there was indeed a market for a 20 gauge Superposed shotgun in the American marketplace.[14] Val Browning worked out the changes necessary to convert his father's original 12 gauge design to a 20 gauge version. He faced problems with getting the dimensions correct on the drafting board, but other than that difficulty, no unexpected complications arose. Val credits the help of his excellent draftsman Mr. Ista with the successful completion of the 20 gauge conversion.[15] Val had a prototype of his 20 gauge Superposed built prior to World War II, but the war interrupted his plans to introduce the gauge into the Superposed product line. No patent was required to convert the 12 gauge Superposed to a 20 gauge because, except for the proportions, the design and function were the same. Browning Arms Company changed some of the model designations for the Superposed after the war. In order to simplify what will later become an increasingly complex list of subvariations, each principal model will be reviewed under the heading Hunting, Trap, and Skeet.

Hunting Models: The Superposed Hunting model was offered in a Standard Weight version and a Lightning version in both 12 and 20 gauge. The 12 gauge guns were fitted with one of three barrel lengths: 30 inches with raised matted rib,[16] 28 inches with ventilated or raised matted rib, and 26-1/2 inches with ventilated or raised matted rib. All 12 gauge guns were chambered for the 2-3/4-inch shell, except for the Magnum, which accepted the 3-inch shell. Superposed in 20 gauge were offered only with a choice of 28-inch or 26-1/2-inch barrels. These 20 gauge barrels were chambered for the 2-3/4-inch shell until around 1957 when all 20 gauge barrels were chambered for 3-inch shells. Listed below are approximate weights published by Browning of its Standard and Lightning Hunting models in both 12 and 20 gauge:

APPROXIMATE WEIGHTS OF BROWNING SUPERPOSED SHOTGUNS

Type	Length/Rib	Weight
12 gauge Magnum	30" vent or raised rib	8 lbs. 4 oz.
12 gauge Lightning	28" ventilated rib	7 lbs. 2 oz.
12 gauge Lightning	26-1/2" ventilated rib	7 lbs.
20 gauge Lightning	28" ventilated rib	6 lbs. 2 oz.
20 gauge Lightning	26-1/2" ventilated rib	6 lbs.
12 gauge Standard	30" raised rib	8 lbs.
12 gauge Standard	28" vent or raised rib	7 lbs. 12 oz.
12 gauge Standard	26-1/2" vent or raised rib	7 lbs. 8 oz.
20 gauge Standard	28" vent or raised rib	6 lbs. 12 oz.
20 gauge Standard	26-1/2" vent or raised rib	6 lbs. 8 oz.

Table 2-1

[14] Val A. Browning, letter to the author, August 15, 1993.

[15] *Ibid.*

[16] This 30-inch barrel length on 12 gauge guns was changed to the Magnum variation in 1955 and was chambered for the 3-inch shell. Superposed guns with 30-inch barrels built before 1955 were chambered for 2-3/4-inch shells.

This photo, taken in November of 1951, shows an FN craftsman working on a Superposed receiver. The gunsmith behind him is fitting a Superposed receiver to a set of barrels. All of this fitting was done by hand and required skill and experience. In the 1950s FN craftsmen were dedicated to their work and proud of their accomplishments, as they are today. Courtesy Fabrique Nationale Archives.

The differences in weight between the Lightning and the Standard Superposed can be attributed to several factors. First, the Lightning buttstock had a lightening hole drilled at the butt end to save a few ounces in weight. The Lightning forearm was slightly slimmer and shorter than the Standard forearm, which also resulted in a small weight saving. Some small milling cuts were performed on the Lightning frame to save weight as well. Lightning barrels also had thinner walls than Standard Weight barrels. In addition, Fabrique Nationale used a higher nickel content in its steel on Lightning barrels to make them as strong as the thicker Standard Weight barrels. The difference in weight between a Standard Superposed with 28-inch barrels and a Lightning model with the same barrel lengths is approximately ten ounces. Superposed guns with 26-1/2-inch barrels saved about eight ounces. This savings in weight came from a combination of weight reducing methods on the buttstock, forearm, and barrels.

Hunting models were available with almost any combination of chokes. Usual combinations were full and modified, and improved cylinder and modified. However, the customer could have any possible choke combination he desired from a selection of full, improved modified, modified, improved cylinder, skeet, and cylinder. Browning chokes were typically tighter than American made shotguns. Choke markings, in the form of stars and dashes, were stamped on the left side of the barrel flats below the ejectors. A comparison of choke constrictions between Winchester shotguns and Browning shotguns may give the reader a better understanding of why the Superposed patterns tighter than a comparable American made gun.

COMPARATIVE CHOKE CONSTRICTION
BROWNING VS WINCHESTER CIRCA 1955

12 Gauge	Browning Bore Dia. – .725	Winchester Bore Dia. – .725
Full	.038	.031
Modified	.024	.016
Improved Cylinder	.013	.007
Cylinder	.000	.000
20 Gauge	**Browning Bore Dia.-.611**	**Winchester Bore Dia.-.614**
Full	.033	.027
Modified	.018	.014
Improved Modified	.008	.005
Cylinder	.000	.000

Table 2-2

This photo, taken about 1957, shows an FN woodworker shaping a Superposed stock to the receiver—a final step before a finish was applied to the stock. Note that the buttplate (the first postwar variation) was in place during this procedure to ensure a proper fit to the wood. Courtesy Fabrique Nationale Archives.

The buttstock and forearm were carved from French walnut with rather plain straight grain wood to which a hand rubbed varnish was applied. The pistol grip was of the half-pistol style with a plain but finely checkered pattern both on the grip and forearm. The forearm was well proportioned with a smooth blunt nose and nicely checkered side panels. It presented a much more trim appearance than the standard forearm found on the prewar Superposed. The forearm on the 20 gauge was smaller and shorter than its 12 gauge counterpart to maintain the smaller scale of the gauge. Browning stated that the pattern on its Grade I Superposed was checkered 22 lines to the inch. On higher grades checkering became progressively more fine and may have reached 30 lines per inch on Grades V and VI. The horn buttplate was no longer of the prewar design with the double circles, but instead "BROWNING" was stamped horizontally on the plate surrounded by a perimeter border. The Superposed 12 gauge 3-inch Magnum was fitted with a Pachmayr Jumbo Trap recoil pad at the factory. The standard stock dimensions for the Hunting model in both 12 and 20 gauge were 1-5/8-inch drop at the heel, 2-1/2-inch drop at the comb, with a 14-1/4-inch length of pull.

The Browning Superposed had two frame sizes, one for the 12 gauge and the other slightly smaller size for the 20 gauge. Like its prewar predecessor, the Superposed frame was machined from solid steel and was overbuilt for safety and dependability. What set the Superposed apart from other mass-produced shotguns was the attention to fit and finish that was found on these over and under shotguns. Val and John Val Browning spent enormous amounts of time and energy struggling to achieve this quality in a production double gun. Their work paid off. The hairline fitting and attention to detail of these guns established the Superposed with an excellent reputation of durability and fine quality.

Fabrique Nationale employed quite a few women. This group is putting the finishing touches on Browning Superposed stocks. Notice the large building that housed several different operations under one roof. These large rooms were sectioned into smaller areas of defined operations. The photo was taken in the mid-1950s. Courtesy Fabrique Nationale Archives.

After World War II, Browning settled on offering only one trigger option, the single selective trigger designed by Val Browning. All postwar Superposed were fitted with this single inertia trigger operated by the recoil of the gun after firing. It was a dependable trigger which worked well. Fabrique Nationale continued to offer the double trigger as an option on its Superposed guns sold elsewhere. After the war, Superposed triggers were gold plated. These early blued triggers were steel, which took the bluing process well. When gold plated triggers were introduced, the plating process did not do as well on steel, so FN changed to an alloy metal to get better, longer lasting results from these plated triggers. The selector was located on the top tang as part of the safety and operated from side to side in selecting the over or under barrel to fire first. The manual safety functioned up and down from safe to fire. Although the system had an excellent reputation for dependability, some shooters disliked this "H" pattern arrangement, which sometimes developed a "hitch" if not operated just right.

When the first Superposed were shipped from Belgium after the war, their barrels were usually stamped on the left side of the upper barrel with the following address:

BROWNING ARMS COMPANY-ST. LOUIS, MISSOURI
SPECIAL STEEL—12 GA. SHELLS 2 3/4"

This left side address was used on all Browning Superposed imported into the U.S. until 1958 when Browning and FN established the separate Canadian operation. The last thirteen months of the decade, a new left side barrel address was used:

BROWNING ARMS COMPANY ST. LOUIS MO & MONTREAL P.Q.
SPECIAL STEEL—12 GA. SHELLS 2 3/4"

On the right side of the barrel the following inscription will often be seen on Superposed built in the late 1940s:

MADE IN BELGIUM-VAL A. BROWNING PATENTS NO. 2203378-2233861

This right side barrel marking is interesting because it uses Val Browning's name and patent numbers as they relate to his prewar patents concerning his improved selective ejector and single selective trigger designs. This was done because Val thought it necessary to distinguish his patents from his father's. When he discovered it was not a legal requirement, FN was instructed to delete his name from the barrel address.[17] For this reason, Browning Superposed barrels with the Val A. Browning name as part of the barrel inscription were used for only a short period after the war. The more common right side inscription will read:

PATENTS NO. 2203378-2233861
MADE IN BELGIUM

A word of caution on interpretation of barrel markings. There were a number of different formats that FN used in marking the Superposed barrels. In some cases "SPECIAL STEEL" may appear as part of the right side inscription and on others it will be seen on the left side. The same situation applies to the gauge and chamber length, as well as "MADE IN BELGIUM." The most important aspect of barrel markings is the actual corporate address, which will show the era in which that particular barrel was built. In the case of the 20 gauge, any reference to three-inch chambers will not appear until 1956 at the earliest. This will help to determine whether the barrel was built and fitted to the gun when it left the factory, or if the gun was sent back to St. Louis or Arnold for rechambering or the addition of a factory barrel at a later date. This may have some significance in helping to ascertain with some degree of certainty if a multibarrel set is factory original.

Trap Model: The Superposed Trap model was first reintroduced into the Superposed product line in 1951. Designed for the competition trapshooter, it featured 30-inch barrels with ventilated rib. The ventilated rib fitted to these Standard Trap guns was the same width and height as those fitted to the Hunting models. It was available choked full and full; improved modified and full; and modified and full, but any combination of chokes was offered on special order. The Superposed Trap was offered in Standard Weight and weighed 8 lb. 2 oz. with its 30-inch barrels fitted with an ivory bead front sight. A Lightning Trap model, introduced in 1955, was also offered with 30-inch barrels and weighed 7 lb. 12 oz.

What really set the Trap model apart from the Hunting model was its stock configuration. The Superposed buttstock had a drop of 1-1/2 inches at the comb, a drop of 1-7/8 inches at the heel, and a length of pull of 14-3/8 inches. Unlike later Trap models, these 1950s guns had a semi-pistol grip with rounded knob. It was a much higher and straighter buttstock than the Hunting model. The Trap forearm was a semi-beavertail type with a full grip contour offering more weight forward. Trap models built between 1952 and 1959 were sold *without* a factory recoil pad as standard.

Other than these specific features the Superposed Trap was identical in every other way to the Hunting model in terms of barrel markings, trigger, type of wood, frame, buttplate, and other small characteristics that were shared by all Superposed models.

Skeet Model: When Browning introduced its Skeet model into the Superposed line in 1956, it was with the express purpose of breaking into the competitive skeet shooting market as it had so successfully done on the trap fields. But between 1956 and 1959 the Browning Skeet model was a special model in name only. Offered in 12 and 20 gauge with a choice of 26-1/2-inch or 28-inch barrels with raised matted or ventilated ribs, these Skeet guns could be ordered in Standard or Lightning weights just like the Hunting models. In fact, the only stipulation to the Skeet model was the chokes: only

[17] Val A. Browning, letter to the author, April 25, 1994.

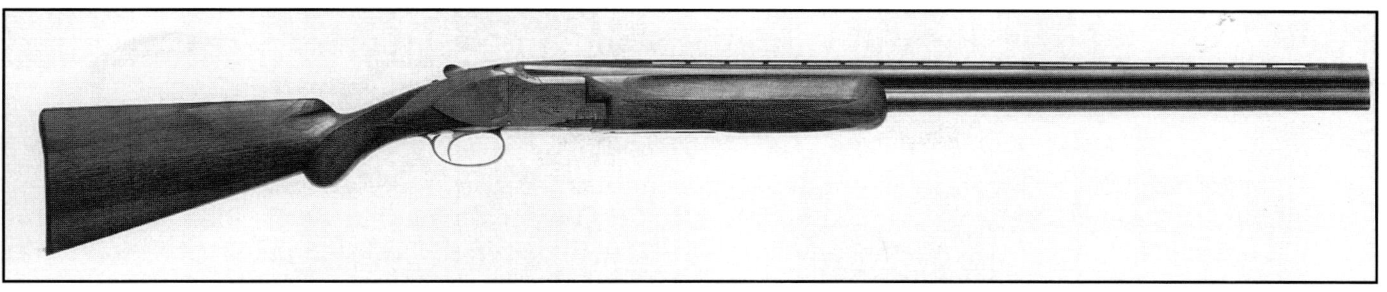

A 1950s Standard Weight Grade I Browning Superposed Trap model with ventilated rib and single selective trigger. Note the rounded semi-pistol grip, semi-beavertail forearm, and no recoil pad. This was the standard configuration for the Trap model during this period. Courtesy Fabrique Nationale Archives.

A close-up view of a 1950s Trap model in Grade I. The only easily seen outward feature is the semi-beavertail forearm. The buttstock was higher and straighter than the Hunting model, but measuring the stock is the only way to verify that Trap feature. Courtesy Fabrique Nationale Archives.

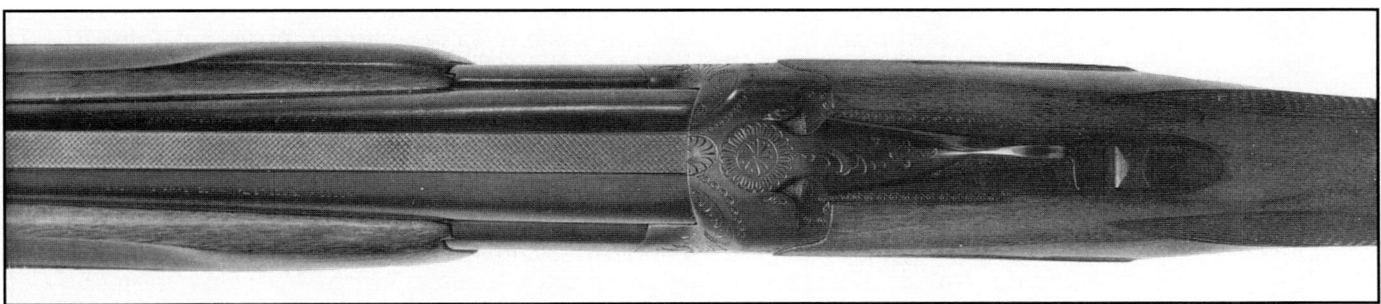

The top of the Grade I Trap model shows that the rib is the same width as the other Browning Superposed models. Courtesy Fabrique Nationale Archives.

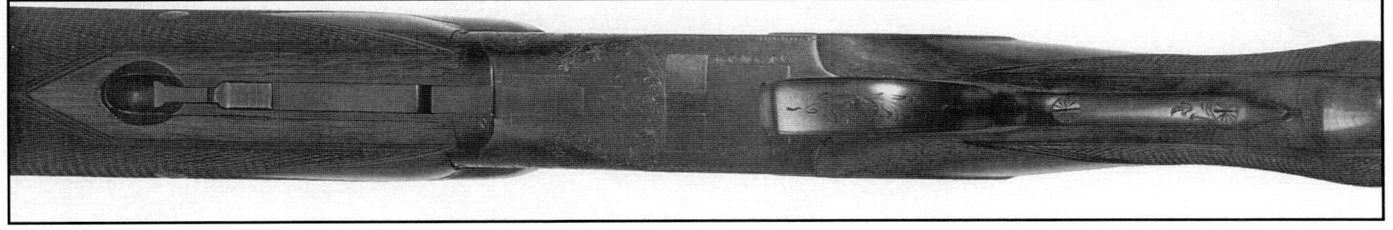

The bottom view of the 1950s Trap model. Because this was a Standard Weight model there is no "Lightning" stamping on the bottom of the receiver. Note the view of the long tang with rounded semi-pistol grip, and the shape of the forearm release latch. All of these features were standard on all 1950s Browning Superposed guns. Courtesy Fabrique Nationale Archives.

Browning Multibarrel Sets and Single Triggers: The Ernie Simmons and Les Freer Episode

In March 1952 Les Freer, an accomplished gunsmith and firearms mechanic, went to work for Ernie Simmons in Ernie's well-known Kansas City workshop. Les had been called on by Ernie to help him solve a complex problem. Several months before, Ernie Simmons had contracted with Cordy & Sons, a Liège concern, to acquire one thousand sets of over and under barrels for the Browning Superposed in 12, 20, and 28 gauge, as well as .410 bore. These barrels were in a rough state, all 28 inches long with excess constriction so they could be custom choked at a later date. Before Les arrived, Ernie had spent several weeks attempting to fit three pairs of barrels to a used Superposed 12 gauge frame. The effort was a total failure, and Simmons was committed to fitting one thousand sets of barrels to Superposed frames without a procedure for doing so. Browning's service facility in St. Louis was not even equipped to do the job, sending its Superposed back to FN for proper fitting of new barrels. Ernie Simmons was ahead of his time, but he was convinced that skeet shooters all over the country would buy his guns fitted with multibarrel sets, if only it could be done.

Les Freer, with his considerable experience and ingenuity, was called upon to solve Ernie's problem. Les approached the task through meticulous hand fitting, and investing large amounts of time in making the necessary jigs and fixtures required to do the job. Les was skillfully assisted by Wylie Jewell and Wilburn Lewis. Together the three men devised a procedures manual, eliminating wasted time and enabling the operations to become standardized. After much trial and error, methods and procedures were established to complete the task in a timely manner that yielded a quality fit at a reasonable price.

One large problem that needed a solution was the operation of .410 barrels on 12 gauge frames. The fitting presented no special problems, but Browning's inertia trigger would not function properly with .410 shells. The recoil was insufficient to set the device for the second shot. The solution lay in developing a different trigger system that would function for all gauges. Les completed three different mechanical trigger devices, and of those three, one was selected based on its simplicity of operation and lower cost of installation. As was the custom of the day, the patent number 2,711,042, was awarded to Ernie Simmons, Sr. Les converted all of the original Superposed triggers fitted with .410 barrels. In some cases Superposed without small bore barrels were converted strictly so they would have the mechanical trigger rather than the inertia trigger.

So that Browning could examine his design, Les installed the third trigger design, which was more expensive but had more desirable features, in a frame furnished by Val Browning. After extensive testing, Val declined to pursue the matter further, but in 1972 Browning modified its Superposed guns with a mechanical trigger very similar in theory to the Freer design.

In the summer of 1954, after installing approximately 224 barrels on 12 gauge Superposed guns, Ernie decided to fit 20, 28, and .410 barrels to 20 gauge Superposed frames. Although the idea sounded easy, it was not. It required an entirely new fitting procedure because of the different dimensions of the 20 gauge frame. Like the original challenge, Les rose to the occasion and accomplished the assignment.

In 1957 Les Freer left Simmons to take over the operation of the Central Gun Shop in Fort Scott, Kansas. During his stay at Simmons, Les fitted 644 barrels to Superposed guns and performed several hundred trigger conversions. Eventually Simmons sold all of his one thousand pairs of barrels and many are still in use today thanks to the quality job executed by Les Freer.

skeet and skeet were offered. The buttstock and forearm were the same dimensions and had the same appearance as the Hunting models. A recoil pad was an extra cost option.

One supplementary feature of Browning Superposed guns should be covered. Superposed with extra sets of barrels are highly coveted by collectors and shooters alike. Guns purchased in the 1950s with one set of barrels could be sent back to St. Louis to have extra sets of barrels fitted. The service facility in St. Louis then sent the complete gun back to FN for the barrel fitting. When the extra barrels were fitted, the gun was sent back to St. Louis and then returned to the customer. Browning often quoted four to six months for this type of work to be completed, but in reality the time was closer to eighteen to twenty-four months. As the years passed, many Superposed had additional sets of barrels added over a period of decades, depending on the whim of the owner. Company policy changed over the years as to the type and style of extra sets of barrels offered to the public. In the 1950s Browning offered as a standard option any combination of barrel weight or choke of the same gauge in either Hunting or Trap configuration. Before 1960, multiple barrel sets containing different gauges were not offered to Browning Superposed customers. All-Gauge Skeet sets were not offered until later. The 1950s represented Browning's attempt to build its multibarrel offerings in a simple, direct method in order to maximize its potential success.

On December 21, 1944, this snapshot was taken of Felix Funken engraving in a basement during a buzz bomb attack by the Germans on the FN plant. Looking over his shoulder was an American general. Funken's other engravers were also hard at work during the attack. This must be the true definition of dedication. Courtesy Liège Arms Museum.

Superposed Engraving of the 1950s

When the Superposed was reintroduced into the United States in 1948, the only grade offered for sale was the Grade I with its light but elegant scroll engraving pattern. The same problems that beset the production of the Superposed also affected Fabrique Nationale's engraving capacity. Felix Funken was still very much in charge of the engraving section at FN and managed to assemble enough engravers to satisfy the demands of engraving the Auto-5 and the Grade I Superposed immediately after the war. In 1946 Funken had about twelve engravers. It was not until 1948 that a formal engraving school was reestablished for students in the factory. By 1950 the FN engraving school had grown to over fifty students and the company employed almost one hundred engravers. But as FN had difficulty meeting production orders, so did Felix Funken in meeting the constantly increasing engraving demands on his shop.

In this 1950 photo, Fabrique Nationale's chief engraver Felix Funken is pictured seated at his desk in the engraving department at FN. On his desk is a photograph of his engravers in that year. Courtesy Liège Arms Museum.

Under the direction of master engraver Funken, new engraving patterns were designed and implemented into the Superposed line, especially for Browning's North American market. Gone for the most part were the old style European patterns. These patterns were modernized and were intended to appeal to American shooters and hunters. By 1950 the capacity to produce a marketable quality engraved Superposed was achieved. Under the critical eye of Felix Funken, Browning offered for sale in the United States four different styles of high grade Superposed guns. Instead of named grades, Browning changed their designation to numbers: Grades II through V. These engraved guns required artisans of skill and experience to

Each FN engraving student was required to complete to Felix Funken's satisfaction a workbook showing their competency with drawing and design work. Before any student could begin practice engraving on metal, this book had to be completed. In 1955 Nelly Watrin, wife of André Watrin, was a Funken student. These are sample pages from her workbook. Courtesy Fabrique Nationale Archives.

LIEGE
BRABANT
HAINAUT
NAMUR
LUXEMBOURG
LIMBOURG
ANVERS
FLANDRE·OR
FLANDRE·OC

The engraving shop inside the FN plant as it looked in 1950. Felix Funken is near the center foreground with the blurred facial features. There are approximately fifty engravers in this photo. An engraver's work not only took skill and artistic ability, but physical endurance as well. Notice there is no one sitting down engraving. Courtesy Fabrique Nationale Archives.

execute the intricate patterns. According to Browning, nine years of experience were necessary to perform the work on the Grade II and twenty-five years of experience to accomplish with deftness the necessary scrolls and game scenes that were part of the Grade V Superposed pattern. Price and coverage increased on each successively higher grade, but all grades shared the same attention to detail. All exposed metal surfaces were polished by hand. Hand polishing was done to internal parts such as the standing breech and breech surfaces of the barrels. Ejectors and ejector extensions were damascened[18] or jeweled. The forearm latch, ejector hammers, trip rods, cocking lever, locking bolt, inertia block, sears, main hammers, and tang piece were all polished to a mirror finish on all high grade Superposed guns.

The vast majority of Superposed guns were built and sold in the Grade I style. The frame was polished and blued to an attractive luster with delicate scroll engraving partially covering both sides of the frame. This grade was most often engraved by craftsmen with less experience than the higher grade guns, but the work was always well executed. The practice of piecework compensation was still in use. A journeyman engraver could execute about four of these Grade I Superposed in one day. As during the prewar years, this grade was affectionately called the "sarma," an indication that it was the lowest grade, more widely available to the average hunter. On the bottom of the frame was stamped, in block letters, "BROWNING." In addition, there was a vignette of the bust of John M. Browning stamped with a roll die. When the Lightning

[18] This term refers to the wavy patterns created on metal by inlaying or etching the surfaces. The term is much more commonly used in Europe, but Browning did include the damascened in its American catalogues.

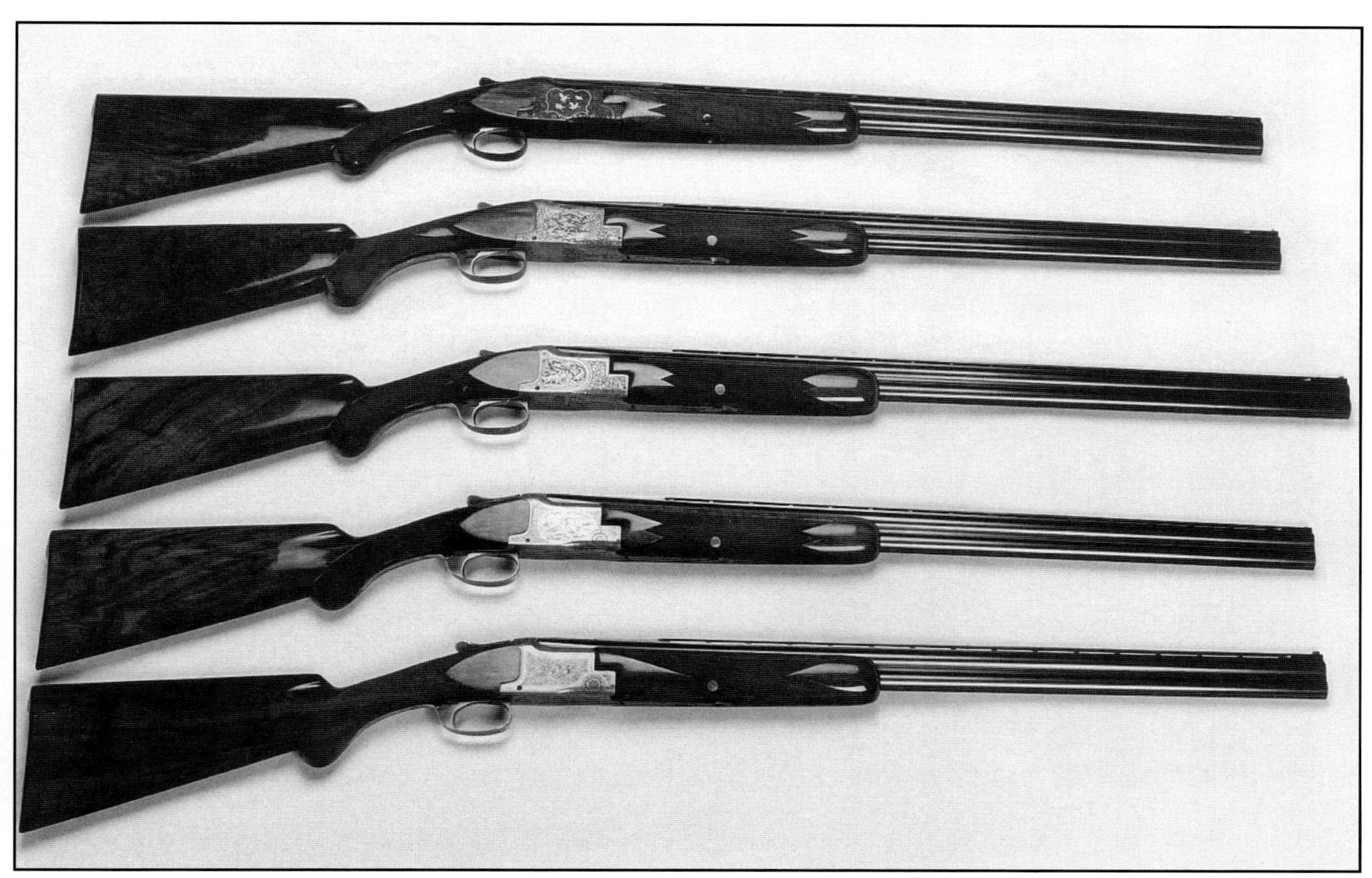

This photo shows five outstanding Browning Superposed Grades II through VI, all in 20 gauge. From top to bottom they are Grade VI, serial number 11367, signed by Müller; Grade V, serial number 6711, signed by V. Doyen; Grade IV, serial number 4325, signed by Felix Funken; Grade III, serial number 10017, signed by Felix Funken; Grade II, serial number 6685, signed by Felix Funken. This grouping captures the feel of each grade and gives an impression of the wood grain and color for each ascending grade. Courtesy Dick DeBruyn Collection.

was introduced in 1956, the word "LIGHTNING" was stamped in script on the bottom of the frame. The trigger was blued from 1948 to 1955 when Browning began to gold plate all Superposed triggers. The Grade I Superposed has always been a gun any hunter or shooter would be proud to take into the field, partly because of the understated elegance of its frame.

The Grade II, almost identical to the prewar Pigeon Grade, remained in the product line because of its relatively modest cost and elegant good looks. In Browning's excellent 1950 Superposed "Special Models" engraving catalogue, the Grade II was described in great detail: "The pigeons in varied positions are represented in meticulous detail from eye to minute feather, as though moving over delicate scrolled background. Flowered rosettes appear ... in which one may barely detect the line between finely fitted steel parts. Screw heads are aligned and engraved." It took approximately fifteen hours for an FN engraver to execute the entire Pigeon Grade pattern. The safety indicator on the upper tang was inlaid with 24 carat gold and the trigger had a blue satin finish until 1956 when it was gold plated. The receiver was not blued but finished in a silver gray tone that helped to bring out the delicate scrollwork. The French walnut utilized on the Pigeon Grade had some figure and was of a better grade than that used on the Grade I. The checkering pattern was similar to the Grade I. The retail price for the Grade II in 1950 was $348.00. By 1959 the price had only risen to $380.00.

Often referred to as the "Fighting Cocks" grade, the Grade III featured a fine line engraved game scene that placed pheasants on one side and fighting cocks on the other. The bottom of the frame displayed a retriever carrying a pheasant. Very fine rosettes were engraved on the hinge pin. Engraving time on the Grade III was about twenty-five hours depending on the skill and speed of the engraver. The safety indicator was inlaid in 24 carat gold and the trigger was a satin blue finish until 1956 when it was gold plated. The receiver on the Grade III was finished in a silver gray. The check-

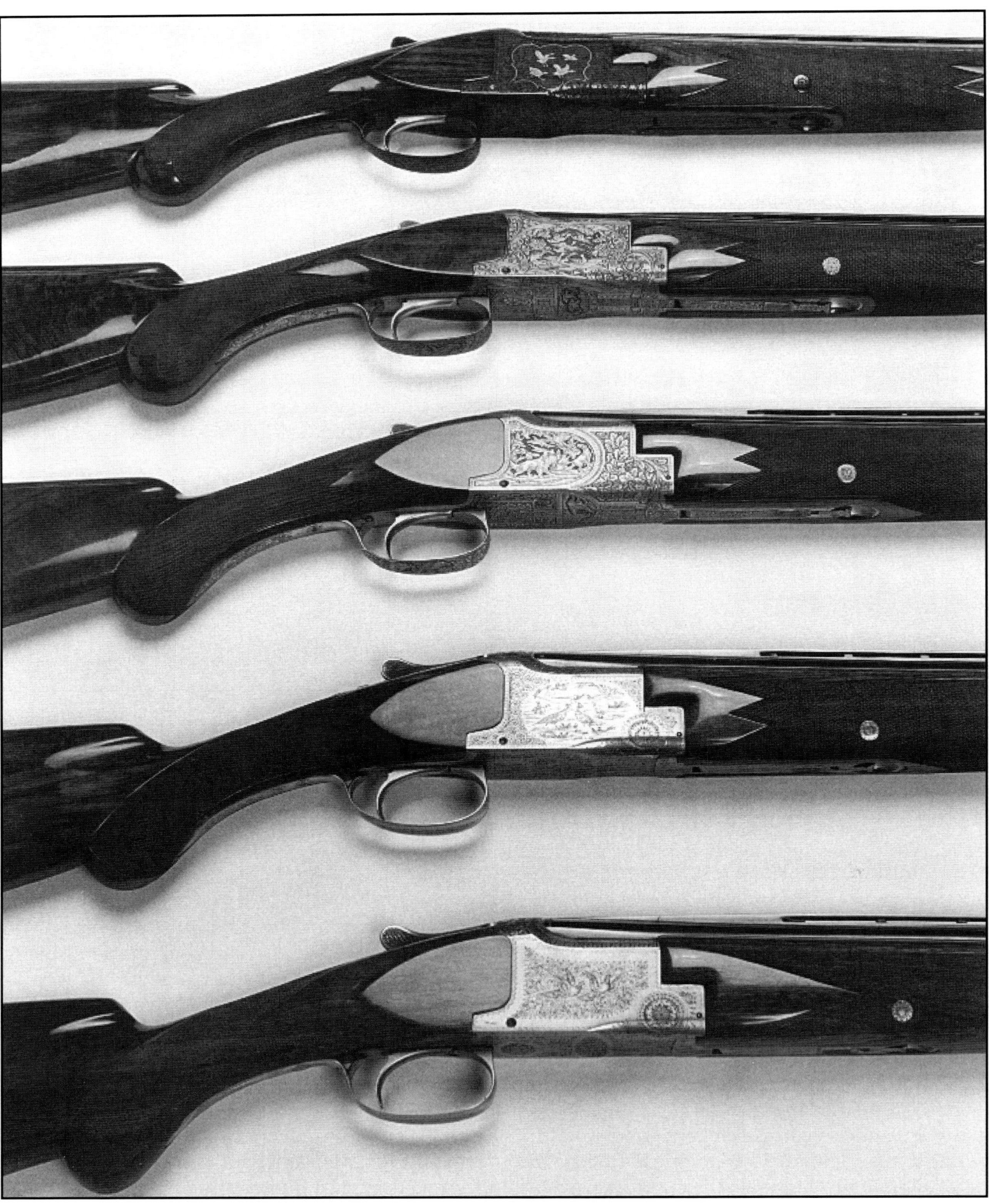

This closer view of the five '50s grades shows the differences in checkering patterns, and illustrates dramatically the wide range of engraving patterns and styles found in these high grade Superposed. One interesting note is the use of small game birds in the Grade VI 20 gauge. In this case rails are used. Courtesy Dick DeBruyn Collection.

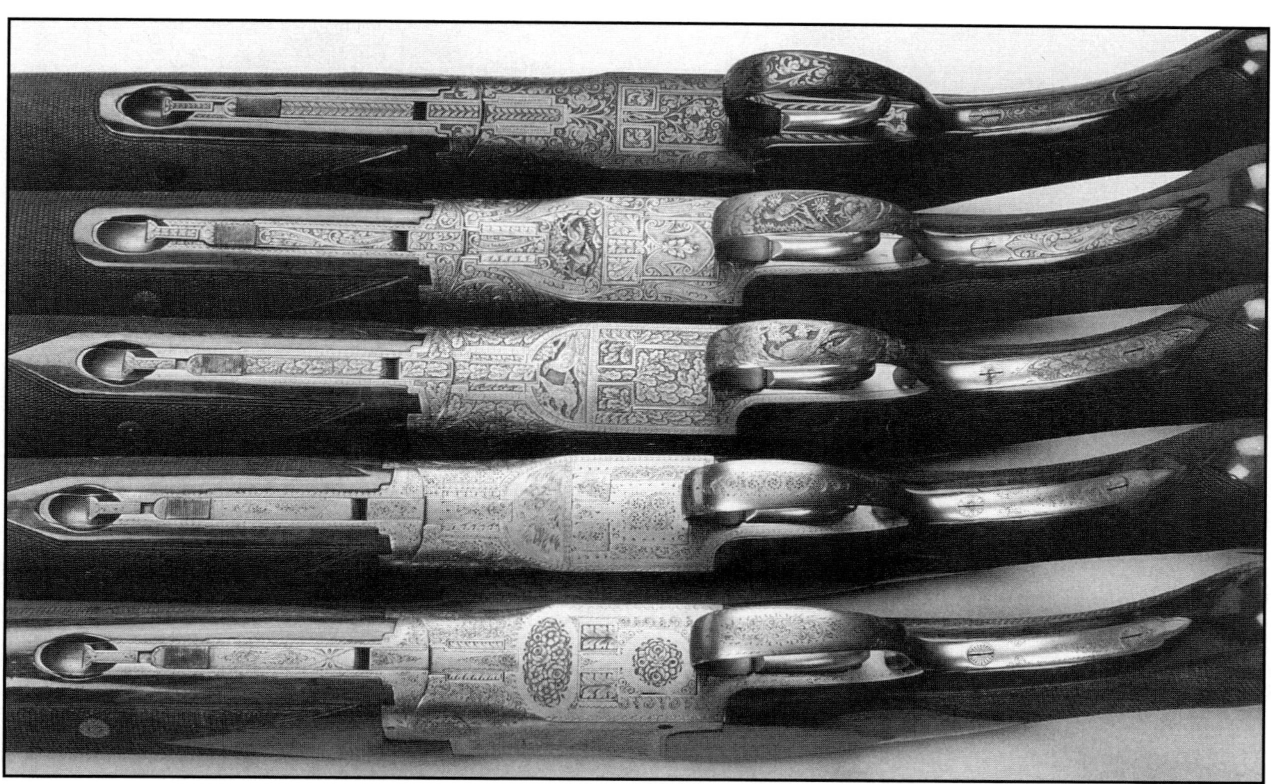

A bottom view of the five '50s Superposed again illustrates the strong contrast between these five high grade patterns. From release latch to bottom tang, each pattern is unique in feel and proportion of line and mass. Courtesy Dick DeBruyn collection.

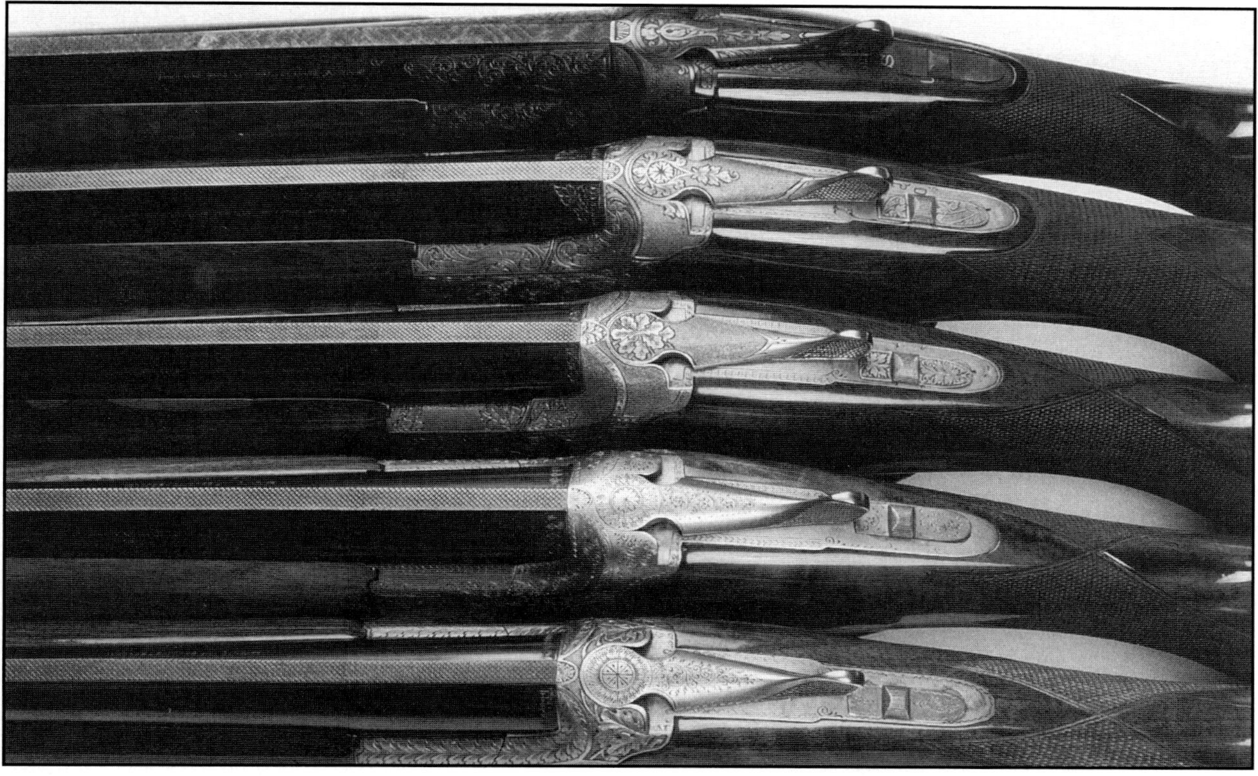

A top view of the five '50s high grade Superposed reveals the same characteristics in treatment and perception as does the bottom view of these guns. Notice how the rib is hand cut on the Grade VI compared to the other high grade Superposed. Even the safety/ selector switch is engraved differently on each grade. Notice, also, how the checkering patterns on Grades II through IV come across the top of the grip where Grades V and VI roll over the top providing greater coverage. Courtesy Dick DeBruyn collection.

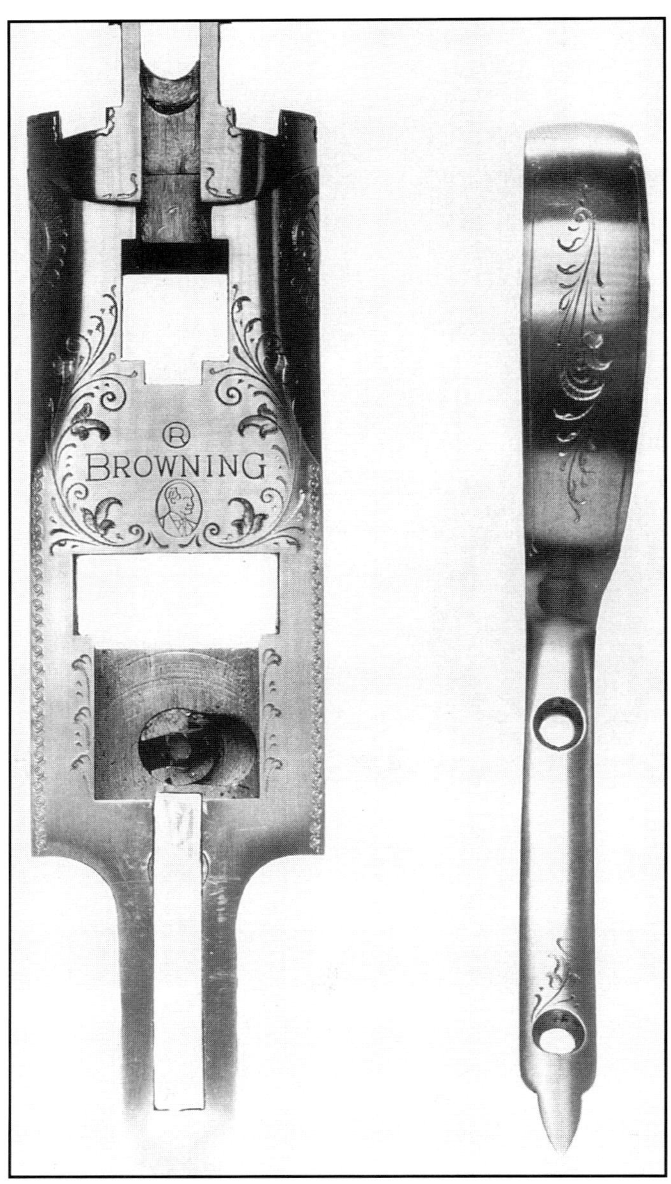

The underside of a Grade I Superposed showing the Browning trademark with John M. Browning's image. This Browning trademark was applied with a roll die and not hand engraved. The balance of the light scrollwork was hand cut. The engraving on the trigger guard was also hand executed. Courtesy Fabrique Nationale Archives.

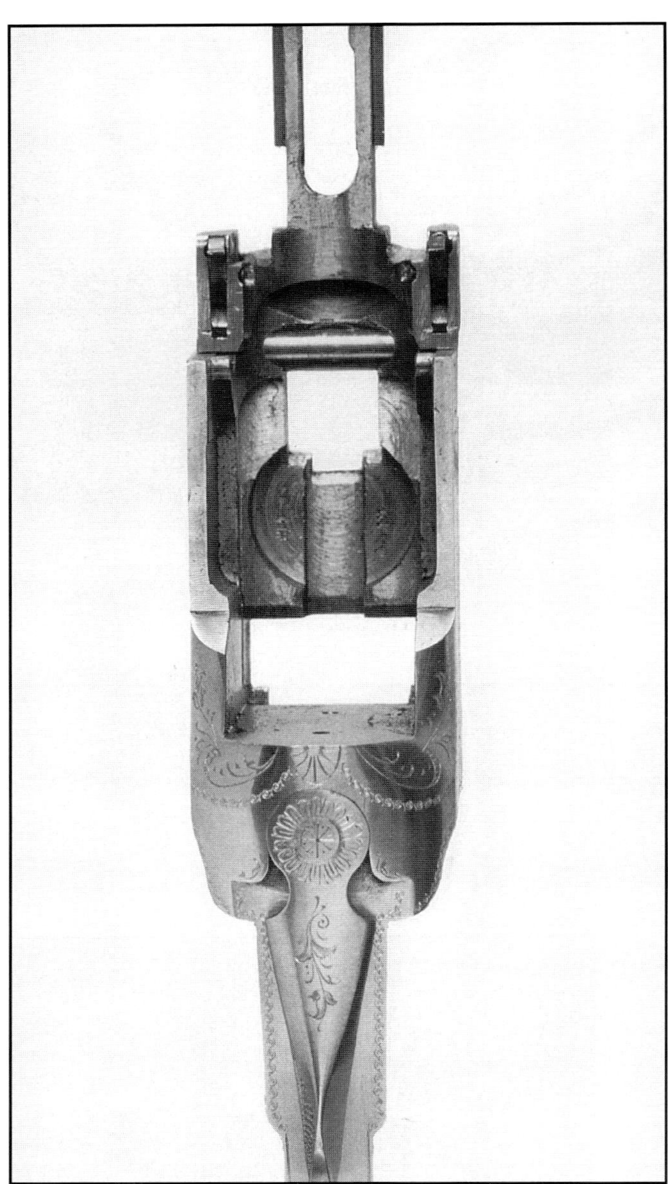

A top view of the Grade I Superposed. Again, this is a representative sample and each Grade I will have subtle differences. Courtesy Fabrique Nationale Archives.

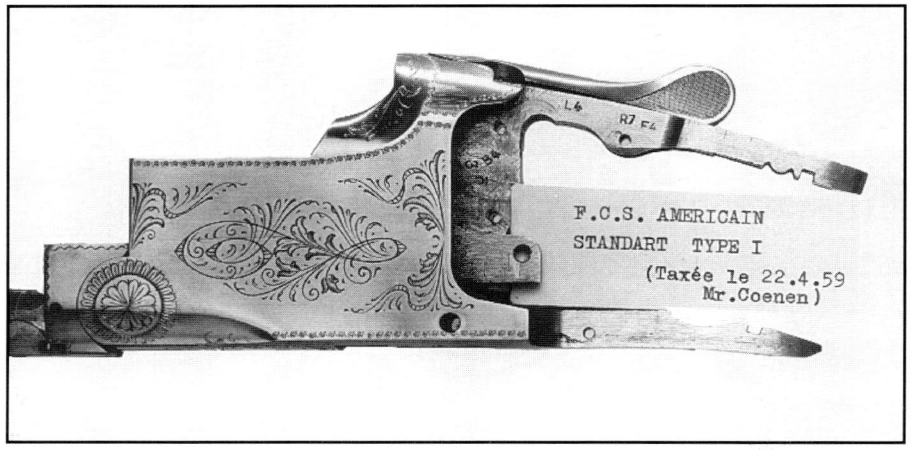

The Browning Superposed Grade I receiver. This is a typical example engraved on April 22, 1959, by Rene Coenen, a veteran engraver who started working at FN in 1948. This was the standard pattern for that era, but all Grade I Superposed were slightly different depending on who executed the engraving. Courtesy Fabrique Nationale Archives.

These two Grade I Superposed were engraved and assembled between 1953 and 1954. Close examination will reveal slight differences between the two guns despite their approximate chronological age. Courtesy Fabrique Nationale Archives.

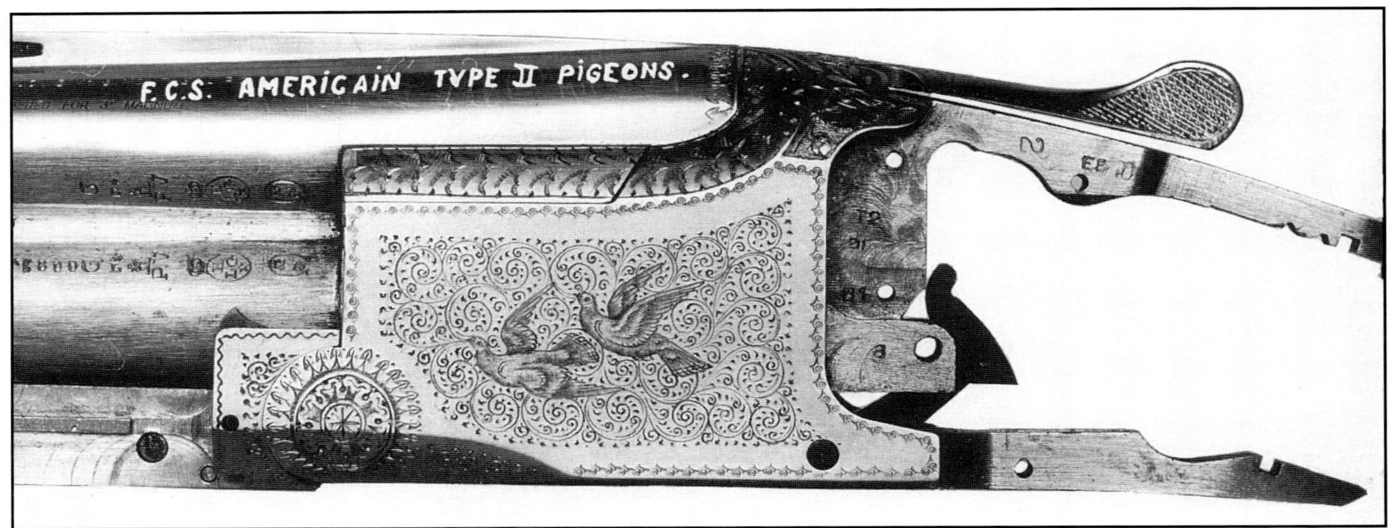

This 1959 FN photograph shows a typical Grade II Superposed from the left side of the receiver. Again, each Grade II will have slight differences, particularly with the composition of the pigeons. This Superposed is not signed, but the engraving work is very well executed. Courtesy Fabrique Nationale Archives.

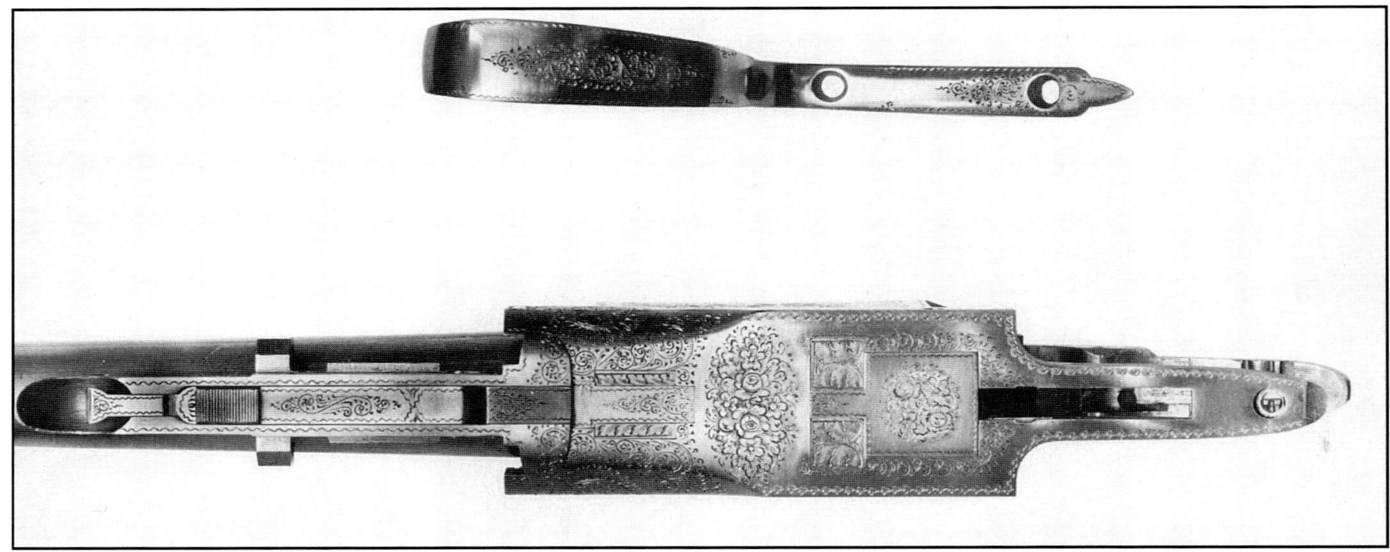

The bottom view of this late 1950s Grade II Superposed. This was the usual engraving style used in the Grade II guns. The view of the trigger guard shows the customary scrollwork executed on the guard and tang. Courtesy Fabrique Nationale Archives.

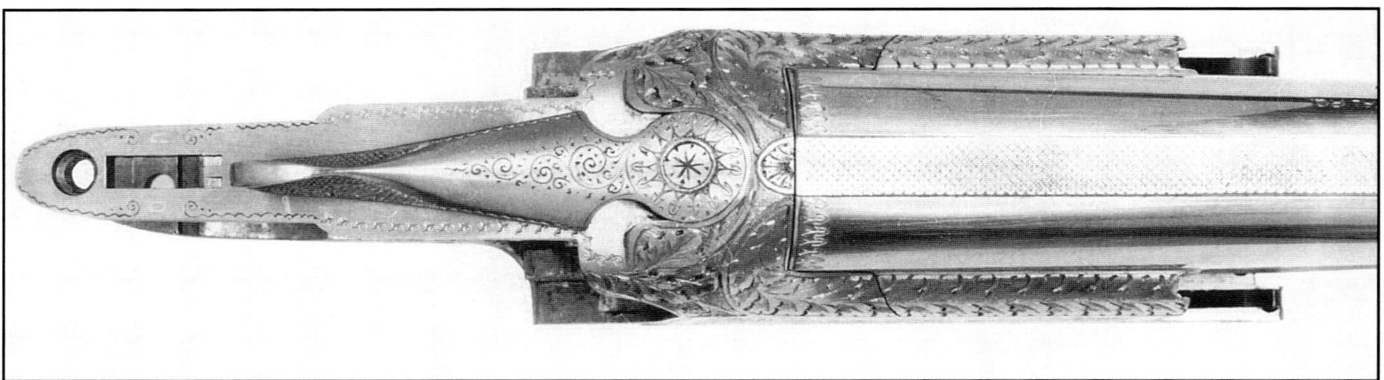

A top view of the typical Grade II styling used on the top lever and the barrel ears. Courtesy Fabrique Nationale Archives.

ering pattern was more elaborate than the Grade II and had finer checkering. The French walnut was dark and well figured. Priced at only $47.00 more than the Grade II in 1950, the Grade III sold for $450.00 by the end of the decade. This is a highly sought after Superposed grade with collectors.

The Grade IV is an interesting engraving pattern. Designed in the European style with deep relief oak leaves and deep relief game scenes, this design displays an unmistakable Germanic influence. On the left side is a fox carrying a bird to its two young, with landscape cut in great detail. On the right side are two setters, one carrying a pheasant and the other flushing two pheasants in another finely detailed landscape. The trigger guard is engraved with two pheasants, one of which is perched in a tree. The bottom of the receiver features two other game birds, one on the ground and the other in flight. A silver gray finish was used on the Grade IV receiver. The fancy, full-figured walnut stock featured fine line checkering with a distinctive checkering pattern. The safety selector was inlaid in 24 carat gold and the trigger was gold plated. In 1950 the retail price for the Grade IV was $520.00 and in 1959 had only increased to $550.00.

The highest catalogued Superposed grade in 1950 was the Grade V. Fitted with full fancy walnut and fine line checkering with a double border pattern, this was the finest production grade that Browning offered to its Superposed customers at the beginning of the decade. The full coverage engraving, which took about thirty-five hours to complete, was a deep relief intricate scroll pattern on the borders with deep relief game scenes of ducks on the right side and pheasants on the left. The bottom of the frame featured a pair of flying pigeons, and two rabbits were engraved in deep relief on the trigger guard. Like Grades II through IV, the Grade V receiver was finished in a silver gray tone. The Grade V retailed for $615.00 in 1950 and ended the decade with a retail price of $650.00.

In the summer of 1957 Browning added another grade to its high grade Superposed line: the Grade VI. There is a certain mystery surrounding the origins of this grade, but we know some of the guns were cut in Germany by an engraver named Müller. The reasons for this were both economic and practical. Gold inlay work was expensive to execute, and factory prices were such that to keep the price of the grade within reason many Grade VIs were contracted outside the factory. The second reason for sending the Grade VI to outside contractors was that there were not enough FN engravers skilled in the art of inlaying.

Finished on a blued receiver, the engraving work was done in deep relief with ducks and pheasants inlaid in 18 carat gold on both sides of the 12 gauge, and smaller game birds on the 20 gauge. Each scene was slightly different on every gun, so all Grade VIs can be considered one of a kind. The engraving work was created by skilled artists with years of experience. The rib was hand matted along the top and the tips of the firing pins were gold plated, as were the ejector pins. The highest grade of walnut was used along with the best checkering cut by the most proficient craftsmen. Grade VI customers were required to wait several months for delivery.

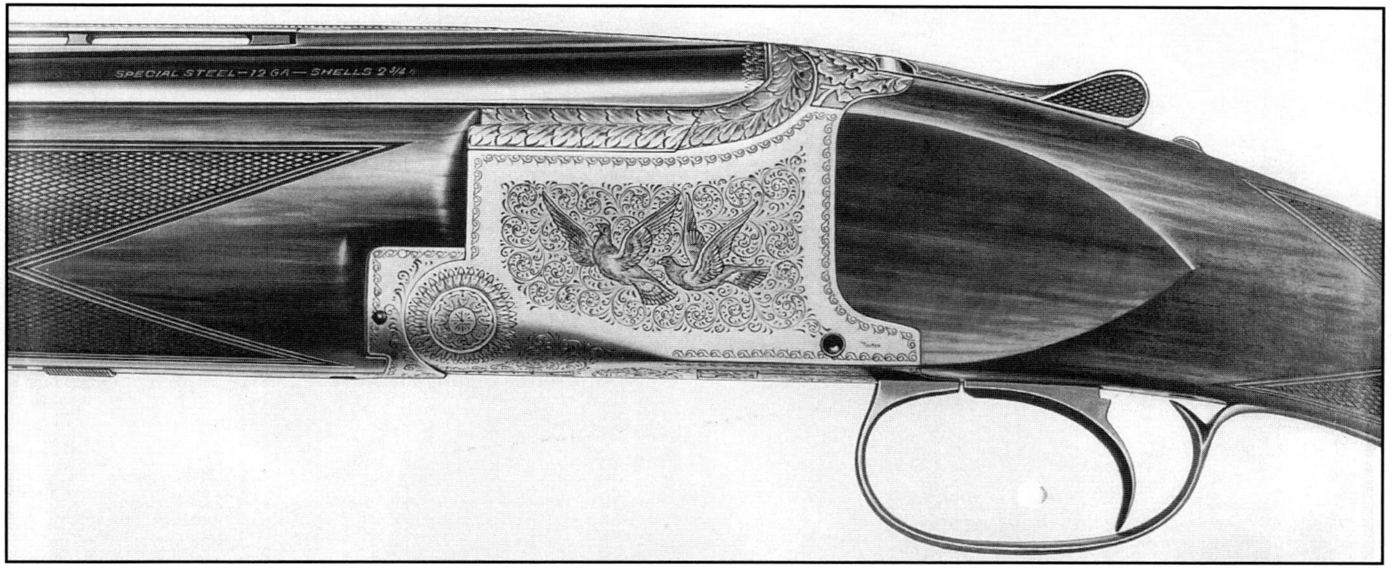

A finished and assembled Grade II done sometime in the early 1950s. The receiver is signed by Felix Funken. Compare the position of the pigeons and their composition to the late 1950s Grade II shown elsewhere in this chapter. Courtesy Fabrique Nationale Archives.

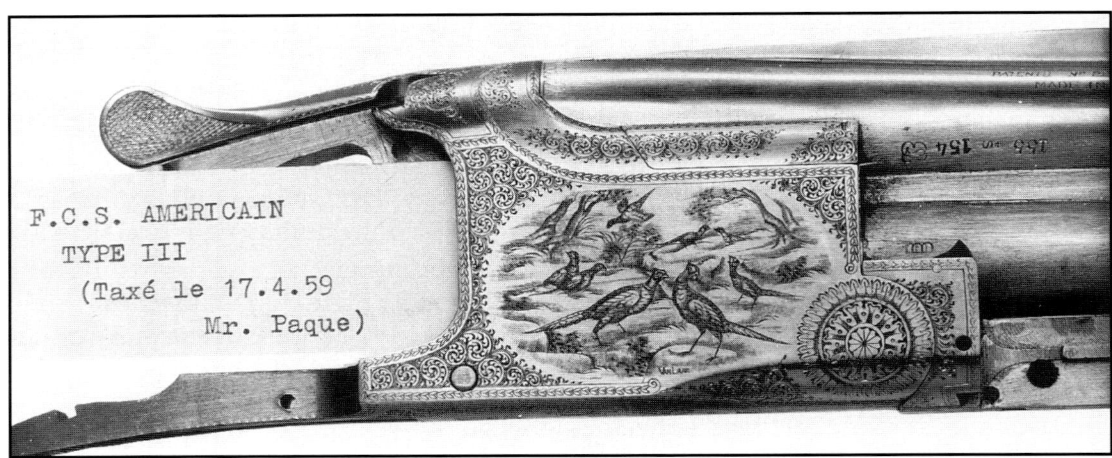

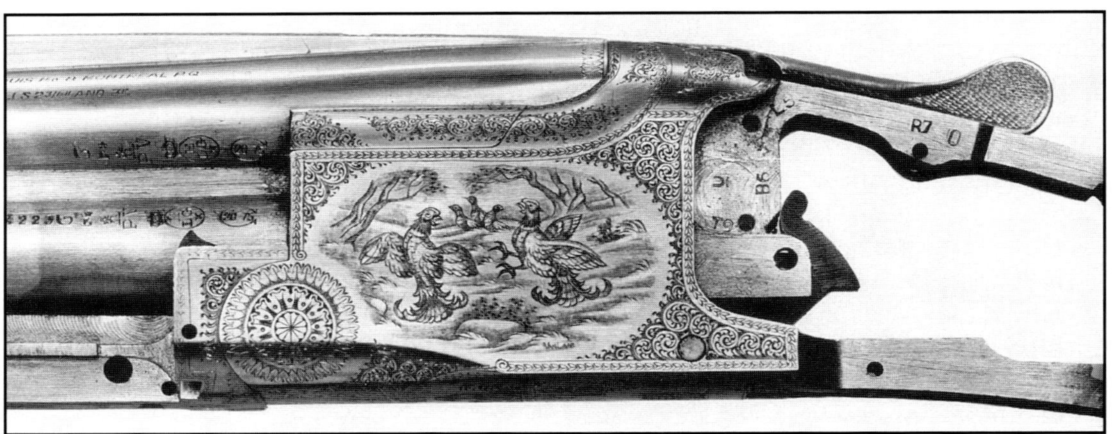

This Grade III Superposed is often referred to as the "Fighting Cocks" grade because of the game scene on the left side of the receiver. The scrollwork was executed by Olivier Paque; the scene itself was done by master engraver Mademoiselle Lea Van Laar. Note the exquisite attention to detail and superb composition of the scene. This is an impressive example of a Grade III Superposed. Courtesy Fabrique Nationale Archives.

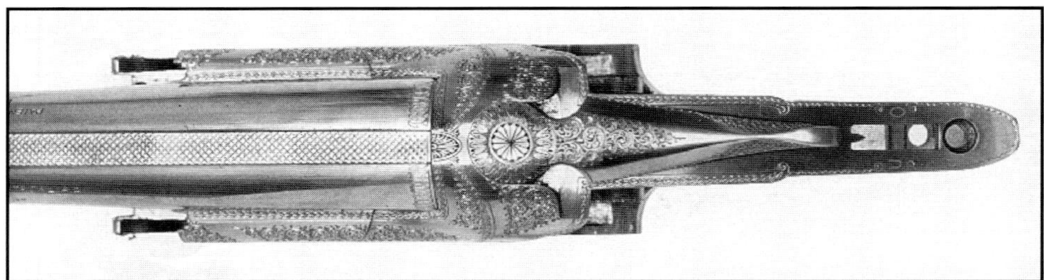

The top and bottom view of the 1959 Grade III Superposed. This grade has some beautifully executed scrollwork which is tastefully done and pleasing to the eye. Notice the vignette on the bottom of the receiver. Courtesy Fabrique Nationale Archives.

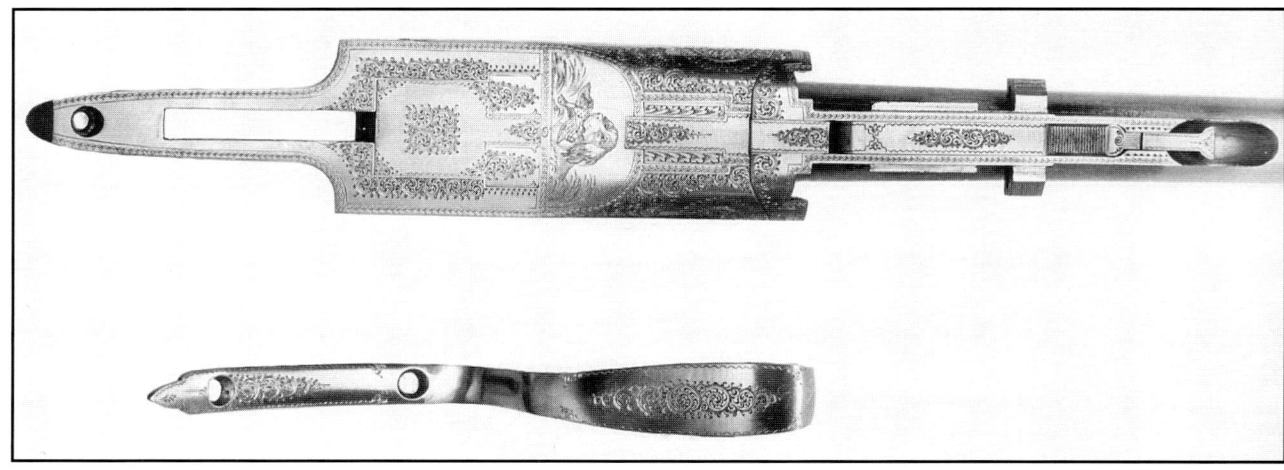

The Grade IV Browning Superposed pattern is seldom encountered today because of its lack of popularity in the 1950s. It featured a heavy Germanic style of deep relief engraving that was not well accepted in North America. This example, serial number 65232, was engraved on April 20, 1959, with the scrollwork executed by one of the Maréchal family, the game animals by Lea Van Laar, and the shading by the master Felix Funken. Notice who signed the receiver on both sides: Felix Funken. Rank does indeed have

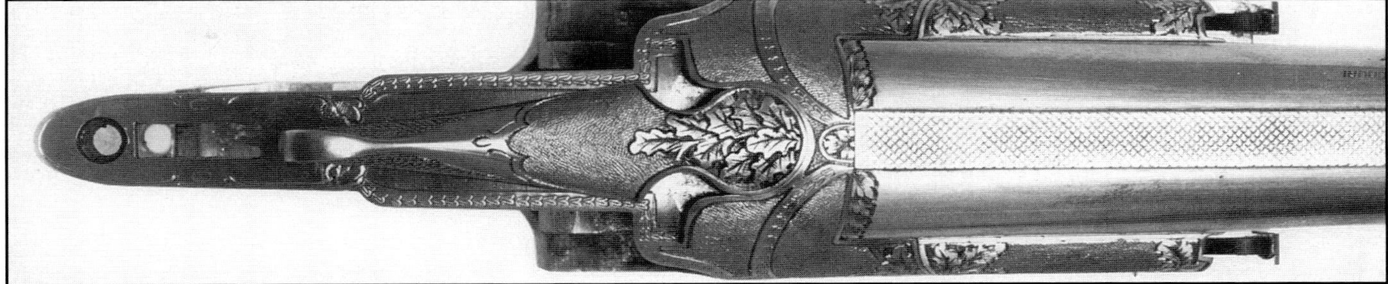

A top view of the Grade IV showing the scarcity of scrollwork, but a profusion of hammered metal. Notice the delicate oak leaves engraved on the breech end of the top barrel. The underside of the Grade IV features a profusion of deeply cut oak leaves with a deep relief game scene. Courtesy Fabrique Nationale Archives.

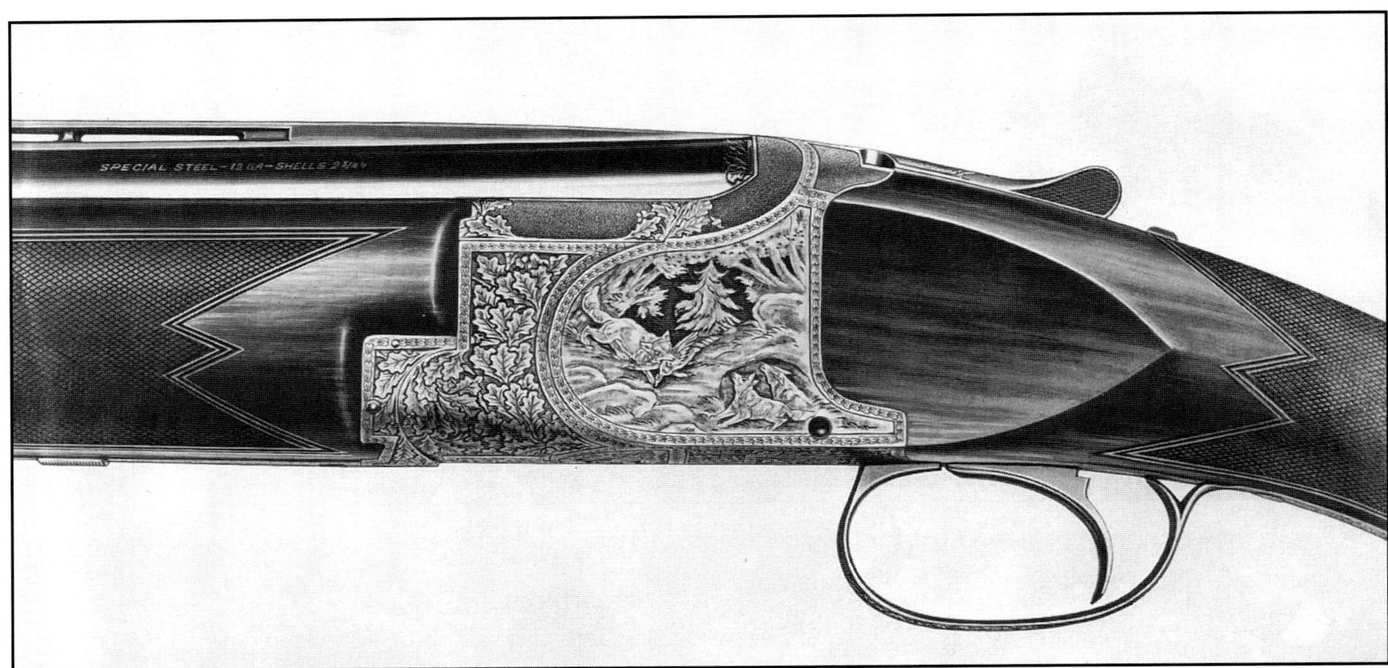

This 1953 Grade IV is signed by Felix Funken. It is interesting to compare this example to the one executed in 1959. Several differences are apparent in the composition of the game scene. This is what makes owning and collecting engraved Superposed so rewarding; each gun has its own unique characteristics. Courtesy Fabrique Nationale Archives.

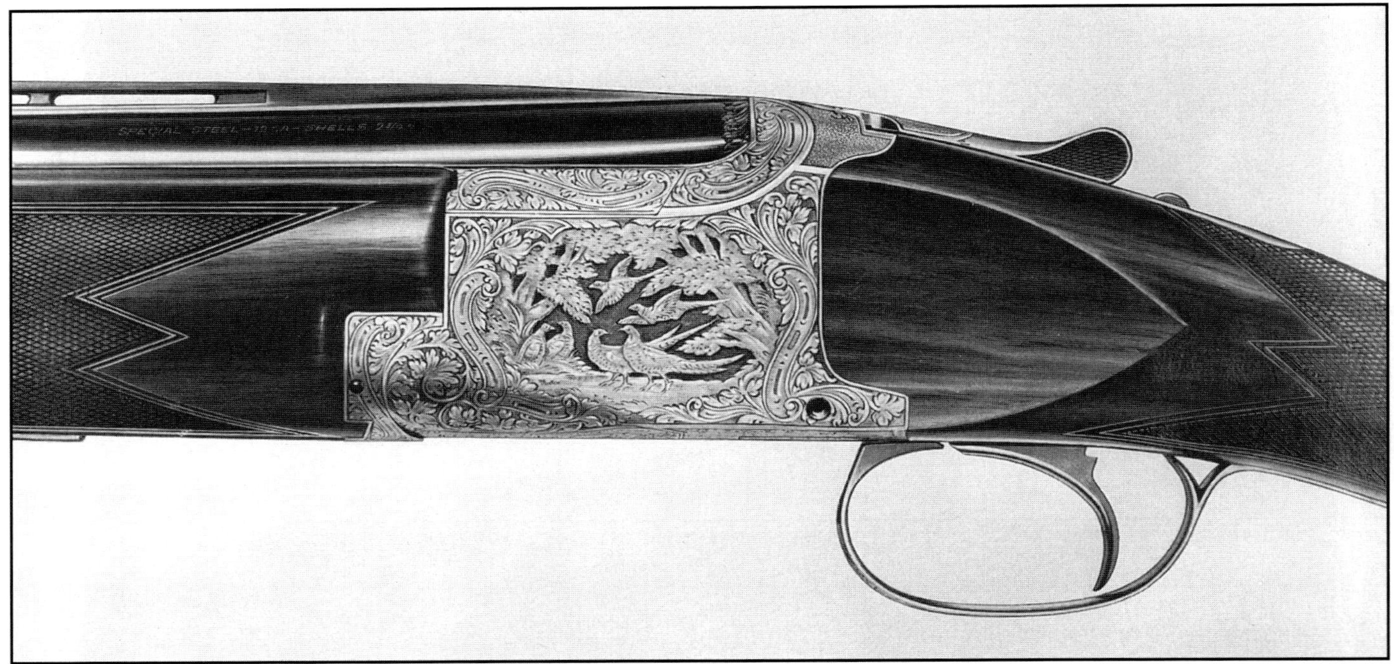

This Grade V was executed in 1953 and signed by Felix Funken. A comparison with the 1959 Grade V shows several differences in game scene composition. Courtesy Fabrique Nationale Archives.

The classic Browning Superposed Grade V. This example was engraved on April 23, 1959, by one of the Maréchal family with game animals executed by master engraver Lea Van Laar, and shading done by master engraver André Watrin. The receiver appears not to be signed. This is not an unusual occurrence. In this case, however, both primary engravers were equal in rank, and perhaps they could not reach an understanding. Thus the gun was left unsigned. Courtesy Fabrique Nationale Archives.

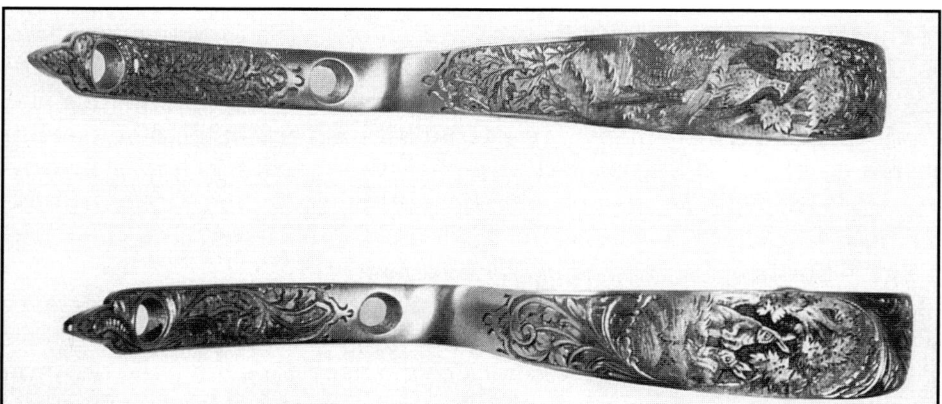

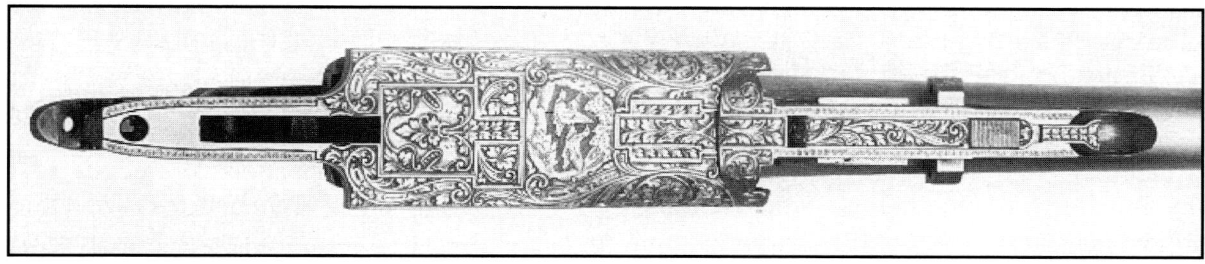

A bottom view of the Grade V showing its extensive scrollwork and small vignette, all cut in deep relief. The trigger guards are shown as well. With the Grade V the trigger guard was furnished either with the pheasant in a tree or rabbits, depending on the customer's request. Courtesy Fabrique Nationale Archives.

Fabrique Nationale had its own Superposed engraving patterns. Also designed by Felix Funken, these patterns reflect European taste. The A1 was the lowest grade and featured a blued finish with acanthus leaves cut into the breech of the barrel and top of the frame. Rosette engraving adorned the hinge pin while a stamped border defined the perimeter of the frame with a graceful curved band through the center. The A2 featured the same sparse engraving pattern but with a case colored finish. These Fabrique Nationale A Grades were referred to by the factory as Standard models. Next in ornamentation and price came the Standard Engraved models. The B1 was engraved with a light English style flower scroll on a gray finish; the B2 also had a gray finish but featured a game scene on a background of light English style scroll. In many ways the B2 closely resembled the American Grade III.

The next group of engraved FN Superposed were designated DeLuxe models. These guns featured certain hand polished action parts and the buttstock was furnished with carved dopper or teardrop points. The C1 featured a case colored finish and a light English style flower engraving. The C2 had a case colored finish and a game scene on a background of light English style scroll. The C3 had a light English style lace engraving on a case colored finish.

The third group of FN engraved Superposed were labeled Super DeLuxe models. The bluing was extra lustrous and all parts of the action were hand polished. The selected dark walnut stock had a special hand polished finish, and the forearm was a three-piece affair. Both buttstock and forearm had diamond point checkering and the buttstock had carved dopper points. The D1 had a finely festooned border engraving with screws and hinge pin finely engraved on a deeply blued frame. This was a rather plain grade, but it did carry a three-piece forearm and special wood. The D2 had a case colored finish with very light English style flower engraving. The D3 had a gray finished frame with very fine English style lace engraving. The D4 was a handsome grade with a gray finished frame and a lightly cut hunting scene on a background of very fine English style engraving. The D5 was the most prestigious catalogued grade offered by FN during the 1950s. It featured a gray finish on the frame with very fine, well executed Louis XVI style engraving.

Although the period following World War II was one of energizing and strengthening the quality control and production process, there were some special engraved and factory custom Superposed. Felix Funken was no stranger to special engraving projects, as many of his most outstanding examples were cut before the war for exhibitions and special occasions. The number of specific types of Superposed guns sold in North America with unique engraving patterns is not known; however, immediately following the war, a number of Superposed were sent to Browning in Ogden for approval of the new postwar engraving patterns that would soon be featured in Browning's 1950 high grade catalogue. FN's best engravers were given general concepts to follow for selecting patterns to adorn the Superposed guns. Many designs and styles were discussed; some were even engraved on Superposed guns. Most of these patterns were discarded, but the guns were sold for nominal sums because their patterns were not part of the Superposed product line. These guns should not be confused with Exhibition Grade Superposed guns which were more often seen in the 1960s and 1970s.

Collectors and shooters should be aware that Browning would custom engrave any pattern the customer desired. It is therefore possible to encounter Superposed guns with unusual or uncommon engraving patterns not catalogued by the company. It is also possible to see European versions of the Superposed with special features such as straight grip stocks, three-piece forearms, checkered butts, oil finishes, double triggers, and other diverse features not usually offered by Browning on guns imported into the U.S. Beginning around 1948, Funken designed and executed a number of special order engraved Superposed. These special guns were sent to countries throughout the world in patterns and styles that make each one unique. Some were sold to well-known individuals, high government officials, and wealthy persons in North America and many foreign countries. Several of these unique Superposed were engraved specifically for Val Browning and members of the Browning family. All are exquisitely rendered by a master craftsman and signed by Felix Funken.

Because Felix Funken was still the chief engraver at FN, the practice of other engravers signing their work was not a common custom, but it did occur on occasion. This resulted in there being only a few pieces during the 1950s signed by FN engravers other than Felix Funken. Funken sometimes stamped his name on one side of the frame with what appears to be a backwards "F." But his principal function was that of supervisor and teacher. As a result, the engraving school at FN continued to grow throughout the decade and each student went through a rigorous training program under the same strict curriculum

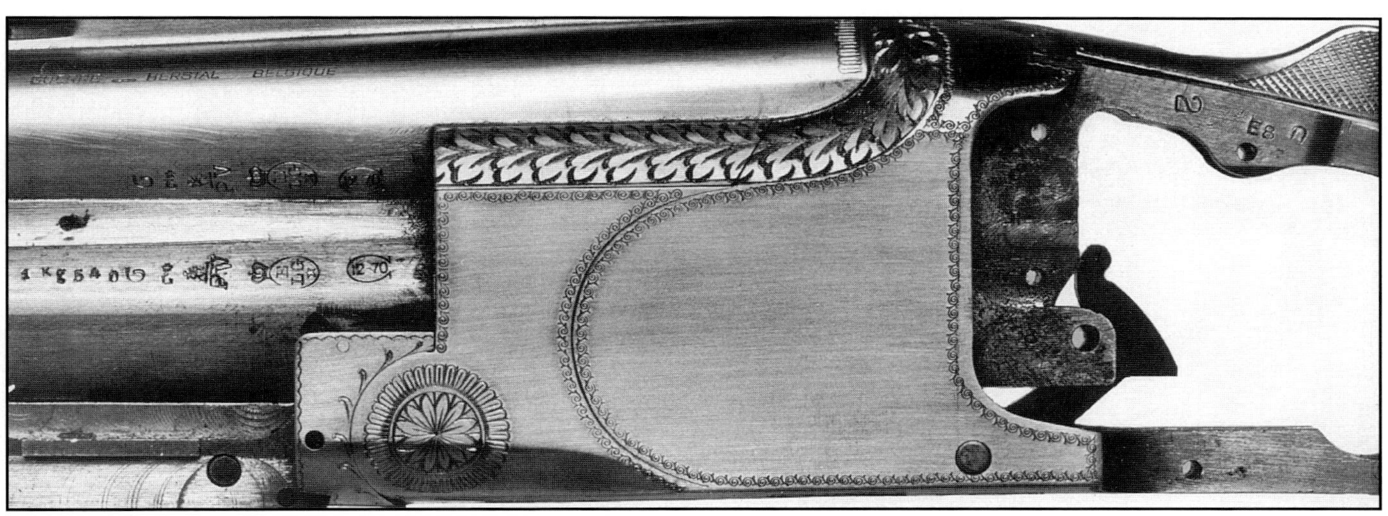

This engraving pattern was the standard European pattern following the end of World War II. FN referred to this pattern as the A1 or A2, the only difference being that the A1 Grade had a blued finish and the A2 was case colored. This pattern is still in use today. The annotation at the bottom of the photo indicates that the engraving work was done on April 28, 1959, in order to establish a mean time to determine how much would be paid for each piece completed. Mr. Scheen was the engraver, and the serial number of the gun was 66732. Courtesy Fabrique Nationale Archives.

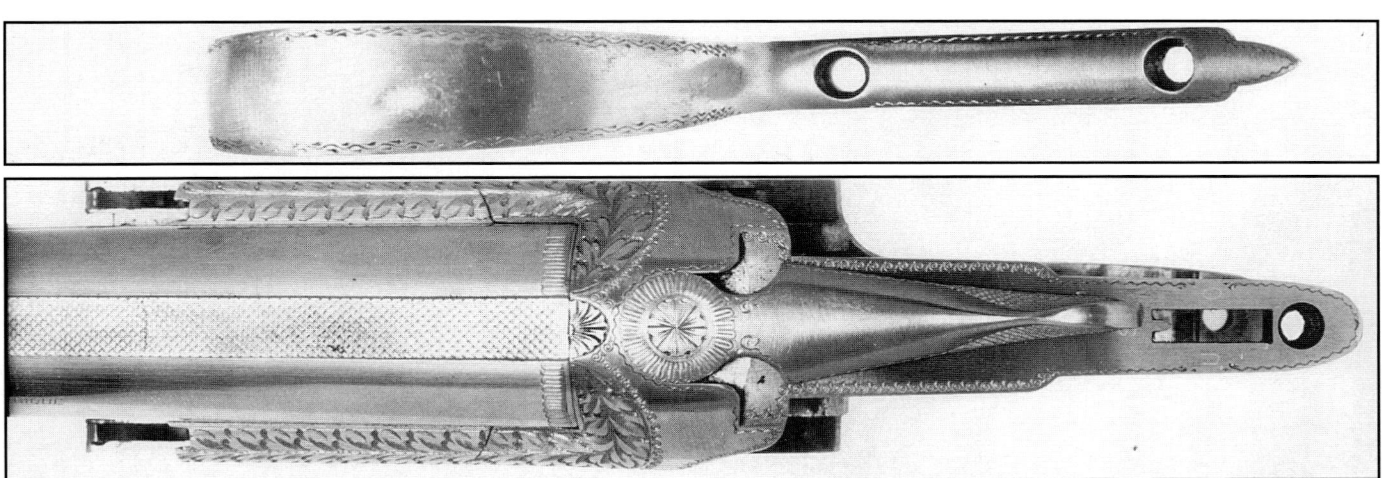

A top view of the A1 Grade. Notice how deeply the barrel ears have been cut. This photo also shows the trigger guard engraving treatment. Courtesy Fabrique Nationale Archives.

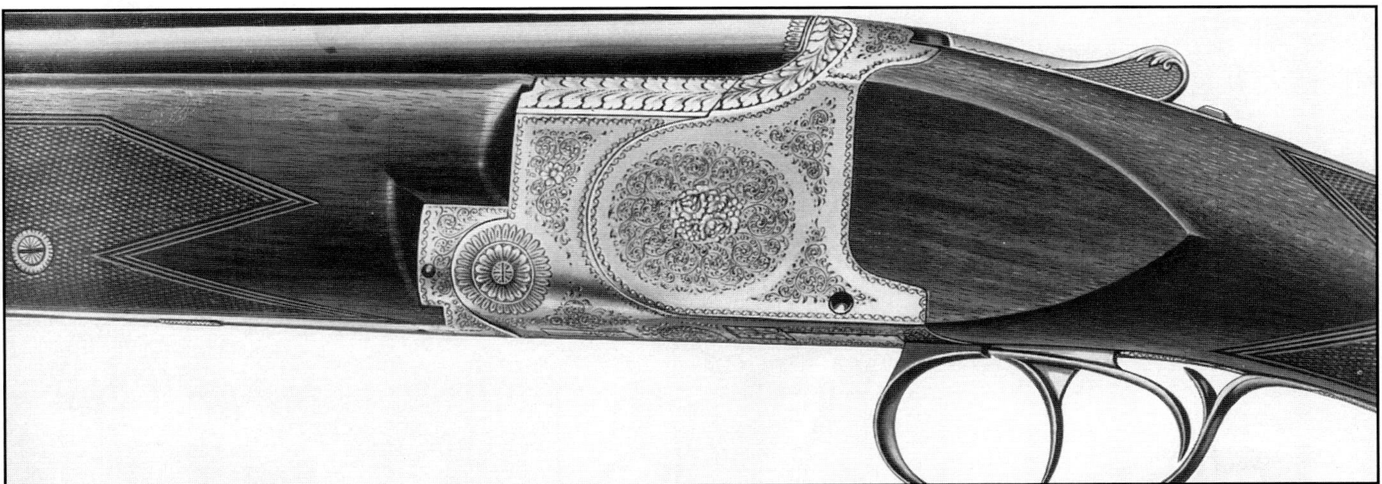

A B1 Grade Browning Superposed intended for FN's world market, circa 1952. This grade featured a gray finish and light English style bouquet engraving. Note the double triggers, a very popular European option. Courtesy Fabrique Nationale Archives.

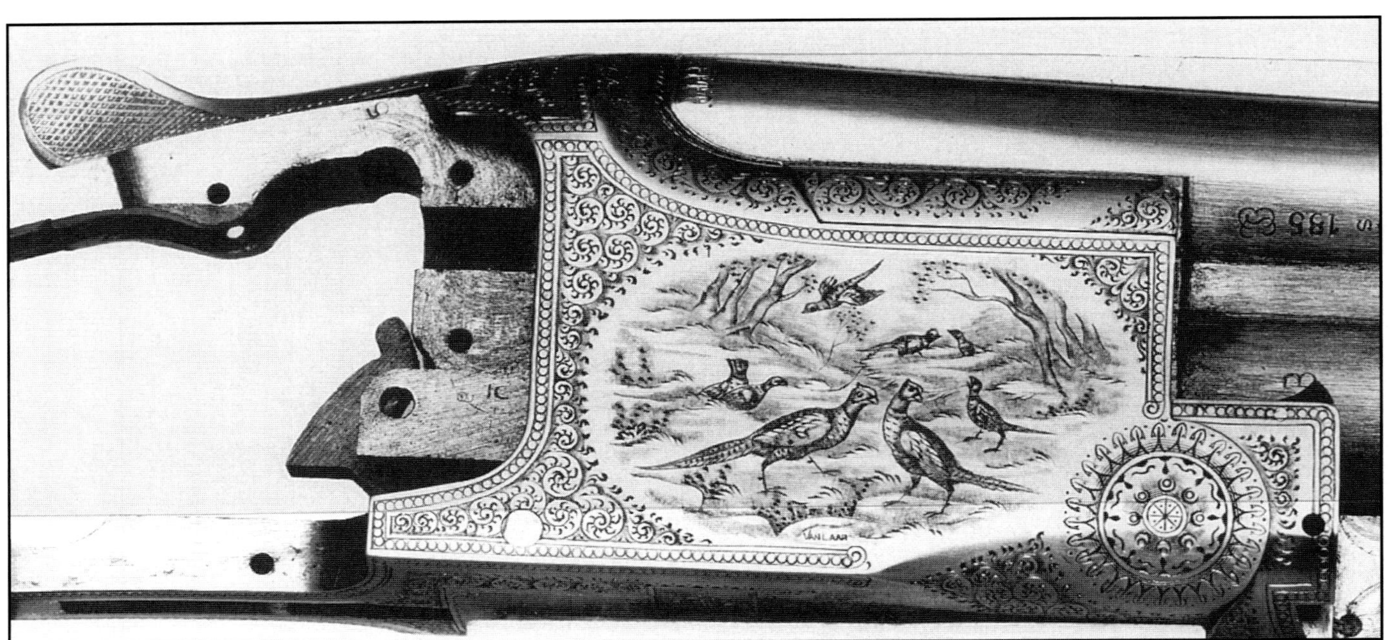

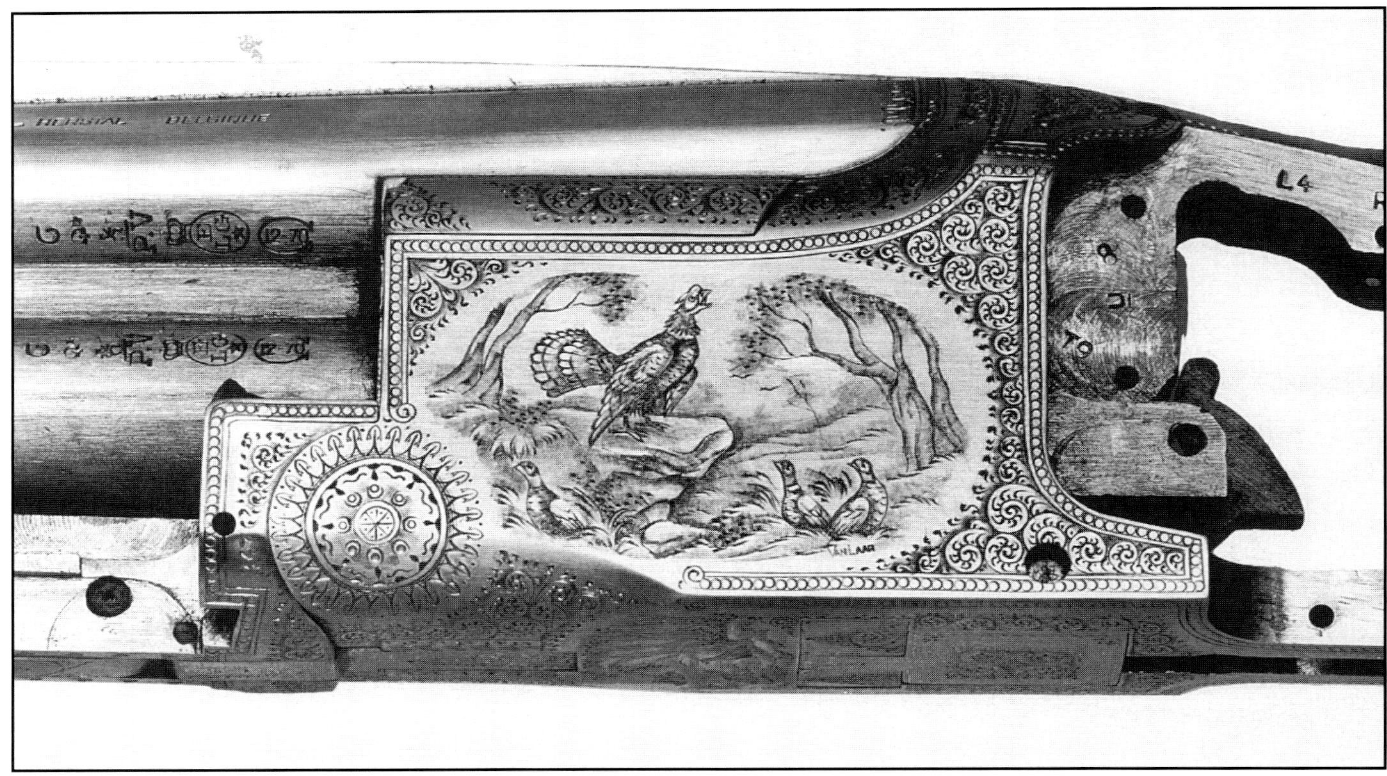

On May 27, 1959, FN engraver Mr. Mativa executed the scrollwork on this B2 Grade Superposed, serial number 66912. The scrollwork on this Superposed is close and tight, with well-executed curves. Master engraver Mademoiselle Van Laar executed the game scenes. Notice that she, as master engraver, has signed both sides of the receiver. Notice, also, the excellent anatomically correct birds, the subtle shading, and the wealth of detail in each scene—the mark of a master. This is an exceptional B2 Superposed. Courtesy Fabrique Nationale Archives.

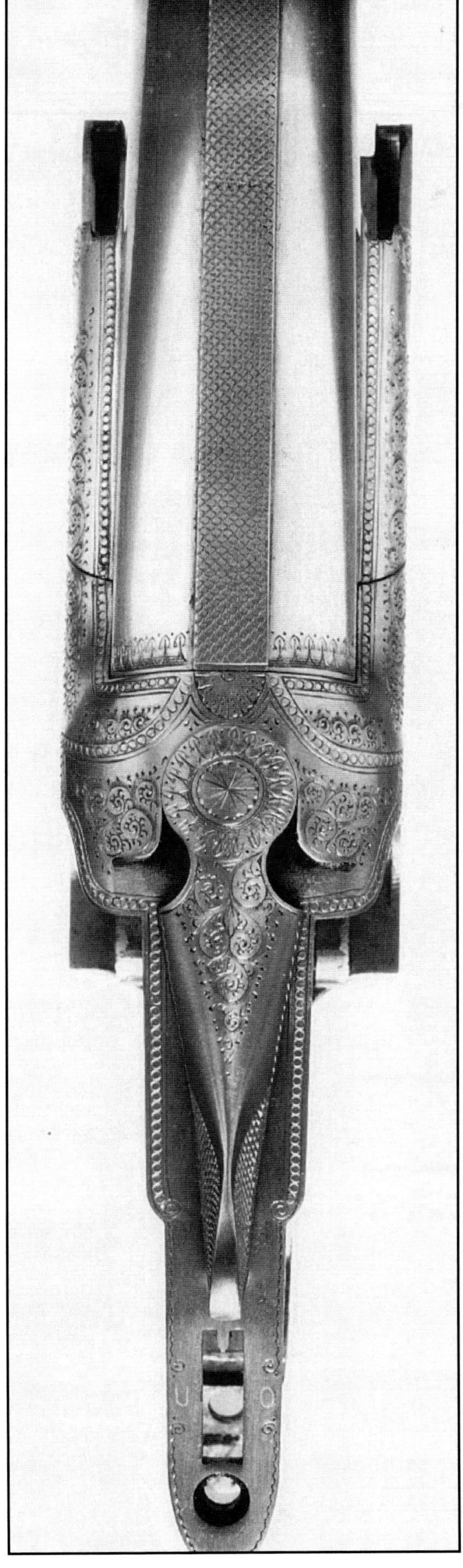

The attention to detail continues on the bottom and top of the B2 Grade serial number 66912. Notice the very fine and delicate work on the breech end of the top barrel. Courtesy Fabrique Nationale Archives.

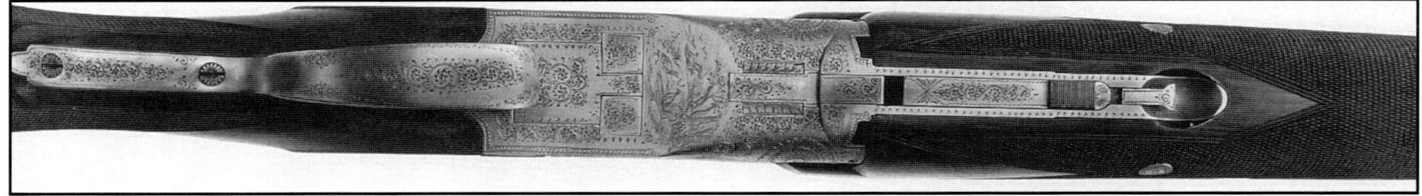

This is a finished B2 Grade which is unsigned. There are several differences between this Superposed and the one signed by Mademoiselle Van Laar. Careful examination will show slight differences between the two patterns in terms of subject placement and background. There is also less detail and composition on both sides of this receiver compared to the Van Laar gun. The scrollwork, although perfectly acceptable, lacks the fineness and balance of the other B2 Grade. Because of the lack of signature and the overall absence of attention to detail, this Superposed was most likely engraved by a journeyman FN engraver. This is a very good but not exceptional B2 Grade. Courtesy Fabrique Nationale Archives.

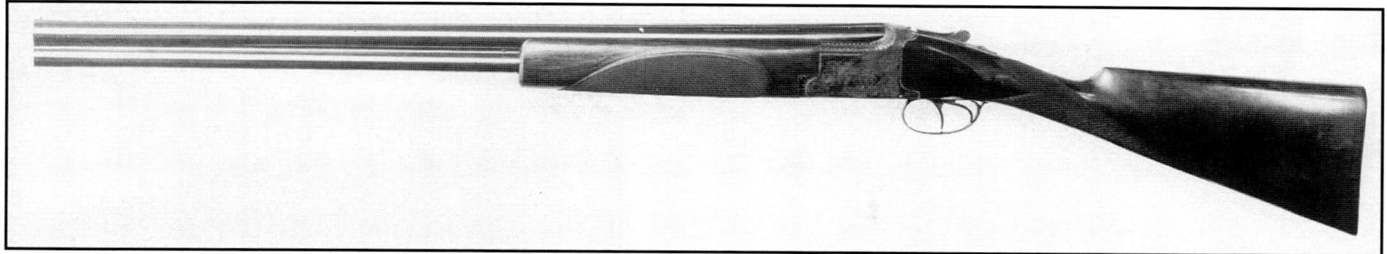

An FN Superposed C1 Grade. The C1 came standard with a case colored finish and light English style scroll. Note the special order forearm. The double triggers and straight grip stock are classic European characteristics. On the close-up photo also note the "FABRIQUE NATIONALE D'ARMES DE GUERRE-HERSTAL" barrel address. This was the standard FN barrel address for guns sold in its exclusive markets. Courtesy Fabrique Nationale Archives.

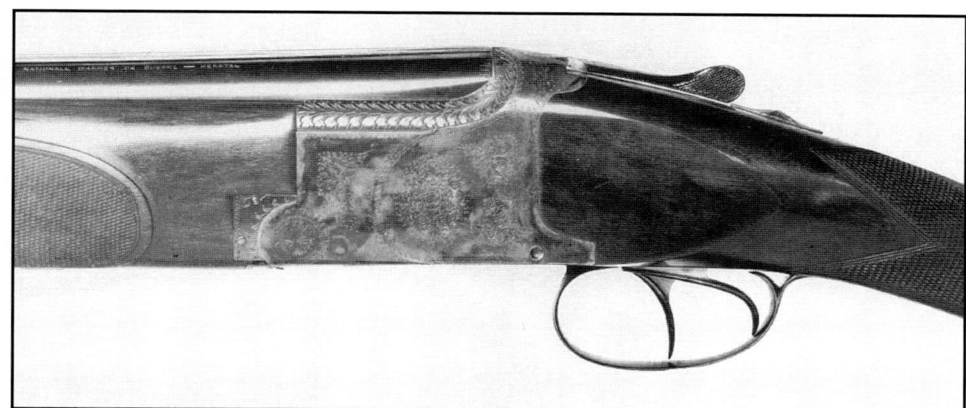

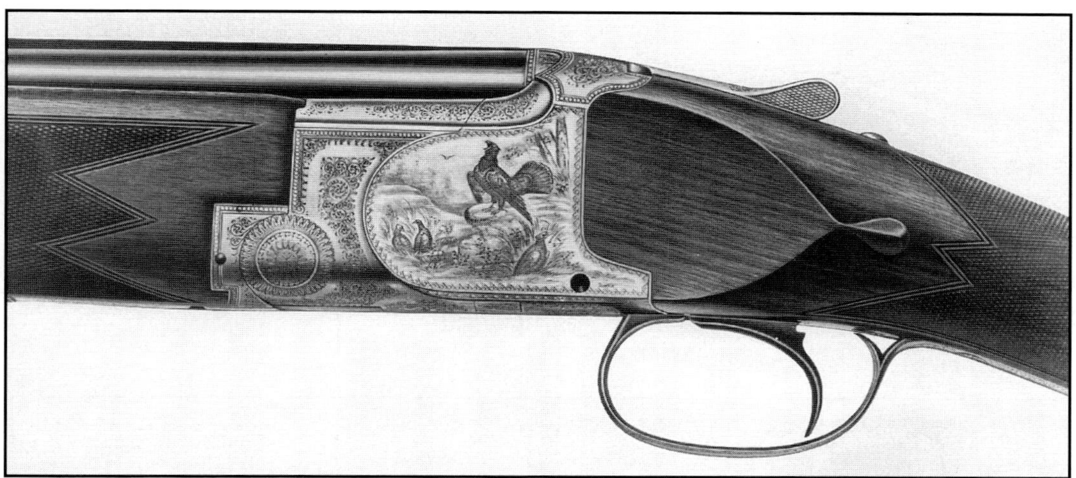

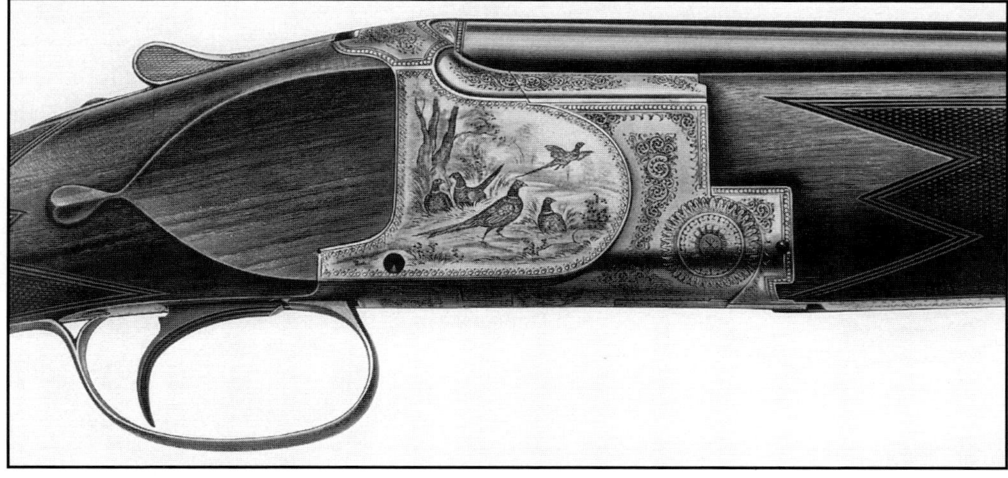

Both sides of an FN C2 Grade Superposed signed by Felix Funken. Whether Funken actually engraved this C2 is open to speculation, but he could very well have. Note the attention to detail and the finely shaded background. This is the work of a real master. This grade also features a sculptured frame, a popular European characteristic in the early 1950s. Courtesy Fabrique Nationale Archives.

The D5 Grade was FN's highest Superposed production engraving pattern. This grade featured a very fine Louis XVI style engraving, and was fitted with a three-piece forearm as standard. The photo was taken in 1950. Courtesy Fabrique Nationale Archives.

A top view of the D5 Grade. The Louis XVI style engraving was beautifully executed. Notice the hand cut matting on the rib and the Fabrique Nationale address on the top barrel. Courtesy Fabrique Nationale Archives.

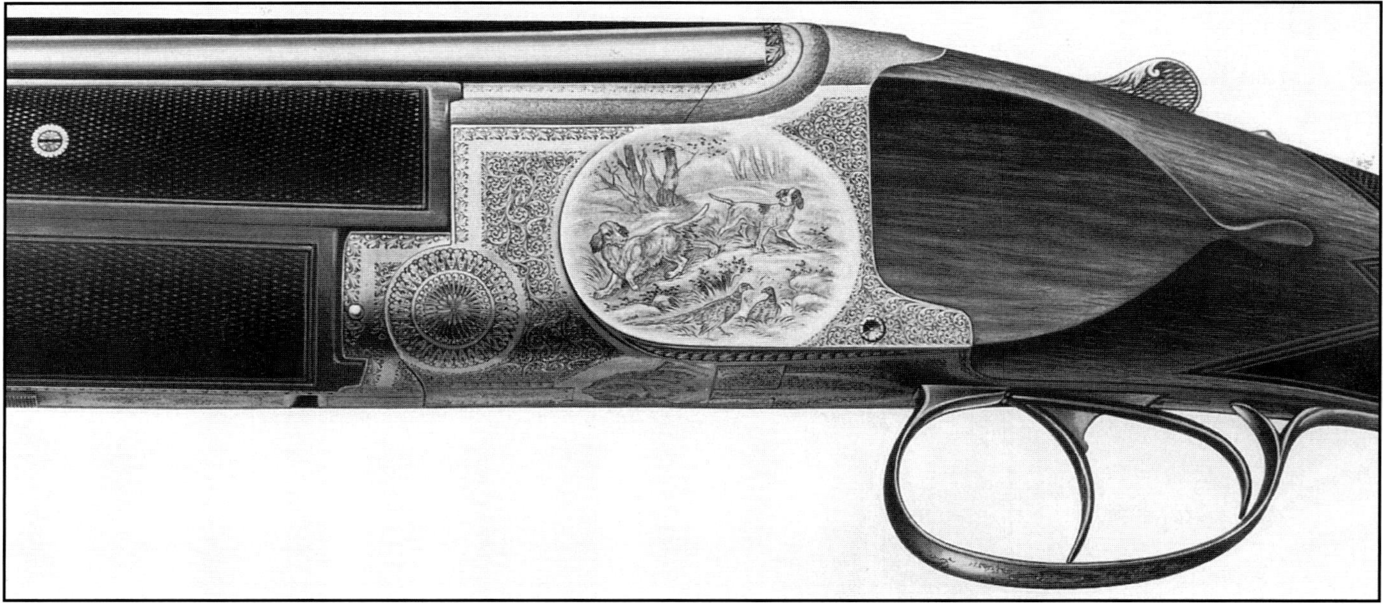

This is an early 1950s D4 FN Superposed also signed by the master Felix Funken. This grade made full use of the sculptured frame in the composition of its game scene. Note the very tight scrollwork. The D4 was fitted with a three-piece forearm as standard. Courtesy Fabrique Nationale Archives.

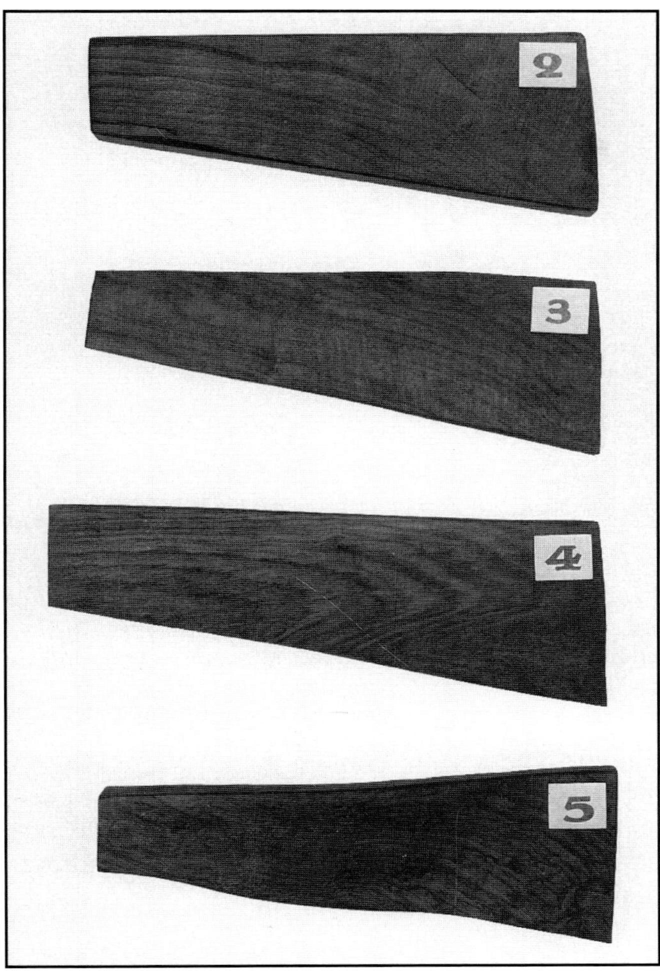

This Fabrique Nationale photo shows a representative sample of wood grades 2 through 5 as they are used on correspondingly numbered grades of Superposed in the early 1950s. Because wood grain and color are subjective traits it is difficult, if not impossible, to categorize wood with any degree of certainty. What this photo does illustrate is FN's attempt to match each grade with an accordingly appropriate class of wood so that the two would complement each other. Courtesy Fabrique Nationale Archives.

prescribed to prewar students. Not all of the engraving students who entered the training program were able to finish. Some did not display the talent necessary and others did not have sufficient motivation to complete the course of study. Felix Funken was not an easy man to work for, and he demanded the best. If a student did not show the promise that Funken required, he or she was promptly dismissed, often quite rudely. The chief engraver had students that were his favorites and others that he did not care for. This partiality was not always founded on talent but sometimes on personality alone. Artistic jealousy was common and Funken seemed to thrive on discord of his own making. But personalities aside, Felix Funken was almost exclusively responsible for the outstanding reputation of engraving during his tenure at Fabrique Nationale.

This snapshot of Funken with some of his engravers at the FN plant was taken during Christmas of 1953. Courtesy Liège Arms Museum.

Similar practices continued from the prewar method of having two or three engravers work on the same Superposed frame. In reality engravers would delegate specific areas among themselves. For example, one would execute only the scroll, another would complete the game scenes, and a third would do only the small parts such as the screws and the trigger guard. This team effort would result in the best execution in all phases of engraving. The practice remained of Funken stamping his name to many of these Superposed,

In September of 1959 a new group of engraving students entered Fabrique Nationale to learn their trade under the master Felix Funken. Funken is the third from the left in the back row. Funken taught hundreds of young men and women the art of engraving. Courtesy Liège Arms Museum.

but there are examples of two engravers signing their names, one on each side of the frame. When this occurred it acknowledged that one executed the scroll and the other the game scenes. If a much more senior engraver stamped his name on the frame, it might indicate that he alone did all of the engraving or it may be an instance where he, being senior, merely signed his name to the frame as Funken did. In many cases there is no name on the frame. There are several explanations for no engraver's signatures on Superposed frames. The first is that he forgot. Remember, the engraver was paid on a piecework basis and time was money. Secondly, a journeyman engraver had to have permission from the master to sign his work. Felix Funken did not often give his consent. Thirdly, engravers sometimes took factory work into their home to earn extra money, and to avoid taxes would not sign their engraving.

The period of the 1950s was one of growth in the number of highly skilled engravers who received their training under Funken, and this instruction would have a significant impact on engraving styles and techniques in the coming decades. The last engraving class to apprentice under Felix Funken was in 1959/1960. There were thirteen students in this class. Some of them were to spend the next thirty years of their working lives engraving Superposed guns for Fabrique Nationale and later the Engravers Co-operative. Richard Kowalski, Charles Severien, Jean Marie Boulanger, and Jean Diet were some of the members of this final group.[19] Through their training under Felix Funken they have passed on the skill and artistry acquired under the great master himself. This last generation would influence others who trained under them to keep the tradition of fine craftsmanship alive.

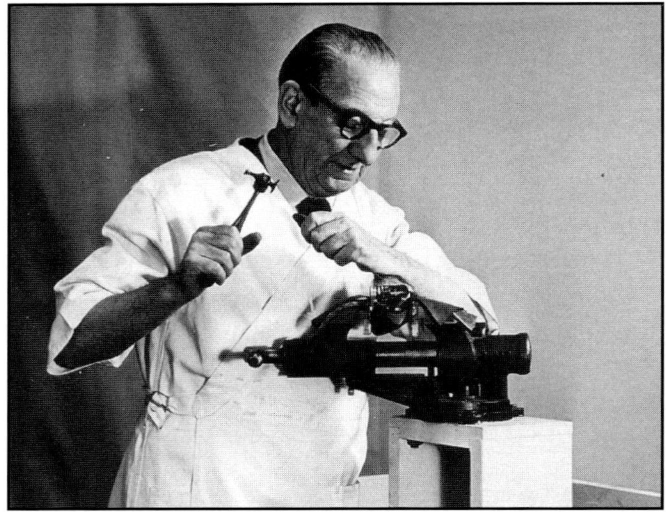

The master himself, Felix Funken as he looked a year before his retirement in 1960. Felix Funken died in 1965. No one had more influence on the style and design of Fabrique Nationale engraving than Funken. His legacy remains strong to this day. Courtesy Fabrique Nationale Archives.

[19] Former FN engraver Jean H. Diet. Personal interview with the author, April 7, 1995.

This photo of the engraving shop inside FN was taken in 1959. Notice the increased number of female engravers compared to the 1950 photo. Notice, too, the game scene motifs painted on the walls surrounding the shop. The number of engravers working under Funken had almost doubled by the end of the decade. Courtesy Fabrique Nationale Archives.

The Artistry of Felix Funken

1945-1960

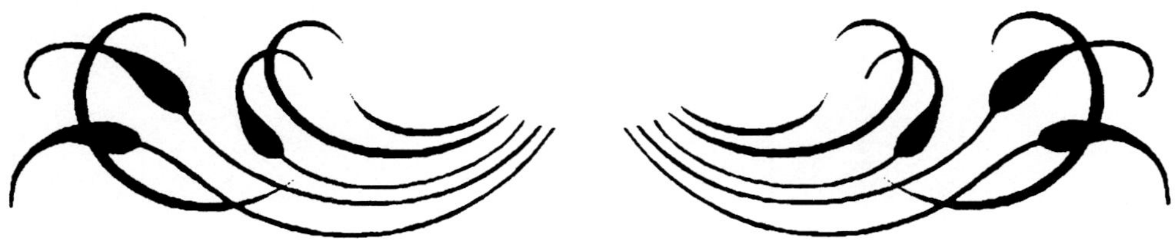

A Photographic Collection

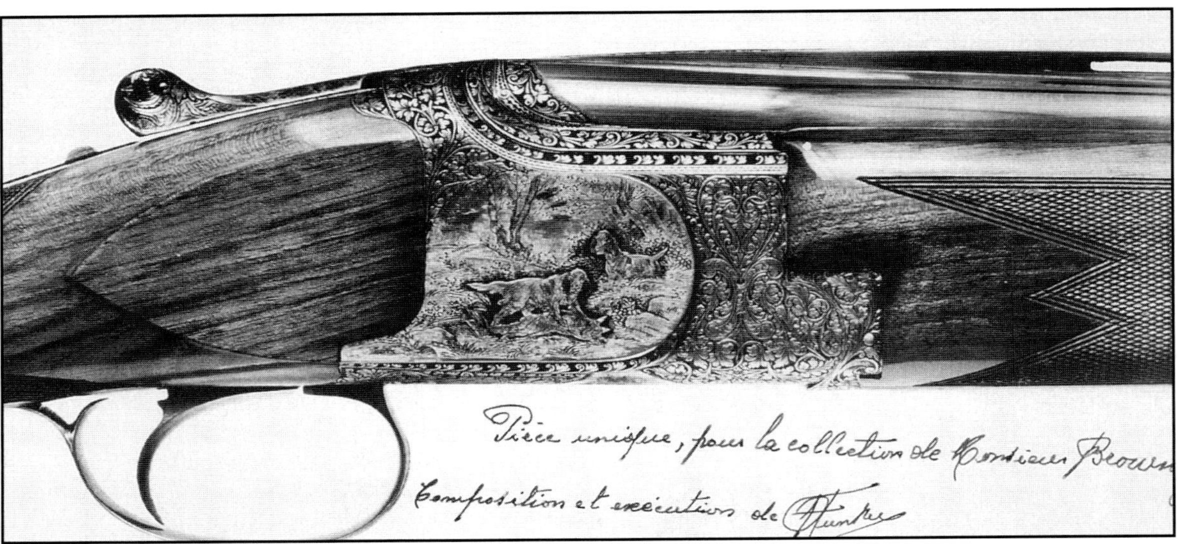

This photo was taken from a page in Felix Funken's diary. The master thought a great deal of his unique design, serial number 39815. This Superposed is a 12 gauge with extra special engraving. This unique creation was executed for Val Browning on June 23, 1954, and the gun was fitted with two sets of barrels, each numbered. Note that the receiver is sculptured in the European style. Courtesy Liège Arms Museum.

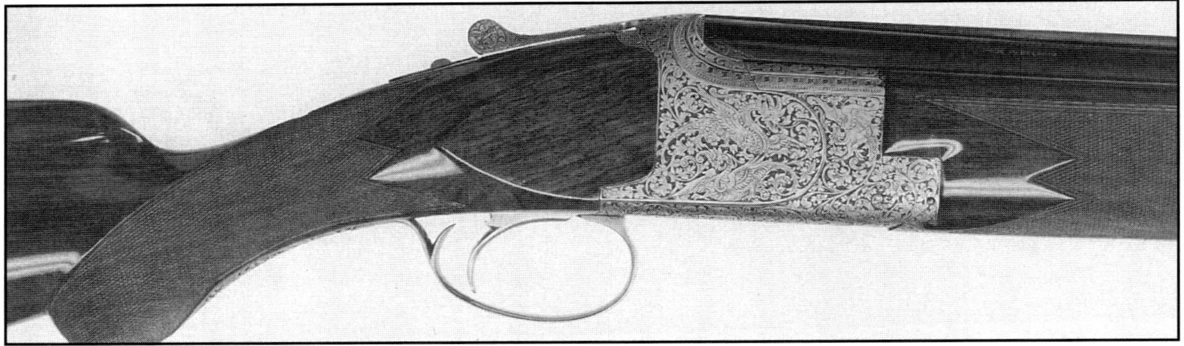

This specially engraved Browning 12 gauge Superposed, serial number 23982, was created by Felix Funken for John Val Browning on June 3, 1953. It is very similar to a later design, also done by Funken, seen elsewhere in this chapter. This early design is slightly less elaborate than the later one principally in the lack of coverage on the breech end of the top barrel and also in the position of the chimeras. Courtesy Browning Company.

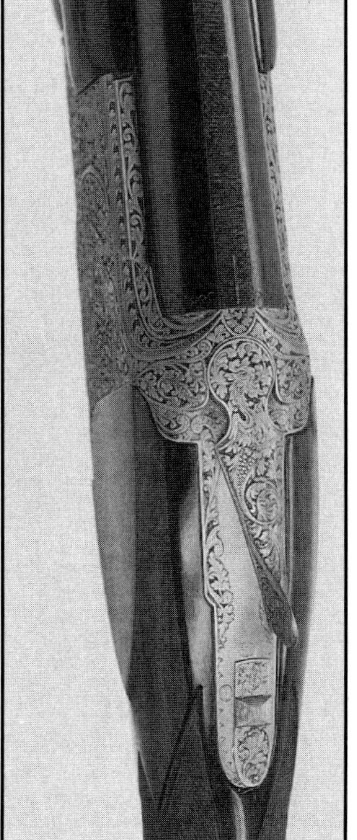

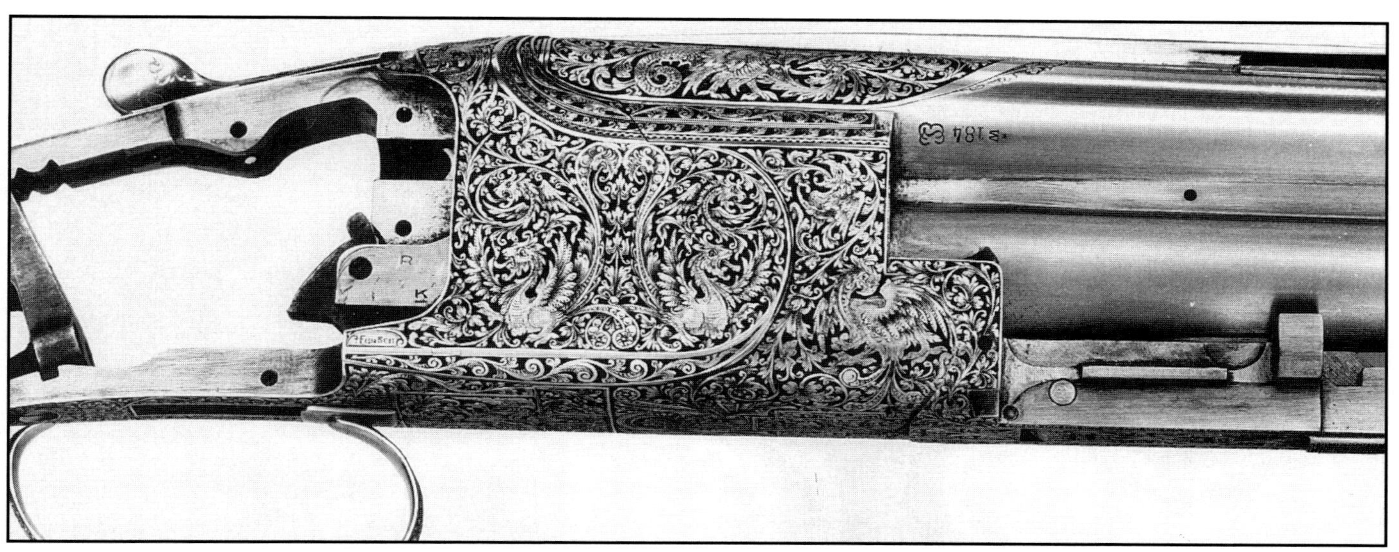

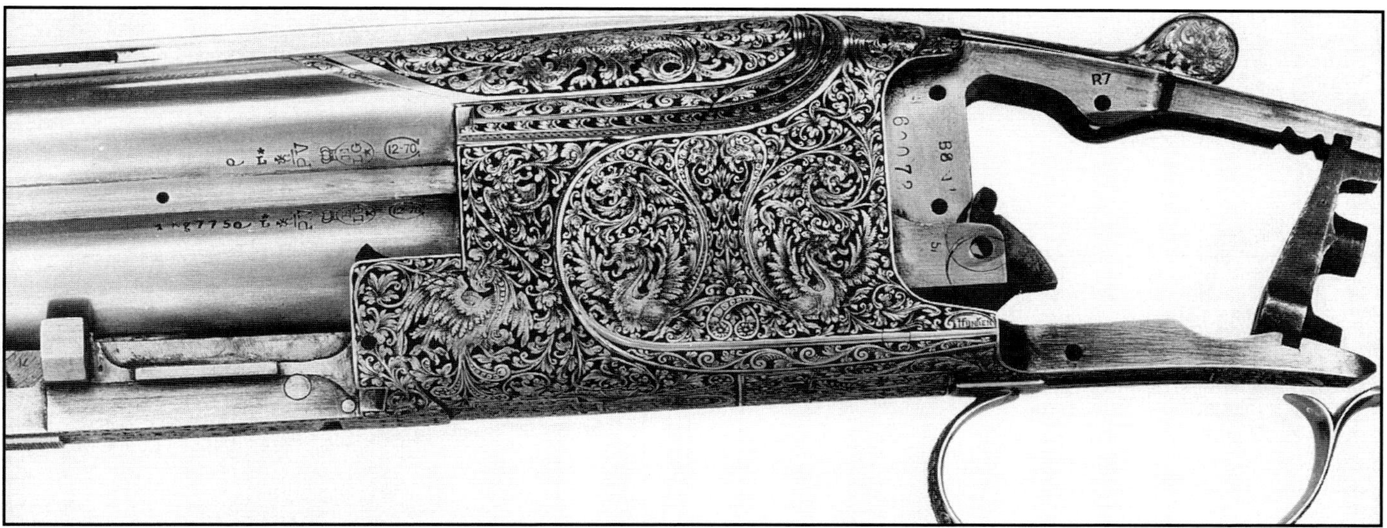

This exceptional 12 gauge Browning Superposed was designed and executed by Felix Funken for Val Browning in 1956. Chimeras surrounded by exquisite scrollwork adorn both sides of the receiver. The engraving on this Superposed is indeed a true work of art. Courtesy Fabrique Nationale Archives.

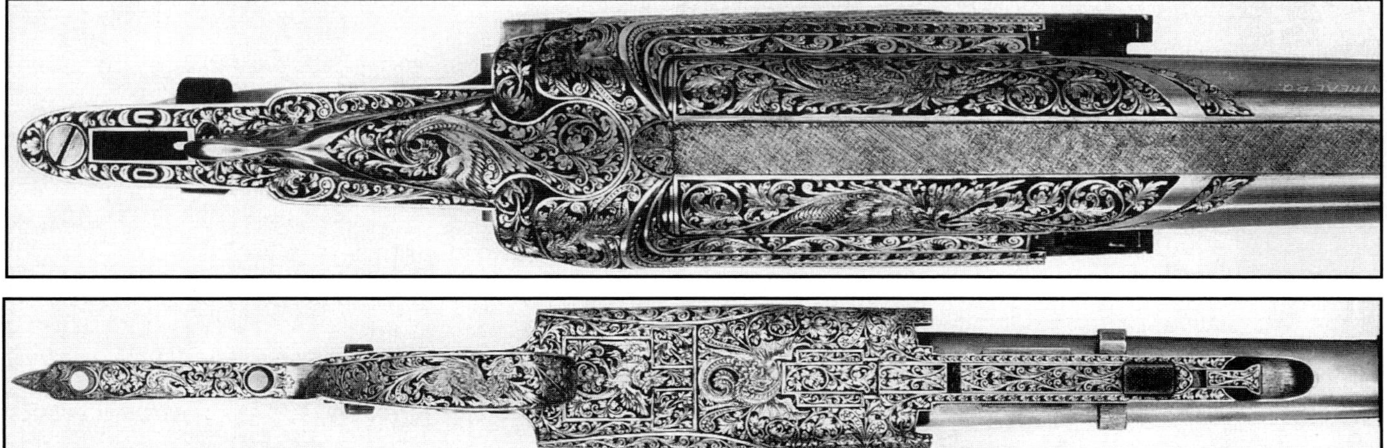

The underside of Funken's masterpiece shows the continuation of the same theme. The top view shows a chimera engraved on the top lever with more executed down the top barrel. The profuse coverage even on the top of the gun is almost overwhelming. Courtesy Fabrique Nationale Archives.

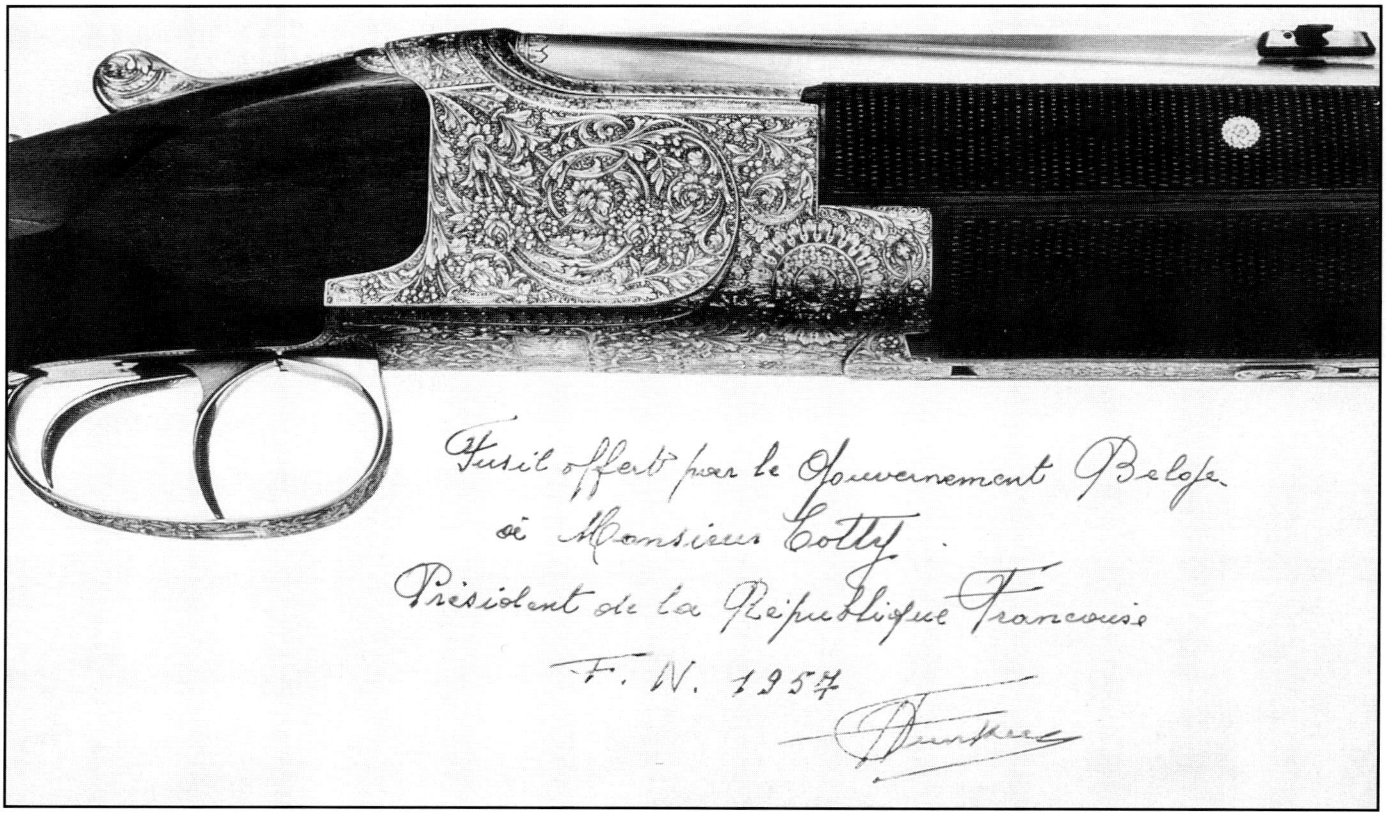

This special FN Superposed double rifle was designed and engraved for the president of France in 1957 by Felix Funken. The inscription on the photo reads, "special creation. Light engraving. Shotgun, presented by the Belgian government to Mister Cotty, president of the French Republic." The name of the French president is misspelled; it should read Mister Coty, for Rene Coty, president of the French Republic from 1954 to 1959. Courtesy Claude Gaier and the Liège Arms Museum.

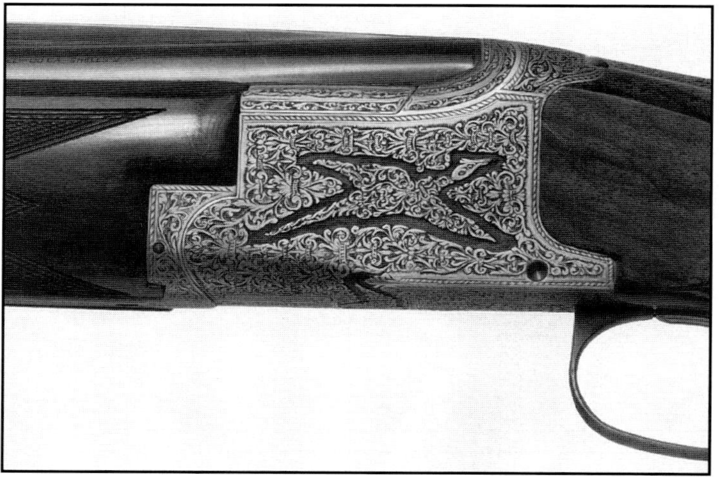

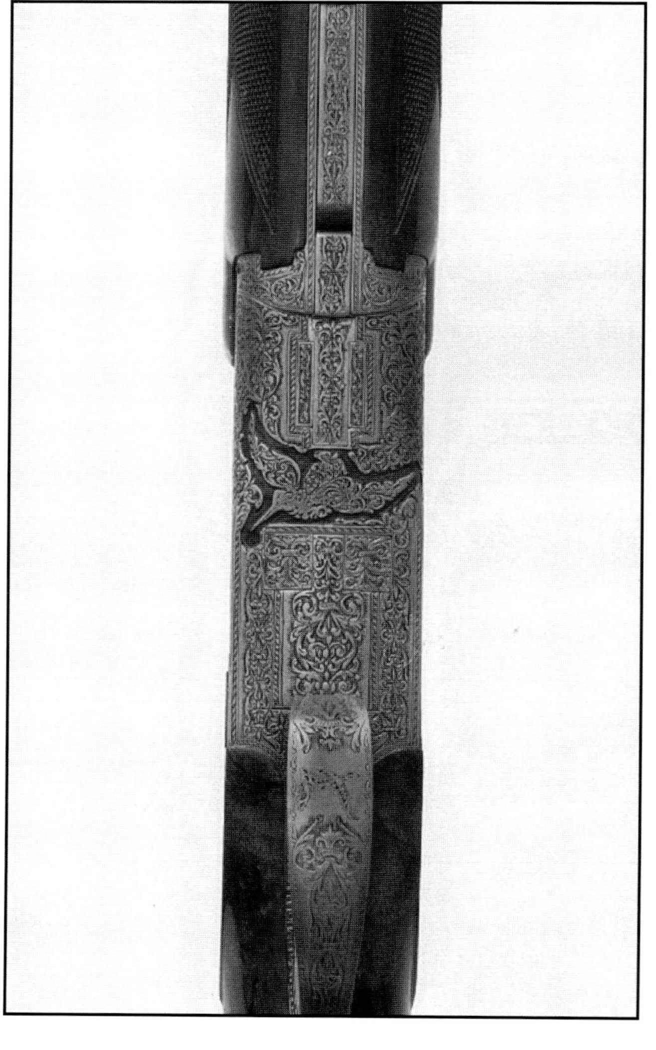

Above and right: This Browning 20 gauge Superposed was built sometime between 1953 and 1954. There is no apparent signature on the receiver, but no doubt the engraving pattern on this gun was designed by Felix Funken. The scroll bird within scroll is classic Funken. The design, with its bouquet scroll and modernistic motif, is a Funken hallmark. The underside of the receiver reveals a continuation of the same mixture of traditional design with art deco. This Superposed may be one of the more unusual Funken creations. Courtesy Fabrique Nationale Archives.

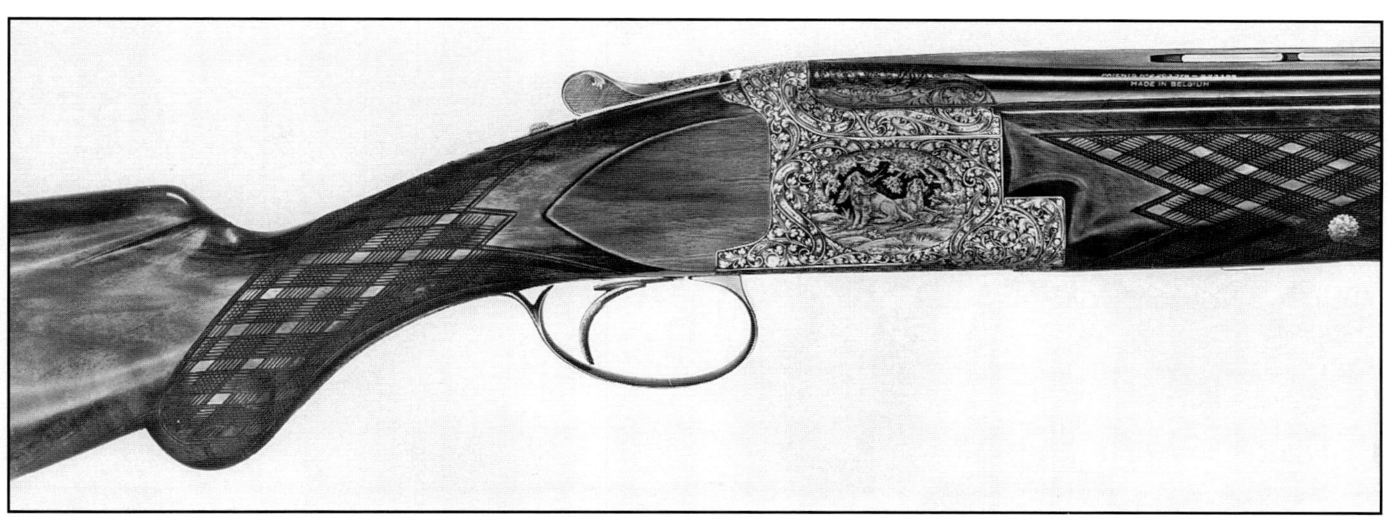

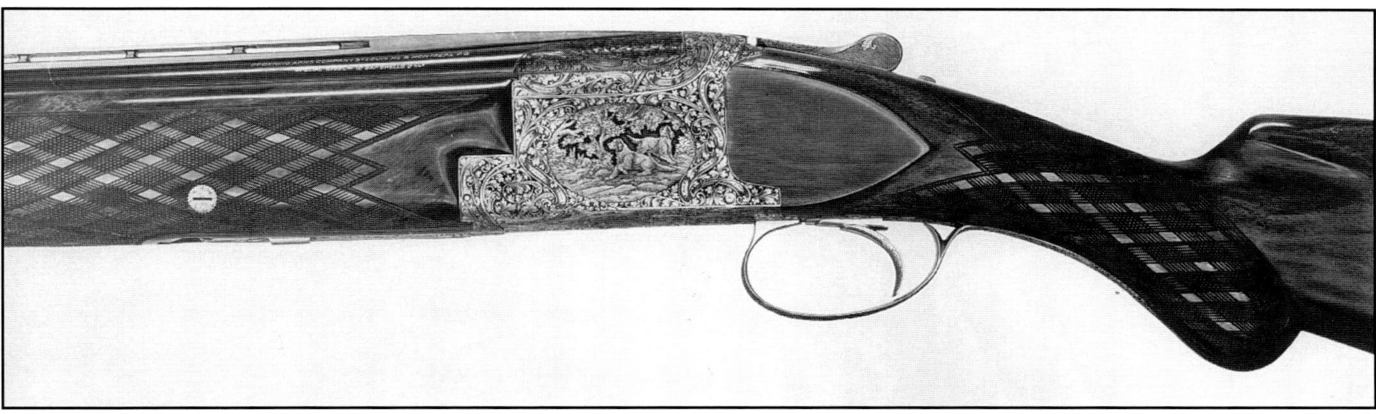

Another spectacular Browning Superposed engraved for the Browning family. The pattern was designed and executed by Felix Funken in the summer of 1959. This design has some vague similarity to the Grade V. Notice the special diamond checkering pattern on this 12 gauge gun. Courtesy Fabrique Nationale Archives.

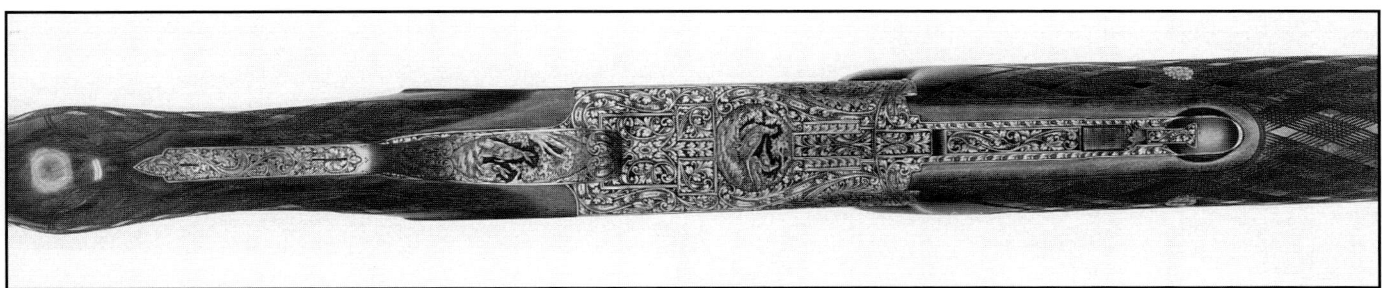

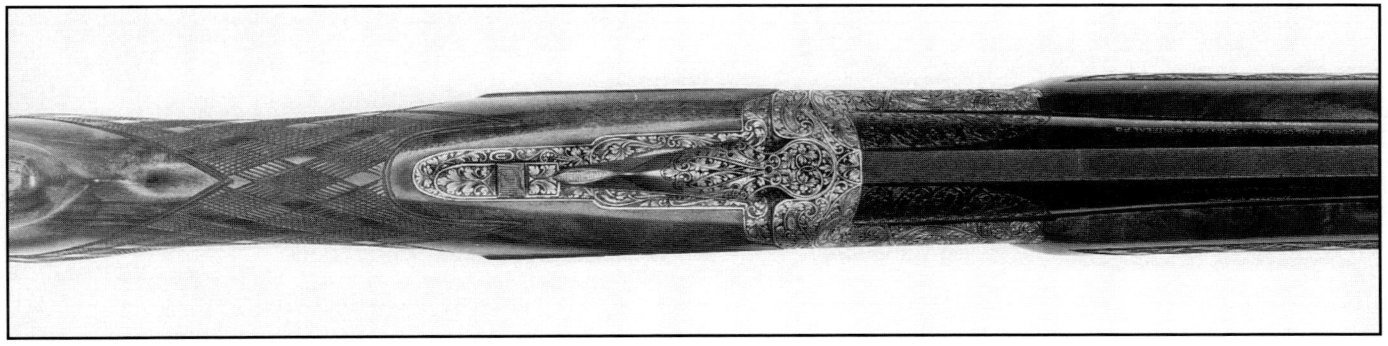

A view of the underside and top of this outstanding special order Superposed. Note the scrollwork coverage down the top barrel. This particular scrollwork and the overall design creates a very elegant effect. Courtesy Fabrique Nationale Archives.

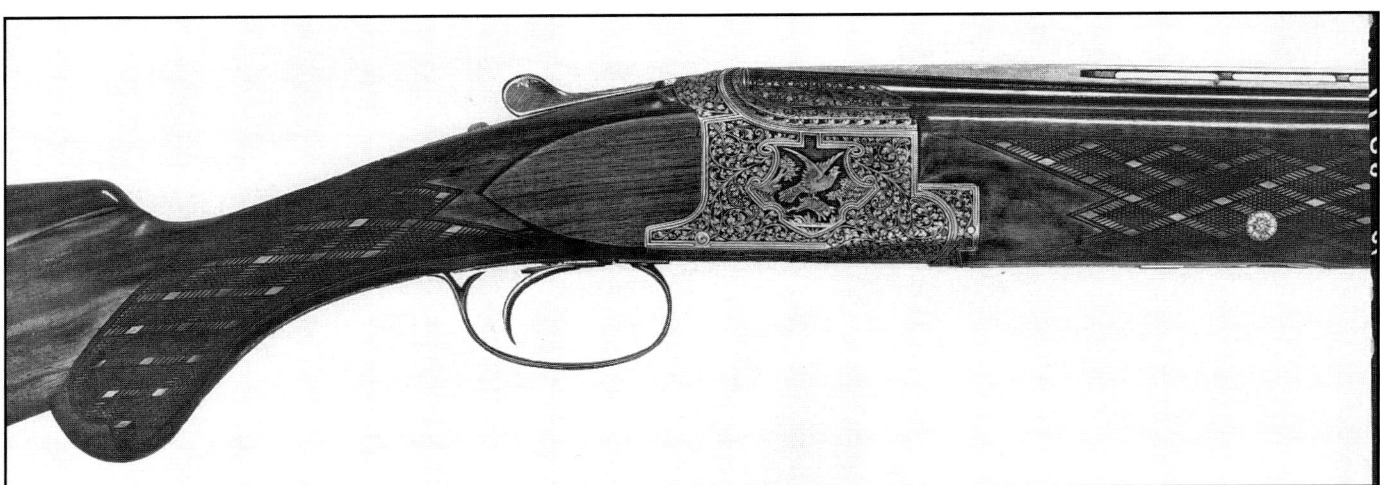

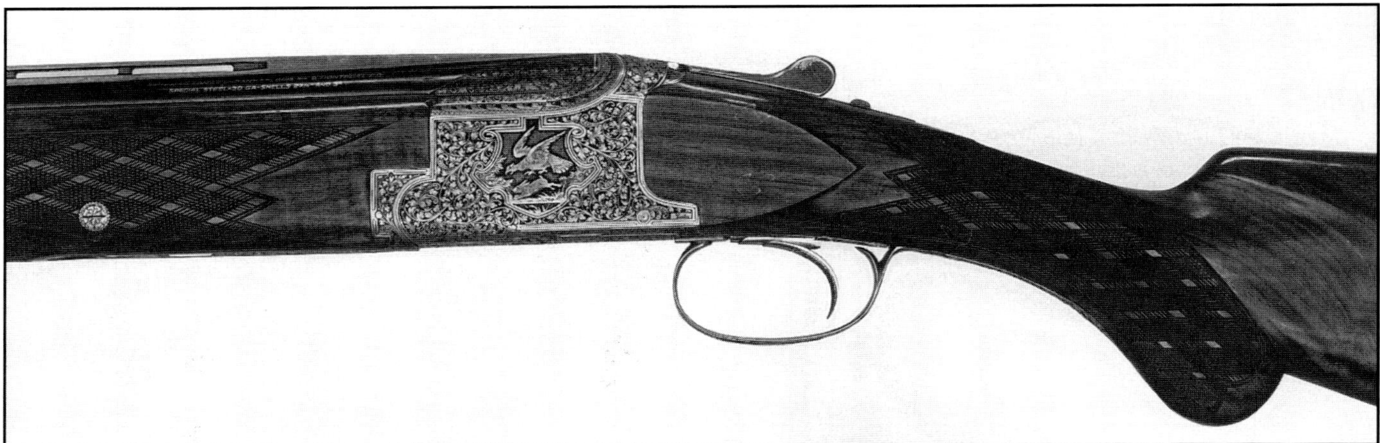

This special engraved Browning Superposed 20 gauge was designed and completed just prior to Felix Funken's retirement in 1960. The left side of the receiver depicts an eagle swooping down on a rabbit and on the right side of the receiver is seen the eagle lifting skyward with his prey. Notice the use of the special diamond checkering pattern. Courtesy Fabrique Nationale Archives.

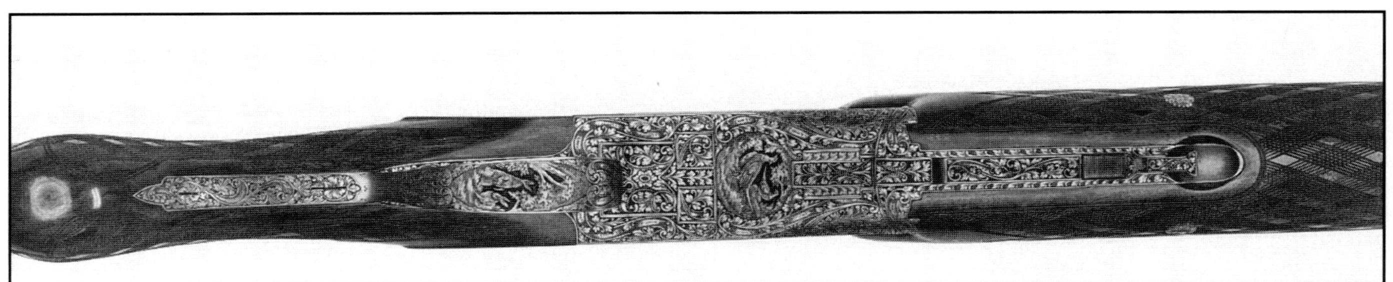

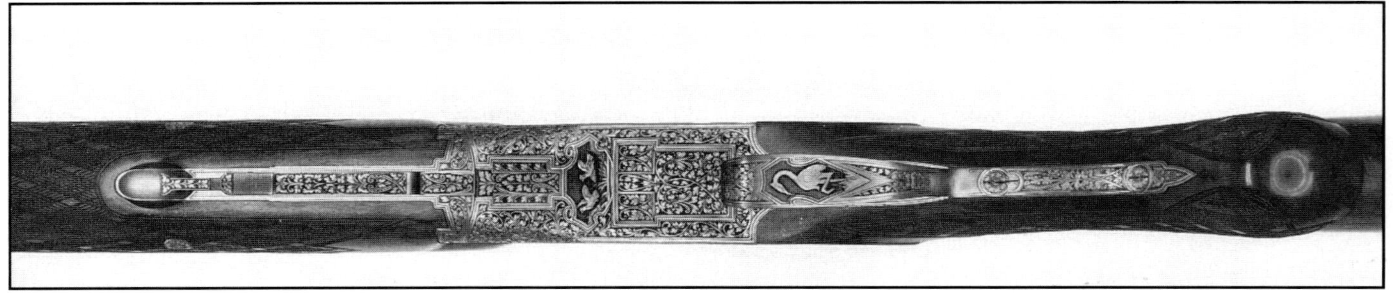

The underside of Funken's special engraved Superposed shows an unusual mix of traditional scrollwork with game scenes; the trigger guard has a gold inlaid shore bird done in an almost "art deco" style. The top of the gun is covered in well-executed scroll with the Roman numeral I inlaid in gold on the rib. Courtesy Fabrique Nationale Archives.

BROWNING ARMS COMPANY - ST. LOUIS, MISSOURI
F. N. le 3 février 1956

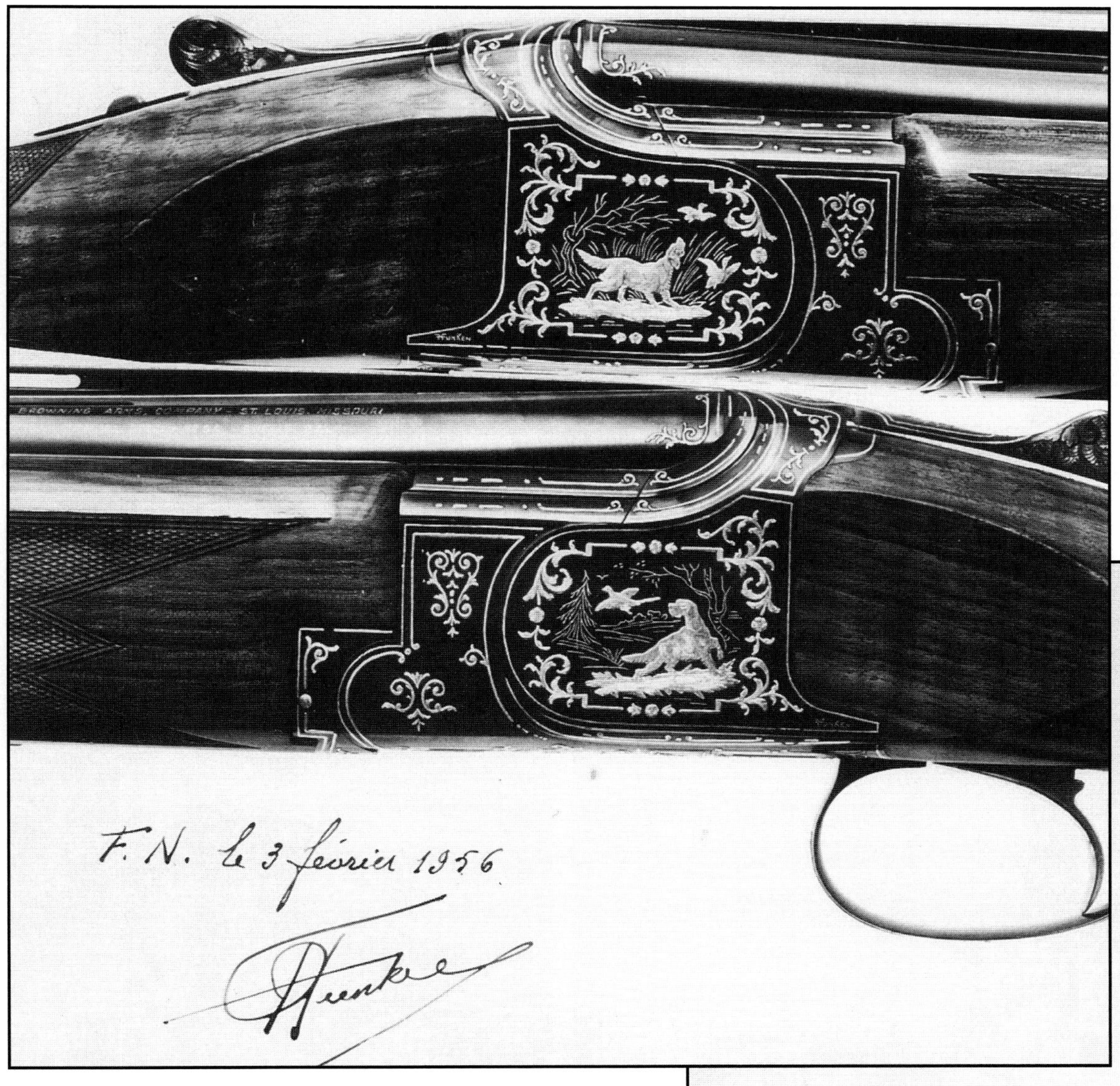

This 12 gauge Superposed Exhibition Grade was signed February 3, 1956, by Felix Funken. These FN photographs were placed in Funken's personal diary as a record of his most memorable designs. Notice that this particular Browning has a sculptured frame. Courtesy Liège Arms Museum.

Cette incrustation en or,
haut relief, a été
spécialement exécutée
pour Monsieur Browning
F. N. le 3 février 1956

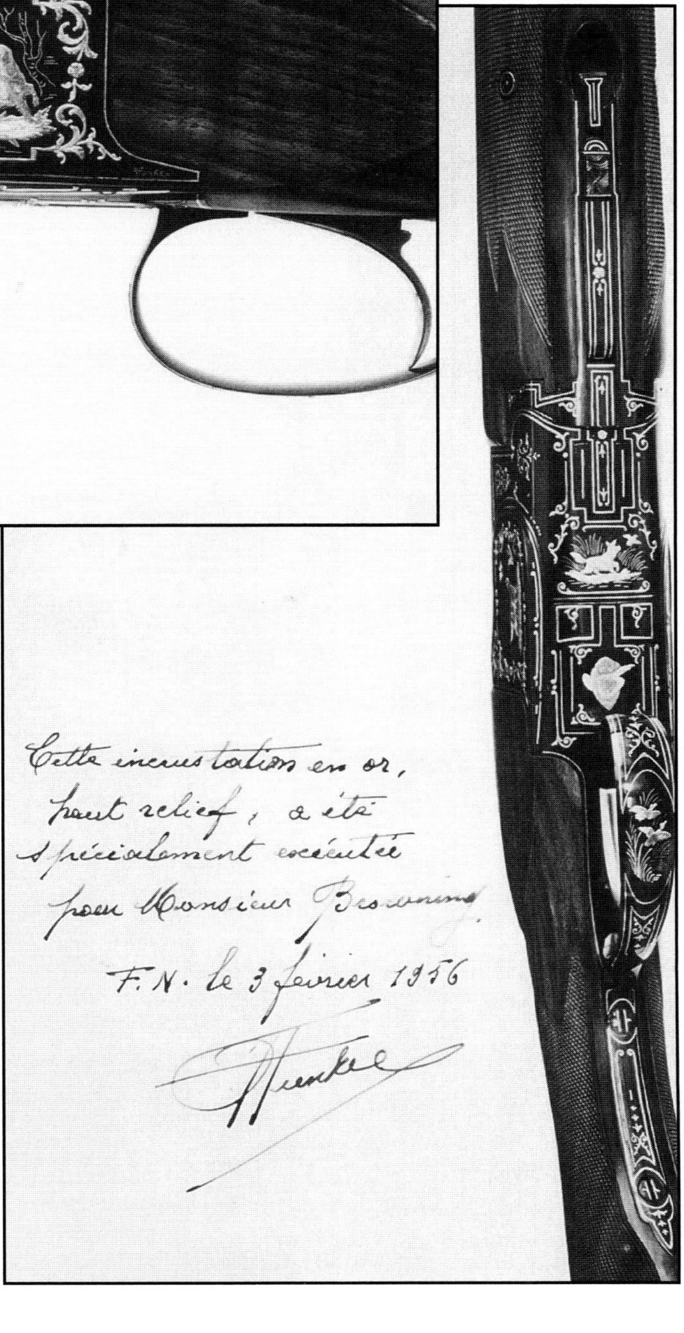

The notation indicates the date (February 3, 1956) and that the gun was executed for Mr. Browning. Mr. Browning could have been either Val Browning or his son, John Val. Many of these special order Superposed were given to family members or special friends of the Browning family. Courtesy Liège Arms Museum.

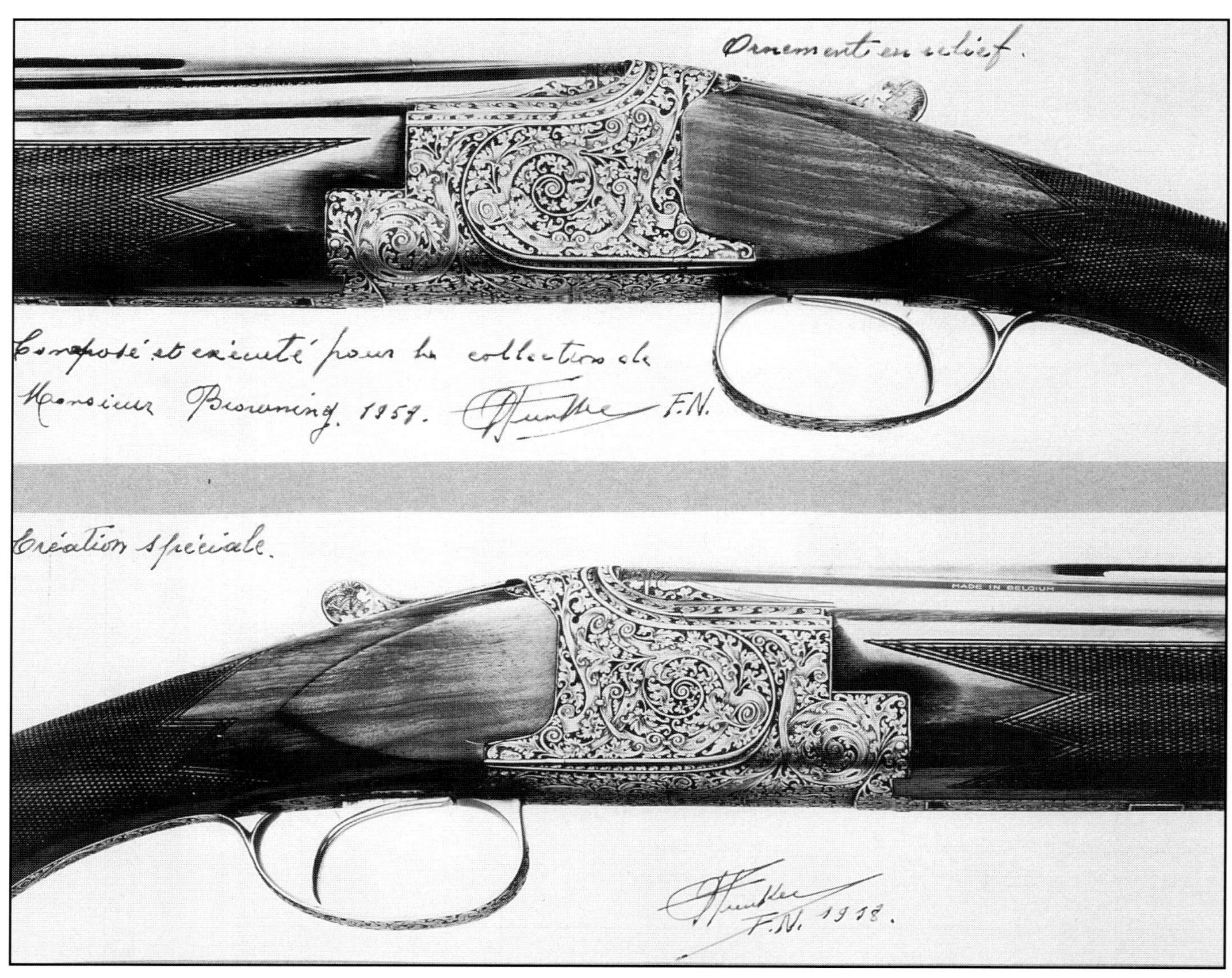

This special design was created for Val Browning in 1959 on a 20 gauge Superposed. Its sculptured receiver and scroll design are very European. The receiver is signed on both sides by Funken. Courtesy Liège Arms Museum.

This early 1960s Browning Superposed Trap model was signed by Felix Funken on both sides of the receiver. Whether or not this particular Superposed was actually engraved by Funken is open to question—his experience with gold inlay was limited. However, close examination of the design reveals Funken's influence with its eclectic mixture of chimera and hunting vignettes. This is a well-designed and beautifully executed piece. Courtesy Fabrique Nationale Archives.

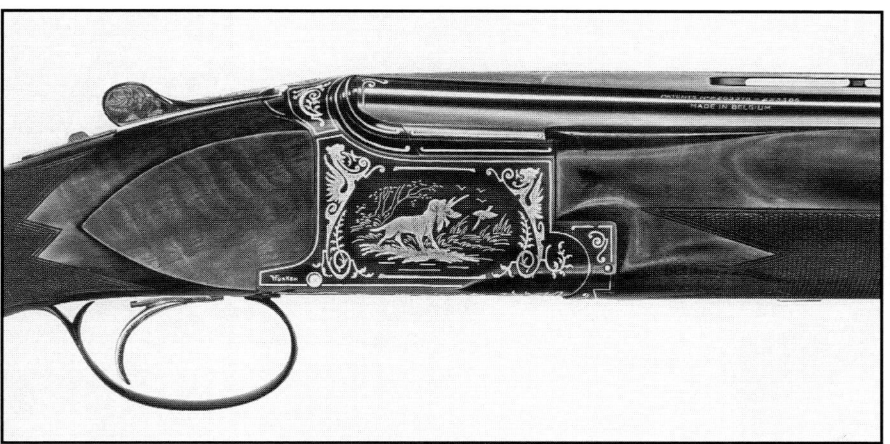

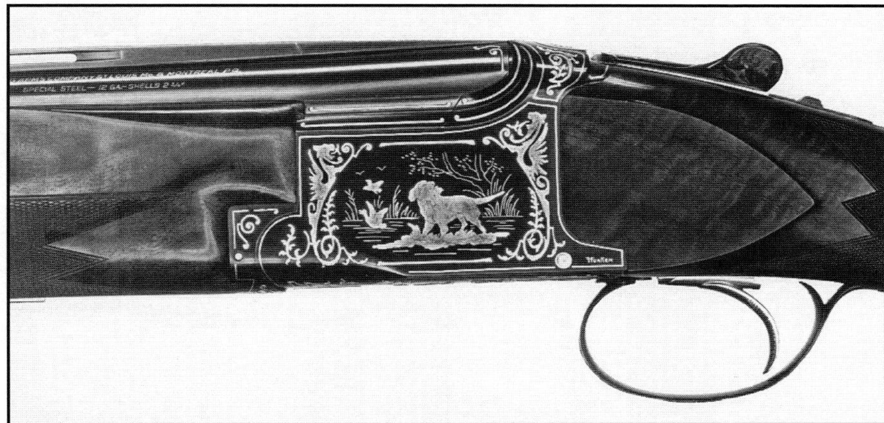

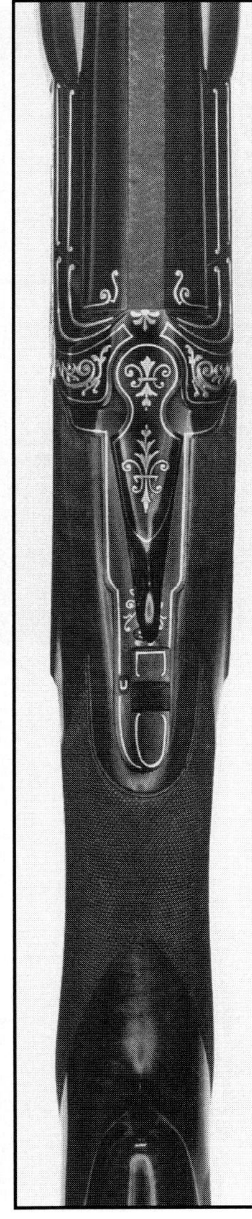

The top and bottom of this Funken designed Exhibition Grade further illustrate his ability to blend new design features with old established ones. Courtesy Fabrique Nationale Archives.

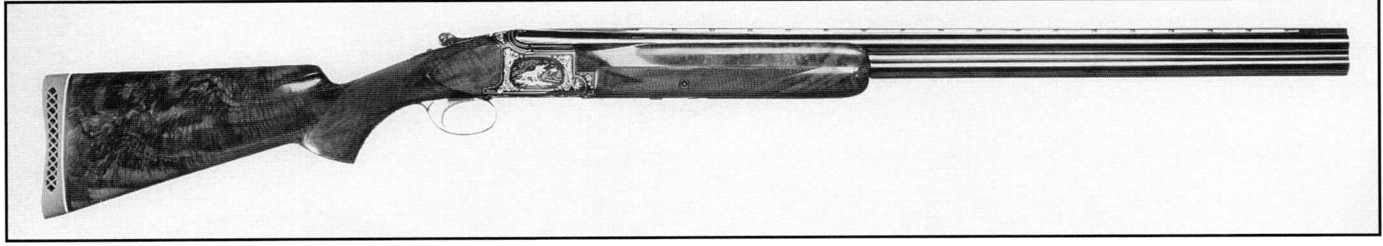

This overall view of the Browning Superposed Exhibition Grade Trap model gives an impression of beauty combined with utility. Many high grade Superposed were used extensively on the trap and skeet fields around the world. Courtesy Browning Company.

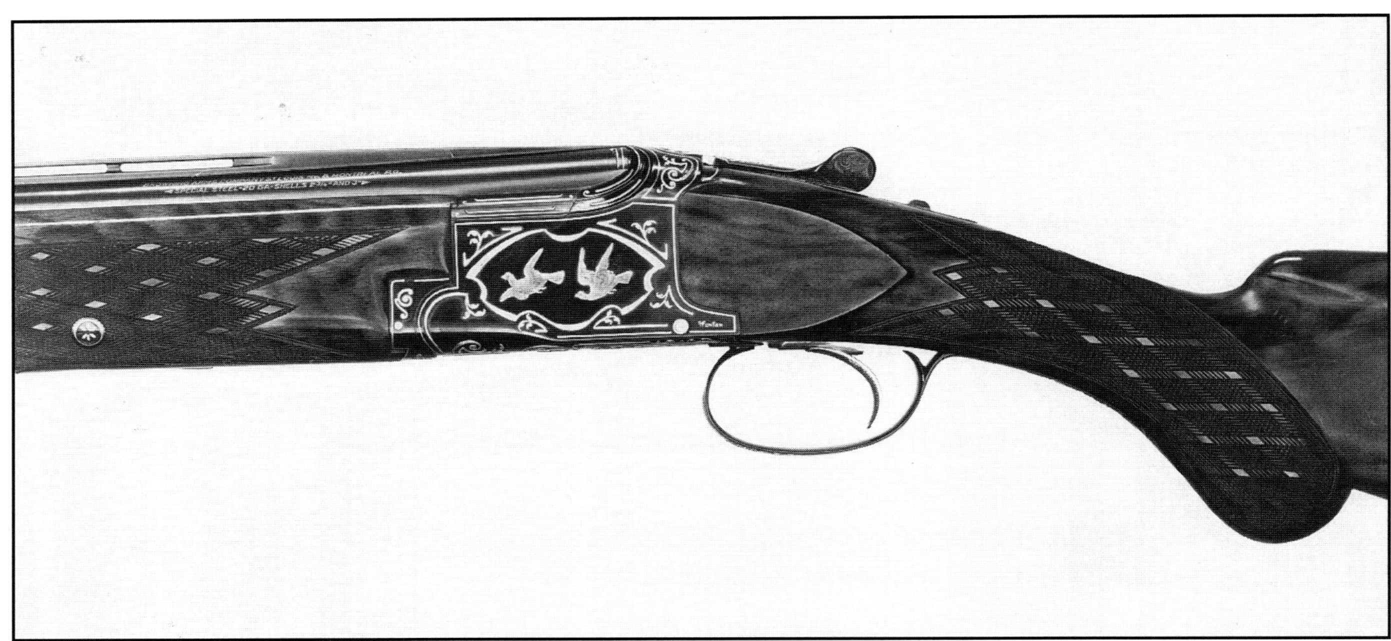

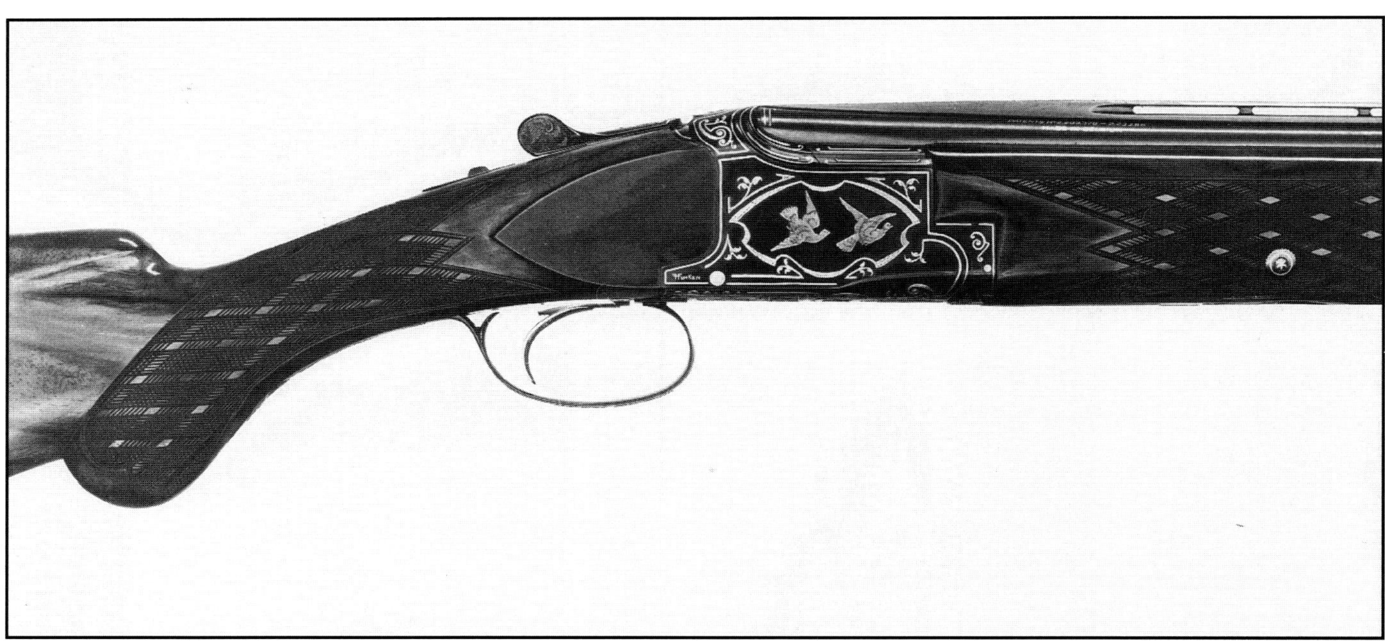

This 1960 Browning 20 gauge Superposed Exhibition Grade is signed by Felix Funken on both sides of the receiver. The design is suggestive of the Grade II or the later Pigeon Grade, but without the scroll. The diamond pattern checkering was often used on these Exhibition Grade Superposed. Courtesy Fabrique Nationale Archives.

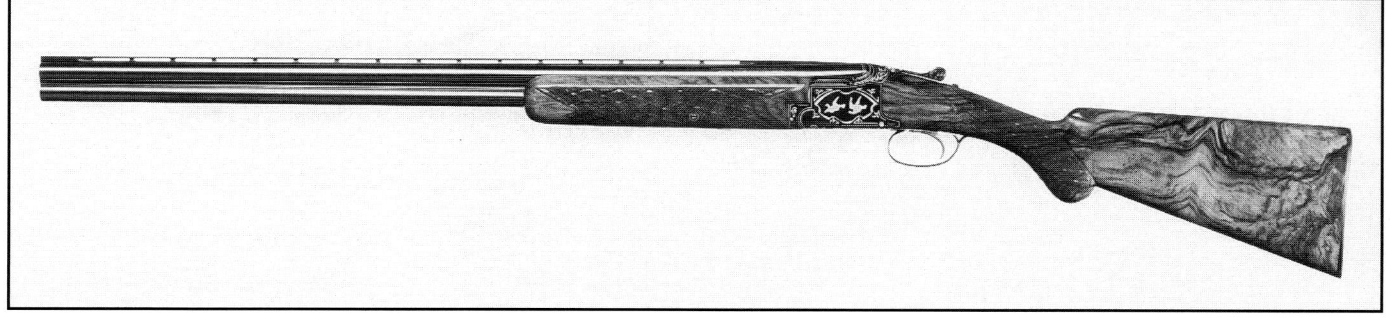

The overall view of the Funken signed Exhibition Grade shows a Field style forearm, rounded pistol grip, and ventilated rib. The wood figure on this Superposed buttstock is extraordinary. Courtesy Browning Company.

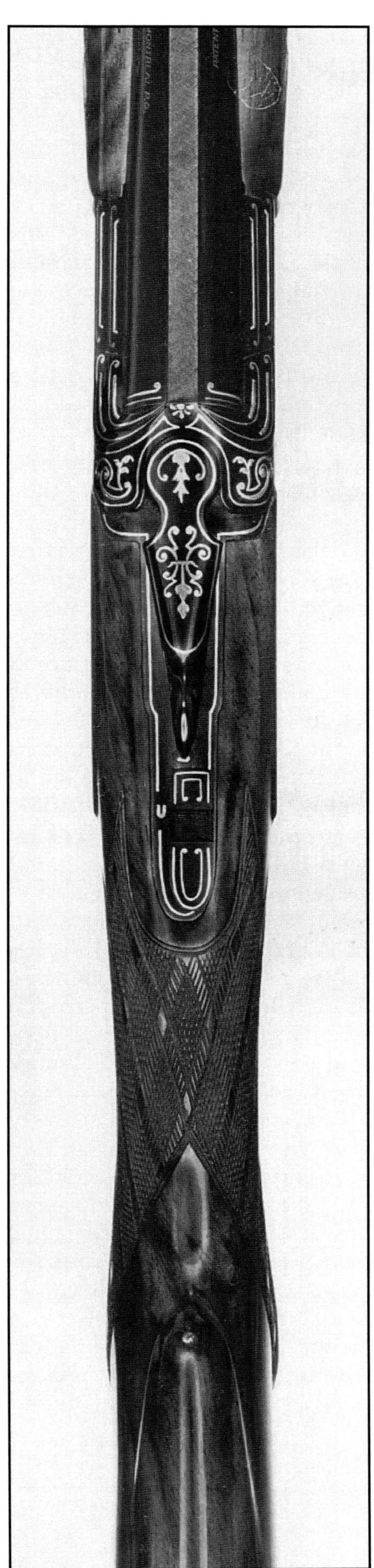

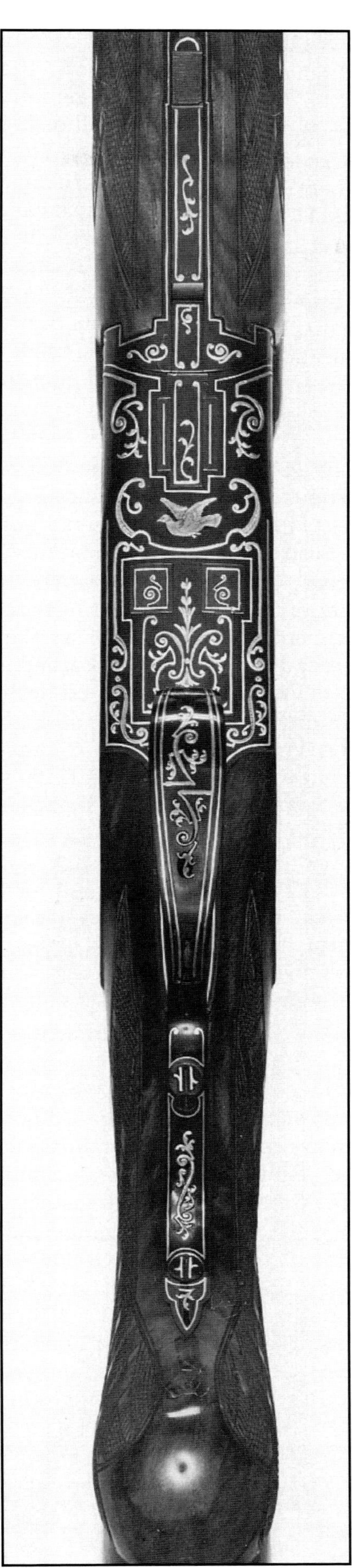

The top view of this outstanding Exhibition Grade shows the delicate gold line work and a hand matted ventilated rib. The bottom view illustrates the gold inlaid work that, while lavish, is well-done and in good taste. Courtesy Fabrique Nationale Archives.

Superposed Production and Sales During the 1940s and 1950s

No discussion of the sales of the Browning Superposed shotguns in the United States, Canada, and around the world can be fully understood without knowledge of the production of the guns in Herstal. A crucial theme throughout the entire production period of the Superposed was Browning's frustration at not having enough Superposed shotguns to sell and FN's inability to meet production levels that Browning requested. This predicament was to become a constant source of irritation and disappointment for Browning during the balance of FN Superposed production. Browning could always sell more Superposed shotguns than it received from Fabrique Nationale.[20] During the 1950s, the previous year's sales provided the basis for the estimates of the next year's orders. A six month notice was given FN so that production could begin for the next year's orders. Instead of placing orders for the number of Superposed guns that the company sales department knew would sell, Browning was forced to order what it knew it would receive from FN. The crux of the problem was Fabrique Nationale's interest in producing high margin military firearms orders. When FN's military business was good, Browning suffered with decreased and imprompt deliveries. Military contracts always seemed to be a priority with FN. The principal source of military contracts came from the Middle East, South America, and Africa. The result of this situation was a decades-long bittersweet relationship between the two companies. When production finally reached adequate levels, there were never enough Superposed produced to satisfy demand. In some years Browning could have sold twice as many Superposed shotguns as they received.[21]

When the American army liberated Liège there had been no Superposed production as such between 1940 and 1944 due to the German occupation. However, a notation in the Fabrique Nationale sales records indicates that the Germans "requisitioned" 183 Superposed during the war. These 183 Superposed may have already been built and assembled, or the German officer in charge of the factory had them built for other German military officers. The FN shipping journals indicate no shipments during the German occupation, so it is possible that these 183 Superposed may not have been stamped with a serial number. When the factory was liberated, the FN shipping journal showed deliveries, beginning in the fall of 1944 and going through the end of the war on May 8, 1945, to American military officers of approximately forty-five Superposed shotguns. For the balance of 1945 and all of 1946 and 1947, a total of only eighteen Superposed 12 gauge guns were assembled at the factory. These guns are in the 17068 to 17100 serial number range. Due to the terrible destruction during the war, Fabrique Nationale made no commercial deliveries of Superposed guns in 1945 and 1946. All Superposed sales recorded during this time span were sold and taken possession of at the factory.

The first commercial 12 gauge shipments after the war were made in December of 1946 to European agents, but a few were sold to representatives in Buenos Aires, Lima, Beirut, and Ethiopia. The first commercial 12 gauge shipments to Browning in St. Louis were recorded in May of 1948 in the 17100 to 17125 serial number range. Serial number 17105 is the earliest recorded 12 gauge Superposed shipped to Browning after the war. The gun was assembled April 1, 1948, and shipped May 31, 1948. A large order of 12 gauge Superposed guns in the 17200 serial number range were shipped to John Inglis and Company in Canada in late 1948.

Because of the terrible bombardment and resultant damage to the factory during the winter of 1944 and 1945, production of Superposed guns following the war began slowly. In 1948 only about 118 Superposed in 12 gauge were built at the FN plant. The following year experienced a significant increase in production with over 1,500 Superposed manufactured in 12 gauge. The first large shipment of Superposed was consigned on February 25, 1949, most in the 19000 to 19200 serial number range. Almost 300 Superposed guns of the newly introduced 20 gauge were shipped as well. Production continued to improve slowly in 1950 for both gauges, and in 1951, 3,600 were produced in 12 gauge and almost 1,000 were built in 20 gauge. The following year marked the first time since the war that Superposed production stabilized. In 1952, 6,400 guns were built in 12 gauge as were almost 1,400 in 20 gauge. The remainder of the decade followed the same pattern, with an average yearly production of 12 gauge Superposed around

---

[20] This information is based on interviews with Mr. Harm Williams, and a thorough study of sales records. Browning had its sales data broken down by the number of back orders at the end of each sales year. During some years, back orders accounted for as much as twenty-five percent of guns actually delivered and sold for the proceeding year.

[21] Harm Williams, interview with the author, July 15, 1993.

5,100 guns and 20 gauge Superposed about 1,600 guns.[22]

Superposed 20 gauge production tells a slightly different story than the 12 gauge. Serial number 1 was assembled and received in the shipping department on April 25, 1949, and was presented to Monsieur Blaise, the governor of the *Société Générale de Belgique*, on June 23, 1949.[23] Serial number 2 was assembled on June 22, 1949, and presented to Serge Lambert, vice president of *Société Générale de Belgique*, on June 24, 1949. Serial number 3 was completed on October 13, 1948, and given to General Quintin on October 17, 1948.[24] Serial number 4 was completed November 4, 1948, and shipped March 4, 1949, to Schroeder Brothers in Liège. Serial number 5 was assembled on November 11, 1948, and shipped to Fusi & Company in Milan on November 20, 1948. The balance of Superposed guns between serial number 6 and 206 were sold to FN's agents throughout the world—most to Europe but some to South America and other locations. The first 20 gauge Superposed assembled and shipped to Browning in St. Louis was serial number 242. This gun was completed May 1, 1949, and shipped May 12, 1949. The earliest serial number shipped to St. Louis was number 207, assembled May 21, 1949, and shipped a few days later.

There were twenty-two 20 gauge Superposed completed May 1, 1949, and shipped May 12, 1949. The following is a list of their serial numbers: 242, 256, 267, 297, 307, 310, 324, 336, 337, 343, 356, 367, 371, 374, 382, 387, 388, 405, 423, 443, 453, and 576. This small list illustrates several important points. First, FN-built Browning Superposed were not assembled on a consecutive serial numbered basis, nor were they shipped on a consecutive serial numbered basis. Out of this single shipment to St. Louis, only two sets of Superposed were assembled and shipped on a consecutive serial numbered basis; 336-337 and 387-388. Secondly, of the missing serial numbers in this shipment, some were sent to Browning at a later date and others were shipped to various agents around the world. Thirdly, it is impossible to establish a definitive date of manufacture for 20 gauge Superposed solely by serial number—the same, of course, is true for the 12 gauge guns.

A number of 28 gauge and .410 bore Superposed were sold by FN to Browning during the latter half of 1959 for Browning's North American market. Announced in May of 1959, these small bore guns were an immediate success, and only six weeks after their introduction, production for late 1959 delivery was sold out. Interestingly enough, the vast majority of 28 gauge and .410 bore Superposed were exported by FN to Browning for its North American market. Serial number 1 for the 28 gauge Superposed was completed September 17, 1959, and shipped to Browning on September 19, 1959. The earliest completed 28 gauge Superposed was serial number 3, finished on August 20, 1959, and shipped September 5, 1959. There were a total of eight 28 gauge Superposed completed on August 20, 1959, besides serial number 3. These guns carried serial number 6 and serial numbers 10 through 16. All were shipped September 5, 1959. According to the FN shipping records, all of these early 28 gauge guns were stamped with the alphanumeric code "9F" preceding the serial number. A total of seventy-six 28 gauge Superposed were sold to Browning by FN in 1959, but many were not received until the early spring of 1960.

FN production of the .410 bore followed a similar pattern. The vast majority of these small bore Superposed were sent to Browning beginning in the fall of 1959. Serial number 1 was completed October 7, 1959, and shipped two days later. Serial number 2 was finished November 12, 1959, and shipped five days later. Serial number 3 was completed October 11, 1959, and shipped to Browning on the 28th of that same month. The bulk of the 1959 .410 Superposed were completed in November and December of 1959 and shipped promptly, all to Browning. As with the 28 gauge Superposed, all of these early .410 bore guns were stamped with the alphanumeric code "9J" serial number prefix. There were a total of eighty-six .410 bore guns sold to Browning by FN in 1959, but again, most did not arrive in the U.S. until the early spring of 1960.

The cumulative effects of postwar production are important to the collector as well as the historian because production patterns closely equate to sales demand. For the years 1948 through 1959, a total of 50,800 12 gauge Superposed were produced by Fabrique Nationale. More than seventy percent of these guns were sold in the United States by Browning. If we compute the prewar production of 12 gauge

---

22 *Tableaux Comparatifs Facturation. Musee d'Armes de Liège.*

23 The *Société Générale de Belgique* was the largest holding company of Belgium and FN's major shareholder. This relationship lasted until November 1990. Claude Gaier, director, *Musee d'Armes de Liège.*

24 General Quintin was a retired general in the Belgian Army who before the war was manager of FN's cartridge manufacturing plant in Bruges. After World War II General Quintin retired because FN had converted the cartridge factory to the production and assembly of vehicles. Claude Gaier, director, *Musee d'Armes de Liège.*

FN YEARLY SUPERPOSED PRODUCTION
12 and 20 Gauge
1945-1959

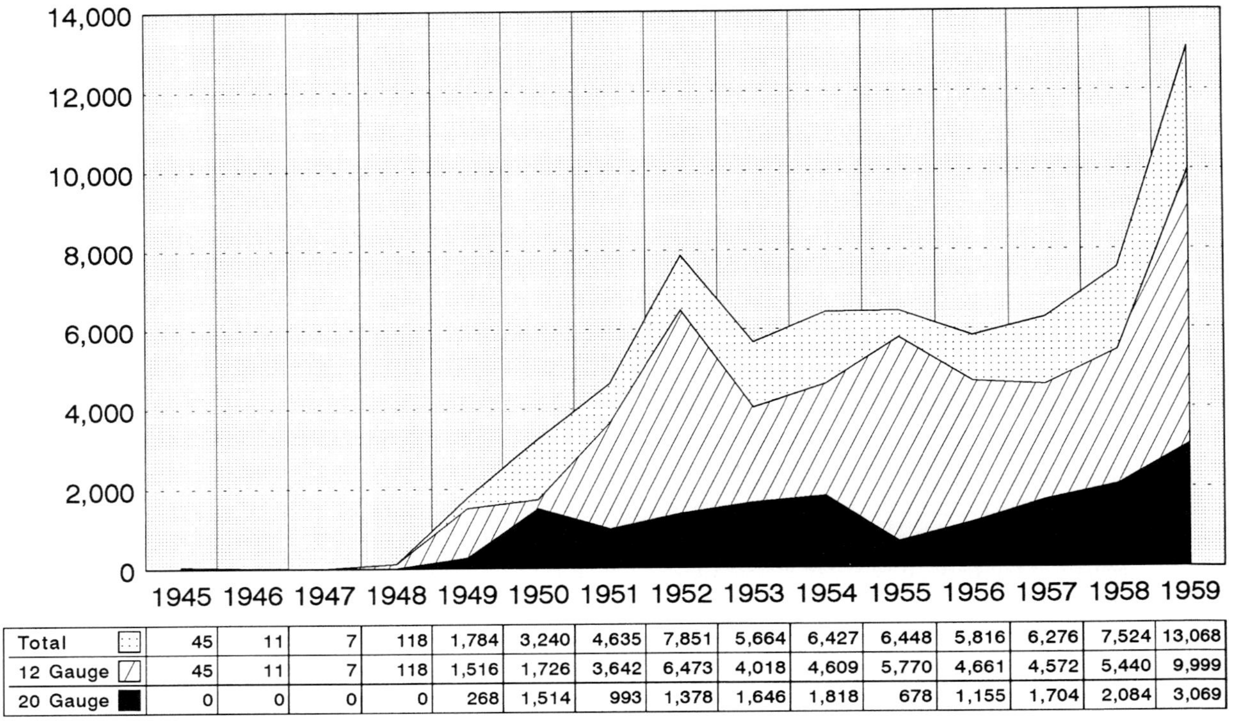

	1945	1946	1947	1948	1949	1950	1951	1952	1953	1954	1955	1956	1957	1958	1959
Total	45	11	7	118	1,784	3,240	4,635	7,851	5,664	6,427	6,448	5,816	6,276	7,524	13,068
12 Gauge	45	11	7	118	1,516	1,726	3,642	6,473	4,018	4,609	5,770	4,661	4,572	5,440	9,999
20 Gauge	0	0	0	0	268	1,514	993	1,378	1,646	1,818	678	1,155	1,704	2,084	3,069

Chart 2-2

FN CUMULATIVE SUPERPOSED PRODUCTION
12 and 20 Gauge
1945-1959

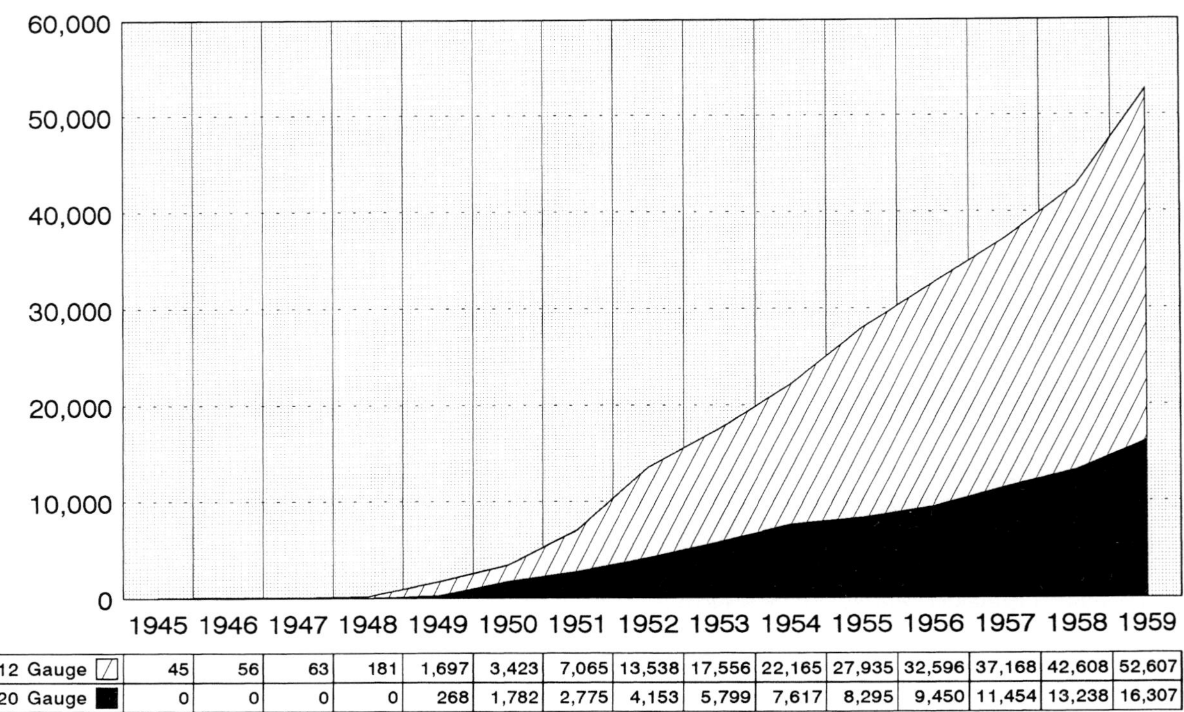

	1945	1946	1947	1948	1949	1950	1951	1952	1953	1954	1955	1956	1957	1958	1959
12 Gauge	45	56	63	181	1,697	3,423	7,065	13,538	17,556	22,165	27,935	32,596	37,168	42,608	52,607
20 Gauge	0	0	0	0	268	1,782	2,775	4,153	5,799	7,617	8,295	9,450	11,454	13,238	16,307

Chart 2-3

guns, we have an aggregate total of almost 68,000 12 gauge Superposed produced and sold since the beginning of production. The total 20 gauge production, which began in 1949, numbers some 16,300 guns through 1959. From the beginning of production through 1959, a total of 86,100 Superposed guns in both 12 and 20 gauge had been built by FN. The result of this production cycle is that 12 gauge guns outnumber 20 gauge Superposed by a four to one margin for this period.

This production data also assists the collector in determining the year a particular Superposed was produced. If we established a base line of 17,032 Superposed built in 12 gauge prior to the occupation of the factory by the Germans in 1940, then a serial number sequence can be established to approximately determine the date of manufacture for 12 gauge guns produced between 1948 and 1959. The same can be accomplished for 20 gauge guns, but much more accurately because production on those guns did not begin until 1949. However, the same warning must accompany these serial numbers as occurred with prewar production and sales. Fabrique Nationale simply did not assemble and sell its Superposed guns on a consecutive serial numbered basis. It is therefore likely that a significant number of postwar Superposed will have serial numbers out of sequence by as much as four or five years. In many cases a Superposed assembled and sent to the shipping department may not have been sold for several years. Due to this, the following table will provide fairly accurate but still imperfect estimates for serial number dates of manufacture.

BROWNING SUPERPOSED 12 AND 20 GAUGE SERIAL NUMBERS, ESTIMATED DATES OF MANUFACTURE[25]

1945-1959

Year	12 Gauge Serial Numbers	20 Gauge Serial Numbers
1945	17033-17078	N/A
1946	17079-17089	N/A
1947	17090-17099	N/A
1948	17100-17218	N/A
1949	17219-18735	1-268
1950	18736-20462	269-1782
1951	20463-24104	1783-2775
1952	24105-30577	2776-4153
1953	30578-34595	4154-5799
1954	34596-39204	5800-7618
1955	39205-44974	7619-8295
1956	44975-49635	8296-9450
1957	49636-52207	9451-11154
1958	52208-57647	11155-13238
1959	57648-70745	13239-16322

Table 2-3

[25] Fabrique Nationale operated on a fiscal year ending June 30. The serial number estimated dates of manufacture are based on this fiscal year with the important exception of 1959, in which these figures include data from fiscal year 1960 to bring sales figures for 1959 to end with the calendar year on December 31. In effect, 1959 represents eighteen months of sales.

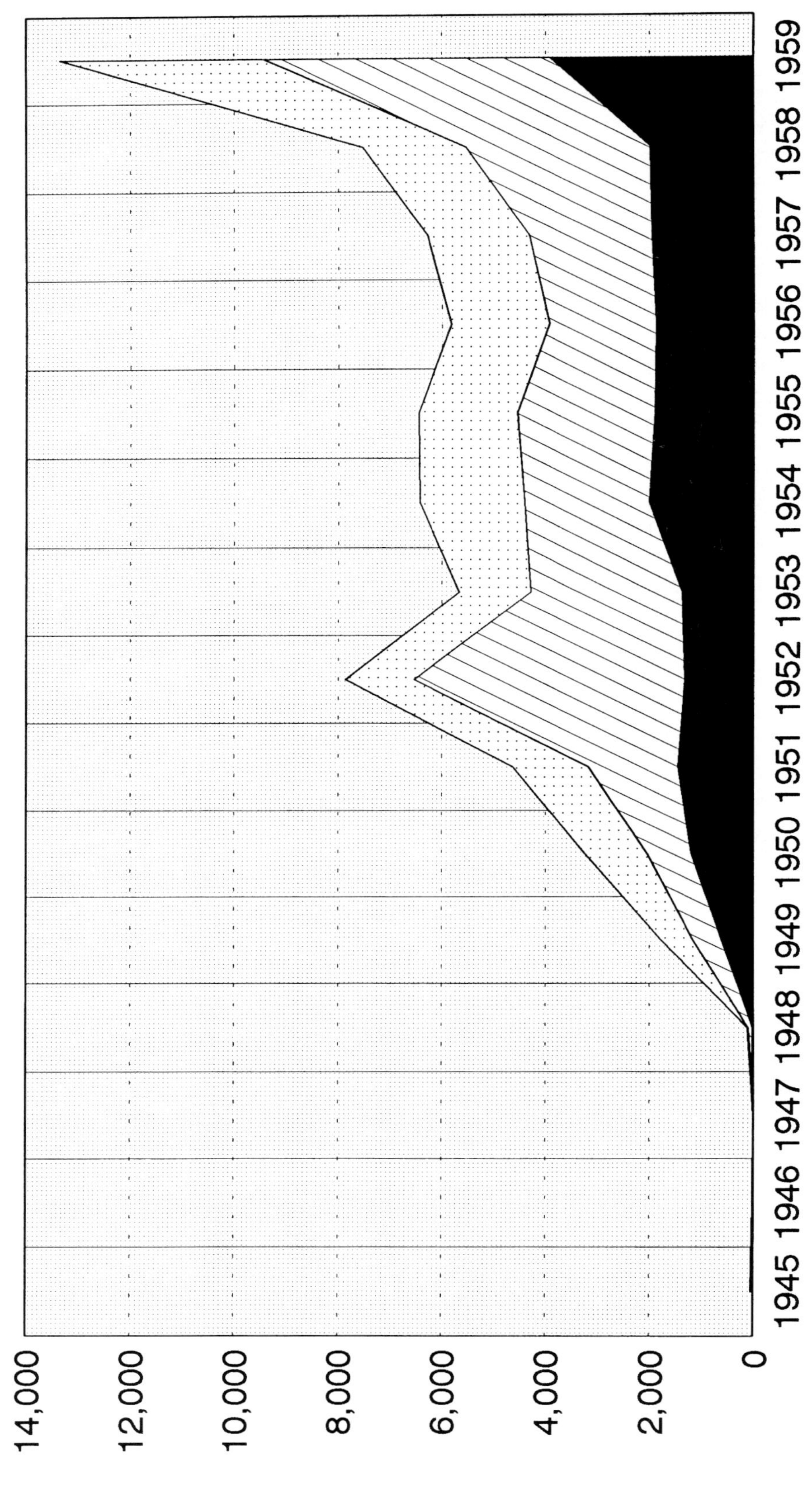

	1945	1946	1947	1948	1949	1950	1951	1952	1953	1954	1955	1956	1957	1958	1959
Total Sales	45	11	7	118	1,784	3,240	4,635	7,851	5,664	6,427	6,448	5,816	6,276	7,524	13,352
Browning	0	0	0	101	1,164	2,046	3,173	6,534	4,282	4,409	4,548	3,930	4,316	5,530	9,442
FN	45	11	7	17	620	1,194	1,462	1,317	1,382	2,018	1,900	1,886	1,960	1,994	3,910

Chart 2-5

Browning Arms Company consistently received more Superposed from Fabrique Nationale than FN sold to its agents throughout the rest of the world, with the exception of the years 1945 through 1947 when FN sold Superposed on a local basis. Between 1945 and 1959 a total of 69,198 Superposed guns in 12 and 20 gauge were sold by FN, both to Browning and FN's agents. Of that sum, 49,475 Superposed were imported into the U.S. and 19,723 were sold elsewhere. Almost seventy-two percent of all Superposed sold by FN between 1945 and 1959 went to the Browning Arms Company for sale to its American market.

Marketing Strategies: Sales and Prices

As early as 1946 a few Auto-5 shotguns had been imported into the United States from a war-crippled factory in Herstal, but no Superposed. By 1948 about one hundred 12 gauge Superposed found their way to St. Louis where they were sold to a few dealers. It was not until 1949 that both the 12 and 20 gauge Superposed reached a large enough inventory to be actively sold. Prior to 1948 Browning had never involved itself in direct marketing efforts. There was always the incredibly short sales year that lasted the first thirty days of

The Browning Arms Company service tent at the Grand American Trap Shoot in Vandalia, Ohio, in August of 1954. Grant Goddard first attended this important sporting event in 1949 with six Browning Superposed and a few spare parts. From left to right are Harry Heiter, shop foreman; Howard Maas, gunsmith; Grant Goddard; Bob Clark, regional sales manager; and Duke Dupree, regional sales manager. Courtesy Grant Goddard.

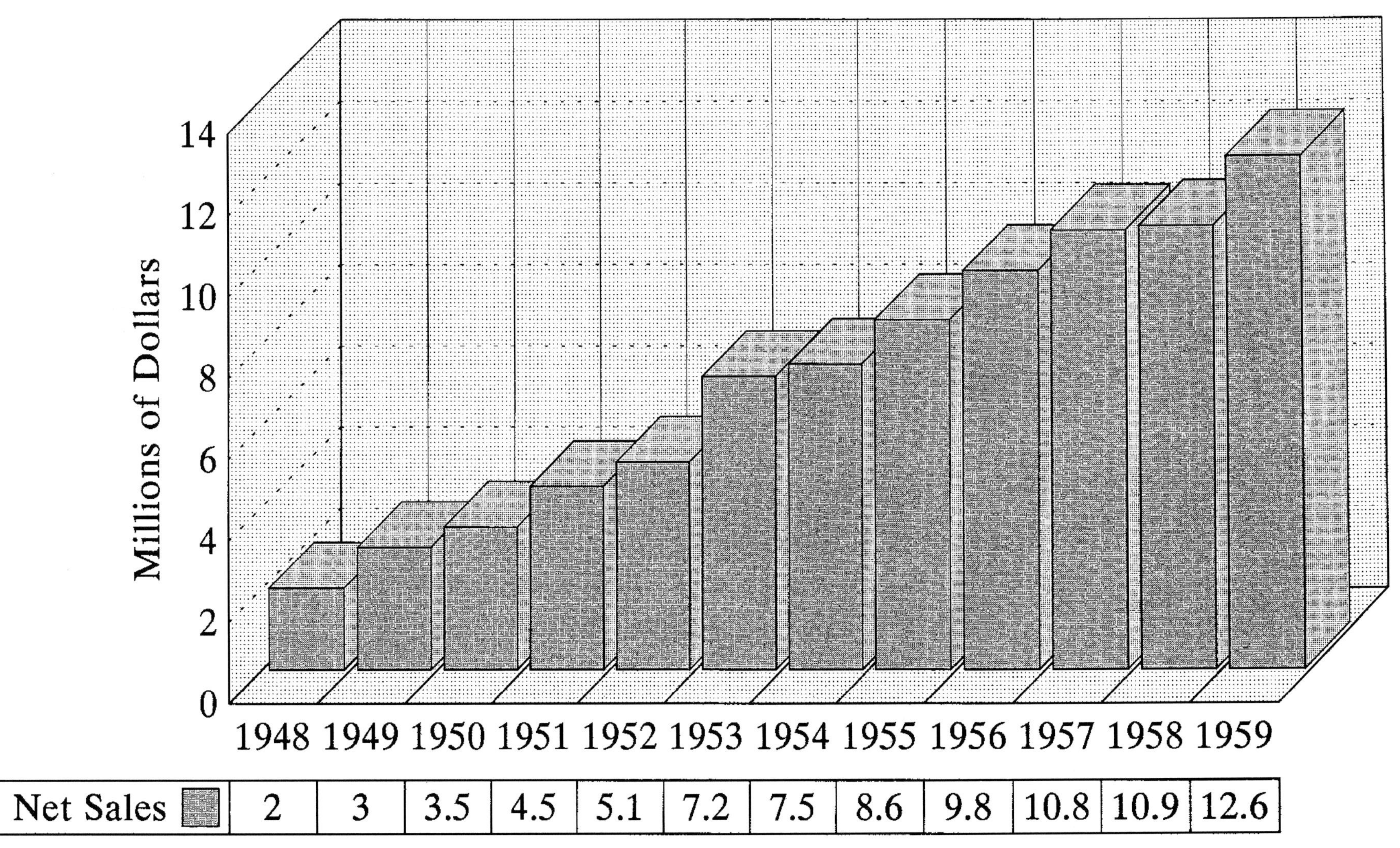

Millions of Dollars

Chart 2-4

each year. In 1950 the Superposed Trap gun was a popular selection among serious competitive shooters, and parts were in short supply. At the suggestion of Grant Goddard, Browning sent Goddard and gunsmith Harry Heiter, along with a quantity of spare parts and six Superposed Trap guns, to the Grand American in Vandalia, Ohio. This was the first time since the Superposed was introduced for sale in the United States that Browning had made an effort to come into direct contact with its customers. As a result, the six Superposed sold in five minutes; the spare parts lasted a little longer.

For Browning this was the beginning of a new and concerted effort to become directly involved not only with its dealers but its customers as well. It was not until the St. Louis facility moved to its newer location at 1706 Washington that a genuine attempt was made to put a sales force in the field. Harm Williams decided the country should be divided into four regions with an individual in charge of sales for each region. These four individuals were called regional sales managers. Contact would be made by telephone and in person, but with sixteen thousand dealers, most of the communications were by telephone and letter. This system stayed in place until it was expanded in 1965 with the addition of a larger sales force that reported directly to the regional sales managers.

With the modernization of the organization in St. Louis came the additional task of trying to spread out the meager supply of Superposed to the dealers who were trying to meet the pent-up demand of the postwar boom. From 1948 to 1955 there was a serious shortfall of Superposed guns to meet demand. Browning and its dealers came to call this interval the "allocation period." It was important that Browning apportion Superposed to the dealers on an equitable basis. Small dealers had to be treated fairly and large dealers could not be allowed to become too demanding. It was during this time period that Sears, Roebuck and Co. purchased $2,000,000 worth of Browning shotguns. Montgomery Ward was the second largest Browning dealer. Still, all dealers could take satisfaction in knowing that Sears paid the same for its Browning Superposed as the small town dealer paid for his. Browning referred to this policy as its Price Maintenance Policy, and it worked.

Dealers liked the system because even though the markup on Browning guns was low at twenty-five percent, the ability to hold prices at the full retail price allowed the dealers to make a fair profit. This was before the advent of the large discount seller that swept the country in the 1960s and 1970s. During this entire postwar decade Browning never had a bad debt from one of its dealers. In 1950 Browning decided to set up a display at the National Sporting Goods Association show in Chicago. Browning was the only major firearms manufacturer at the show that year. In 1951 all of the major American manufacturers attended the Chicago show. From then on Browning Arms Company stood toe to toe with the rest of America's firearms manufacturers and competed enthusiastically for its share of the marketplace.

Company sales for the Superposed shotgun for the years immediately following the war were almost nonexistent. It was not until 1948 that the sales of a few 12 gauge Superposed guns were made. In 1948 total net firearms sales of approximately $2,000,000 were recorded by Browning.[26] Net sales data support the state of affairs as they existed at Fabrique Nationale. Production of the Superposed was painfully slow to return to dependable levels and even then, as we have seen, satisfactory production of Superposed shotguns never materialized to Browning's satisfaction. Despite these difficulties, 1951 sales for the company doubled to $4,000,000.

The balance of the decade saw a steady increase in total net sales for all Browning firearms. This increase can be attributed in part to increased sales of Superposed shotguns, but in a larger sense this increase must be regarded as an outgrowth of the expansion of the company's product lines. Indeed, as Browning's product lines expanded so did its sales. In 1954 Browning introduced its semiautomatic pistols in .25ACP, .380ACP, and 9mm calibers. The following year Val Browning's Double Automatic shotgun was introduced. In 1956 the .22 caliber semiautomatic rifle was imported into the United States. In 1958 the Auto-5 line was expanded to include a 20 gauge version as well as a 12 gauge 3-inch Magnum model. By the end of the decade Browning's total net sales were $12,600,000, an increase of over four hundred percent from its estimated 1949 sales.

---

[26] Net sales for 1948 through 1951 are estimates based on interviews with Harm Williams and Grant Goddard. Records for actual net years are not available until the year 1952 and are based on financial information supplied by the company to *Moody's Industrial Manual*. Early financial reports provided to the stockholders also support these estimates.

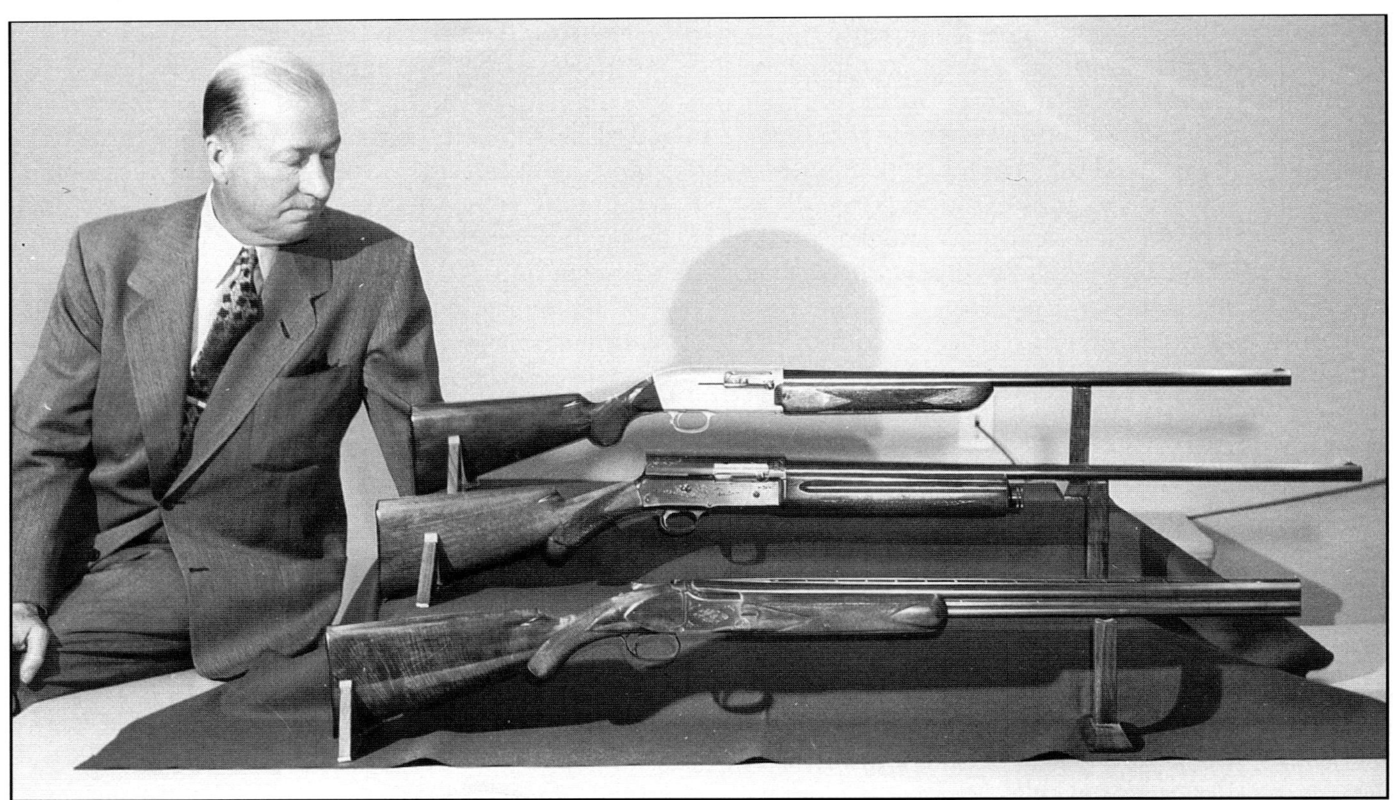

Val Browning with three of the company's most important shotguns. From the top is the Double Automatic, his own invention; his father's Auto-5 shotgun; and the flagship of the Browning firearms line, the Superposed, which he helped bring to production. Courtesy Browning Company.

The decade of the 1950s was marked by a strong economy working hard to meet the flourishing demand of postwar America. A pleasant derivative of this strong economy was a relatively stable consumer price index. Between 1950 and 1959 the Consumer Price Index rose by about twenty-one percent. Prices for a Grade I Browning rose only about eight percent during the same period. When the Superposed was reintroduced into the United States after the war, the retail price was $261.00. The price was reduced to $250.00 in 1951 but increased back to the 1950 level the following year, where it remained until 1957 when the retail price was increased to $270.00. The price for the Grade I was raised again in 1958 to $280.00, where it remained for the ensuing year.

Browning management faced a constant struggle during the 1950s to keep prices stable despite the ever-increasing manufacturing costs that were passed on to the company by Fabrique Nationale. In spite of the increasing volume, FN management kept raising prices to Browning for the Superposed. The more Superposed guns Browning ordered, the more FN raised its prices. The reason for this price escalation lay with FN's inability to deal effectively with its trade unions. There was constant pressure to increase wages, and management relented. During the 1950s, however, there was a reduction of custom duties and a favorable exchange rate between the dollar and the Belgian franc, and these two circumstances helped to offset the persistent price increases imposed by Fabrique Nationale, thus lowering the cost pressure on Browning's retail prices in the United States.

The period following the war was one fraught with frustration. The dedication of Val Browning and his son John Val, along with an expanded management team, enabled Browning to grow and prosper during the 1950s. The Superposed also did well, and its catalogue offerings expanded from a single 12 gauge Hunting model in 1948 to a large number of varied models and styles by the end of the 1950s. This decade is considered by many to have produced some of the finest Browning Superposed shotguns collectors and shooters can own. Despite production difficulties, Browning always placed quality foremost, and the Superposed of the 1950s is the company's highest example of excellence.

Chapter 3

The Beginnings of Change: The Decade of the 1960s

The decade of the 1960s was marked by expansion, growth, and change. After firmly establishing itself as a leader in the double gun market in the United States, Browning's management embarked on a new era. With the positive Browning name identification, the company expanded into other outdoor related fields. Convinced that the hunting market was finite due to increased government regulation and diminishing game populations, Browning Arms Company embraced the popular 1960s notion of aggressive business expansion and diversification. This expansion, begun by Val Browning and carried forward by his oldest son, John Val Browning, was a desire to move the company into product lines that did not rely solely on firearms sales or foreign manufacturers. As we will observe, some of the expansion plans were successful; others were not. Despite these overall successes, Browning's firearms production problems became increasingly more troublesome. It was primarily for this reason that the company decided, in concert with Fabrique Nationale, to begin making noticeable internal and external changes to the Superposed throughout the course of the decade.

Browning Arms Company Moves into the Modern Era

This period in the company's history witnessed not only the expansion of Browning's product lines, but also the foundation through which this was accomplished. In 1961 Browning Arms Company went public after thirty-four years as a privately held company. The officers of the company were Val A. Browning, president; John Val Browning, executive vice president and treasurer; Harmon G. Williams, vice president; Grant F. Goddard, secretary; and Richard L. Beckstead, assistant secretary and assistant treasurer. There were approximately 2,564 shareholders. Net sales were $13,080,011, up from $12,483,860 in 1960. Net income for 1961 was $1,001,615, compared to $852,416 the previous year. Browning Arms also earned $34,562 Canadian dollars in 1961 from its seventy percent ownership in its Canadian subsidiary. On November 27, 1961, a semiannual dividend of $.25 per share was declared.[1]

The company's first annual report refers to its business philosophy in simple and straightforward terms: "The past year marked the start of the program of expansion and diversification which your company has undertaken." The report goes on to declare that this will not interfere with Browning's sales of its firearms line, but rather will build on its reputation as a leader in the sporting goods field. Management decided to enter the archery market with a complete line of bows, arrows, and accessories. The year 1962 also marked the introduction of the Silaflex line of fishing rods, vaulting poles, and ski poles through Browning's acquisition of that company. In the summer of 1962 a full line of hunting telescopes and mounts were offered for sale. New firearms development was not forgotten. Early in 1962 a new .22 caliber semiautomatic pistol was introduced in three models: Challenger, Nomad, and Medalist. This new pistol was designed and developed by Val A. Browning's son, Bruce Browning.

[1] Browning Arms Company, 1961 Annual Report.

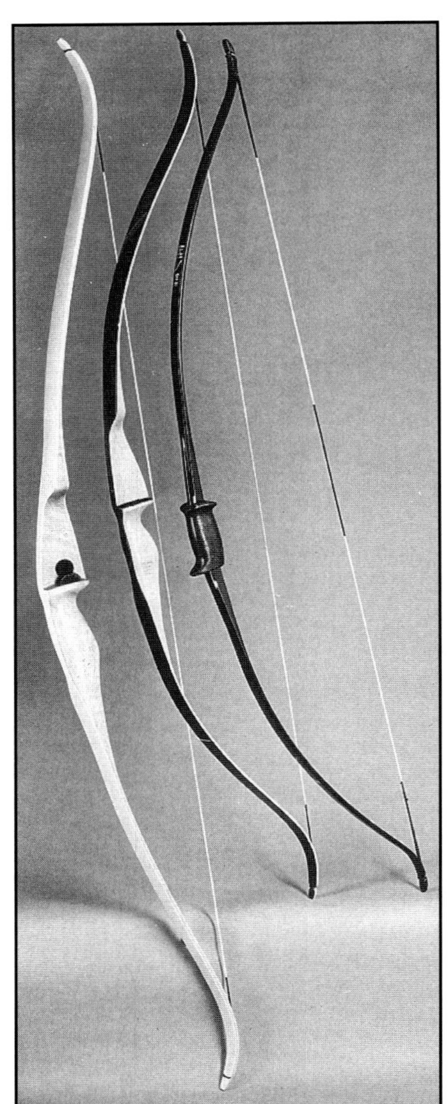

In 1962 the Browning Arms Company began a determined start on its expansion plans into related sporting goods fields and its own firearms lines. Its new offerings included archery equipment, fishing rods, hunting telescopes, and the new .22 caliber semiautomatic pistols, the Nomad, Challenger, and Medalist. Courtesy Browning Company.

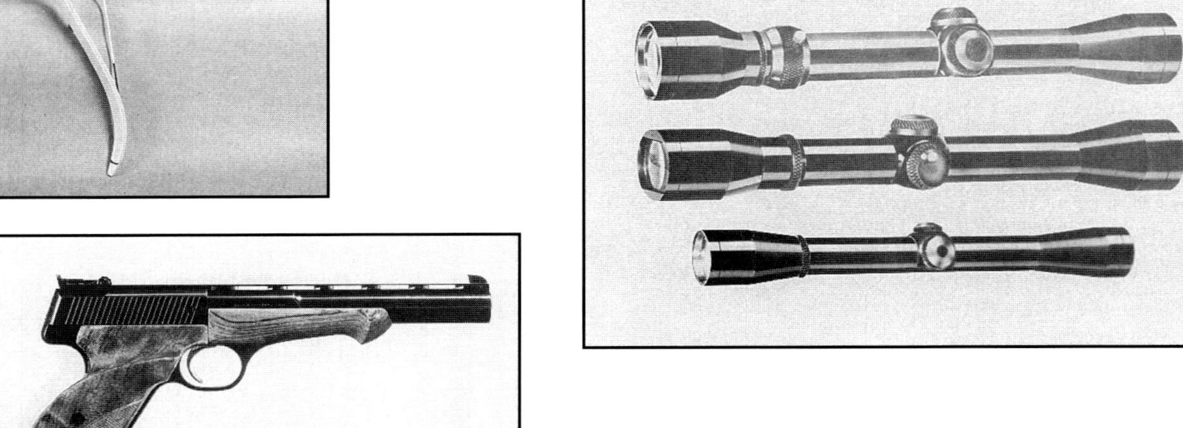

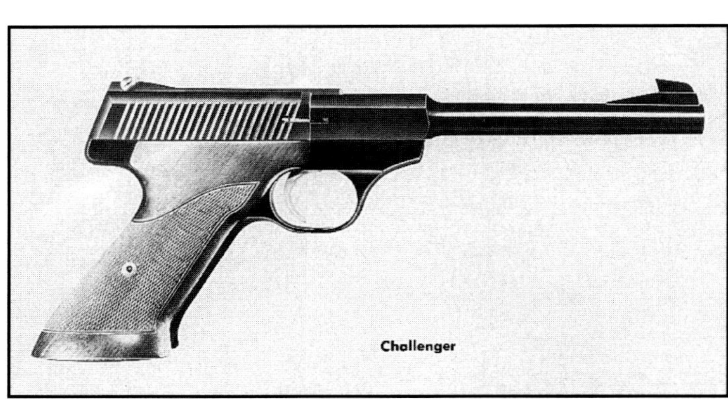

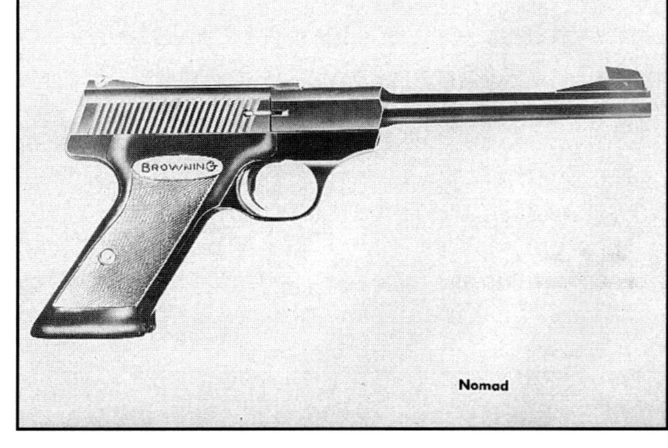

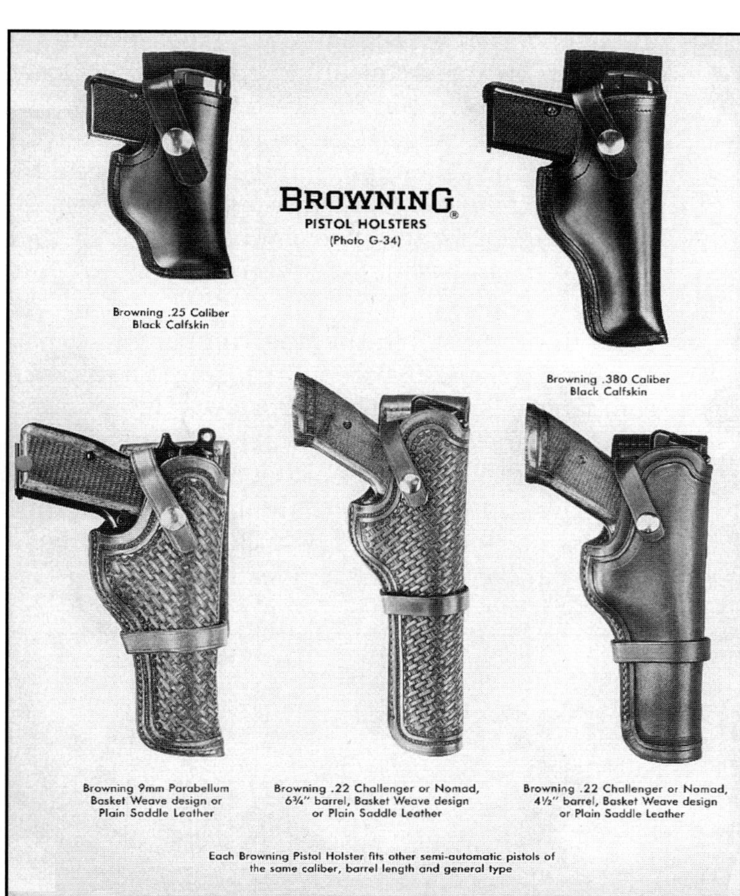

By the middle of the 1960s Browning expanded into leather goods, making a complete line of leather pistol holsters and flexible gun cases for its shotguns, rifles, and pistols. Browning also developed a new .22 caliber bolt action rifle, the Browning T-Bolt. Courtesy Browning Company.

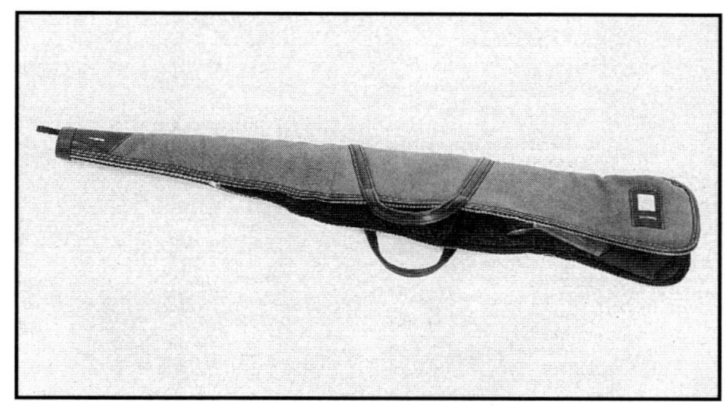

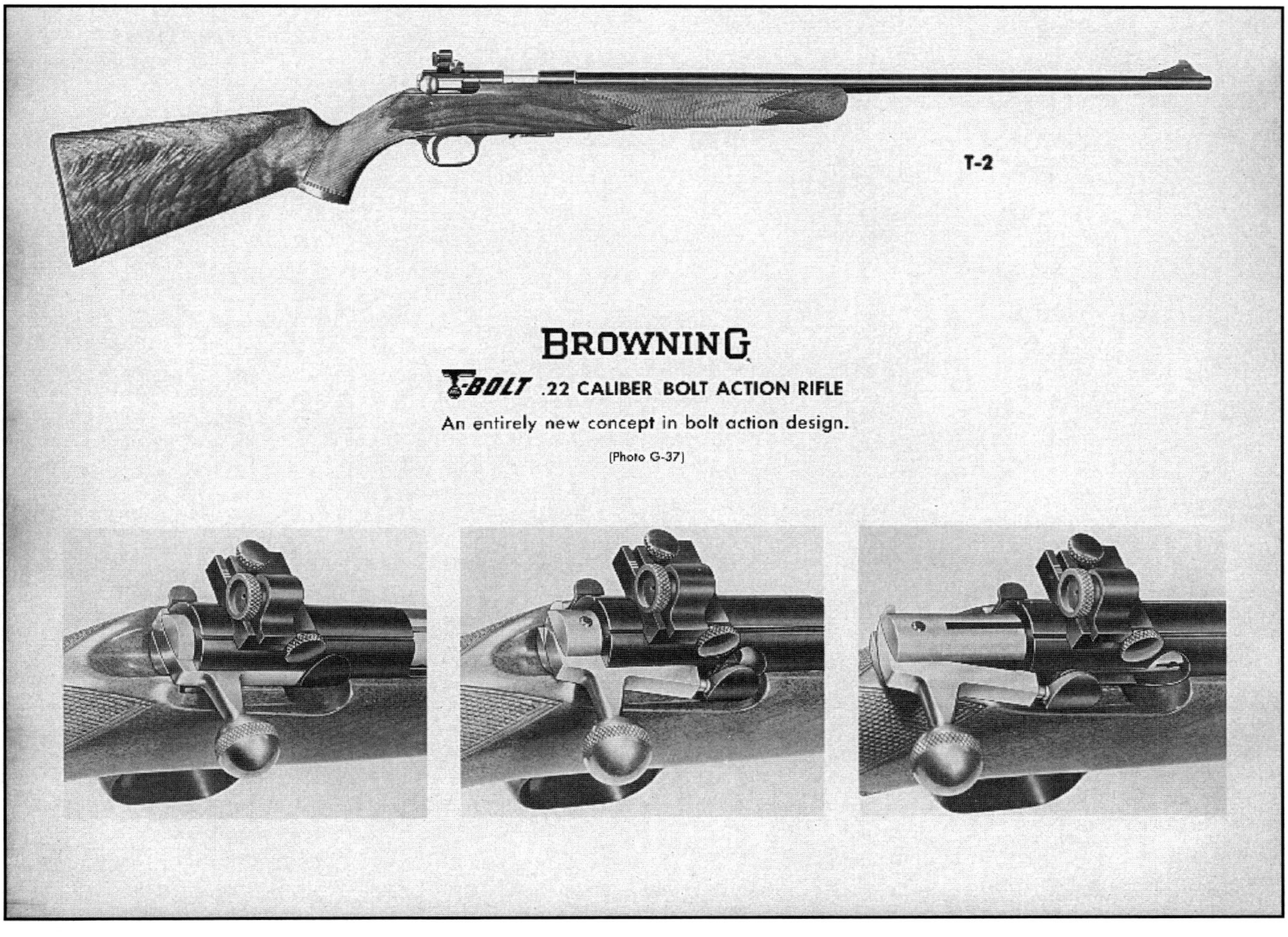

T-2

BROWNING

T-BOLT .22 CALIBER BOLT ACTION RIFLE

An entirely new concept in bolt action design.

(Photo G-37)

The company's profits were helped with the successful negotiations of the General Agreement on Tariffs and Trade (GATT). Duties on imported firearms like the Superposed were reduced twenty percent. This helped to counterbalance the upward pressure on costs that FN passed on to Browning in the form of higher prices.

As the decade progressed, Browning management continued their aggressive growth policies. Upon the retirement of Val Browning as president of the company in 1963, the new president, John Val Browning, continued to implement his family's long-range goals of growth and diversification. The corporate offices in Ogden, where the sales and day-to-day management decisions had been shaped since the company was incorporated in 1927, were moved to Morgan, Utah. In reality the new corporate headquarters were located on 640 acres in the small unincorporated village of Mountain Green, eight miles from Morgan. Nestled in a small valley at the head of Weber canyon in the Wasatch mountains, this new corporate location gave the company the opportunity to establish shooting facilities, expand its research and development capabilities, and have room to grow in future years.[2]

By the middle of the decade, company sales had risen to $21,000,000. Browning acquired additional companies such as Newport Boats of California and that company's subsidiary, Mobjacj Manufacturing Company of Virginia, a sailboat manufacturer. The company also expanded its traditional firearms line with the addition of the T-Bolt .22 caliber rifle and a line of flexible gun cases and leather goods.

The reception room on the second floor of the Monogram Building on Washington Street in St. Louis in 1960. Pictured are Eddie Koehrer (standing), sales manager, and Perry Farrow (seated), chief accountant. The location in downtown St. Louis had outlived its usefulness by 1968 when the parts, service, and distribution departments were moved to Arnold, Missouri. Photo courtesy Grant Goddard.

[2] John Val Browning, letter to the author, August 23, 1993.

BROWNING ARMS COMPANY AND SUBSIDIARY

CONSOLIDATED BALANCE SHEET, DECEMBER 31, 1961

ASSETS

Current Assets:		
Cash		$ 478,747
U.S. Treasury bills-at cost plus accrued interest		397,655
Accounts receivable-trade	$ 2,032,553	
Less allowance for doubtful accounts and reserve discounts	144,284	
Notes receivable plus accrued interest		607,914
Inventories-at lower of cost of market		2,263,820
Prepaid expenses		41,578
Total current assets		5,677,983
Property and Equipment-At Cost:		
Land	73,942	
Buildings, equipment, and leasehold improvements	324,813	
Total	398,755	
Less accumulated depreciation and amortization	142,987	
Property and equipment-net		255,768
Investments and Advances-At Cost:		
Browning Arms Company of Canada Limited:		
Capital stock	36,353	
Advances	222,524	
Fabrique Nationale d'Armes de Guerre-capital stock	366,325	
Total investments and advances		625,202
Cash Surrender Value of Life Insurance and Other Assets		76,862
TOTAL		6,635,815

LIABILITIES

Current Liabilities:		
Accounts payable	$ 544,069	
Federal income tax payable		767,000
Dividends payable		235,613
Other liabilities		119,874
Total current liabilities		1,666,556
Stockholders' Equity:		
Capital stock-authorized 2,500,000 shares of a par value of $1 each; issued 942,450 shares	$ 942,450	
Paid-in surplus	118,991	
Retained earnings	3,907,818	
Total stockholders' equity		4,969,259
TOTAL		6,635,815

Table 3-1

BROWNING ARMS COMPANY AND SUBSIDIARY

STATEMENT OF CONSOLIDATED INCOME AND RETAINED EARNINGS
For The Years Ended December 31, 1961 and 1960

	Year Ended December 31 1961	1960
Net Sales	$13,080,011	$12,483,860
Cost of Goods Sold	9,549,645	9,220,715
Gross Profit on Sales	3,530,366	3,263,145
Operating Expenses:		
Salaries, advertising, and other office and general expenses exclusive of items shown below	1,375,894	1,227,994
Provision for doubtful accounts-net	38,886	39,589
Provision for depreciation and amortization	41,633	27,880
Rents	44,475	43,841
Taxes (other than income)	46,040	39,447
Total	1,546,928	1,378,751
Operating Profit	1,983,438	1,884,394
Other Income:		
Dividends on foreign investment	39,531	42,736
Interest income	4,431	16,415
Miscellaneous	9,355	4,524
Total	53,317	63,675
TOTAL	2,036,755	1,893,590
Other Deductions-Interest	13,850	54,479
Income Before Income Taxes	2,022,905	1,893,590
Income Taxes:		
Federal	955,000	1,014,890
State and city	14,000	12,998
Foreign	12,290	13,286
Total	1,021,290	1,041,174
Net Income	1,001,615	852,416
Retained Earnings At Beginning Of Year	6,156,188	5,398,017
Dividends:		
Cash	(235,612)	(94,245)
Stock	(879,620)	
Retirement of Treasury Stock	(2,134,753)	
Retained Earnings At End Of Year	$3,907,818	$6,156,188
Earnings Per Share	$1.06	$.90
Cash Dividends Per Share	$ .25	$.10

Table 3-2

BROWNING ARMS COMPANY NET SALES
1960-1969
Millions
$50
$40
$30
$20
$10
$0
1960 1961 1962 1963 1964 1965 1966 1967 1968 1969
Net Sales
$12.5 $13.1 $15.1 $16.8 $21.8 $25.4 $29.6 $34.4 $43.2 $42.6

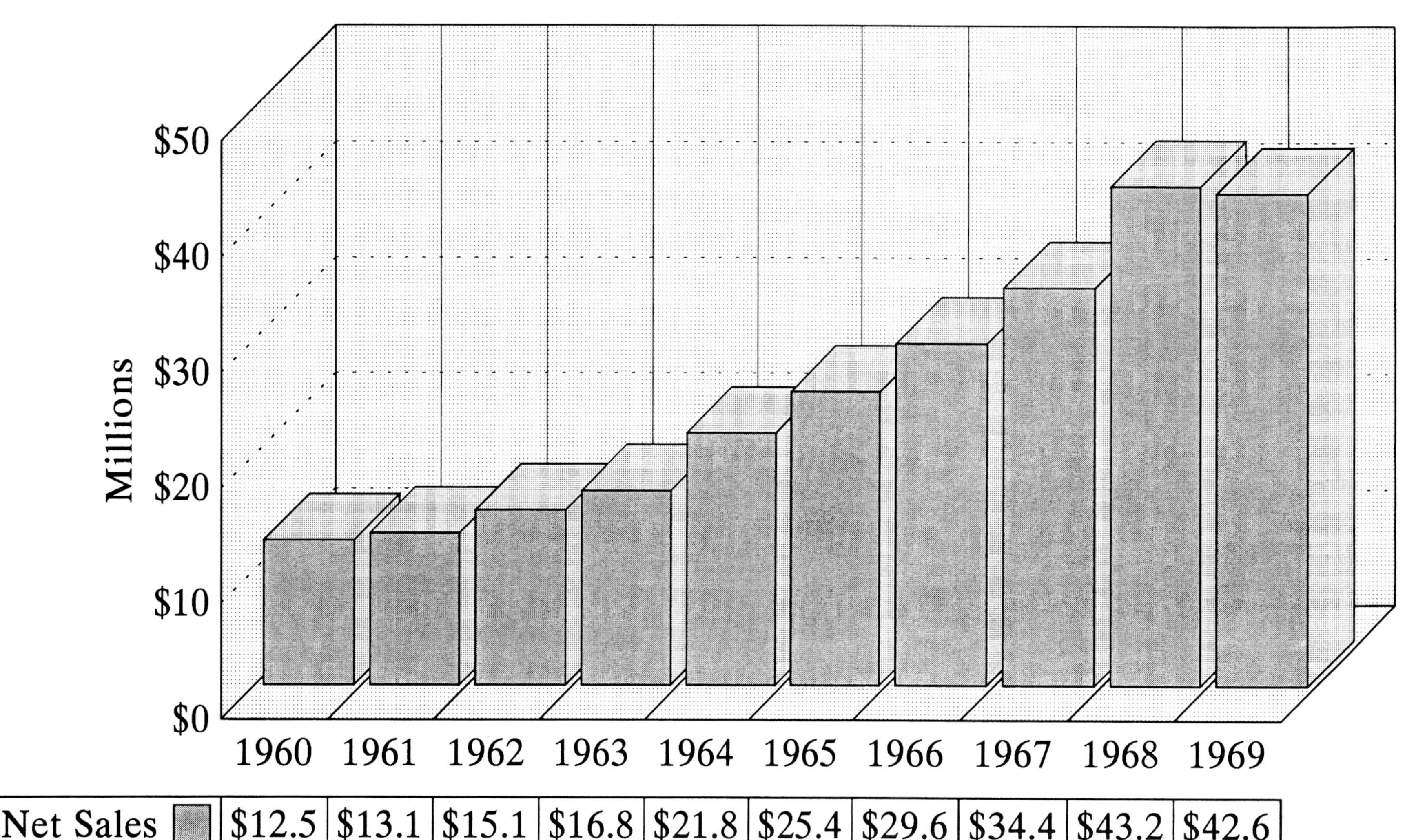

Chart 3-1

In 1967 Browning Arms Company introduced its new centerfire semiautomatic rifle, the BAR, (above) as well as a new addition to its Auto-5 line, the new 3-inch Magnum 20 gauge (opposite). Courtesy Browning Company.

The year 1966 marked the first time in Browning's history that the company sent out a sales force to contact dealers directly. The company trained eleven salesmen in its products and policies, and each was given a specific geographical area of responsibility. There was positive acceptance of this new policy on the part of dealers and it allowed each Browning salesman to build his own territory. This new selling tool gave the company an opportunity to establish comprehensive direct contact between the corporate entity and its dealers.[3] This sales force stayed in place until 1980. The four original regional sales managers, Warren Jenks, Bob Clark, Vern Peterson, and Arthur "Duke" Dupree, remained in place to administer and guide the new sales force.

The effects of this rapid expansion were beginning to have consequences. In 1966 sales rose eighteen percent from the previous year to $25,640,611, but costs of goods sold rose twenty percent. Part of the increase was due to losses sustained in the company's sailboat subsidiaries and the establishment of its new sales force. The boat subsidiaries were to be a constant source of frustration. Despite repeated attempts to infuse new management, better sales policies, and cost cutting policies, they were never profitable. However, the company reported gains in its fishing rods, archery equipment, boots, and vaulting poles.[4]

In 1967 Browning sales rose twenty percent to $30,023,316. The company introduced its new

[3] Richard Bauter, personal interview with the author, March 15, 1994.

[4] Browning Arms Company, 1966 Annual Report.

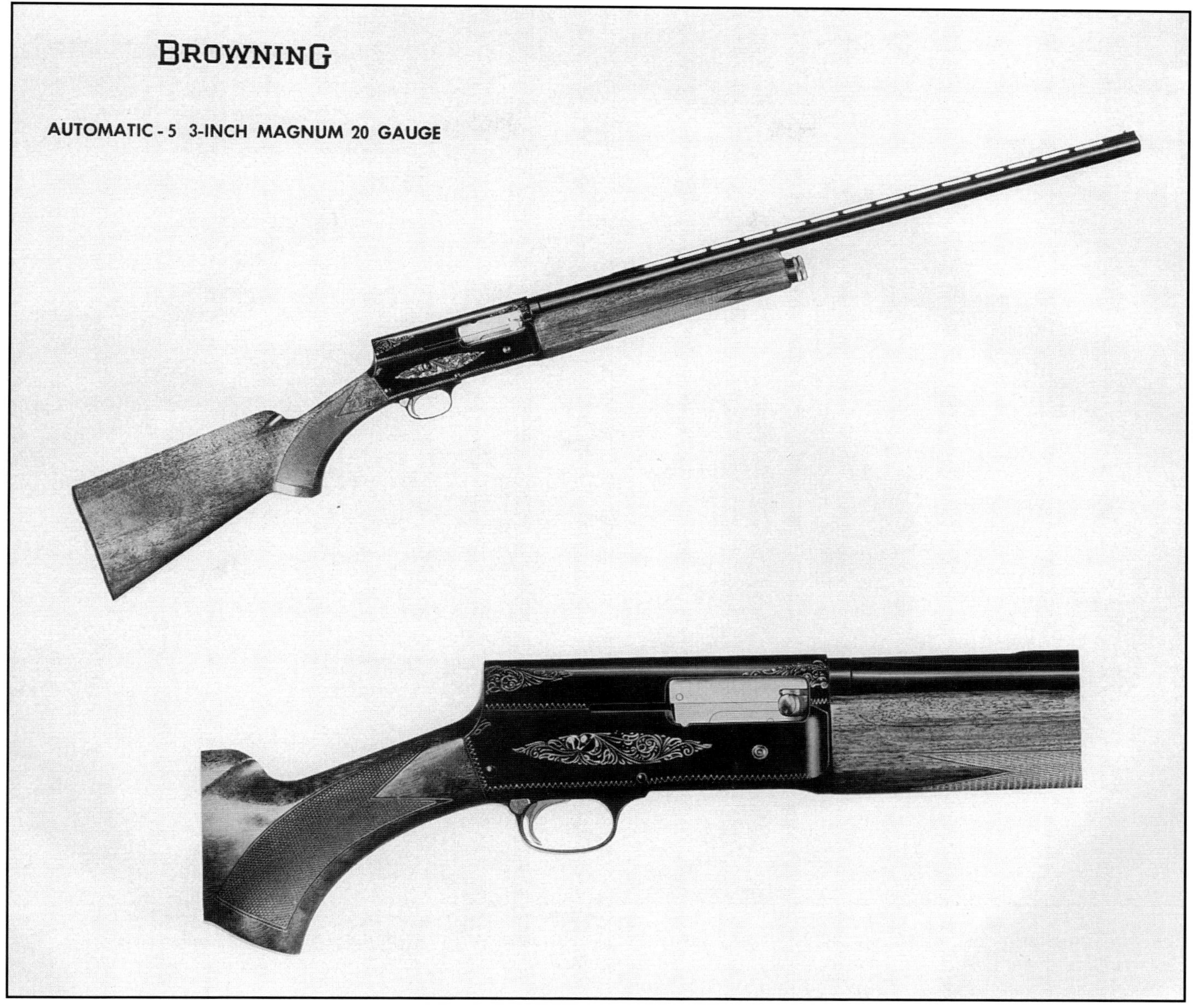

Browning Semiautomatic Rifle (BAR) and the Auto-5 20 gauge chambered for the 3-inch Magnum shell. Business was good and sales were improving despite difficulties with FN's failure to meet delivery schedules for its sporting firearms. The decision to expand into domestically produced sporting goods was responsible for the company's continued growth despite these problems with FN.

After thirty-eight years in St. Louis, in the spring of 1968 the warehouse, distribution, service, and parts departments were moved to a new eighty thousand square foot building in Arnold, Missouri, a small town south of St. Louis. Bob Clark, one of the regional sales managers, stayed behind to manage the facility. This move was long overdue, as the company had outgrown the old St. Louis location several years earlier. With its rail capacity, the Arnold site would finally enable the company to unload its guns directly into the warehouse. The larger quarters would make function testing of firearms safer and more efficient as well. New equipment was added to the repair department also. In effect, this move brought the parts, repair, shipping, and warehouse facilities of Browning into the modern era and enabled the company to operate more effectively.

Sales, accounting, data processing, and the general administrative offices were moved to Mountain Green, Utah, on August 1, 1968. These departments now had closer cooperation with top management, resulting in better efficiency between them.[5] Of the thirty or so St. Louis employees,

[5] John Val Browning, letter to the author, August 23, 1993.

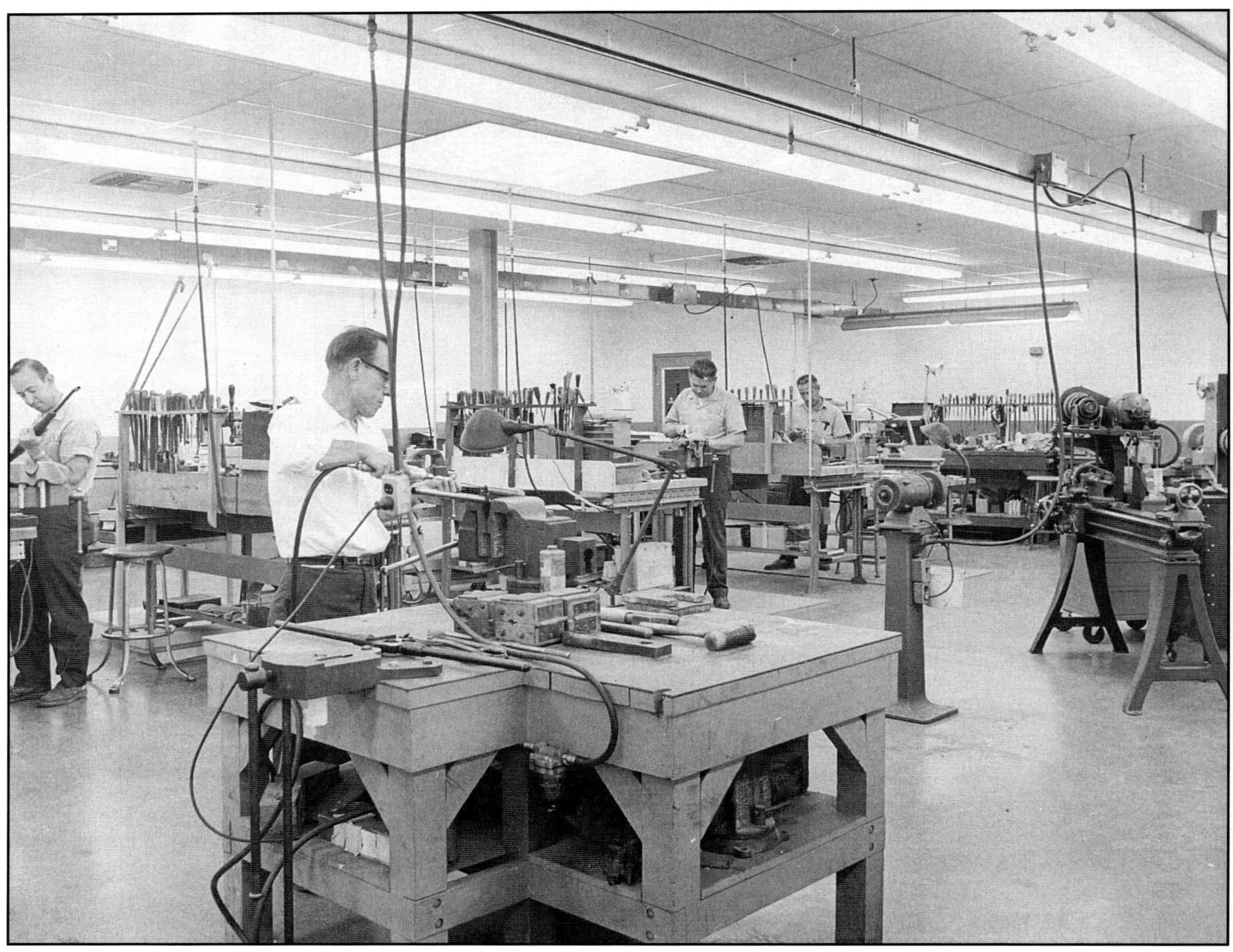

Browning gunsmiths in the new Arnold, Missouri, repair department. From left to right are Vearl Brown, Lloyd Gastreich, Dick Heiter, and Norman Pyeatt. This new location gave the company much more room in which to operate and made all of the functions in Arnold much more efficient. Courtesy Browning Company.

about ten or twelve made the move to Mountain Green. An additional twenty employees were hired in the new Utah location to help support a growing and expanding parent company. Grant Goddard, the general manager at St. Louis, moved to Mountain Green and assumed new responsibilities over personnel policy and insurance acquisition, and as liaison between Browning and its ever-growing number of subsidiaries.

Three additional acquisitions were made in 1968. The first was the exchange of stock for Caldwell and Barth Companies, which made specialty leather products such as footballs, baseball gloves, ski bindings, golf bags, and rifle slings. The second purchase was the Jarman Company, which produced golf carts, golf clothing, and related accessories. The third acquisition was Harwill Incorporated, a pleasure boat company with sales of approximately $3,000,000 annually. The acquisition of these nonfirearms related companies reduced the percentage of Browning's total sales derived from sporting arms to about seventy percent. At its peak, the number of Browning employees, including those who worked in its subsidiaries, was almost nine hundred.[6]

Continued problems with FN forced Browning to look elsewhere for a reliable supplier of firearms. The result was the first Japanese-built shotgun produced for Browning, the BT-99, introduced in 1968. Built by Miroku, this was to set a new course for Browning firearms for years to come and have a profound impact on the future of the Superposed.

---

[6] Grant Goddard, personal interview with the author, November 25, 1994.

This photo of the Browning service personnel was taken at the company's new facility in Arnold, Missouri, on August 15, 1968. This group is gathered at the back of the building. The open door leads to the shop. In the front row from left to right are Dick Heiter, Norman Pyeatt, Ed Frillman, Fred Haunold, Wilbert Walter, Ken Shriell, Keith Neubauer, and Paul Fuchs. In the back row from left to right are Herman Stengel, Vearl Brown, Jack Callahan, Earl Womble, John Cowie, Gary Annelick, John Woesthaus, Roy Nobbe, Marty Ryan, George Sieber, Ed Fuchs, Howard Maas, Harry Heiter, Lloyd Gastreich, and Charles Kelsay. Not pictured is Al Sargent, who was on the phone at the time the picture was taken. Courtesy Browning Company, Arnold, Missouri.

This aerial photo was taken of Browning's new corporate facility in Mountain Green, Utah, in 1968. The move from Ogden to Mountain Green gave much more flexibility and room for operations such as research and development, accounting, and sales. Courtesy Browning Company.

The front entrance of the new Mountain Green facility. Nestled in Weber Canyon in the Watatch mountain range, this is a very attractive work environment. Courtesy Browning Company.

Many of the Browning catalogue photos were taken at or near Mountain Green. This duck hunter is holding a 12 gauge 3-inch Magnum Superposed for one of the company's promotional pictures. Courtesy Browning Company.

Browning would no longer have to rely on Fabrique Nationale for a substantial proportion of its firearms production.

The last year of the '60s proved to be a difficult one for Browning. Both sales and earnings declined for the first time since the company went public. Net sales for 1969 were $42,620,519, down from $43,253,031. Net income for 1969 fell to $1,261,791 from $2,215,281. Higher interest rates, poor performance from the company's boat subsidiaries, and a generally slower national economy caused this poor financial showing for 1969.

For the decade of the 1960s, Browning sales had grown an impressive 350 percent. Much of this was due, of course, to the expansion and diversification of the company, but firearms sales did commendably well for the same period, and demand for the Superposed continued to grow at a rate the company was unable to meet. This inability to meet demand was a constant source of disappointment for Browning management and its sales staff. Knowing that the demand for the Superposed was strong, but being unable to satisfy that demand was difficult on morale. As we shall see, this troublesome situation was a complex one for both Browning and Fabrique Nationale.

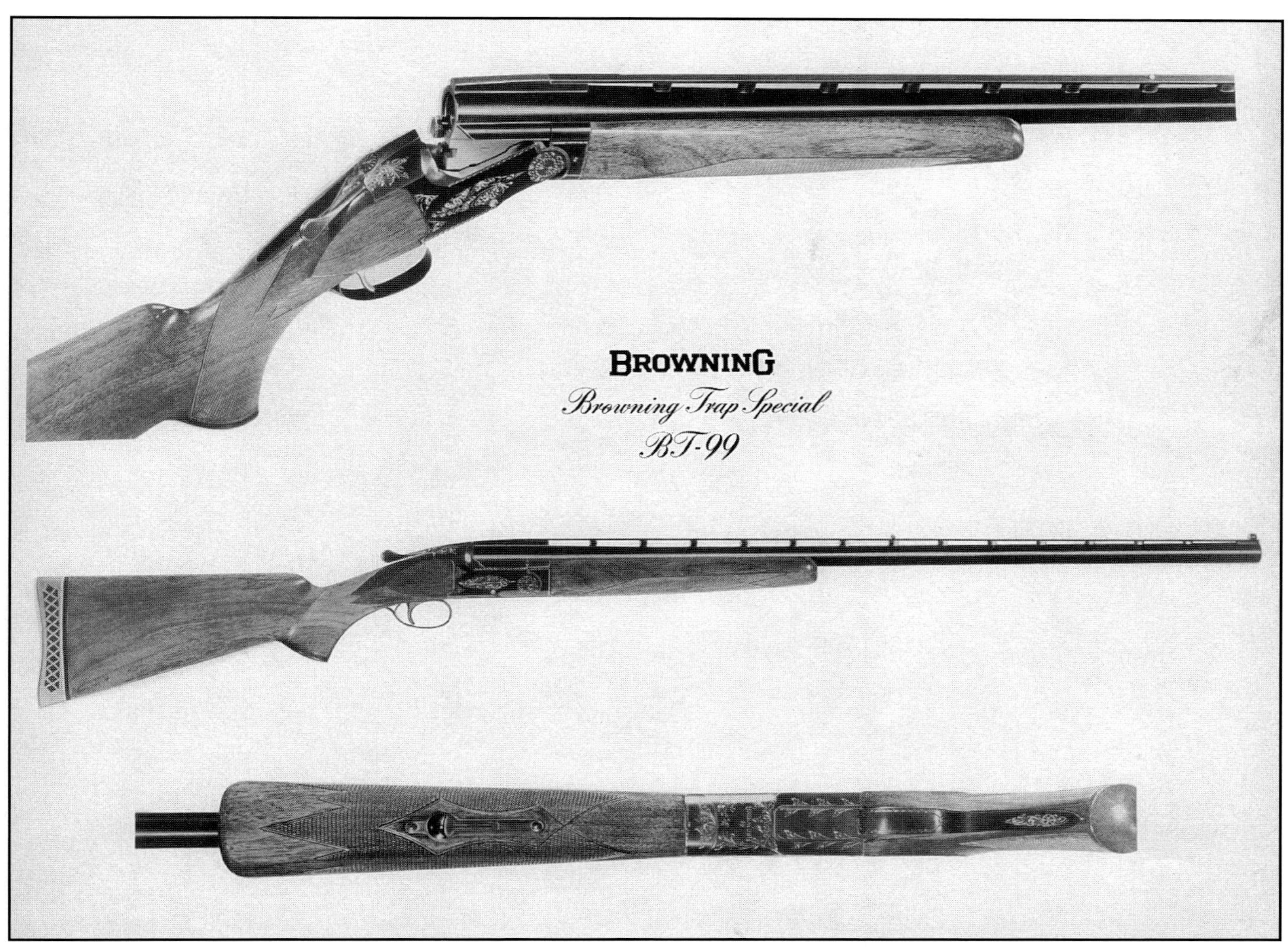

The first Japanese built shotgun in the Browning Arms Company firearms line was the BT-99, introduced in 1968. This would mark the beginning of a trend toward Japanese built firearms that would lessen the company's reliance on Fabrique Nationale produced guns. Courtesy Browning Company.

Browning versus FN: Mounting Frustration

Browning's relationship with Fabrique Nationale, although built on mutual respect and trust of long standing, was one of enormous frustration for the American company. Since the end of World War II, a small but perceptible change in the connection between the employer and its employees had transpired in the Herstal company. A combination of high demand for Fabrique Nationale's products, and a small skilled worker base created pressure to increase wages in order to attract and retain skilled workers. During the 1950s several programs were put into place that helped to insure high expectations on the part of FN workers. A substantial bonus system was implemented, free medical care was provided to all FN employees, and a scholarship fund, pension fund and survivorship annuity were instituted. These benefits added appreciably to FN's cost of doing business, and workers expected them to continue to grow in scope and value. Business was good, however, and productivity was high, especially in the production of military weapons and sporting arms. Contrary to common belief, Fabrique Nationale was not a state-owned enterprise, but was privately owned by shareholders around the world.[7] These workers' benefit packages were not the result of state inspired socialism, but an attempt by management to retain a stable and skilled workforce.

By the beginning of the 1960s FN employed almost thirteen thousand workers in all of its pro-

[7] Part of the company's name, "Nationale," referred to the fact that the original order was produced for the Belgian government, thus it was a "National" order.

These photographs, taken much earlier in the century than the photo on the next page, show the general working conditions women experienced at Fabrique Nationale. It took until the 1960s before FN was forced by strikes to acknowledge and alter its turn of the century working conditions. There was much resistance on the part of management, but the female workers were equally determined to see the necessary changes made. By the end of the decade, working conditions began to improve for all workers. Courtesy Fabrique Nationale Archives.

The Fabrique Nationale plant as it appeared in 1961. This was an enormous facility, employing over thirteen thousand workers and manufacturing a variety of small arms for governments all over the world as well as the Browning Company. Courtesy Fabrique Nationale Archives.

duction facilities. Of this figure there were approximately seventeen hundred salaried staff: executives, foremen, designers, and other office workers. The balance of the workforce was comprised of machine operators and other personnel who were not engaged in highly skilled capacities. These largely unskilled positions consisted of thirty percent women. Roughly six hundred workers made up the highly skilled workforce, which was composed of toolmakers, mechanical specialists, gunsmiths, engravers, and woodworkers who did all the handwork necessary to produce quality firearms and other close tolerance components.

All of this was controlled by one man: the managing director and chairman of the board, René Laloux. Trained as an engineer, Laloux was a "gun man." He knew what it took to produce and sell firearms, both military and civilian. His control and power were considerable, and according to Claude Gaier, "The style was authoritarian: everybody knew his place and his job ... the rigidity of the system gave rise to a certain routine and failed to liberate the energies in accordance with the available potential."[8] In spite of these problems within FN, workers considered the company a stable employer that paid well.

The production difficulties that had plagued Browning before the war and a few years after, were to take on a new and more troublesome aspect. The rise of the trade unions in the Liège region was to have a profound impact on the Browning Superposed in terms of both price stability and availability. Liège was an industrial area upon which the trade unions could have a tremendous impression. Suspicious of management and eager to build their political power, a pattern of disputes broke out during the 1960s that would have a direct effect on Browning's Superposed

---

8 Auguste Francotte and Claude Gaier, *FN 100 Years: The Story of the Great Liège Company, 1889-1989*, p 116.

This Fabrique Nationale craftsman at his polishing lathe is putting the finishing touches on the barrels of a Browning Superposed. All Superposed barrels were choked full and full until chokes were cut to size with a hone. The barrels were then polished. Courtesy Fabrique Nationale Archives.

production and price structure. The unions constantly pressed for higher wages. Strikes and partial walkouts became common.

Fabrique Nationale faced additional dilemmas as well. Business was good and growing, and by the middle of the decade sporting firearms exceeded military weapons production for the first time. Browning Arms accounted for sixty-six percent of this sporting firearms production. But the ever-increasing prices, brought on by constant union demands, created an atmosphere that no longer made the Superposed competitive in the American marketplace. The effect of the wage and price spiral on Fabrique Nationale can best be followed by examining its effects on delivery and prices of the Superposed in the U.S.[9]

Browning reported in 1962 that increased wages at FN pushed its prices to a point beyond which the company could recover in price increases without jeopardizing its competitive position. Wages for comparative workers in the U.S. were not increasing as fast as those in Belgium. What saved the company from this untenable situation was the reduction of import duties, which was to take effect in 1963.[10]

In 1963 the company experienced record demand for its shotguns including the Superposed. But Browning stated in no uncertain terms, "... sales could have been appreciably higher if deliveries of several of our most popular models from Belgium had not been hampered by labor difficulties at the factory there. The most serious problem confronting the company in 1963 was the continuing pressure on firearm margins as a result of increased wages and other costs at FN."[11]

By 1964 the company began looking for ways to counteract the increasing costs at Fabrique Nationale. Two distinct consequences flowed from this situation, one short-term and the other long-term. The short-term was to reduce production cost of Browning firearms produced at FN. This manifested itself by the myriad of production modifications that began to appear on the Superposed in the mid to late 1960s. The long-term was the opening of negotiations with the Japanese firm Miroku to produce a more competitively priced over and under shotgun.

Browning was able to provide a better inventory of its Superposed guns by 1965 and this contributed greatly to increased sales. But a strike which began February 9, 1966, led exclusively by female Fabrique Nationale workers, was not settled until May 10 of that year. This strike cut off deliveries to Browning of all its FN produced firearms. With increased production at FN following the strike, and the expensive airfreighting of firearms to meet the fall demand, Browning was able to have a satisfactory sales year. However, the result of the strike was another round of price increases which again forced Browning to raise its retail prices to protect its margins.[12]

In November of 1966 Browning Arms Company formed a new company, Browning SA, for the purpose of distributing nonfirearm products in Europe. This was a result of a natural outgrowth of Browning's product line expansion in North America. The company felt that this European connection would provide an additional outlet for its products. Prohibited from selling Browning fire-

[9] *Ibid.*, pp. 116-118. Claude Gaier gives a thorough and balanced look at the difficulties FN management faced during the 1960s. The rise of trade unions in Europe after World War II plays an important role in FN's inability to hold the line on costs. Whether or not the Belgian company could have dealt with the unions more effectively is subject to debate.

[10] Browning Arms Company, 1962 Annual Report.

[11] Browning Arms Company, 1964 Annual Report.

[12] Browning Arms Company, 1966 Annual Report.

Fabrique Nationale produced a variety of sporting firearms, not only for Browning, but for its own markets as well. From top to bottom is the FN Mauser hunting rifle produced from 1922 to 1978; the Browning Superposed produced from 1930 to the present; the Auto-5 shotgun produced from 1903 to 1976; the Hammerless Anson double barrel shotgun produced from 1920 to 1949; the Browning slide action Trombone .22 caliber rifle produced from 1920 to 1974; and the Browning Automatic rifle in .22 caliber produced from 1914 to the present. Courtesy Fabrique Nationale Archives.

arms in Europe by the original 1927 agreement between Browning and FN, Browning Arms Company had been selling its firearms to American military personnel on American bases in Europe since the early 1950s. The creation of Browning SA nonfirearms products was an attempt to capitalize on the company's positive name recognition and history of selling quality products.[13]

In 1967 Browning negotiated with FN to hold prices steady. Wages continued to escalate, but were held to moderate levels. Further reductions of import duties eased the effects of price increases on the retail level to about one percent.

In its 1968 annual report, Browning revealed that negotiations to build sporting firearms had been underway with the Japanese manufacturer Miroku since 1965. The ever-increasing costs spiral for Browning firearms at FN had compelled the company to look elsewhere for a more stable manufacturing base. This year was marked by another round of price increases by FN, which resulted in a three percent increase in retail prices for Belgian produced firearms. Once again, despite these difficulties, sales of Browning firearms produced at FN increased, including the Superposed. The decade ended with another round of price increases, due again to FN's continued wage increases.

[13] John Val Browning, interview with the author, November 15, 1994.

The constant upward pressure on prices in the decade of the '60s would in fact be a warning for the future. The American market could only absorb so much in the way of price increases. Costs and delivery problems were to take their toll on Browning's sales force and management team. The Superposed was the flagship of the company's product line, but it was always in short supply, and now the price was increasing at a rate that threatened to depress demand. With the introduction of the Japanese produced Browning Citori over and under shotgun in 1973, the importance to the Browning line of the Belgian made Superposed began to diminish, not in terms of prestige, but in terms of economic significance.

Superposed Engraving of the 1960s

Fabrique Nationale's chief engraver Felix Funken retired in 1960, ushering in a changing of the guard. Since 1926 the old master had directed FN's engravers with his Germanic influences and nineteenth century work ethic. A new generation of artisans—André Watrin, José Baerten, Jean Diet, Lucien Ernst, Lea Van Laar, and Louis Vrancken—was prepared and eager to lead. Of these engravers it was Louis Vrancken and André Watrin that became the chief engravers during the 1960s. Louis Vrancken was perhaps the leading force in new designs and innovation at FN, while André Watrin's strengths lay in his artistic ability and impeccable taste. Funken appointed master engraver Lea Van Laar to lead FN's female engravers.

Louis Vrancken was born near Liège in 1930 and joined FN as an engraving student under Felix Funken soon after World War II. By the late 1950s Vrancken had captured the attention of management at both FN and Browning, and was asked by John Val Browning to create new designs for the 1960s. Vrancken was instrumental in creating the Pointer Grade and in improving the design of the Midas Grade.[14] Vrancken was also responsible for designing and executing many of the Exhibition Grade Superposed sold in the 1960s. His preeminence as an engraver is unchallenged among experts.

The task of modernizing Browning engraving patterns fell to Vrancken and Watrin. The Grade I, with its deep bluing and sparse but tasteful scroll, remained unchanged. The Grade II, with its pair of flying pigeons, would now be known by its prewar name, the Pigeon Grade, and would remain essentially unchanged except for the reduced size of the pigeons. The Grade III, sometimes referred to as the "Fighting Cocks" grade, would be replaced by the Vrancken-designed Pointer Grade. The Grade IV with its deep cut oak leaf border and European style game scenes was dropped from the new engraving designs and was not replaced by a new pattern. The Grade IV was considered too European in appearance for American tastes. The Grade V with its classic deep cut game scenes was changed to the Diana Grade, another prewar designation, and redesigned with minor changes. The Grade VI, which was not introduced into the Browning Superposed line until 1957, was redesigned by Louis Vrancken and named the Midas Grade.

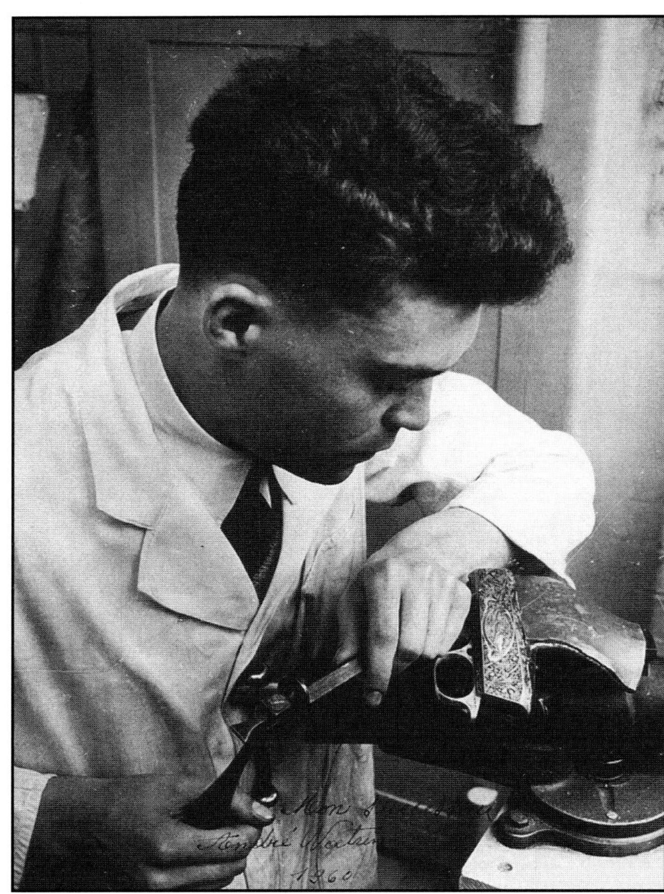

Felix Funken wrote in his diary that André Watrin was his successor. Watrin was known for his artistic abilities and impeccable taste. This photo was taken June 30, 1960, shortly before Funken retired. The dedication reads, "My successor André Watrin, my most dedicated and best pupil. For a long time in pains and now honored." The reference to pains was in regard to Watrin's long service as Funken's assistant. Courtesy Liège Arms Museum.

[14] Thomas Koessel, *Browning Collectors Association Newsletter*, Vol. VIII, No. 5, March-April, 1986. Koessel was a close personal friend of Louis Vrancken and wrote a brief narrative of Vrancken and his influence during his tenure at FN.

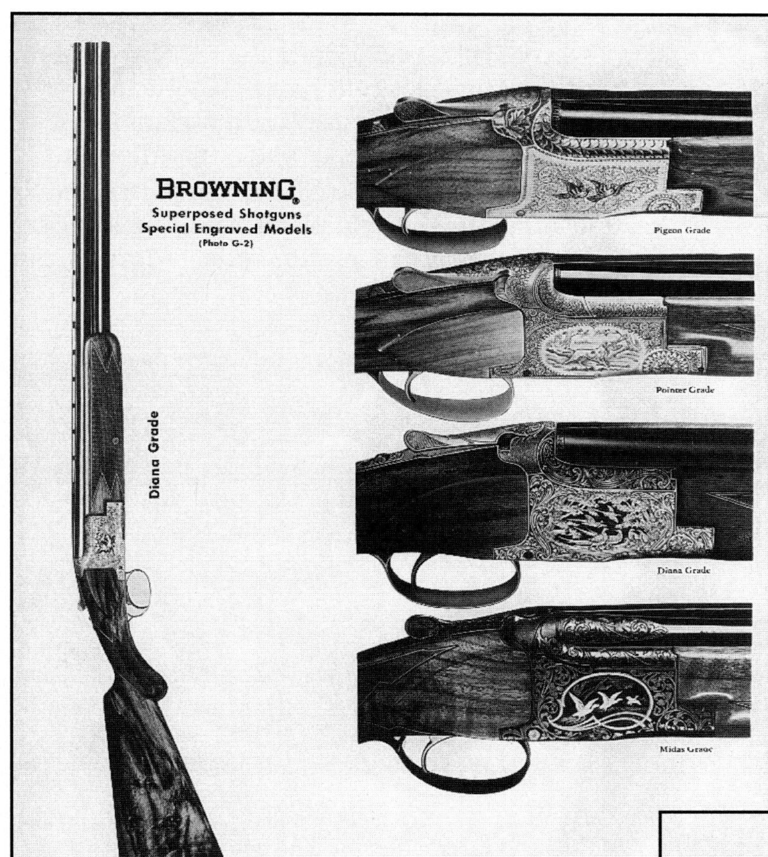

SPECIALLY ENGRAVED MODELS — The genius of the United States mass production talent, which makes such a variety of luxuries available to so many, has brought about nearly total abandonment of certain richly satisfying crafts. One of these is the artistic hand-engraving of steel. The makers of Browning shotguns have consistently tried to foster and preserve this fine art and in the process have gathered a large and unique group of qualified engravers.

Steel engraving of the sort we present is done with a light hammer tapping against chisels that are moved about in a continuous action. By this means the design is developed much as one might draw it. The engraver begins his work on bare metal; mind, eye, and hand are unassisted by pre-placed patterns.

To acquire the engraving skill represented in the Midas Grade, for instance, takes years of painstaking experience. Consistent with traditional pride in craftsmanship, the engaver signs each gun on which he has labored. This is a craft demanding nearly the ultimate, not only of artistry, but of flawless execution. One does not erase steel.

The Midas Grade incorporates every refinement known to shotgun making. The receiver and trigger guard have inlaid hunting scenes in 18 carat gold, sparkling as on jeweler's velvet, against a specially blued and deeply carved background. No two scenes are alike. Each gun is the only one of its exact kind. The rib is hand-matted along the sighting surface to give a finer grained, non-reflecting surface. The ejector rods and the tips of the firing pins are gold plated.

Only the finest grade matched walnut is used on these specially engraved models, the quality ascending with the various grades. The checkering is meticulously done by hand in correspondingly more intricate patterns using finer checkering tools than those for the Grade I Models.

The Superposed Magnum 12 gauge is provided in standard weight in all grades. All 28 and .410 gauge models, whether Grade I or the specially engraved grades are also provided in but one weight. All other 12 gauge and all 20 gauge models in these specially engraved grades come only in Lightning weights. It should be noted that because the finer, figured walnut used on these grades is generally denser they will nearly always be some heavier than the weights shown for Grade I Lightning models under Specifications on the next page.

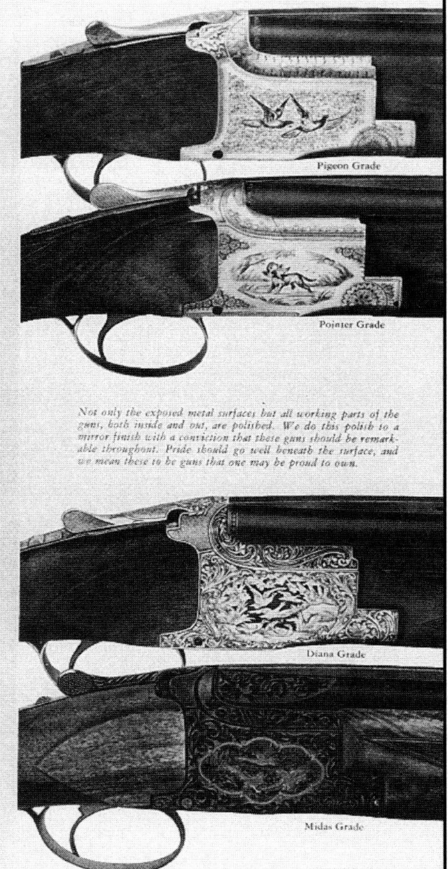

In December of 1960 Browning printed its general retail catalogue (top) showing Superposed engraving patterns that in fact were out-of-date. The Pigeon Grade, Diana Grade, and Midas Grade were in reality the old Grades II, V, and VI respectively. The Pointer Grade shown was an early version that was changed the following year. In December of 1961 the new engraving patterns were accurately shown. Courtesy Russ Church.

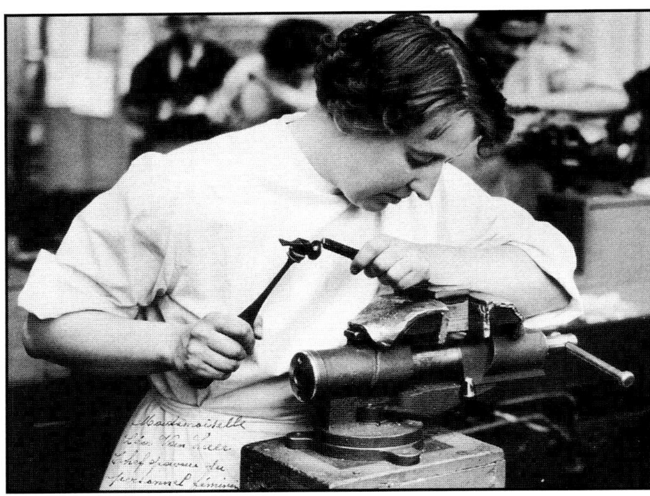

Mademoiselle Lea Van Laar was the chief engraver of women at FN. She was appointed to this position by Felix Funken, who thought very highly of her as an engraver, but misspells her name. This photo is also in Funken's diary and bears the date of June 30, 1960. The inscription reads, "My good and dedicated assistant thus finds her reward for her numerous qualities." Courtesy Liège Arms Museum.

Because the Midas Grade was the best of the production high grade Superposed, it received the finest treatments. The hunting scenes were inlaid in 18 carat gold against a specially blued and deeply carved background. Pheasants and ducks adorned the 12 gauge Superposed Midas, while smaller game birds were inlaid on the 20 and 28 gauges and .410 bore. Despite the fairly consistent use of bird types, no two scenes were exactly the same. It took Louis Vrancken about sixty hours of handwork to produce the Midas Grade pattern. The ventilated rib on the Midas Grade was hand matted along the sighting plane, resulting in a very fine grain surface. The ejector rods and firing pin tips were gold plated.

This photo was taken at Felix Funken's retirement party in 1960. Funken is in the front marked with an "X." To his right are Sylvain Dorval and Joseph Gerard, two of the original FN engravers who started under Funken in 1930. The woman in the foreground is Annie Vlodarzack, Louis Vrancken's wife. Courtesy Angelo Bee.

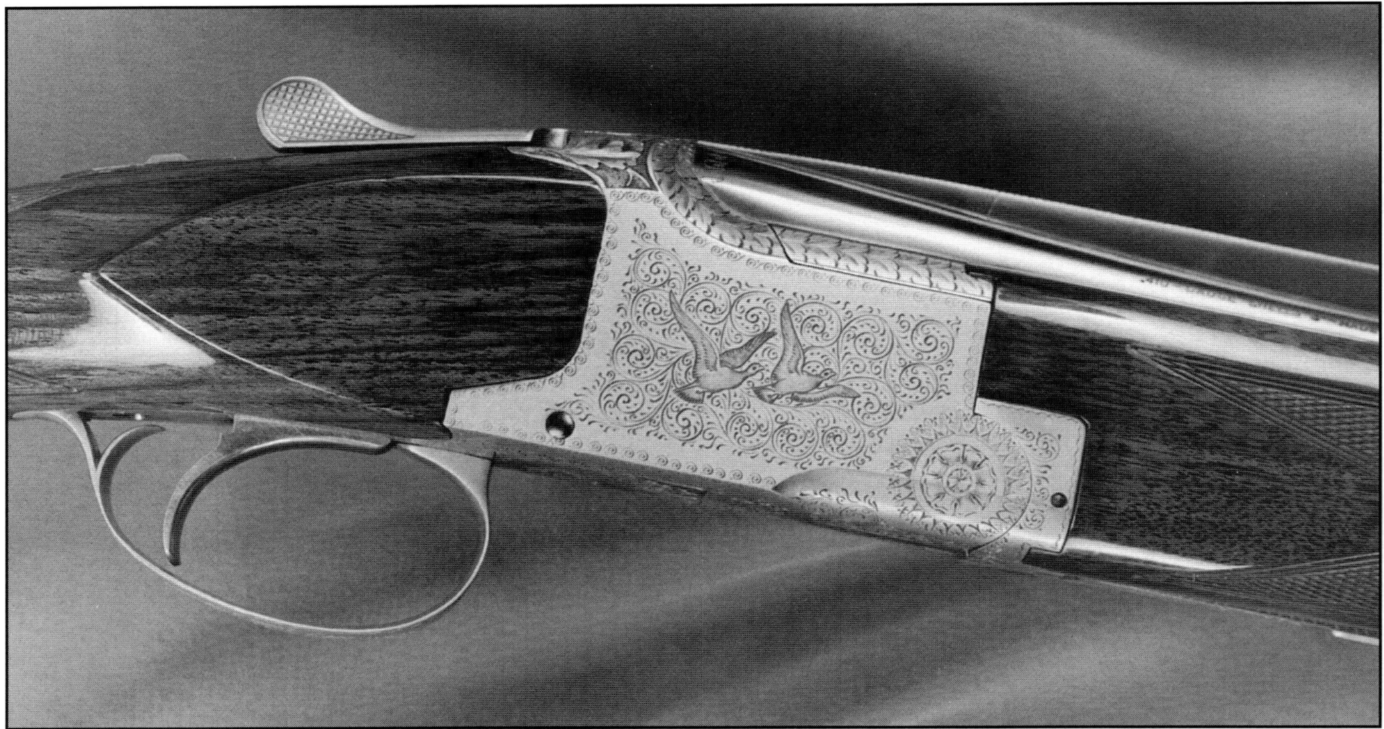

This .410 bore Superposed was engraved in the Pigeon Grade pattern. This was the entry level grade for high grade Superposed and was very popular in all models and gauges. Courtesy Browning Company.

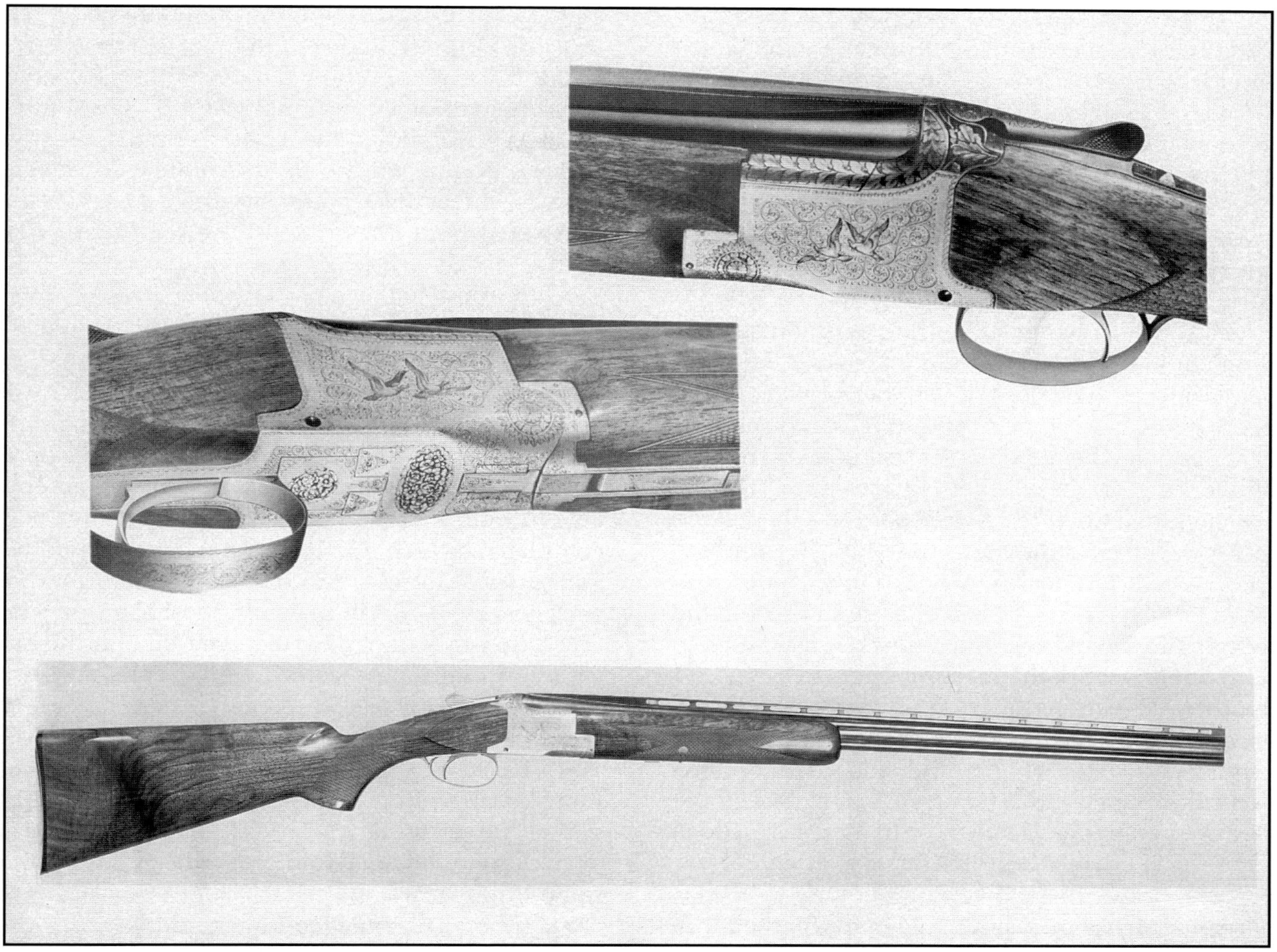

This page is taken from a 1960s Browning Arms Company catalogue picture showing three views of the Pigeon Grade. Note the square knob on the pistol grip, a certain indication that this is a post 1966 photo. Courtesy Browning Company.

This is a 20 gauge Browning Superposed Grade I. This was the standard pattern used during the 1960s. FN engravers referred to this grade as the "sarma" or affordable grade. Courtesy Browning Company.

Between 1960 and 1969 well over one thousand Midas Grades were sold by Browning in its North American market.[15] When the Grade VI was introduced in 1957, Felix Funken had difficulty meeting the demand due to the lack of experienced engraving inlay specialists like Gaston Vandersmissen. One or two inlay experts could not produce enough Midas Grades, as they took some sixty hours to execute. Vrancken faced the same difficulty as Funken had before him and he was instructed by Louis Nicolaï to find solutions to this problem in order to meet the increasing demand. Vrancken resolved the problem in two ways. First, in order to keep the price within reason he offered FN engravers the opportunity to earn extra money by working on these Midas Grades at home during their own time. They were paid less than at the factory, but paid no taxes on this off-premises work. Midas Grades engraved in this fashion will frequently have no engraver's signature on the frame. The second method Vrancken used was to send out this work to other engravers in Liège and in other countries. This contract method had been used by FN before the war to provide assistance to factory engravers when workloads were too burdensome. Some Midas Grades were signed by the German engraver Müller. Whether the Midas Grade was engraved at the factory, at an FN engraver's home, or by a contract engraver, all underwent intense inspection by FN for high quality and proper execution.

On all high grade Superposed stocks, FN used only matching walnut with corresponding finer grain and color. The hand checkering was increasingly finer the more ornate the grade, as was the pattern itself.

An interesting anomaly appears in 1960 with Pointer Grade engraving pattern variances. When introduced in 1960, the Pointer Grade illustrated in the company's catalogues featured pointers and setters engraved in a light fine line style with excellent background detail. On the right side was a retriever positioned toward the buttstock, an unusual position on a Superposed. The game scene vignette was oval in shape, surrounded by light scrollwork covering approximately fifty percent of the frame. The result was a very classic but relatively sparse engraving pattern. This first extremely early Pointer Grade pattern appeared in the June 1960 and December 1960 Browning catalogues. But in the Browning catalogue of March 1961 the Pointer Grade engraving pattern was revised. This new Pointer Grade pattern featured the same working dogs, but in slightly greater detail. This version had the retriever on the left side and the pointer on the right. Another noticeable difference was the greater coverage of scroll engraving around the vignette. The scrollwork was tighter and the coverage was almost one hundred percent of the balance of the frame. This was the final Pointer engraving pattern and remained consistent until the grade was discontinued in 1966.

The final Pointer Grade design involved a number of attempts over many months to develop a Pointer Grade engraving pattern that was acceptable to John Val Browning. The first attempt was completed March 11, 1959, on a Superposed 12 gauge, serial number 68308, based on information supplied by John Val Browning to FN engravers. This design was not adopted even though the design and engraving were done by Felix Funken. The next effort was done by master engraver Marie Louise Magis and completed on August 23, 1960, based again on instructions received from John Val Browning. The serial number of this 12 gauge Superposed was 77871. This design was very close to the final Pointer Grade layout. At the same time, master engraver Louis Vrancken executed a pattern similar to the one done by Magis. The serial number of this 12 gauge Superposed was 73616.

The final Pointer Grade pattern was approved on November 28, 1960. This pattern was executed on a 12 gauge Superposed, serial number 79845, with game scenes engraved by Marie Louise Magis and scrollwork cut by Jacques Lodewyc. This final Pointer Grade pattern is the one that appears in the 1961 Browning catalogue.

The reason for these various attempts was most likely some disagreement as to which design was the most attractive Pointer Grade pattern. Fabrique Nationale photographic archives display a remarkable number of Pointer Grade examples executed by a number of different FN engravers. There are subtle differences in each pattern, with the final version adopted late in 1960. It is likely that these demonstration frames were assembled into finished Superposed and sold to various FN or Browning agents.

---

[15] This number is an estimate based on Browning sales between 1964 and 1969 of 985 Midas Grades sold in North America. If we interpolate these official company figures of 1964 through 1969 to include the entire decade, the number of Midas Grades sold might be approximately 1,500 guns.

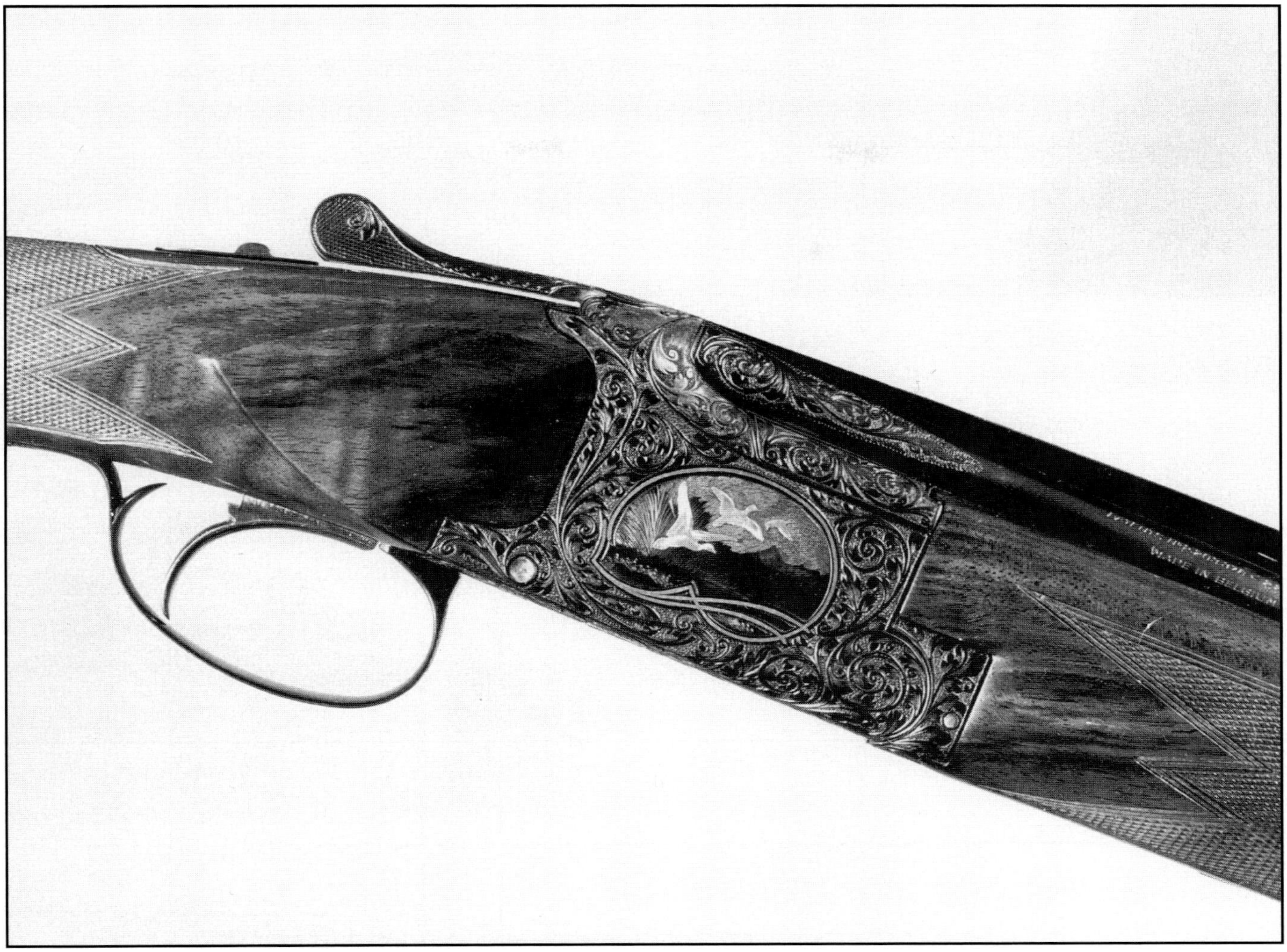

André Dierckx was a master engraver at FN for many years. This superb example of a Midas Grade Superposed is the reason he was considered a master engraver. Each Midas Grade was different in some way from any other Midas, and Dierckx's interpretation is very interesting and attractive. Courtesy Browning Company.

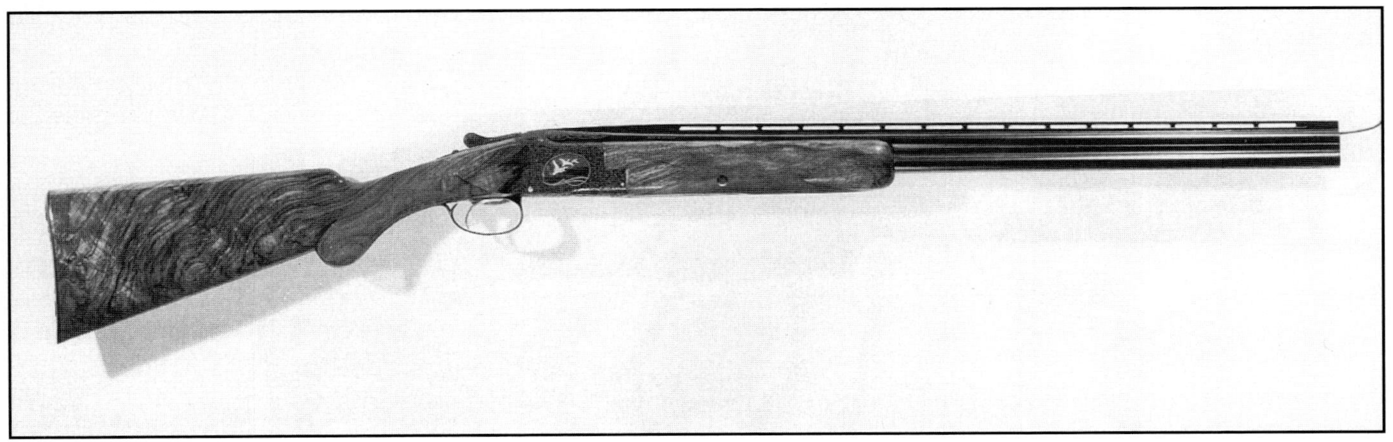

The overall view of Dierckx's Midas Grade Superposed is remarkable. The color and grain of the buttstock is magnificent. This is truly a remarkable Midas Grade Superposed. Courtesy Browning Company.

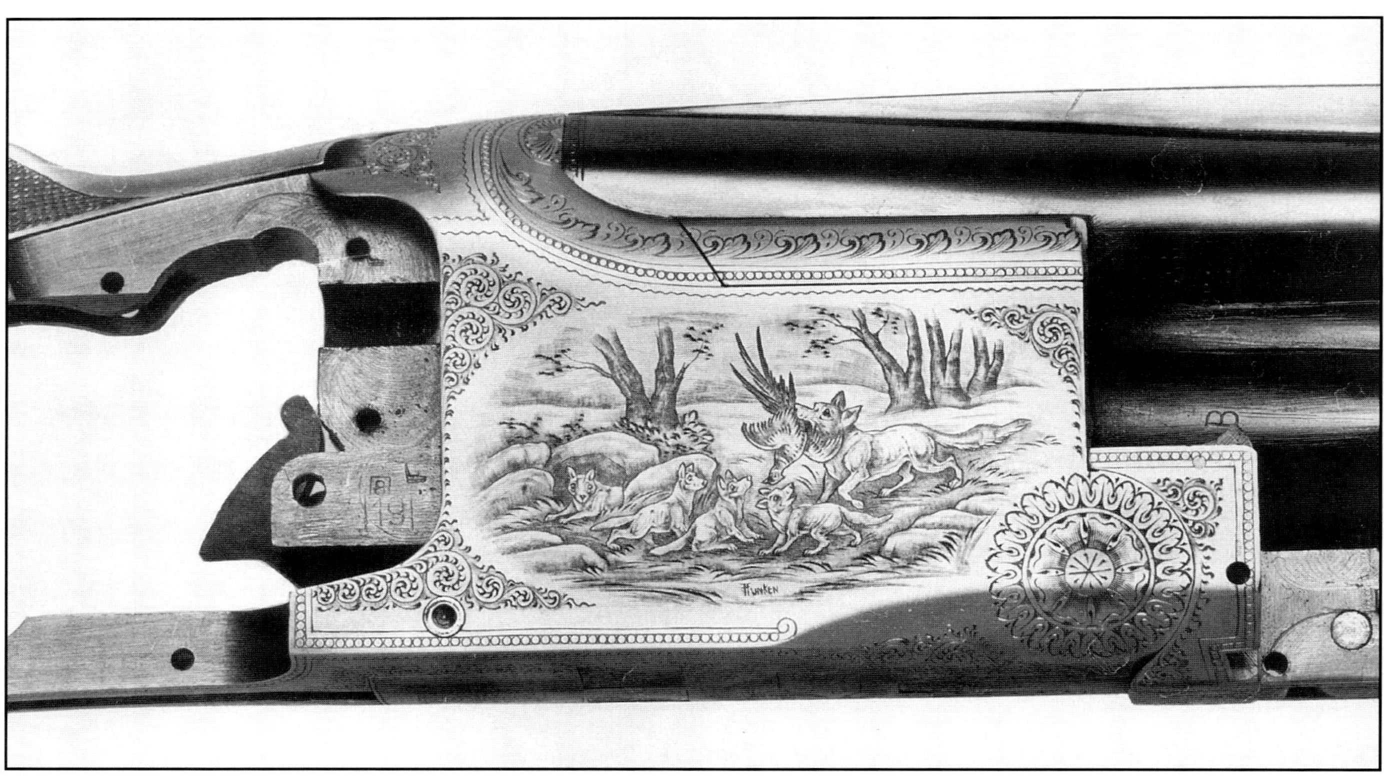

In 1959 there was some discussion between John Val Browning and Mr. Pirard, an FN administrative officer in charge of the engraving department, about a new design for the Pointer Grade which was soon to replace the Grade III. The correspondence between the two men took place on March 11, 1959, and was placed into a formal FN internal document, number 7524, on March 12, 1959. Both sides of this 12 gauge Superposed, serial number 68308, are signed by Felix Funken and were most likely designed by him as a preliminary design for the Pointer Grade. Courtesy Fabrique Nationale Archives.

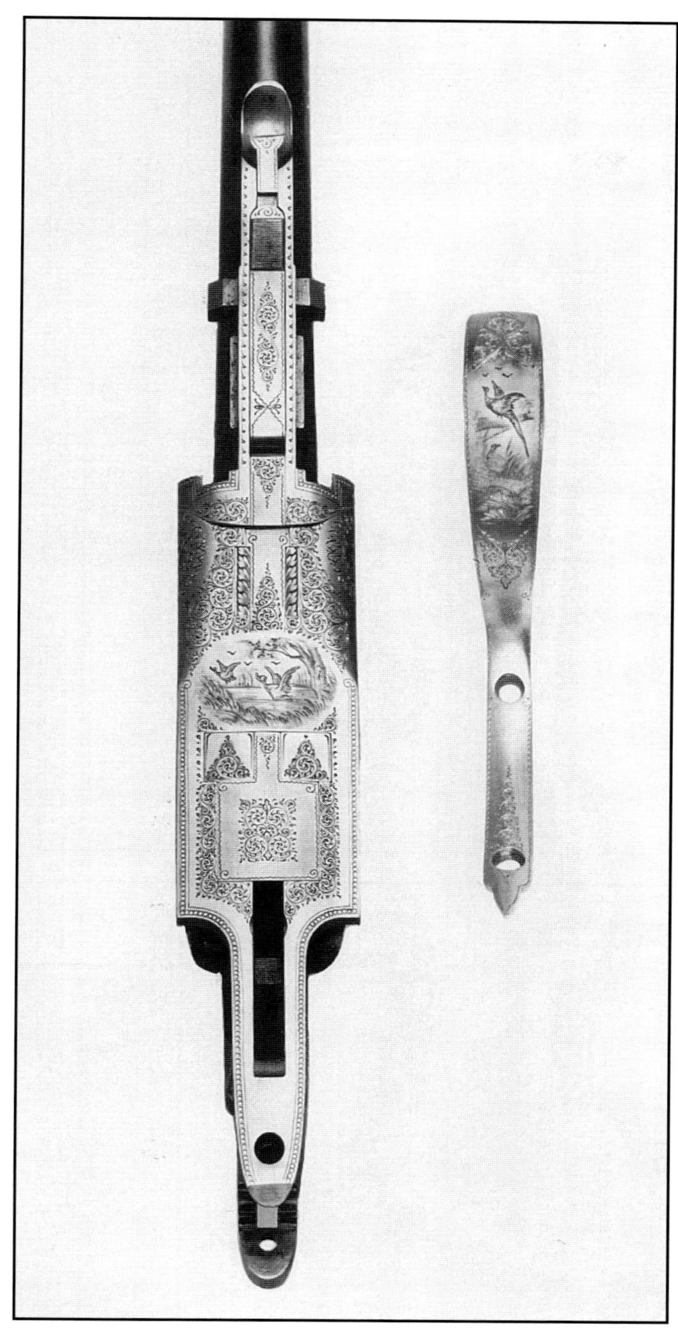

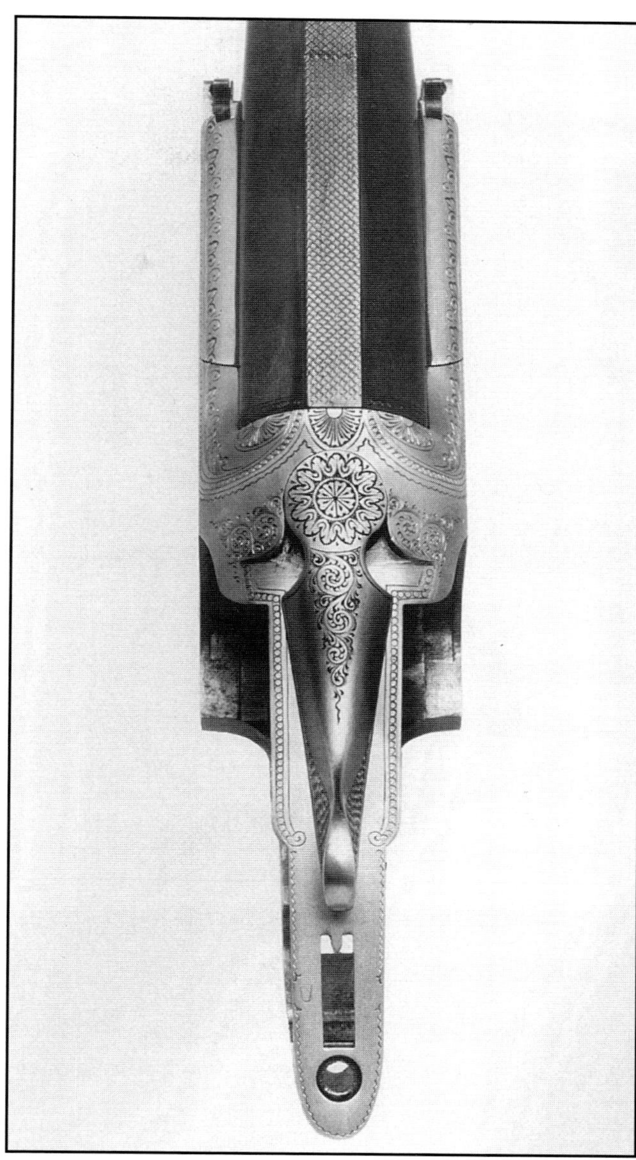

A top and bottom view of this preliminary new design for the Pointer Grade. The scrollwork on the top is tastefully done but sparse in coverage. The underside of this new design is very close in composition to what would be the final design completed in 1960. Courtesy Fabrique Nationale Archives.

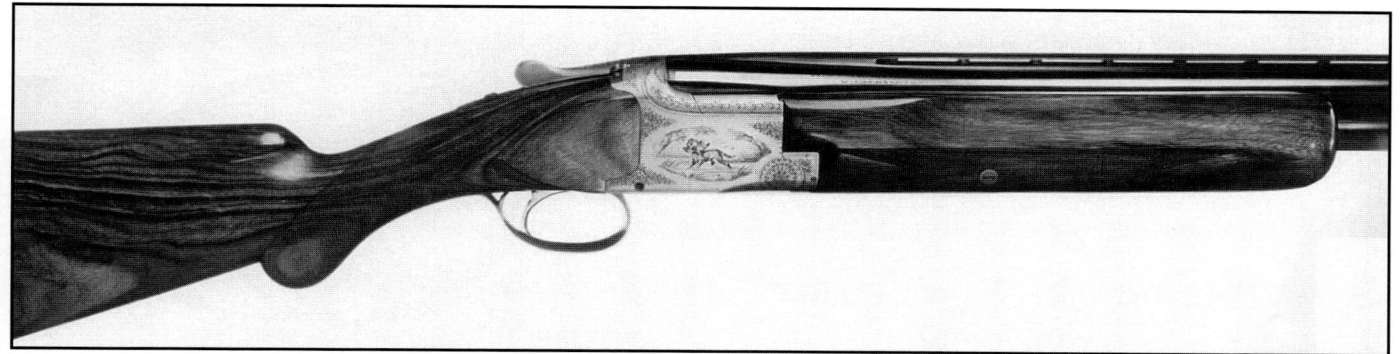

In the December 1960 Browning catalogue, the company used this Superposed Pointer Grade to illustrate the new grade. Notice the meagerness of the scrollwork surrounding the game scene. This is the only time this particular version of the Pointer Grade was used in the catalogue, and in all likelihood only a very few Superposed were engraved with this variation. The forearm indicated that this particular Superposed is a Trap model. Courtesy Browning Company.

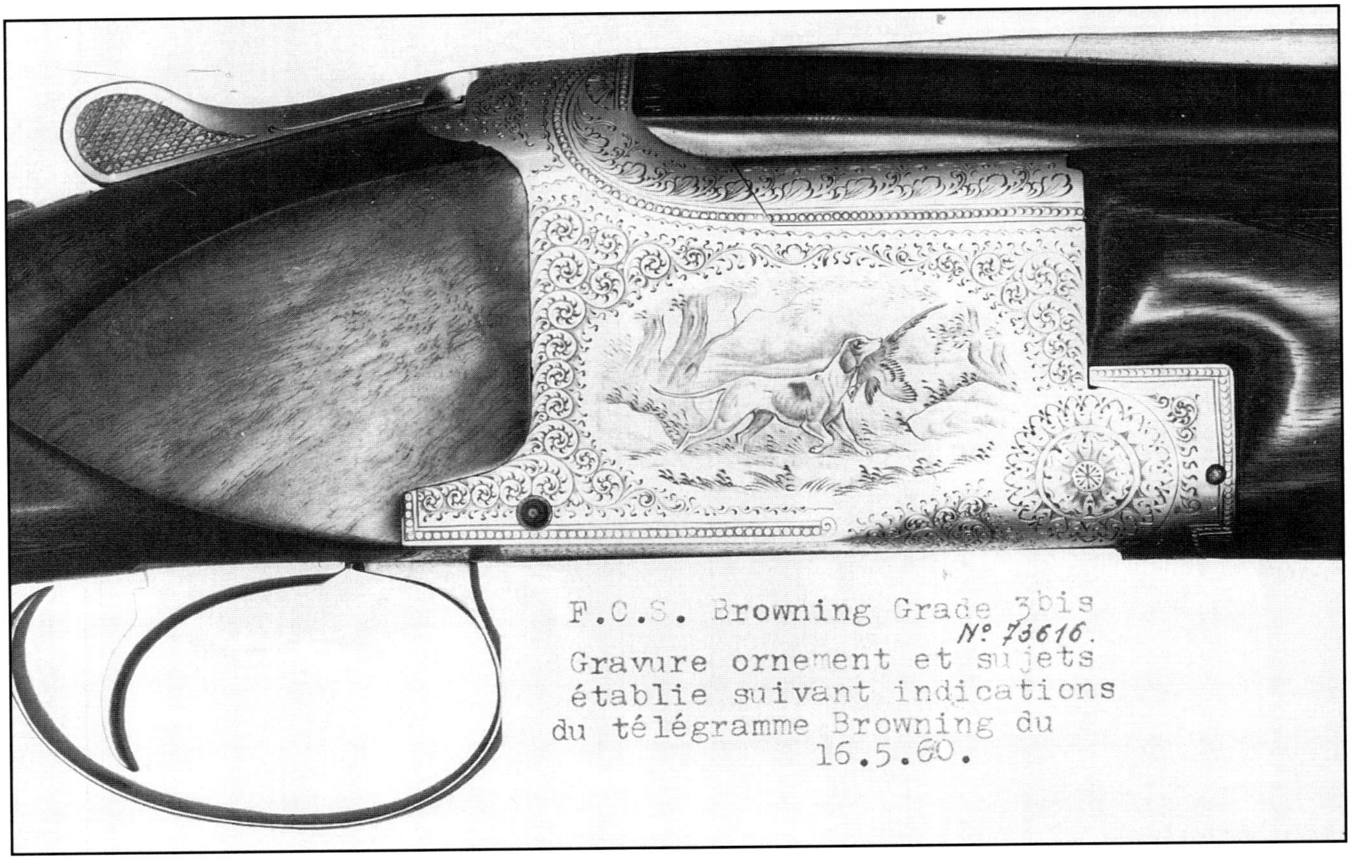

F.C.S. Browning Grade 3bis
Nº 73616.
Gravure ornement et sujets
établie suivant indications
du télégramme Browning du
16.5.60.

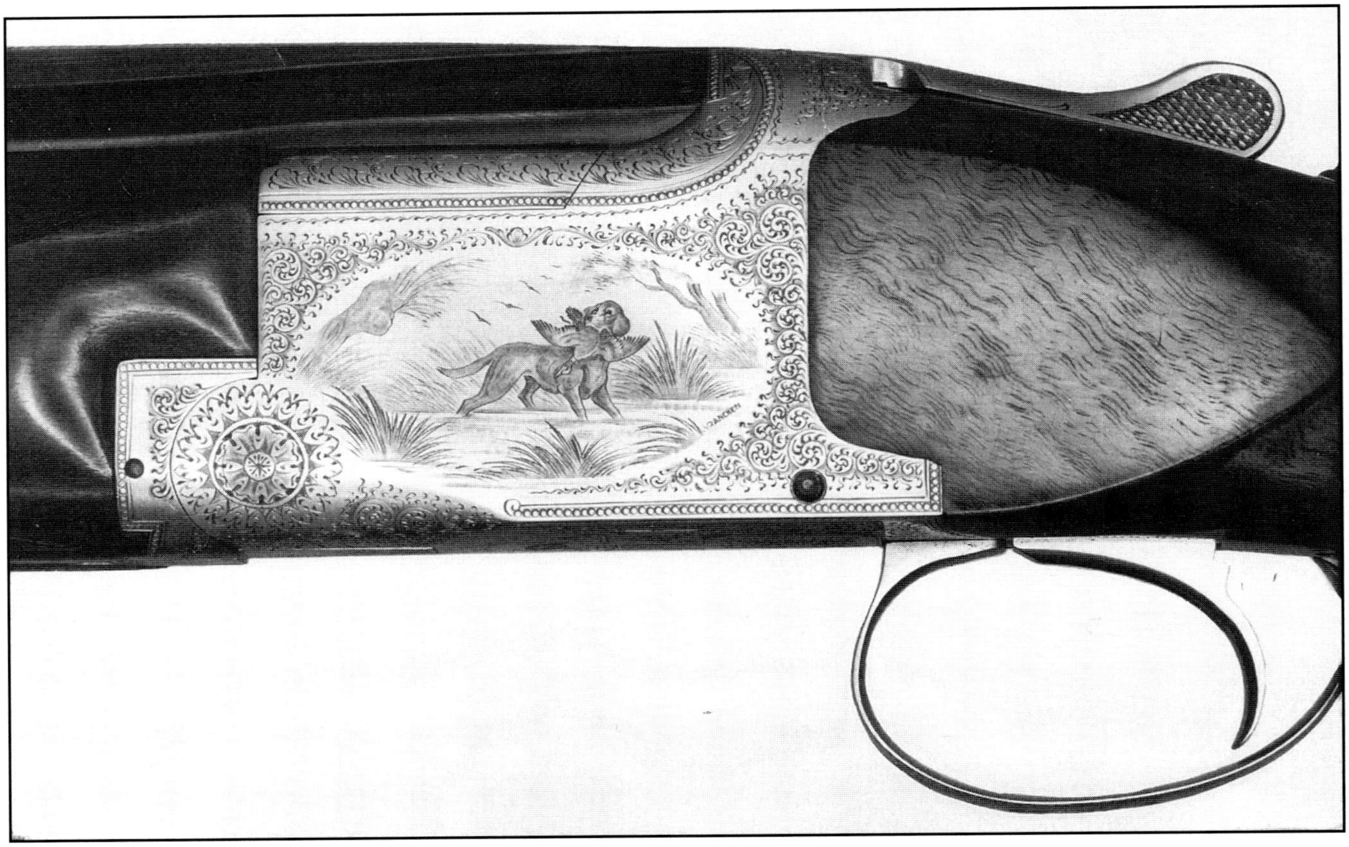

This Browning Superposed, serial number 73616, was designed and engraved by Louis Vrancken at the instruction of John Val Browning in a telegram dated May 16, 1960. This was probably an attempt by Browning to decide on a final pattern for the Pointer Grade. This design was very, very close to the conclusive design, the only differences being the scroll treatment and layout of the outline surrounding the game scenes. Courtesy Fabrique Nationale Archives.

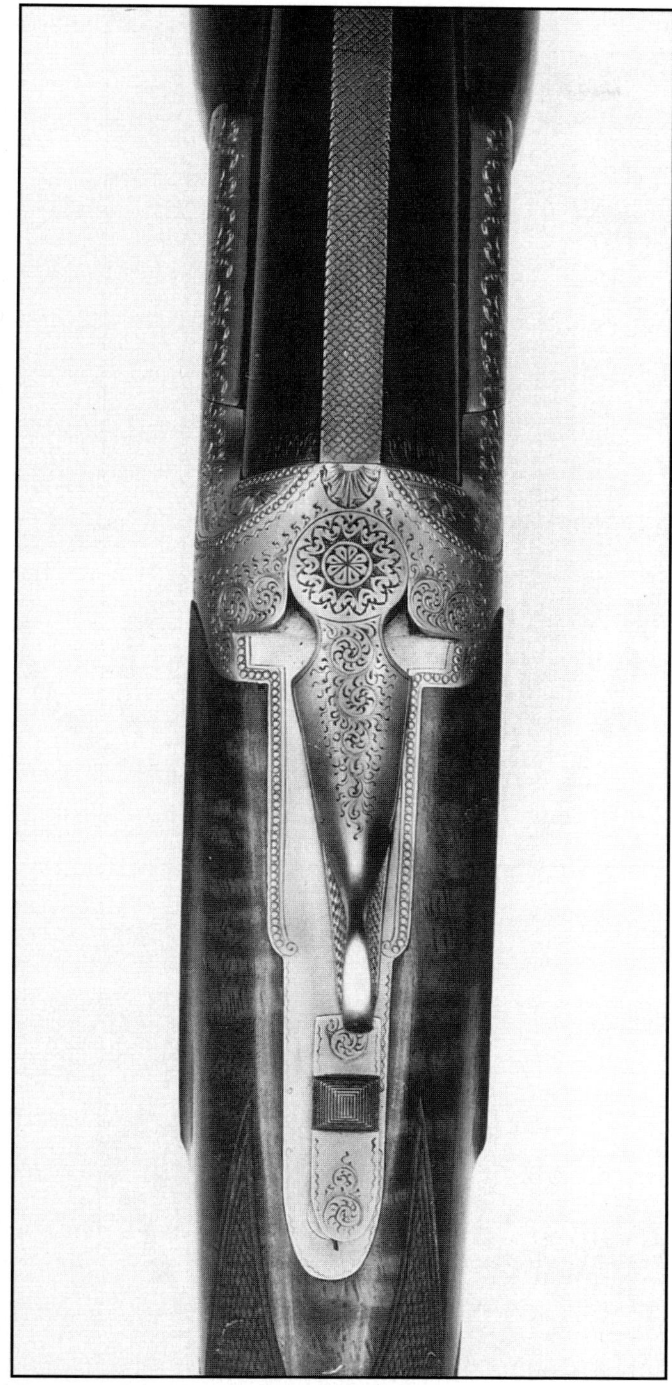

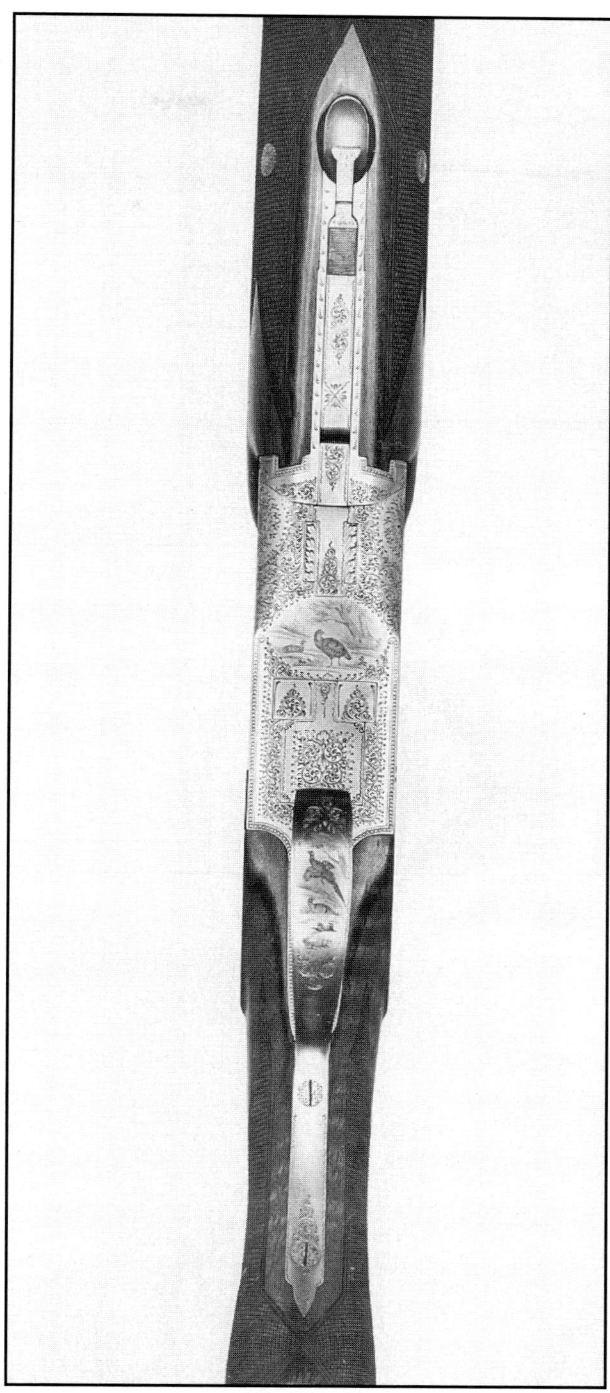

The top and bottom view of Vrancken's Pointer Grade. Again, the principal difference is found in the scrollwork coverage and layout. Courtesy Fabrique Nationale Archives.

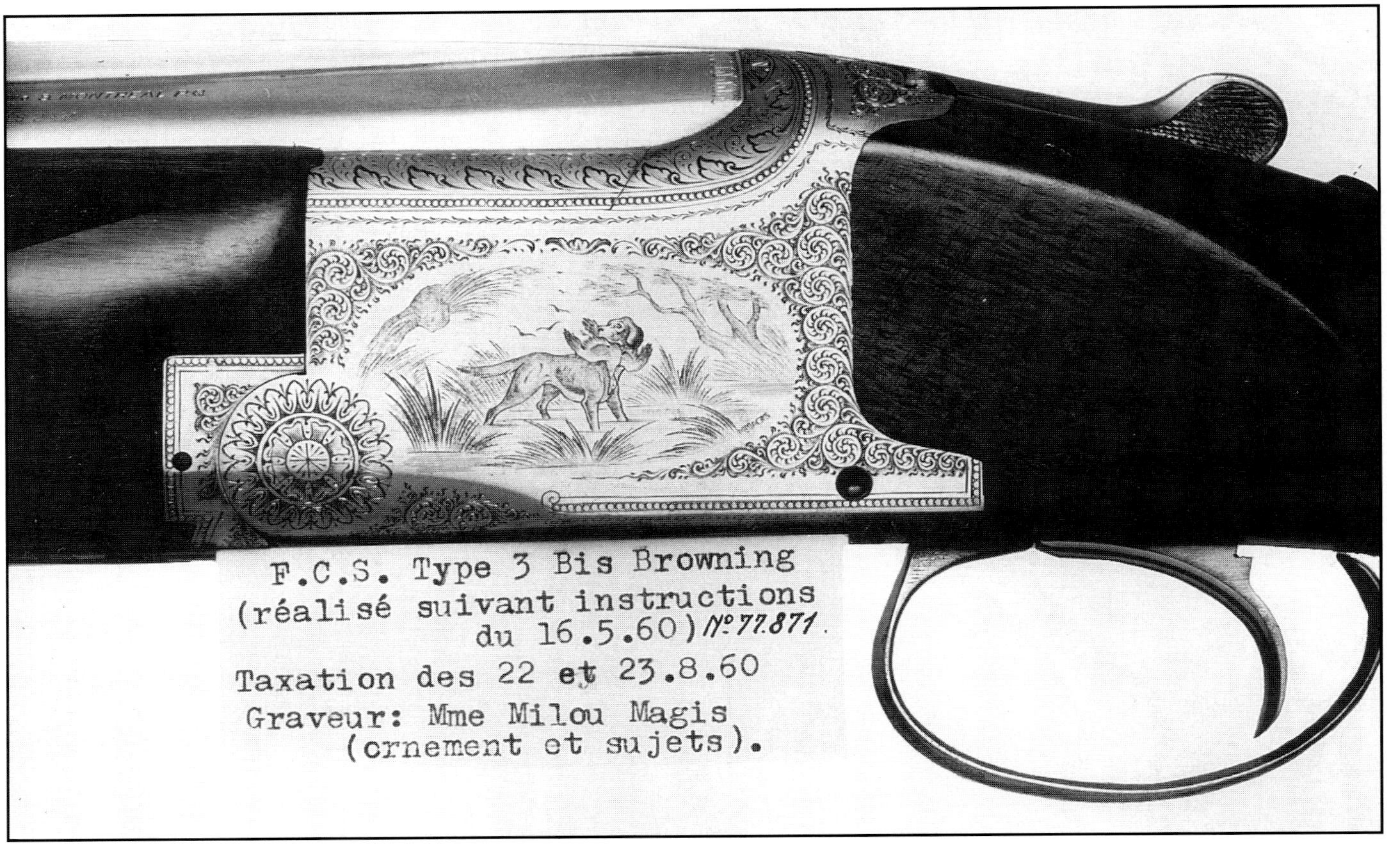

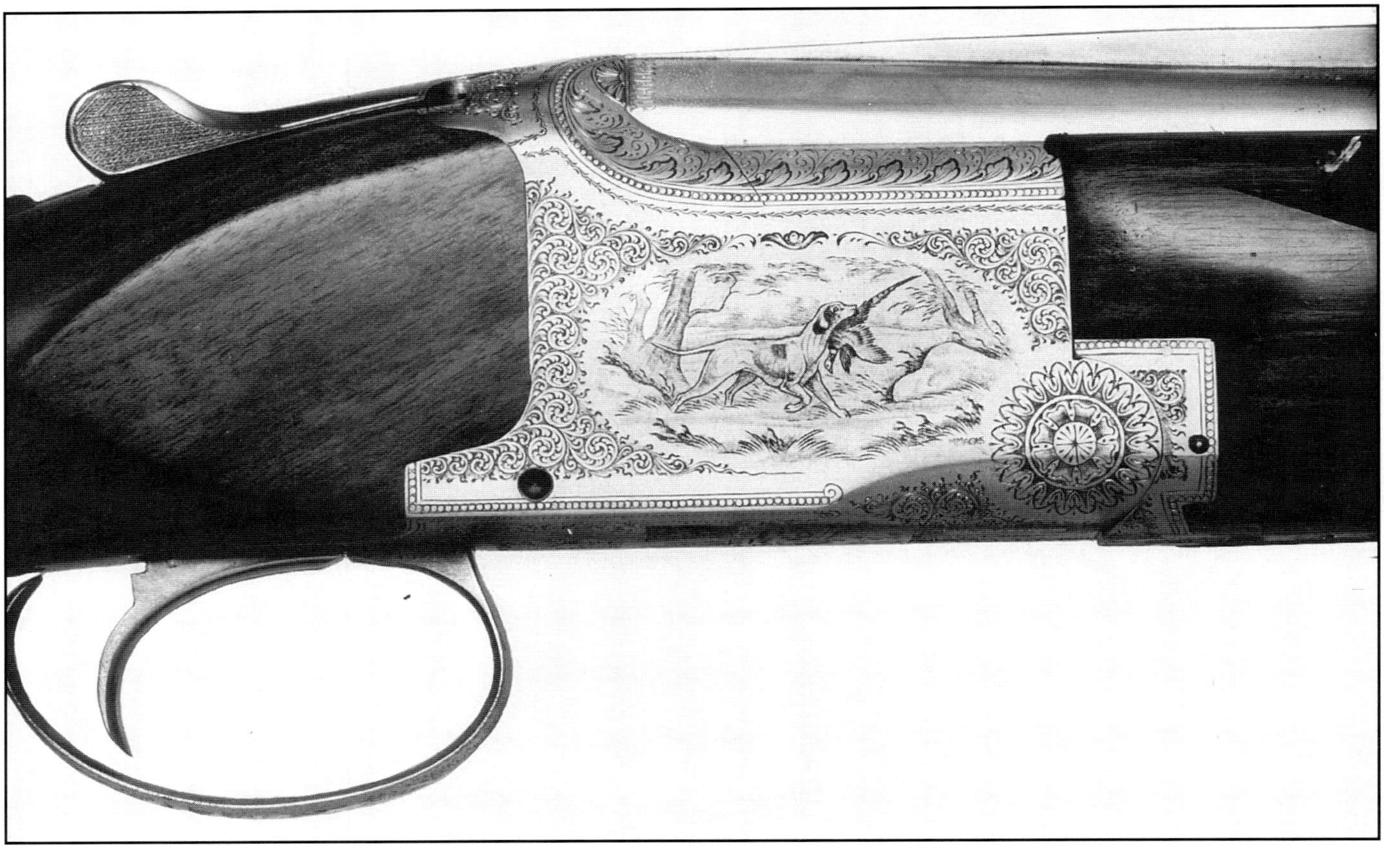

On May 16, 1960, John Val Browning again sent instructions for the new Pointer Grade. Browning Superposed serial number 77871 was engraved by Madam Milou Magis on August 22 and 23, 1960, to determine a time rating for this grade. Magis engraved both the scroll and the game scenes. Close examination will show strong similarities between the Magis gun and the Vrancken gun, with the exception of the scrollwork and borders. Courtesy Fabrique Nationale Archives.

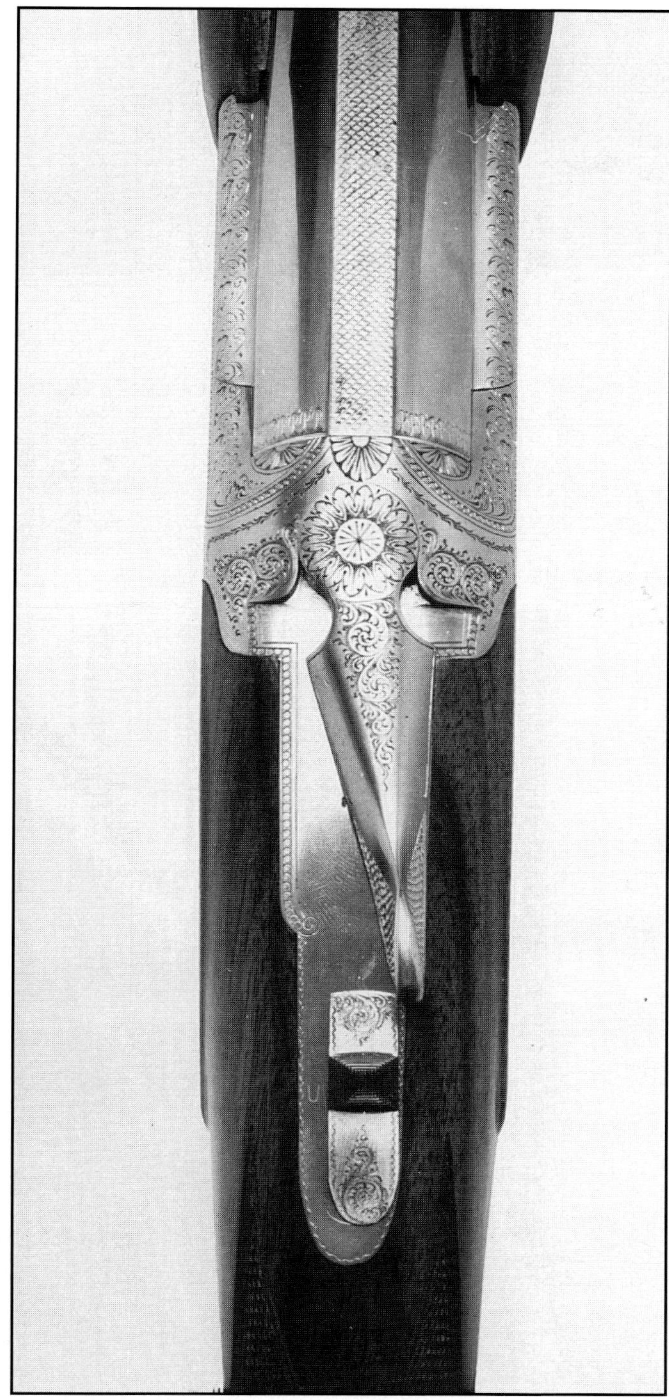

A top and bottom view of the Magis Superposed Pointer Grade. Scrollwork treatment and coverage are the main differences between this gun and the Vrancken gun. Note the interesting scrollwork treatment of the game vignette on the underside of the Magis Superposed. Courtesy Fabrique Nationale Archives.

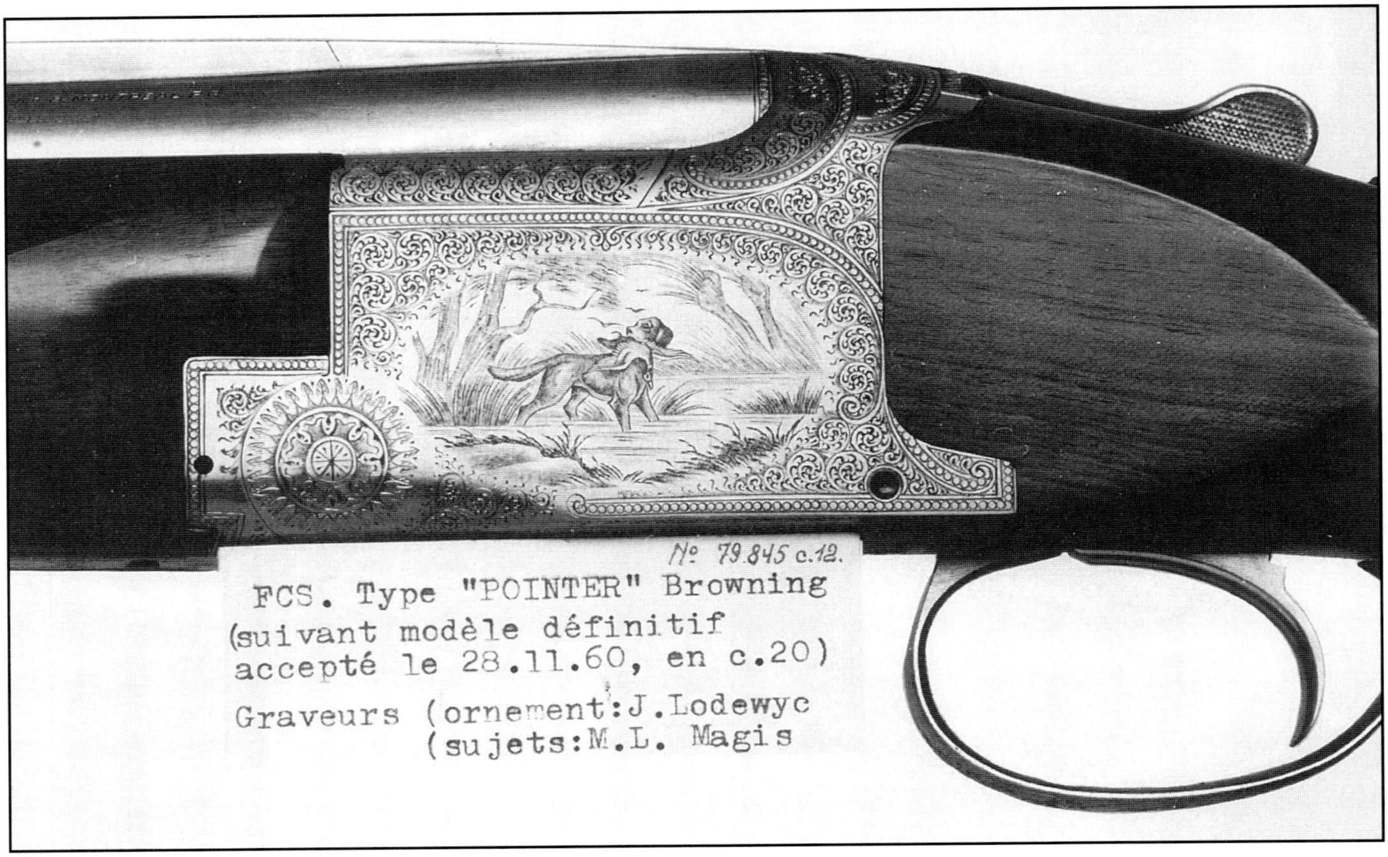

Nº 79.845 c.12.
FCS. Type "POINTER" Browning
(suivant modèle définitif
accepté le 28.11.60, en c.20)
Graveurs (ornement:J.Lodewyc
(sujets:M.L. Magis

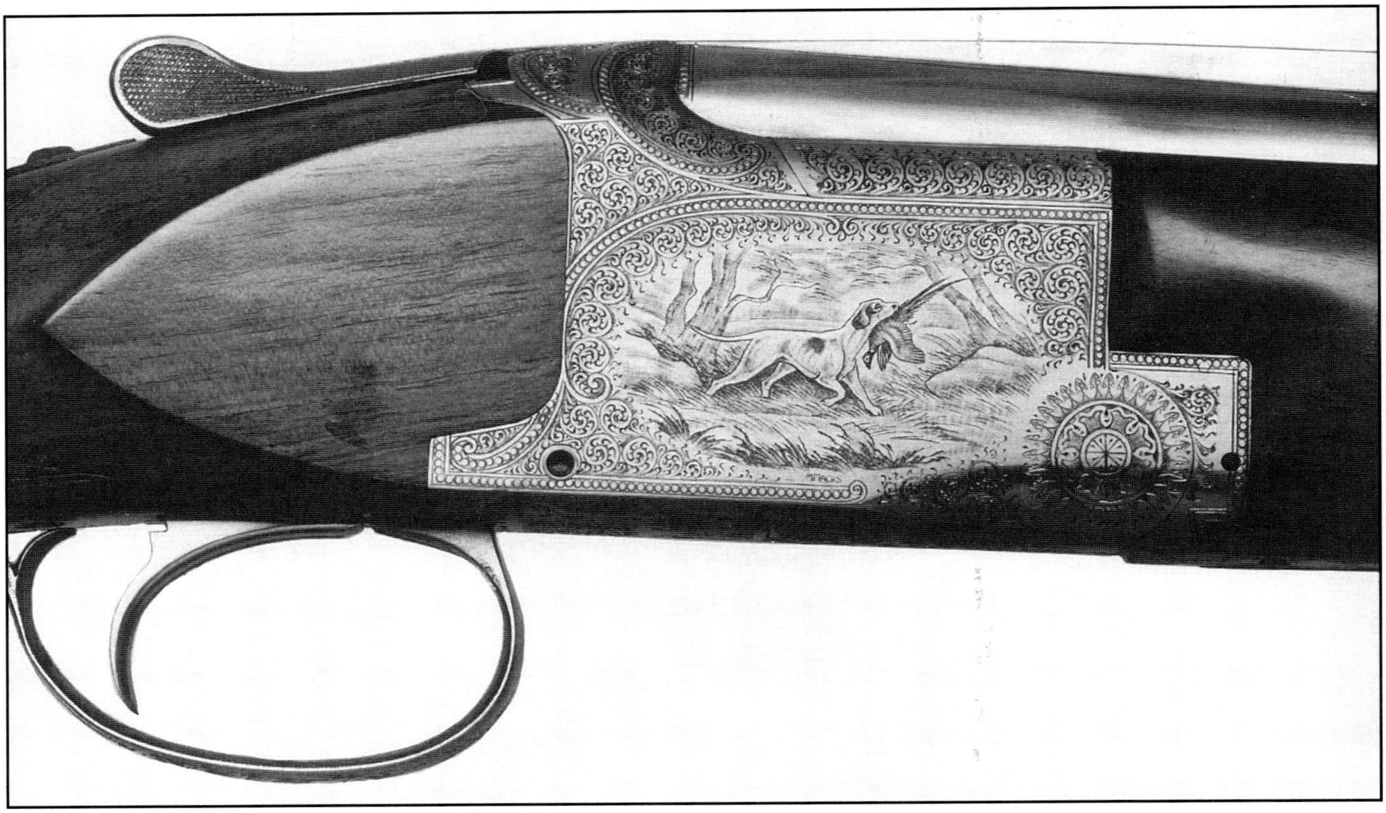

The final version of the Pointer Grade was accepted on November 28, 1960, for the 20 gauge. This photo shows a 12 gauge, serial number 79845, with game scene engraved by Milou Magis and scrollwork executed by Jacquez Lodewyc. Notice that the game scenes are very similar to an earlier version of this grade, but the scrollwork and borders are much different. These areas show increased and tighter scroll coverage more closely incorporated into the vignette itself. This is an outstanding example of a master engraver's work. Courtesy Fabrique Nationale Archives.

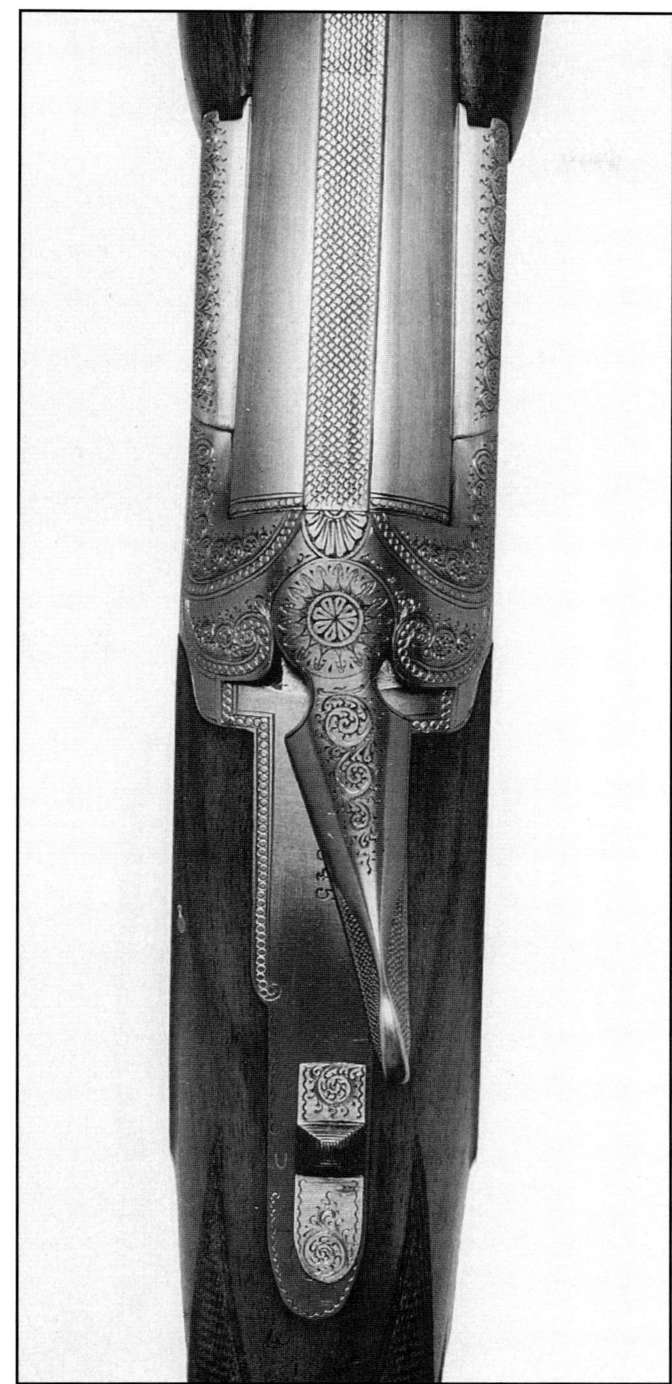

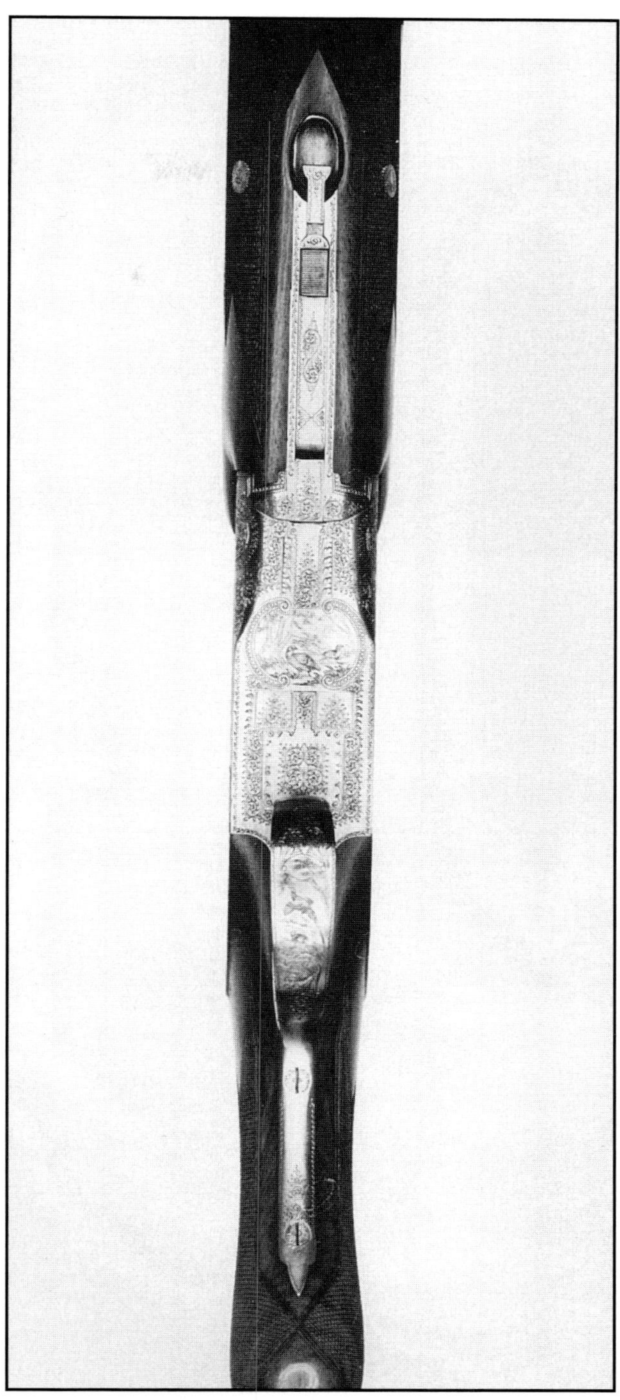

The top and bottom view of the final version of the Browning Pointer Grade. Notice the border surrounding the game vignette on the bottom. Courtesy Fabrique Nationale Archives.

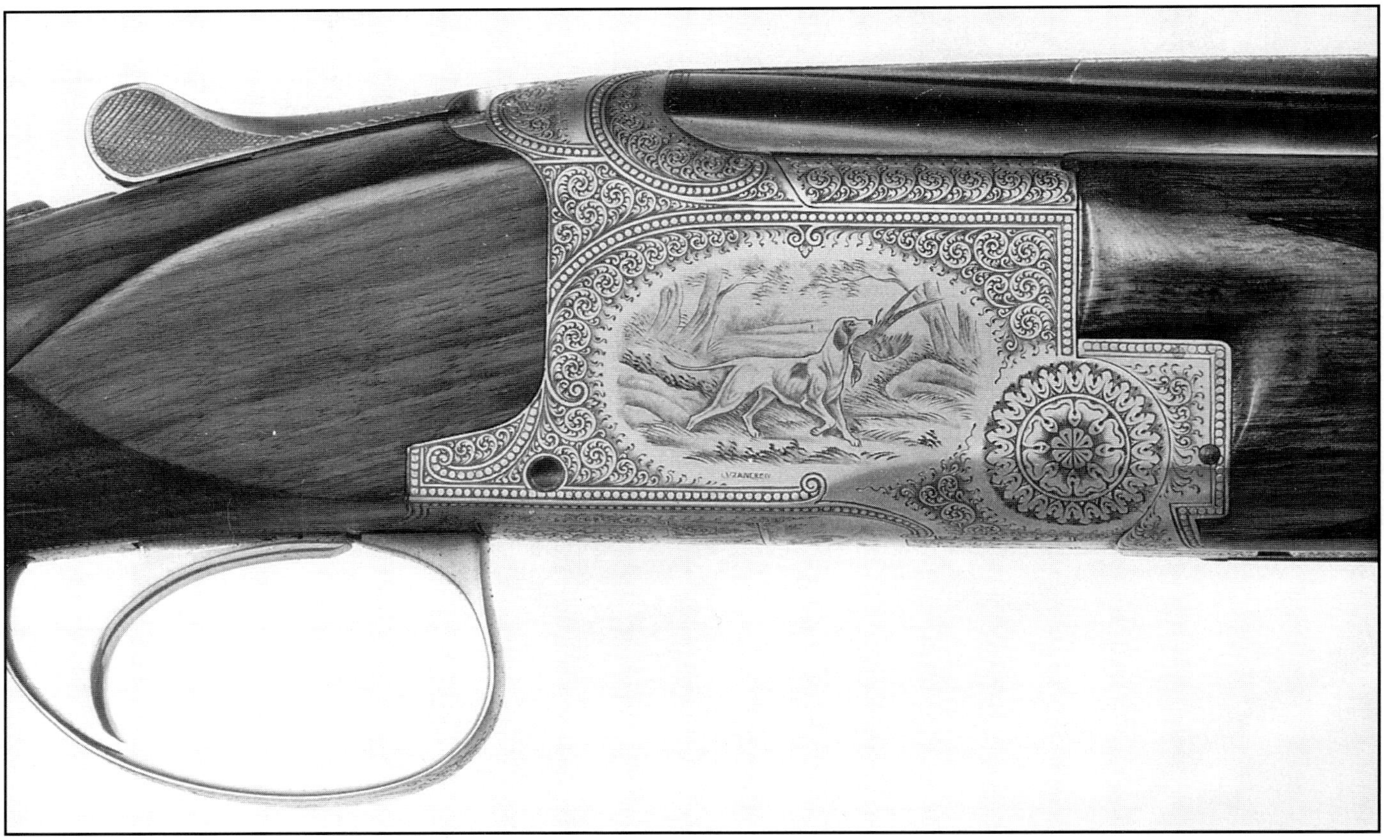

An example of master engraver Louis Vrancken's design and execution of this 1960 Pointer Grade. While Vrancken follows the standard pattern for this grade, his anatomically correct animals and birds coupled with his subtle use of shading and background detail make this Pointer Grade come to life. Courtesy Fabrique Nationale Archives.

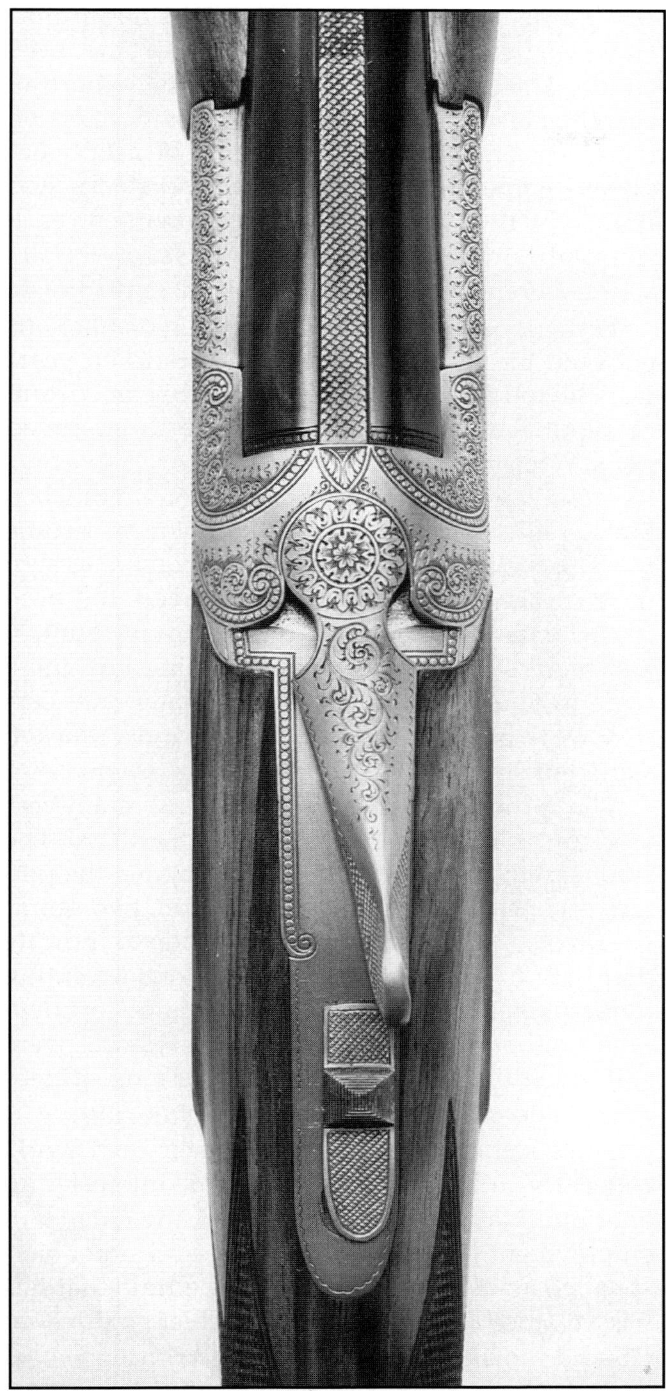

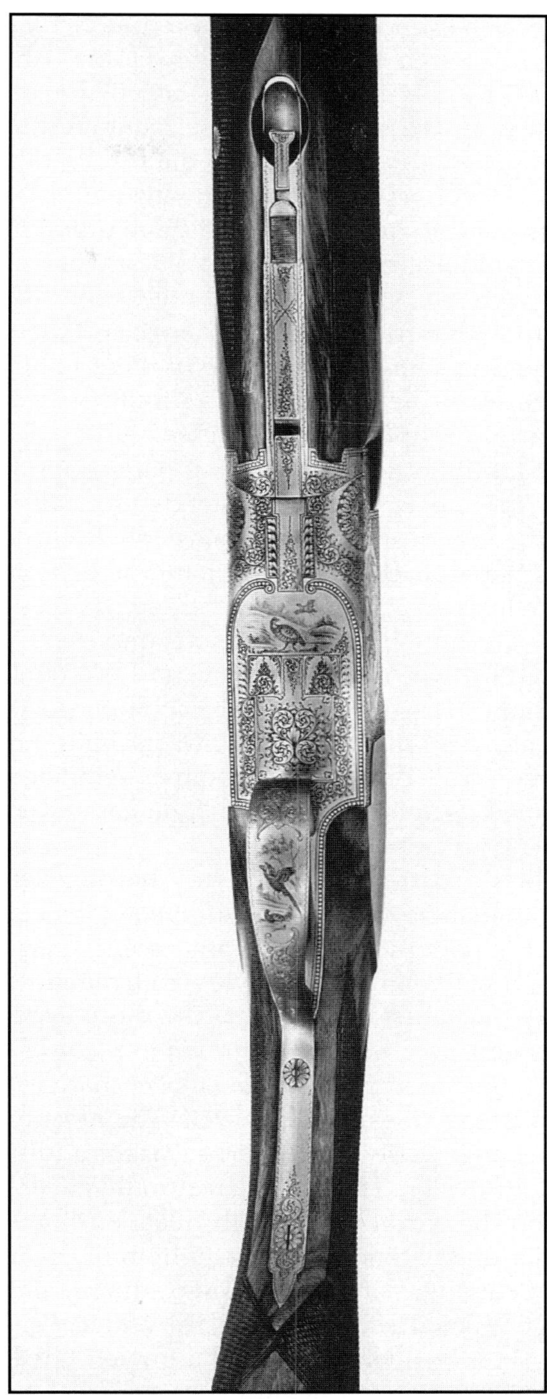

The top view of Louis Vrancken's outstanding Pointer Grade shows little that is unusual, but the bottom view reveals Vrancken's own interpretation of the game scene, scrollwork, and border treatment. Courtesy Fabrique Nationale Archives.

Special order and uniquely engraved Superposed, referred to as Exhibition Grades and inspired by Louis Vrancken, began to appear midway in the decade.[16] These Exhibition Grade Superposed guns represented the finest efforts of FN master engravers. The engraving patterns were unique and frequently utilized three different colors of gold. Fabrique Nationale's best wood craftsmen were encouraged to add their expertise and did so with intricate wood carvings and the finest checkering. Only about fifteen of these Exhibition Grades were built each year—a tribute to the talent of Europe's superlative craftsmen.

In addition to the engraving pattern modifications for Superposed guns intended for sale in the North American market, revisions occurred in FN's Superposed engraving patterns exported to its exclusive markets. Most of these changes were minor, although there were two important additions. The two A grades, the A1 and A2, remained the same. These were FN's basic Superposed engraving patterns. The B1, with its light English flower scroll on a grayed frame, remained unchanged, as did the B2 with its light game scene engraving on a grayed frame.

The C1 pattern, with its case hardened frame and English flower scroll, continued in the FN line. The C2 pattern, with its game scene engraving framed with fine English style scroll, remained virtually unchanged except that the more expensive recessed frame was discontinued in favor of a less costly flat-sided frame. The subject matter of the game scene was altered as well. The most noticeable change in the "C" patterns was the addition of the C2G design. This pattern featured light engraving on the barrel wings with fillets outlined by a border on the fences and the bottom of the frame. Deep cut engraving of pheasants, ducks, and partridge was framed by heavy scroll and leaf engraving. The flat-sided frame had a grayed finish and the selected French walnut buttstock was carved with dopper or teardrop points. The C3 design remained the same except that the recessed frame was abandoned for the less expensive flat-sided frame.

Fabrique Nationale's Browning Superposed "D" patterns also remained unchanged apart from the alteration of the recessed frame, used on all "D" frames prior to 1960, to the flat-sided frame. However, there was the addition of the D4G Grade. This grade featured a very fine pattern of acanthus leaves on the barrel wings with fillets on the fences and bottom of the frame. A deeply engraved game scene of pheasants and ducks was framed by heavy scroll and leaf engraving on each side of the grayed frame. The wood was a specially selected French walnut with a natural matte finish.

Perhaps one of the most interesting distinctions between the Funken era and the Vrancken years was the modification of the old European custom of signing only the master's name to engraved guns. While this practice was not an exclusive one, it certainly was the most common. Louis Vrancken took a more modern approach, and it now became more prevalent for experienced engravers to sign their names to guns they had engraved. But both Vrancken and Watrin had trained under Funken and were strongly influenced by him, and there were instances where, after performing only cursory work on a Superposed, Watrin and Vrancken signed or stamped their names on the frame.

The procedure of having several engravers work on a single Superposed was still utilized. The lead or senior engraver frequently signed the pattern on one or both sides. On occasion, two senior engravers signed a frame on each side to indicate that both had worked on that gun, one executing the scrollwork, the other the game scenes. Journeyman engravers, those of lesser experience, were still given the task of engraving the tang, trigger guard, and other less critical areas of the gun.

Since some engravers signed their own work, collectors and shooters have become interested in Fabrique Nationale engravers and their dates of employment, level of experience, and other personal characteristics. Because of the time that has passed since Funken became the chief engraver at FN and the loss of records suffered during World War II, most of the early information is missing. FN employment records are not available, so only a general list has been compiled of engravers who have worked on Superposed guns since the beginning of production in 1930. Our best and most accurate information covers those individuals who are still alive or who were known personally by surviving engravers or FN employees.

---

[16] The term Exhibition Grade was sometimes used interchangeably with the term Exposition Grade. During the decade before World War II, Felix Funken engraved special Superposed and Auto-5 shotguns for specific regional expositions. These guns were sometimes referred to as Exposition Grades. This term remained in use compatible with Exhibition Grade for some time after the end of the war. In reality, FN used the two terms together without reference to a specific event. All of these special order grades were referred to as Exhibition Grades during the 1960s in Browning's catalogues.

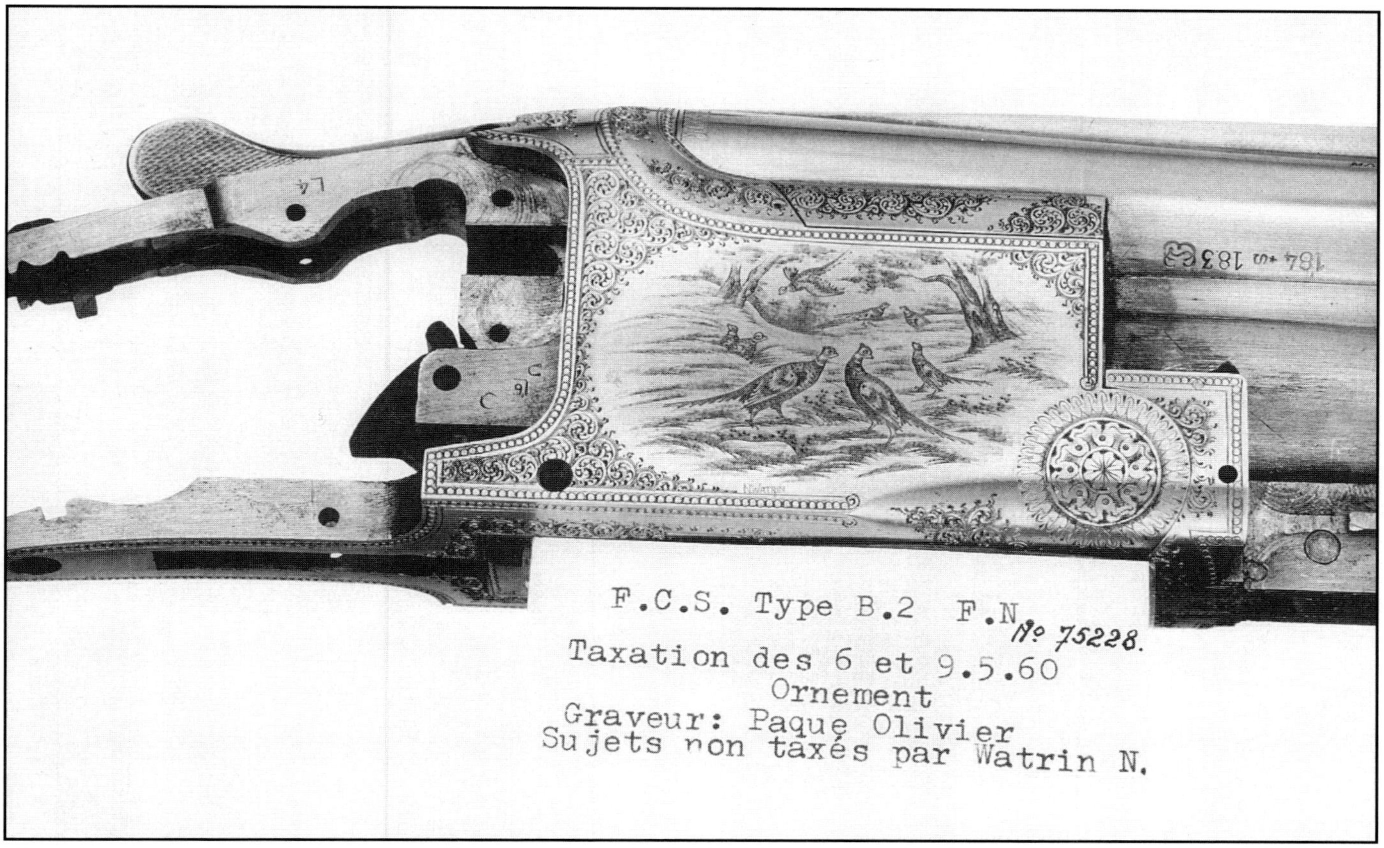

F.C.S. Type B.2 F.N. Nº 75228.
Taxation des 6 et 9.5.60
Ornement
Graveur: Paque Olivier
Sujets non taxés par Watrin N.

This 12 gauge Superposed executed in the FN B2 style, serial number 75228, was engraved on May 5 and 6, 1960. The scrollwork was performed by Olivier Paque and the game scenes were executed by Nelly Watrin without a working time recorded. This was a very popular grade for FN's worldwide Superposed sales. Notice the absence of the sculptured frame. This feature was discontinued from some of the regular production FN high grade guns during the 1960s. Courtesy Fabrique Nationale Archives.

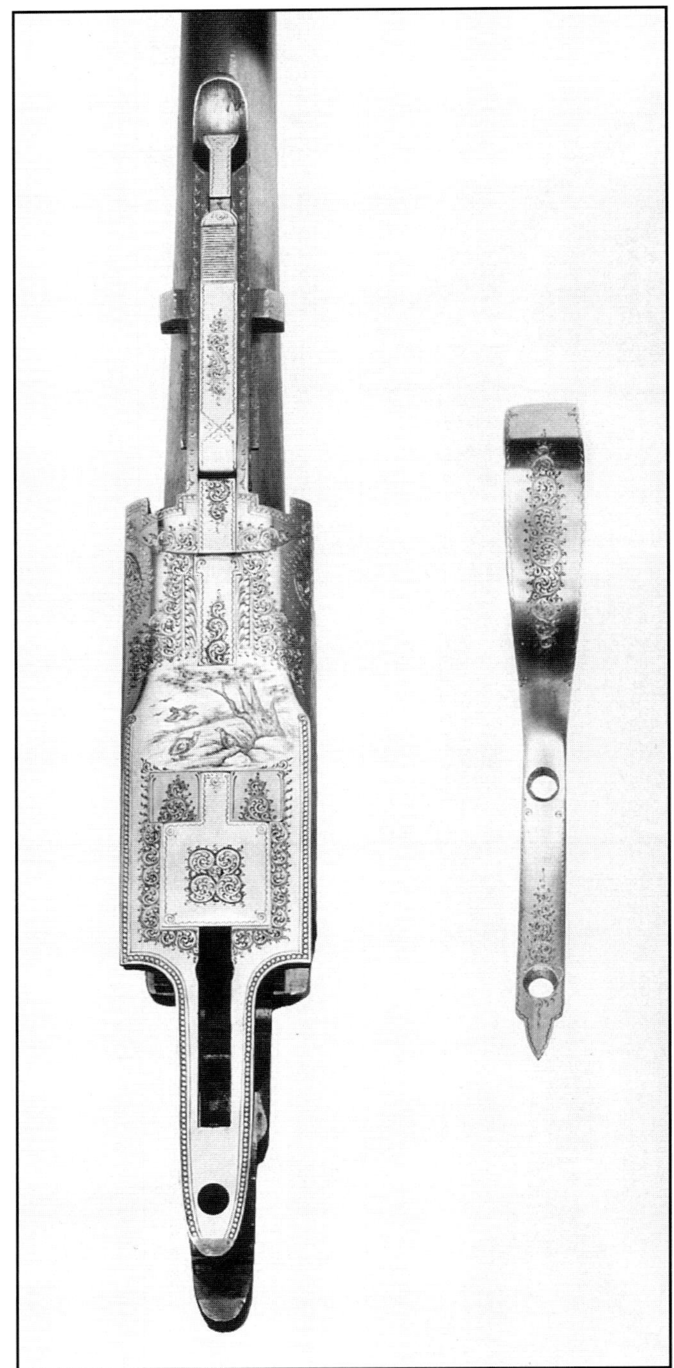

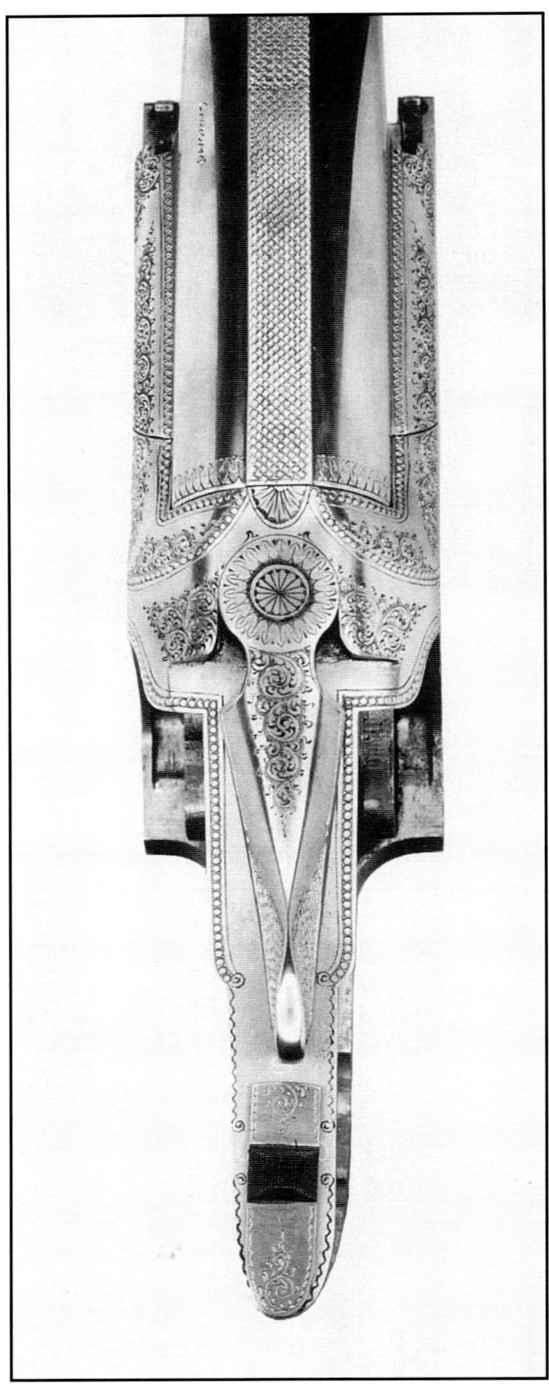

A top and bottom view of the FN B2 Grade. The scrollwork is very well-done, as is the game scene on the bottom of the receiver. Both scroll and vignette seem to complement each other, which is the mark of a well-executed composition. Courtesy Fabrique Nationale Archives.

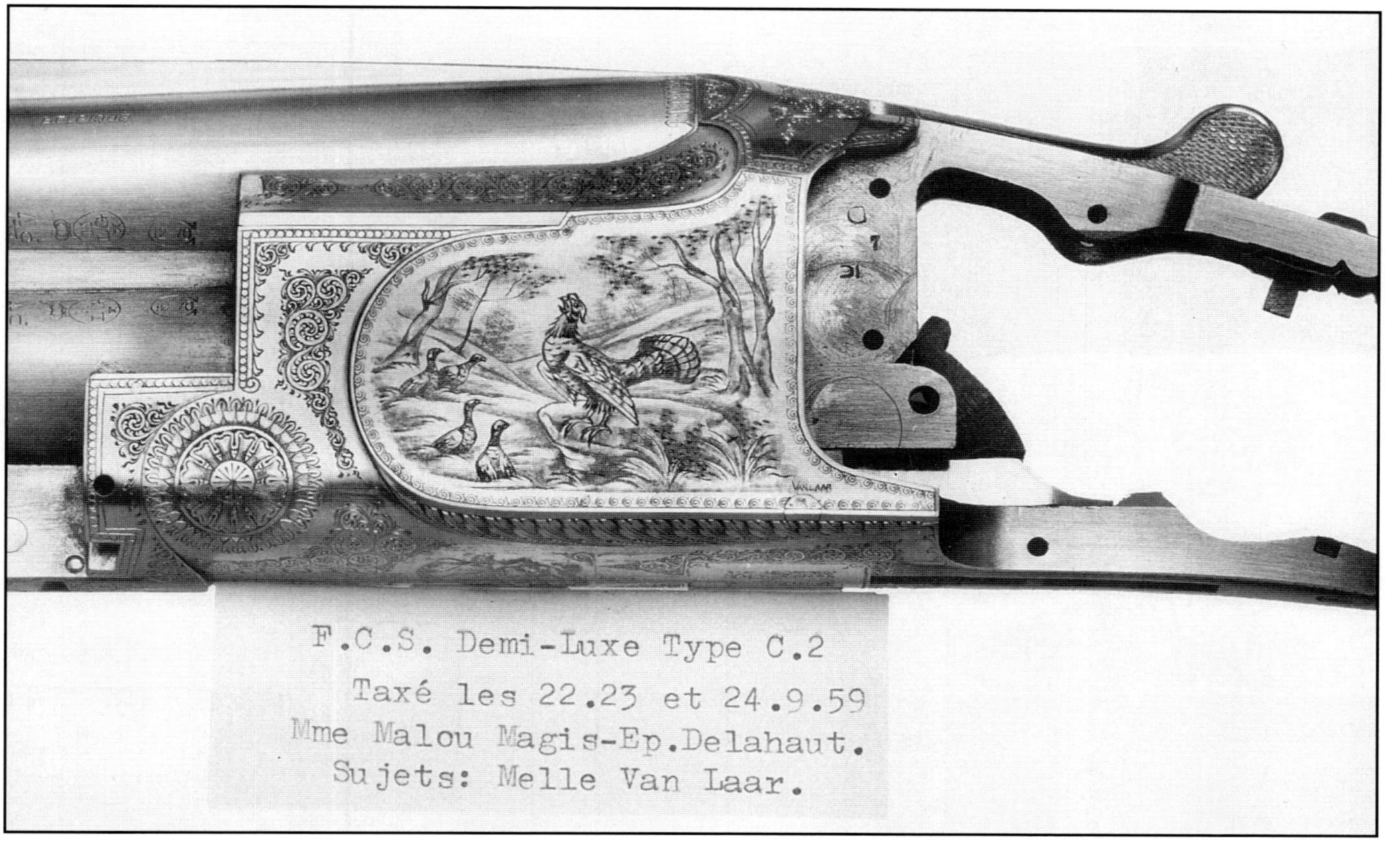

F.C.S. Demi-Luxe Type C.2
Taxé les 22.23 et 24.9.59
Mme Malou Magis-Ep.Delahaut.
Sujets: Melle Van Laar.

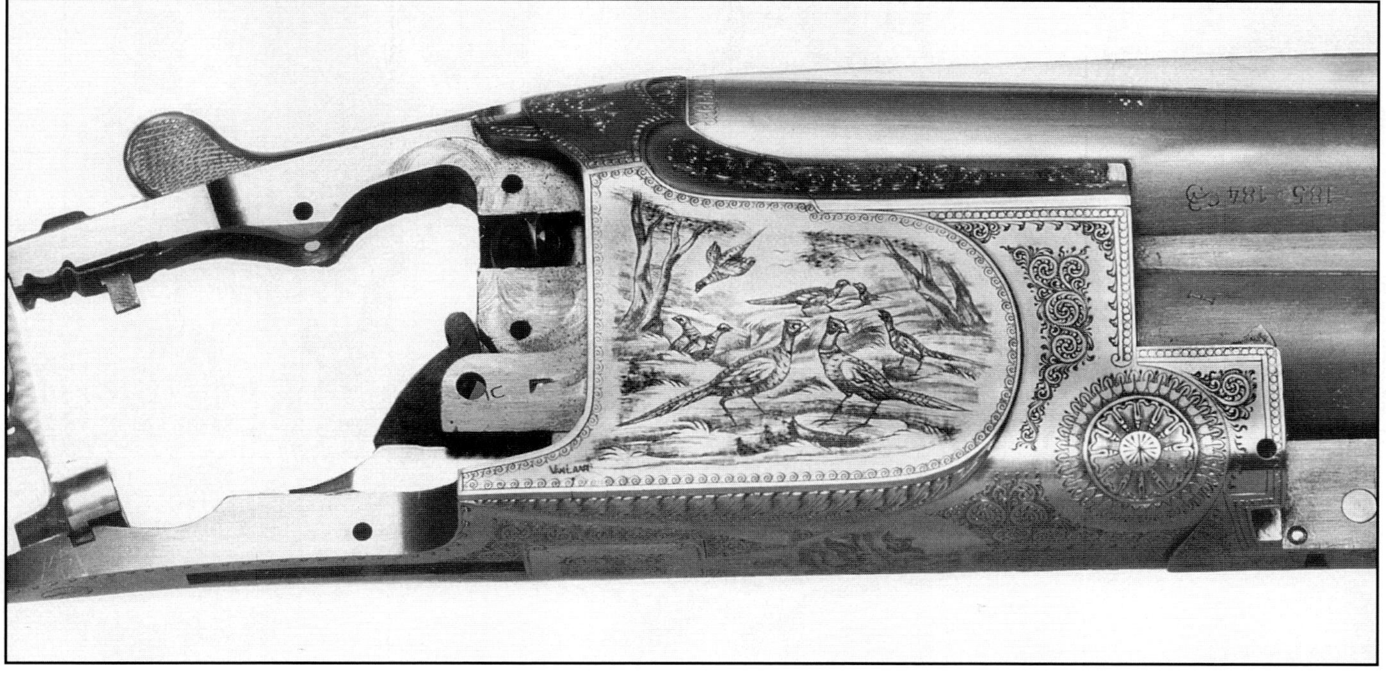

This 12 gauge FN Superposed, serial number 65740, is engraved in the C2 pattern. It was completed over a period of three days from September 22 to September 24, 1959. This work was performed in order to establish a mean engraving time rate for this grade. What is interesting about this particular Superposed is that the work was done by two master engravers, Marie Louise Magis, whose married name was Delahaut; and Lea Van Laar, chief of female engravers at FN. Notice who signed both sides of the receiver. Van Laar was the senior engraver, even though Magis was a master. Courtesy Fabrique Nationale Archives.

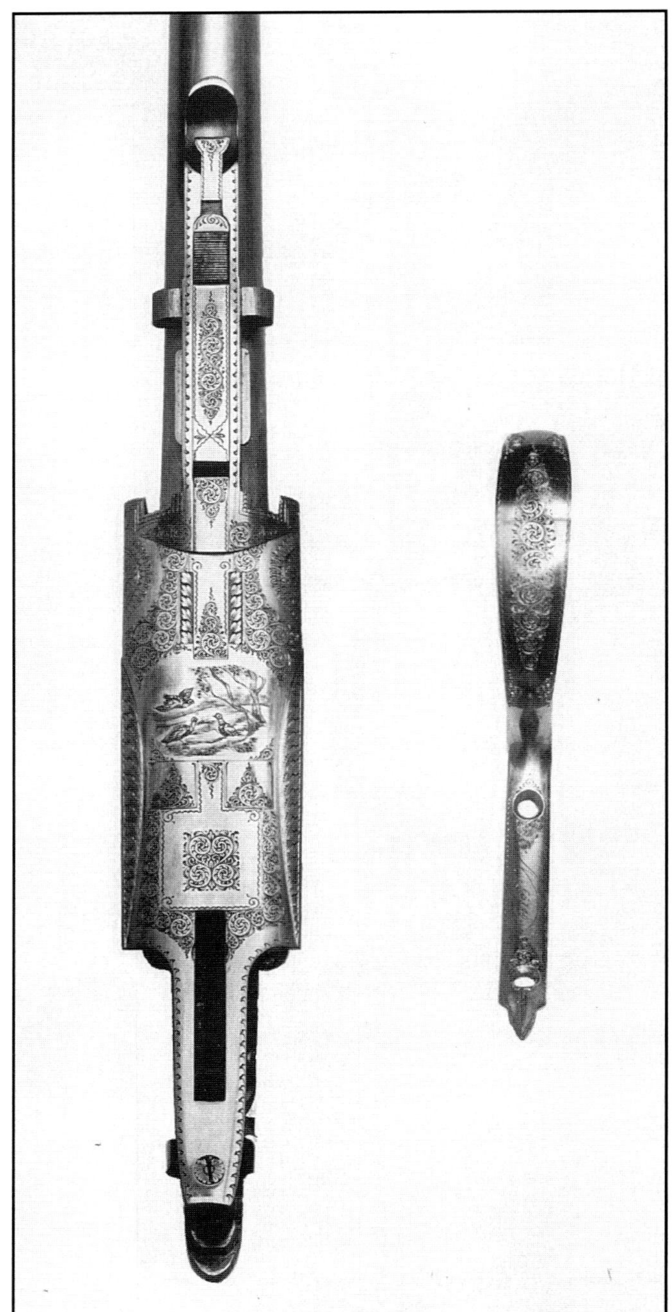

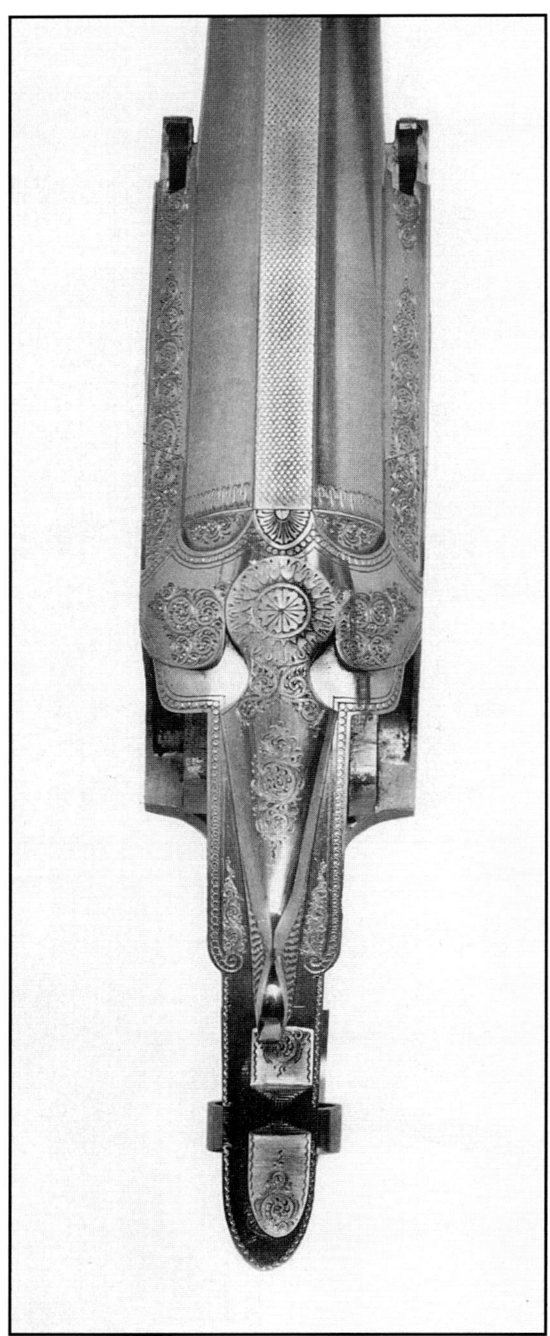

The top and bottom views of the Magis/Van Laar C2 Superposed. The scroll was tastefully executed with proper geometric flow. The vignette on the bottom of the receiver is nicely incorporated into the scrollwork. This is a real jewel of a Superposed executed by two outstanding FN engravers. Courtesy Fabrique Nationale Archives.

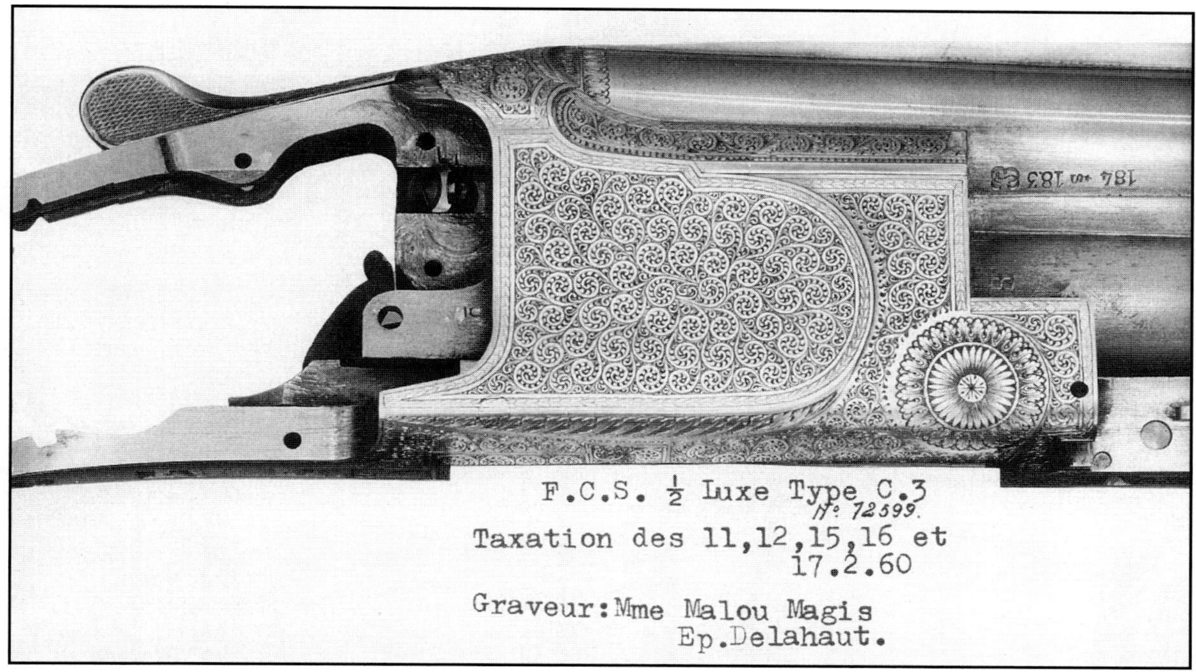

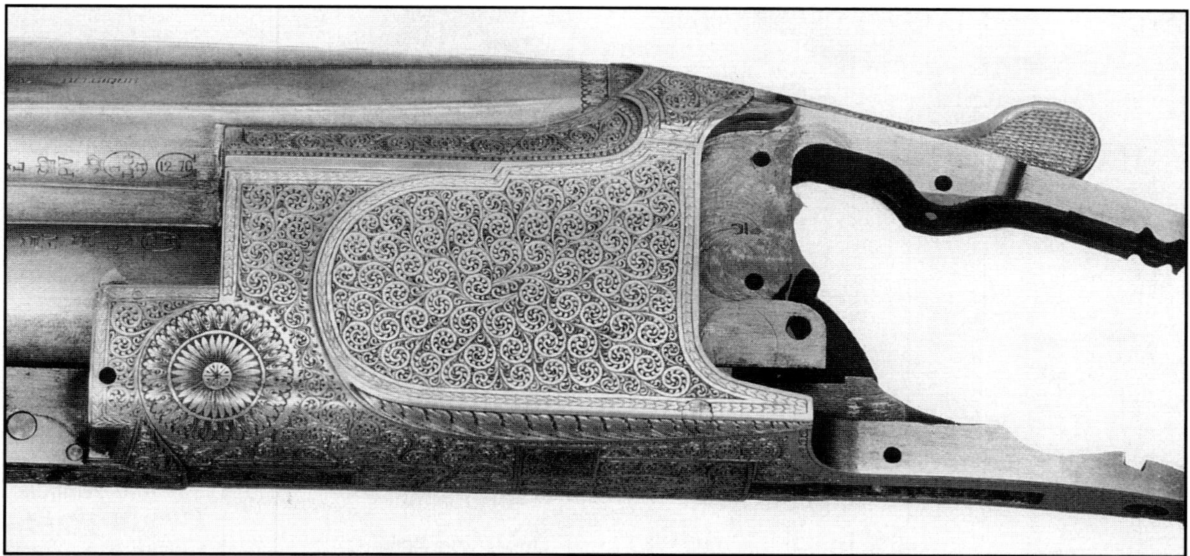

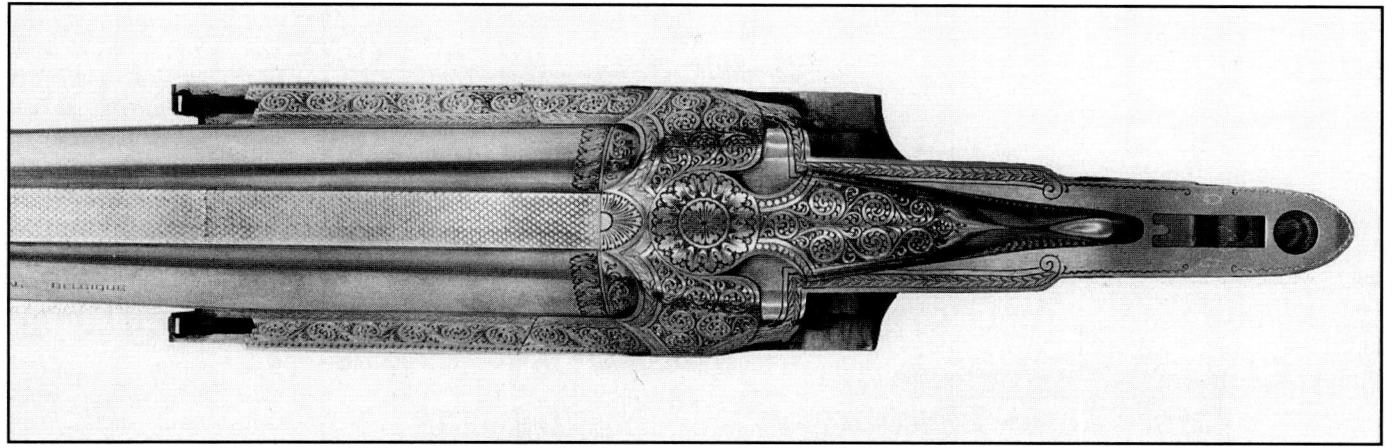

Master engraver Marie Louise Magis executed this impressive FN C3 Grade on this 12 gauge Superposed, serial number 72599. This pattern is even more impressive with the knowledge that the scrollwork was done freehand. This is truly a masterpiece of concentration, perception, and artistry. Married female workers kept their maiden names while employed at FN. Marie Louise Magis was married to Mr. Delahaut, who was also an FN engraver. Courtesy Fabrique Nationale Archives

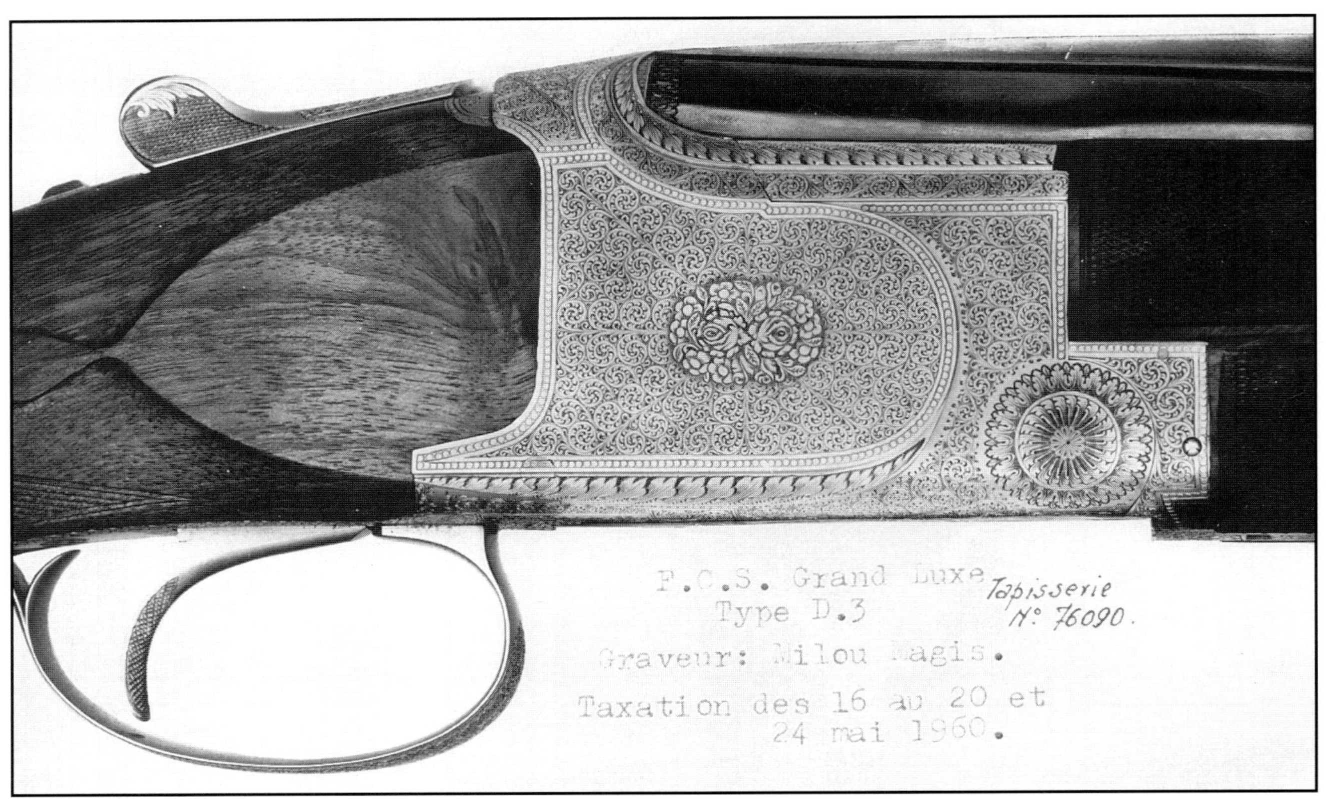

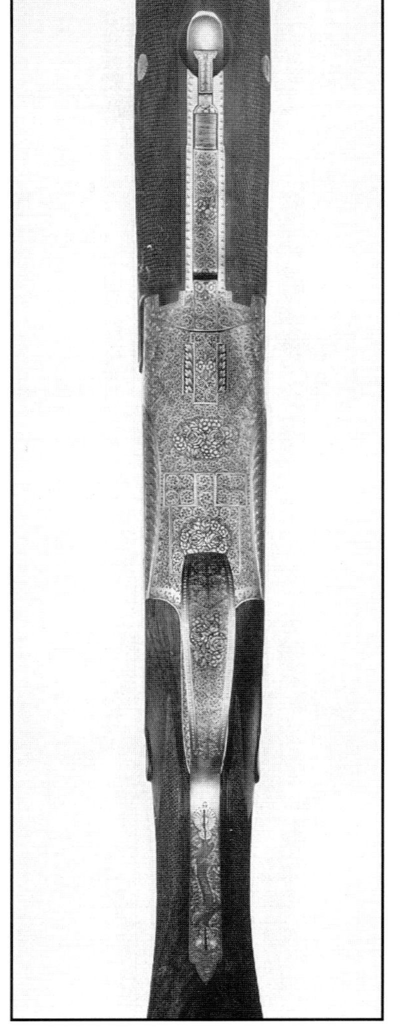

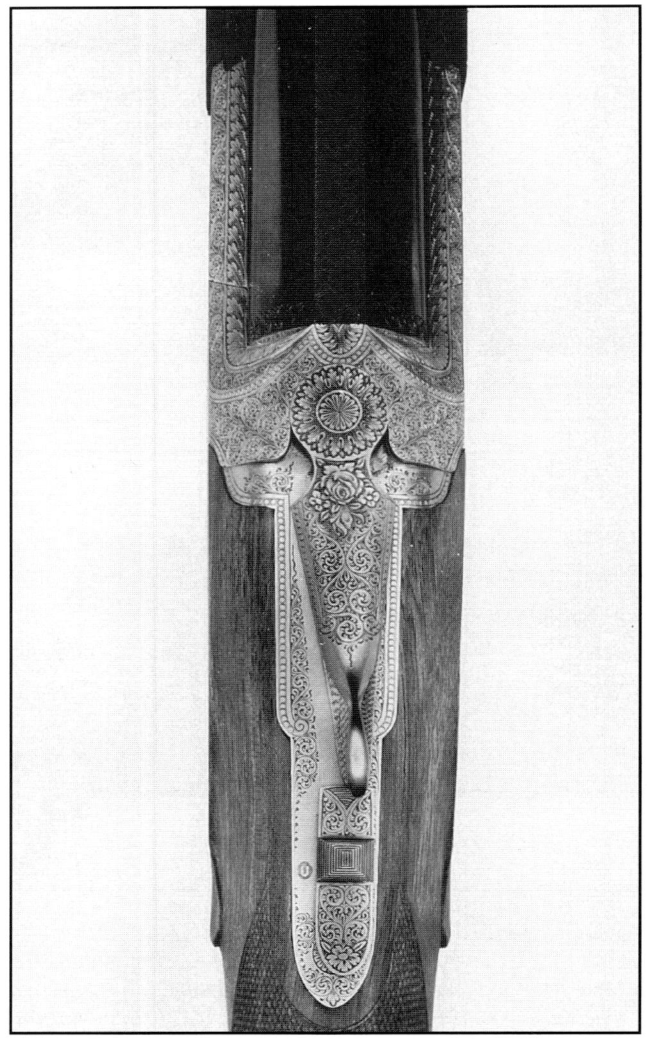

This FN Superposed D3 Grade, serial number 76090, was executed by master engraver Marie Louise Magis. She worked on this gun from the 16th to the 20th of May and also on the 24th of May, 1960. FN engravers were paid on a piecework basis and the custom of "taxation," or mean work time, to engrave a particular grade of Superposed was performed in order to establish how much time it would take to engrave a certain type pattern. Since this Superposed D3 Grade was one hundred percent scroll engraved it took quite a bit longer to execute than if the pattern was made up of game scenes and scroll. This was one of FN's highest production grades and featured a sculptured frame. Courtesy Fabrique Nationale Archives.

A PARTIAL LIST OF FN ENGRAVERS

Acampo, Louis
Baerten, Claude – *active*
Baerten, José – 1955 to 1987 – *master engraver*
Bailley, Jean Pierre
Baptiste, Raymond
Bleus, Louie
Bodson, Mario
Bee, Angelo – 1951 to 1975 – *active in USA*
Bee, Rosa – 1955 to 1980 – *active in USA*
Bertrand, Charles
Blanvelet, Henri
Boulanger, Jean Marie
Calabrese, Maria
Capece, Lucien
Cargnel, Gino – 1951 to 1977 – *active in USA*
Cockran, G
Coenen, Rene – 1948 to 1980
Corombelle, Lyson – *(outside contract) – deceased* 1972
Cortis, Lilly
Crousse, André
Debrus, Jean Marie
Delahaut, E.
Delcour, Rene – 1946 to 1963 – *engraving teacher* 1963 to 1992
Delcour, Louis
Denard, Georges
Deprez, Henri
DeWil, Rene – 1950 to 1980
Dewaer, Georges
Diet, Jean – 1959 to 1992 – *master engraver – active in Liège*
Dierckx, André – *master engraver*
Dorval, Sylvain – *one of the original FN engravers – deceased*
Doyen, Rene
DuBois, Raymond
Dujardin, J.
Dumond, Jules
Ernst, Lucien
Florent, Jean Marie – *self-employed* – 1970 to 1994
Funken, Felix – 1926 to 1960 – *master engraver – one of the original FN engravers – deceased* 1965
Gillet, A.
Gerard, Joseph – 1930 to 1965 – *one of the original FN engravers – deceased*

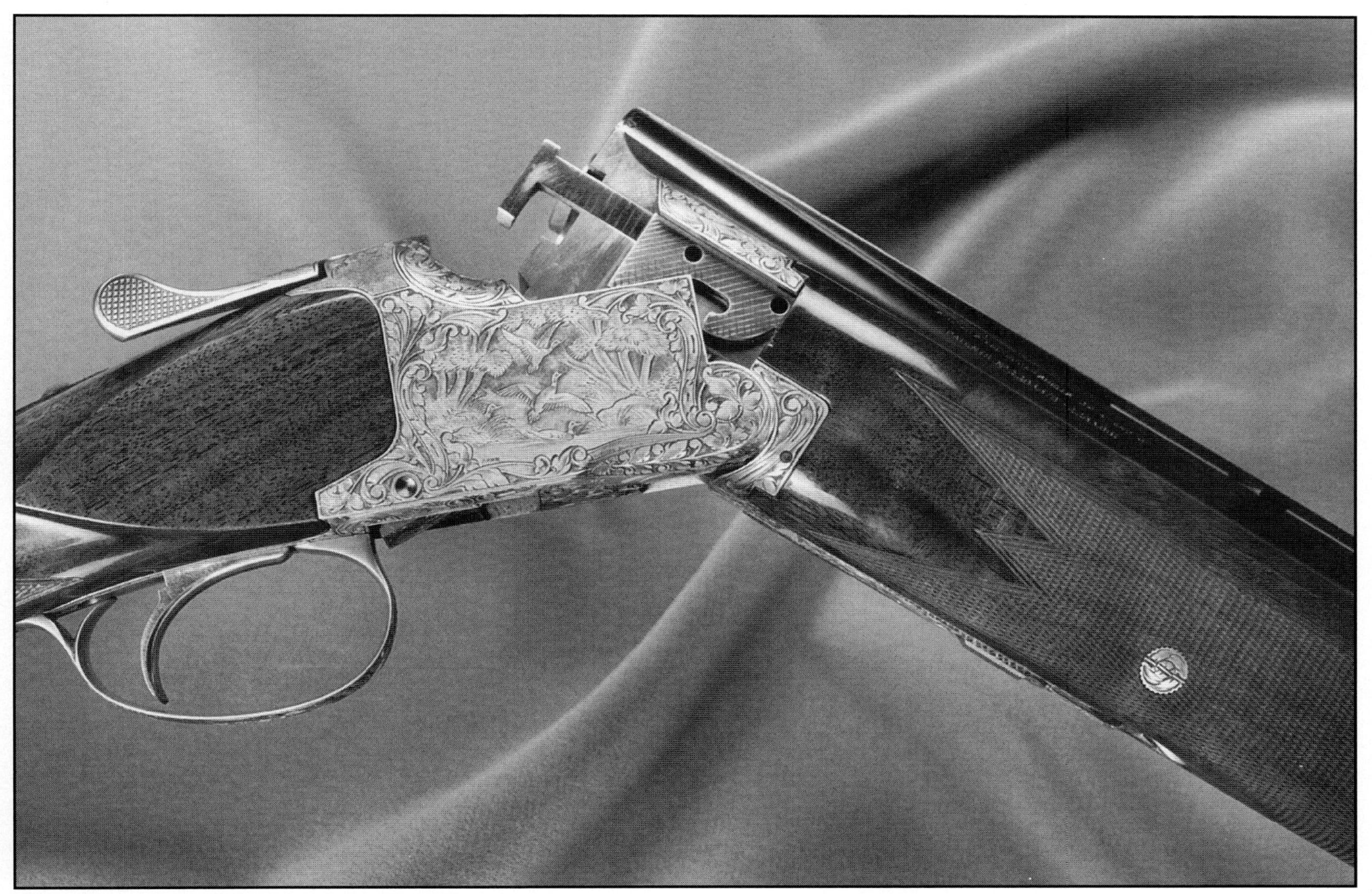

The Diana Grade was a very popular high grade Superposed and is much in demand by collectors and shooters today. This Browning Superposed was engraved by Angelo Bee. Courtesy Browning Company.

Geysen, Maurice
Goffard, Louis
Goffin, Jean
Greco, Reno – *active in Italy*
Greco, Nina
Greco, Cesario
Haugustaine, J.
Jansens, Willy
Kowalski, Richard
Kozlowski, George
Lallemand, Pierre
Legiers, Charles – 1969 to 1993 – *self-employed*
Lamaire, Jack
Lambert, Lilly – 1946 to 1980
Lewanczvk, Jules
Lodewyc, Jacquez
Loïse, Jean Marie
Magis, Marie Louise – 1946 to 1965 – *master engraver – deceased*
Maréchal, Alfonse – *deceased*
Maréchal, Florent – *deceased*
Maréchal, Francoise – *deceased*
Maréchal, Peter – *deceased*
Maréchal, Georges – 1960 to 1977
Mativa
Merringer, Jenny
Mouton, O.
Mouton, Roland
Müller – (*outside contract*)
Nicolai, Marcel
Olivier, Julien
Oukelinse, C. – (*outside contract*)
Paque, Olivier
Paussart, Jean
Perfido, Claudia
Pirotte, Jeannine
Pirotte, Lillian – 1955 to 1980
Pöes, Augusta – *active*
Purgal, Sophie
Recule, Jean
Richelle, Denise
Risak, Raymond
Scheen
Seeberg, Jean Marie
Seimen, Joseph
Severien, L.
Servais, Charles
Sexton, Dommique
Sollemond, Pierre
Vanderspiegel, J.
Vandersmissen, Gaston
Van Laar, Lea – *master engraver and chief of female engravers*
Vos, Edovard
Vossen, Pierre
Vrancken, Louis – 1946 to 1977 – *master engraver – deceased* 1983
Watrin, André – 1946 to 1985 – *retired – master engraver*
Watrin, Nelly – *wife of André Watrin*
Wilkinson, Jerry
Wilmot, Robert
Victor Inchusti – 1946 to 1980 – *engraver's toolmaker*

Although this list is not and perhaps never will be complete, it does in some cases give us some information about each engraver and when he or she may have worked for FN. It should be pointed out that it was the custom at Fabrique Nationale for married female engravers to register their last names as their maiden name for payroll purposes. For example, the married female engraver Marie Louise Magis was married to the FN engraver E. Delahaut; however, she signed her work with her maiden name, Magis. An important exception to this is that of Nelly Watrin, wife of André Watrin. She signed her name as N. Watrin. Some of the engravers on this list only worked at the factory for a short time, while others spent their entire careers engraving for FN.[17] Some engravers are considered by collectors to be superior to others. Superposed guns engraved by Vrancken, Watrin, Baerten, Funken, and others will bring a premium over lesser known engravers. However, beauty is indeed in the eye of the beholder, and all engraved Superposed are true works of art.

---

[17] This list of engravers is compiled from several sources, most of whom are retired FN engravers. Fabrique Nationale master engraver Jean Diet provided a comprehensive list based on his thirty-two years at FN. Other sources are Rene Delcour, Angelo Bee, Homer Tyler, and Claude Gaier.

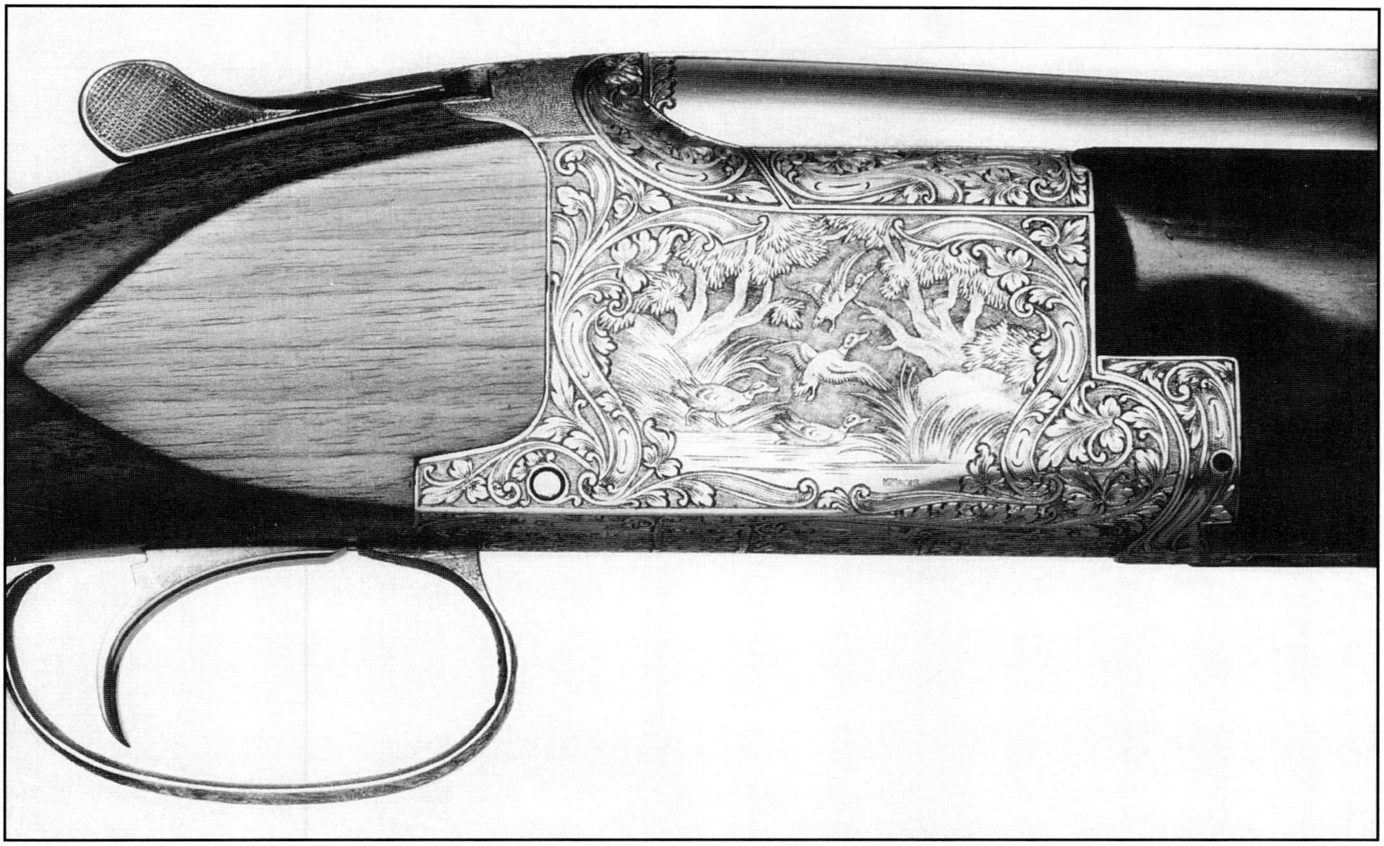

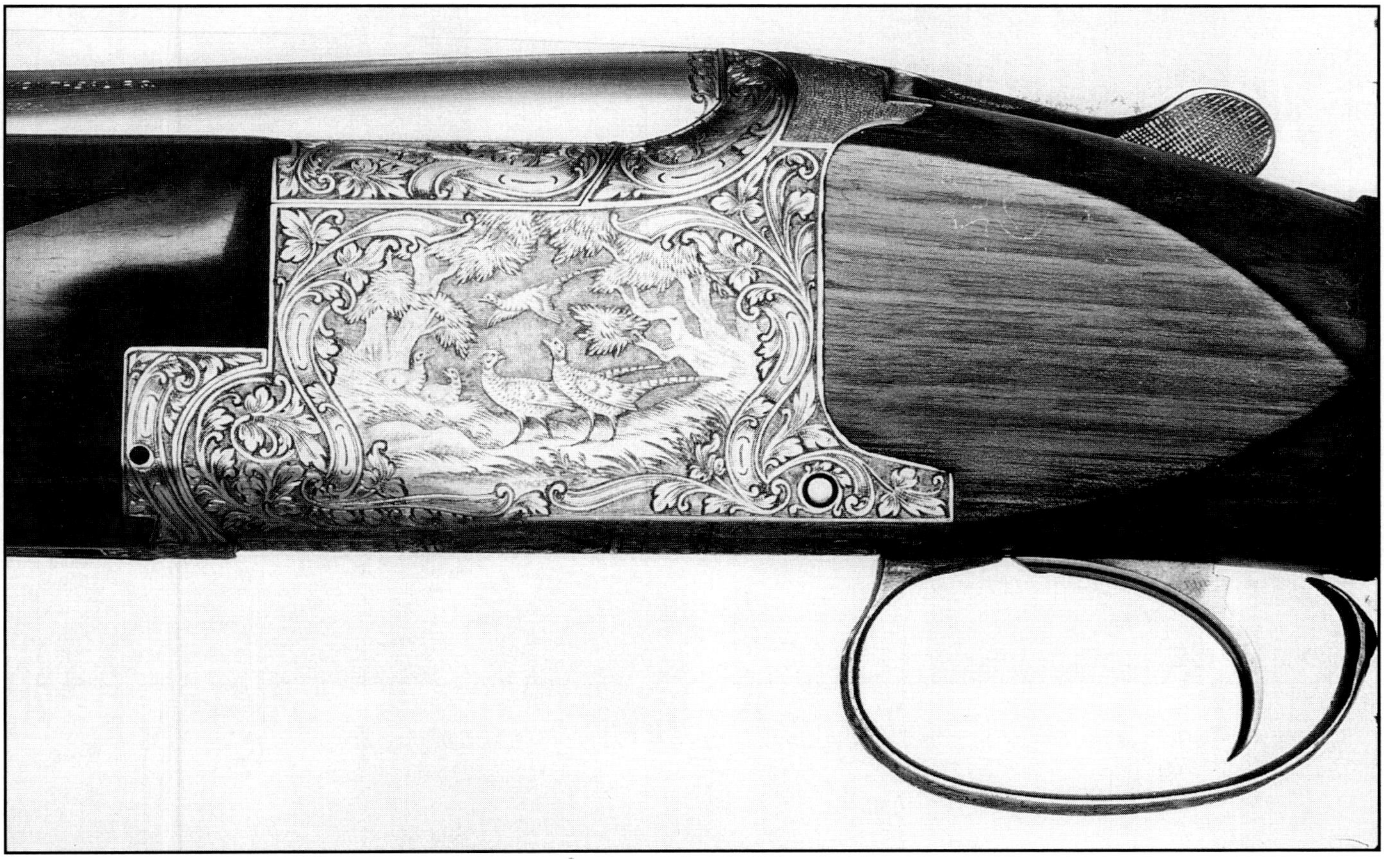

This early 1960s Superposed was engraved by master engraver Marie Louise Magis. This is the standard Diana Grade pattern, but many subtle variations will be seen in this grade depending on who engraved the gun and when. Only the most experienced engravers executed the Diana Grade. Courtesy Fabrique Nationale Archives.

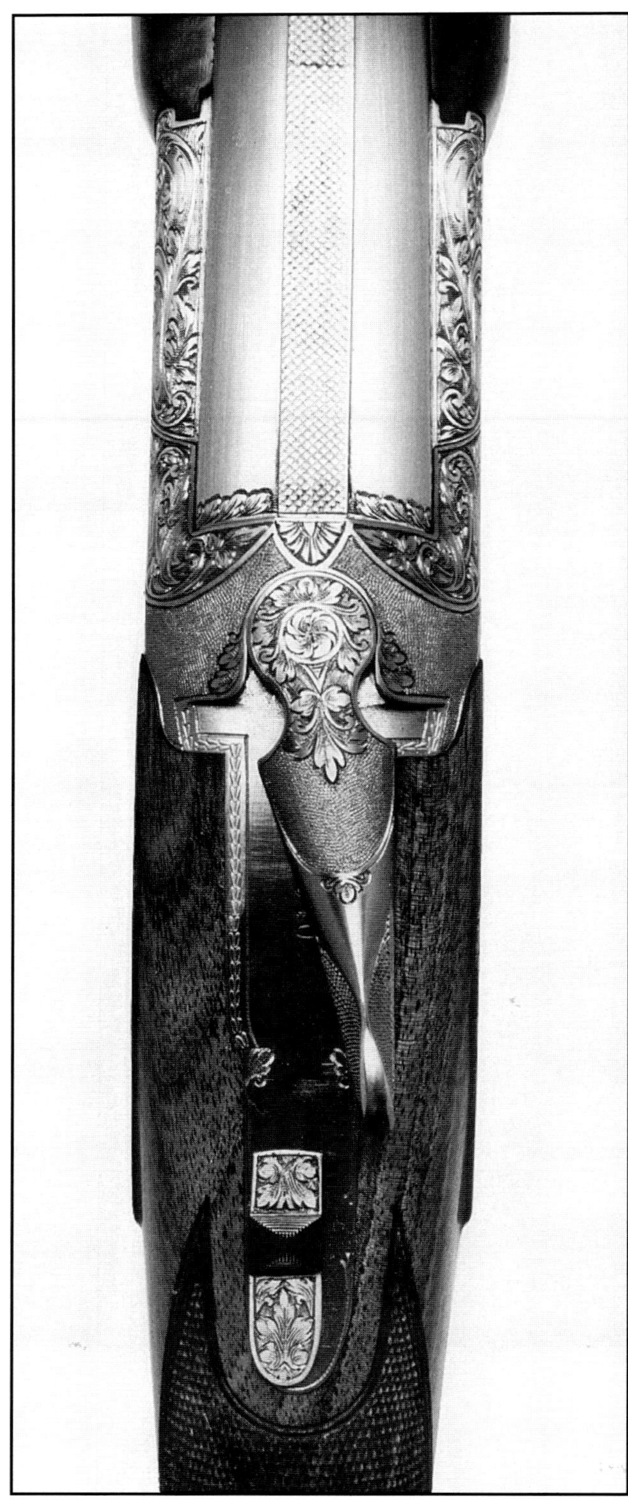

The top and bottom of the Magis engraved Diana Grade. Courtesy Fabrique Nationale Archives.

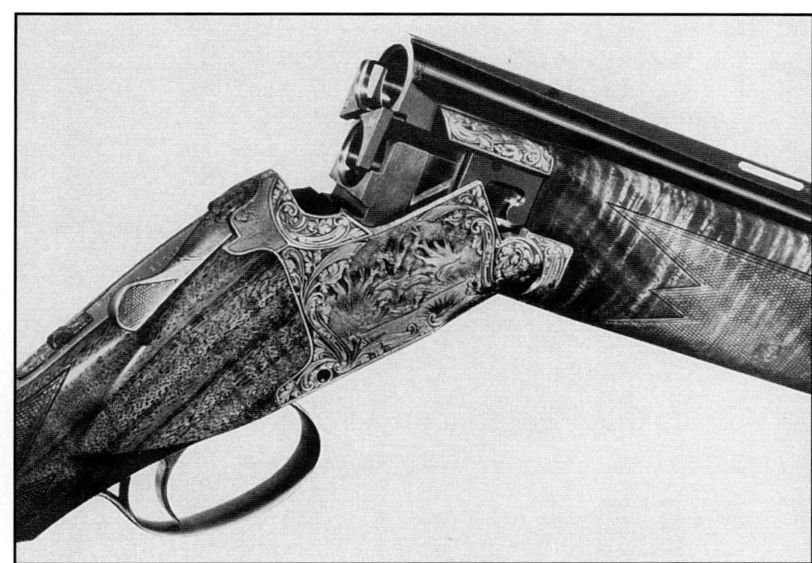

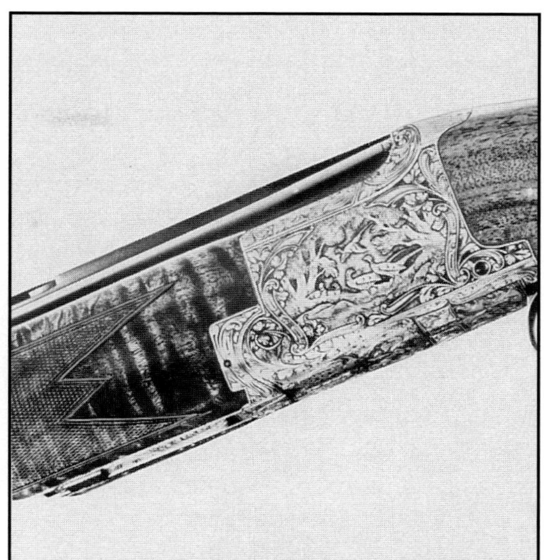

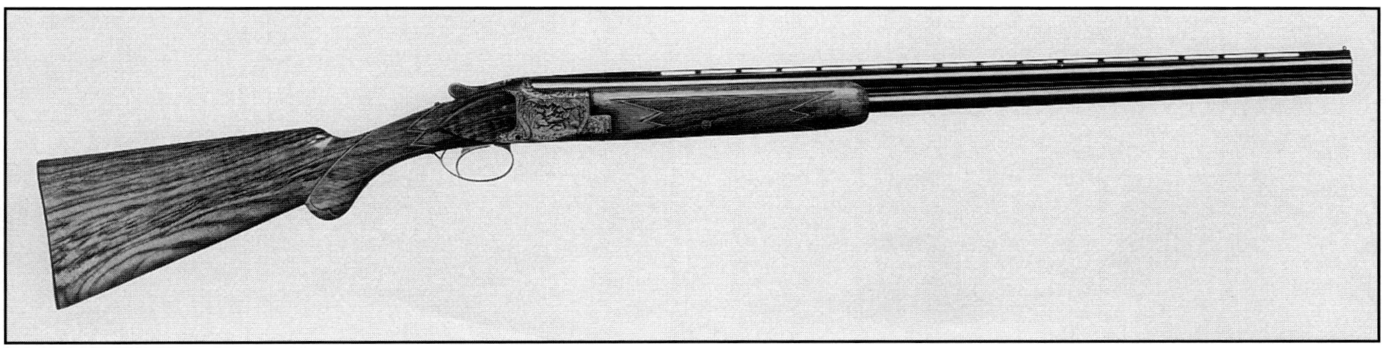

A Browning Arms Company promotional photograph showing both sides of the Diana Grade and the overall view. The checkering pattern was different on the Diana Grade compared to the Pigeon and Pointer Grades, and the quality of wood was superior as well. Courtesy Browning Company.

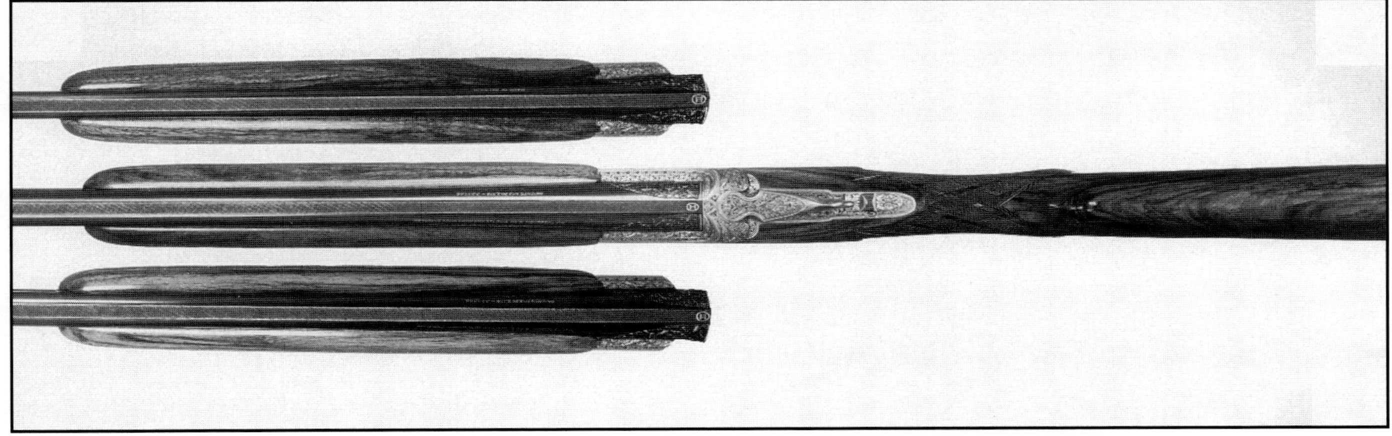

This specially engraved Browning Superposed three-barrel set has its barrels numbered with Roman numerals, a popular option for extra high grade Superposed. Courtesy Browning Company.

Fabrique Nationale used a system of grading wood that would ensure a fairly close match in grain and color between its various grades. This photograph illustrates six different grades of wood plus two additional grades that might be considered for very special applications such as Exhibition Grade Superposed. FN used primarily French walnut on its guns and American black walnut on Superposed intended for sales in North America. Later in the 1960s, Claro walnut was used to meet the growing demand for high grade wood. Courtesy Fabrique Nationale Archives.

Browning Exposition Grades

1960-1970

A Sampling of the Engraver's Art

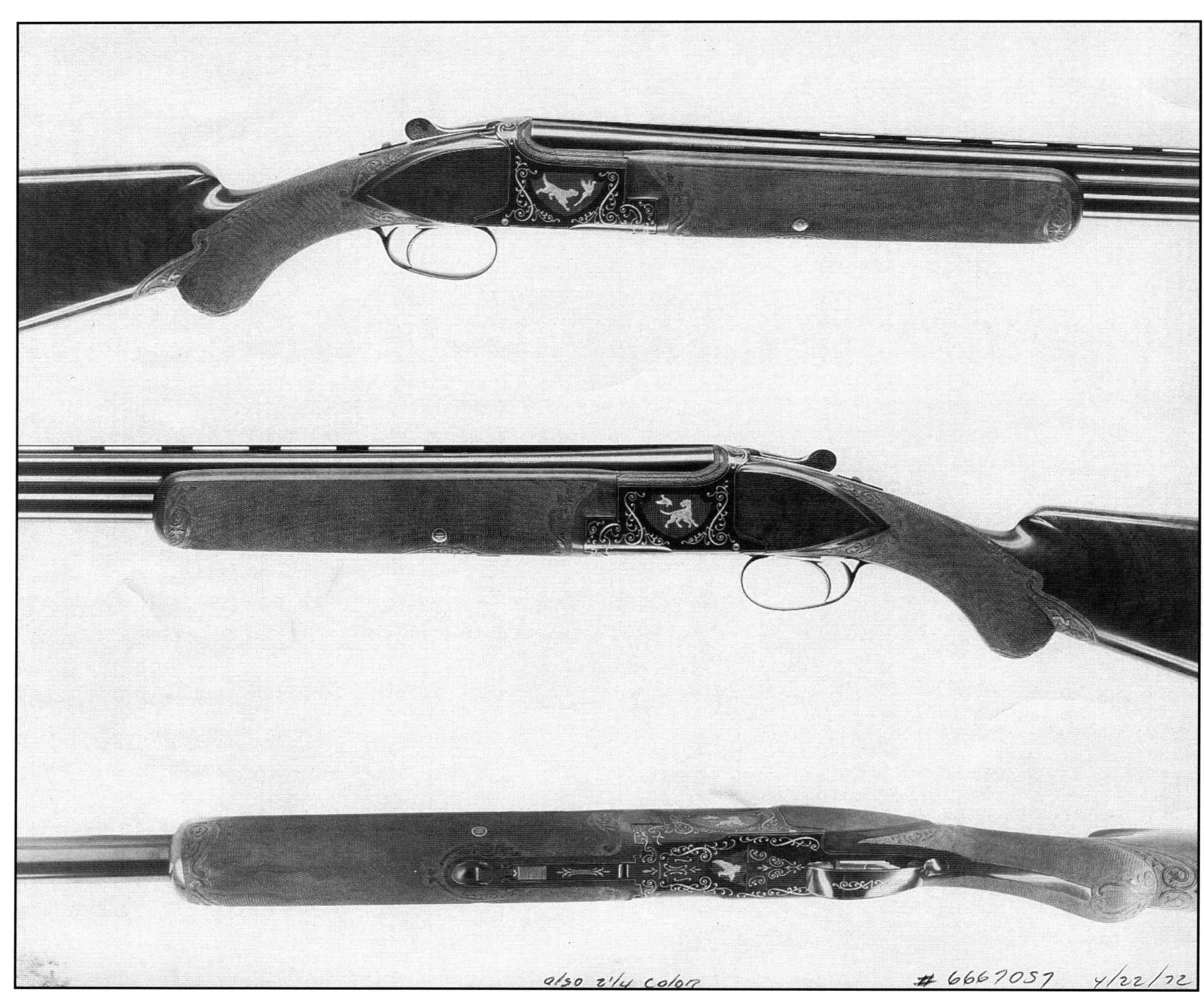

This 12 gauge Browning Superposed Exhibition Grade, serial number 66670S7, was built on April 21, 1969, and shipped to Browning May 23, 1969. The engravers are unknown but it was probably the work of either Louis Vrancken or André Watrin. Note the fine line checkering with a small, but tastefully executed, wood carving on both the buttstock and forearm. Courtesy Browning Company.

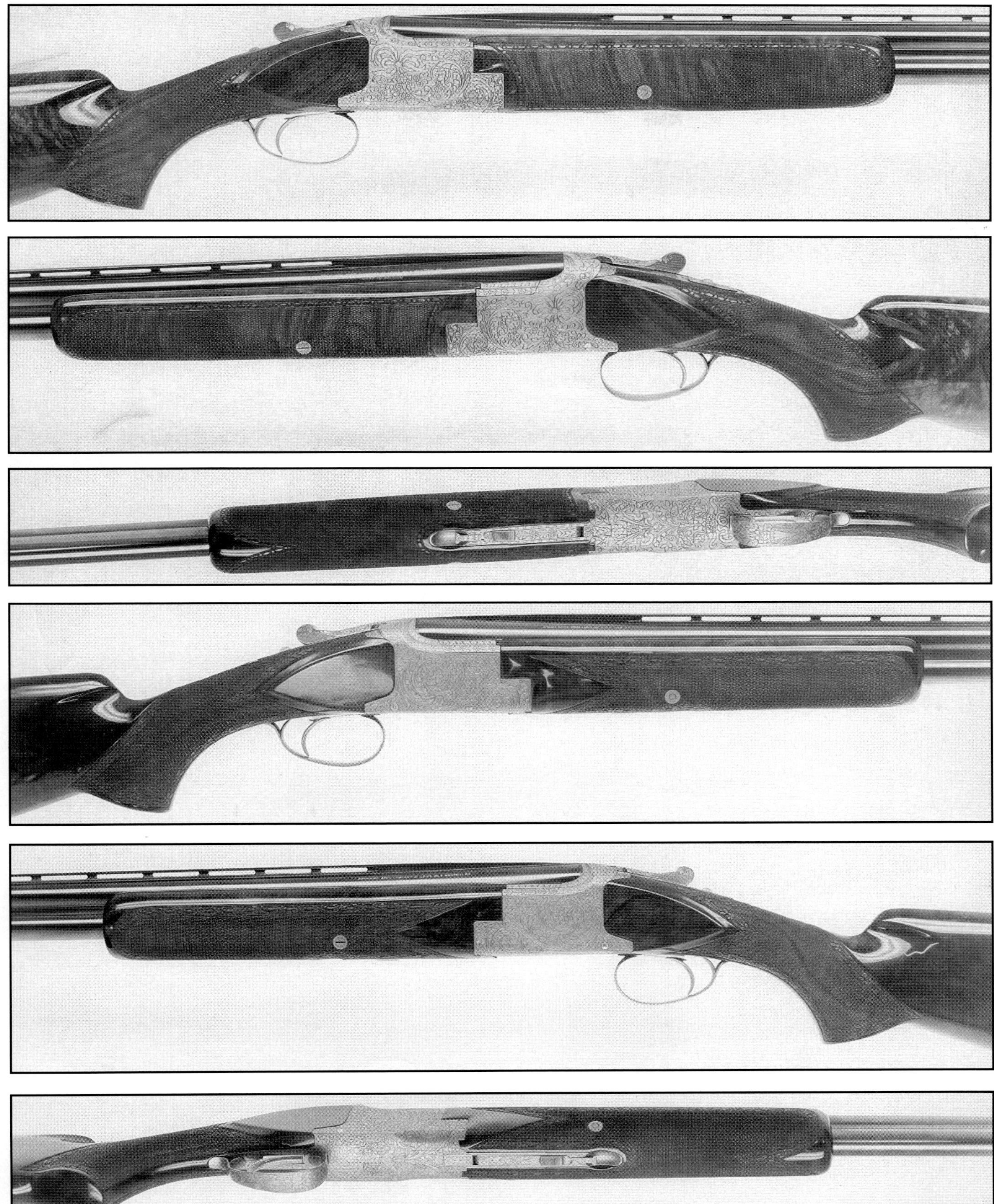

This consecutive serial numbered pair of 20 gauge Browning Superposed Exhibition Grade, serial numbers 44880V7 (bottom three) and 44881V7 (top three), was engraved by André Watrin. Watrin was noted for his intricate and beautifully executed scroll-work. Notice the interesting border design on the buttstock and forearm on both guns. Courtesy Browning Company.

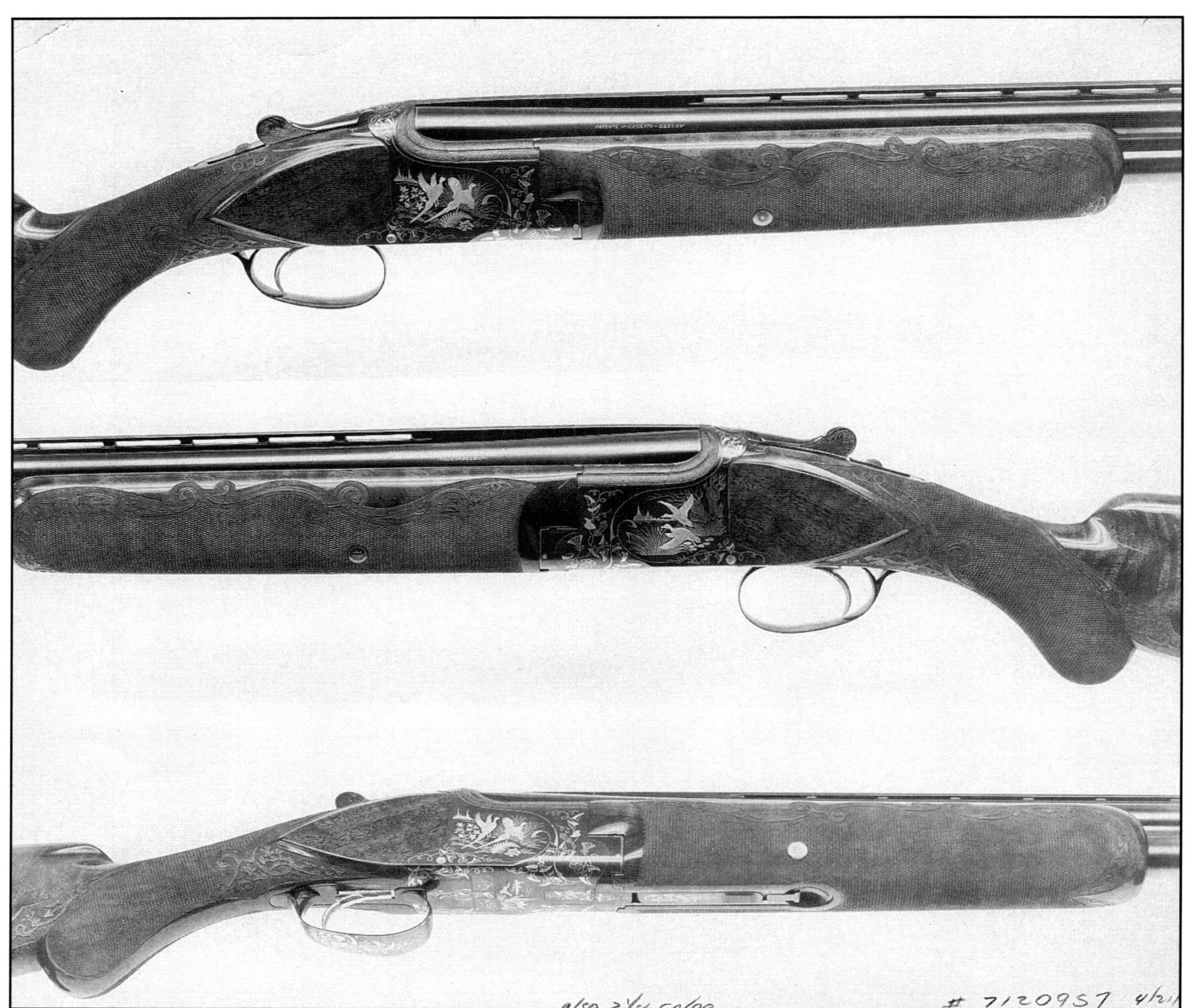

This Vrancken engraved 12 gauge Superposed Exhibition Grade, serial number 71209S7, features ducks on one side and pheasants on the other—traditional subjects. However, the overall design is modernistic, which combines both the old and the new. This is a direct result of the new generation of engravers in leadership roles at FN during the 1960s. Courtesy Browning Company.

This 12 gauge Browning Superposed Exhibition Grade Trap model, serial number 71198S7, was engraved by Louis Vrancken and Rene DeWil. This modern design was executed in two colors of gold. The wood carving complements the engraving design and gives the gun a completed and unified look. Courtesy Browning Company.

Serial number 71197S7, another Louis Vrancken engraved Superposed Exhibition Grade 12 gauge, again features traditional game scene subjects combined with modern scroll design and backgrounds. Vrancken displayed a wide range of talents. Courtesy Browning Company.

The Elegance of André Watrin

A Photographic Essay

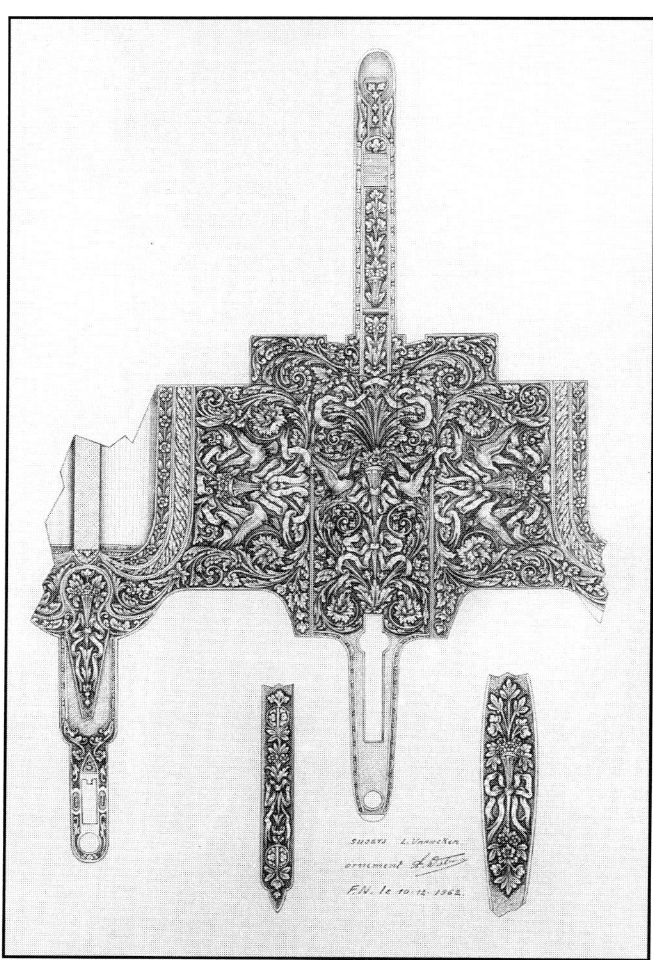

Master engraver and co-chief engraver of the FN facilities with Louis Vrancken, André Watrin is considered by many to have outstanding artistic ability. His strengths lay in design, as this 1962 sketch so impressively illustrates. The subjects of this engraving design were executed by Louis Vrancken, while the intricate scrollwork and overall design was done by André Watrin. Courtesy Fabrique Nationale Archives.

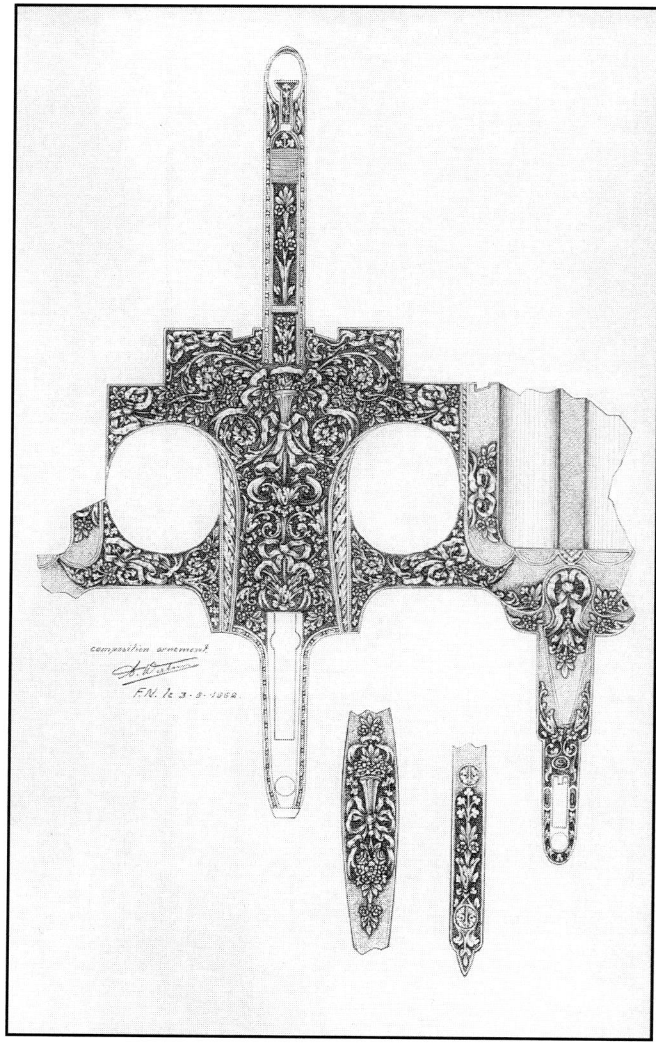

This design drawing was completed in September of 1962 and shows the incredible detail that Watrin put into his work. The panels on either side of the receiver are for game scenes, perhaps designed and executed by another master FN engraver. Courtesy Fabrique Nationale Archives.

This Watrin sketch was executed on November 16, 1962, and illustrates an almost perfect blending of scroll and birds in an imperceptible motion of swirls and flowers. This design is art in its purest form. The game birds were executed by Louis Vrancken; the balance of the piece was engraved by Watrin. This was a common practice at FN. Courtesy Fabrique Nationale Archives.

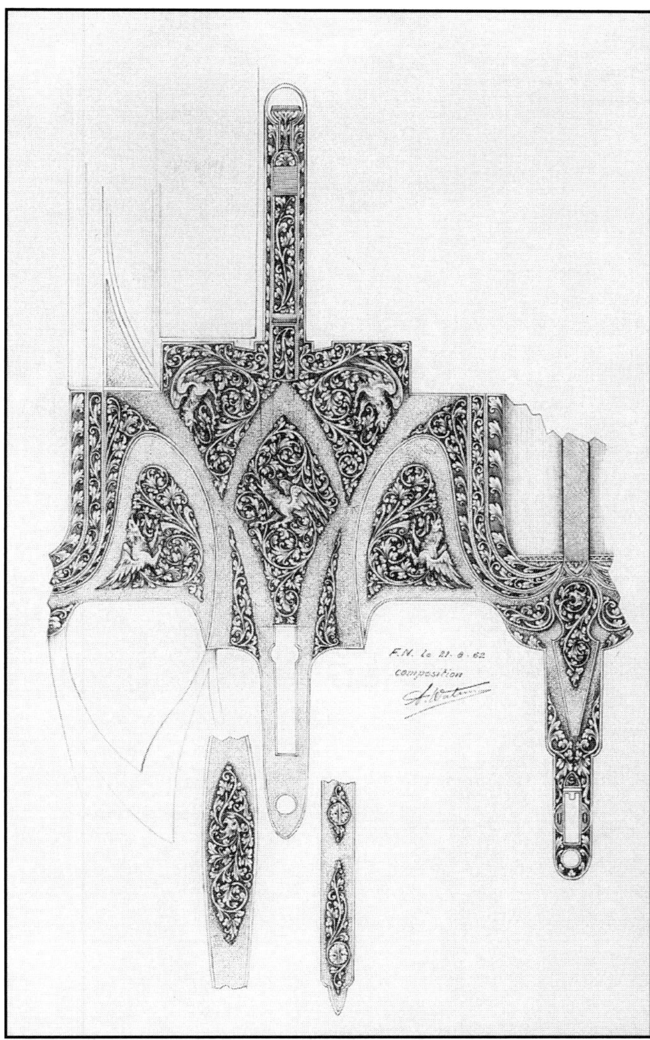

This unusual composition was designed and drawn by André Watrin on August 21, 1962. Whether this design was commissioned or not is unknown, but it is certainly a distinctive pattern. The position of the chimeras blends well with the scrollwork. Courtesy Fabrique Nationale Archives.

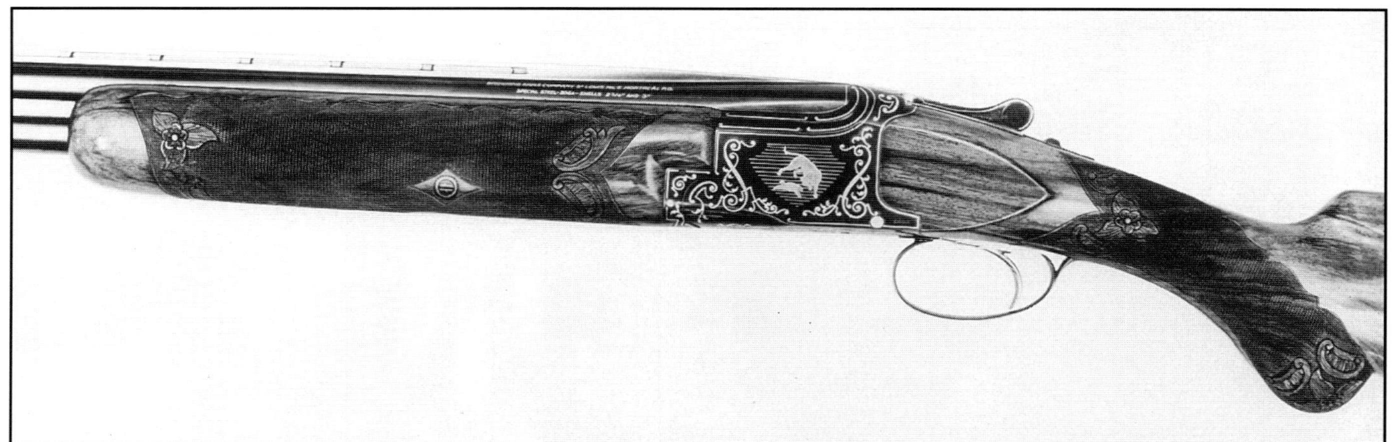

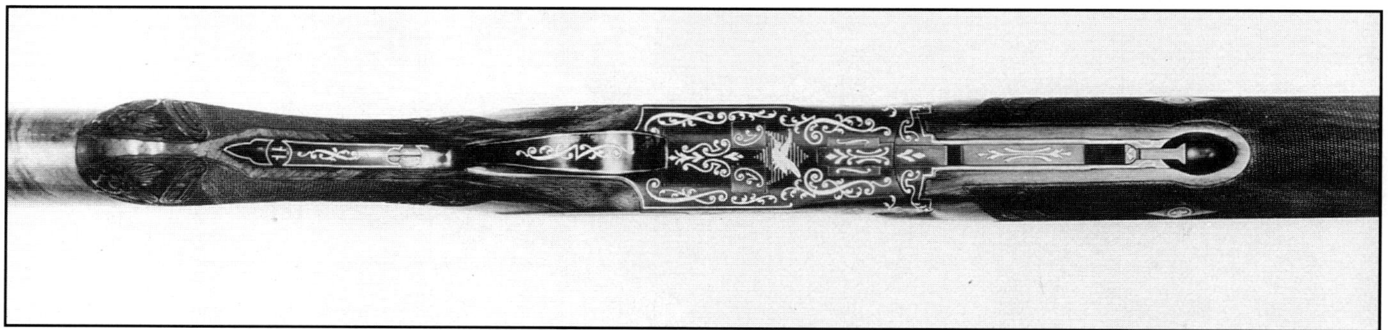

These two photographs of 20 gauge Superposed, serial number 23186, shown elsewhere in color, gives a view of the intricate wood carving that was executed on both the pistol grip and forearm. The bottom view shows a snipe in flight surrounded by carefully executed gold work. Courtesy Fabrique Nationale Archives.

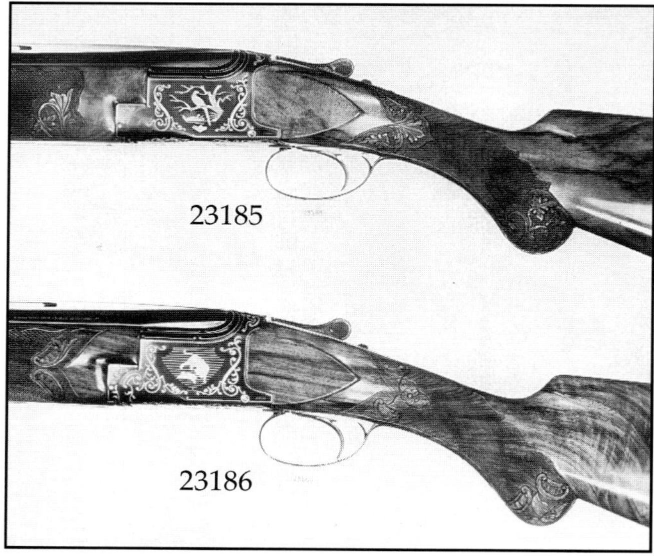

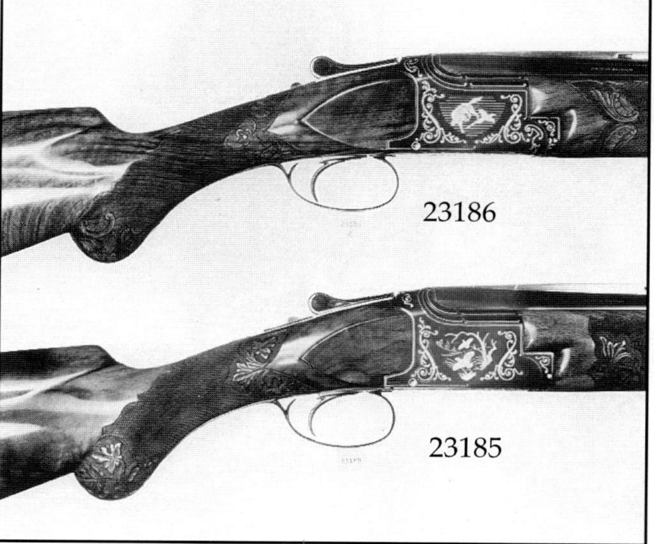

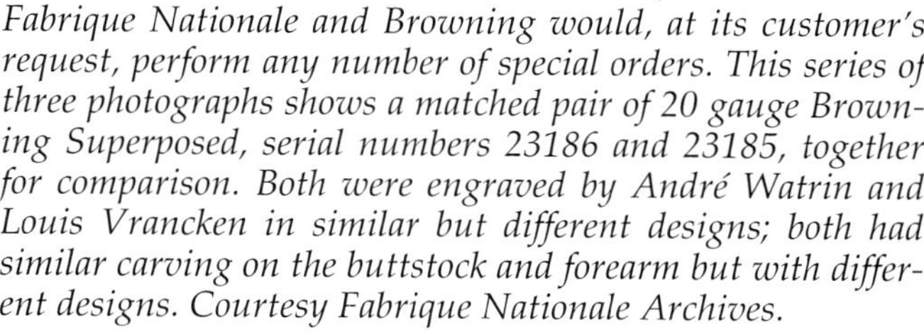

Fabrique Nationale and Browning would, at its customer's request, perform any number of special orders. This series of three photographs shows a matched pair of 20 gauge Browning Superposed, serial numbers 23186 and 23185, together for comparison. Both were engraved by André Watrin and Louis Vrancken in similar but different designs; both had similar carving on the buttstock and forearm but with different designs. Courtesy Fabrique Nationale Archives.

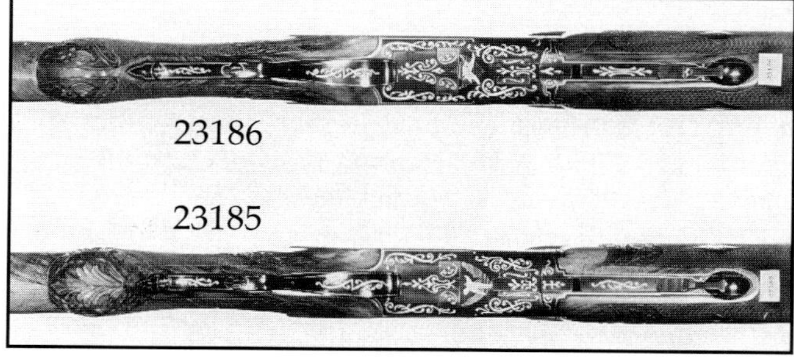

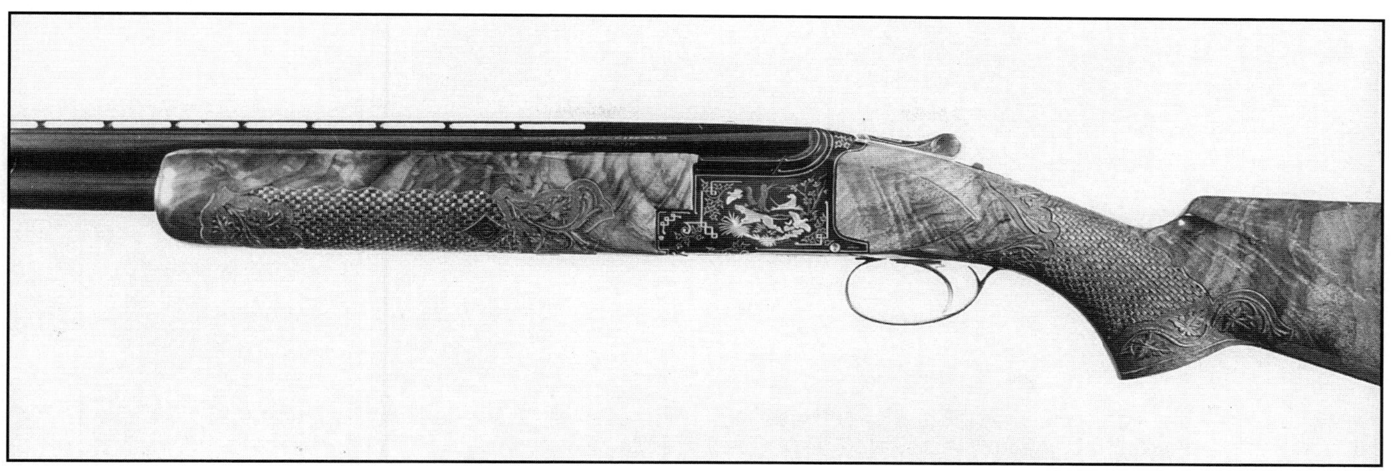

André Watrin collaborated with Louis Vrancken on this 12 gauge Browning Superposed. It has a large number of animals in its game scene and while the background is traditional, the border treatment is geometric in design. The checkering pattern is also unusual with a basketweave pattern coupled with a leaf carving motif. This is a very unique Superposed. Courtesy Fabrique Nationale Archives.

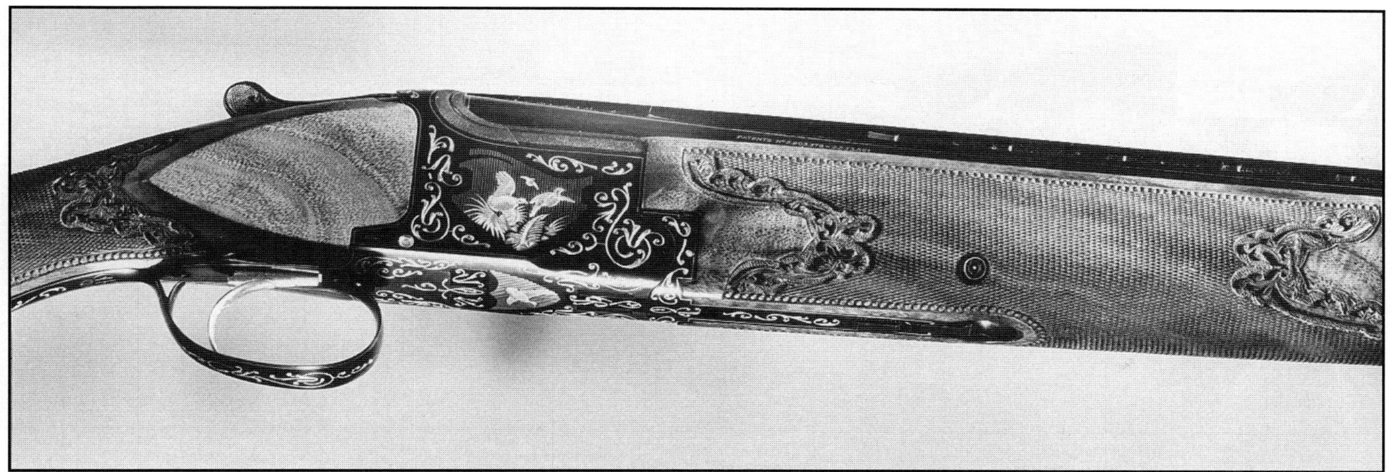

This is another outstanding example of a Watrin designed and executed Superposed. This particular Exhibition Grade was featured in the 1970 Browning general catalogue where it was referred to as an Exposition model. Both Browning and FN routinely interchanged the terms Exhibition and Exposition for its highest grade Superposed. Courtesy Browning Company.

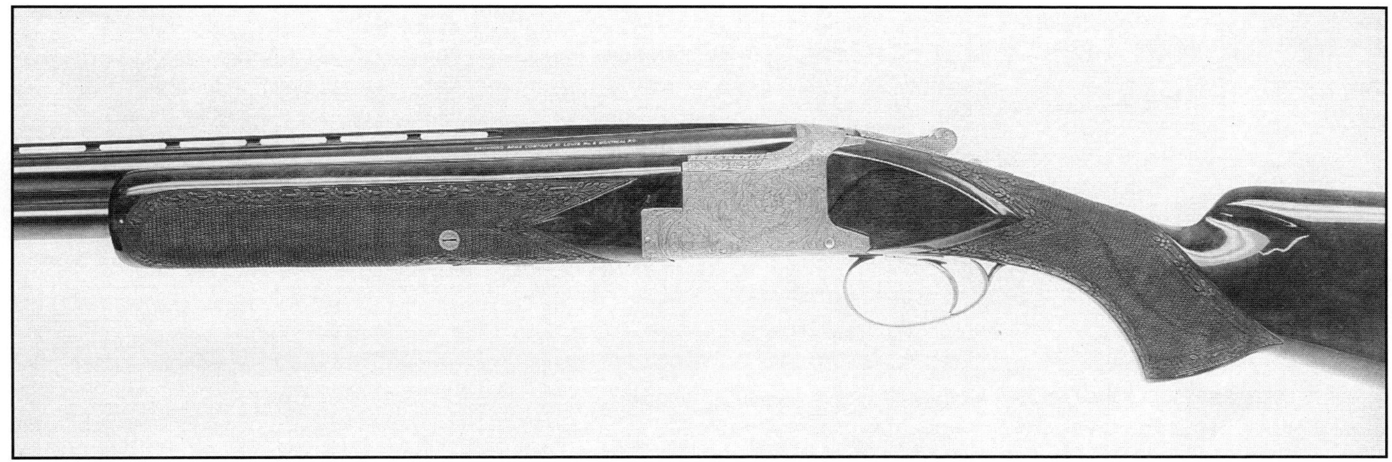

This specially engraved 20 gauge Browning Superposed was executed by André Watrin in the late 1960s. Its complex scrollwork is a Watrin attribute. This Superposed is signed on the bottom left side of the frame near the trigger root. Courtesy Browning Company.

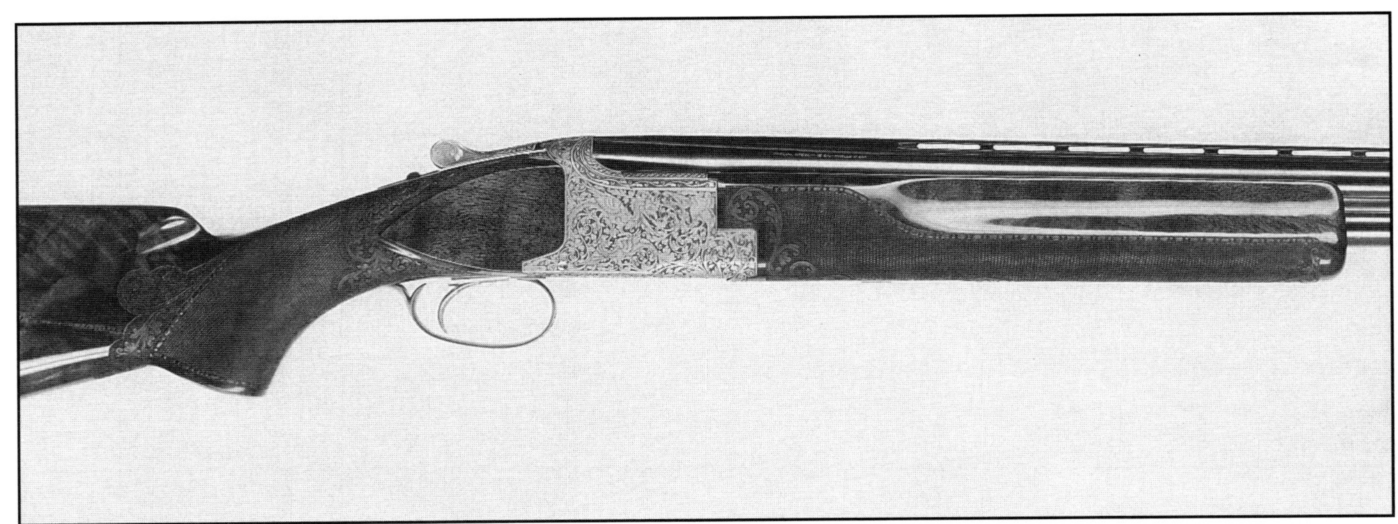

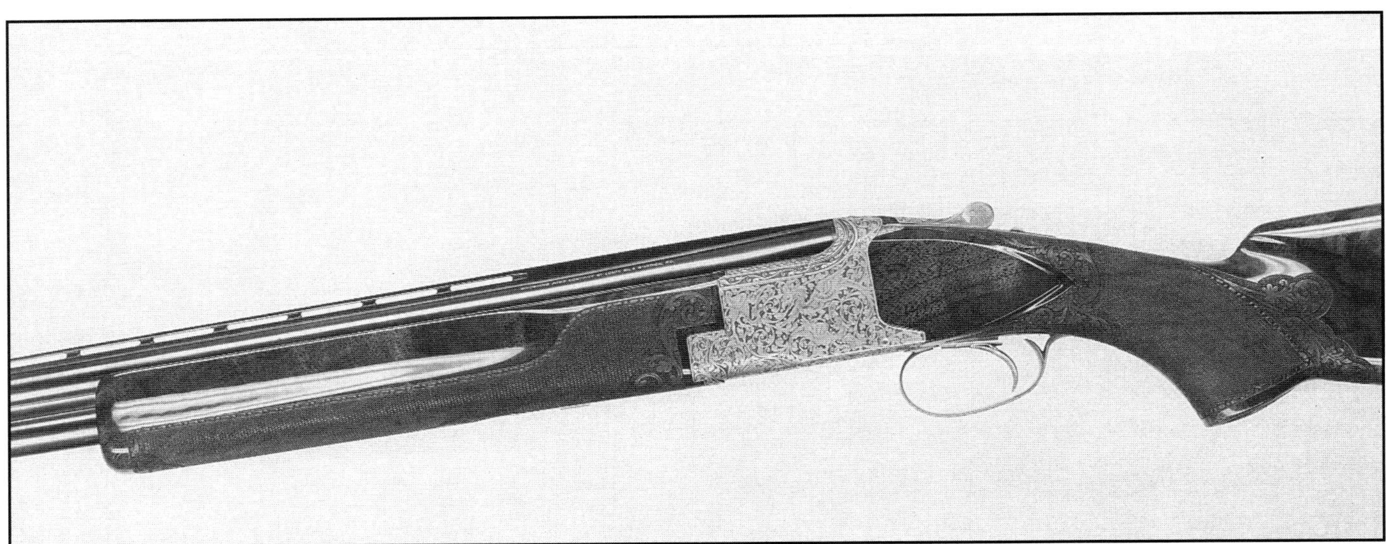

This Browning Superposed Trap model, serial number 71208S7, is engraved by André Watrin. What is interesting about this particular gun is that the pattern Watrin used is almost identical to one used by his mentor, Felix Funken, in 1953 on a Superposed engraved for John Val Browning. Courtesy Browning Company.

Browning Superposed Catalogue Offerings: 1960-1969

Like the company that gave it its name, in 1960 the Browning Superposed was ready to expand its offerings to the shooting public far beyond anything that had come before. With its acceptance well established in North America and production capabilities considerably improved from the beginning of the 1950s, Browning was enthusiastic about expanding the Superposed line to broaden its appeal and create even more demand. In a letter to its dealers at the beginning of 1959, Browning requested information and suggestions from its large retail network. Some of the suggestions were implemented very quickly, such as the inclusion of the 28 gauge and .410 bore Superposed as well as a new Lightning Trap model; other dealer recommendations were carried out later in the decade. Browning management was interested in improving and expanding its Superposed product line and wisely availed themselves of input from dealers, who were more attuned than the company to consumer desires. The catalogue offerings for the 1960s reflect Browning's commitment, through a cooperative effort with its dealers, to the establishment of a comprehensive Superposed product line built on quality.

1960: The company began the decade with an aggressive expansion of the Superposed line while at the same time consolidating some of its long-time offerings. The venerable raised matted rib on the Superposed was discontinued as a standard feature due to limited demand. The raised matted rib could, however, be obtained on special order. The Standard Weight Superposed was now offered in Grade I only, with the exception of the 12 gauge 3-inch Magnum, which continued to be offered in all grades. The retail price of the Standard Grade I Superposed was $300.00. The company decided to discontinue the Superposed Standard Trap model and replace it with a new improved model.

The biggest news for the Superposed in 1960 was the addition of the 28 gauge and .410 bore. These new gauges were available in all grades in Standard Weight only. The announcement for these new guns came from Browning to its dealers on May 21, 1959. Dealers who ordered these small bore Superposed were promised delivery in late fall of 1959. In a letter to its dealers dated July 23, 1959, Browning confirmed that the response to the 28 gauge and .410 bore Superposed was greater than anticipated. The company went on to state, "In just one and a half months our production is fully obligated until December of this year [1959]. We regret that no further orders can be delivered before that date."[18]

The year 1960 was also the beginning of a new series of engraving patterns for the Superposed. The numbered grades, Grades I through VI, were discontinued and the new designs, Pigeon, Pointer, Diana, and Midas, were introduced.

> **An interesting fact:** In the June 1960 Browning general catalogue, photos of the new high grade Superposed were in fact photos of the older pre-1960 numbered grades. Browning merely changed the grade designation without updating the photos. It was not until the March 1961 catalogue that the new designs were accurately shown.

Browning also expanded the extra sets of barrels offered. Previously only same gauge barrels were available for the Superposed. For 1960 it was now possible to have a 12 gauge Superposed with an extra 20 gauge set of barrels or a 20 gauge with an extra 28 gauge or .410 bore set of barrels. The Superposed was also offered in a 28 gauge configuration with an extra set of .410 bore barrels. The 1960 Browning price list shows a large number of categories for Superposed with extra sets of barrels. There were eight different plans for ordering these extra barrel sets, and they were lettered A through H. It was a very complex arrangement and caused some confusion with Browning dealers.

The Superposed product line for 1960 featured the Hunting models in Standard Weight in 12 and 20 gauge in Grade I only. These were furnished with either 26-1/2-inch barrels or 28-inch barrels with ventilated rib. The 28 gauge and .410 bore were also built in Standard Weight, but were offered in all grades. These small bore guns were fitted with either 26-1/2-inch barrels or 28-inch barrels with ventilated rib. The retail price for a Grade I 28 gauge or Grade I .410 bore Superposed was $400.00, thirty-three percent more than the Grade I in 12 or 20 gauge. The 12 gauge 3-inch Magnum model remained in the line and was offered in all grades with 30-inch ventilated rib barrels.

The Superposed Lightning was available in 12 and 20 gauge in all grades with 26-1/2-inch or 28-inch barrels with ventilated rib. Retail prices of the Lightning model started at $300.00 and increased

---

[18] Browning Arms Company sales letter to "Authorized Browning Dealers," July 23, 1959, p. 3.

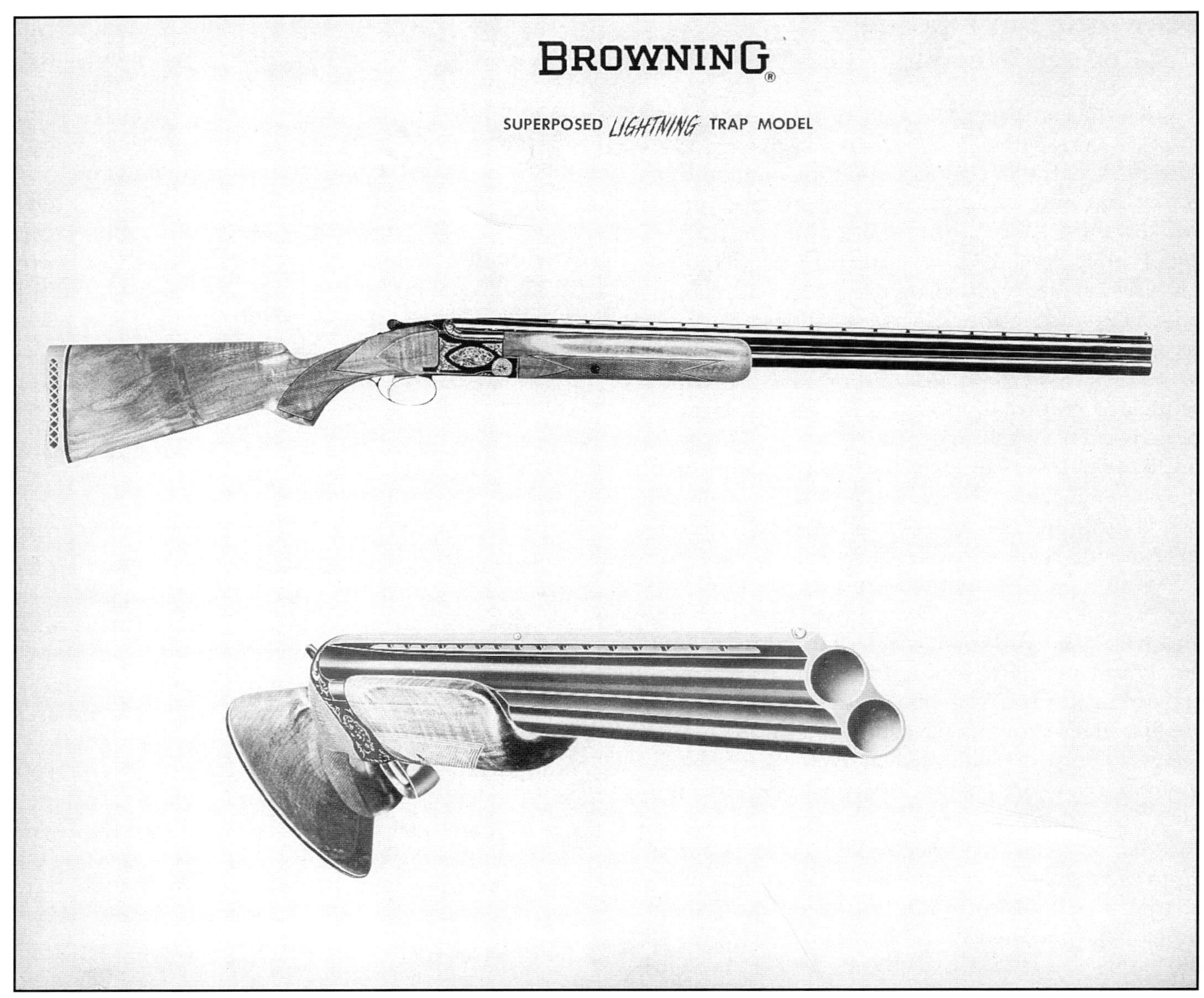

A redesigned Browning Superposed Lightning Trap model was introduced in 1960. It featured a special trap recoil pad, a redesigned pistol grip with flat bottom, a semi-beavertail forearm, and special dimensions on the buttstock. The standard barrel length was 30 inches. Courtesy Browning Company.

to $1,000.00 for the Midas Grade. The 28 gauge and .410 bore Superposed were not offered in the Lightning configuration.

The Skeet model remained unchanged from its introduction in 1956. It was, for all intents and purposes, a Hunting model with skeet chokes offered in either the Standard Weight or Lightning weight configuration. Additional sets of barrels in 28 gauge and .410 bore made the Superposed Skeet model a more attractive alternative for the competitive skeet shooter.

For the competitive trapshooter, the introduction in 1960 of the newly redesigned Superposed Lightning Trap model was welcome news. This latest Trap model featured a special dimension trap stock with full pistol grip, flat on the bottom instead of rounded as before, with a contoured ventilated recoil pad as standard equipment. The forearm was redesigned to offer better control in the hands of the shooter. Front and center ivory sights were furnished on a ventilated rib that was 5/16 of an inch wide. The standard barrel length for the new Lightning Trap was 30 inches. Extra sets of barrels in the same gauge or 20 gauge could be ordered for the Lightning Trap if desired.

For the customer who desired extra barrels for his Superposed the choice became more complicated. In general, the price of a 12 or 20 gauge gun with an extra set of barrels in the same gauge was $465.00. For two extra sets of barrels in the same gauge the retail price was $615.00. For the 20 gauge Superposed with an extra set of barrels in either 28

In 1961 Browning introduced the new BROADway Trap model. This small brochure was printed by Browning to obtain maximum exposure among its dealers and trapshooters. Courtesy Russ Church.

gauge or .410 bore, prices started at $615.00. For two extra sets of barrels the retail price was $910.00. A 28 gauge .410 bore combination retailed for $715.00 for a Grade I. Lightning and Standard barrels could still be interchanged on all models.

An interesting fact: In 1961 Browning experienced a 48% increase in orders for its Lightning Trap model through the first six months of the year. All subsequent orders for the Lightning Trap model were suspended for that year because production could not keep up with demand.

1961: The new addition for 1961 was the introduction of the Superposed BROADway Trap model on July 7, 1961. Fitted with the same trap stock and forearm as the Lightning Trap model, including contoured recoil pad, the BROADway Trap was fitted with an extra large ventilated rib 5/8 of an inch wide. Besides its width, the BROADway rib had a distinctive look that featured small grooves on either side of the line of sight to flatten and break up reflections. These grooves were slightly diagonal transverse cuts intended to aid the eye in focusing and tracking the target. The sight radius on a BROADway Trap was a full 32 inches; the Lightning Trap model had a sight radius of only 26-3/4 inches with its 30-inch barrels. The BROADway Trap was available with all high grade engraving patterns. It was offered with 32-inch barrels only, although other barrel lengths in 12 or 20 gauge were available without the BROADway rib, and carried a retail price of $350.00 for a Grade I, compared to $315.00 for the Lightning Trap model. Browning was prepared to ship the new BROADway Trap models during July and August of 1961. The reason for the delay in the introduction of the BROADway Trap was the desire on the part of management to have the new model ready for shipment at the time of introduction.

The balance of the Superposed product line remained the same with the exception of prices, which were increased slightly for most models and grades. The exception was the 28 gauge and .410 bore, which were reduced from $400.00 to $375.00 for Grade I. Retail prices for higher grades in these two small gauges were reduced as well.

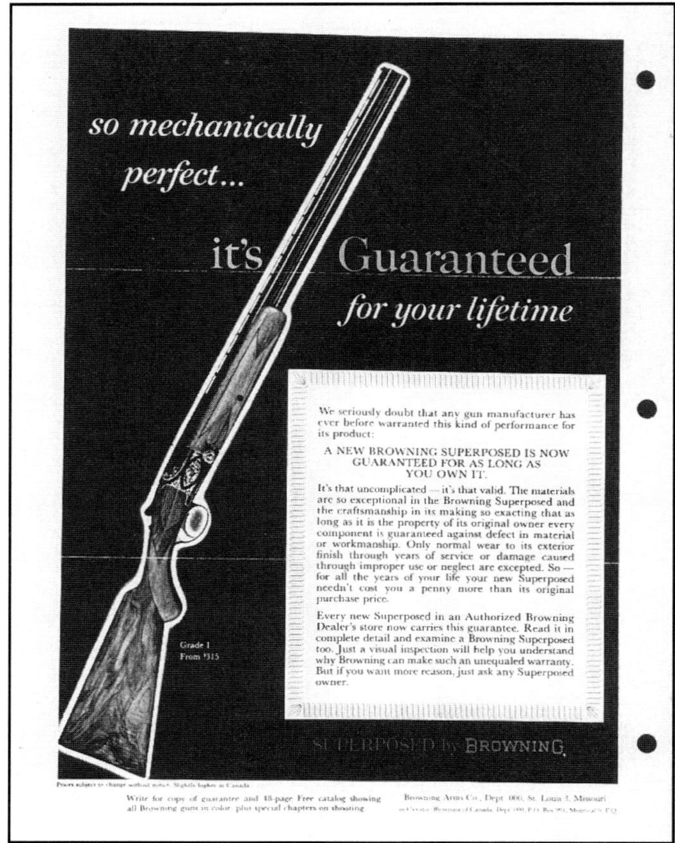

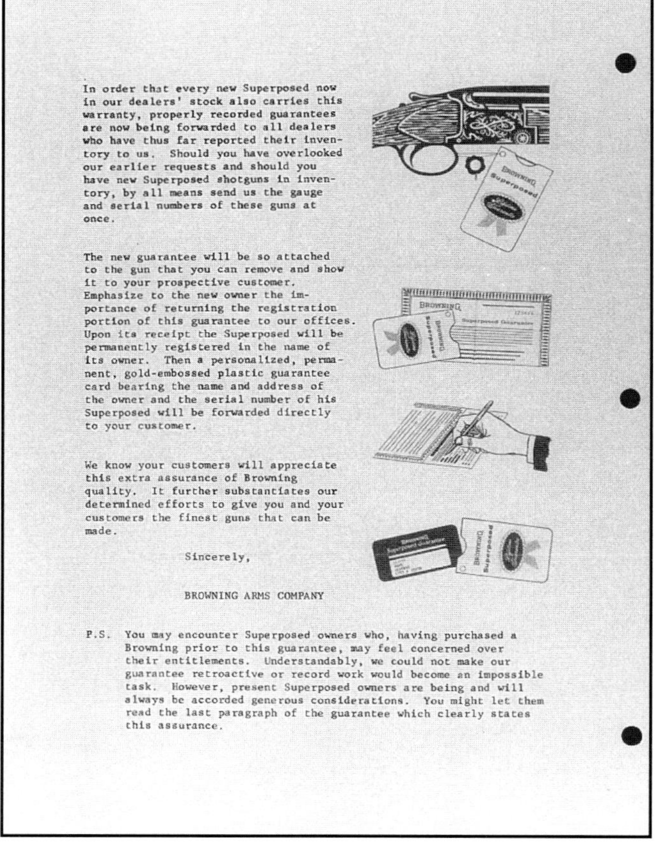
In order that every new Superposed now in our dealers' stock also carries this warranty, properly recorded guarantees are now being forwarded to all dealers who have thus far reported their inventory to us. Should you have overlooked our earlier requests and should you have new Superposed shotguns in inventory, by all means send us the gauge and serial numbers of these guns at once.

The new guarantee will be so attached to the gun that you can remove and show it to your prospective customer. Emphasize to the new owner the importance of returning the registration portion of this guarantee to our offices. Upon its receipt the Superposed will be permanently registered in the name of its owner. Then a personalized, permanent, gold-embossed plastic guarantee card bearing the name and address of the owner and the serial number of his Superposed will be forwarded directly to your customer.

We know your customers will appreciate this extra assurance of Browning quality. It further substantiates our determined efforts to give you and your customers the finest guns that can be made.

Sincerely,

BROWNING ARMS COMPANY

P.S. You may encounter Superposed owners who, having purchased a Browning prior to this guarantee, may feel concerned over their entitlements. Understandably, we could not make our guarantee retroactive or record work would become an impossible task. However, present Superposed owners are being and will always be accorded generous considerations. You might let them read the last paragraph of the guarantee which clearly states this assurance.

Browning's decision to offer a lifetime guarantee was introduced with a great deal of fanfare. The company's guarantee was a novel one for the firearm's industry and an impressive promotional campaign was launched. The company literature was careful to point out each step necessary for new Superposed owners to be assured they would have this guarantee. Previous Superposed owners were also given consideration. Courtesy Russ Church.

BROWNING®

SUPERPOSED SERIAL NUMBER

Superposed Guarantee

We are proud that you have chosen a Browning Superposed shotgun. It is made of the very finest materials and every phase of the manufacture and assembly of your new shotgun has been dedicated to crafting a sporting arm which will provide exceptional performance and an abundance of shooting pleasure, not for years but for your lifetime. It is because this Browning Superposed has been manufactured under such exacting processes that we can make the following guarantee to you as the original owner, in whose name it must be registered with our Company:

THIS BROWNING SUPERPOSED SHOTGUN IS GUARANTEED FOR AS LONG AS YOU OWN IT, AGAINST ANY AND ALL DEFECTS IN MATERIALS OR WORKMANSHIP

This guarantee does not cover such conditions as normal wear to bluing or stock finish resulting from years of service or damage resulting from accident, negligence, misuse or unauthorized alteration, or wherein the serial numbers of this Superposed have been altered, defaced or removed.

Our obligation assumed under this guarantee is limited to the repair or replacing of any part or parts which prove upon our examination to have been defective. The complete shotgun must be returned to our Service Department at the address listed below.

This guarantee shall apply only to Browning Superposed shotguns purchased in the United States, its territories and possessions, and Canada. It also applies to any of these shotguns purchased from military exchanges in foreign countries when such guns have this guarantee attached thereto.

This guarantee is in lieu of all other guarantees, expressed or implied. No representative or other person is authorized or permitted to make any guarantee or to assume for us any liability not strictly in accordance with the foregoing.

We wish to point out to you as a Superposed owner some of the more serious causes of damage, which are entirely unrelated to the quality of a fine shotgun, for which we could not assume responsibility:

Damage from barrel obstruction or through the use of ammunition generating pressure in excess of those in regular commercial loads designated for this gauge.

Damage caused through the use of shot, slugs, or ball loads of materials other than those used in regular commercial loads.

Damage caused through improper rechambering or reboring. Rechambering, if ever considered, should be approved and performed by Browning Arms Company personnel.

Damage resulting from improper repairs or alterations by others than our own Service Department personnel. Please do not construe this caution to mean that repairs and/or alterations by competent gunsmiths other than our own necessarily voids our guarantee. There are many gunsmiths throughout the country well qualified to work on a Browning Superposed shotgun, and only in cases of negligence would we fail to recognize their services as legitimate. Of necessity, however, we can only assume repair costs applicable under our guarantee when performed by our own Service Department.

— PLEASE NOTE —

Since the introduction of the Browning Superposed, our Company has had only a fractional percentage of instances where correction of any type was necessary. However, on any such occasion there was no hesitation in correcting any deficiencies, without question and without charge. Though it shall continue to be at the discretion of our Company, there is no intention in the future to be less considerate of Browning Superposed owners who acquired their guns prior to the adoption of this guarantee. Neither is it our intention to disregard any just problem in the future, even though the Superposed owner may not be the original owner.

BROWNING ARMS COMPANY

In order that this guarantee be valid, it is essential that you fill out and return the registration form. It will be permanently recorded. You will in turn receive a handsome wallet size guarantee card of durable plastic on which your name and the serial number of your Superposed will be embossed.

FORM S82063 PRINTED IN U.S.A.

The complete Browning Superposed guarantee as it was written in 1963 and published in the company's advertisements. Courtesy Russ Church.

One of Browning's many promotional photographs showing its new lifetime guarantee with the owner's card beside a new Browning Superposed. Courtesy Browning Company.

1962: Superposed catalogue offerings for 1962 remained unchanged except for slightly higher retail prices.

1963: Superposed catalogue offerings remained unchanged from 1962. Retail prices for 1963 remained at 1962 levels. This was the only year out of the decade that recorded no retail price increases.

There was, however, a supplementary feature added to the Superposed line that helped to set it apart from other double guns offered for sale in North America: the lifetime guarantee. On August 23, 1963, Browning offered a lifetime guarantee for all Superposed purchased after that date. "Every new Superposed is now guaranteed to the person in whose name it is registered for as long as he owns it—even for his whole lifetime." The Browning Superposed Guarantee was announced with a national advertising campaign that continued throughout the fall hunting season. From this point forward Browning warranted that every new Superposed was free of defects in materials or workmanship as long as it was in the possession of the original owner. All the owner of a new Browning Superposed had to do was complete and return to the company a registration form which was permanently recorded. The company sent its new Superposed owners a plastic wallet size card with the name of the owner and serial number of the gun embossed in gold.

The new guarantee was not retroactive, but the company stated in its new warranty that, "...there is no intention in the future to be less considerate of Browning Superposed owners who acquired their guns prior to the adoption of this guarantee."

1964: Other than a sweeping price increase, the only change for this year was the addition of options for the BROADway Trap model. Beginning in 1964 the BROADway Trap buyer was no longer limited to 32-inch barrels with the BROADway rib; 30-inch barrels were offered as well. The BROADway Trap could also be special ordered with the BROADway rib installed on 12 gauge guns with 26-1/2-inch or 28-inch barrels at an extra charge of $40.00.

Prices on the retail level were increased substantially in 1964, reflecting the pressure of increased costs passed on to Browning by Fabrique Nationale. The retail price of a Grade I 12 or 20 gauge was raised from $335.00 to $380.00, an increase of more than thirteen percent. Substantial price increases were seen in the Pigeon and Pointer Grades but lessened somewhat for the Diana and Midas Grades. The BROADway Trap in Grade I was now the same price as the 28 gauge and .410 bore in the same grade.

1965: Superposed catalogue offerings for 1965 remained the same with regard to models and grades, but a few new accessory items were added. Browning offered the Hydro-Coil® stock and forearm for its Superposed shotguns. This device, for 12 gauge Superposed only, was designed to reduce recoil by about eighty-five percent. It used an internal pneumatic cylinder to absorb the recoil energy. The stock was made from a synthetic material called Cycolac and had an appearance similar to wood. It was offered as a kit for an $80.00 charge. Browning would fit the Hydro-Coil® stock and forearm to new or used Superposed for a charge of $115.00. The Hydro-Coil® stock and forearm was available in Trap or Hunting/Skeet dimensions. The drop at the heel and comb could be increased on special order as well as cast-off or cast-on added. Additional length of pull was also obtainable on request in lengths as short as 13-1/2 inches and as long as 14-1/2 inches. When this option was selected Browning required that a mechanical trigger be installed in place of the standard inertia trigger to insure dependable operation.

-4-

Hydro-Coil Stock & Forearm for the Browning Superposed

The Hydro-Coil stock, in our opinion, is the solution for the person who is at all sensitive to recoil. Hydro-Coil operates like a car shock absorber utilizing a pre-loaded pneumatic cylinder to absorb as much as 75% of the peak recoil. When the gun is fired, the comb portion of the stock remains stationary while the remainder of the gun recoils against the pneumatic cylinder. Thus a cushion of air is always between the shooter and the gun accomplishing an unbelievable reduction in kick.

The Hydro-Coil unit is made of a new synthetic called Cycolac, finished to simulate walnut in appearance. It is extremely strong and durable and weather has no affect on it. It has a weight and feel comparable to wood, thus the balance of the gun is not significantly altered.

The Hydro-Coil stock and forearm are fitted much the same as wood. In addition, some minor adjustments are required to the trigger mechanism. Hydro-Coil is offered to Browning Dealers in 12 gauge models only, and in these different ways:

1. As a complete kit to be installed by the dealer's gunsmith.
2. A customer's gun can be forwarded to our Service Department for the installation.
3. It is available on a new Superposed.

PRICES

	Dealer Price	Suggested Retail
1. Hydro-Coil Kit, Delivered	$ 56.00	$ 80.00*
2. Installed by Browning on a used Superposed	91.00	115.00
3. Installed by Browning on a new Superposed		
a. Standard 12 ga. Grade I	308.00**	385.00
b. The gun above with original fitted wood stock & forearm also included extra	369.10**	465.00
c. Lightning 12 ga. Grade I	324.00**	405.00
d. The gun above with original fitted wood stock & forearm also included extra	385.00**	485.00

*Plus dealer installation charge.
**Dealer purchase discounts also apply to these prices.

SPECIFICATIONS

	Trap	Skeet/Field
Drop at Comb*	1 3/8"	1 7/16"
Drop at Heel*	1 3/4"	2 1/8"
Length of Pull**	14 3/8"	14"

*Drop can be increased up to a maximum of 1 1/2 x 2 1/2 and reasonable cast can also be provided on request.
**Other lengths of pull can be provided on request: 13 1/2", 13 3/4", 14", 14 1/4", 14 3/8", 14 1/2".

In 1965 Browning offered a new accessory for its Superposed guns called the Hydro-Coil stock. The idea was to reduce recoil and the company felt that the competition shooter would be interested in such a device. This expectation proved to be false and the unit was dropped from the product line the following year. Courtesy Browning Company.

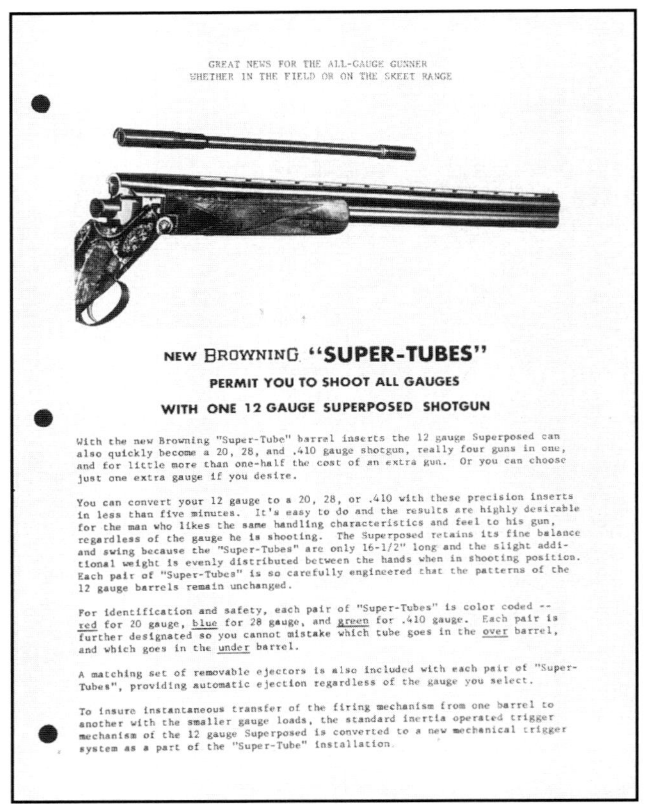

GREAT NEWS FOR THE ALL-GAUGE GUNNER
WHETHER IN THE FIELD OR ON THE SKEET RANGE

NEW BROWNING "SUPER-TUBES"

PERMIT YOU TO SHOOT ALL GAUGES

WITH ONE 12 GAUGE SUPERPOSED SHOTGUN

With the new Browning "Super-Tube" barrel inserts the 12 gauge Superposed can also quickly become a 20, 28, and .410 gauge shotgun, really four guns in one, and for little more than one-half the cost of an extra gun. Or you can choose just one extra gauge if you desire.

You can convert your 12 gauge to a 20, 28, or .410 with these precision inserts in less than five minutes. It's easy to do and the results are highly desirable for the man who likes the same handling characteristics and feel to his gun, regardless of the gauge he is shooting. The Superposed retains its fine balance and swing because the "Super-Tubes" are only 16-1/2" long and the slight additional weight is evenly distributed between the hands when in shooting position. Each pair of "Super-Tubes" is so carefully engineered that the patterns of the 12 gauge barrels remain unchanged.

For identification and safety, each pair of "Super-Tubes" is color coded -- red for 20 gauge, blue for 28 gauge, and green for .410 gauge. Each pair is further designated so you cannot mistake which tube goes in the over barrel, and which goes in the under barrel.

A matching set of removable ejectors is also included with each pair of "Super-Tubes", providing automatic ejection regardless of the gauge you select.

To insure instantaneous transfer of the firing mechanism from one barrel to another with the smaller gauge loads, the standard inertia operated trigger mechanism of the 12 gauge Superposed is converted to a new mechanical trigger system as a part of the "Super-Tube" installation.

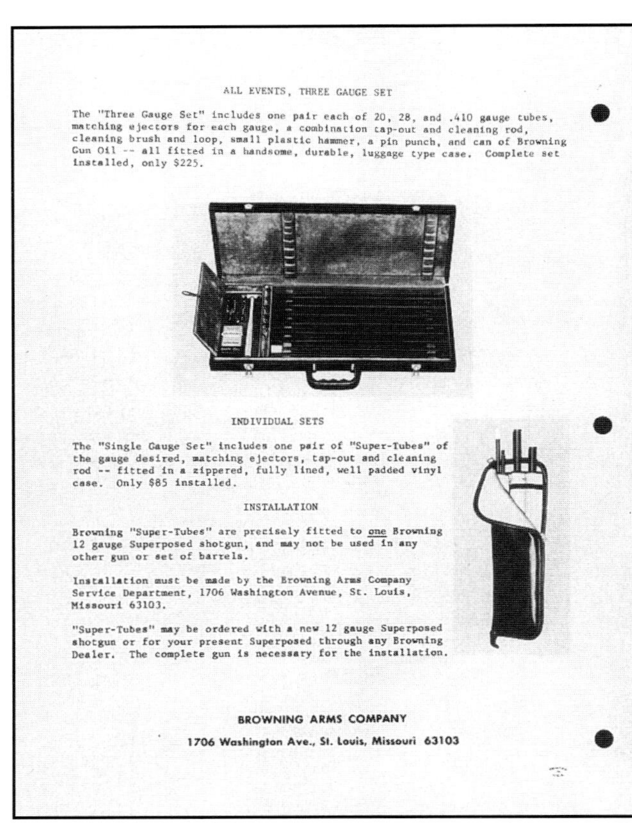

ALL EVENTS, THREE GAUGE SET

The "Three Gauge Set" includes one pair each of 20, 28, and .410 gauge tubes, matching ejectors for each gauge, a combination tap-out and cleaning rod, cleaning brush and loop, small plastic hammer, a pin punch, and can of Browning Gun Oil -- all fitted in a handsome, durable, luggage type case. Complete set installed, only $225.

INDIVIDUAL SETS

The "Single Gauge Set" includes one pair of "Super-Tubes" of the gauge desired, matching ejectors, tap-out and cleaning rod -- fitted in a zippered, fully lined, well padded vinyl case. Only $85 installed.

INSTALLATION

Browning "Super-Tubes" are precisely fitted to one Browning 12 gauge Superposed shotgun, and may not be used in any other gun or set of barrels.

Installation must be made by the Browning Arms Company Service Department, 1706 Washington Avenue, St. Louis, Missouri 63103.

"Super-Tubes" may be ordered with a new 12 gauge Superposed shotgun or for your present Superposed through any Browning Dealer. The complete gun is necessary for the installation.

BROWNING ARMS COMPANY

1706 Washington Ave., St. Louis, Missouri 63103

The idea of having a shotgun capable of firing different gauges from the same barrels was an appealing concept, especially for the skeet shooter. These two pages are taken from a Browning promotional flyer extolling the virtues of the company's new "Super-Tubes." Courtesy Russ Church.

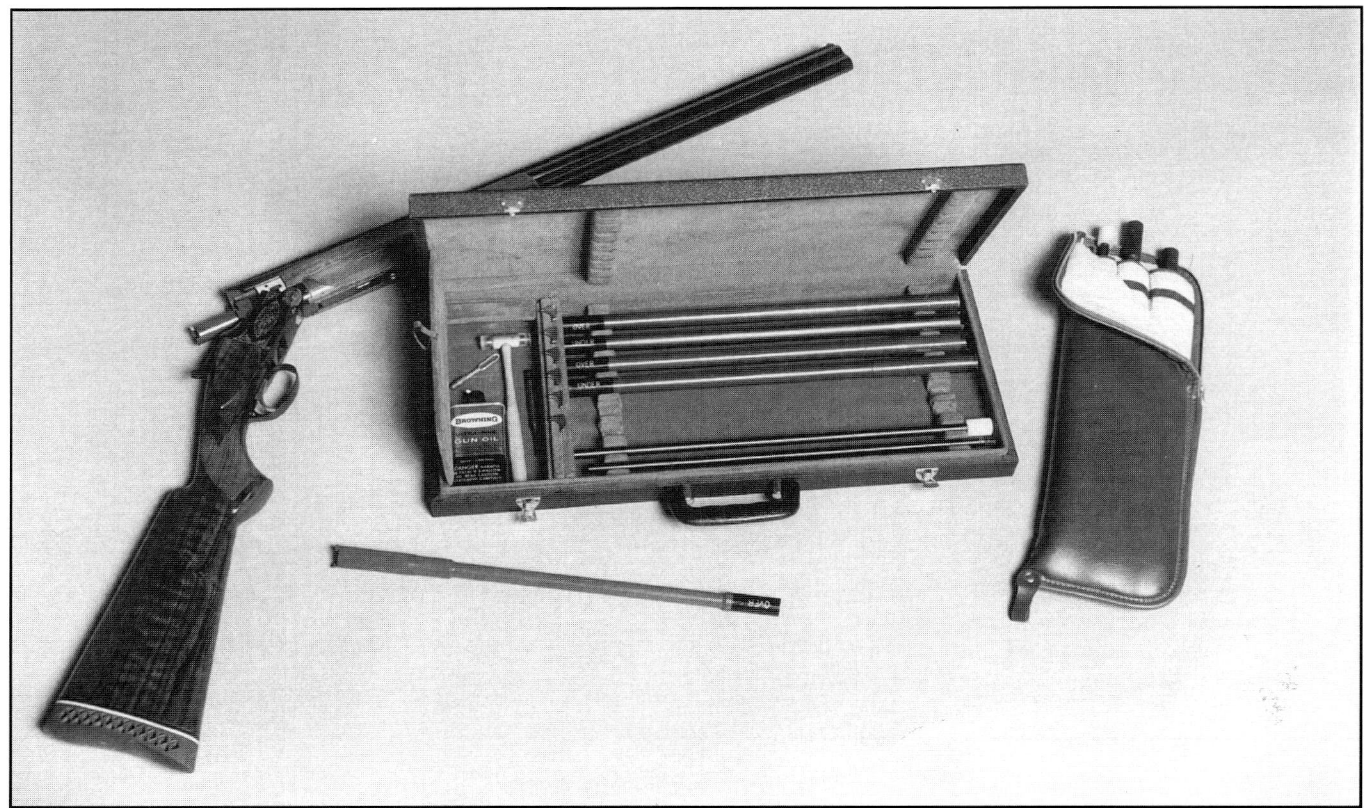

The new "Super-Tubes" were offered either individually or in a set. Factory installation was required. The all gauge set was offered in a fitted case with accessories, while the individual set was sold in a soft case. Courtesy Browning Company.

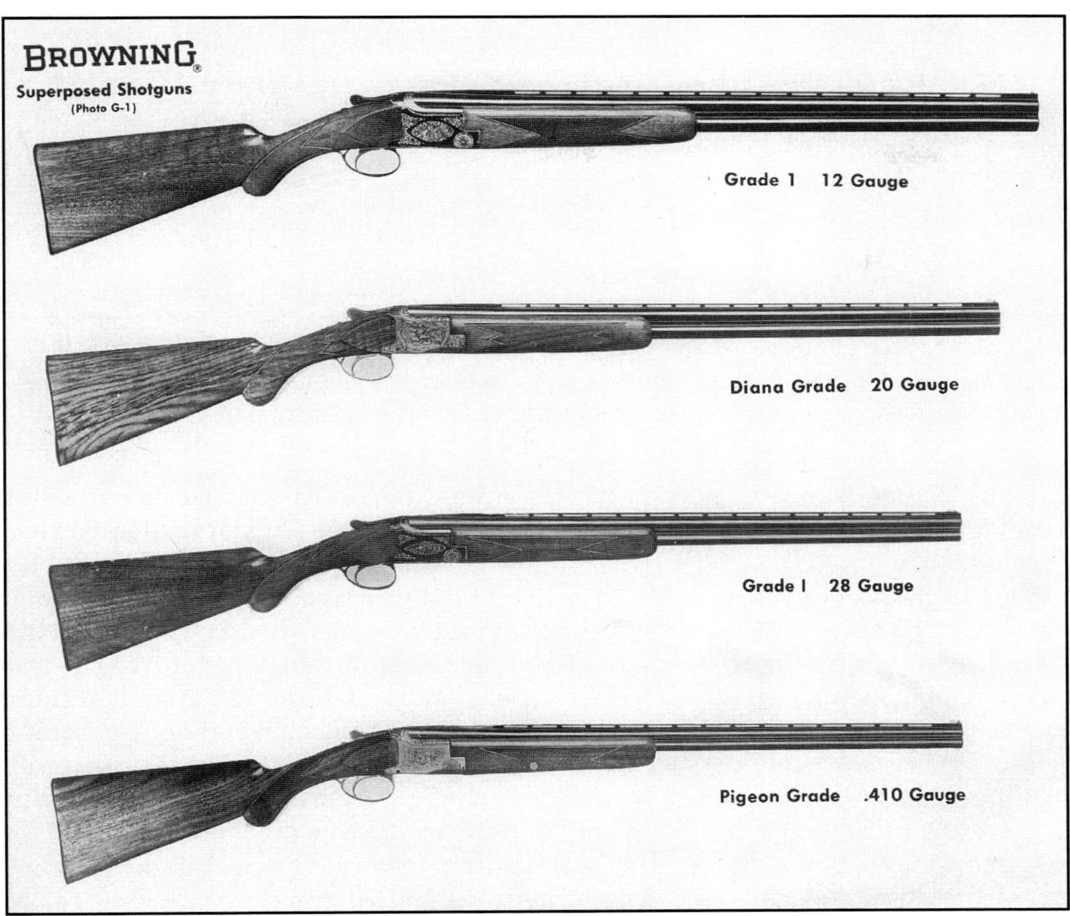

These two Browning Arms Company photographs, circa 1960 to 1966, show the general configuration of several different Superposed models. Photographs such as these are useful in learning about different exterior modifications and appearances during certain eras. Courtesy Browning Company.

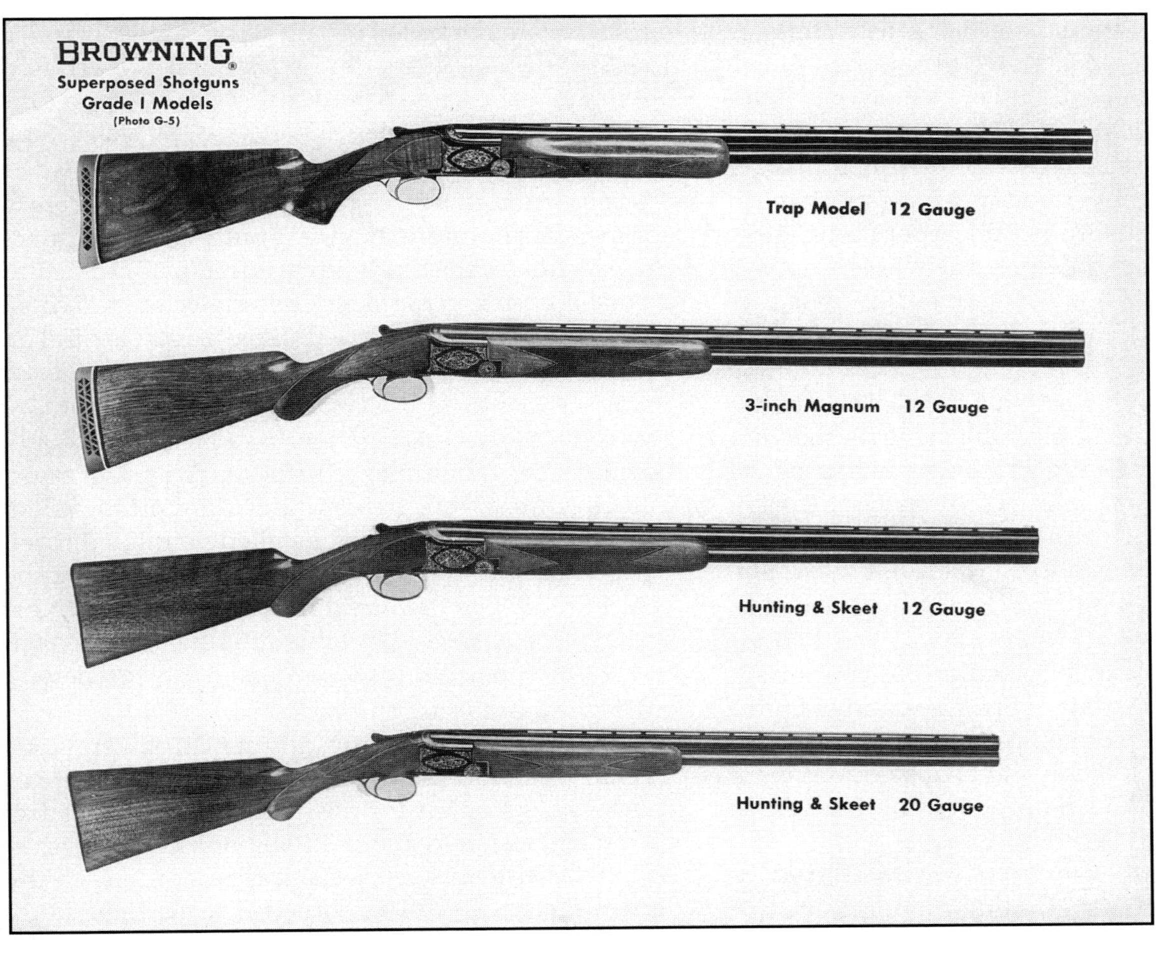

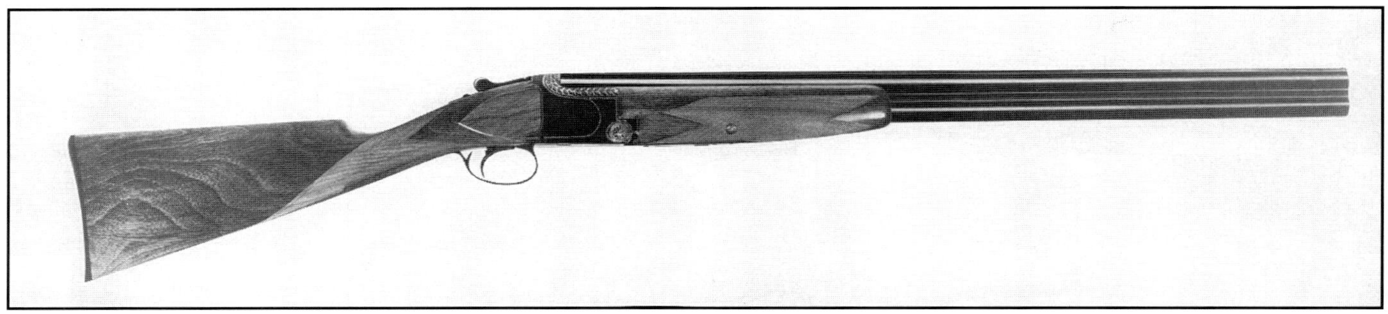

In 1967 Browning introduced its new 12 gauge Superlight Hunting model. In its initial configuration the Superlight was offered with 26-1/2-inch barrels with solid tapered rib and slim forearm. The Superlight in this photo represents this initial appearance. The weight was listed in the company catalogues as 6 pounds 6 ounces. Courtesy Browning Company.

Browning also introduced its "Super-Tubes" inserts on July 15, 1965. Offered for 12 gauge Skeet or Hunting models, these inserts converted a 12 gauge Superposed into a 20 or 28 gauge, or even a .410 bore, in about five minutes. The three-gauge set was priced at $225.00 and required Browning Service Department installation. Single-gauge sets were also offered in 20 gauge, color coded red; 28 gauge, color coded blue; and .410 bore, color coded green, for $85.00 each. The tubes were 16-1/2 inches long and weighed 5-3/4 ounces in 20 gauge, 8 ounces in 28 gauge, and 10 ounces in .410 bore. The single-gauge tubes came in a fitted padded vinyl case with matching ejectors, tap-out, and a cleaning rod. The three-gauge set came in a luggage type case with all of the above accessories plus a cleaning brush, loop, and gun oil. When these "Super-Tubes" were installed at the service facility in St. Louis the standard inertia operated trigger mechanism was converted to a new mechanical trigger system to insure reliable operation. These "Super-Tubes" were not interchangeable.

Retail prices were raised again in 1965, but only moderately. The Lightning Grade I retail price increased $15.00 to $395.00 while the Pigeon Grade price was raised by $30.00 to $550.00 The Pointer Grade retail price remained the same as the year before. The Diana Grade price was increased by only $5.00 to $750.00, and the Midas Grade retail price was raised $30.00 to $1,100.00.

1966: A few changes were made for 1966. The unpopular Hydro-Coil® stock and forearm was dropped from the catalogue as was the Pointer Grade. Prices were again raised due to continuing cost increases on the part of FN. The Grade I Lightning 12 and 20 gauge retail price was increased by only $5.00, and the Pigeon and Diana Grades were raised by $25.00. The retail price for the Midas Grade remained at 1965 levels.

1967: The big news for 1967 was the introduction of the Superposed Hunting model in the Superlight configuration in August. Designed with a straight grip buttstock and slim tapered forearm, it was offered in 12 gauge Grade I only with 26-1/2-inch solid tapered rib barrels choked modified and improved cylinder, or modified and full. The suggested retail price for the new Superlight was $448.50, $36.00 more than the 12 gauge Lightning Grade I. Browning claimed a weight of 6 pounds 6 ounces for its new Superlight model. All other models and configurations remained the same as the previous year. Prices were increased again for 1967—a familiar pattern. Prices for the Grade I Lightning in 12 and 20 gauge were raised $12.50 and for the Pigeon, Diana, and Midas Grades retail prices were increased $25.00 across the board.

1968: Catalogue offerings for the Superposed remained the same for 1968 with the very important exception of the "New Model" Skeet gun. Browning's Superposed "New Model" Skeet was a significant departure from past Superposed Skeet guns. Never more than a Hunting model with skeet chokes, the Skeet Superposed had not distinguished itself on the Skeet stations as its Trap cousins had done since 1960. Offered in 12, 20, and 28 gauge, as well as .410 bore, the "New Model" Skeet was available in both Standard and Lightning weights for 12 and 20 gauge; Standard Weight only for the 28 gauge and .410 bore. A special skeet stock with a full, hand filling flat-bottom pistol grip fitted with a factory installed ventilated recoil pad combined with a beavertail forearm gave the Skeet model its distinctive appearance. The "New Model" Skeet was available in either 26-1/2-inch or 28-inch barrels with ventilated rib fitted with front and center ivory beads.

The year 1968 was no different from previous years when it came to price increases. Retail prices were raised again for all models and grades but only amounted to about a two percent increase.

1969: Browning closed out the decade with the introduction of the Superposed Superlight in 20

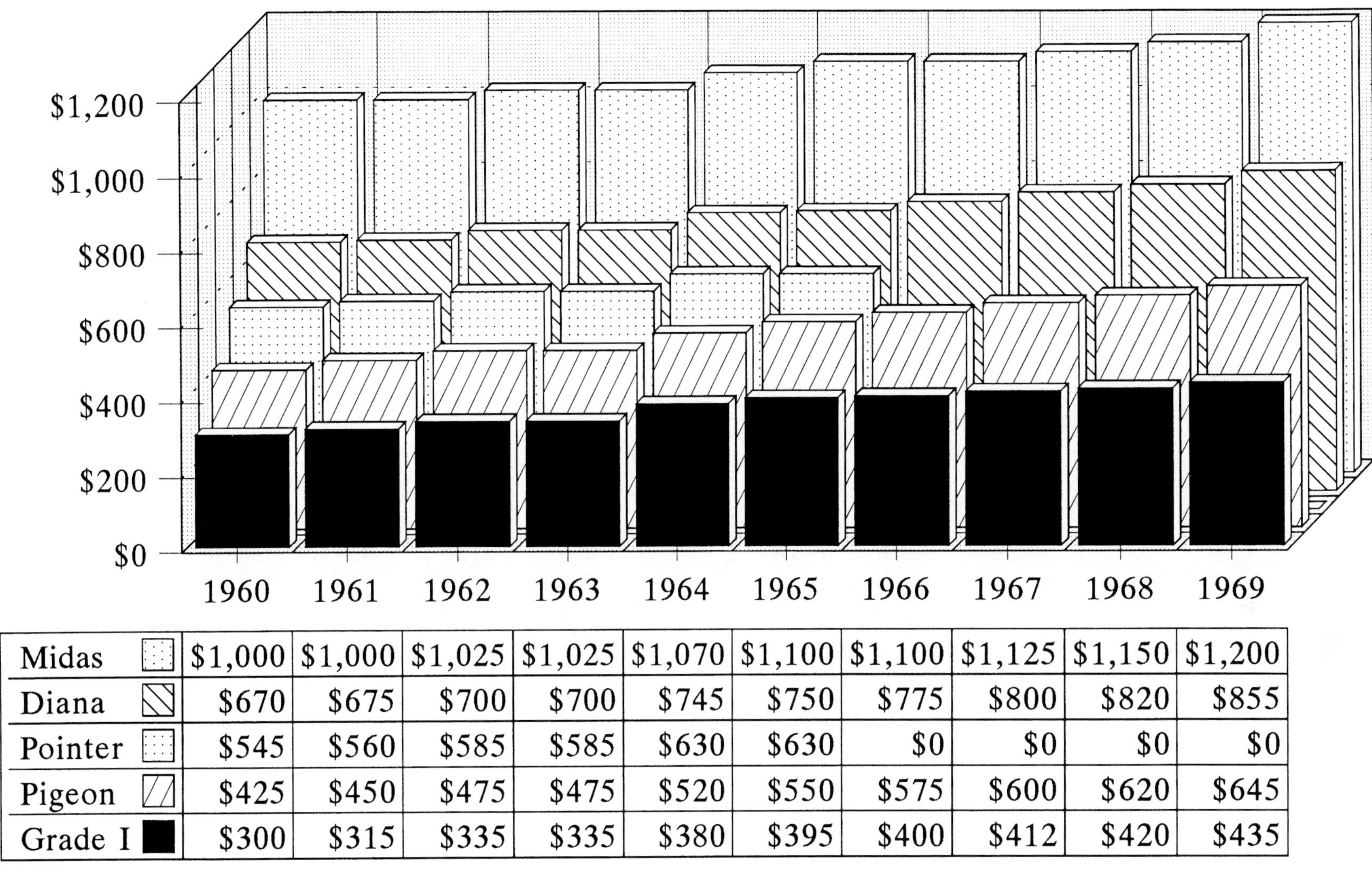

	1960	1961	1962	1963	1964	1965	1966	1967	1968	1969
Midas	$1,000	$1,000	$1,025	$1,025	$1,070	$1,100	$1,100	$1,125	$1,150	$1,200
Diana	$670	$675	$700	$700	$745	$750	$775	$800	$820	$855
Pointer	$545	$560	$585	$585	$630	$630	$0	$0	$0	$0
Pigeon	$425	$450	$475	$475	$520	$550	$575	$600	$620	$645
Grade I	$300	$315	$335	$335	$380	$395	$400	$412	$420	$435

Prices are based on Lightning 12 gauge
Hunting model with ventilated rib.
Pointer Grade discontinued in 1966.

Chart 3-2

gauge. Offered in Grade I only with 26-1/2-inch solid rib barrels, it was a natural addition to the 12 gauge Superlight introduced in 1967. In its standard configuration the 20 gauge Superlight was choked modified and improved cylinder.

For the first time, Browning published retail prices for fitting extra barrels to used Superposed guns. Same gauge barrels for 12 and 20 gauge guns in Grade I were $334.00, while extra 20 gauge barrels for 12 gauge guns were priced at $371.00. Extra barrels in 28 gauge or .410 bore for 20 gauge Superposed were $356.00 for Grade I guns.

Like preceding years, retail prices were raised for all models and grades. In 1969 the retail price of a Grade I Lightning 12 or 20 gauge was $435.00 compared to $300.00 in 1960, an increase of forty-five percent. Every year during the decade, with the exception of 1963, prices were increased for Grade I Lightning Superposed guns.

The Superposed product line grew during the decade of the 1960s, but so did the prices. These price increases were the compelling force behind the manufacturing modifications made to the Superposed during this time period.

The 1960s Superposed: A Decade of Modifications

The Browning Superposed entered the 1960s in many ways unchanged from its predecessor in the prewar era and the years following the war. Production levels had been increased while still keeping quality high, but as the decade progressed the difficulties at Fabrique Nationale forced Browning management to face the realities of the situation and think seriously of methods to keep the Superposed a viable product despite the constant need to raise prices. To keep prices as low as possible during the course of the decade, Browning, in conjunction with Fabrique Nationale, began to make significant engineering changes to the Superposed with the hope of cutting costs. Reducing quality was never considered by Browning, but they did feel certain changes could be made to decrease cost without sacrificing excellence. These manufacturing changeovers did not occur on a precise date because the inventory of earlier parts was used until exhausted. This meant that there was a transition period where new and old parts were used concurrently. This changeover may have occurred over a period of several months or even years, depending on the size of the previously utilized parts inventory. For this reason, the dates of modifications are approximate only.

General Appearance: These modifications appear in all models and gauges. The first noticeable change occurred in the type of buttplate used on Superposed guns. About 1961 the Superposed was fitted with a plastic buttplate similar in appearance to the horn butt which had been in use since the beginning of production in 1930. In 1964 the ejector was modified to cut cost. A pin called the ejector extension stop pin replaced the ejector stop screw, simplifying assembly, saving labor, and strengthening the overall mechanism.

In 1966 the most noticeable modification occurred with the redesign of the pistol grip. The long trigger guard tang was discontinued and a short tang replaced it. The shape of the grip itself was also altered. The grip was originally a half-pistol grip, rounded on the bottom; the new arrangement created a fuller grip with tighter radius and flat bottom with no cap. These modifications accomplished several things. First, some savings were achieved by reducing the cost of bluing. Secondly, the time and expertise required to fit the long tang to the stock was reduced. With a change in the shape of the pistol grip, checkering was somewhat easier and quicker to complete with less handwork than required to carve the older rounded pistol grip.

During this same production period another manufacturing change occurred to the upper tang. The old style "Y" shaped tang was rede-

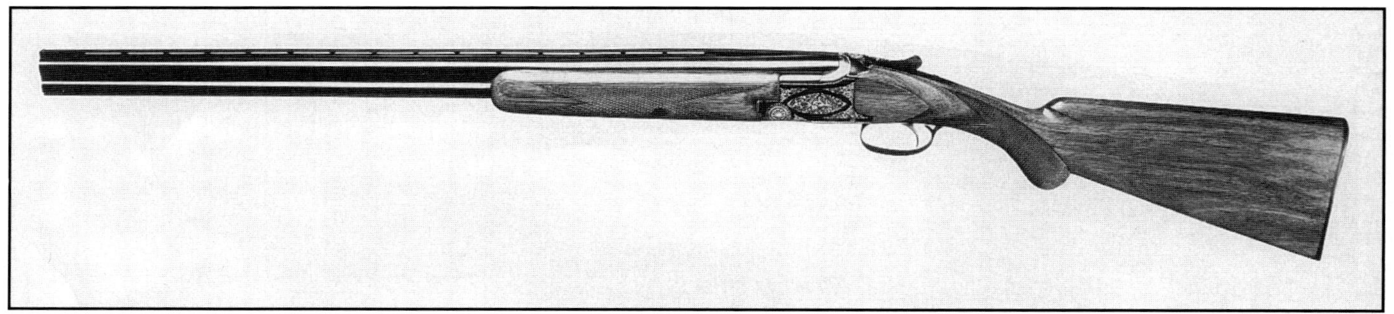

This was the Browning Superposed Lightning model in Grade I as it might have looked in the early to mid-1960s. Courtesy Browning Company.

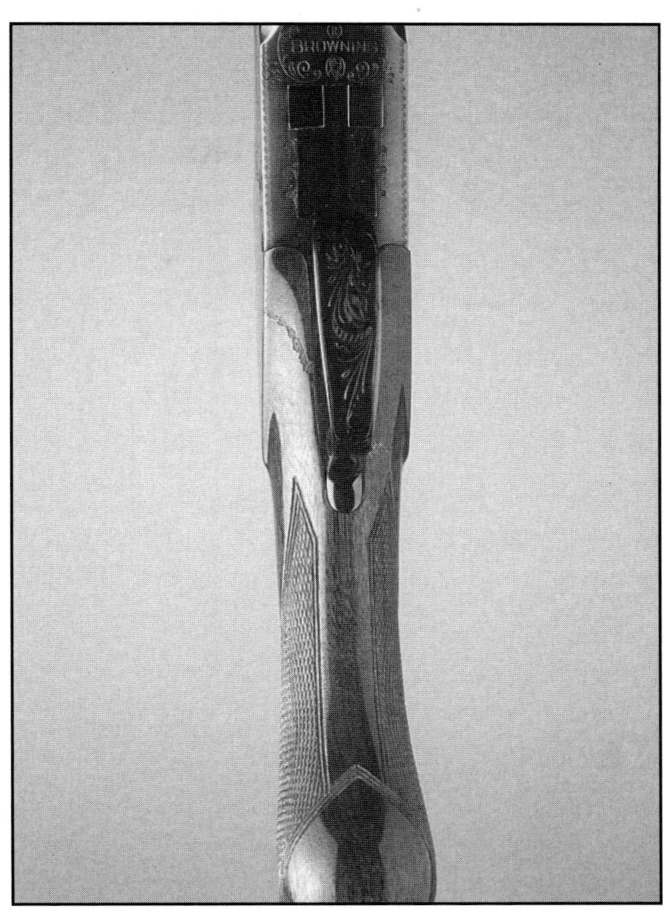

In 1966 Browning modified the lower trigger guard tang and pistol grip configuration. The photo on the left shows the long tang arrangement; the photo on the right shows the new short tang configuration adopted in 1966. Courtesy Browning Company.

signed to a "U" shaped tang to make fitting easier. This changeover between the older "Y" style and the newer "U" style seems to have occurred over a relatively long period of time. It is possible to see both styles of upper tang used between 1966 and 1968.

In 1968 the necessity for further cost reduction continued. Fabrique Nationale suggested, and Browning Arms concurred, that a change in the wood finishing process could be used to reduce costs. After World War II, FN used a Browning-supplied Sherwin Williams commercial non-yellowing lacquer. This gave the wood a flat "oil finish" look, similar to the more expensive hand applied French polish used before the war. FN suggested using a new wood finish known as "Texacryl," an acrylic. This synthetic finish gave the wood much better protection and was faster, easier, and less expensive to apply. The more expensive FN-applied oil finish was still available at an extra charge.

At the beginning of the decade FN continued to use French walnut for all grades of Superposed wood. As the decade progressed, the supply of high quality French walnut became increasingly difficult to acquire. By the mid-1960s California Claro walnut began to appear, especially on high grade Superposed guns. By the end of the decade Claro walnut was used almost exclusively on all Superposed models.

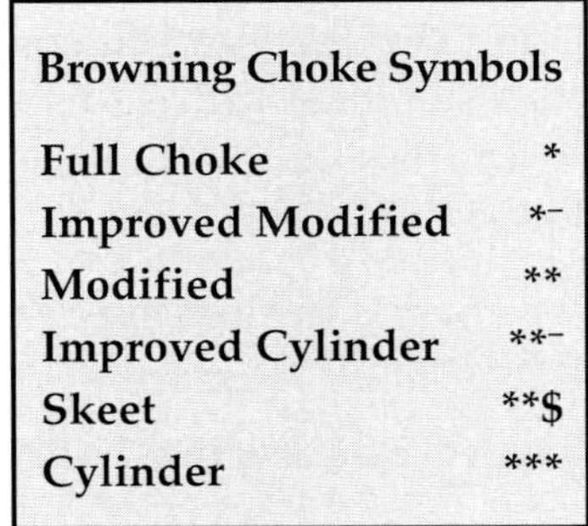

Browning Choke Symbols	
Full Choke	*
Improved Modified	*-
Modified	**
Improved Cylinder	**-
Skeet	**$
Cylinder	***

Another subtle change was made around 1968 with the discontinuation of the two different widths of barrel channels in the Standard Weight Superposed and the Lightning Superposed forearms. Previously, Standard Superposed barrels were fitted with thicker barrel walls that required a wider barrel channel in the forearm to accommodate them. The Lightning Superposed barrels, with narrower barrel walls, could make use of a smaller barrel channel. Gradually Browning adopted one barrel channel width to fit both Standard and Lightning barrels in 12 and 20 gauge.

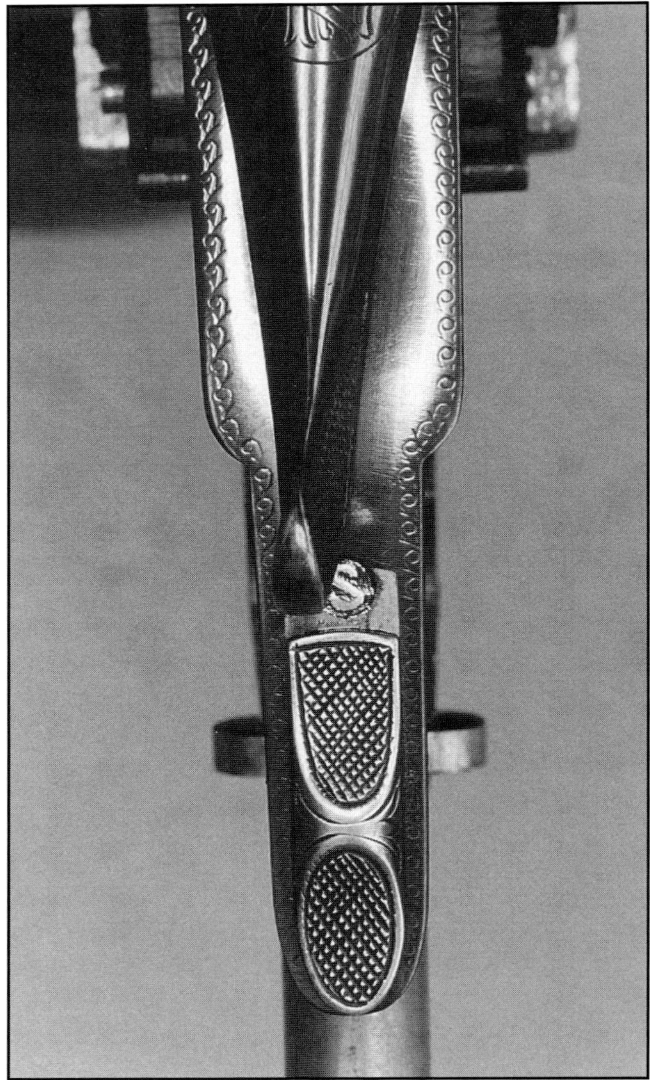

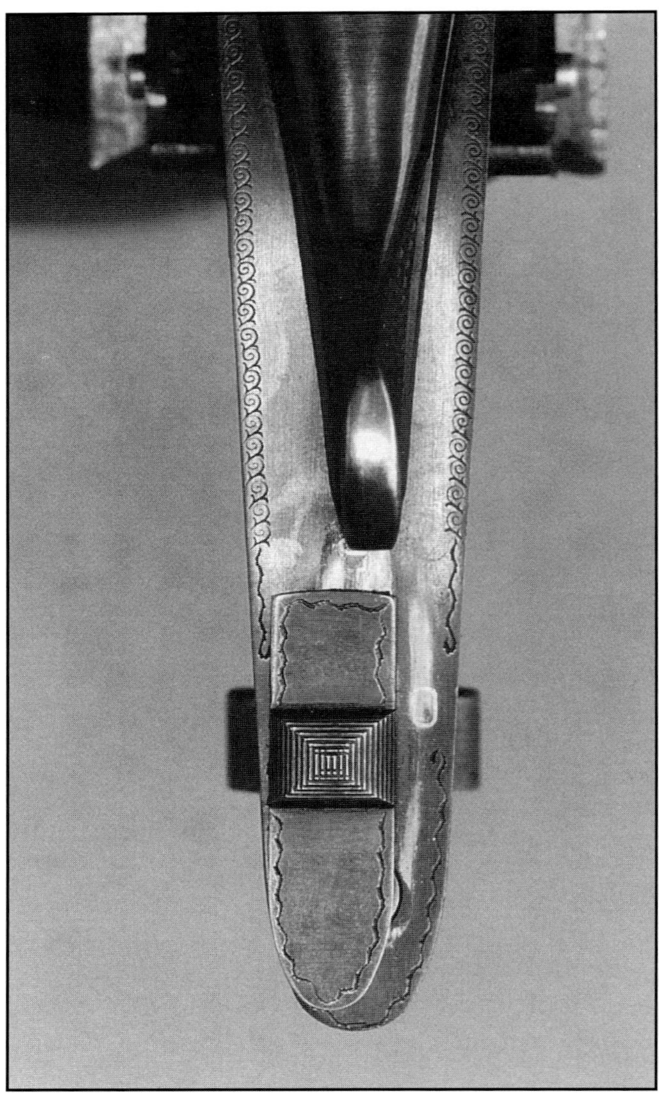

About 1966 Browning and FN decided to modify the top tang to reduce cost. The older "Y" shaped top tang is pictured on the left, while the new "U" shaped style is pictured on the right. It is possible to see both styles from 1966 until about 1968. Photo courtesy Vearl Brown.

From 1960 until late 1968, barrel inscriptions for both the right and left side were the same in content and appearance as the last barrel address used in the 1950s. The left side address that will be seen during the '60s is as follows:

**BROWNING ARMS COMPANY ST. LOUIS MO & MONTREAL P.Q.
MADE IN BELGIUM**

On the right side, the barrel address most often seen is as follows:

**SPECIAL STEEL-12 GA-SHELLS 2 3/4"
PATENTS NO. 2203378-223386**

In place of the patent numbers the following shortened version was sometimes used:

**SPECIAL STEEL-12 GA-SHELLS 2 3/4"
BROWNING PATENTS**

A new barrel inscription began to appear at the end of 1968 or very early in 1969 after the St. Louis sales office moved to Morgan, Utah. On the left side the barrel address will read:

**BROWNING ARMS COMPANY MORGAN UTAH & MONTREAL P.Q.
MADE IN BELGIUM**

The right side address remained the same for the last year of the decade. Some of these barrel inscriptions will be seen on three lines while others may be seen only on one line. The number of lines used for these barrel addresses changed back and forth over the years.

All Superposed guns were fitted with gold triggers regardless of model and grade. All triggers were single selective triggers despite that FN still built Superposed for its markets with a choice of single trigger or double triggers. The Val Browning inertia type were the Standard single triggers used throughout the decade for all gauges including the 28 gauge and .410 bore guns.

Hunting Models: The most noticeable change at the beginning of the decade was the introduction of the Superposed in 28 gauge and .410 bore. These new gauges were in fact built on a 20 gauge frame, so the only new aspect was the addition of the barrels. Both the 28 gauge and .410 bore Superposed barrels were referred to by Browning as Standard Weight. These two small gauges were not offered in a Lightning configuration. Both the 28 and .410 were fitted with ventilated ribs one quarter of an inch wide, the same as the 20 gauge Superposed. The customer had a choice of 26-1/2-inch or 28-inch barrels with any combination of chokes. The 28 gauge was chambered for the 2-3/4-inch shell, and the .410 bore was chambered for both 2-1/2-inch and 3-inch shells. The buttstock and forearm on the Hunting 28 and .410 models were also the same dimensions as those used on the 20 gauge Hunting model. In essence, the 28 gauge and .410 bore Superposed were 20 gauge guns fitted with small bore barrels. Because they were fitted to 20 gauge frames, these small gauge guns were actually heavier than the 20 gauge Lightning Superposed with identical barrel lengths.

It should be noted that high grade Superposed will most likely be heavier than those weights listed below due to the finer figured wood, which is generally denser and therefore heavier than the walnut used on Grade I Superposed.

APPROXIMATE WEIGHTS FOR 20 AND 28 GAUGE, AND .410 BORE SUPERPOSED HUNTING MODELS

20 ga. Standard	20 ga. Lightning	28 ga. Standard	.410 bore Standard
28"	28"	28"	28"
6 lb. 12 oz	6 lb. 4 oz	6 lb. 6 oz	6 lb. 9 oz
26-1/2"	26-1/2"	26-1/2"	26-1/2"
6 lb. 8 oz	6 lb.	6 lb. 3 oz	6 lb. 5 oz

Table 3-3

The 12 gauge and 20 gauge Hunting models did not change with the arrival of the '60s except for buttstock dimensions. Prior to 1960 these dimensions were the same for both gauges. After 1960 these dimensions were changed in the drop at the heel and the comb. The 12 gauge proportions remained the same but the 20 gauge dimensions were altered to be 1-1/2 inches at the comb and 2-3/8 inches at the heel, compared to 1-5/8 inches at the comb and 2-1/2 inches at the heel for the 12 gauge. Length of pull was the same for both gauges, 14-1/4 inches. Checkering patterns remained unchanged, with Grade I Superposed having twenty lines to the inch. Higher grades had progressively finer checkering. The forearm on the Hunting models continued to feature the blunt nose configuration that was a hallmark of the Lightning model.

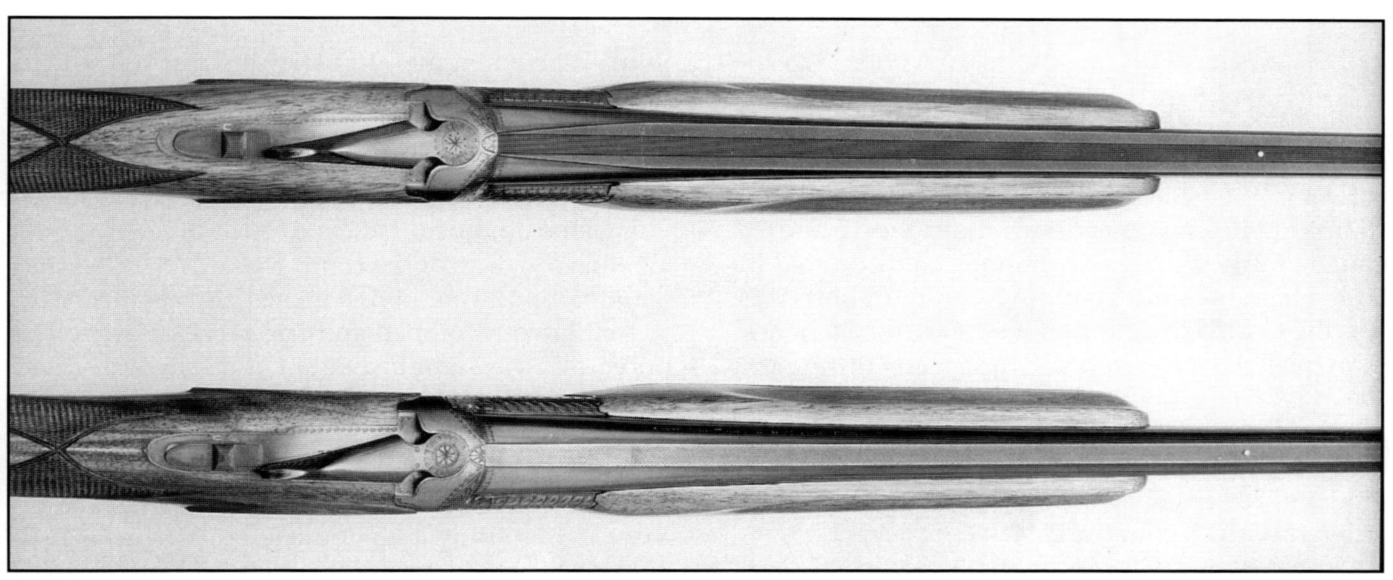

This top view of a Lightning Trap model on the bottom and a BROADway Trap model on the top gives graphic evidence of the difference between the two ventilated rib designs. The width of the standard Trap rib was 5/16 of an inch; the BROADway rib was 5/8 of an inch wide. Courtesy Fabrique Nationale Archives.

Browning went to great lengths to explain and sell the concept of its new Superposed BROADway Trap model. The gun sighting plane was longer than comparable Trap guns and the extra width helped the eye to quickly align itself to the target. The new ventilated BROADway rib dissipated heat faster without distortion. Courtesy Russ Church.

The 12 gauge Hunting model was offered in 26-1/2-inch or 28-inch barrel lengths, and with 30-inch barrels in the 12 gauge 3-inch Magnum model. The 20 gauge Hunting model buyer had a choice between 26-1/2-inch or 28-inch barrels with any choice of choke combinations. Both the 12 and 20 gauge Hunting models continued to be offered in both Standard and Lightning configurations. As was the case during most of the 1950s, the Standard Superposed was offered in Grade I only during the 1960s, while the Lightning model was offered in all grades. For the first time, Superposed Hunting models could be ordered with extra sets of barrels in 12 and 20 gauge. Twenty gauge models could be ordered with 28 gauge and .410 bore barrels.

Trap Models: The Standard Superposed Trap model, introduced in 1951, was dropped from the line in 1960, leaving the Lightning Trap, introduced in 1955, as the only Trap model available until 1961 when the BROADway Trap was added to the product line. The Lightning Trap featured a 30-inch set of barrels with a width rib of 5/16 of an inch, the same width as the 12 gauge Hunting model. The Lightning Trap had special trap dimensions on the buttstock: drop at the heel was 1-3/4 inches, drop at the comb was 1-3/8 inches and length of pull was 14-3/8 inches. It was fitted with a ventilated recoil pad and special semi-beavertail forearm. The semi-beavertail forearm was fitted with a crossbolt screw. In 1966 this forearm was replaced by a full beavertail forearm fitted with an extended longitudinal screw with a crescent shaped end piece on the front of the forearm to secure it. Lightning Trap models built prior to 1960 had a semi-pistol grip with rounded bottom knob similar to the Hunting models. In 1960 the grip was changed to a full pistol grip with square knob and no grip cap.

In 1961 the BROADway Trap model was introduced. What set this model apart from the Lightning Trap was the wider rib fitted to its barrel. All other aspects of the model were identical with the Lightning Trap. This BROADway rib was 5/8 of an inch wide and had distinctive grooves on either side of the line of sight. The BROADway Trap was offered with a choice of either 30-inch or 32-inch barrels choked to the customer's specifications. Later in the decade Browning made the special BROADway rib available on 26-1/2-inch or 28-inch barrels. The BROADway Trap weighed the same as the Lightning Trap with 30-inch barrels: 7 lb. 12 oz. The 32-inch barreled BROADway Trap weighed in at an even 8 pounds. Like the Lightning Trap, it too was fitted with a contoured ventilated recoil pad and had the same buttstock dimensions. The recoil pad was installed by FN and supplied by Pachmayr. It was a Jumbo #550 Trap pad, brown with white line spacer. Both Trap models were furnished with front and center ivory sights, and both models were offered in all high grade engraving patterns.

Skeet Models: The Browning Superposed Skeet models remained as they had been during the decade of the 1950s—essentially Hunting models with skeet chokes. It was not until 1968 that Browning redesigned its Skeet model to become a distinct model. Browning called its new skeet gun the "New Model" Skeet, and it was offered in 12,

In 1968 Browning Arms Company redesigned its Skeet model Superposed into a dedicated Skeet model. Features of this new model were a Pachmayr recoil pad, beavertail forearm, and special skeet dimension buttstock. Notice the short tang and flat bottom pistol grip, or knob, that was standard for all Browning Superposed after 1968. Shown here is the Grade I Skeet model. Courtesy Browning Company.

SUPERPOSED NEW MODEL SKEET APPROXIMATE WEIGHTS

Gauge and Style	Barrel Length/Weight
12 ga. Standard New Model Skeet	28" – 7 lb. 14 oz. 26-1/2" – 7 lb. 12 oz.
12 ga. Lightning New Model Skeet	28" – 7 lb. 11 oz. 26-1/2" – 7 lb. 9 oz.
20 ga. Standard New Model Skeet	28" – 6 lb. 15 oz. 26-1/2" – 6 lb. 13 oz.
20 ga. Lightning New Model Skeet	28" – 6 lb. 12 oz. 26-1/2" – 6 lb. 8 oz.
28 ga. Standard New Model Skeet	28" – 6 lb. 14 oz. 26-1/2" 6 lb. 11 oz.
.410 bore Standard New Model Skeet	28" – 7 lb. 26-1/2" – 6 lb. 13 oz.

Table 3-4

20, and 28 gauge, as well as .410 bore. It possessed several new features that made it stand apart from the Hunting model for the first time. The Superposed "New Model" Skeet was furnished with a skeet style buttstock and forearm. The pistol grip was full with a square knob and no cap. The buttstock on all Skeet models had a drop at the heel of 2 inches, a drop at the comb of 1-1/2 inches, and a length of pull of 14-3/8 inches. The forearm was a full grip beavertail that did not utilize a crossbolt screw for support but used instead a longitudinal screw with crescent shaped end piece. This was the same forearm used on both Superposed Trap models. Skeet models in all gauges used the same length forearm, the only difference being in the width of the barrel channel dictated by the gauge of barrels used and their weight. All Skeet models were fitted with a noncontoured ventilated recoil pad. Like the Trap models, Pachmayr supplied FN its large size #325 Skeet pad, brown with white line spacer. The Browning logo was molded on the face of the pad.

The buyer had a choice of 26-1/2-inch or 28-inch ventilated rib barrels with front and center ivory bead sights. Chokes were, of course, skeet and skeet. These Skeet models weighed more than the Hunting models, most likely because of the recoil pad and the forearm style.

Superlight Models: Introduced in 1967 in 12 gauge Grade I only, and in 1969 in 20 gauge Grade I only, this Superposed model represented a sharp departure from the usually traditional and conservative Superposed product line. Superposed guns with straight grip stocks had been available in Europe for FN customers for many years because of the popularity of straight grip guns there. The Browning Superlight that was introduced in the U.S., however, was more than just a Lightning Superposed with a straight grip stock. Browning designed this new model to appeal to the upland bird hunter and built it as an ultralight field gun.

The frame began as a 12 gauge Lightning frame but the bottom edges of the frame were rounded to save weight. There was no engraving on the frame itself with the exception of a small area on the barrel wings. The buttstock was fitted with a straight grip and plastic buttplate. These early Superlight buttstocks had no flutes in the comb, as was the European preference. The buttstock dimensions were the same as those for the 12 gauge Hunting model: 1-5/8-inch drop at the comb, 2-1/2-inch drop at the heel, and a 14-1/4-inch length of pull. The forearm was a slim tapered style with crossbolt, shorter in length overall than the Lightning forearm. Both the 12 gauge and, in 1969, the 20 gauge were offered with 26-1/2-inch barrels fitted with a solid tapered rib. During the latter part of the 1960s about two hundred 12 gauge Superlights were sold with 28-inch barrels.

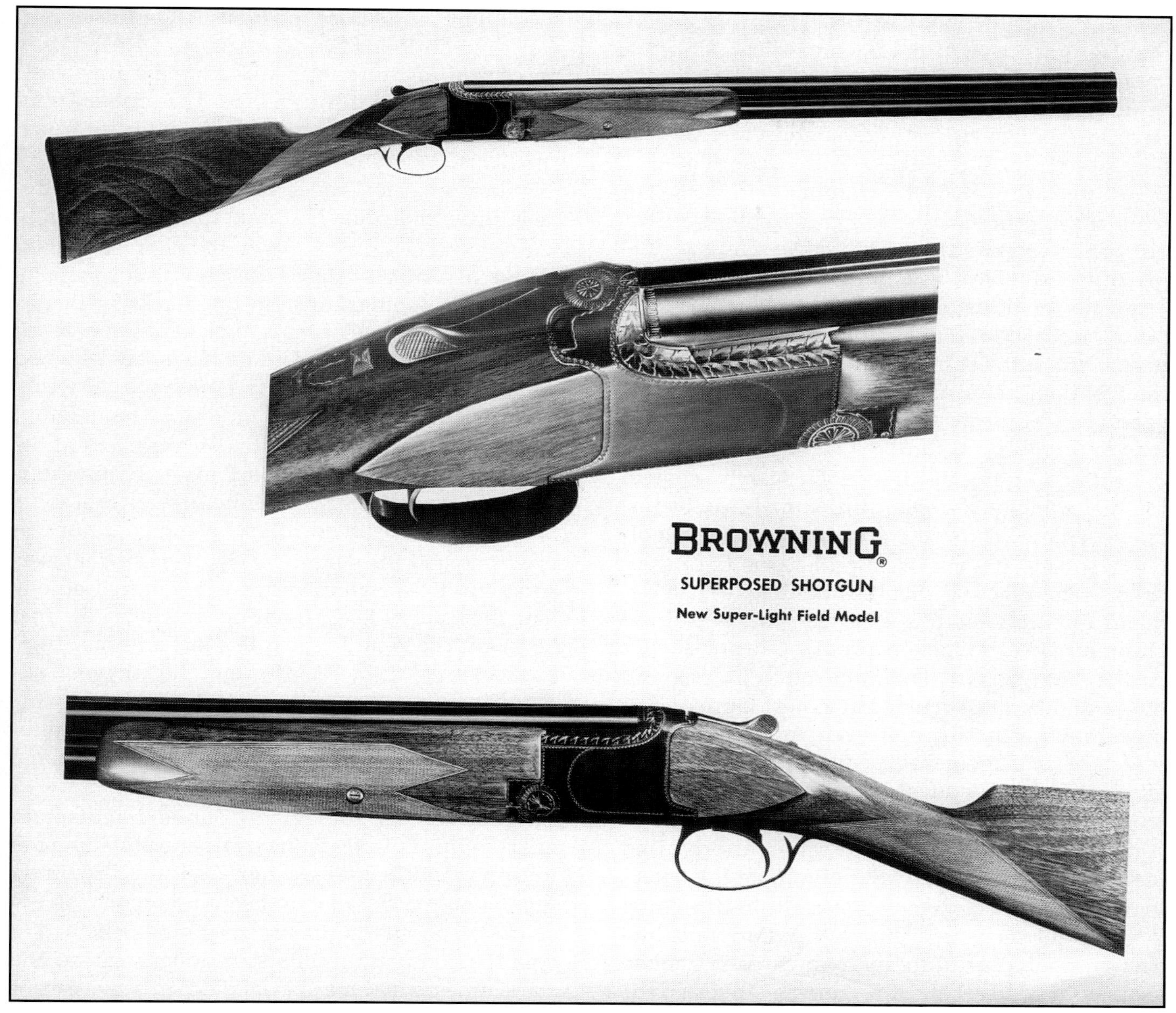

These three views of the late 1960s Browning Superlight show detail of the slim forearm, straight grip stock, rounded frame, and engraving treatment on the receiver. It was not until 1969 that the Superlight was offered in 20 gauge. Courtesy Browning Company.

Both the 12 and 20 gauge Superlights were chambered for 2-3/4-inch shells. There is no record that any engraved Browning Superlights were sold in North America during the 1960s, but it is possible that a few special order guns may have been engraved. The 12 gauge Superlight with 26-1/2-inch barrels weighed approximately 6 lb. 6 oz. while the 20 gauge Superlight weighed about an even 6 lb.

The Salt Wood Debacle

Perhaps no other American gun company managed a potentially disastrous situation better than the Browning Arms Company. Much has been written about the salt wood problem on Browning guns but it seems fitting to present the whole account, including background, in this history of the Superposed. The story begins in the mid-1960s. Because of the ever-increasing demand for the Browning Superposed, especially in the high grade guns, Fabrique Nationale was having difficulty finding acceptable high grade French Walnut for buttstocks and forearms. By this time even fancy American black walnut was in short supply. The solution lay in finding an alternate supply of high grade fancy walnut at reasonable prices and with a reliable inventory. Harm Williams, Browning's vice president of sales, heard about a man named Joe Oakley who was in the business of clearing trees from power line right-of-ways in the Sacramento, California area. This region of California has a high concentration of Claro walnut trees. The wood has a beautiful, highly figured grain, and there was an ample supply. Joe Oakley had accumulated a large inventory of Claro walnut over the years from cutting these trees, so Harm Williams went out to Sacramento to see Mr. Oakley and his supply of wood. Harm was impressed with what he saw, and the decision was made to have Joe supply Claro wood blanks for all of Browning's needs. Browning promptly set up a kiln to air dry the wood and consulted with experts at the University of California at Davis to determine the best way to do this procedure.

This new source of Claro wood supply seemed, for the moment, to solve Browning's problems. However, the kiln drying process took time and often resulted in over-drying the wood, causing cracks. These new difficulties occurred when demand for Browning Superposed guns was at an all-time high. Production problems were always part of the Superposed manufacturing process, but this new dilemma occurred at a most inopportune time, slowing production even further. Another search by management discovered a better, more efficient process and faster method of curing these wood blanks.

The new method involved salt, and promised to speed up the process and eliminate the cracking problem. This process was sold to Browning by the Morton Salt Company in 1965 and had been in use by furniture manufacturers for many years with good results. Browning even tested the process independently with no indication of any problems. In an area roughly the size of a football field, five-foot by five-foot by eight-foot stacks of stock blanks were covered with salt. The salt was supposed to leach out the moisture and dry the wood quickly. The process did accomplish its purpose but the moisture that was drawn out of the blanks on top of the stacks ran down into the blanks below, resulting in a brine solution that soaked the lower wood blanks. Although the blanks appeared superficially to be dried, they did in fact contain salt that would react to metal, destroying it after a period of time. The time this took and the extent of the damage depended on the amount of salt in the wood. All of this curing was done in the U.S. and affected at least ninety percent of all stocks for all Browning firearms[19] for the years 1967 through 1969. The problem continued to show up as late as 1972, but in much smaller numbers.

When the salt wood problem first began to appear, Browning and FN sought to correct the problem by trying to wash away the salt. The wood blanks had been shipped to Belgium for installation on Browning guns, so the stacks of blanks were loaded on pallets and trucked down to River Meuse where cranes picked up the pallets of wood and dunked them into the river in hopes of washing away the harmful salt buildup. This attempt appeared to have only limited success, and at the suggestion of several chemical experts, numerous other solutions were tried. Browning felt that some of these remedies were effective and continued to use the wood for its gun stocks. The disaster was compounded when it was discovered that no one had thought to keep track of which blanks had been salt cured and which blanks had not. Errors seemed to create more errors and the salt wood situation continued over the course of several years. Finally, around 1972 the entire supply of walnut blanks was burned and replaced with traditional kiln dried walnut.[20]

What sets the Browning Company above and apart in this episode is the company's willingness to honor its lifetime warranty on any Browning gun damaged by salt cured wood by replacing the stocks at no charge to the customer. This action cost the company millions of dollars, but at the same time earned it a special place in the hearts of its customers. Even today the company is continuing to replace salt cured stocks on Superposed guns owned by the original owner with a registered warranty card. Secondary owners with no warranty card are currently directed to other repair sources.

The best method of determining whether or not a Superposed is fitted with a salt wood stock is to first carefully examine the outward appearance of the gun for discolored wood or dark spots. Slide the forearm away from the breech end of the barrels to look for signs of rust on metal parts. For a more definitive determination, remove the buttplate, scrape away a small amount of exposed

---

[19] The salt wood problem was originally discovered on T-Bolt rifles. It appeared on all Browning firearms including Mauser rifles and even Hi-Power pistol stocks.

[20] The above account of the salt wood problem was told to the author in a personal interview with Mr. Harm Williams, July 15, 1993, and in a separate interview with Mr. John Val Browning, August 23, 1993.

wood and apply a one percent solution of silver nitrate to the fresh wood.[21] If the silver nitrate remains a light purple then there is no evidence of salt in the buttstock, but if the solution turns white that is a clear warning that salt has contaminated the buttstock or forearm.

As a general rule, higher grade Superposed guns are more likely to have salt cured stocks than Grade I guns. This is due to the scarcity of highly figured French and American black walnut, making the need for high grade wood greater. Also as a general rule, buttstocks appear to be more susceptible to the salt wood problem than forearm wood. The best advice for anyone considering purchasing a Superposed produced between 1966 and 1972 is to check the gun over carefully before purchase, regardless of outward appearances.

1960s Superposed Production

The 1960s were a decade of change not only for the Browning Arms Company but also for Fabrique Nationale's production procedures. The use of separate serial numbers on its 12 and 20 gauge guns continued, along with separate sets of serial numbers for the newly introduced 28 gauge and .410 bore. In 1960, 12 gauge Superposed production began approximately with serial number 70746 and 20 gauge production numbers started around serial number 16322. The 28 gauge and .410 bore serial numbers began somewhere in the mid double-digit range. The years 1960 through 1962 are critical for the individual who wants to date the production of a particular Superposed, and the table below will provide a rough estimate of the dates of manufacture.

BROWNING SUPERPOSED SERIAL NUMBERS, ESTIMATED DATES OF MANUFACTURE[22] 1960-1969

Year	12 Gauge Serial #s	20 Gauge Serial #s	28 Gauge Serial #s	.410 Bore Serial #s
1960	70745-79543	16322-19340	50-281	50-282
1961	79544-89554	19340-22851	282-319	283-340
1962	89555-99999 1-2000	22852-25676	320-421	341-476
1963	2001-11960	25677-29057	422-572	477-625
1964	11961-24296	29058-32054	573-718	626-800
1965	24297-38977	32055-36677	719-929	801-987
1966	38978-52332	36678-40850	930-1191	988-1363
1967	52333-69252	40851-45064	1192-1583	1364-1835
1968	69253-84730	45065-50319	1584-2053	1836-2261
1969	84731-99999 1-4881	50320-55212	2054-2439	2262-2890

Table 3-5

[21] There was some disagreement between FN and Browning on how best to test for salt. The Browning service facility in Arnold, Missouri, uses a one percent solution of silver nitrate while FN used a five percent solution. The thinking was that if a one percent solution performed well, then five percent would do even better. In fact, the one percent solution is the much more accurate formula to test for salt content.

[22] FN switched from a fiscal year ending June 30 to a calendar year at the end of 1960. These serial number dates of manufacture reflect that changeover. For the sake of clarity, the alphanumeric code has been deleted from these estimated dates of manufacture.

The reader must be cautioned that, like the years before 1960, production of Superposed frames and assembly of those frames into complete guns did not follow a consecutive serial numbered pattern. Moreover, the assembly of a Superposed on a specific date does not indicate the date of sale. In most cases sales occurred in the year the gun was completed, but there are numerous exceptions to this practice. There are many, many deviations from the norm, making dating of Superposed by serial number very complex and uncertain. Using a combination of FN shipping records and FN sales data, an approximate date of manufacture may be estimated. Remember these dates are imprecise because FN did not assemble Superposed on a consecutive serial numbered basis. In certain instances Superposed with consecutive serial numbers may have been assembled as many as two or three years apart. What sets the 1960s apart from prior decades is demand. Greater demand for the Superposed resulted in more consecutive serial numbered guns being shipped to Browning and other agents throughout the world in relatively large groups of guns. Despite this demand, it is not unusual for consecutive serial numbered Superposed to be six months to one year apart in assembly.[23]

To illustrate the increased demand for the Superposed during the 1960s, Chart 3-4 offers a clear picture. Between 1960 and 1969 FN sold 132,167 Superposed in 12 gauge and 38,841 in 20 gauge worldwide. The company also sold 2,439 guns 28 gauge and 2,890 in .410 bore during the same period. The total of these four gauges is 176,337, or an average of 17,638 Superposed sold by FN each year. Chart 3-3 reveals the strong, almost constantly rising, yearly sales for the 12 gauge Superposed throughout the decade. The 20 gauge Superposed displayed steady sales but did not show the dramatic yearly increases of the 12 gauge.

On October 10, 1962, the number of Browning 12 gauge Superposed produced by FN reached 99,999. The company decided to restart the serial numbers beginning with serial number 1, assembled October 11, 1962. It is therefore possible to see two 12 gauge Superposed guns with the same serial number between 1 and 2000; one built between 1930 and 1934 and the second produced in 1962. However, the second set of serial numbers will have the alphanumeric suffix "S2" as part of the serial number.

Both Browning and Fabrique Nationale could foresee the confusion that this system was bound to cause, and a decision was made to implement a new serial number arrangement. On January 22, 1963, a memorandum from John Val Browning to Grant Goddard outlined a new serial numbering system. Beginning January 1, 1963, FN would now officially use a series of alphanumeric codes in conjunction with its serial numbers. This code would identify the year and gauge in which the Superposed was produced by Fabrique Nationale. In actual practice the code was introduced on the production line in September of 1962. The alphanumeric code stamping began in the fall of 1962 with the designation "S2" for the 12 gauge and "V2" for the 20 gauge, and so on. This new serial numbering system resulted in the following classifications:

BROWNING SUPERPOSED ALPHANUMERIC SERIAL NUMBER SYSTEM: 1962-1969

Gauge	1962-1969
Superposed 12 gauge	—S2, S3, S4, etc.
Superposed 20 gauge	—V2, V3, V4, etc.
Superposed 28 gauge	—F2, F3, F4, etc.
Superposed .410 bore	—J2, J3, J4, etc.

Table 3-6

For the first time, Browning Superposed owners could tell at a glance the year and gauge of their Superposed. This new system was used through 1976. In the latter part of 1969 Browning and FN altered the alphanumeric designation slightly with the addition of two digits for the year instead of just one. Obviously, when the year 1972 arrived a whole new problem would occur if this change were not implemented. For the years 1969 to 1976, a 12 gauge Superposed, for example, would have a serial number code that looked something like this: 1234S69 or 1234S74.

The new serial number system had to begin with one Superposed. Research of the FN shipping records reveals an interesting occurrence. As early as serial number 23200V2, FN stamped the alphanumeric code on 20 gauge Superposed. The practice

[23] See Chapter 1, footnote number 12, for a detailed example of inconsistency in date of assembly from one group of Superposed to another in the same serial number range.

FN SUPERPOSED YEARLY SALES WORLDWIDE 12 AND 20 GAUGE 1960-1969

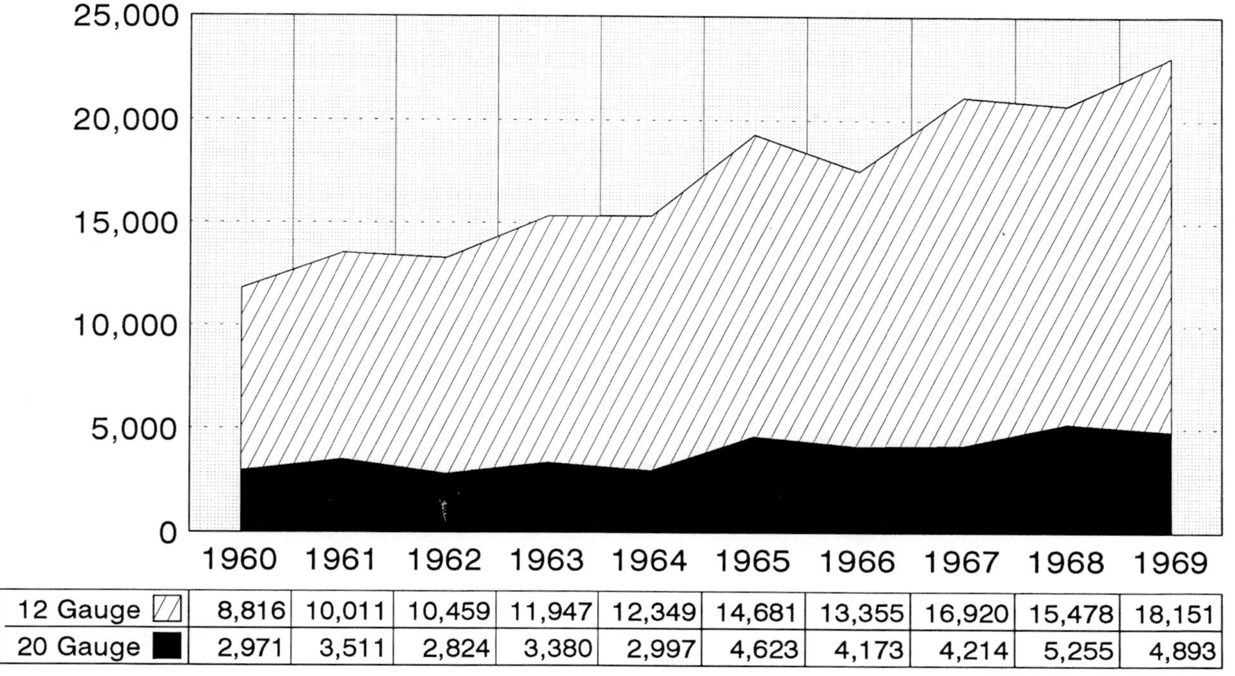

	1960	1961	1962	1963	1964	1965	1966	1967	1968	1969
12 Gauge	8,816	10,011	10,459	11,947	12,349	14,681	13,355	16,920	15,478	18,151
20 Gauge	2,971	3,511	2,824	3,380	2,997	4,623	4,173	4,214	5,255	4,893

Chart 3-3

FN SUPERPOSED CUM. SALES WORLDWIDE 12 AND 20 GAUGE 1960-1969

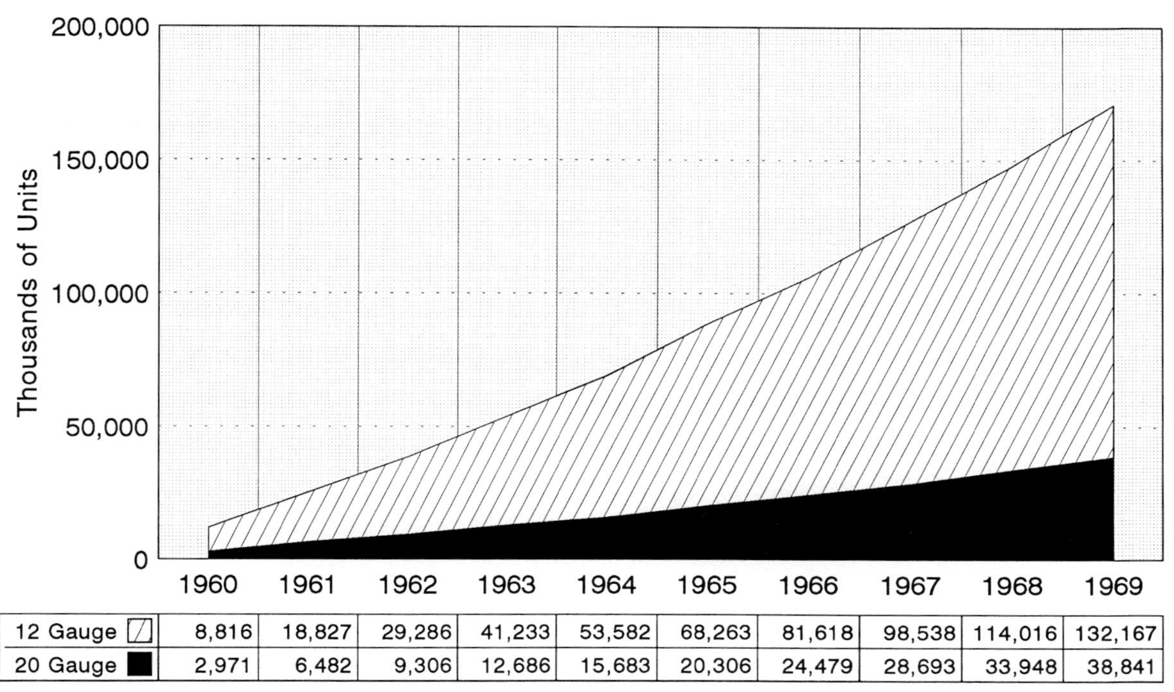

	1960	1961	1962	1963	1964	1965	1966	1967	1968	1969
12 Gauge	8,816	18,827	29,286	41,233	53,582	68,263	81,618	98,538	114,016	132,167
20 Gauge	2,971	6,482	9,306	12,686	15,683	20,306	24,479	28,693	33,948	38,841

Chart 3-4

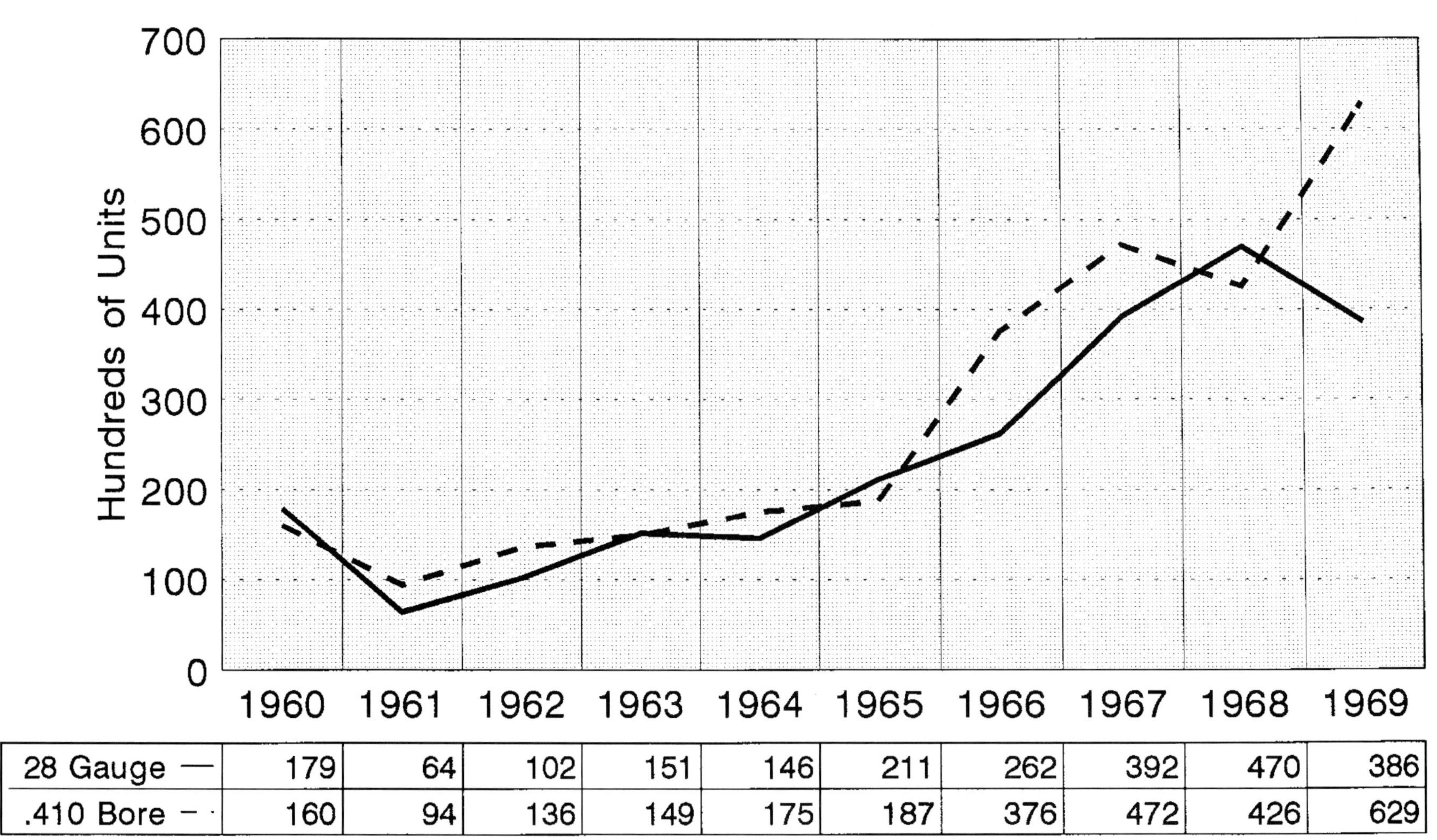

	1960	1961	1962	1963	1964	1965	1966	1967	1968	1969
28 Gauge —	179	64	102	151	146	211	262	392	470	386
.410 Bore - ·	160	94	136	149	175	187	376	472	426	629

Chart 3-5

did not become common until serial number 23500V2 during the winter of 1962. For 12 gauge Superposed the first recorded use of the new system was serial number 92509S2, completed November 1962. The practice of stamping all 12 gauge Superposed with the alphanumeric code did not begin entirely until serial numbers were restarted with number 1S2, completed October 11, 1962. The earliest known 1963 marked frame is serial number 5868S3, completed on July 11, 1963, and shipped to Schroeder Wagner in Germany on November 18, 1963.

Demand for the Superposed was so exceptional during the 1960s that FN faced a second turnover of serial numbers for the 12 gauge. On August 22, 1969, serial number 99999S69 was assembled and sent to FN's shipping department where it was sent to Browning on September 3, 1969. Serial number 1S69 was assembled June 13, 1969, and shipped to Browning on June 27, 1969.

There is one important additional exception to this new alphanumeric system that Browning implemented on all its Superposed guns in 1962, and that is the unique alphanumeric code utilized on the 28 gauge and .410 bore when these small gauges were first produced in the fall of 1959. This small bore system was used through 1962, and if not understood can create confusion. Instead of placing the single-digit year of production after the gauge letter code as was done in the fall of 1962, the single-digit production year was placed ahead of the letter code, with the alphanumeric code becoming the prefix to the serial number. Thus, for a 28 gauge produced in 1959 the alphanumeric code would appear as "9F12." The system was the reverse of the one adopted for all gauges in 1962. Late in 1962 the serial number would look something like this: 123F2. With the adoption of the alphanumeric system for the 12 and 20 gauge Superposed, FN may have used both variations of the system for the 28 gauge and .410 bore. That is, during the early part of 1962, 28 gauge and .410 bore Superposed are stamped with the year number preceding the letter code, with the alphanumeric code as a prefix. Beginning in the early fall of 1962 the process was reversed. The letter code now preceded the year number, and the alphanumeric code became a suffix, as on the 12 and 20 gauge guns. Table 3-7 illustrates the early numbering system.

The number of small bore Superposed sold during the decade of the 1960s closely corresponds to production. If we keep in mind the delay between frame production and assembly it is possible to construct an approximate number of 28 gauge and .410 bore Superposed produced and assembled in each year. Chart 3-5 represents an attempt to create an imprecise delineation of small bore production and sales from 1960 to 1969.

BROWNING SUPERPOSED ALPHANUMERIC SERIAL NUMBERING SYSTEM: 1959-1962 28 GAUGE AND .410 BORE

Gauge	1959-1962
Superposed 28 Gauge	9F, 0F, 1F, 2F/F2—
Superposed .410 Bore	9J, 0J, 1J, 2J/J2—

Table 3-7

One final word about FN's new alphanumeric code: While the single-digit number designating the date a particular Superposed was manufactured is fact, a clarification should be made concerning its significance. Fabrique Nationale stamped the serial number on the Superposed frame on the production line when the frame had completed its journey through the manufacturing process. The date code does not indicate when the frame was assembled into a completed gun, nor does it show when the gun was sold. It is therefore common for Superposed frames built at the end of the year to have a date code stamped on the frame that is one year earlier than when the gun was actually assembled. In a few cases Superposed frames may not have been assembled into complete guns for several years. This is rare during the 1960s due to strong sales of the gun, but it did take place.

Fabrique Nationale stamped its serial numbers on the Browning Superposed in several locations. The most obvious place is under the top lever on the upper tang. Serial numbers were also stamped under the trigger guard on long tang guns. On the forearm the serial number is stamped on the side of the take-down lever and the underside of the cocking lever lifter. FN also stamped the serial number on one or both sides of the barrels just under the ejector extension. These numbers were stamped on the frame at the time the frame completed its final inspection prior to bluing, not when the frame was assembled into a complete gun. The serial number stampings on the barrels and other component parts were in fact stamped at the time of assembly, or at the very least in anticipation of assembly.

1960s North American Superposed Sales

Under the careful management of Harm Williams, Superposed sales grew at a dramatic rate throughout the 1960s. Sales averaged about 11,500 units per year. This success occurred in spite of the difficulties the company had with Fabrique Nationale. According to then vice president of sales Harm Williams, "The Superposed has been a rather unusual product for us in that it was not the type of gun we had expected to so consistently accelerate in demand. Our assumption had been that the repeater or automatic type shotgun was generally preferred in the American market and that the Superposed volume would be restricted to a rather selective portion of the market. But in spite of consistent and quite sizable production increases every year since 1948, we have yet to fully meet the demand each year."[24]

About 115,000 Superposed shotguns were sold in North America during the 1960s. That reflects about sixty-five percent of the total worldwide sales. During that same time period Fabrique Nationale sold 176,000 Superposed worldwide. (See Chart 3-4.) Of this total, Browning has computerized sales records for the years 1964 through the end of the decade. These sales records (see Table 3-8) account for about 78,000 Superposed sold by Browning in North America, or sixty-eight percent of the company's total sales for that period. This gives a fairly good idea not only of the types of Superposed the company was selling in the U.S. and Canada, but also the type of Superposed guns Browning was able to coax out of FN.

These sales records, while complete, are not comprehensive as to specific types of special order features. For the purposes of this book, all records that list both Standard and Lightning weights were calculated in the aggregate of both weights and not broken down further. Therefore, any 12 gauge Hunting models available in either Standard or Lightning weights are represented in their aggregate total. Also, Browning records list Skeet guns by choke and not style. In the early 1960s there was no differentiation between a Skeet model and a Hunting model except choke. This poses no problem until 1968 when the company introduced a dedicated Skeet model, the "New Model" Skeet. From that point on, it was the author's determination to include any Hunting gun with skeet chokes as a Skeet gun despite its Hunting configuration.

These sales records also do not take into account FN Superposed guns imported into North America outside the Browning corporate sales structure. This includes returning servicemen and individuals bringing their own personal Superposed into the country. These guns will not be reflected in these totals.[25] One final word regarding this data: These records reflect the sales figures of the Browning Arms Company and do not in any way represent Fabrique Nationale production totals.

Special order Superposed guns are those that were sold with features considered not standard to that particular model. For example, a recoil pad on a Hunting model would be a special order feature while that same feature was standard on the Magnum model. Special engraving, fancy wood, special stock dimensions, or any other special order feature not found on the standard models were considered special order.

Regardless of the type, model, gauge, and barrel lengths, the Superposed sold very well during the 1960s. These years were the apex of Browning Superposed sales. No other period in Superposed history can even come close to matching its popularity with the shooting public. But storm clouds were forming on the horizon in the shape of constantly higher retail prices, and by the end of the decade sales had fallen from their highs achieved in 1968. Browning was under continual pressure to cut costs and seek alternate products and manufacturing sources. With this dilemma facing the company, the Superposed product line moved cautiously into the decade of the 1970s.

---

[24] Jack Denton Scott, "The Supermen." *SAGA*, November, 1959.

[25] For a complete year-by-year sales analysis see Appendix A.

BROWNING SUPERPOSED SALES
NORTH AMERICA
1964-1969

Type	Grade I	Pigeon Grade	Pointer Grade	Diana Grade	Midas Grade	Exhibition Grade	Total
Broadway	10,051	1045	57	426	220	26	11,826
Trap	4,809	463	24	233	99	6	5,634
Total Trap	*14,860*	*1,508*	*81*	*659*	*319*	*32*	*17,459*
12 ga. Skeet	5,809	455	27	201	80	0	6,572
All ga. Skeet Set	0	0	0	0	0	0	0
Total Target	*20,669*	*1,963*	*108*	*860*	*399*	*32*	*24,031*
Magnum	4,131	99	11	69	27	0	4,337
12 ga. Hunting 28"	11,057	443	43	228	86	19	11,876
12 ga. Hunting 26.5"	7,296	581	67	248	59	5	8,256
Total 12 ga. Hunting	*18,353*	*1,024*	*110*	*476*	*145*	*24*	*20,132*
12 ga. Superlight 28"	201	0	0	0	0	0	201
12 Superlight 26.5"	1,490	0	0	0	0	0	1,490
12 ga. Superlight Special	4	0	0	0	0	0	4
Total 12 ga. Superlight	*1,695*	*0*	*0*	*0*	*0*	*0*	*1,695*
12 ga. Special Order	962	301	51	228	114	1	1,657
Total All 12 gauge	**45,810**	**3,387**	**280**	**1,633**	**685**	**57**	**51,852**
20 ga. Skeet	2,703	250	18	119	21	0	3,111
20 ga. Hunting 28"	6,108	318	23	126	48	3	6,626
20 ga. Hunting 26.5"	10,399	653	55	303	75	4	11,489
Total 20 ga. Hunting	*16,507*	*971*	*78*	*429*	*123*	*7*	*18,115*
20 ga. Superlight 26.5"	1	0	0	0	0	0	1
20 ga. Superlight Special	0	0	0	0	0	0	0
20 ga. Special Order	528	230	34	199	48	7	1,046
Total All 20 gauge	**19,739**	**1,451**	**130**	**747**	**192**	**14**	**22,273**
28 ga. Skeet	544	69	5	29	10	0	657
28 ga. Hunting 28"	280	55	11	41	16	0	403
28 ga. Hunting 26.5"	333	86	10	41	22	0	492
Total 28 ga. Hunting	*613*	*141*	*21*	*82*	*38*	*0*	*895*
28 ga. Special Order	71	21	5	16	13	0	126
Total All 28 gauge	**1,228**	**231**	**31**	**127**	**61**	**0**	**1,678**
.410 Skeet	943	78	4	41	12	0	1,078
.410 Hunting 28"	306	65	8	29	17	0	425
.410 Hunting 26.5"	360	89	10	41	16	1	517
Total .410 Hunting	*666*	*154*	*18*	*70*	*33*	*1*	*942*
.410 Special Order	2	0	25	0	2	0	29
Total All .410 bore	**1,611**	**232**	**47**	**111**	**47**	**1**	**2,049**
Grand Total	**68,388**	**5,301**	**488**	**2,618**	**985**	**72**	**77,852**

TABLE 3-8

Chapter 4

The Beginning of the End: 1970-1977

The period from 1970 to 1977 in Browning Arms Company history represents a dichotomy of two separate directions, yet each reaches the same destination. One road represents the role of the company as a publicly held dynamic entity, its very success leading to decline. The other road is represented by a premier product line slowly but inexorably pricing itself out of the reach of the very consumer who made it the most popular over and under shotgun in North America. These two paths converged in 1977, and both the company and the Superposed were forever transformed. John Val Browning and his management team were faced with the task of guiding the company through rough and treacherous waters with the rocks of recession on one side and the shoals of inflation on the other.

The Browning Company and the Difficulties of the 1970s

The decade of the 1970s began inauspiciously for the Browning Arms Company. Large losses by the boat and golf divisions amounted to $1,300,000 and $400,000 respectively. This almost $2,000,000 loss affected earnings by forty-three percent and resulted in after tax net earnings of $802,537 compared to $1,562,537 in 1969, a thirty-six percent decline. Total sales were slightly ahead of 1969 with $43,163,530. Sales were off in sporting arms but up in archery, fishing rods, clothing, and leather goods. These lower sales in sporting arms were offset by increased margins. Superposed sales amounted to 10,609 guns for 1970, down from 13,262 sold the year before, a twenty-five percent decline. Browning managed to pass on more of its cost increases forced on it by escalating wages supported by Fabrique Nationale.

Despite the obstacles encountered in 1970, Browning kept forging ahead, attempting to expand its product lines into profitable fields. Browning introduced Bruce Browning's Belgian made Medalist .22 caliber target pistol in 1970, and in February the company announced the introduction of a comprehensive line of centerfire metallic ammunition. It was hoped that this new ammunition line would have long-term positive effects on earnings. Browning also announced to its shareholders that it was lowering its inventory of FN supplied firearms, including the Superposed, with the expectation that such a move would reduce borrowing cost. This prudent business decision was to be the harbinger of the future for the Superposed. The continued price increases of the 1960s were beginning to take their toll on FN produced firearms, namely the Superposed.[1]

The following year marked an improvement for the company's earnings. Sales for 1971 reached a historical high with total net sales of $52,234,828. The boat division experienced a complete turnaround, with demand far outpacing supply. The ammunition business, however, was hampered by poor deliveries and a shutdown by the supplier at year's end. A new supplier was found and the company was determined to stay with its ammunition venture. Generally, business was improved for every subsidiary. Even the golf cart division was profitable for 1971.

---

[1] Browning Arms Company, 1970 Annual Report.

At the beginning of the decade of the 1970s the Browning Company was at the high point of its expansion. From sporting firearms to sailboats, Browning was no longer dependent upon its Belgian-made firearms line for the bulk of its yearly sales. This rapid growth culminated in 1971 with sales of over $52,000,000. Courtesy Russ Church.

Superposed sales almost managed to keep pace with the previous year's results despite the devaluation of the dollar abroad. In 1971 some 10,089 Superposed were sold, down 520 guns from the previous year, a decline of about five percent. The reduction in the value of the dollar forced prices up, causing Browning to increase its firearms prices fifteen percent across the board. Browning hoped to counterbalance the loss of volume with the introduction to its sporting arms line of a new .380ACP caliber pistol, and the BLR lever action high power rifle.[2]

In 1972 Browning emphasized for the first time in its annual report the growth of nonfirearms related products in relation to the company's sporting arms and ammunition sales, and their influence on overall sales. The drive for diversity that began in 1961 when the company went public was beginning to pay dividends, both literally and figuratively. In 1968 nonfirearms products accounted for approximately twenty-three percent of net sales. By 1972 this figure had risen to thirty-five percent, a substantial increase. Net sales for 1972 amounted to $54,006,000, up almost $2,000,000 over 1971 despite the devaluation of the dollar against the Japanese yen and the Belgian franc. Although demand remained strong for Browning's sporting arms generally, Superposed sales for 1972 fell to 7,444 guns from 10,089 in 1971, a decrease of more than twenty-five percent. Browning management was alarmed enough about the continued fall of the dollar that it predicted lower firearms sales for the following year.

---

[2] Browning Arms Company, 1971 Annual Report.

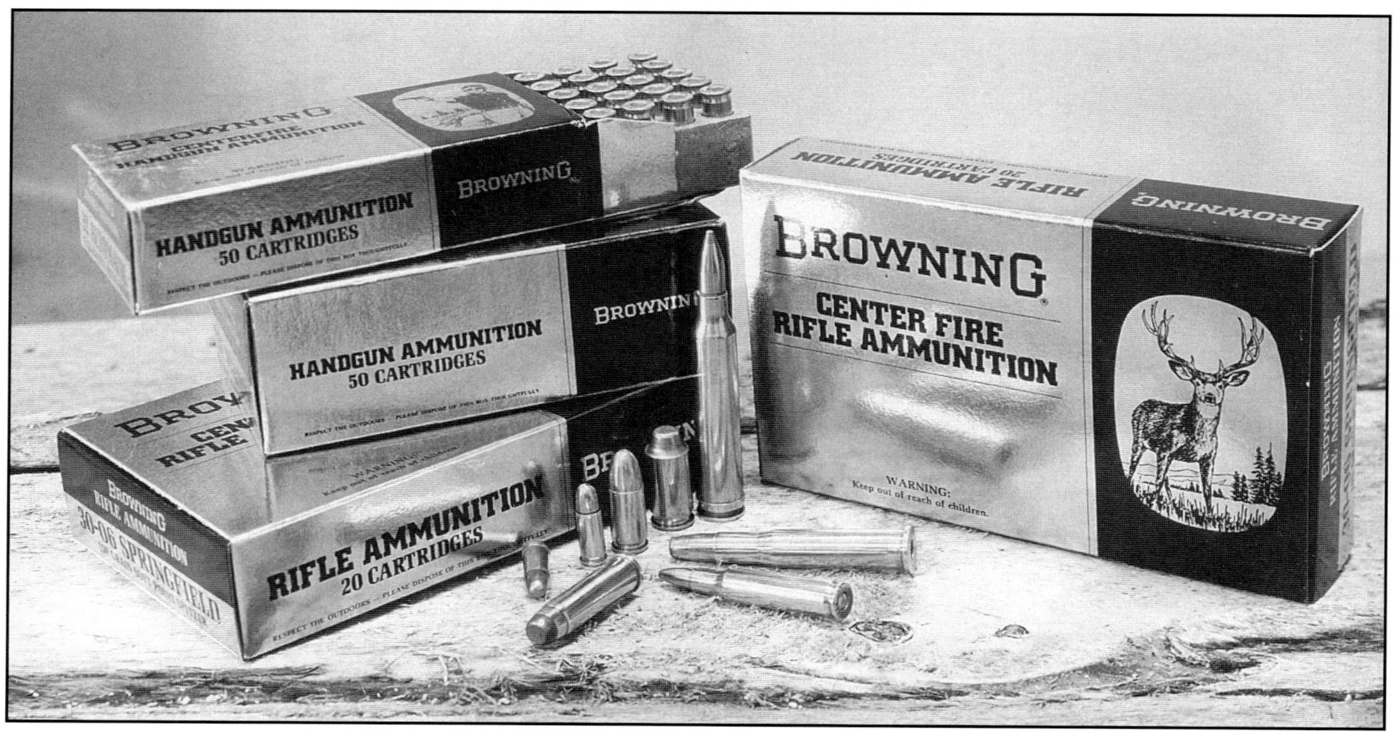

Browning entered the ammunition business in what would seem to be a logical extension of its sporting firearms line. The venture failed but left behind another Browning collectible. Courtesy Browning Company.

Browning sold its vaulting pole manufacturing facilities to a group of private investors in 1972, and it sold its Microflite arrow shaft manufacturing plant and inventory to the Bear Archery Company. Neither of these companies fit in well with Browning's distribution channels, and the customer base lay outside Browning's usual dealer network. Browning attempted to take advantage of the other side of the dollar devaluation by establishing a wholly owned subsidiary in Belgium to handle European sales to its Japanese supplier. The company planned to increase exports to Europe and Japan with its archery, fishing, and golf equipment.

In 1972 Browning also completed construction on a new plant near Morgan, Utah, for the manufacturing of bows and fishing rods. The old Costa Mesa and Chula Vista, California, plants where these products were originally produced were shut down. At its Arnold, Missouri, facility the company built a new forty thousand square foot building to warehouse its ammunition line. There

Some of the company employees were used as models for various products lines. Here vice president Grant Goddard shows off a Browning vest while reloading a Superposed at the company skeet range in Mountain Green. Courtesy Browning Company.

The Superposed of the 1970s

Outstanding examples of the two remaining high grade Superposed that were offered in the Browning catalogues from 1975 to 1977, the Diana Grade (top) and the Midas Grade (bottom). The Diana Grade was executed by George Maréchal, an experienced and talented engraver who did a superb job. Notice the detail in the ducks and their correct conformation. He may have also engraved the Midas Grade because the same attention to detail and appearance is in evidence. Courtesy Browning Company.

Above and opposite: Browning introduced a special Superposed to commemorate the 200 year anniversary of the United States. FN built fifty-three Bicentennial Superposed for this purpose. Fifty of the guns represented each state in the union; the fifty-first represented the District of Columbia. The two additional guns were given to the Smithsonian Institution in Washington, D.C. and the Musee d'Armes in Liège. The Bicentennial shown is number 51, serial number DC-1776-51.

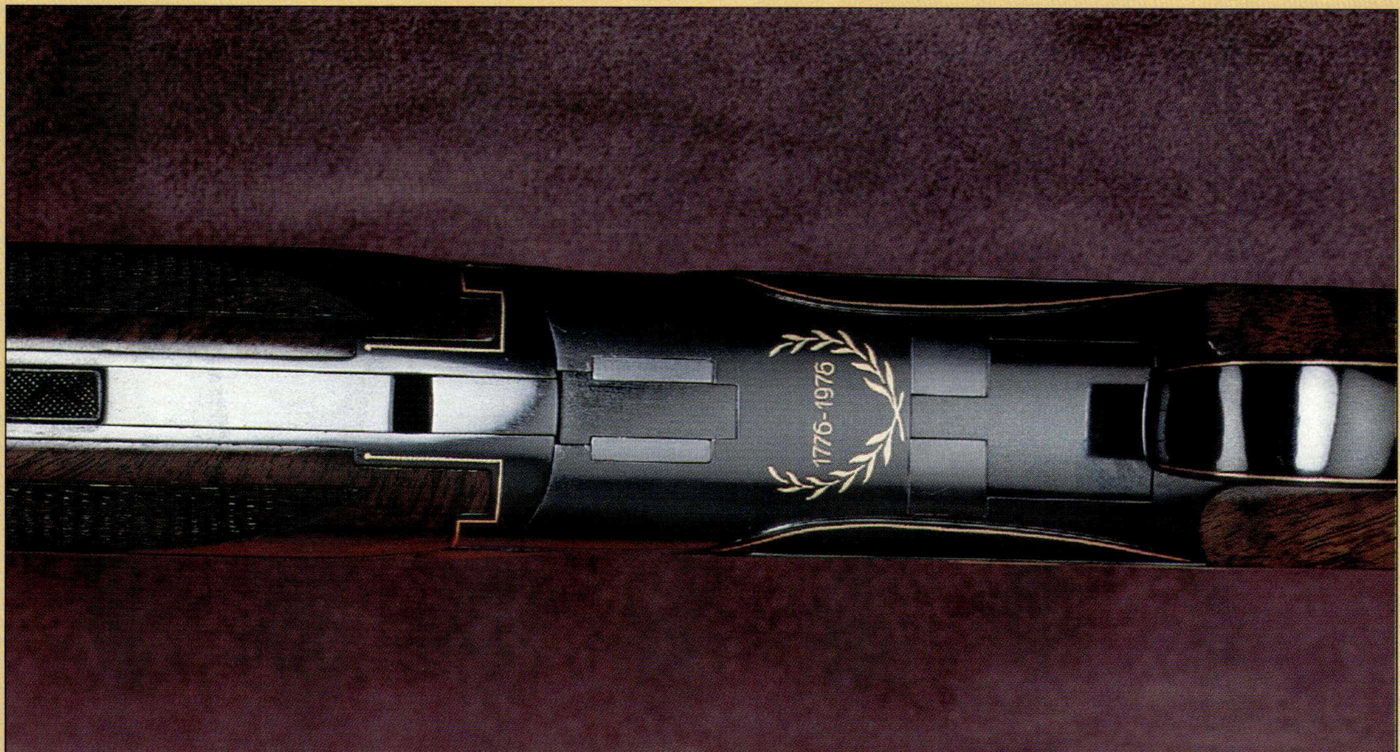

It is a 12 gauge with 28-inch barrels choked full and modified. The engraver is Richard Kowalski. On the left side of the receiver the "District of Colombia" is misspelled. It should read "District of Columbia." This is a rare error that may enhance the value of the gun. Courtesy Robert Hawkins Collection.

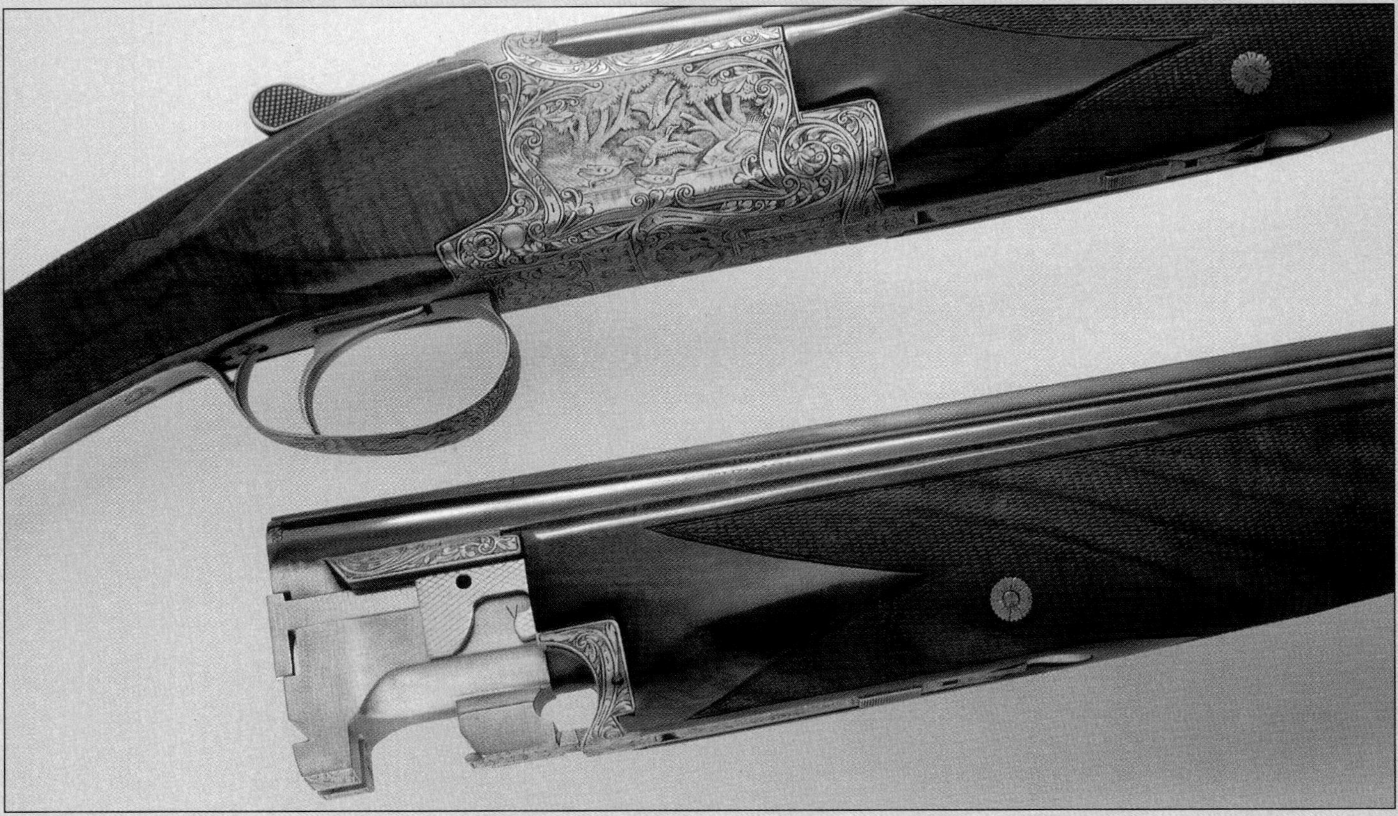

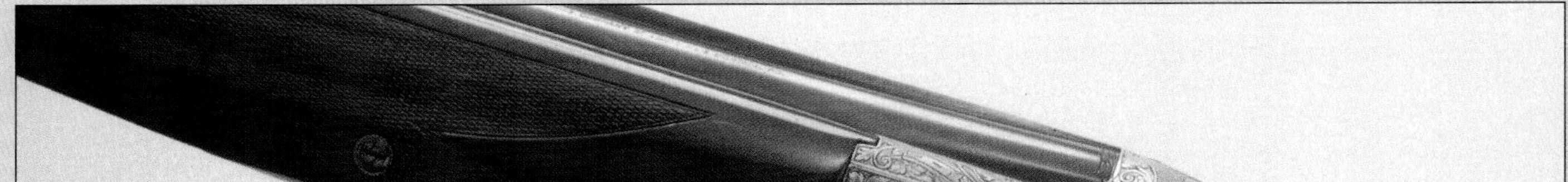

This very early Browning Diana Grade Superposed Superlight, serial number 90295S8, is fitted with two barrels, a rare factory option. This Superlight is also notable for being a special order engraved gun before that option was catalogued in 1971. Lloyd Crede Collection.

Browning "C" Grade Exhibition Grades

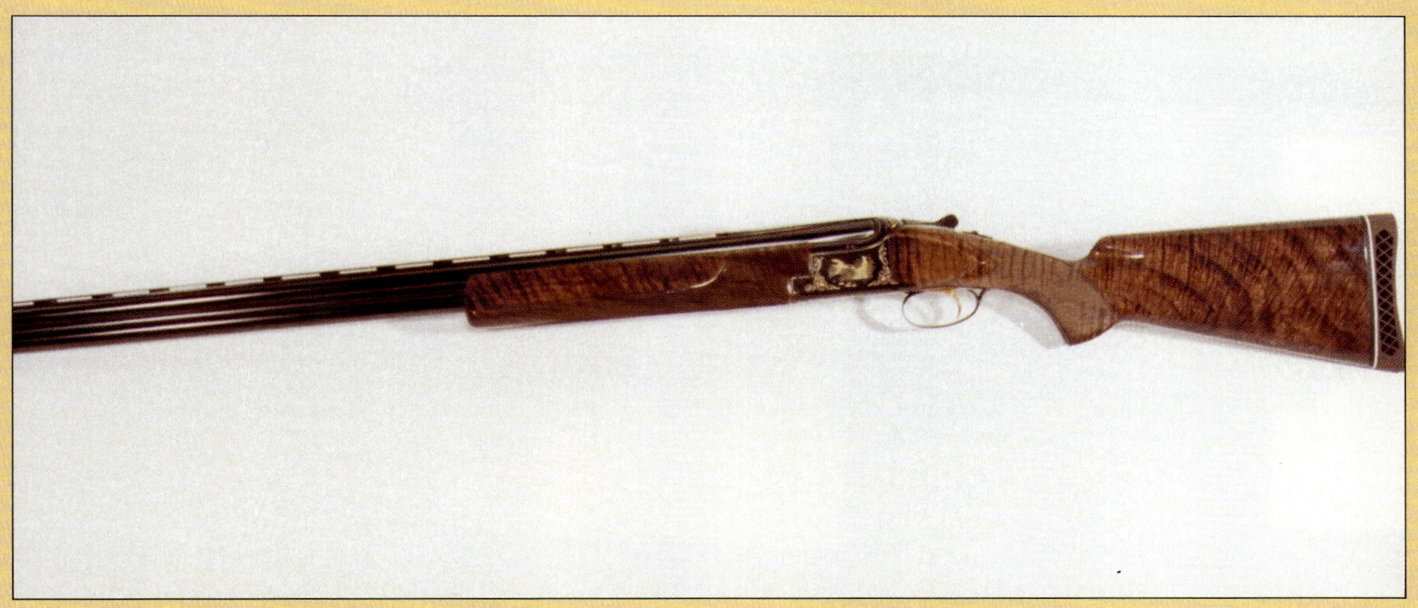

A Group F-6 C Grade Exhibition Superposed. This particular gun was engraved by José Baerten and features somewhat sparse, but elegant, gold inlays. This was the most expensive of the C Grade guns with a retail price of $9,375. According to factory records, all Group F-6 guns sold in North America were 12 gauge. Courtesy Browning Company.

The Group F-3 C Grade Exhibition Grade Superposed were slightly less expensive with a retail price of $8,125. This particular Group F-3 gun was engraved by José Baerten. With its straight grip stock, Schnabel forearm and solid rib, it conveys a very elegant European appearance. Courtesy Browning Company.

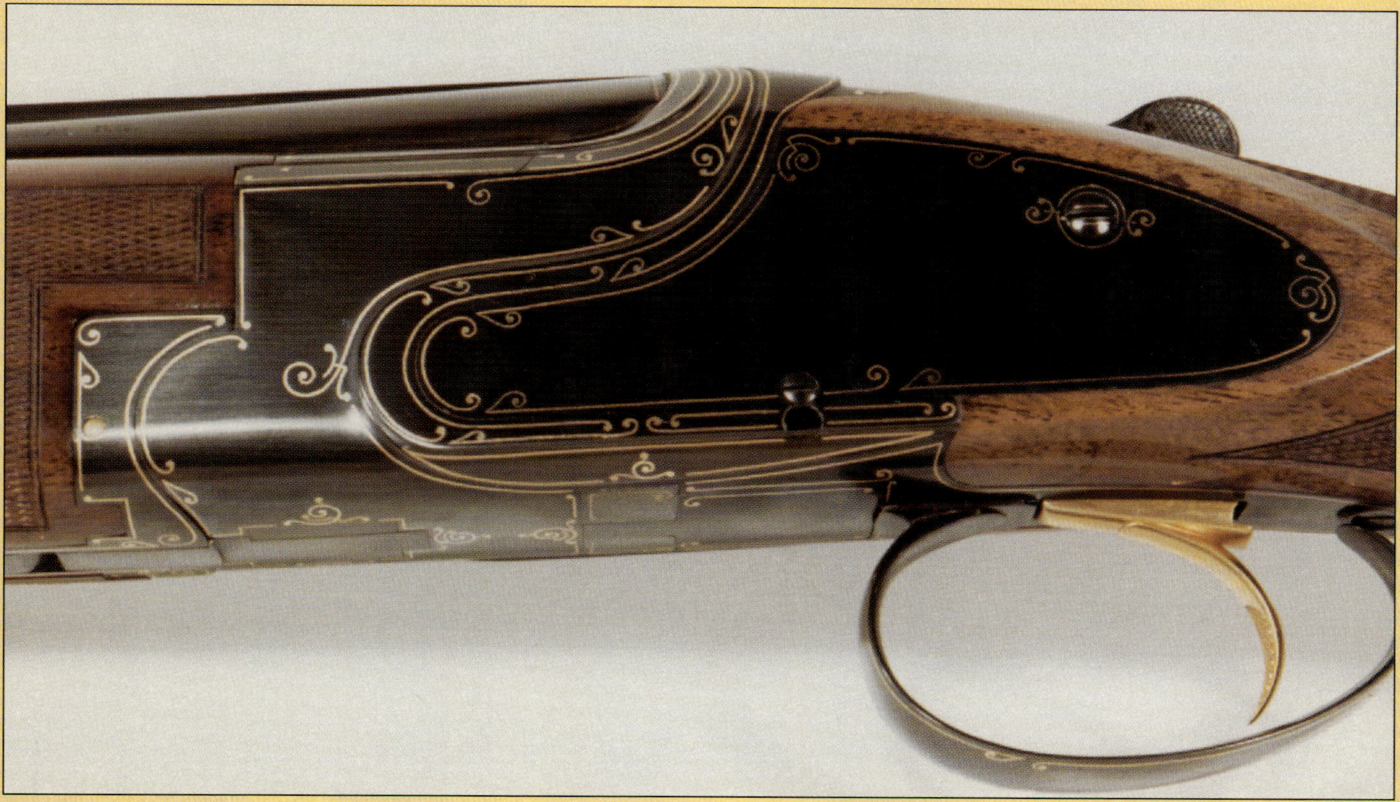

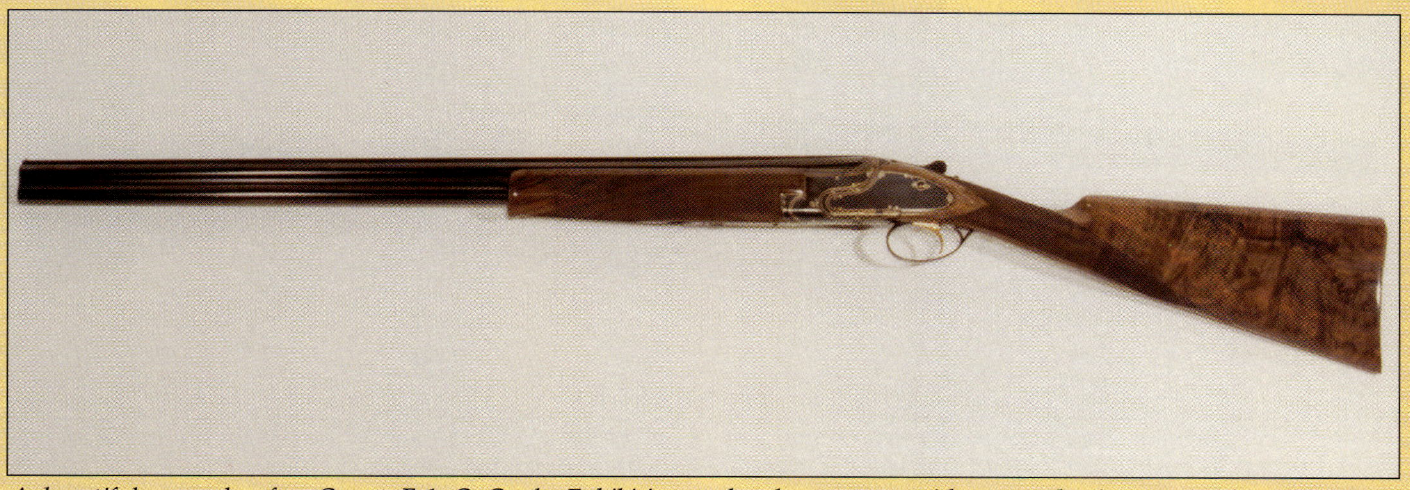

A beautiful example of a Group F-1 C Grade Exhibition Superposed. As a result of its fine, delicate gold wire work, an understated elegance is achieved. The overall view shows a handsome gun with very pleasing proportions. Courtesy Browning Company.

This C Grade Exhibition Grade Superposed is representative of the A-1 Group. This particular gun is a Trap model. Engraved by José Baerten, this Group A-1 carried a retail price of $4,375. Courtesy Browning Company.

The Genius of Louis Vrancken

In 1962 André Watrin designed a custom engraving pattern much like this one for a Superposed, but without sideplates. About ten years later Louis Vrancken built on that original pattern and executed a dramatic design on this 20 gauge Browning Superposed, serial number 282V72. The Watrin inspired scrollwork blends beautifully with the elegantly executed birds. This is Vrancken's work at its most dramatic. Courtesy Browning Company.

This .410 bore Browning Superposed, serial number 066J72, was engraved by Louis Vrancken in a banknote style that shows his wide range of talents. On this particular Superposed, scrollwork is kept to a minimum while the game scenes dominate the receiver. A tastefully executed gold inlay adorns the trigger guard. Courtesy Fabrique Nationale Archives. The Robert Hawkins Collection.

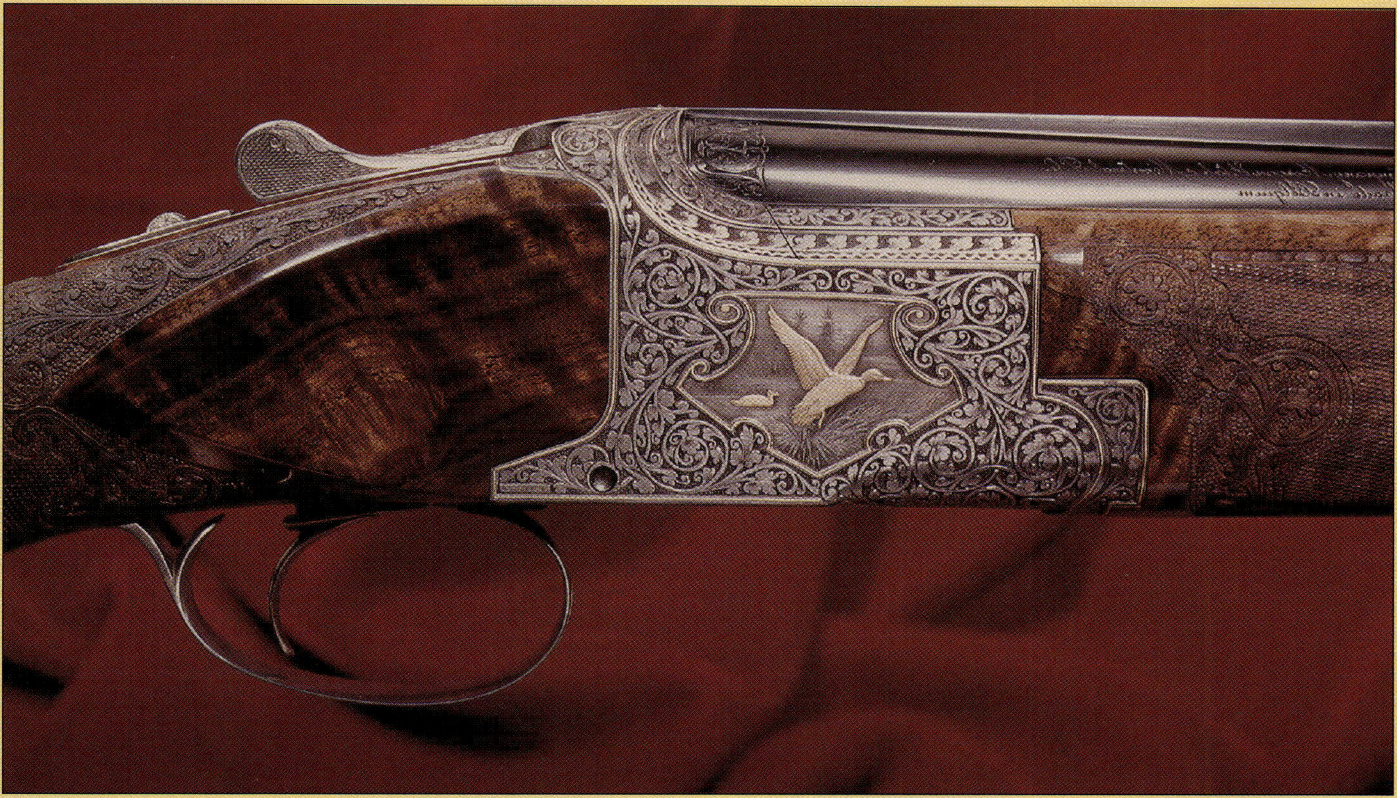

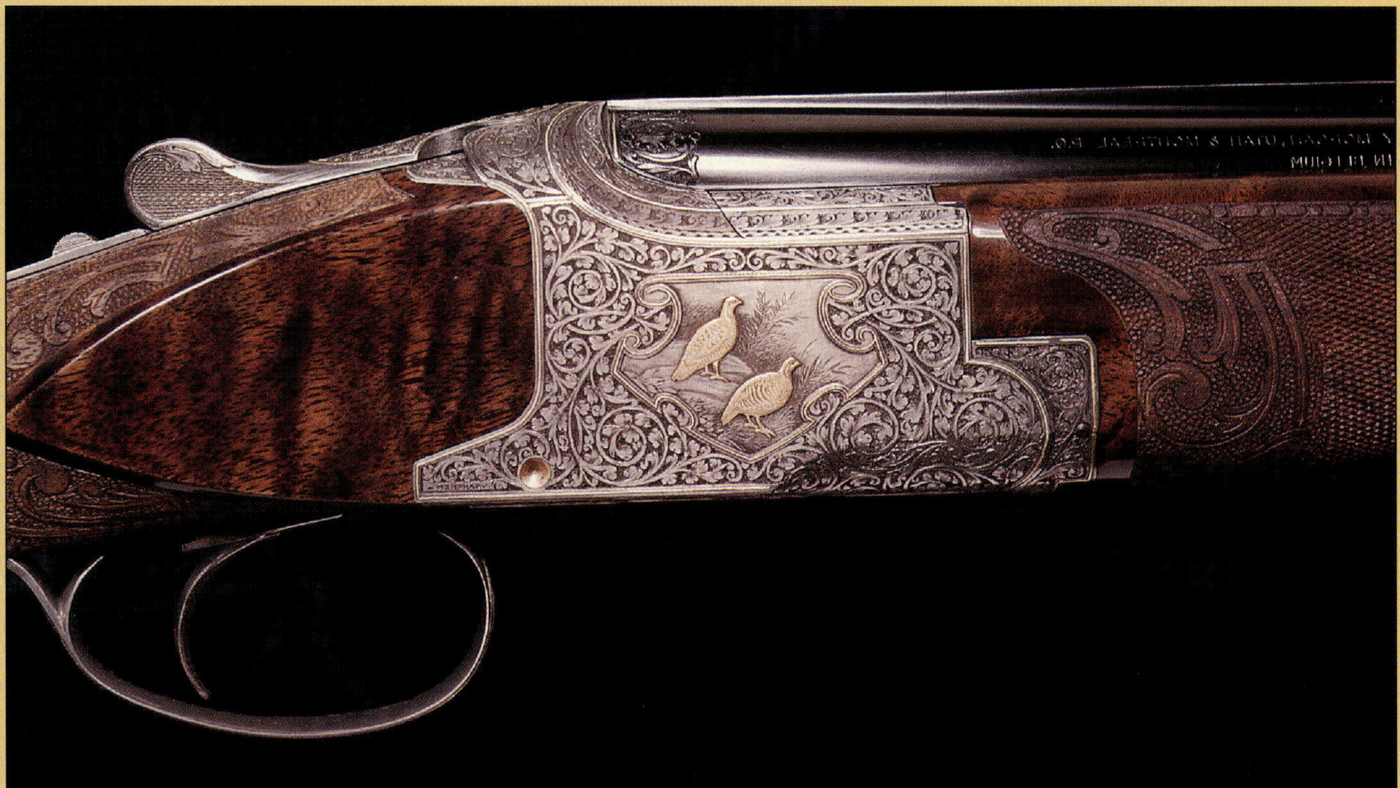

These two Browning Exhibition Grade Superposed were engraved by Louis Vrancken in the early 1970s, and while similar in overall design, they are in fact two separate patterns. Occasionally, if an engraver liked a specific pattern or design he would use it again with subtle changes to insure uniqueness. Notice that the wood carving on both of these guns is different as well. Courtesy Browning Company.

In 1975 Louis Vrancken designed this modernistic creation that features Diana, the Roman goddess of hunting. Its embellishments are a blend of deeply cut scroll and gold encrustation. The gold inlay was executed by José Baerten. Courtesy Browning Company.

Designed in 1974 by Louis Vrancken, this Browning Superposed follows a traditional FN engraving theme used many years ago by Felix Funken. These chimeras are gold inlaid on a blue background, which imparts an elegant appearance. Notice how the wood carving complements the engraving design. Courtesy Browning Company.

The Creativity of José Baerten

This is a Baerten engraved Browning Superposed Exhibition Grade. Baerten had a talent for working with gold. That talent combined with his artistic ability resulted in outstanding compositions such as this. Courtesy Fabrique Nationale Archives.

This is another example of the elegant design and exceptional engraving work of José Baerten on a 20 gauge Browning Superposed Exhibition Grade. Courtesy Fabrique Nationale Archives.

Two 1980s examples of José Baerten's design and execution are shown here to illustrate his wide range of talent in different types of design. The gold inlay work on the sideplated Superposed is simple yet elegant and expertly executed, while the other Superposed has received an entirely different treatment of a dog's head with a tight scroll border. Both are custom patterns executed on special order Browning Superposed guns. Courtesy Browning Company.

There are two specially engraved Midas Grades that were part of the .410 Superlight special order of 1984. These Midas Grades were distinctly different from the production Midas Grades of the earlier era. At the top is the right side of Superposed Superlight serial number 500J83, engraved by Baerten. In the middle is the left side of serial number 500J83. At the bottom is the left side of Superlight serial number 600J83. The right side is the same as serial number 500J83. Courtesy Browning Company.

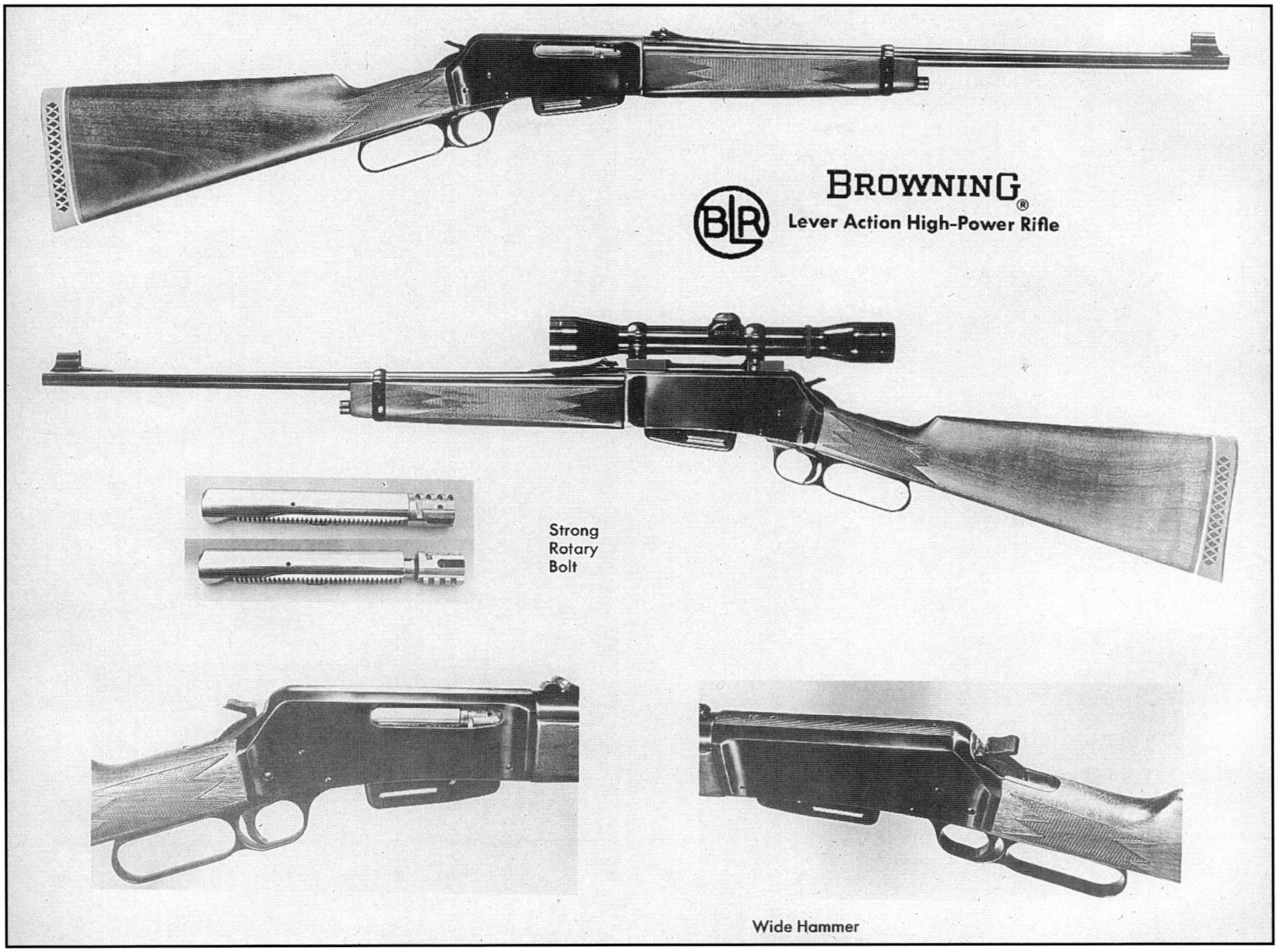

BROWNING®
Lever Action High-Power Rifle

Strong Rotary Bolt

Wide Hammer

In 1971 Browning introduced a new semi-automatic pistol chambered for the .380ACP cartridge. The company also introduced a new centerfire lever action rifle, the BLR. Courtesy Browning Company.

Browning's Research and Development Shop at the Mountain Green facility. New ideas were created here, and because of the extra space, testing was done here as well. Courtesy Browning Company.

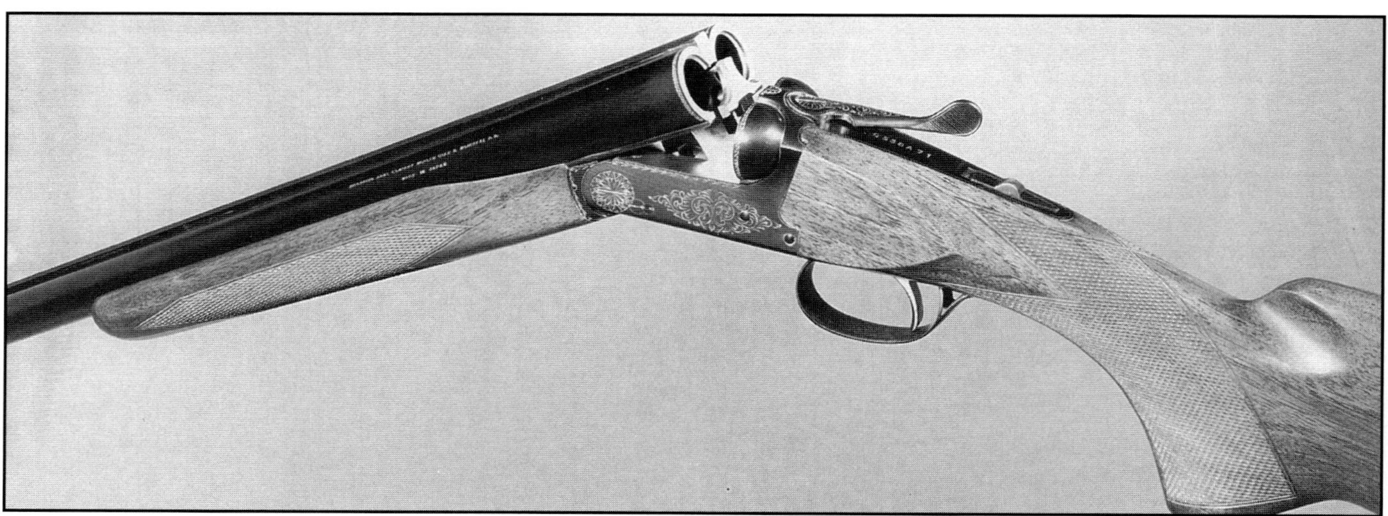

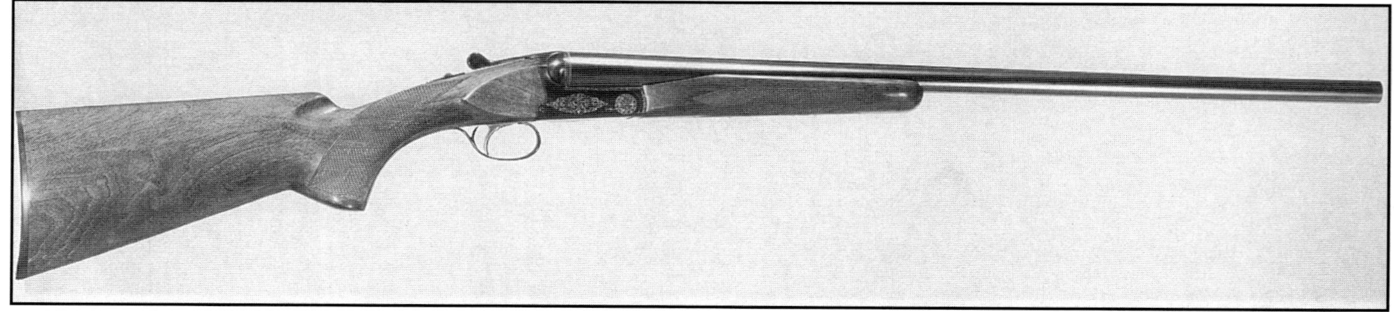

The new Browning side by side. Introduced into the company's product line in 1972, this shotgun was built in Japan by Miroku. Courtesy Browning Company.

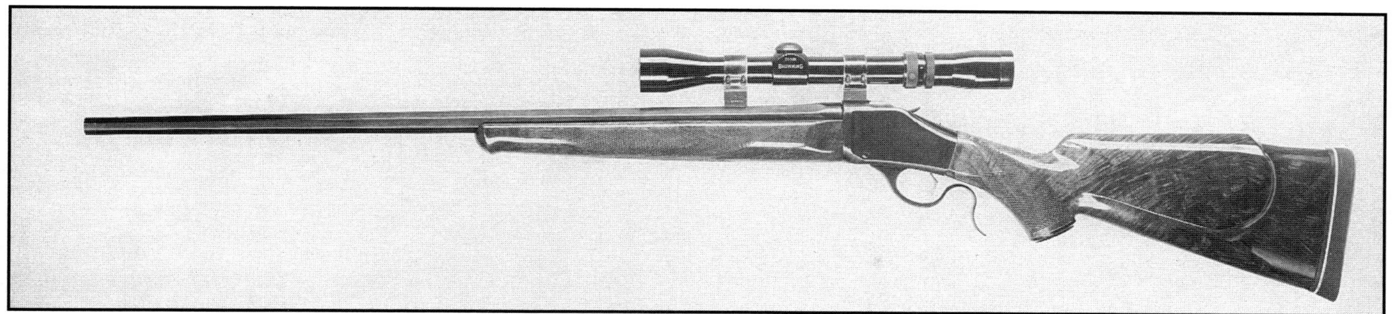

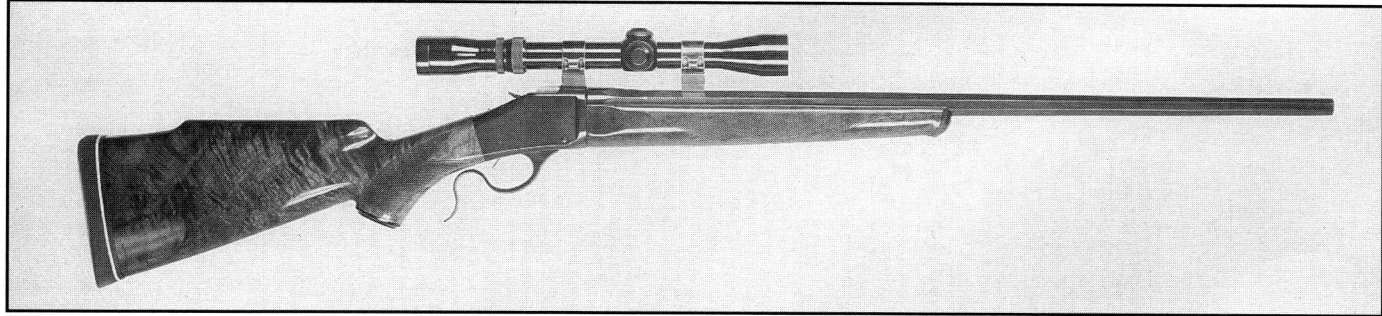

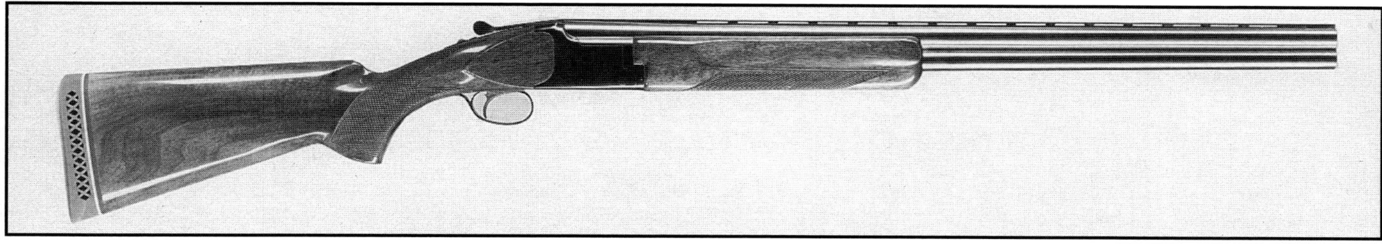

One of the company's new firearms products for 1973 was the B-78 single shot rifle. Note that the company's promotional photo has a Browning scope mounted on its new rifle. Perhaps the most important new model for the company was the Citori shotgun. This new over and under was introduced as a more affordable alternative to the Superposed. It was hoped that the Citori would help fill the demand for the Browning over and under market, which the company was having difficulty holding because of price increases and uncertain deliveries on its premium Superposed line. Courtesy Browning Company.

were now almost thirty gunsmiths employed in the repair department with thousands of Browning guns being serviced each year. The company also introduced a new BSS side-by-side shotgun, produced in Japan, to its firearms line in 1972.

In keeping with these moves toward diversity, the company abbreviated its name to "Browning" in 1972. The company stated in its annual report that the name change reflects, "... its growing commitments to other sporting equipment besides hunting arms."[3]

Fishing, archery, outdoor clothing, and golf lines continued to grow. The company added bicycles and camping equipment for 1973. The new Citori over and under 12 gauge shotgun was an important addition to its firearms line, as were the Liège over and under, the BSS side-by-side shotgun in 20 gauge, and the B-78 single shot rifle. Despite these new additions to the product line, the company suffered its worst earnings since going public in 1961. While sales did increase slightly, profit margins were depressed. One of the reasons for this decline was management's decision to accept lower margins in order to preserve markets for its sporting arms until new sources of supply could be found in Portugal, Korea, and Japan. The continued fall of the dollar against the Belgian franc and the Japanese yen made a bad situation worse. Some price increases were made, but they could not offset the large decline in the dollar. A four-month strike in Belgium against Fabrique Nationale during the second half of the year seriously crippled gun sales during the peak season. This was a devastating blow to the company's firearms sales—to the Superposed in

[3] Browning Arms Company, 1972 Annual Report.

BROWNING ARMS COMPANY AND SUBSIDIARY

CONSOLIDATED BALANCE SHEET, DECEMBER 31, 1977

ASSETS

Current Assets:		
Cash		$ 3,216,344
Accounts and notes receivable		11,932,539
Inventories-at lower of cost of market		20,128,027
Prepaid expenses		449,675
Total current assets		35,726,585
Property and Equipment-At Cost:		
Land	240,121	
Buildings and improvements	3,611,257	
Equipment and autos	3,368,446	
Fixtures and leasehold improvements	696,289	
Total	7,916,113	
Less accumulated depreciation and amortization	3,750,164	
Property and equipment-net		4,165,949
Investments		396,166
Other Assets		227,878
TOTAL		40,516,578

LIABILITIES

Current Liabilities:		
Notes payable		$ 6,428,250
Current installments on long term obligations		1,661,029
Accounts payable:		
Affiliated companies		1,996,849
Trade		863,834
Income taxes		210,756
Duty and excise taxes		675,542
Payroll		251,272
Other accrued liabilities		583,037
Total current liabilities		12,661,569
Long Term Obligations		3,177,080
Minority Interest		564,179
Stockholders' Equity:		
Common stock-authorized 2,500,000 shares of a par value of $1 each	1,612,168	
Paid-in surplus	6,350,901	
Retained earnings	16,150,861	
Total stockholders' equity		24,113,750
TOTAL		40,516,578

Table 4-1

BROWNING ARMS COMPANY AND SUBSIDIARY

STATEMENT OF CONSOLIDATED INCOME AND RETAINED EARNINGS
For The Years Ended December 31, 1977 and 1976

	Year Ended December 31 1977	1976
Net Sales	$61,239,815	$56,534,607
Cost of Goods Sold	48,091,270	43,244,327
Gross Profit on Sales	13,148,545	13,290,280
Operating Expenses:		
Salaries, advertising, and other office and general expenses exclusive of items shown below	8,518,502	7,927,938
Provision for doubtful accounts-net	590,316	843,575
Provision for depreciation and amortization	194,174	191,653
Rents	326,691	395,566
Taxes (other than income)	355,109	315,631
Research and development	261,363	340,644
Total	10,246,155	10,015,007
Operating Profit	2,902,390	3,275,273
Other Income:		
Royalty income	329,417	58,272
Dividends on foreign investment	12,927	12,029
Interest income	183,247	149,351
Miscellaneous	(69,011)	288,965
Interest Expense	(1,376,032)	(1,600,849)
Excise Tax Settlement	(354,917)	
Total	(1,274,369)	(1,152,232)
Income Before Income Taxes, Minority Interest, and Extraordinary Item	1,628,021	2,123,041
Income Taxes	711,440	1,037,385
Minority Interest	(39,991)	107,012
Net Income Before Extraordinary Item	956,572	978,644
Extraordinary Item-Federal Trade Commission Civil Judgment		(155,127)
Net Income	$ 956,572	$ 823,517
Per Share of Common Stock	$ .61	$ .63
Extraordinary Item		(.10)
Net Income	.61	.53
Cash Dividends Paid	None	None
Average Shares Outstanding	1,573,168	1,547,168

Table 4-2

Browning Service personnel at the entrance to the company facility in Arnold, Missouri, in the Spring of 1976. In the front row from left to right are Howard Mass, Vearl Brown, Fred Haunold, Norman Pyeatt, Dave Praul, Ed Frillman, Charles Kelsay, Wilbert Walter, Jack Callahan, Tommy McGhee, Kent Sutton, and Paul Fuchs. In the back row from left to right are Lloyd Gastreich, Herman Stengel, Marcel Olinger (FN), Willy Bertran, George Sieber, Marty Ryan, Ray Suesserman, Mike O'Brien, Earl Womble, John Woesthaus, Roy Nobbe, Tom Wayer, and Gene Smugala. Dan Warren is not pictured. Courtesy Browning Company, Arnold, Missouri.

particular. Only 5,290 Superposed were sold in 1973 compared to 7,444 in 1972, a thirty percent decrease. Generally 1973 was a very poor year for gun sales, particularly those firearms produced in Belgium, and the company's gains in other product lines were unable to offset this decline.[4]

The year 1974 saw a strong increase in overall net sales with a total of $60,414,809 compared to $51,834,189 for 1973. Browning made the decision to divest itself of its marine division, which had been consistently losing money since its acquisition in 1969. This divestiture was made with the hope of investing the liquidated assets in other divisions of the company. Browning management also resolved to divest itself of its ammunition enterprise. Desired volume and profits did not materialize and the company decided to cut its losses.

Such moves were made to strengthen the company's financial position and they were successful. Cash on hand increased by $1,400,000, inventories declined over $6,000,000, as did plant and equipment by about $2,000,000. Short-term borrowing was $4,600,000 lower than the previous year. Long-term debt was also reduced by over $1,200,000.

In 1974 Browning introduced its new B-2000 semiautomatic shotgun in 12 gauge, assembled in Portugal with FN manufactured parts. The Citori 20 gauge over and under was added, as were various models of the Citori Trap and Skeet guns. Sales of the Superposed declined again to about 3,689, another precipitous drop of thirty percent.

By the year 1974 Browning had a total of eleven thousand active retail dealers in the United States selling its sporting arms. In Canada, where Browning owned seventy percent of its subsidiary, Browning Canada, over fifteen hundred dealers sold the company's sporting goods products. This Canadian subsidiary had always been a small but profitable operation for the parent company.[5]

In 1975 the value of the dollar against the Belgian franc was at its lowest point since World War II. Such was the ominous beginning to the year. Browning sales were down for all product lines, primarily due to a weak domestic economy. Total net sales for 1975 were $53,302,269, down $7,000,000 over the previous year. Sporting arms declined the most, and the Superposed recorded sales of only 1,276 guns, a depressing sixty-five percent decrease over the previous year.

The company felt the problems could be traced to three distinct areas. The first problem focused around the poor value of the dollar in Belgium, and FN's continued increase in cost. The second difficulty lay with credit restrictions

[4] Browning Arms Company, 1973 Annual Report.

[5] Browning Arms Company, 1974 Annual Report.

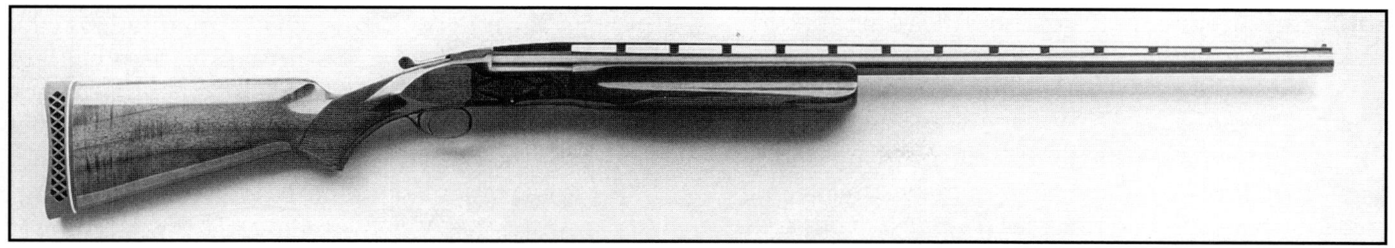

In 1976 Browning added the BT-99 Competition model to its already vastly expanded firearms line. The company expected that by the end of the decade of the '70s it would no longer be dependent upon Fabrique Nationale for its sporting arms sales. Courtesy Browning Company.

imposed on many Browning dealers because of cash flow difficulties brought about by the poor U.S. economy. The final troublesome area was that most of the sporting arms were unavailable at the right time of the year. Late deliveries missed the hunting season and resulted in higher than normal inventories. Browning did manage to introduce two additions to its firearms product line in 1975: the Citori 20 gauge Skeet model and the B-2000 20 gauge.[6]

Legal troubles also plagued the company in 1975. In June the Tenth Circuit Court of Appeals reversed a ruling of a district court concerning alleged violations of price fixing at the retail level. This action by the federal government was a blow to Browning's long-standing custom of assuring its dealers of a fair profit on all Browning firearms sold. Most dealers liked the establishment of a firm retail price because each knew that all Browning dealers were selling the company's firearms for the same price. With the advent and popularity of discount chains, what was once a consistently and fairly priced firearms line was now subject to who could sell them for the lowest price. This legal action effectively ended Browning's pricing policy, hurting small dealers the most, and making the Superposed even more difficult to find in dealers' inventories across the country. In September of 1975 the court granted a motion for partial summary judgment and set a hearing to determine the amount of penalties assessed to Browning Arms Company.[7]

The United States Customs Service demanded payment of $249,800,000 for alleged violations of certain customs laws. The company estimated a contingency of approximately $939,000 to settle the dispute.[8] This situation came about as a result of an alleged conspiracy between Fabrique Nationale and John Val Browning to falsify U.S. Customs forms by claiming a lower value on FN manufactured .22 caliber semiautomatic rifles imported into the U.S. under the Browning name. By reducing the cost of the rifle below $25.00, Browning could avoid a higher

Mr. Harm Williams assumed the presidency of Browning in 1976 from John Val Browning. Harm was a former vice president and director of sales since 1952. Courtesy Browning Company.

[6] Browning Arms Company, 1975 Annual Report.

[7] *Ibid.*, Notes to Financial Statements 1975.

[8] *Ibid.*

duty, thus keeping its .22 caliber rifle competitive in the North American market. This particular legal action brought by the federal government was the result of a five-year investigation, and was to have far reaching ramifications for the company and its president, John Val Browning, in the years to come.

The year 1976 began as the previous year ended, with poor sales and a sluggish economic recovery. But by August sales had improved, and demand for Browning products increased as the year progressed. Even sales for the Superposed, suppressed for the last several years, exhibited a small increase in sales with a total of 2,653 guns sold in 1976 compared to only 1,276 the previous year, a better than fifty percent improvement.[9] Sales for 1976 were $56,534,607, up slightly from $53,302,269 the previous year. Net income grew from $621,057 to $823,517, an impressive thirty-two percent increase over 1975.

This was the year for several new additions to Browning's sporting arms line. The Challenger II .22 caliber pistol was added, as was the BT-99 Competition. The single shot B-78 rifle was now offered in 45-70 caliber and 7mm Magnum. In the BLR the .358 caliber was added, and for the first time, the Citori became available with extra sets of barrels. Also in 1976, the Auto-5 was discontinued in 16 gauge, and the production of the Auto-5 moved to Japan in the latter half of the year.

With the financial situation seeming to stabilize and sales in all product lines poised to improve, another serious development occurred that had momentous far-reaching consequences. In the company's annual report, the following announcement was made to the stockholders:

> On March 30, 1976 the Browning Company, one of its subsidiaries and its then President were indicted by a Federal Grand Jury in the United States District Court for the Eastern District of Missouri for alleged obstruction of justice and irregularities concerning the entry and payment of customs duties from Belgium and Japan. On April 5, 1976 the companies and Mr. John Val Browning entered pleas of not guilty in the District Court. On April 9, at a special meeting of the Board of Directors of the company, the Board reluctantly accepted the resignation of Mr. Browning as President and Director of the Company as well as all his offices and positions with the Company's subsidiaries. Mr. Browning's resignations were made in order that he might devote full time to his defense against the allegations of the indictment referenced above.

Mr. Harmon Williams was appointed by the board to succeed John Val Browning as president of the company. Regarding the customs duties suit, in September of 1976 the United States District Court for the District of Utah dismissed all counts of the government's indictments against Browning Arms and John Val Browning. The government filed an appeal in district court and the company filed an appeal for dismissal of the government's appeal. The company's appeal was denied. The appeal of John Val Browning was also denied.

In 1977 sales increased to $61,239,815, up from $56,534,607 the year before. A total of 1,563 Superposed guns were sold in the very year they were discontinued in their original, traditional configuration. The significant event for 1977, however, was not the total sales of the company or its net earnings, but its sale to Fabrique Nationale.

Clearly Browning was having difficulty with its Belgian-made sporting arms product lines. Management's decision to move shotgun production to Japan in the late 1960s and the subsequent introduction of the Citori over and under shotgun to replace the Superposed in 1973 was sound business judgment. Battered by a recession, plagued by legal problems, and continually besieged by higher costs from FN, the company made its move to Japan too late. The Superposed product line in North America simply could no longer sustain higher prices. Demand fell, not only for the Superposed, but for all the FN built firearms. The company's weakened financial position could not fight off a hostile takeover bid by A-T-O Inc., a Cleveland-based conglomerate. A-T-O's bid of $12.50 per share was countered by FN's $13.00 bid, and the sale was concluded. In August of 1977 *Fabrique Nationale Société Anonyme Holding*, a subsidiary of Fabrique Nationale Herstal, SA, made a tender offer of $13.00 per share for outstanding shares of the Browning Company. This offer amounted to about $20,000,000. Approximately ninety-one percent of the outstanding shares were acquired by Fabrique Nationale as a result of the tender.

After the sale was concluded, FN, the new owner, pleaded no contest to the Browning Company's role in the conspiracy case and paid a penalty of approximately $1,000,000. In June of 1979 a trial was held in Salt Lake City where John Val Browning was charged with two counts of defrauding the government of its customs duties and one count of obstruction of justice. Mr. Browning was found not guilty of defrauding the government but was con-

[9] Browning Arms Company, 1976 Annual Report.

victed on the single count of obstruction of justice. On July 20 he was sentenced to two years probation, fined $5,000, and assessed the government's estimated court cost of between $30,000 and $40,000. He appealed. The appeal was denied. Later the Supreme Court refused to hear the case.

The Browning family's control of the Browning Arms Company, which had lasted fifty years, was terminated. The reasons for this sale have been the subject of much speculation over the years. Val Browning's decision to move the company into other parallel product areas was farsighted and prudent. John Val Browning's energy and enthusiasm proved to be a compelling force. Nevertheless, the road to diversification and growth was an arduous one filled with many uncertainties. Several of the company's acquisitions were profitable, but others, such as its boat and ammunition additions, did not prove to be. But such are the vagaries of business. If we consider that John M. Browning began business in 1878 in his small shop in Ogden, Utah, then the Browning family's influence over its designs and the sales of those designs lasted almost one hundred years. Few families and companies could have sustained themselves for such a prolonged period without profound changes, both internally and externally. If Browning succumbed to changing conditions and difficult times, Fabrique Nationale was not to be spared either.

Fabrique Nationale: A Period of Transition

Fabrique Nationale emerged from the 1960s with a strong record of accomplishment. The company, like Browning, had diversified its interest into allied areas. Some of these ventures had been successful, but others had not. FN faced many of the same difficulties as Browning. From an annual profit of 200,000,000 francs in 1965, the company suffered losses by 1971. Falling sales culminated with the end of the postwar arms expansion, the fall of orders for the J79 turbo-jet engine, and the end of the military vehicles division. Perhaps the most damaging of all were the tremendous increases in labor cost. This labor expenditure amounted to sixty-six percent of cost of goods sold in 1970 and increased to eighty percent in 1974. Between 1960 and 1975 wages increased four hundred percent while productivity was, according to Claude Gaier, "...one of the lowest in the entire Belgian metallurgical industry... ."[10]

In an attempt to counter the two most pressing problems—declining sales and increasing wages—Fabrique Nationale expanded into other compatible areas. In 1972 FN acquired thirty-six percent of the capital of the famous Italian gunmaker Beretta. In 1973 construction began on an arms assembly plant in Portugal. That same year the Belgian company acquired the former Dumont-Sclaigneaux Company to design and build industrial hydraulics. In 1977 FN purchased one of its oldest customers, the Browning Arms Company.

The problem of how to deal with rapidly increasing wages was perhaps the most troublesome to FN. The period of the late 1960s and the early 1970s was one in which great advances were made in automating production methods. This resulted in some reduction in hand labor and in the overall number of skilled workers required to create its manufactured products. As we have seen, the 1960s was a difficult time with regard to labor disputes for FN, with numerous strikes occurring during that decade. The 1970s, however, offered no shelter from labor troubles. The fallout from the women's strike of 1966 was still very much a part of the underlying conflict between labor and management. In 1974 another serious strike affected FN. It began as a grassroots movement over which union representatives had little control. The conflict spread and management was faced with a profound situation in which workers wanted to be treated as valuable assets and work in conditions that were not reminiscent of the nineteenth century, but were more modern and compassionate. In other words, there was a fundamental shift in the relations between labor and management at Fabrique Nationale that brought both sides into the modern era.[11]

Fabrique Nationale underwent another more superficial alteration brought about by changing attitudes throughout the world toward the manufacture and sale of arms. In October of 1971, FN management decided to change the name of the company from "Fabrique Nationale d'Armes de Guerre" to "Fabrique Nationale Herstal." The company was attempting to disassociate itself from a past that was, "... traditional, bureaucratic, and old fashioned," where working conditions were obsolete, and the company was the center of the so-called "Belgian militaro-industrial complex." FN did not want to be known as a "gunmer-

[10] Gaier, *FN: 100 Years*, p 119.

[11] *Ibid.*, pp. 129-130.

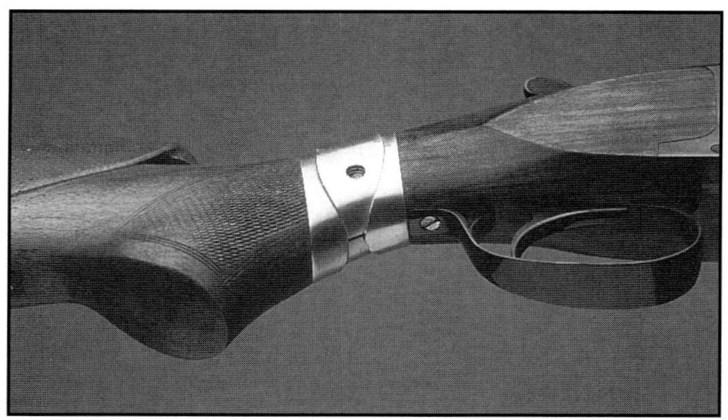

Many high quality double gun manufacturers employed a Try Gun to get the best fit possible for its customers. Such a gun is usually associated with English and European makers, but Winchester had several Try Guns for its Model 21 customers, and Browning was no exception. This Browning Superposed Try Gun was used by Browning when customers wanted to order special dimension stocks. All of the important measurements are adjustable on this stock, from length of pull to drop at the comb. Courtesy Browning Company.

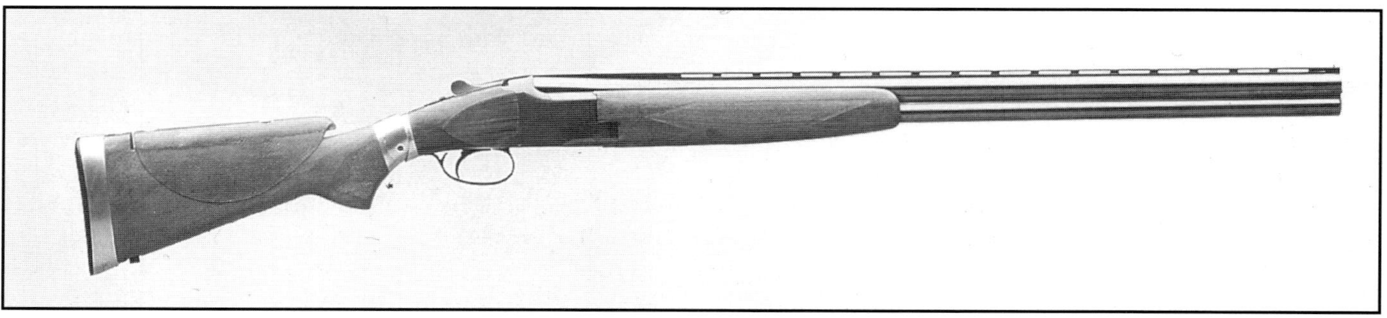

chant," but rather as a modern enlightened industrial company.[12]

Just as the Browning Arms Company experienced the vicissitudes of a recession in the U.S., so did Fabrique Nationale experience similar economic hardships. The slowdown in sales seemed to escalate, as did wages, along with the ravages of inflation. In order to survive, FN had no choice but to turn toward the contemporary world and, if it hoped to survive, become a modern-day company. The new general manager, Michel Vandestrick, was responsible for FN's recovery.

Vandestrick intended to solve the company's problems in two ways. He wanted to revitalize the corporation by moving it away from the old ways. There would be a refurbishing not only of the physical plant, but also of the relationship between worker and management. This new partnership would be a radical departure for Fabrique Nationale. The next obstacle would be to implement a new growth strategy and become a truly international company. This new approach would occupy FN for the balance of the 1970s and into the 1980s.

What is important to understand about the Browning chronicle and the history of the Superposed is to what extent FN was affected by both internal and external forces. These forces, and FN's handling of them, have a direct bearing on Browning's ability to sell its FN produced sporting arms in a timely manner and at competitive prices in its North American marketplace. Unreliable production and constantly rising prices from FN were the nexus of Browning's difficulties with its Belgian produced sporting arms line. Simply put, FN's inability to produce Superposed shotguns in a timely manner for a relatively stable price was to eventually be responsible for the decision to drop the Superposed shotgun from the Browning product line as a production gun. In order to stave off the inevitable for as long as possible, manufacturing modifications made to the Superposed during the course of the 1970s were a direct result of FN's inability to hold the line on its cost and its failure to make deliveries.

---

[12] *Ibid.*, pp. 130-131.

A Pictorial Chronicle of the Fabrique Nationale Custom Shop

Above: These are the tools used for barrel making and finishing in the Custom Shop. Great skill is required to fit and finish a set of barrels. Courtesy Fabrique Nationale Archives.

Left: All of the work to assemble and build the Superposed was performed in the Custom Shop. Here a set of barrels is checked for trueness. Courtesy Fabrique Nationale Archives.

Above left: Here an FN Custom Shop craftsman drills a set of barrels during one of the many operations required to complete a pair of Superposed barrels. Courtesy Fabrique Nationale Archives.

Above right: After each operation is performed, a gauge is used to measure the barrel to determine that the exact tolerances are maintained. Courtesy Fabrique Nationale Archives.

This finished set of Superposed barrels complete with ventilated rib is checked for straightness. Courtesy Fabrique Nationale Archives.

In order to achieve an exact fit between barrels and receiver it is necessary to chisel or cut away metal from the frame around the barrel ears. This operation is often done by hand, and requires great skill and experience. Courtesy Fabrique Nationale Archives.

To make certain that the barrels fit the receiver perfectly, lamp black is used in order to see that the breech end of the barrels do not bind against the standing breech of the receiver. Courtesy Fabrique Nationale Archives.

Here Superposed barrels are polished to make certain a perfect fit exists between the barrels and the receiver. Courtesy Fabrique Nationale Archives.

At last, after several hand fittings, the receiver and barrels have attained the precise alignment. Courtesy Fabrique Nationale Archives.

After numerous operations involving hand fitting, the Superposed receiver is visually checked. Courtesy Fabrique Nationale Archives.

Buttstock wood begins as a solid blank. The Custom Shop craftsman must cut the blank along a pre-drawn outline of the stock in order for the shaping operations to start. Once that has been accomplished, he measures the stock to insure accuracy. Courtesy Fabrique Nationale Archives.

Once the contours of the stock have been cut, the final shaping takes place using hand tools and a keen eye. Courtesy Fabrique Nationale Archives.

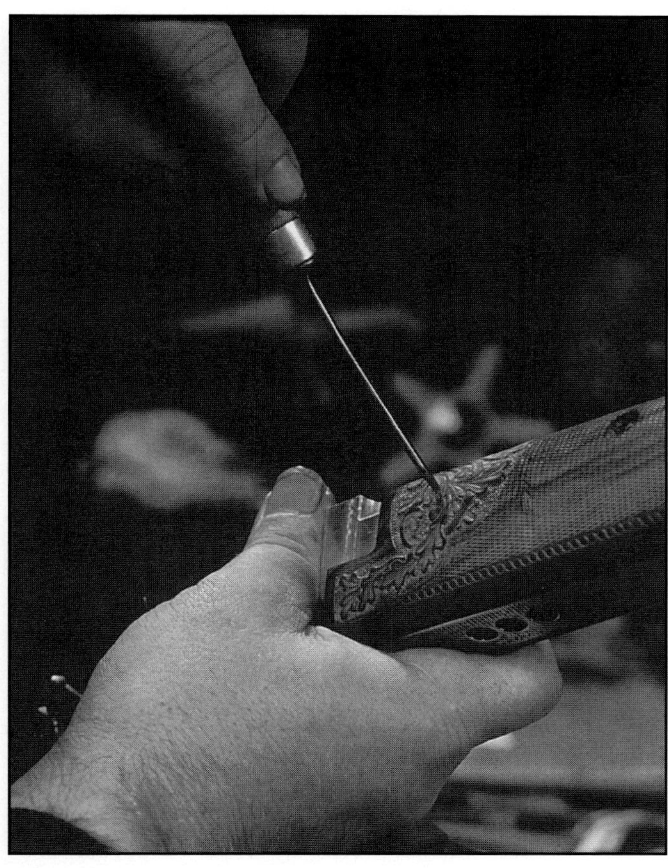

Wood carving requires the same skill and artistry as engraving. Here a craftsman carves an intricate pattern of oak leaves into a Superposed forearm. Courtesy Fabrique Nationale Archives.

This Custom Shop artisan is cutting a border into a Superposed forearm. He uses a special jig to hold his work in place. Courtesy Fabrique Nationale Archives.

This Custom Shop craftsman is shaping the bottom tang to the surrounding wood in order to obtain a flawless fit between metal and wood. Courtesy Fabrique Nationale Archives.

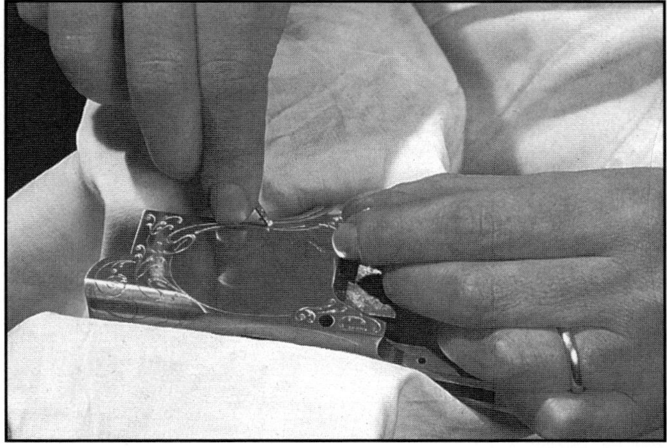

Here a Superposed receiver is having gold wire placed into engraving cuts. This process is known as inlaying and yields spectacular results. Courtesy Fabrique Nationale Archives.

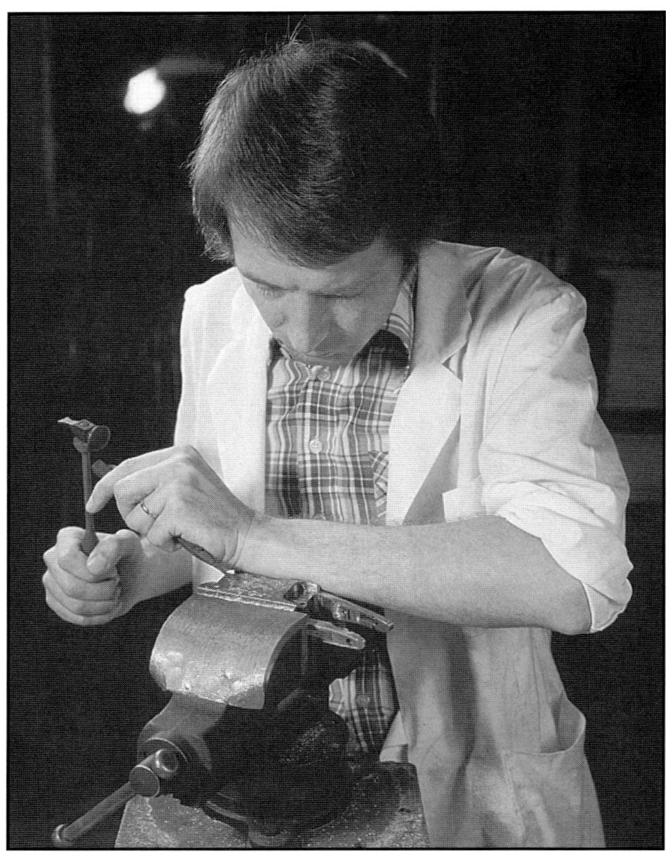

Working with gold inlays requires skill, patience, and a dexterity different from engraving steel. Courtesy Fabrique Nationale Archives.

Here a Custom Shop gunsmith performs the final assembly on this special order Superposed. The gun is checked not only for proper fit and finish, but also for proper functioning. Only when it works perfectly does the Custom Shop allow the gun to be shipped to the customer. Courtesy Fabrique Nationale Archives.

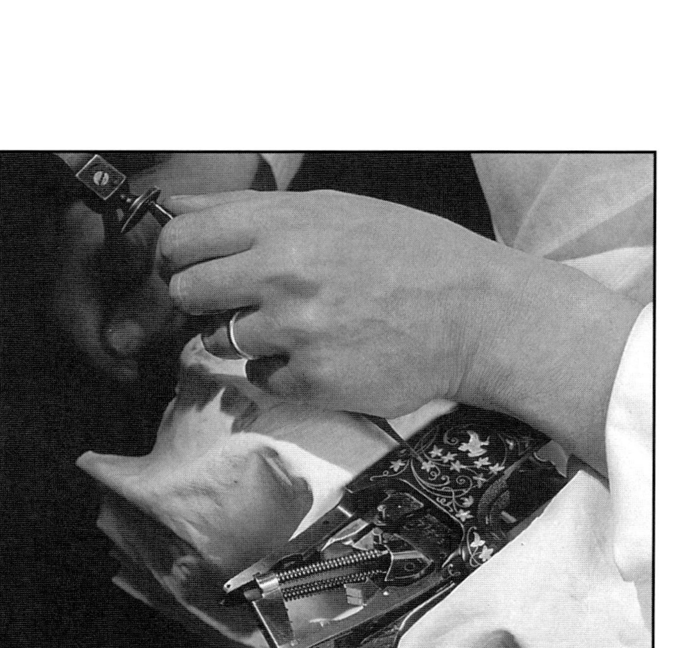

The engraver, Gaston Vandersmissen, puts the finishing touches on his masterpiece, a superbly executed Custom Shop Exhibition Grade Superposed. Courtesy Fabrique Nationale Archives.

Superposed Engraving of the 1970s

There were approximately 7,206 engraved Superposed sold in North America from 1970 through 1977. This is an average of nine hundred guns a year that were embellished by the engravers at Fabrique Nationale. Led by Louis Vrancken and André Watrin, the engraving shop continued to produce spectacular results.

The Grade I Superposed pattern remained the same during this period, as did the Pigeon Grade, Pointer Grade, Diana Grade, and Midas Grade. The Pigeon Grade was discontinued in 1975, as the Pointer Grade had been in 1966, because the price of

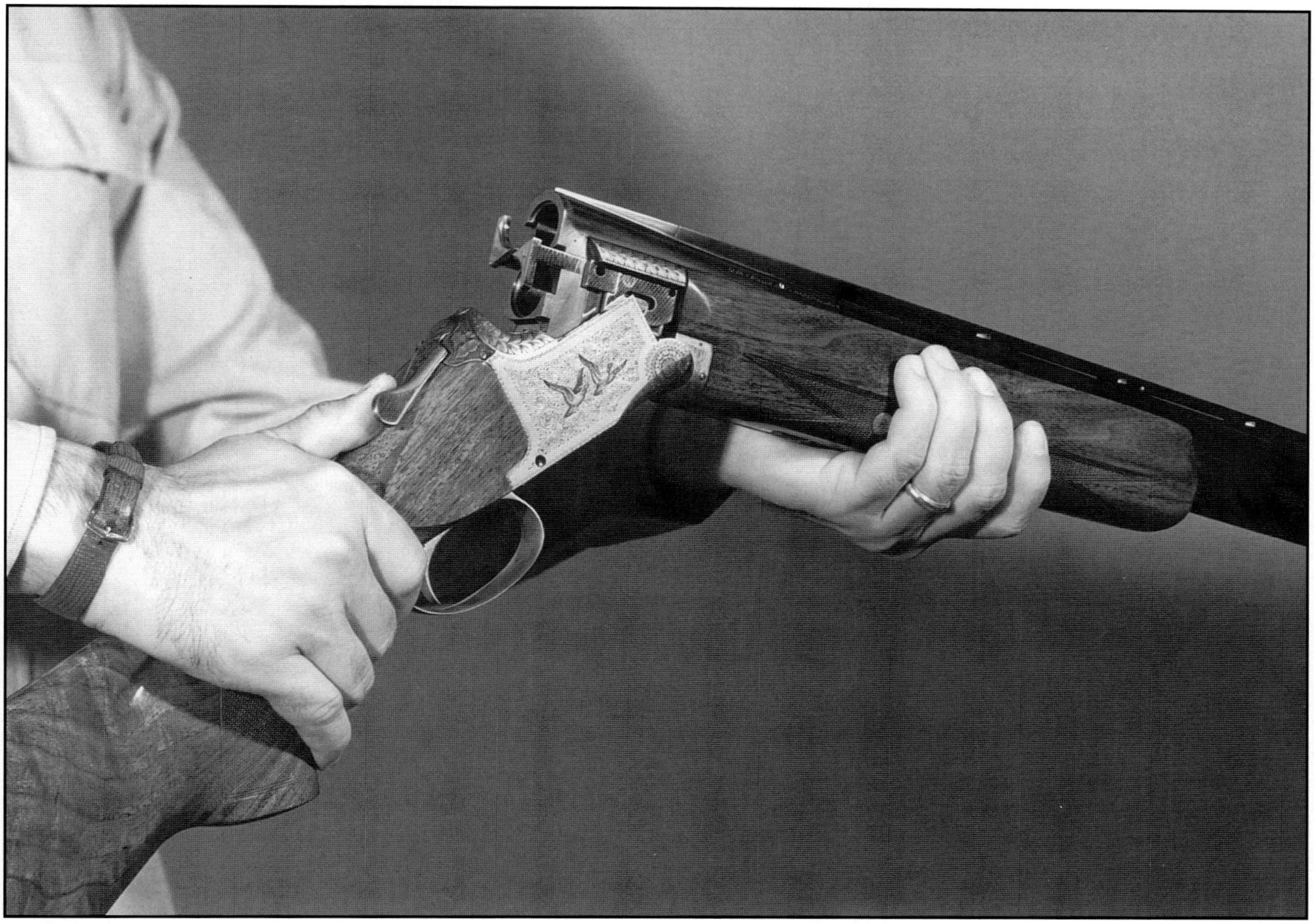

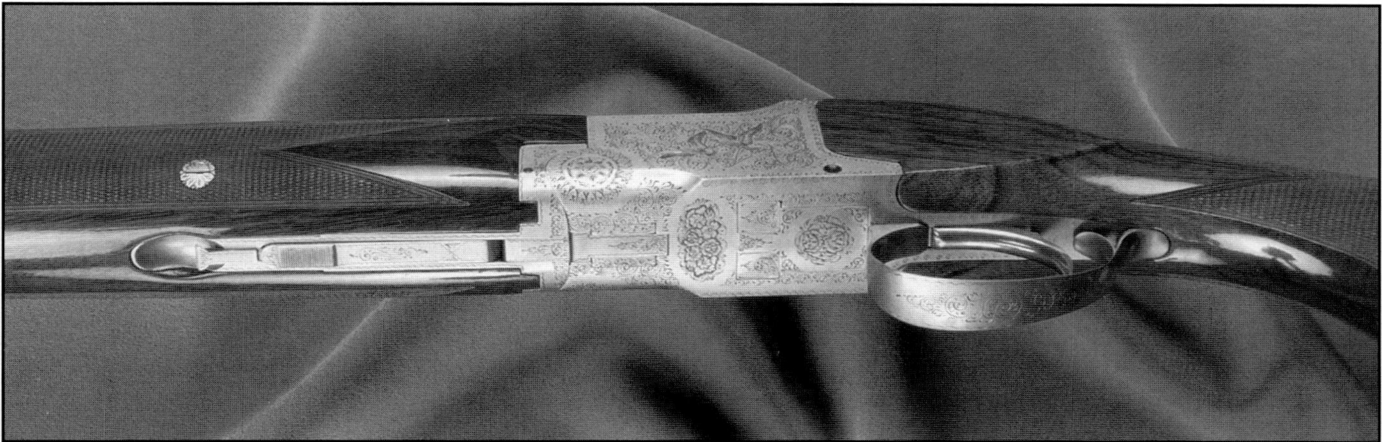

The Pigeon Grade was discontinued from the Browning catalogue in 1975. It had been in the Superposed engraving family since 1930, and was a very popular grade. Pricing pressures and delivery schedules forced the Pigeon Grade to be dropped from the Superposed line. Courtesy Browning Company.

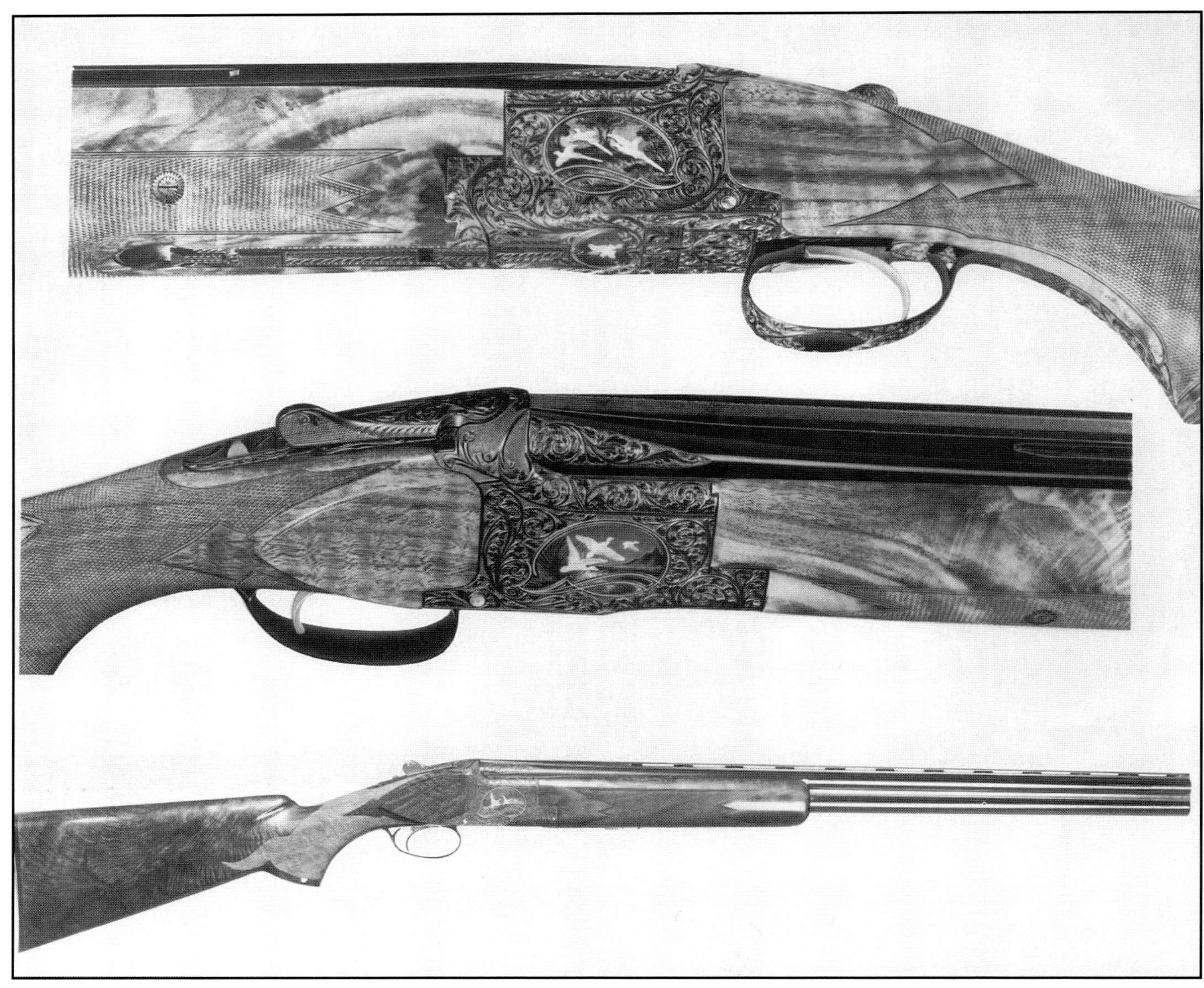

A 1970s Midas Grade, the top of the line production high grade Superposed. The basic pattern remained the same from its inception in 1960 until it was dropped in 1977, but each Midas Grade was different in composition to some degree. Courtesy Browning Company.

engraving had risen at the same rate as the rest of the component parts of the Superposed, and some cuts were required to reduce inventory costs and keep the available supply of engraved Superposed within reasonable delivery limits. Both the Pigeon Grade and the Pointer Grade were available on a special order basis only. This was a time of change not only for the FN engraver but also in regards to the wide range of new engraving styles that would be imported into North America by Browning.

"C" Grade Exhibition: During the '70s Browning purchased from Fabrique Nationale a number of specially engraved Superposed created primarily for the European market. FN had a large inventory of these distinctive guns on hand due to declining sales in its European markets. FN offered these guns to Browning at very tempting prices. Browning management felt that the sales of these unusual Superposed throughout North America might stimulate interest in engraved Superposed in all of its grades. These guns were referred to as "C" Grade Exhibition Superposed in the U.S. because of the "C" prefix of the serial number.[13] These Exhibition Grade guns began to appear for sale in North America in the mid-1970s and numbered around 230

[13] Harmon Williams, "Exposition/Exhibition Superposed," *Browning Collectors Association Newsletter*, Jan.-Feb. 1985, Vol. VI, No. 4., pp. 2-4.

guns. The known serial numbers of these guns range from C1 to as high as C254.[14] These specially engraved Superposed were divided into different levels, or groups, to designate the price range, array of features, and level of ornamentation.

Group A-1 consisted of 12 and 20 gauge guns with a retail price of $4,375. They featured 28-inch barrels, some with Schnabel forearms and checkered butts. The engraving was a deep, heavy scroll consisting of flowers and leaves on a silver gray frame.

Group A-2 was composed of 12, 20, and 28 gauge guns with a retail price of $5,000. Barrel lengths were 26-1/2 or 28 inches with either ventilated or solid ribs. Most had Schnabel forearms and checkered butts. One of these guns, a 28 gauge, was fitted with a straight grip stock with oil finish, solid rib, and double triggers. The engraving patterns were similar to the A-1 Group.

Group B-1 and B-2 were less expensive than the A Group, carrying a retail price of $3,000 and $3,125 respectively. These guns had fewer features and the scroll engraving was not as fine, nor did it have as great a coverage, as the A Group.

Group C had a suggested retail price of $4,125. This group was made up of 12 and 20 gauge guns with barrel lengths of 26-1/2, 28, and 32 inches. The 32-inch barrel guns were BROADway Trap models. The 26-1/2 and 28-inch barrel guns were choked skeet and skeet. Most of these guns were fitted with recoil pads and beavertail forearms. The frame was recessed or scalloped, a popular European option used by FN for its sales on the continent. The engraving was a finely executed scroll with flowers and leaves on a silver gray frame.

Group D-1 carried a retail price of $4,375 and was similar in appearance to the C Group with the exception of the Schnabel forearm and checkered butt.

Group F-1 had a retail price of $6,250. This group featured 12 and 20 gauge guns with barrel lengths from 26-1/2 to 28 inches, Schnabel forearms, and straight grip stocks with checkered butts. The frame was fitted with sideplates and blued with gold inlay linework.

Group F-3 was offered for $8,125 retail and featured 12 and 20 gauge guns with 26-1/2 and 28-inch ventilated rib barrels. Straight grip stocks with Schnabel forearm and checkered butts were fitted to guns in this group. The engraving was done on a blued frame with gold inlay linework and gold inlay game birds.

Group F-6 was priced at $9,375 retail and featured primarily 12 gauge guns with 26-1/2 and 30-inch ventilated rib barrels. Most of the long barrel guns had beavertail forearms and recoil pads while the short barrel guns were fitted with Schnabel forearms and checkered butts. The engraving featured gold inlay linework on the borders with finely executed game birds against delicate gold backgrounds.

Group F-7 was priced the same as the F-1 Group, having a retail price of $6,250. It featured primarily 20 gauge guns with 28-inch ventilated rib barrels. Buttstocks had straight grips with oil finish and checkered butts. Schnabel forearms were also featured on this group of guns. The engraving was seventy-five percent coverage of fine line scroll against a blued frame fitted with sideplates.

The final group was Group G, which had a suggested retail price of $5,625. This group perhaps more nearly met the taste of the North American market than the other groups. It consisted of 12 and 20 gauge guns choked full and full, or skeet and skeet with barrel lengths of 26-1/2, 28, and 32 inches. Some were fitted with straight grip stocks, Schnabel forearms, and checkered butts; others had pistol grips, beavertail forearms, and recoil pads. The engraving resembles the Diana Grade to some extent with deeply cut game scenes and scroll borders on grayed frames.

---

[14] There were actually 256 "C" Grade Exhibition guns built. There were two pairs of guns with the same serial numbers, each of the pair had one gun with an "A" suffix. Serial numbers C12 and C12A were built as a matched pair, as were C13 and C13A. Both sets of guns were 12 gauge with double triggers, Schnabel forearms, and checkered buttstocks with straight grip. The barrels were 28 inches on one pair and 26-1/2 inches on the other. Both were from Group B-1. Set C12 and C12A were assembled January 21, 1974, and shipped to Browning February 17, 1974. Set C13 and C13A were assembled April 22, 1974, and shipped to Browning May 13, 1974. These two sets are the only known matched pair of "C" Grade Exhibition Superposed produced. This information is derived from the official Fabrique Nationale shipping records.

Below is a partial listing of engravers whose names will appear on some of these "C" Grade Exhibition Superposed guns:

Mario Bodson	Georges Maréchal
Lucien Ernst	Jean H. Diet
André Crousse	Jean Marie Debrus
Richard Kowalski	Louis Vrancken
José Baerten	

The "C" Grade Exhibition guns were not particularly successful in Browning's marketplace. A great deal of time and effort was required to sell the guns, and the company was finally forced to lower prices to clear out its inventory.

Of the 256 "C" Grade guns produced, approximately 231 were sold in North America. The balance of the "C" Grades were sold in Europe and Australia. Fabrique Nationale shipping records show that most of these guns were produced between 1974 and 1977. The "C" Grade guns were called thus because of their serial number configuration, therefore the gauges of most of these special Superposed are recorded in FN's shipping records. The table below illustrates the breakdown of "C" Grade Superposed by gauge.

BROWNING SUPERPOSED "C" GRADE TOTAL FN PRODUCTION[15]

Gauge	Number Produced
12 gauge	133
20 gauge	85
28 gauge	17
.410 bore	19

Table 4-3

[15] The total of this listing is 254 guns, 2 short of the 256 produced. Shipping personnel neglected to record the gauges of two of the guns.

Browning "C" Grade Exhibition Grades

A Photographic Survey

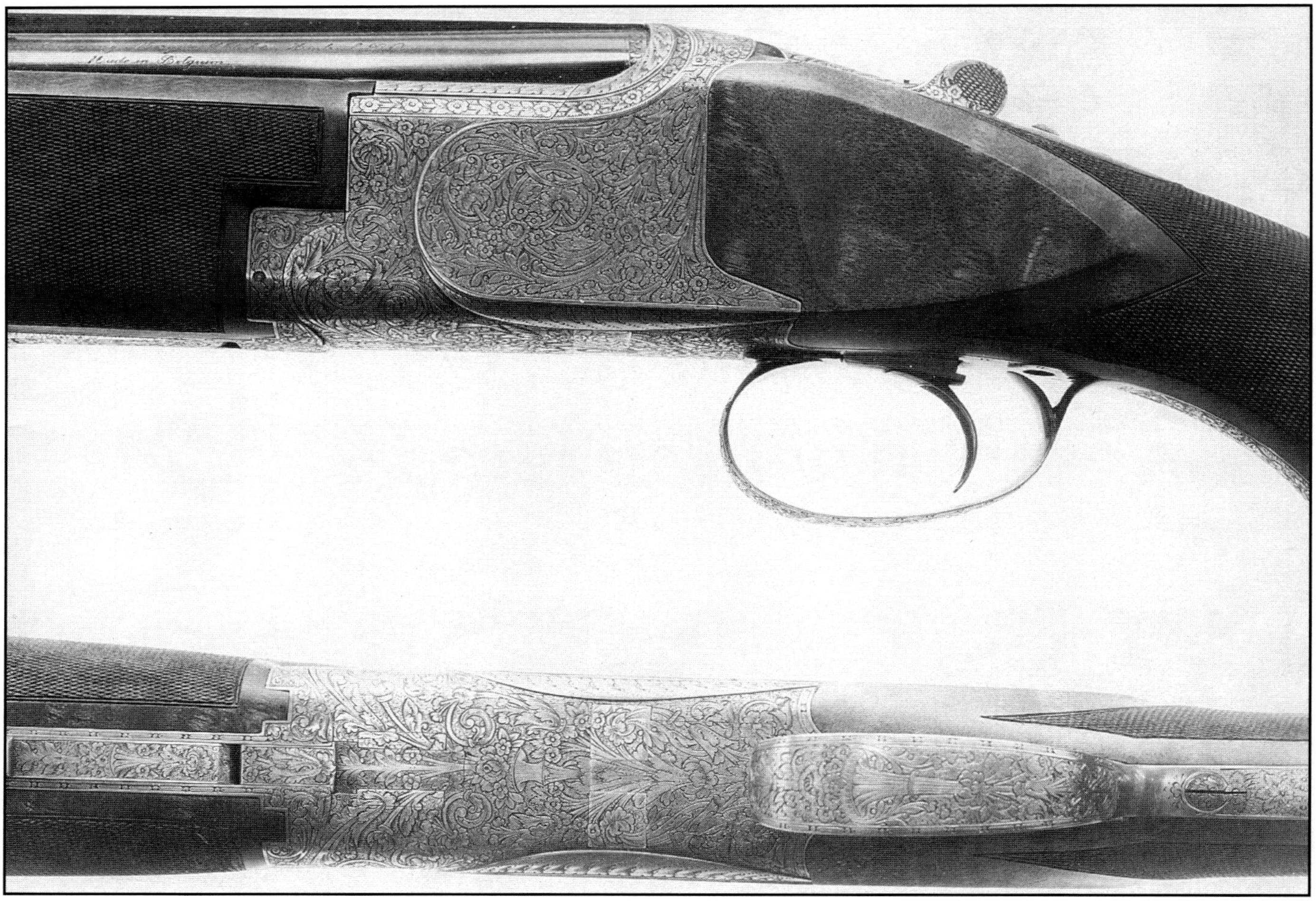

This C Grade Exhibition was engraved by FN master engraver Jean Diet. It is part of Group C and according to factory records this particular pattern was used on only eight guns. Note the sculptured frame and the barrel address in script. Courtesy Browning Company.

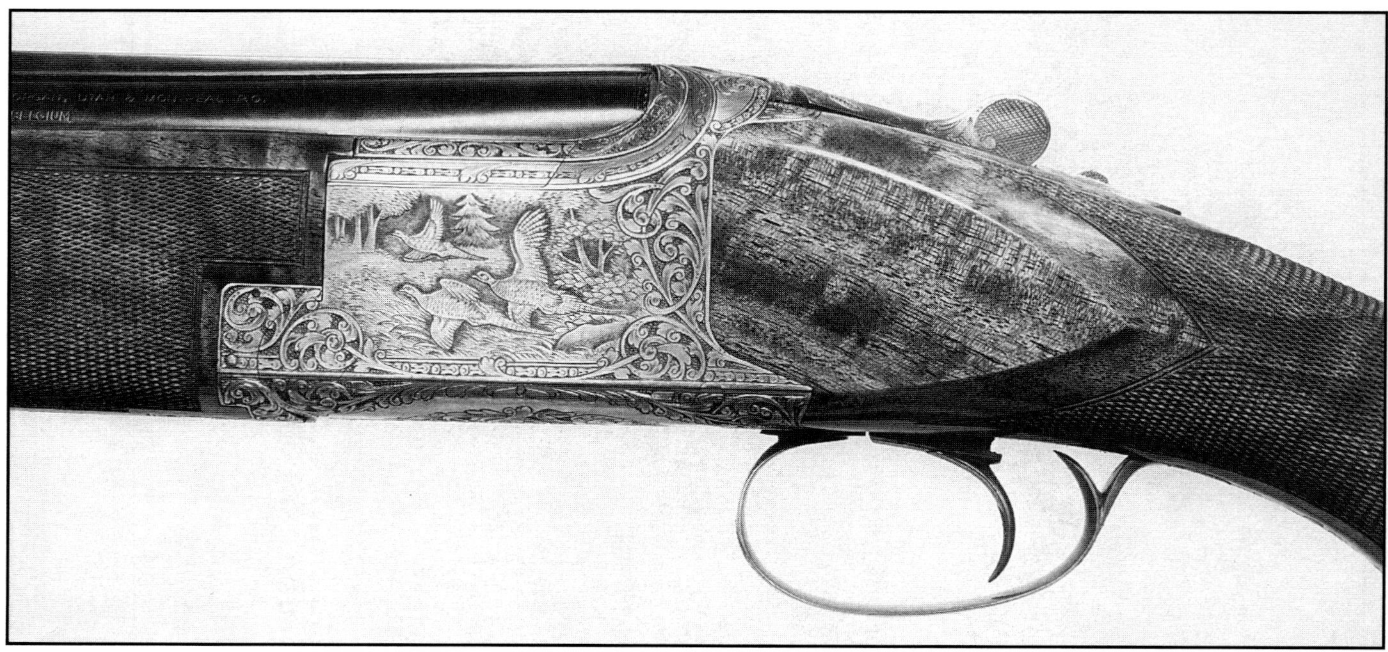

This is an example of a Group G C Grade Exhibition engraved by Mario Bodson. This particular pattern resembles in some respects the Diana Grade that was so popular in North America. Courtesy Browning Company.

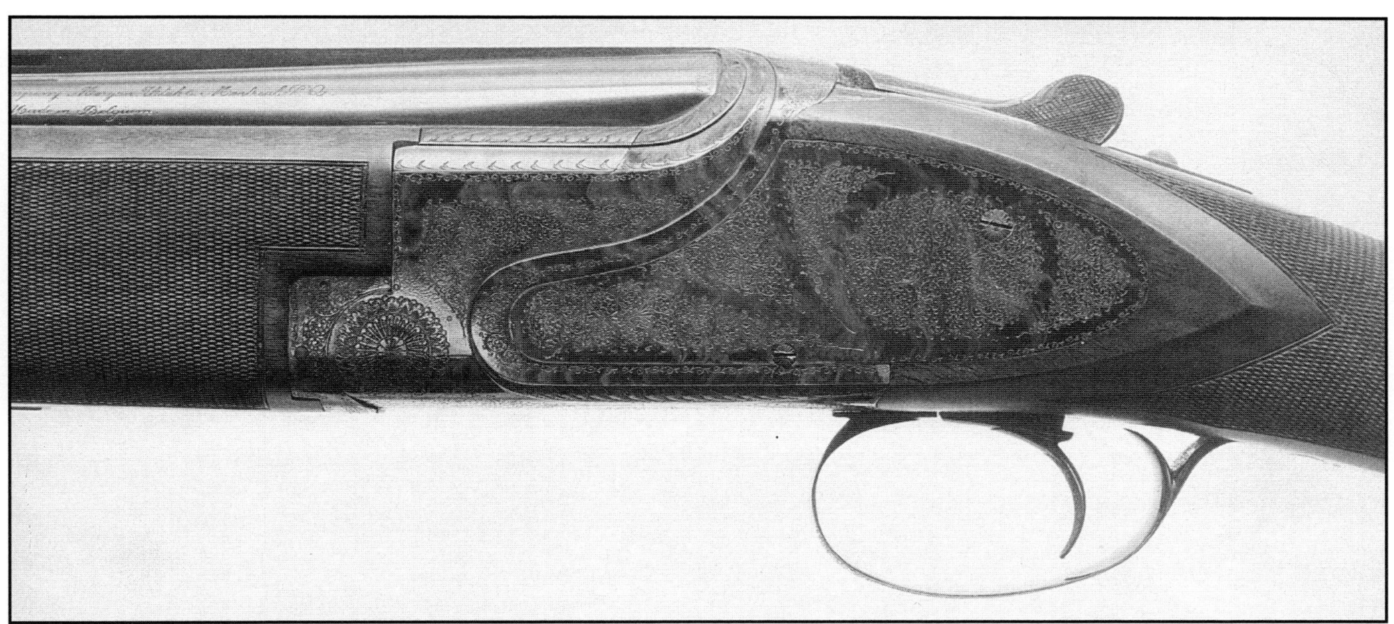

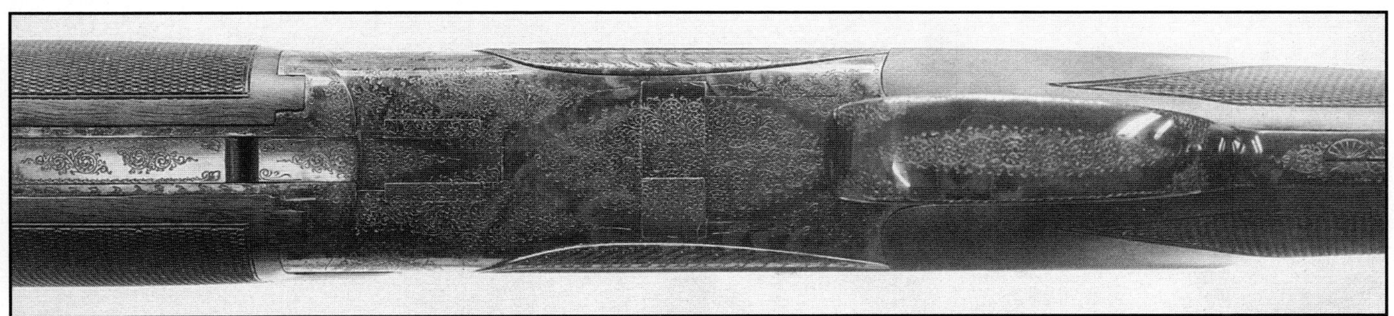

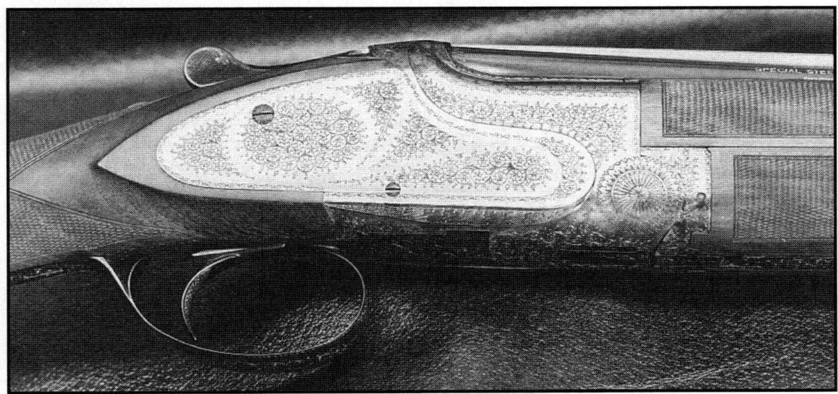

A Group F-7 C Grade Exhibition. Fitted with false sideplates, this Superposed was engraved with a very fine line scroll on a blued or case colored frame. This is a 20 gauge Group F-7 Superposed with blued frame and three-piece forearm. The bottom photo shows the overall view of the Group F-7 gun with its straight grip stock. The overall appearance is very European. Courtesy Browning Company.

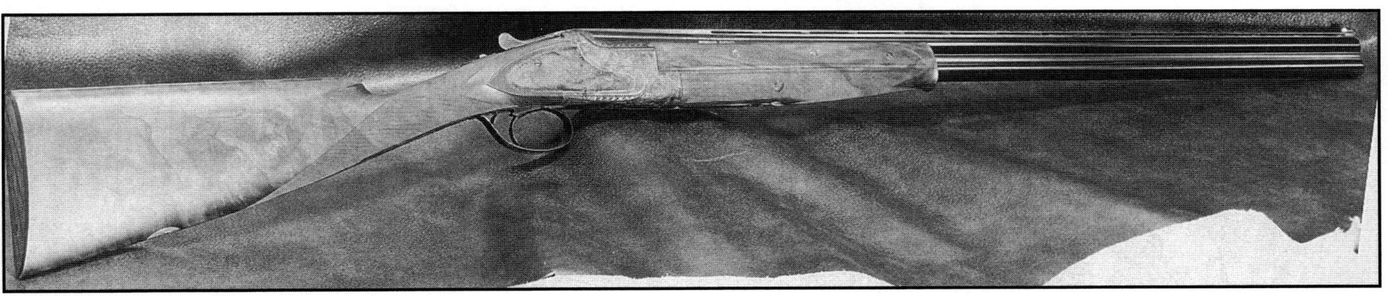

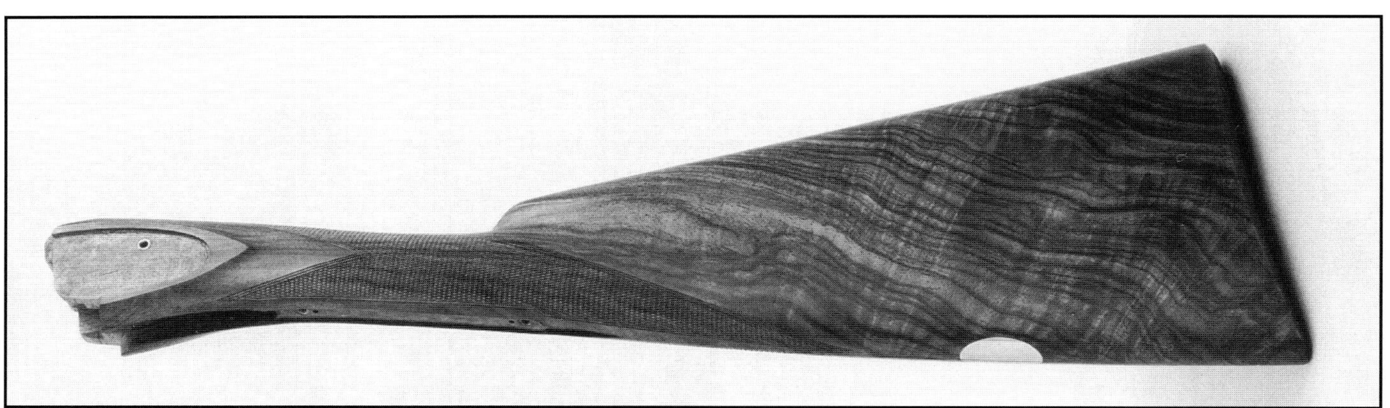

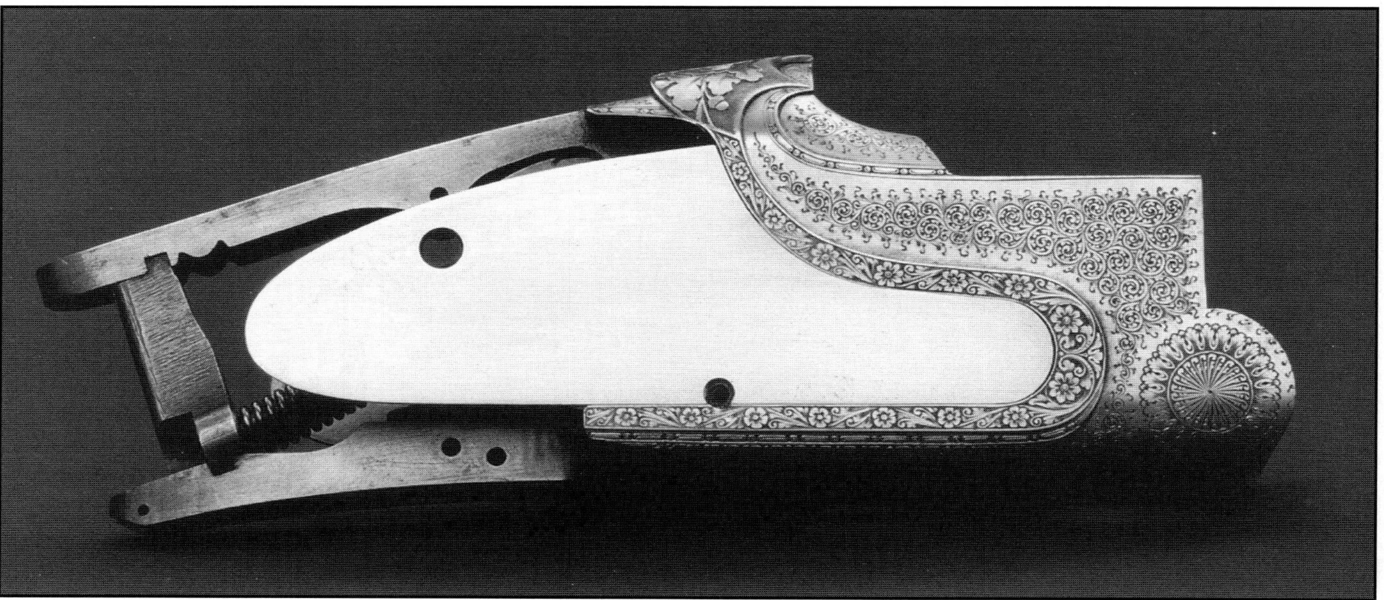

This is an exquisite example of a Custom Shop straight grip stock of outstanding grain and color cut for a Superposed with false sideplates. The Superposed receiver example at the bottom could very well be the same receiver that was fitted to this beautiful straight grip buttstock. The sideplate has been left blank for the game scene that was to be engraved at a later time. Courtesy Fabrique Nationale Archives.

The '70s were a period of uncertainty for the FN engravers themselves. In 1971 a small number of engravers led by Louis Vrancken left the engraving shop at FN and moved to a small commercial building at 13 Rue Faurieux, about a quarter-mile from the main factory. Located only a few yards from the town center of Herstal, near the small chapel of St. Aurelius, this new facility was called the Custom Shop and operated under the direct control of both Fabrique Nationale and Browning. The original purpose for creating the Custom Shop was to concentrate the efforts of FN's best engravers and craftsmen on FN's high grade guns, namely the Superposed. The idea of separating FN engravers from the main plant was management's, however, and their purpose was also to reduce some of the influence engravers as a labor group had built over the years at FN.

At first only eight engravers made the move to the Custom Shop at the invitation of Louis Vrancken . Some of these were José Baerten, André Crousse, Jean Diet, Jean Marie Debrus, Georges Maréchal, and Richard Kowalski. About six months later another eight engravers transferred from the factory to the Custom Shop. Some of these were Louis Bleus, Edouard Vos, Claudy Baerten, Jean Marie Deprez, and Lucien Ernst. Thus, by the end of 1972 there were a total of sixteen engravers working under the direction of Louis Vrancken. In addition, all custom work was performed under one roof. This included engraving, wood carving, checkering, bluing, and assembly work. Inspection was performed by the formidable Louis Nicolaï for Browning and Edmond Werys for FN. Custom work was defined as any high grade FN produced gun. In Superposed

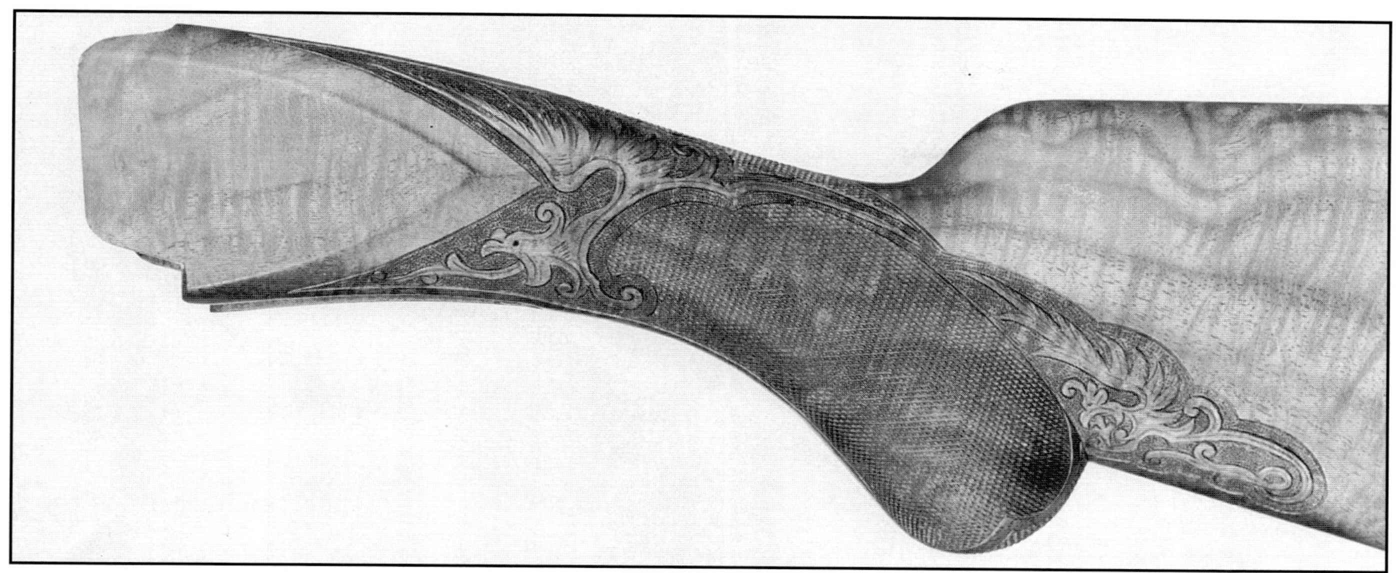

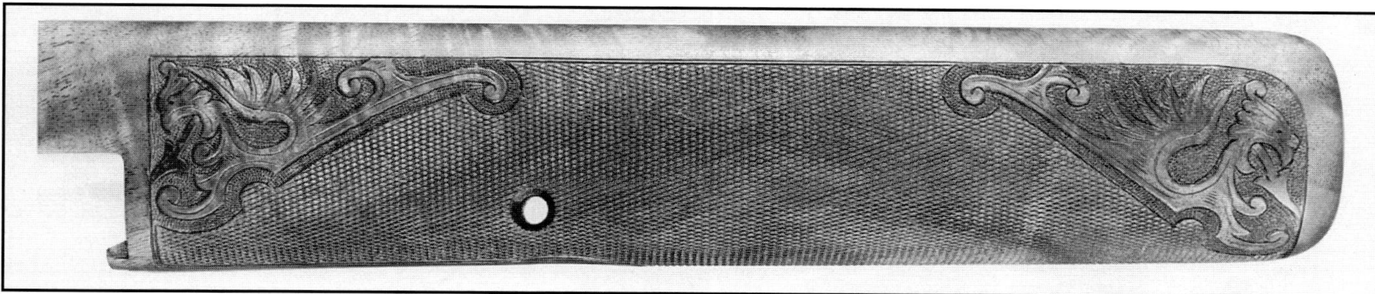

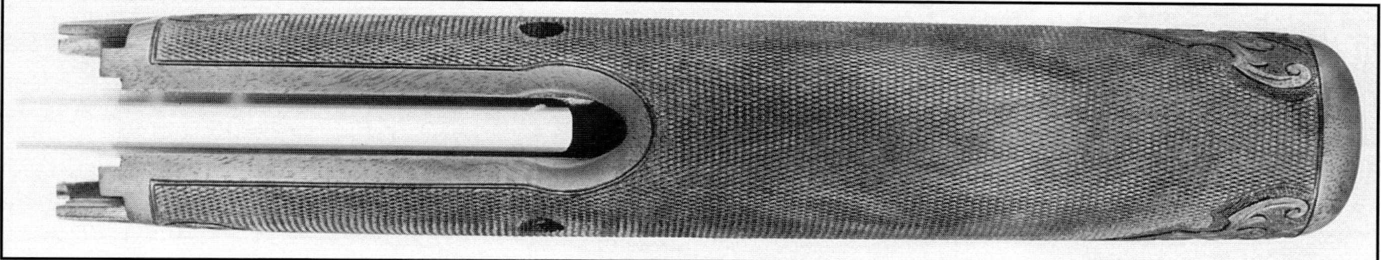

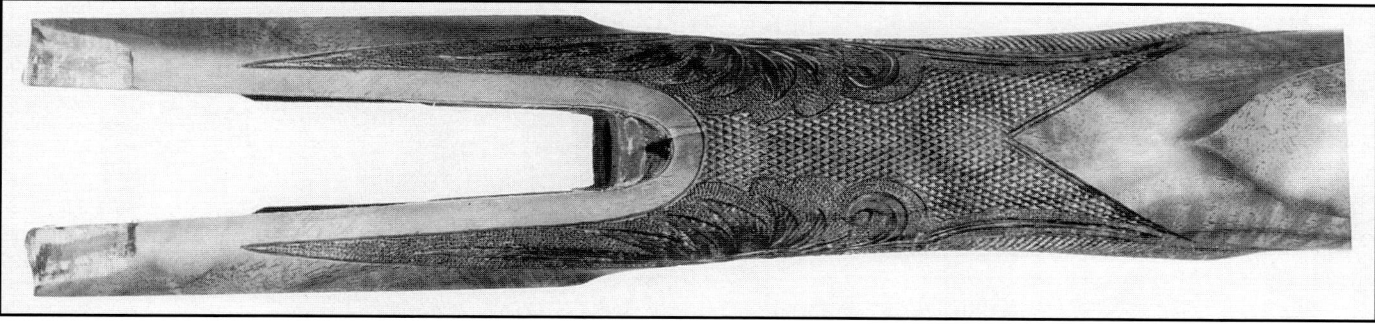

While FN engraving received the bulk of attention on the part of the Custom Shop and its customers, an often overlooked special order feature of the Superposed was wood carved buttstocks and forearms. Wood carving is found more often on European Superposed than those sold in North America, but it is nevertheless an art form as sought after as the engraver's art. This series of FN photographs illustrates several different views of a special order carved buttstock and forearm. The theme is chimeras cut into extremely fine checkering with a double line border. This Superposed stock, while cut with a round pistol grip knob, is inlaid for a short tang, an early 1970s Superposed modification. Courtesy Fabrique Nationale Archives.

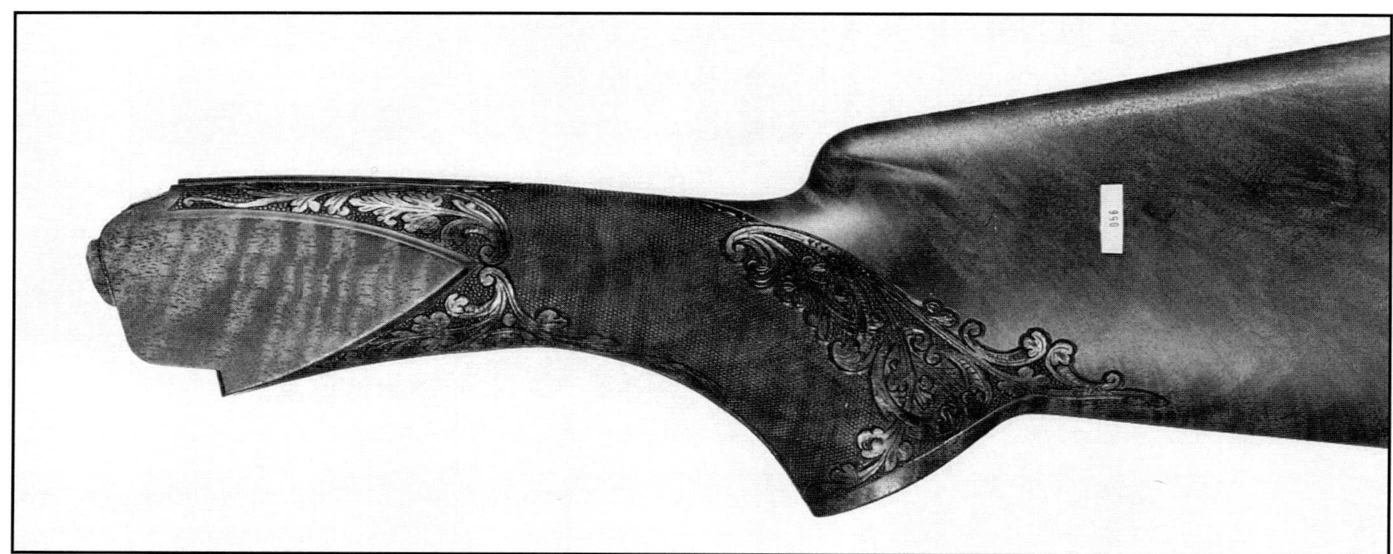

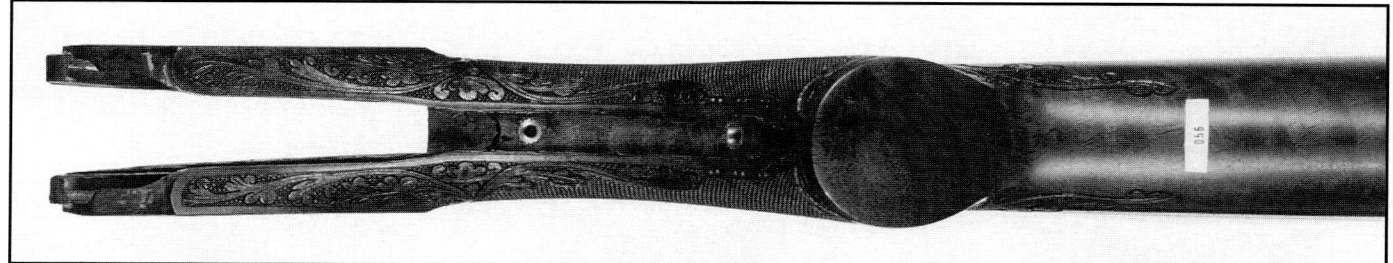

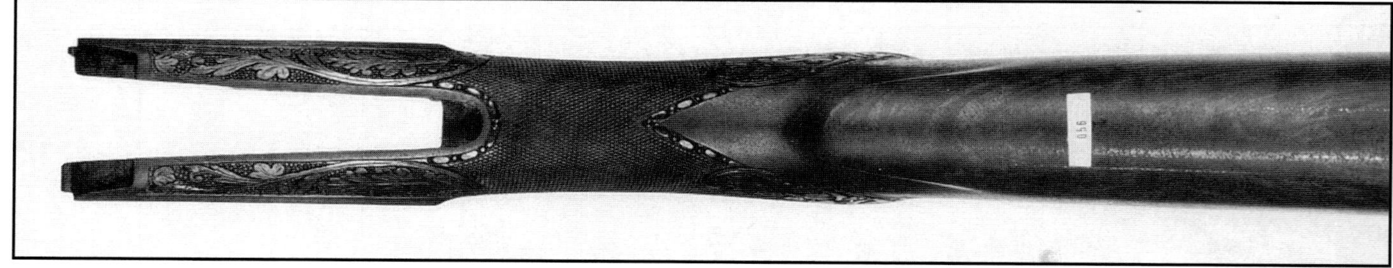

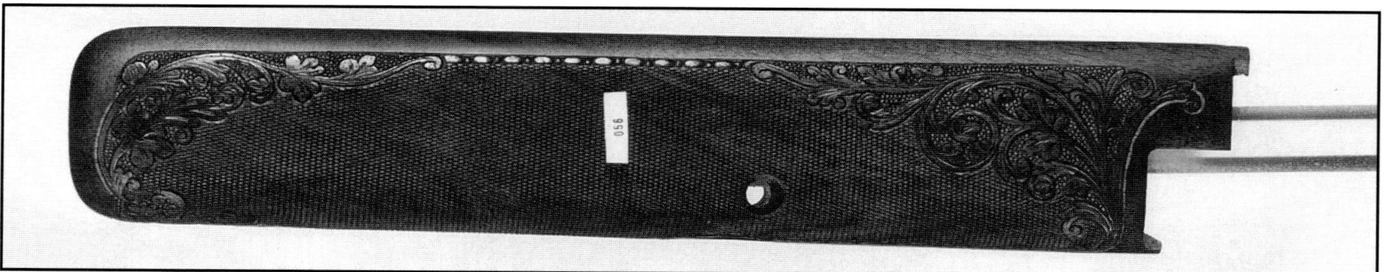

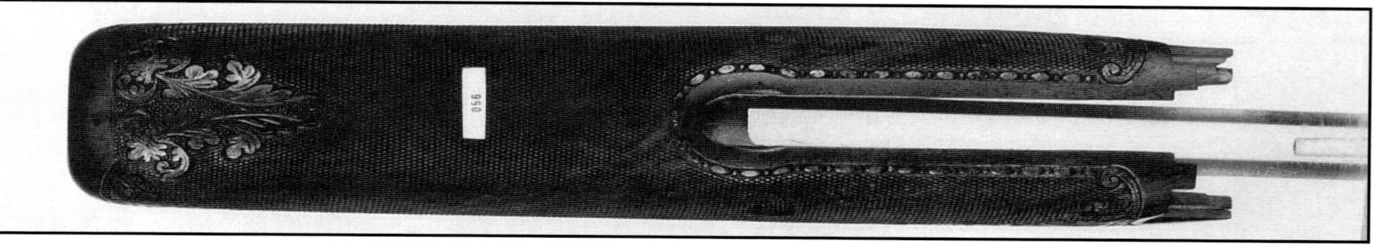

Another series of FN photographs showing a special order custom carved buttstock and forearm. A leaf motif with scroll is a more conventional theme for FN carved stocks. Note the fine line checkering. This particular buttstock has been cut for a long tang, while the pistol grip bottom is square. Courtesy Fabrique Nationale Archives.

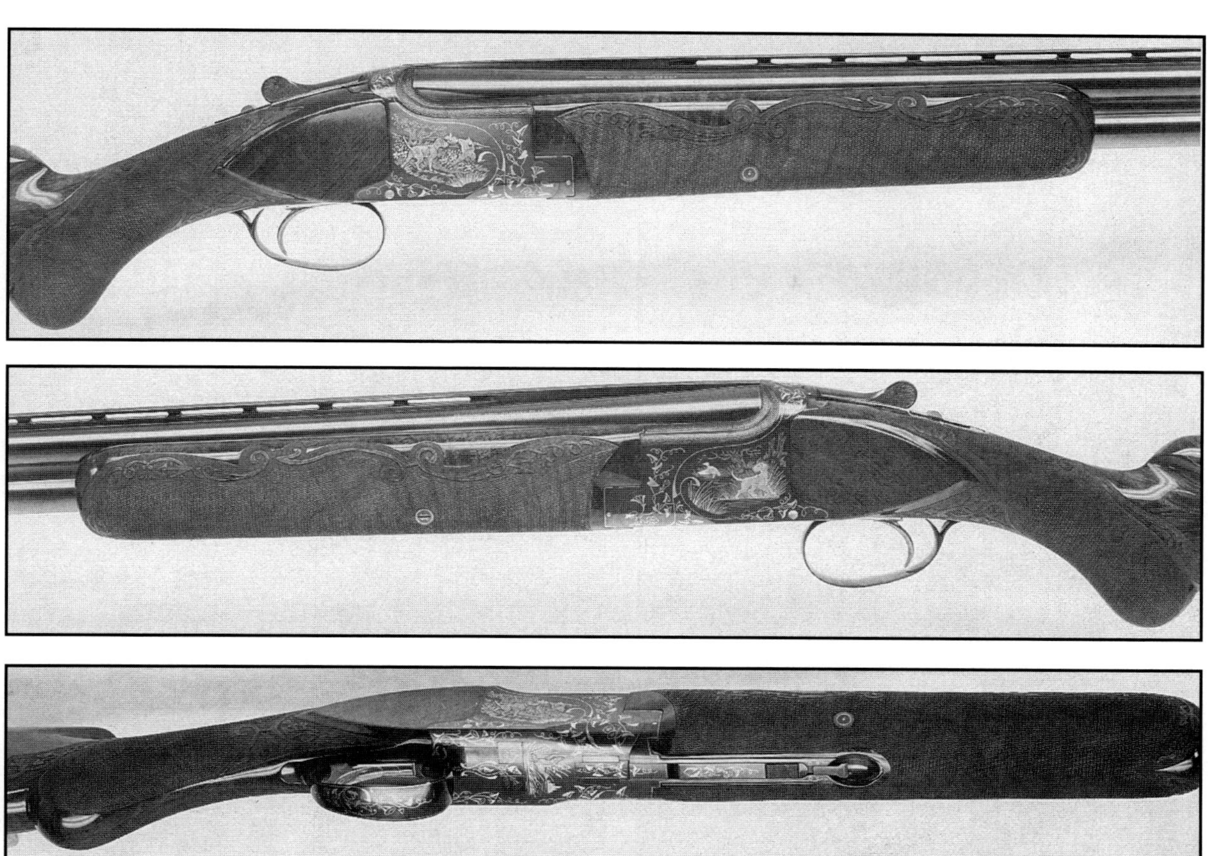

Although the decade of the 1970s represented an era of declining Superposed sales, it also represented an era of outstanding custom engraving and wood carving from the Custom Shop. This Browning 12 gauge Superposed Exhibition Grade, serial number 71197S71, exemplifies this outstanding '70s production. Courtesy Browning Company.

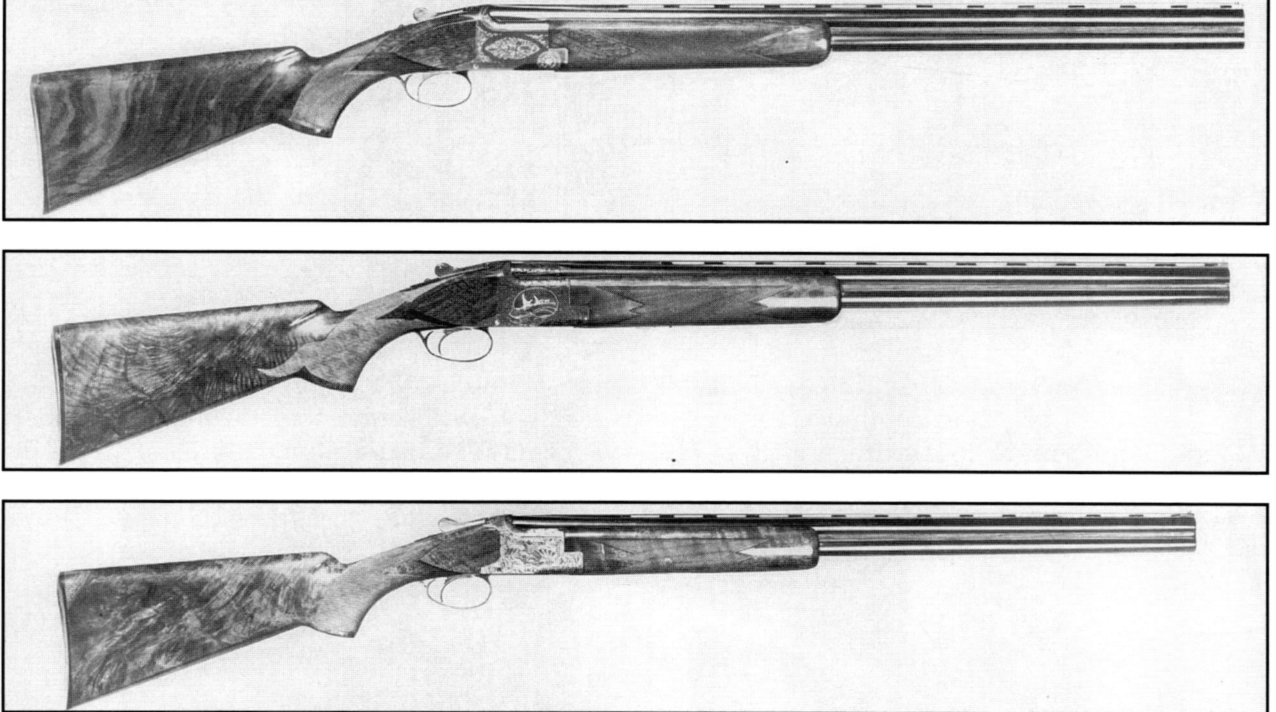

The last Superposed grades of the 1970s. From top to bottom, the Superposed Grade I, Midas Grade, and Diana Grade were the only grades to remain in the Superposed product line when the traditional Superposed was discontinued in 1977. Courtesy Browning Company.

A Browning lover's dream. Courtesy Browning Company.

terminology it meant any gun from Pigeon Grade or higher. Grade I Superposed continued to be assembled and engraved by journeyman engravers in FN's main facility.

It was in the Custom Shop at 13 Rue Faurieux that FN engravers produced numerous outstanding examples of the gun engraver's art. If that result is any indication, then the move from the main Fabrique Nationale plant to the Custom Shop must be judged a success.

The Genius of Louis Vrancken

A Photographic Tribute

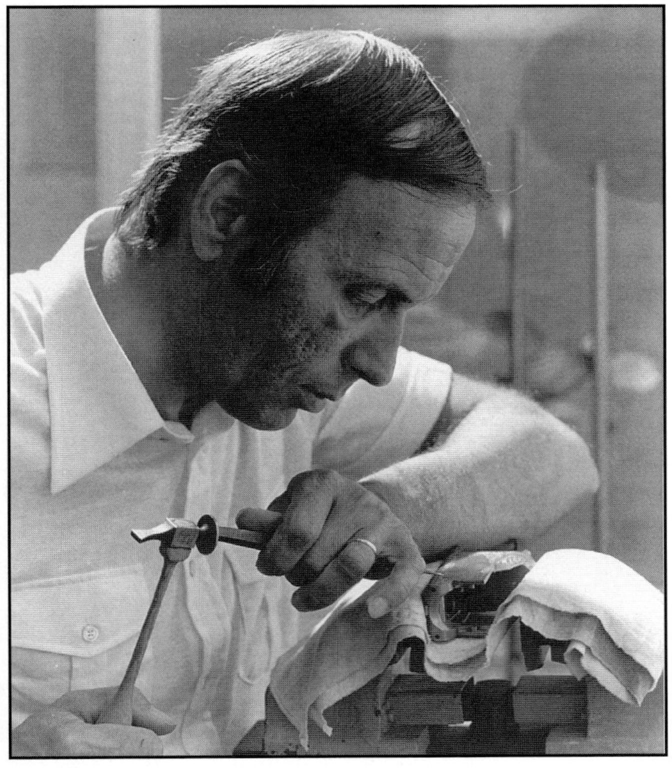

Louis Vrancken is considered by many to be one of the finest gun engravers of the twentieth century. He was blessed with a wide range of skills. His artistic talent was considerable, and his ability to create and execute game scenes in metal may be unsurpassed. He was one of the leaders of the Custom Shop and in many ways was responsible for its creation. Many collectors value his work more than that of the great master Felix Funken, André Watrin, or José Baerten. Louis Vrancken died in December of 1983. Courtesy Fabrique Nationale Archives.

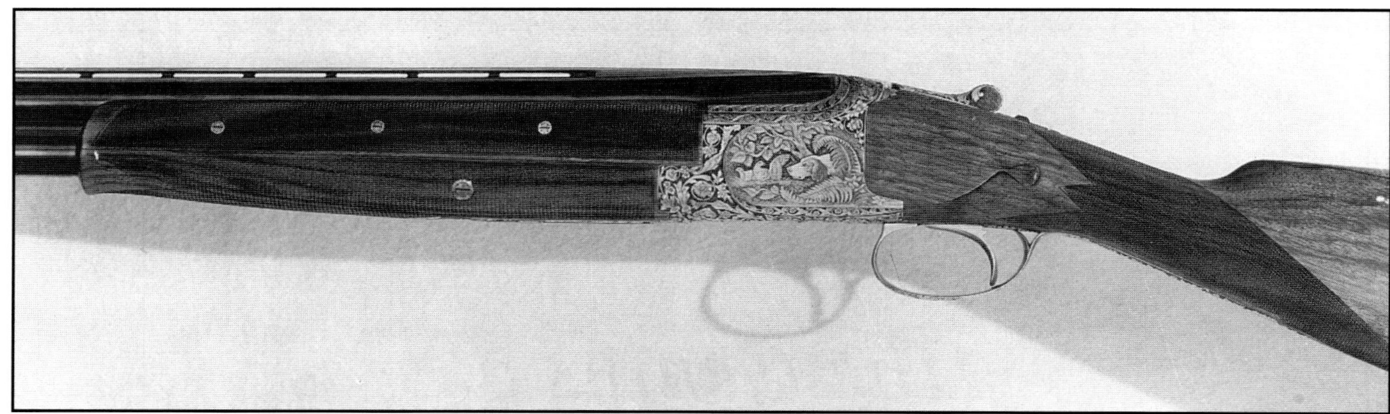

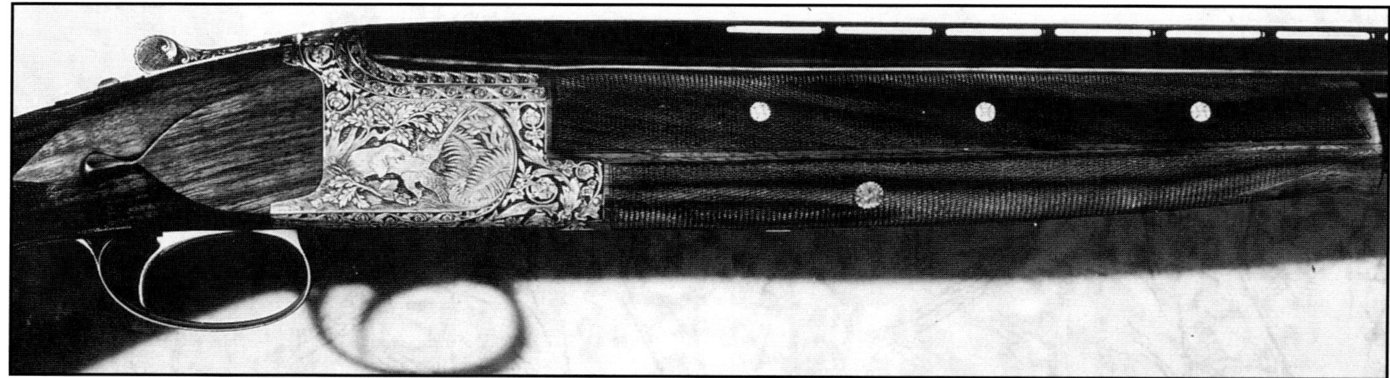

This early 1960s FN Browning Superposed is a special creation by Louis Vrancken. It features a sculptured frame and deeply cut scrollwork that incorporates the game scene so well that both appear to coalesce. This was one of Vrancken's early creations, and is a significant indicator of his future prominence. Courtesy Fabrique Nationale Archives.

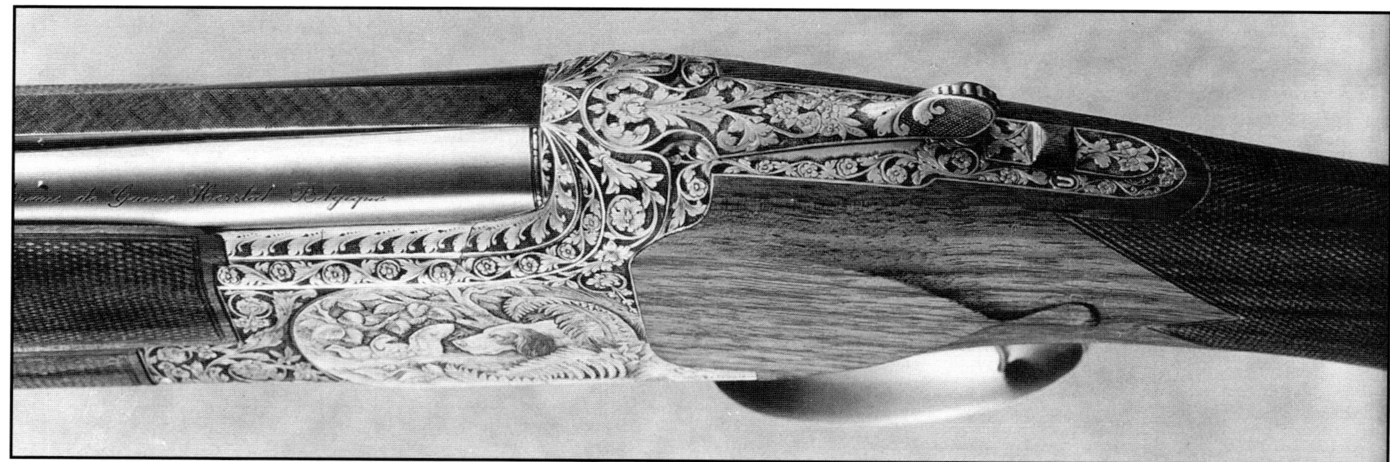

A top and bottom view of this early Vrancken creation. The black background accentuates the depth of the scroll and makes the scroll more dramatic. The bottom shows complete coverage with a scroll and flower motif and a vignette executed on the trigger guard that blends perfectly with the rest of the composition. Courtesy Fabrique Nationale Archives.

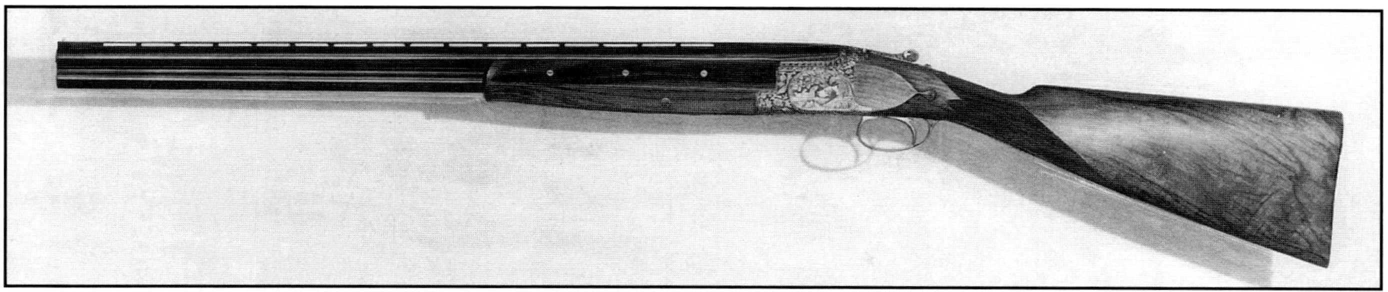

An overall view of Vrancken's masterpiece showing the left side. The straight grip stock, three-piece forearm, and teardrop points on the buttstock behind the receiver all contribute to the impressive appearance of this magnificent Superposed. Courtesy Fabrique Nationale Archives.

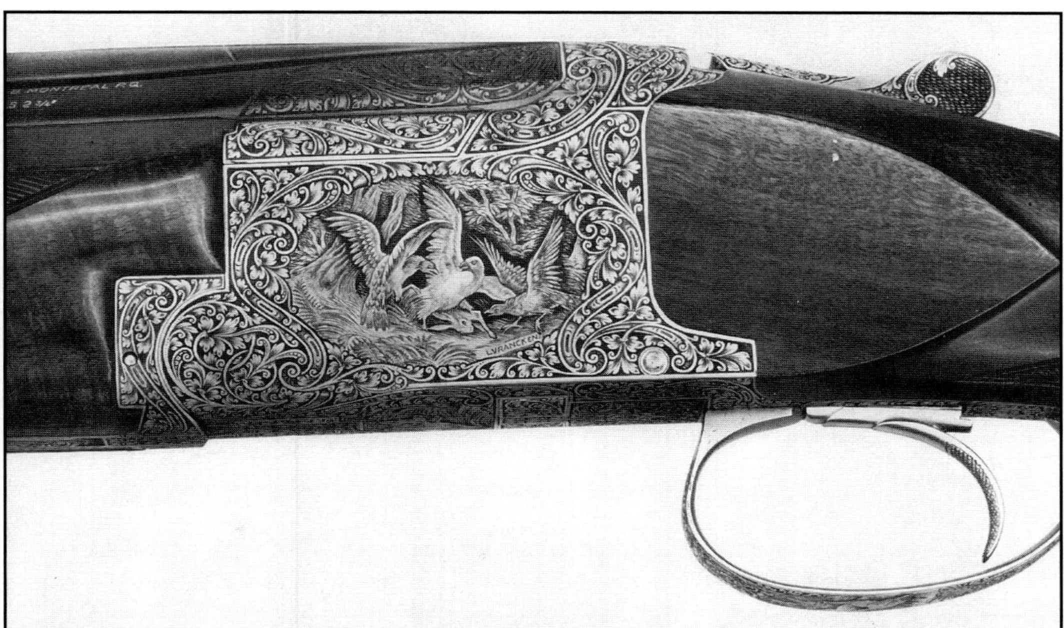

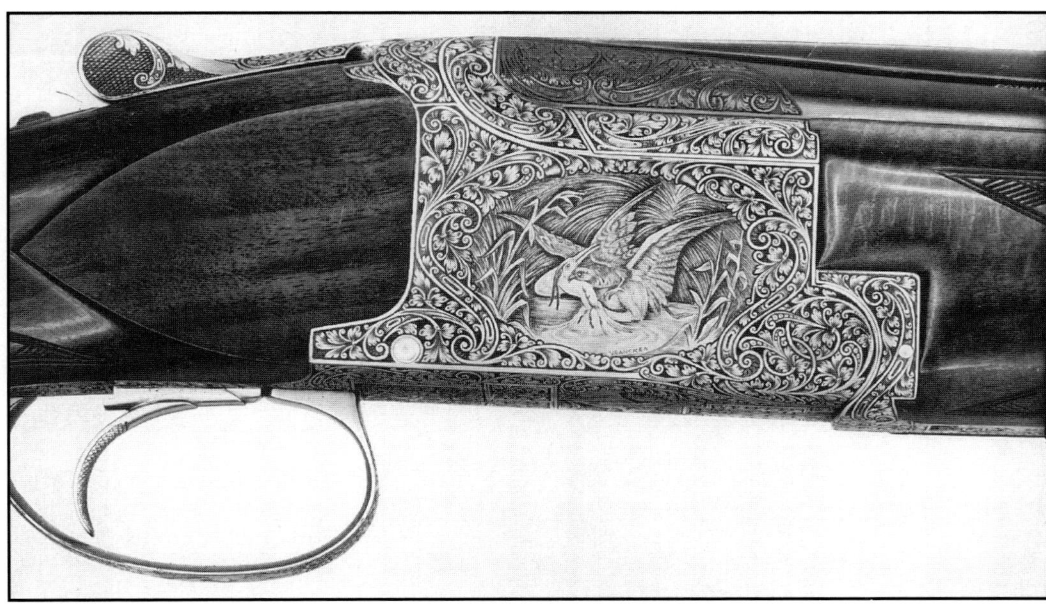

Another early Louis Vrancken Browning Superposed that he created in 1960. The theme is ominously beautiful with great attention to detail and composition. His shading of the subjects and the background is exceptional. Note the scrollwork on the breech end of the top barrel. Courtesy Fabrique Nationale Archives.

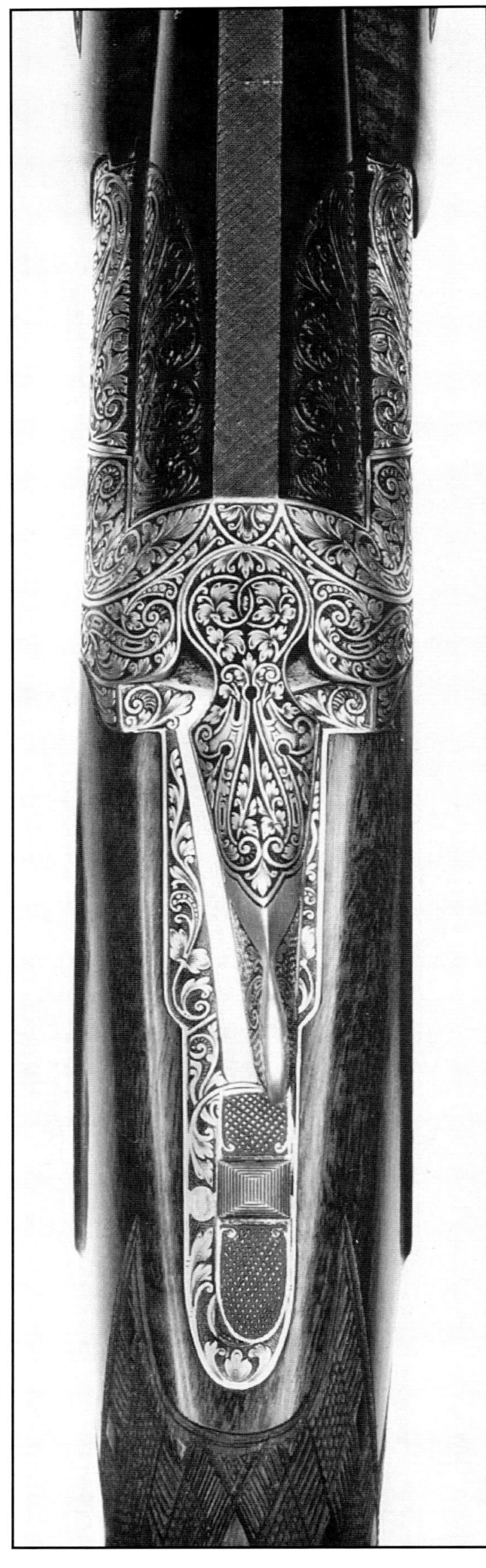

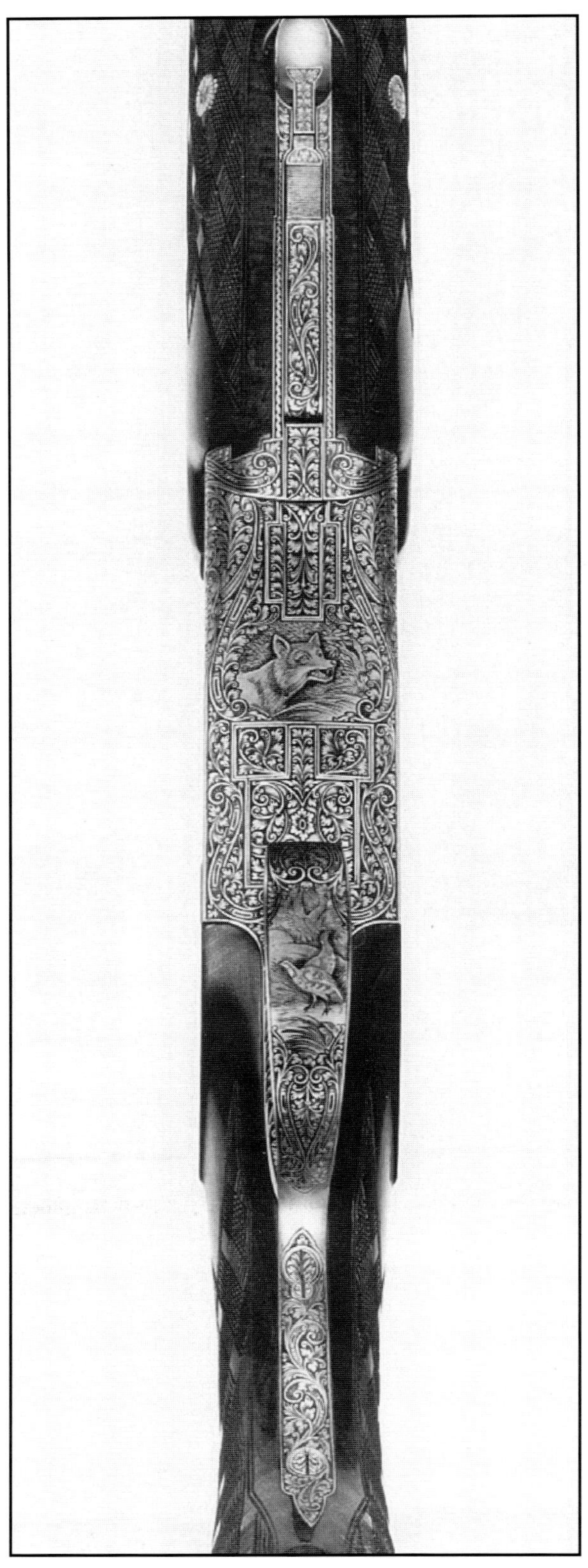

The top and bottom view of the Vrancken Superposed-shown on the previous page. His use of deep, heavy scrollwork continues while on the bottom a fox eyes his prey engraved on the trigger guard. His design is very dramatic and is not easily forgotten. Courtesy Fabrique Nationale Archives.

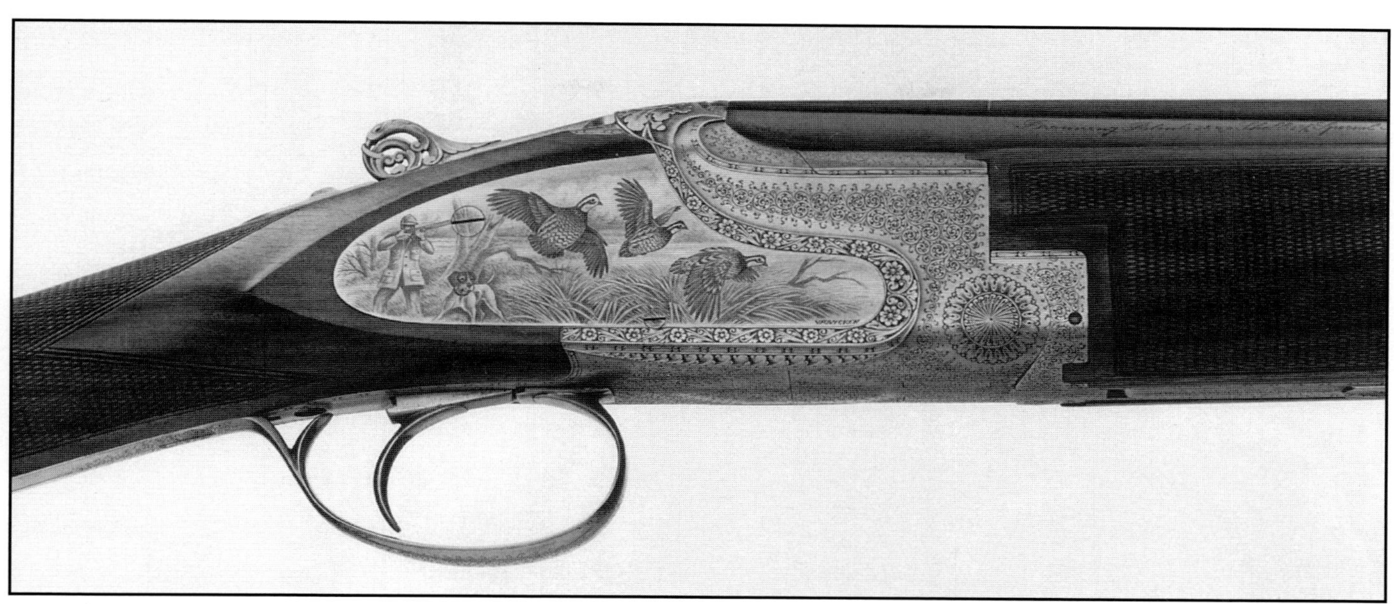

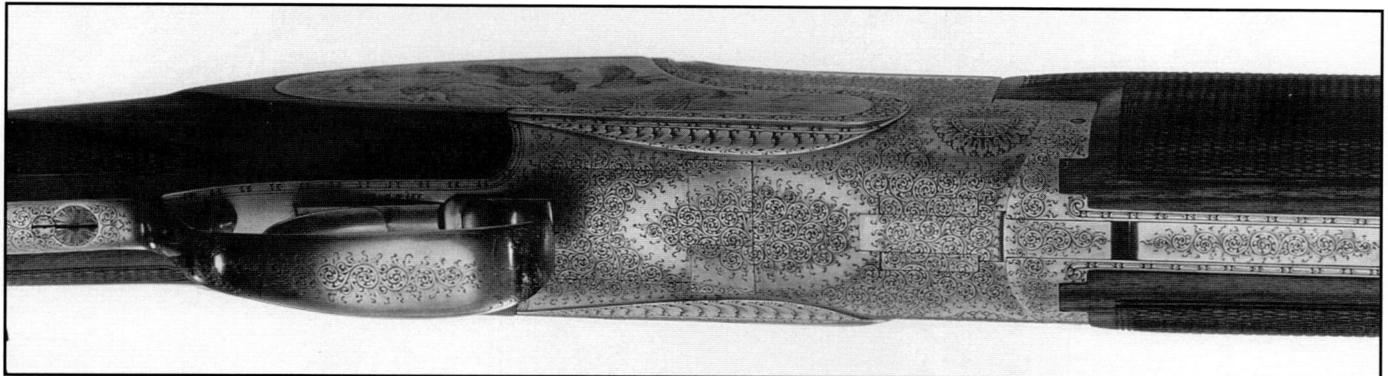

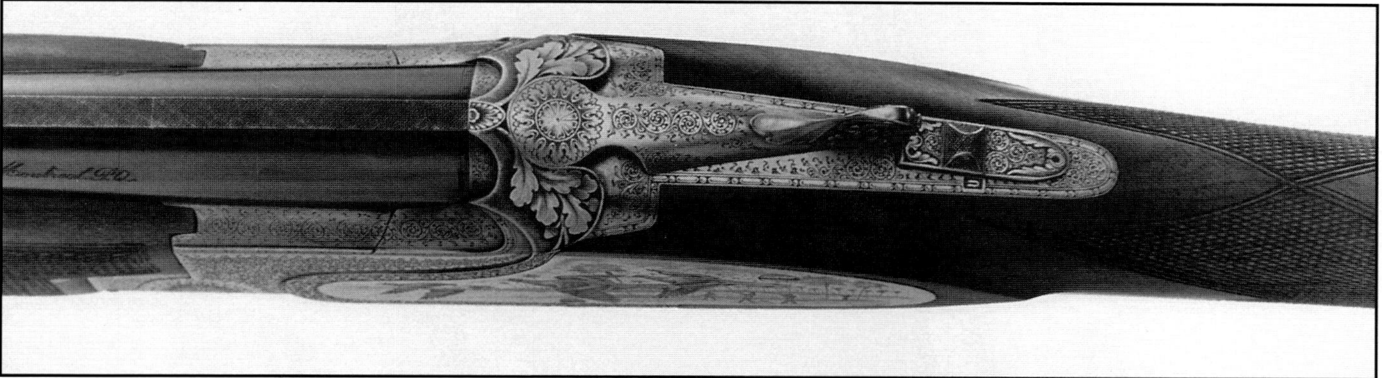

This custom engraved 28 gauge Browning Superposed was executed by Louis Vrancken shortly before he left Fabrique Nationale in 1977. His skill by this time in his career had reached a high level of refinement, as this Superposed so vividly illustrates. Notice the sculptured top lever and the overall composition of the design. Courtesy Fabrique Nationale Archives.

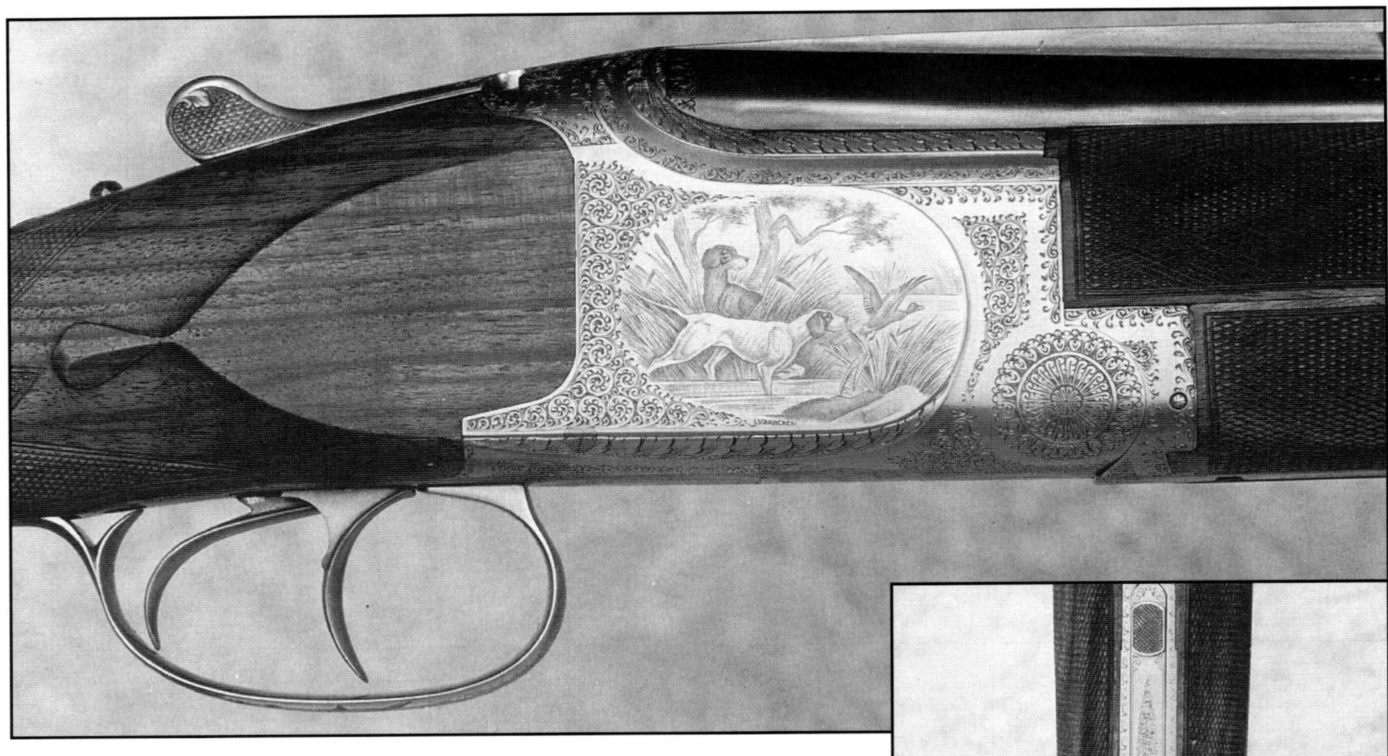

Above and opposite: This FN Browning Superposed D4 Grade was engraved by Louis Vrancken about 1961. Both sides reveal Vrancken's artistry with game scenes. The composition, shading, and the technical aspects of his work are all signs of his future success. Notice the three-piece forearm and fine line checkering on this grade. Courtesy Fabrique Nationale Archives.

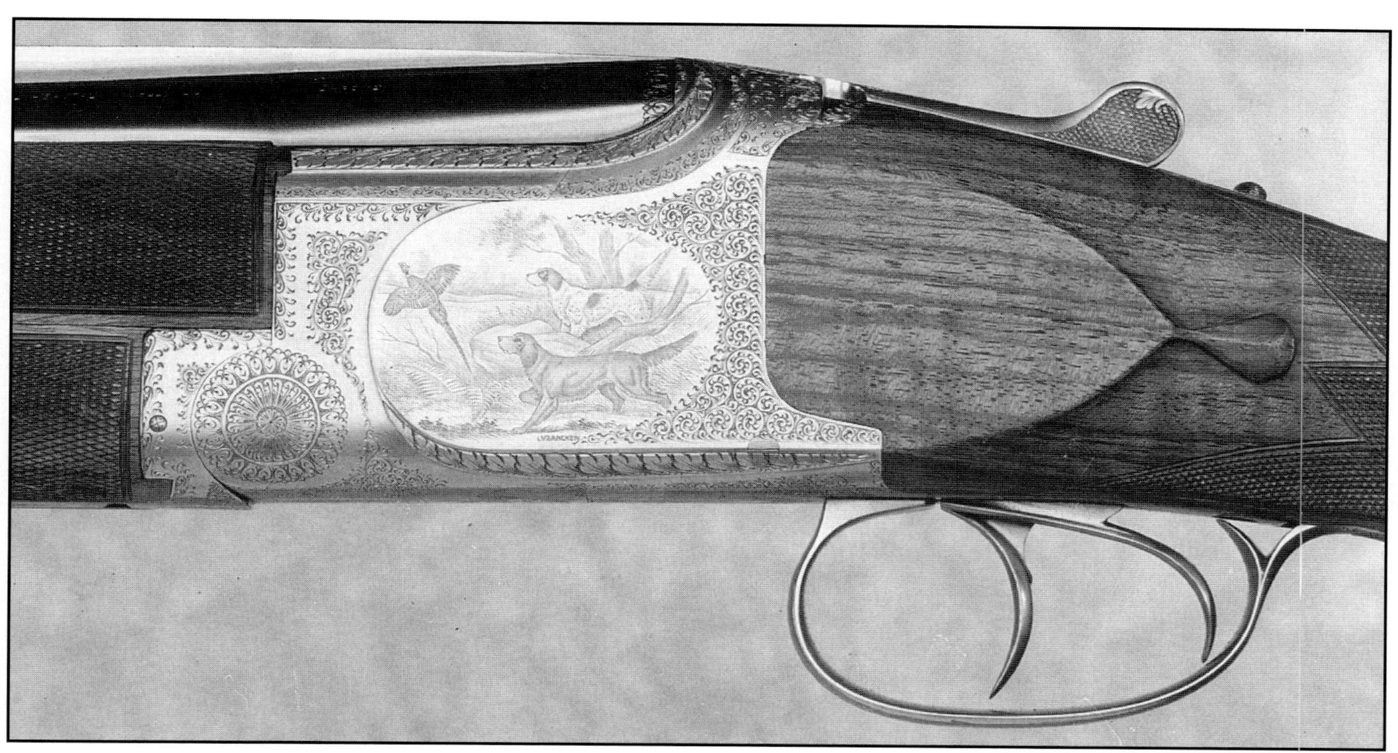

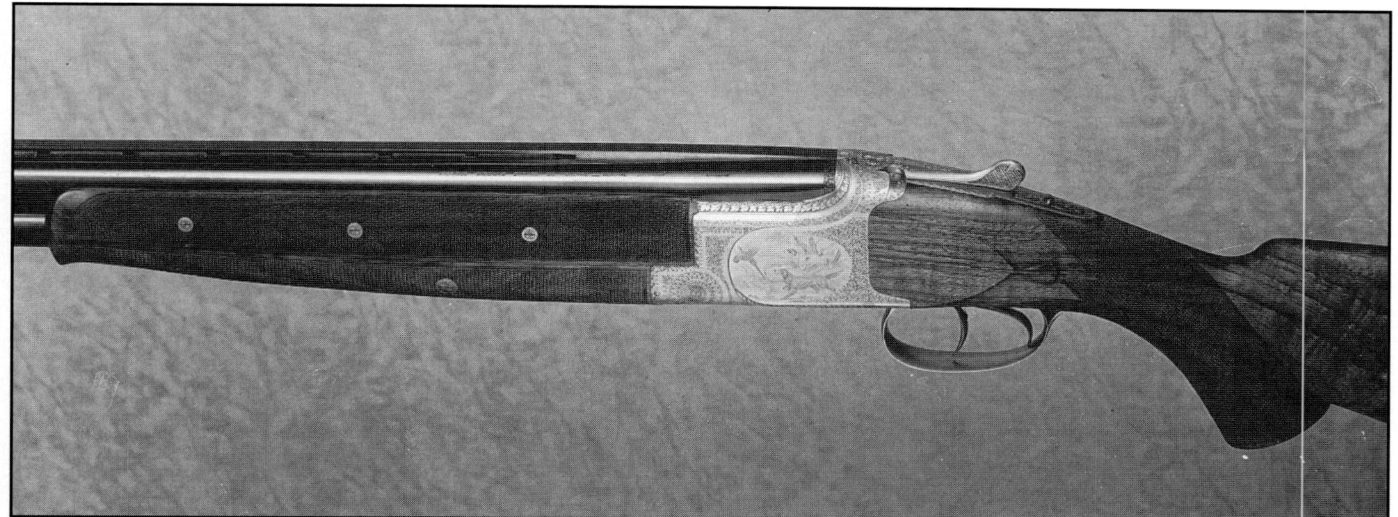

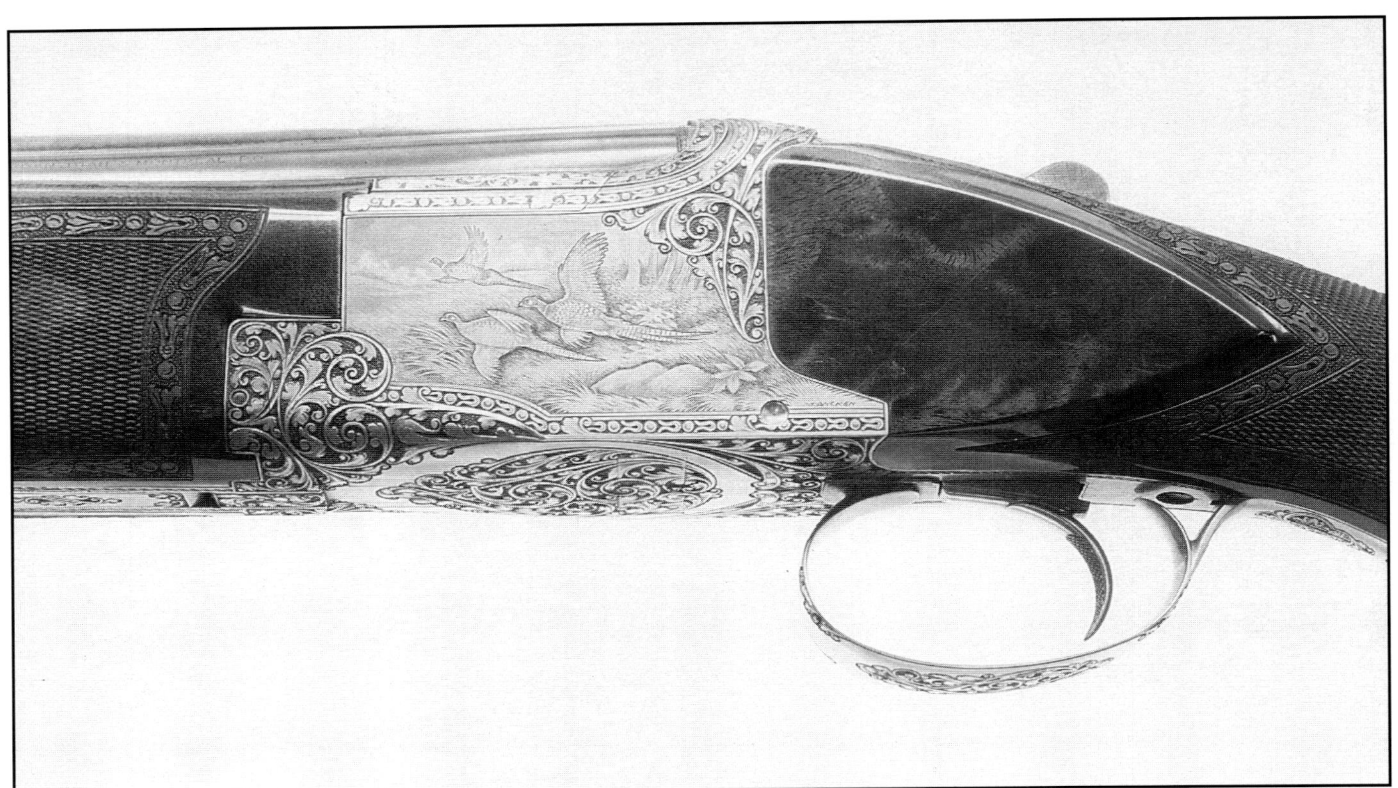

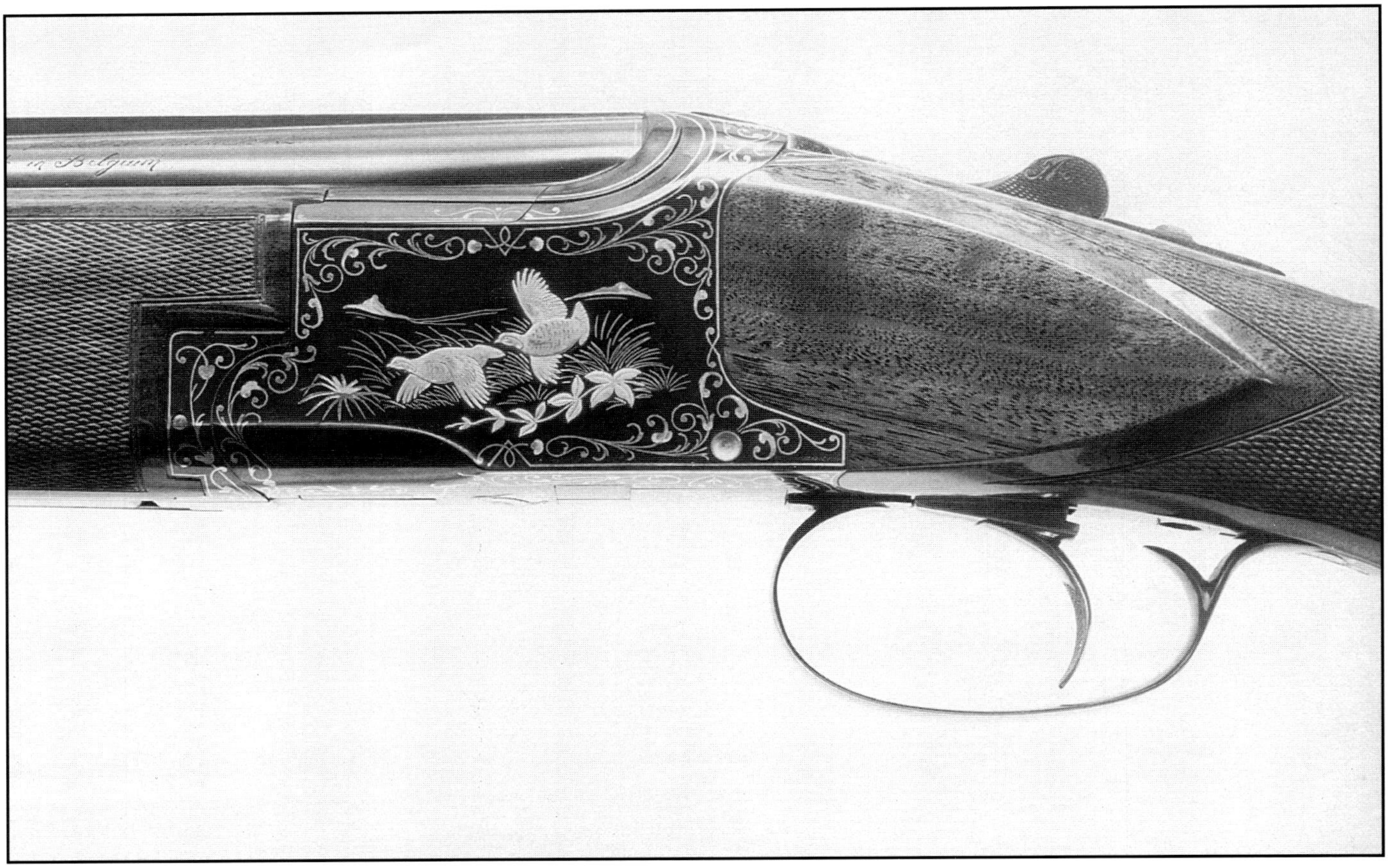

Above and opposite: Two Browning "C" Grade Exhibition Superposed engraved by Louis Vrancken. His skill with game scenes and composition were extraordinary. Courtesy Browning Company.

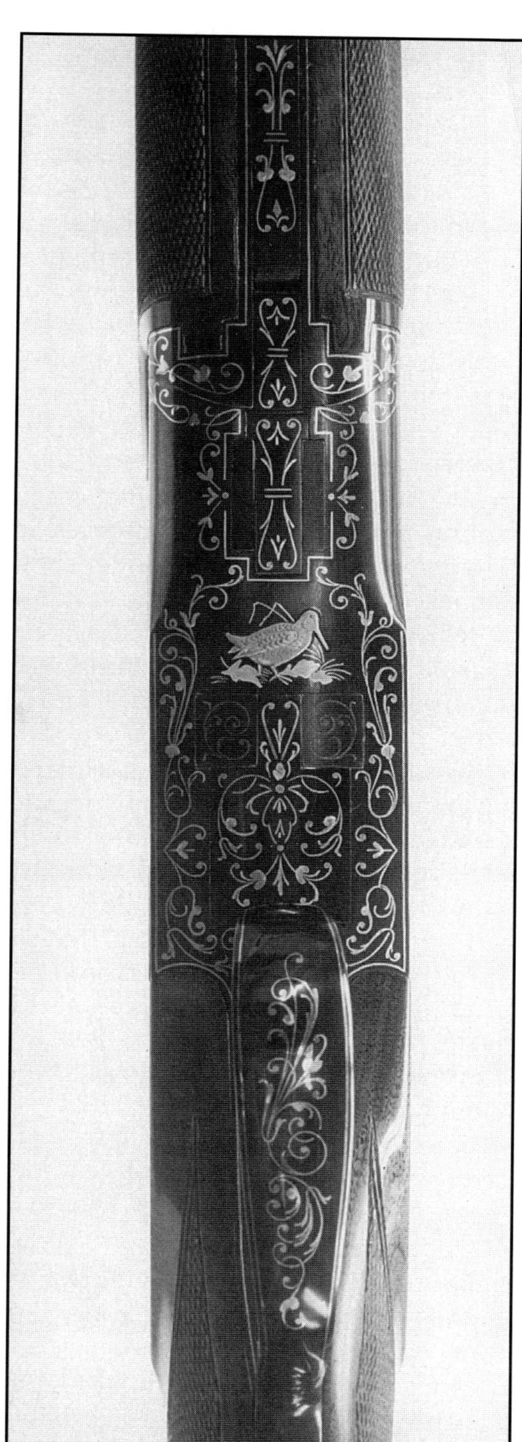

Superposed Catalogue Offerings: 1970-1977

Perhaps the most portentous indicator found in Browning's catalogues between 1970 and 1976 is the clear prologue to the cessation of production of the Superposed in its original, traditional configuration. The two signs that will appear throughout this period are yearly price increases and a somewhat steadily diminishing selection for the prospective Superposed customer. These two themes will spell the beginning of the end of production of the Browning Superposed as it was first built in 1930.

Another noticeable change in Browning's catalogues during this period is the subtle increase in catalogue coverage of Citori over and under shotguns and other Japanese produced shotguns in the section once reserved for the celebrated Superposed. This was a clear sign that Browning was moving away from its dependence on FN produced firearms.

1970: The decade began for Superposed catalogue offerings much in the same way the decade of the 1960s ended. First, there were no changes from the 1969 Superposed offerings, and secondly, there was a retail price increase. In 1969 the Superposed Grade I with ventilated rib was priced at $435.00. In 1970 the retail price was increased almost five percent to $455.00. All models received price increases for 1970, in keeping with the constant, almost unrelenting cost increases passed on to the company by Fabrique Nationale.

1971: Superposed shotgun choices for 1971 again faced increased retail prices. The Grade I Lightning in 12 or 20 gauge increased in price to $480.00, slightly over five percent. The largest price increase among the Lightning models occurred in the Midas Grade with a price increase of $125.00, ten percent over 1970 prices. All other Superposed models experienced price increases equivalent with the Lightning guns. The only change in the Superposed line for 1971 was the expansion of the high grade options to the Superlight model. Beginning in 1971 the customer for the first time had the choice of purchasing his Superlight engraved in the same patterns as the other Superposed guns. The prices of these engraved Superlights were from $25 to $30 higher than comparable Lightning models.

1972: In 1972 the first in a series of small but significant reductions in catalogue offerings for the Superposed occurred. For the first time since 1930, the Superposed in 12 gauge Standard Weight configuration was no longer offered in Browning's catalogues. The Standard 20 gauge was also dropped, as was the 28 gauge and .410 bore Superposed. However, the small bore guns were replaced with the Lightning configuration. Browning retained both the 12 and 20 gauge in the Standard configuration in its Skeet models. Of course, the Superposed in 12 gauge 3-inch Magnum was still offered with its Standard Weight features.

The company did manage to add another innovation to its Superposed line with the introduction of its All Gauge Skeet Set. This set was offered with four sets of matched barrels: 12, 20, and 28 gauge, and .410 bore in either 26-1/2-inch or 28-inch lengths. Each set of barrels was hand fitted to a 12 gauge frame with a single removable beavertail forearm. According to Browning, "Each set of barrels features 2 'instant align' ivory sight beads atop a quick to point 1/4 inch ventilated rib, each barrel choked to give target smashing patterns at any skeet station." The All Gauge Skeet Set was sold with a fitted luggage case and was offered in Grade I through Midas Grade. The retail price of this set in Grade I was $2,150.00, increasing to $3,900.00 for the Midas Grade.

Retail prices were again raised for the Superposed line. In 1972 the retail price for the Grade I Lightning model was increased to $530.00, a growth of ten percent over the previous year. This ten percent increase was generally applied to all the Superposed models across the board.

1973: In 1973 the most significant occurrence in the Superposed line was the burdensome retail price increase affecting all Superposed models. The Grade I Lightning model retail price was raised from its 1972 price of $530.00 to $650.00, an increase of almost twenty-three percent. This large price increase was the harbinger of further substantial increases in the years to come that would have a major and lasting impact throughout Browning's Superposed market.

In an attempt to counterbalance this large price increase, Browning introduced a new over and under shotgun called the "Liège." Built by FN in its Herstal plant, this 12 gauge shotgun was offered with a choice of 30-inch barrels with 3-inch chambers, or 26-1/2-inch and 28-inch barrels with 2-3/4-inch chambers. The introduction of the Liège was an attempt to build an economy version of the famed Superposed. The Liège had a retail price of $472.50 in the May 1973 Browning price list, but by August 1973 Browning was forced to raise the price to $494.50. Even the Liège model, the economy Superposed, could not hold the line on prices for more than three months. The FN catalogues refer to the Liège as the Browning 26, later shortened to the B-26, to differentiate it from the Superposed.

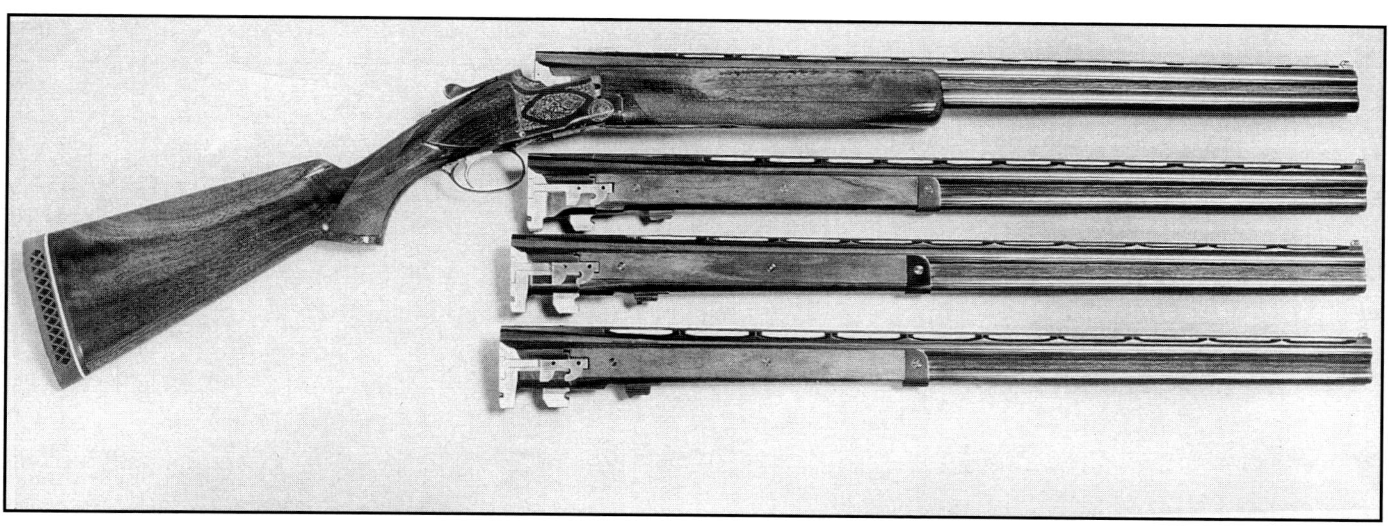

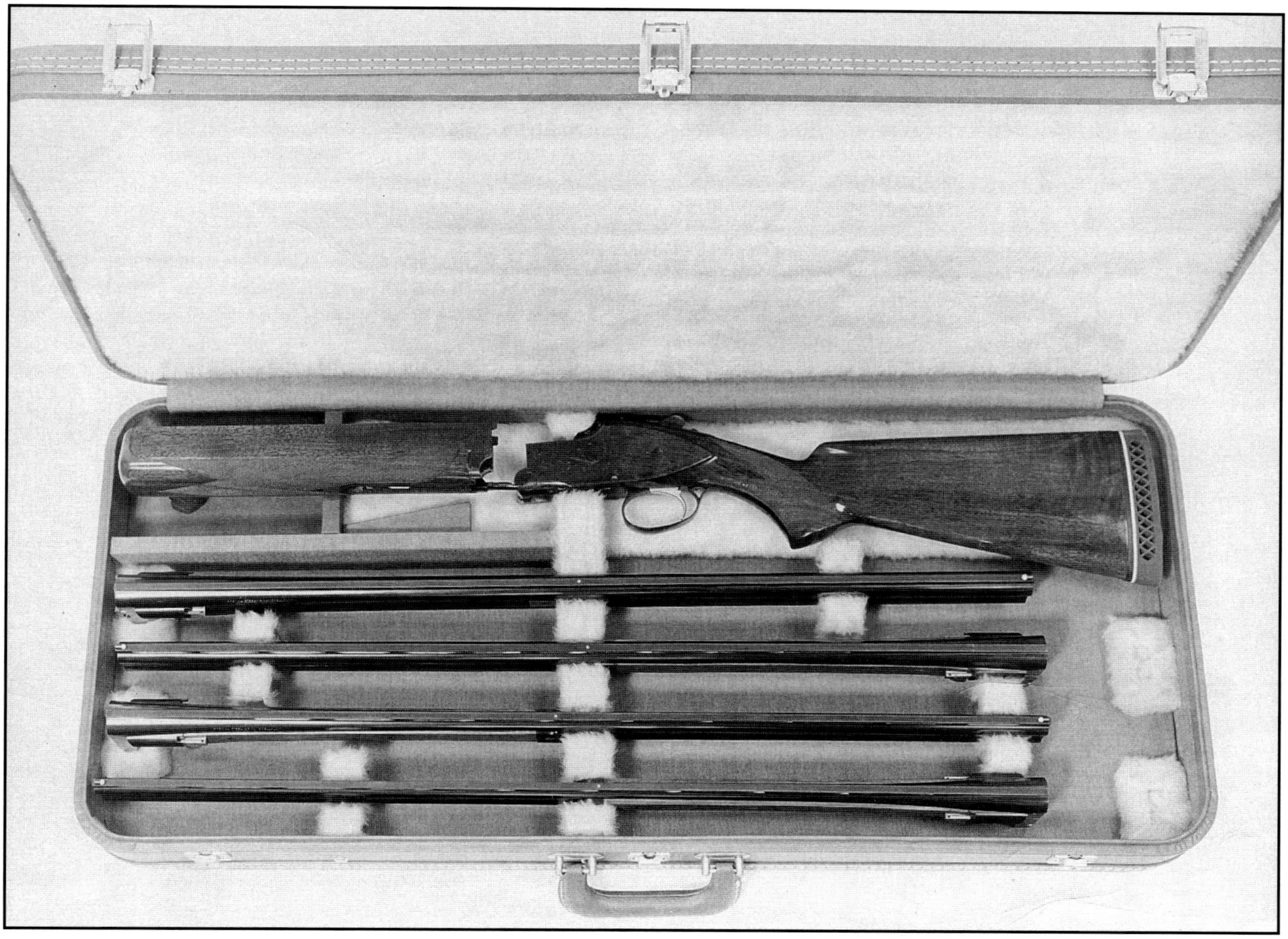

In 1972 Browning introduced the All Gauge Skeet Set. A 12, 20, and 28 gauge set of barrels, as well as a set of .410 barrels, was fitted to a 12 gauge receiver with a single forearm. The set was sold in a fitted luggage case. Courtesy Browning Company.

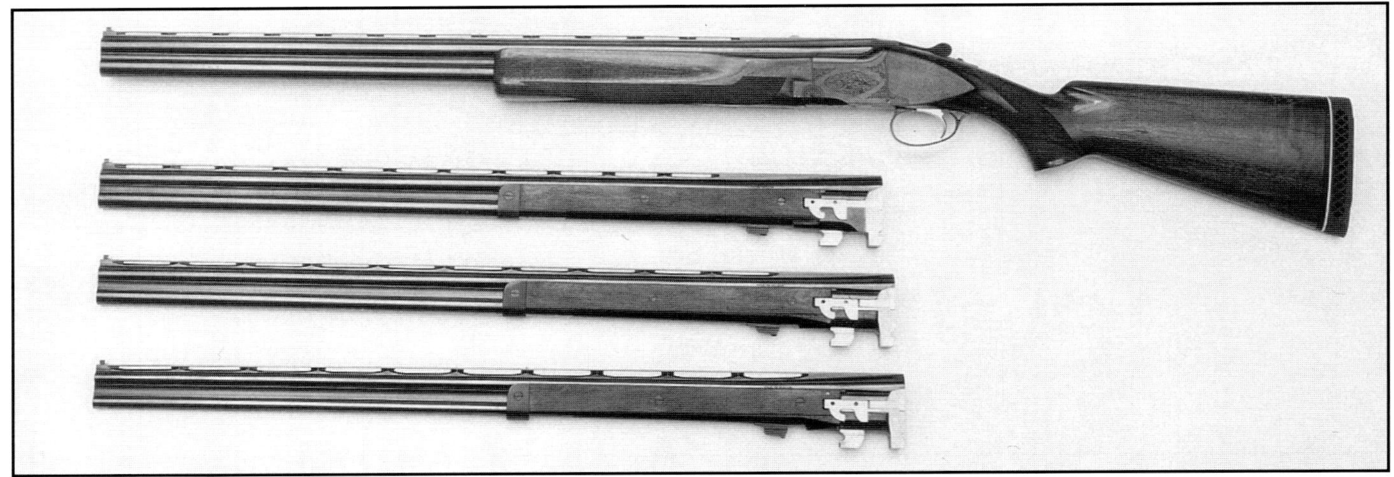

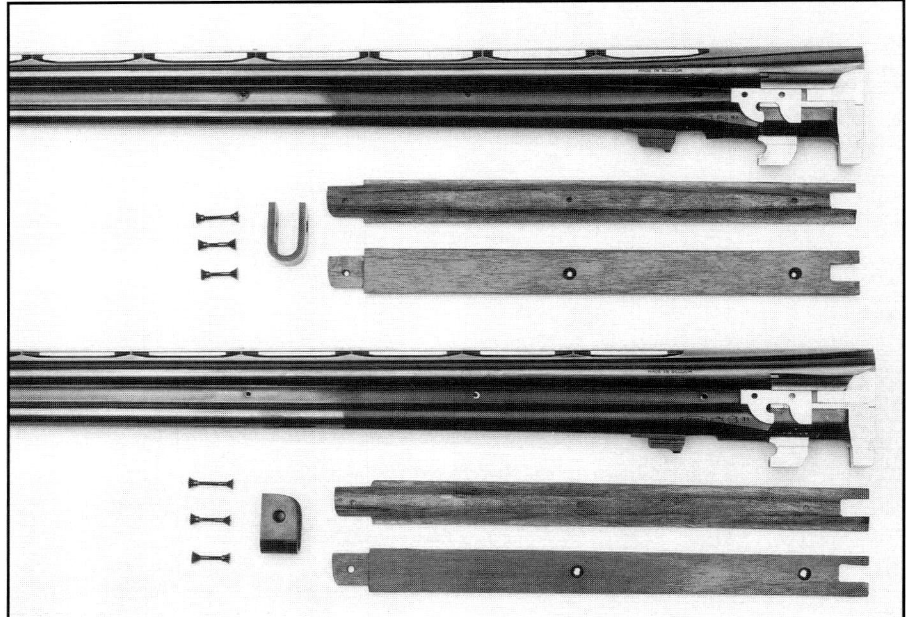

This series of three FN photographs shows the major component parts of the All Gauge Skeet Set. The concept was for the competitive skeet shooter to have an all gauge set that would handle and weigh the same. Notice how the height of the rib has been adjusted to offer the same sighting plane for all gauges. Each set of barrels has been adjusted to weigh the same as the 12 gauge set. With a single forearm fitted to all the barrels, the shooter had the same handling qualities with all barrels. Courtesy Fabrique Nationale Archives.

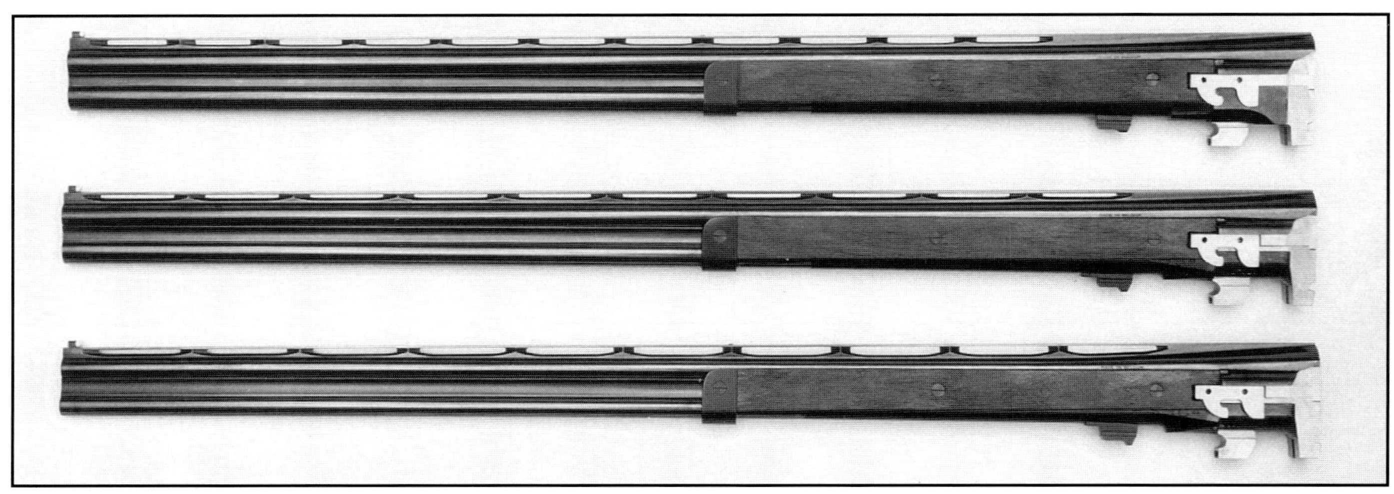

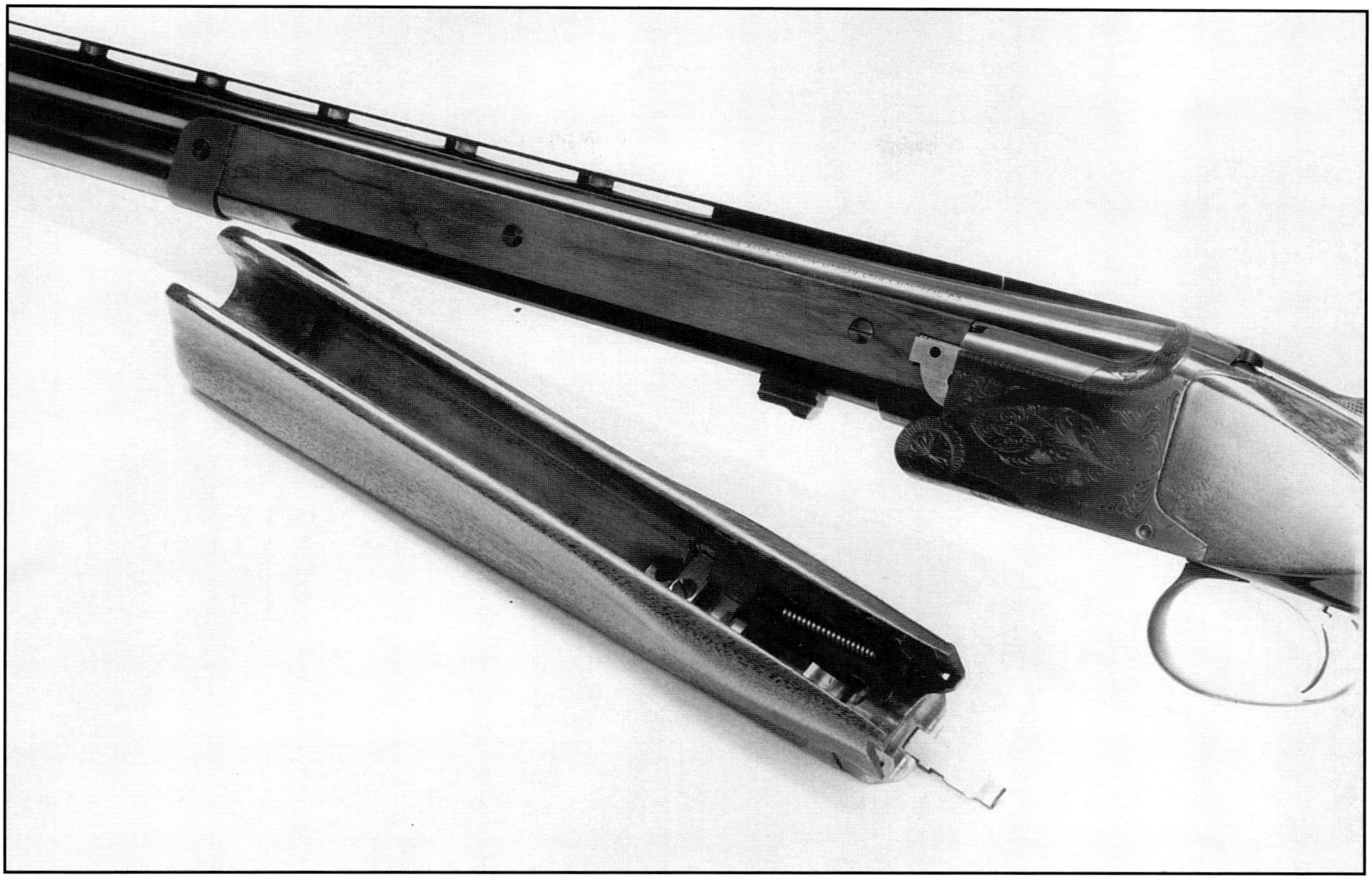

The single forearm on the All Gauge Skeet Set was the only removable forearm FN built for its Superposed. All other Superposed forearms remained joined with the barrels when the barrels were removed from the receiver. Courtesy Fabrique Nationale Archives.

FN then assigned the original Superposed the number designation of B-25.

Browning's Super-Tubes were dropped from the company's catalogues in 1973, replaced by the more expensive All Gauge Skeet Set introduced the previous year.

1974: This was the last year Browning offered any Superposed models in Standard Weight with a lone exception. From now on the Standard Weight Superposed was no longer available in any configuration except the 12 gauge 3-inch Magnum model.

If the retail price increases of the previous year were considered substantial, then the price increases for 1974 might be thought of as catastrophic. The retail price of the Lightning Grade I in 12 and 20 gauge was raised from $650.00 to $840.00, a whopping twenty-nine percent. This price increase moderated somewhat in the higher grades with the Midas Grade receiving the smallest increase,

Introduced in 1973, the Liège over and under shotgun was supposed to offer a low cost alternative to the more expensive Superposed. Built by FN in its Herstal plant, the Liège failed to attract many customers. Courtesy Browning Company.

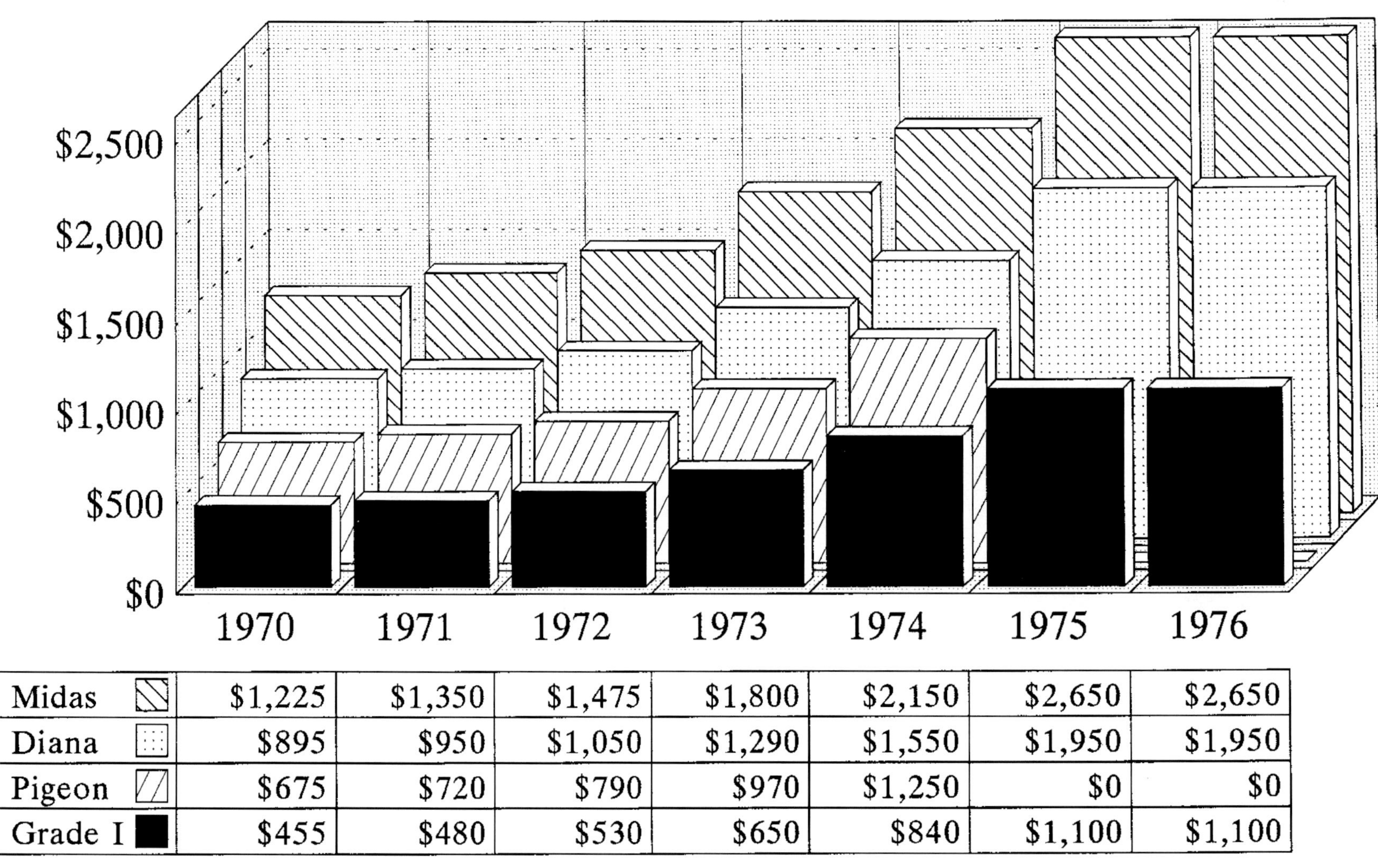

	1970	1971	1972	1973	1974	1975	1976
Midas	$1,225	$1,350	$1,475	$1,800	$2,150	$2,650	$2,650
Diana	$895	$950	$1,050	$1,290	$1,550	$1,950	$1,950
Pigeon	$675	$720	$790	$970	$1,250	$0	$0
Grade I	$455	$480	$530	$650	$840	$1,100	$1,100

Prices are based on Lightning 12 gauge Hunting model with ventilated rib.
Pigeon Grade discontinued in 1975.

Chart 4-1

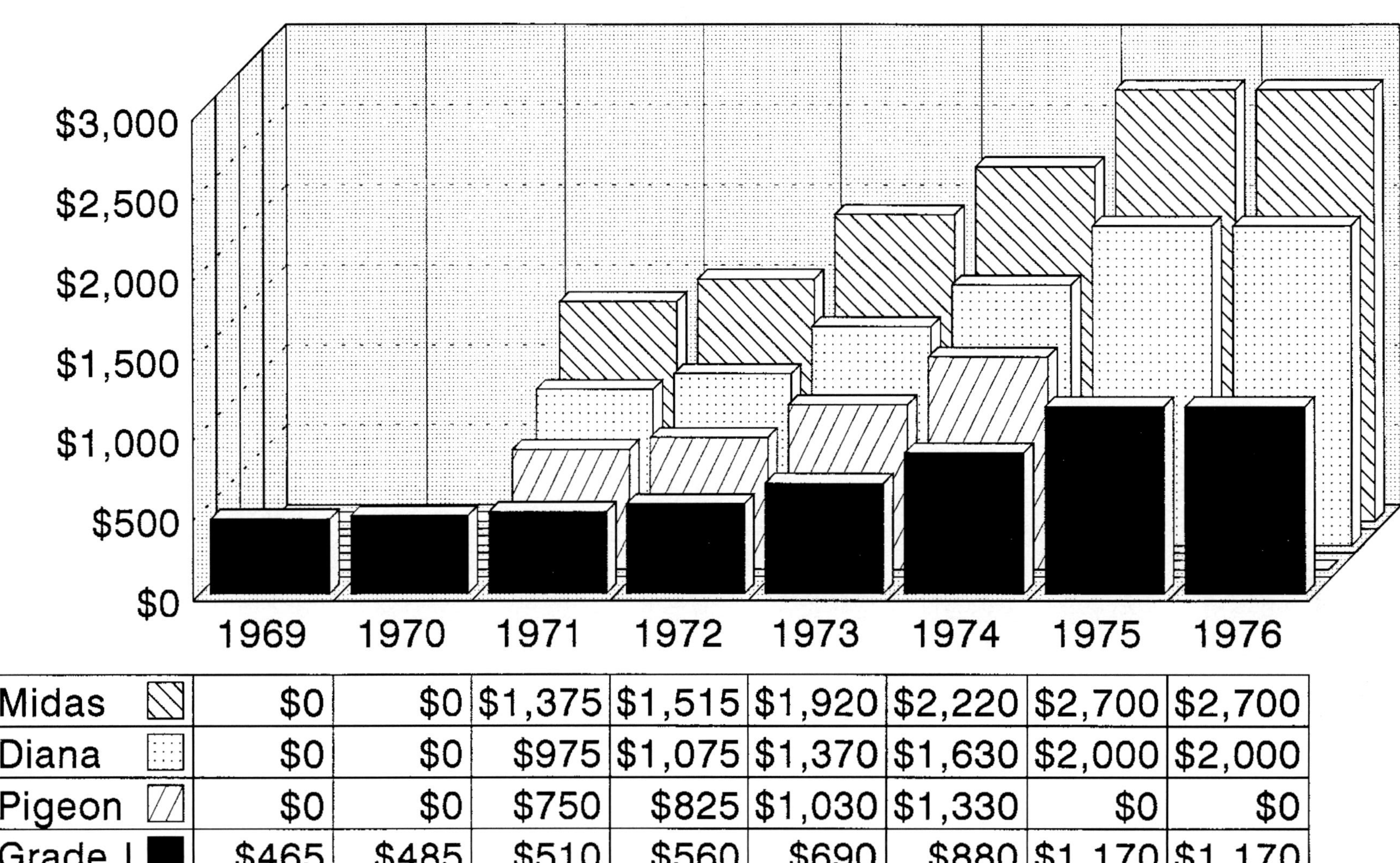

	1969	1970	1971	1972	1973	1974	1975	1976
Midas	$0	$0	$1,375	$1,515	$1,920	$2,220	$2,700	$2,700
Diana	$0	$0	$975	$1,075	$1,370	$1,630	$2,000	$2,000
Pigeon	$0	$0	$750	$825	$1,030	$1,330	$0	$0
Grade I	$465	$485	$510	$560	$690	$880	$1,170	$1,170

Chart 4-2

nineteen percent. The Superlight line also received the same high price increases throughout its grades. The Liège model was listed in Browning's catalogue for the last time in 1974 and it, too, saw a slight price increase to $497.50, a $3.00 increase over the previous year.

1975: With retail price increases almost out of control, the price of the Superposed Lightning Pigeon Grade in 12 and 20 gauge reached a retail price of $1,250 in 1974. Browning made the decision to drop the Pigeon Grade from its Superposed line. The Pigeon Grade represents perhaps the longest and most consistent ties to the past. First offered in 1931, the Pigeon Grade was as easily recognized as a Superposed as was the Grade I itself. Beginning in 1975 the Superposed was now offered in only three grades: Grade I, Diana Grade, and Midas Grade.

Retail prices took another huge jump in 1975 with the Grade I Lightning in 12 and 20 gauge priced at $1,100, an enormous thirty-one percent increase. The Superposed Lightning Diana Grade saw a price increase of twenty-six percent, and the Midas Grade had a twenty-three percent increase. The Grade I Superlight retail price increased from $880.00 in 1974 to $1,170.00 in 1975, a gigantic thirty-three percent increase.

1976: This marked the final year for the production Superposed in its traditional configuration. For the first time during the decade of the 1970s there was no price increase, nor were there any changes in the Superposed catalogue offerings. There was, however, a hint of changes to come. Browning offered to its customers the opportunity to have their Superposed built as a custom gun. Customers could select special stock dimensions, engraving patterns, and even different styles of engraving, as well as grades of wood, buttstock styles, forearm styles, and type of grip. A choice of wood finish was offered to the customer as well, which shows the level of detail Browning was willing to allow the customer to control.

1977: This year represented a new departure for Browning with the introduction of the "P Series" Superposed guns. Essentially this new series was genuine Superposed from a mechanical perspective, but its outward appearance was altered. Most noticeably, the engraving patterns and styles, as well as checkering patterns and other fine points, were changed or modified. These P Series catalogue offerings will be covered in great detail in the following chapter.

Browning did offer in its 1977 catalogue the traditional Superposed shotgun in all models, including the Superlight, in Grade I only. The 1977 Browning catalogue stipulated that:

> Although some Browning Dealers may still have a few Superposed Grade I shotguns on their shelves, only a very limited number of Superposed Grade I models were still in our inventory at the time this catalog went to press in late 1976. When the supply of these Grade I shotguns is exhausted, only Presentation Grade Browning Superposed will be offered.

This was the last mention by Browning in its catalogues of the classical Superposed shotgun as a production gun. Future catalogue references would designate the Browning Superposed as a special order shotgun requiring a deposit and a lengthy wait for delivery. No more would Browning inventory the Superposed for sale in its North American markets.

The Superposed in Its Penultimate Configuration

The period from 1970 to 1976 witnessed the next to last phase in production changes for the Superposed. In some ways there was little Browning could do to cut cost further without sacrificing quality, and this the company would not consider. There were some changes made that did involve cost savings, but others were implemented to increase reliability. In spite of the salt wood problem, the Superposed was the same high quality, hand fitted over and under shotgun that it was when first introduced in 1931. Its overall appearance, handling qualities, dependability, and character remained unchanged during this period.

General Appearance: These external changes appear in all gauges and configurations except the Superlight. Most of these external changes took place during the first two years of the decade and represent a continuation of the manufacturing design changes begun during the mid-1960s.

The most noticeable change to occur, and perhaps the most discussed among collectors, was the modification made in 1966 from the traditional long tang trigger guard to the short tang. This saved some fitting time, but evoked criticism for its cost cutting appearance. This same criticism was aimed at the modified shape of the pistol grip from the classic half pistol grip style to the more American closed and square-bottom grip. This was the so-called "round knob" and "square knob" modification. Browning decided to revert back to the long trigger guard tang in 1970 because it was stronger than the short tang; however, the squared bottom, or "square knob," pistol grip modification was retained. The tang modification

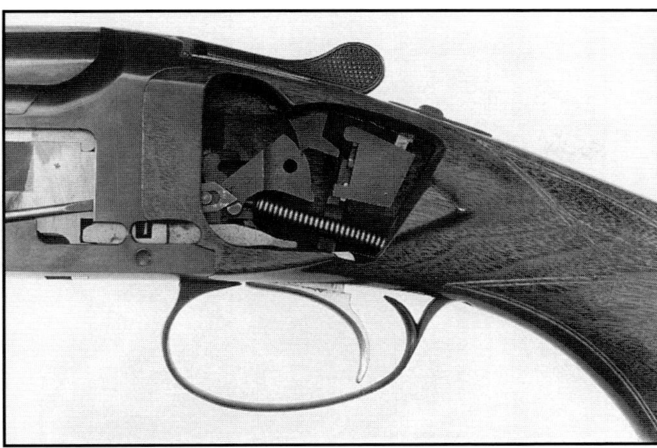

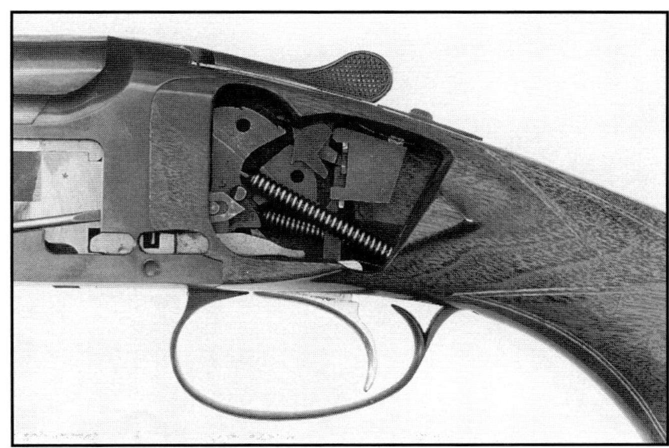

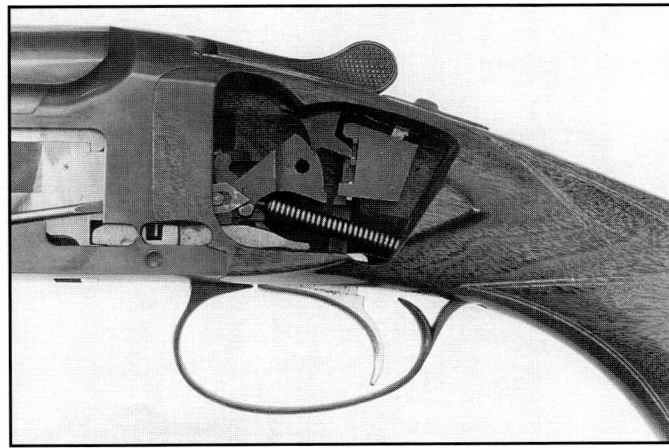

On this special Fabrique Nationale Superposed cutaway is seen the inertia type trigger system developed by Val Browning in the 1930s. Browning used this trigger until the early 1970s when the small gauge Superposed barrels, mounted on 12 gauge receivers, failed to activate the second set of barrels due to lack of inertia. This series of photos reveals the firing sequence in the inertia system. At the top left is the first sequence with hammers cocked safety on, bottom left is hammers cocked safety off, and at the top right is the first barrel fired, second hammer cocked ready to fire. Courtesy Fabrique Nationale Archives.

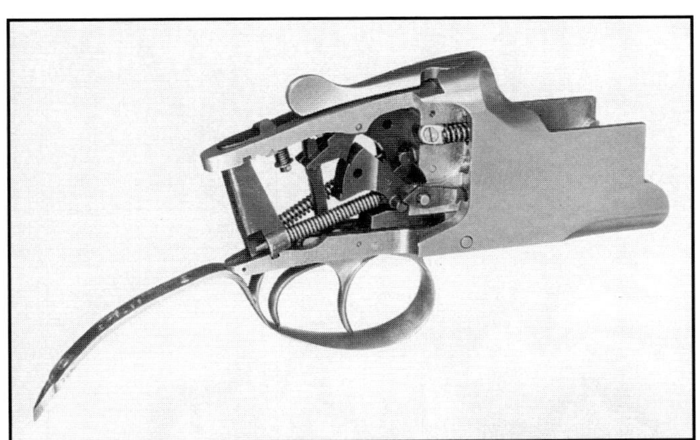

In Europe FN sold quite a few of its Superposed with double triggers. This photo, taken in 1969, illustrates an FN long bottom tang with a "U" shaped upper tang. This is the equivalent to the modern version of the double trigger receiver. Courtesy Fabrique Nationale Archives.

began in 1970 and continued through 1971, and for a period of about two years both short and long tang trigger guards will be seen.

It was during this same time period that another modification took place: the replacement of the old style inertia trigger, developed by Val Browning, with a mechanical trigger. This change resulted because the inertia trigger would not function reliably in small bore Superposed, namely the 28 gauge and the .410 bore. There was almost no problem with the trigger working correctly on 12 and 20 gauge guns because the force of recoil against the shooter would be sufficient to set the trigger for the next shot. Some difficulty with the inertia trigger first began to surface when the small gauges were introduced into the Superposed line in 1959. FN gunsmiths were able to adjust the trigger in such a way that it would almost always function properly in these smaller gauges.

More trouble appeared when the Super-Tubes were introduced in 1965. The mass of the 12 gauge frame coupled with the relatively low forces exerted by the recoil of the 28 gauge and .410 bore were not enough to reset the trigger to fire the second

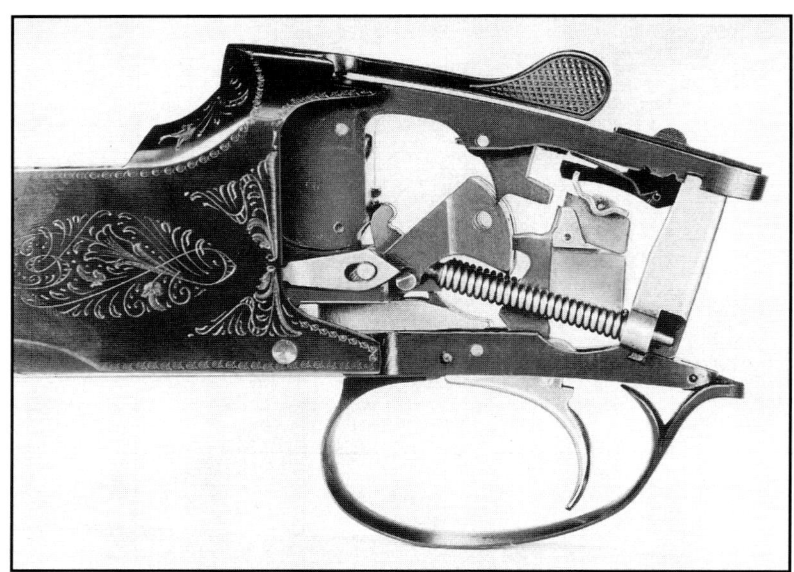

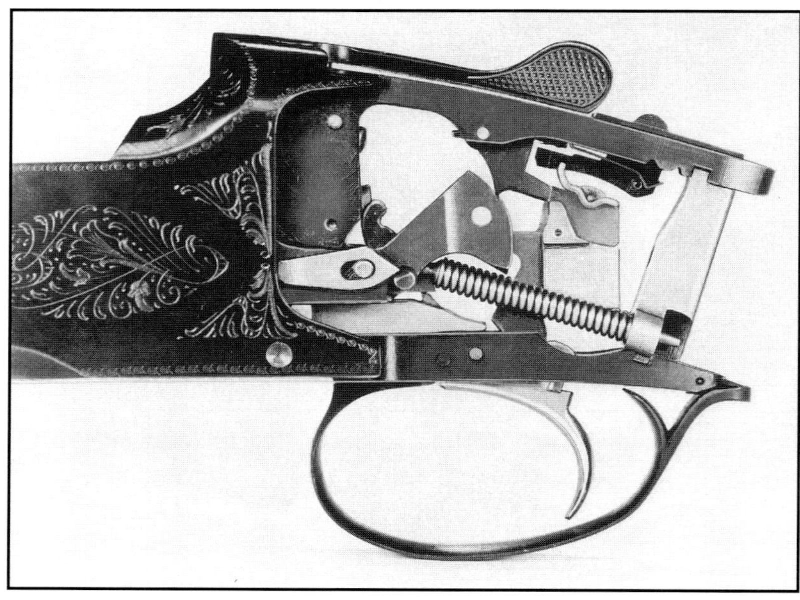

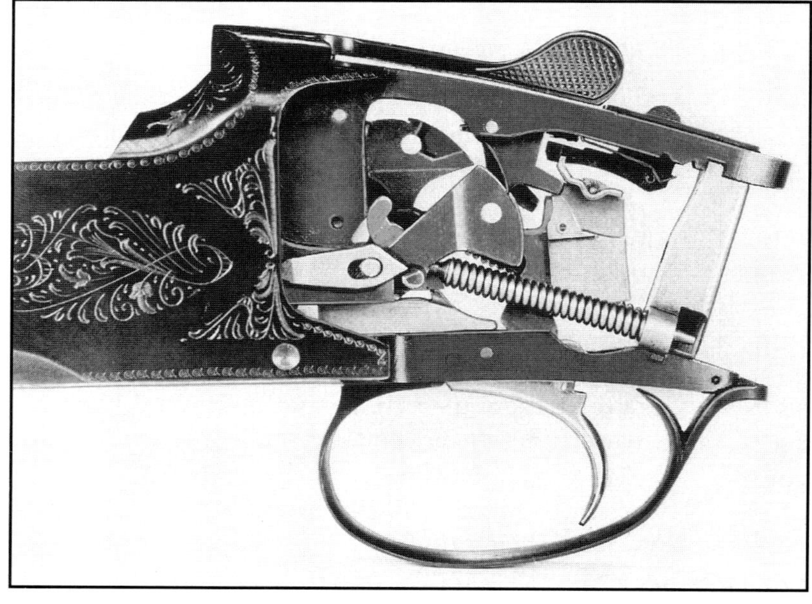

A new trigger system was developed that would offer a more flexible alternative to the inertia system. The Browning mechanical trigger system was more costly to build, but it could be used with a wider variety of gauges with more reliability. In this series of photos, the top shows both hammers cocked with the safety on, in the middle the safety is released, hammers still cocked, and at the bottom the first barrel has been fired, safety still off and the second barrel ready to fire. Courtesy Fabrique Nationale Archives.

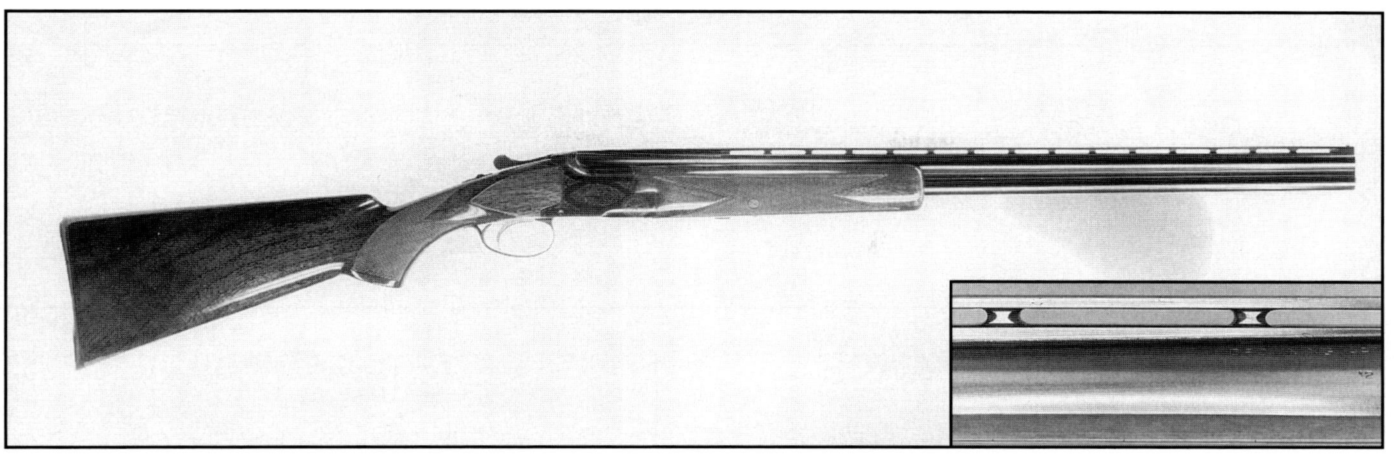

This Browning Superposed Grade I is fitted with the old style ventilated rib post. In the inset is a close-up view of these old style posts. Browning used these small ventilated rib posts from the late 1930s until the early 1970s. Courtesy Browning Company. Inset photo courtesy Vearl Brown.

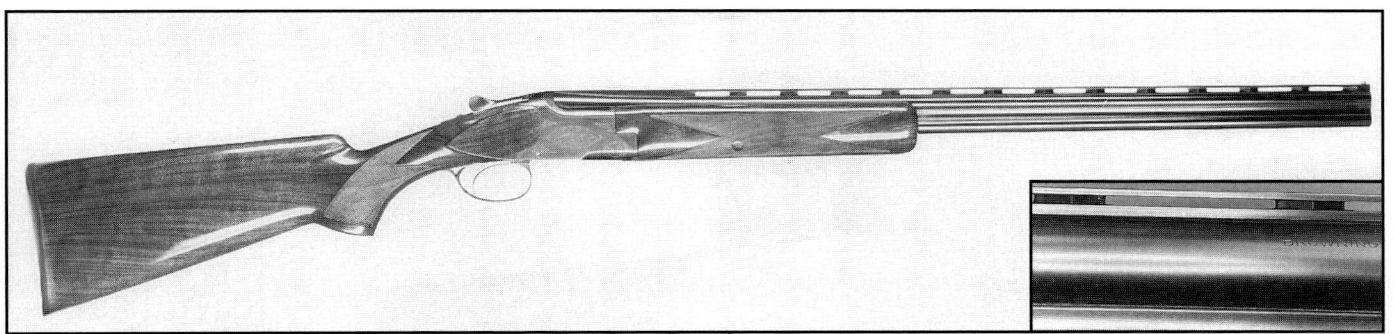

In the early 1970s Browning and FN decided to change the design of the ventilated rib in order to achieve a lower rib that was also stronger. This new design, called the diamond posts rib, accomplished that goal and is still in use on today's Superposed. The inset clearly shows this new ventilated rib post design. Courtesy Browning Company. Inset photo courtesy Vearl Brown.

barrel. Part of the installation required the removal of the inertia trigger and the installation of a mechanical one. Further difficulties occurred with the introduction of the All Gauge Skeet Set in 1972. This four-barrel set would not function reliably with the inertia trigger and so used a mechanical trigger in its place. On the whole, the mechanical trigger was a more reliable and dependable trigger mechanism than the traditional inertia trigger even though it was more expensive to produce because of the large number of interconnecting parts requiring close tolerances.

Also about this same time, or perhaps as early as 1970, a modification was made pertaining to the ventilated rib. The old style rib that had been used for so many years on the Superposed was altered from its small square post design to a larger diamond shaped post, which resulted in a flatter, lower rib. With this change in the post design came the replacement of the earlier soft tin solder with silver solder to fasten the top rib post to the barrel. The result of these rib modifications was a stronger, lower ventilated rib that was much less likely to loosen over time. It was also less expensive to produce the new rib because machining time was greatly reduced. Soft solder continued to be used on the side ribs with no loss of strength.

During the early 1970s, probably around 1973, a forearm modification was introduced on all Browning Superposed. From the very first production guns built in 1930, a forearm screw or crossbolt was used to hold the forearm to the barrels. It was referred to in Browning's parts list as a side fastening forearm screw. The discontinuance of this forearm screw around 1973 was made possible by the utilization of a two-piece barrel lug. This lug provided the added strength and stability needed to hold the forearm securely in place.

One final change was incorporated into the Superposed at about the same time that the side fastening screw was discontinued. Around 1973 FN engineers made the decision to change the forend

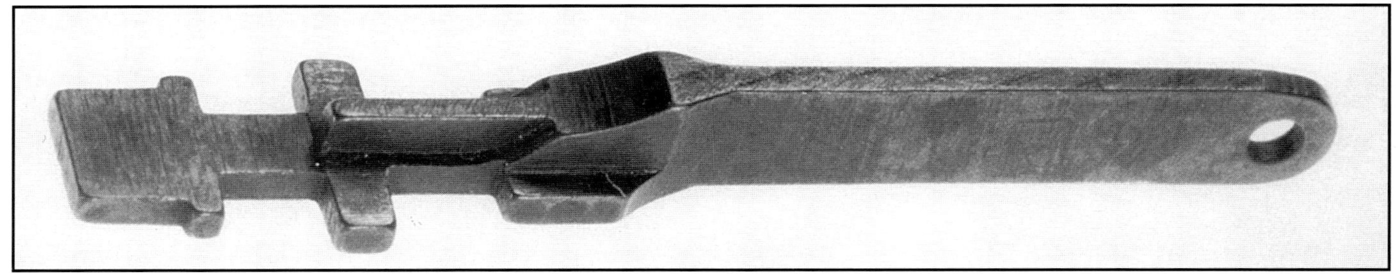

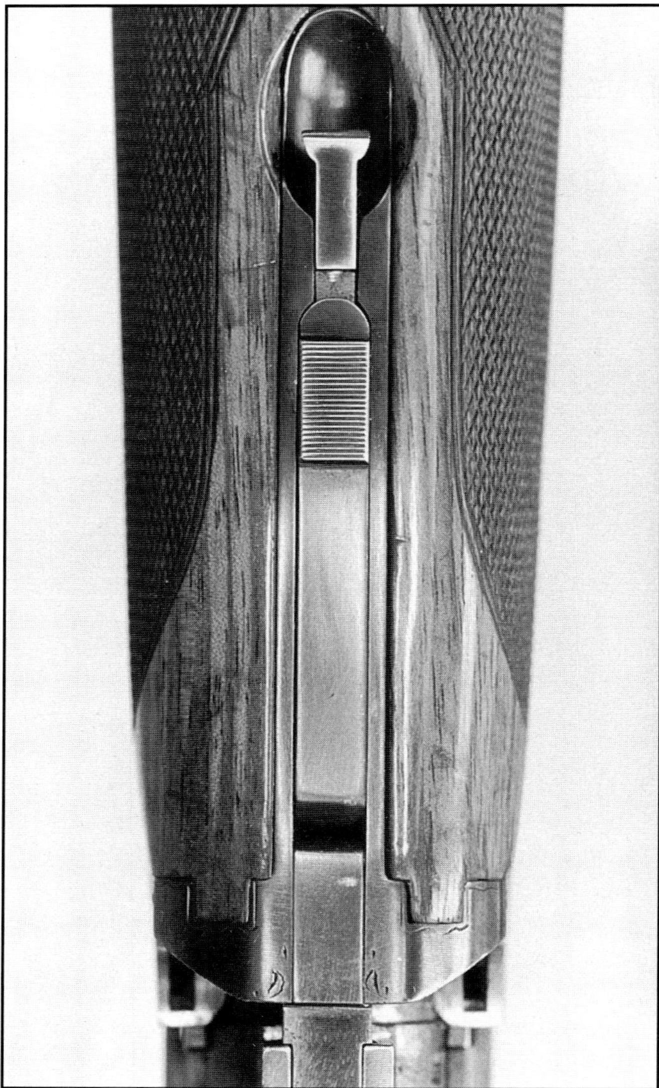

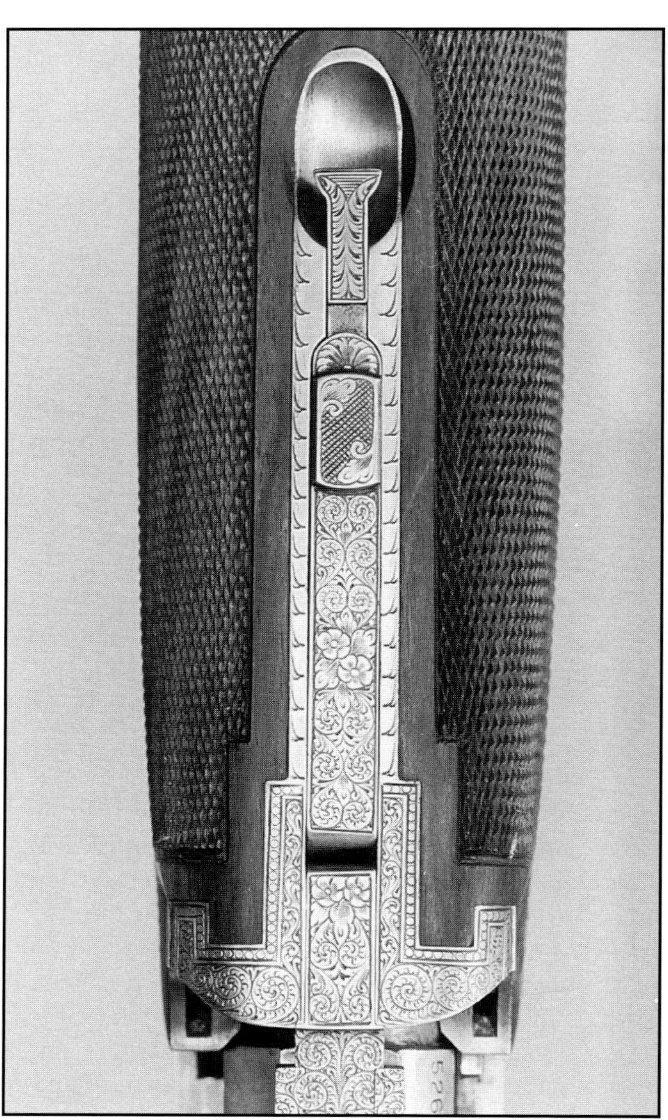

The Superposed forearm iron was composed of a system of components that held the forearm to the barrels and allowed the forearm to be released, and slid forward to facilitate breaking the gun down. This forearm release latch design was modified about 1973 to provide for a stronger design. The original forearm latch began as a forging. Through a series of hand machining operations, this forearm latch became a finished integral part of the forearm mechanism. On the bottom left is the forearm release latch that was in use for most of the postwar period. On the bottom right is the newly designed forearm release latch that is still in use on today's Superposed. Courtesy Fabrique Nationale Archives. Forearm release latch close-up photos courtesy Vearl Brown.

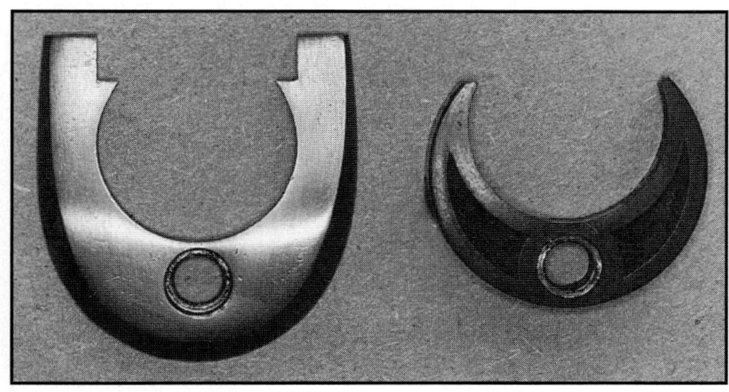

This photograph illustrates the two styles of forearm end pieces. The example on the left was used on prewar beavertail forearms. It was milled out of solid steel. The sample on the right was used on beavertail forearms beginning in the early 1970s. This later forearm piece was a metal casting, and in some cases black plastic was used. Photo courtesy Vearl Brown.

iron in such a way that the new configuration would be stronger and less prone to breakage. The force required to snap the forearm iron closed using the take-down lever and its latch could sometimes provoke a failure in the forearm bracket. This bracket and the cocking lever lifter were reinforced to prevent any further failures.

From 1970 through 1976, one barrel address predominates on the Superposed. On the right side of the top barrel will often be seen the following inscription:

BROWNING SUPERPOSED
SPECIAL STEEL-12 GA-SHELLS 2 3/4"
BROWNING PATENTS

On the left side of the barrel the most often seen address will appear as follows:

BROWNING ARMS COMPANY MORGAN UTAH & MONTREAL P.Q.
MADE IN BELGIUM

Barrel inscriptions on the left side will sometimes be seen with the information stamped on three lines instead of two. During this time period a number of Superposed guns built and sold by Fabrique Nationale were brought into North America by individuals directly from Belgium. Many of these Superposed were engraved in the FN patterns and had features offered only by FN, such as 12 gauge guns with 27-1/2-inch barrels, and swan neck stocks. These Fabrique Nationale Superposed do not have the Browning address stamped on the barrel, but instead make use of their own Fabrique Nationale inscription. An example of an early 1970s FN barrel will be seen as follows:

FABRIQUE NATIONALE D'ARMES DE GUERRE HERSTAL-BELGIQUE

A later version of this barrel address will occur after the company changed its corporate name late in 1971. This address may appear as follows:

FABRIQUE NATIONALE HERSTAL-BELGIQUE

In any event, the barrel address can offer some clues as to the era that a particular Superposed was built and whether or not it was imported into North America through Browning or sold in others parts of the world directly from Fabrique Nationale.

Hunting Models: No substantive changes for the period 1970 through 1977, except those mentioned in the "General Appearance" section on page 316. All mechanical and outward features remained unchanged from the 1960s.

Trap Models: No substantive changes for the period 1970 through 1977, except those mentioned in the "General Appearance" section on page 316. All mechanical and outward features remained unchanged from 1968.

Skeet Models: No substantive changes for the period 1970 through 1977, except those mentioned in the "General Appearance" section on page 316. All mechanical and outward features remained unchanged from the 1960s.

Superlight Models: Before a discussion of the manufacturing changes affecting the Superlight can begin, it is necessary to clarify precisely what constitutes a Browning Superposed Superlight. Purists consider Superlights to be true Superlights only if they have the following features:

1. A tapered solid or ventilated rib;
2. A slim or Schnabel forearm;
3. A straight grip stock;
4. A rounded frame.

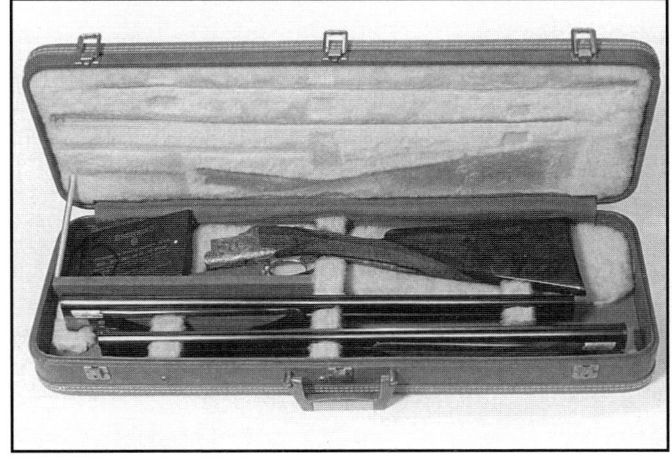

This very early Browning Diana Grade Superposed Superlight, serial number 90295S8, is fitted with two barrels, a rare factory option. This Superlight is also notable for being a special order engraved gun before that option was catalogued in 1971. Lloyd Crede Collection.

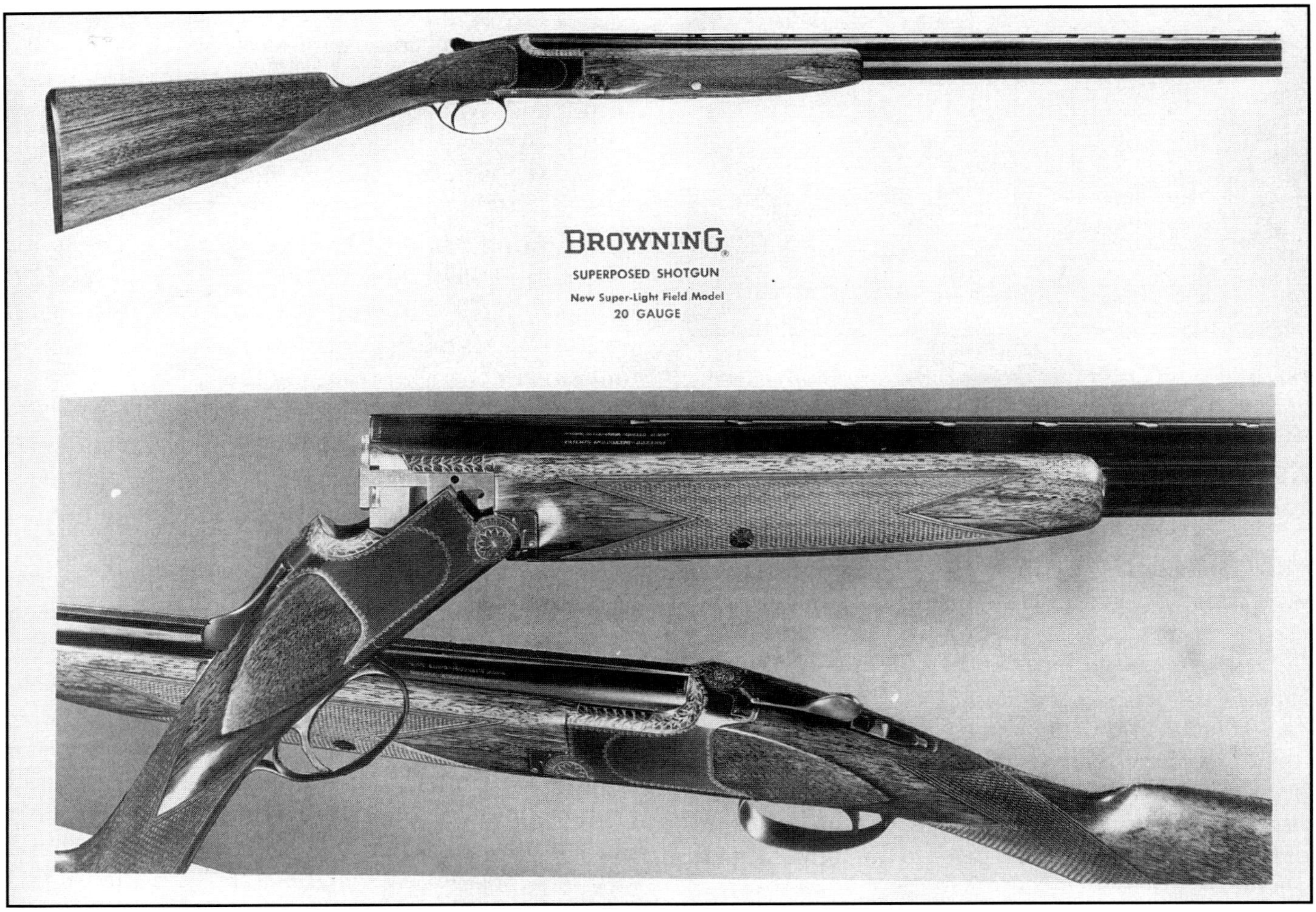

BROWNING
SUPERPOSED SHOTGUN
New Super-Light Field Model
20 GAUGE

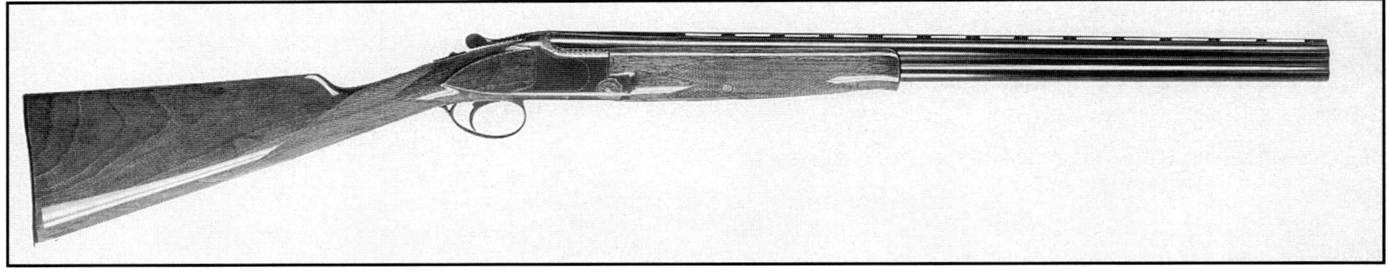

Introduced in the late 1960s, the Browning Superposed Superlight was offered in both 12 and 20 gauge. It too underwent a few subtle modifications during the early 1970s. The top photo represents a 20 gauge Superlight with rounded frame, slim forearm, and tapered ventilated rib. The bottom photo shows the same model with the same features except for the addition of a Schnable forearm. Courtesy Browning Company.

Of these features, the two that are most often missing are the rounded frame and the tapered rib. Some Superlights may have square frames, but that is inconsistent with Browning catalogue offerings, which state otherwise. The reader may encounter Superposed with straight grip stocks that were ordered from the factory, but with other characteristics that are those of a Superposed Hunting model or some other Superposed configuration. A straight grip stock alone does not earn a Superposed the right to be titled a Superlight model.[16]

Superlight models stayed fairly consistent during the 1970s, with little in the way of mechanical

[16] The author knows personally of a 28 gauge Superposed with 26-1/2-inch ventilated rib barrels that was ordered from the factory in 1972 with a straight grip stock, Exhibition Grade wood, checkered butt, Schnabel forearm, and no engraving on a square frame. This is not a Superlight, but instead a special order 28 gauge Superposed Hunting model.

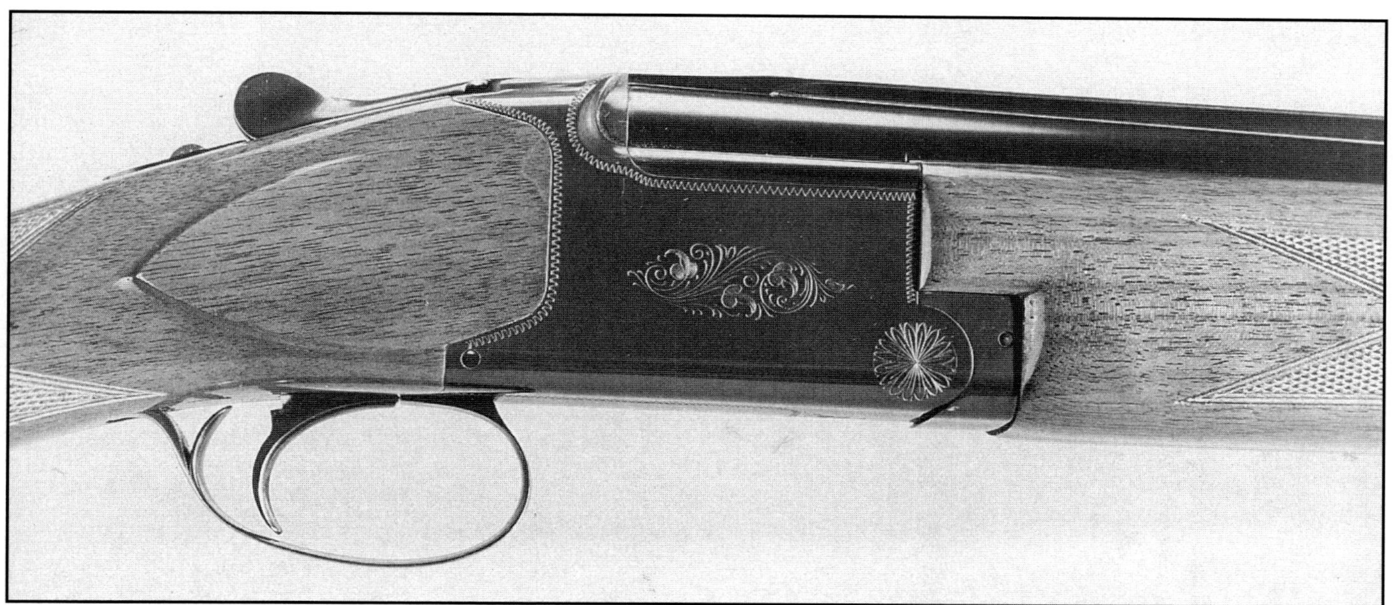

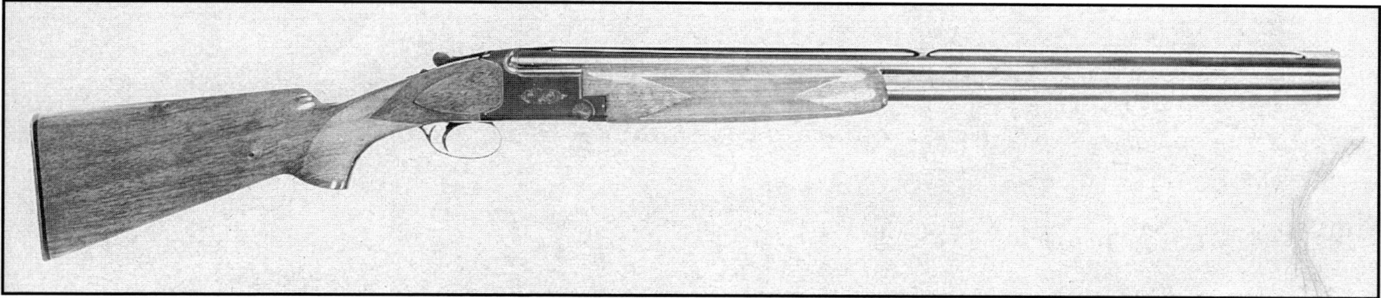

The Liège over and under shotgun was introduced to the Browning product line in 1973. It was to offer a lower cost alternative to the Superposed. Using modern manufacturing techniques, such as castings and a different locking design, the Liège was still considered too expensive by American shooters. These two photos show a 1971 prototype of the Liège. Courtesy Browning Company.

modifications. The mechanical trigger alteration did affect the Superlight as it did all other Superposed models. Perhaps the most noticeable changes occurred to the forearm. The early Superlights were fitted with a small, plain, slim forearm with crossbolts. Beginning in approximately 1970 and continuing until about 1973, the classic Schnabel forearm was introduced to the Superlight. This variation of the Schnabel forearm was fitted with a crossbolt like the earlier Superposed models. Late in 1973 and beginning in earnest in 1974, the Schnabel forearm was no longer fitted with a crossbolt since a two-piece barrel lug made the crossbolt unnecessary. It was also around 1970 that the Superlight buttstock was fitted with a fluted comb similar to the traditional Superposed style buttstock.

In 1971 both the 12 and 20 gauge Superlights were offered with engraving patterns in Pigeon, Diana, and Midas Grades. These patterns were identical to the traditional Superposed patterns. Perhaps the most noticeable engraving feature on the Superlight is the sparsity of it on Grade I guns. Only the shoulders of the frame had an engraved border, while the hinge pin received a light rosette. The frame itself acquired only a finely cut line gracefully curved from the top of the frame to the bottom rear of the frame just above the trigger guard.

Barrel lengths remained at 26-1/2 inches for both the 12 and 20 gauge Superlights, and there continued to be no mention in Browning's catalogue of Superlights available in 28 gauge or .410 bore.[17]

---

[17] There were in fact a very few, probably less than ten, Superlights with 28-inch barrels sold in North America during this period. These 28-inch guns were special order guns. There were also 28 gauge and .410 bore Superlights sold in North America. These special order Superlights are discussed in greater detail in the section on Superposed sales found later in this chapter.

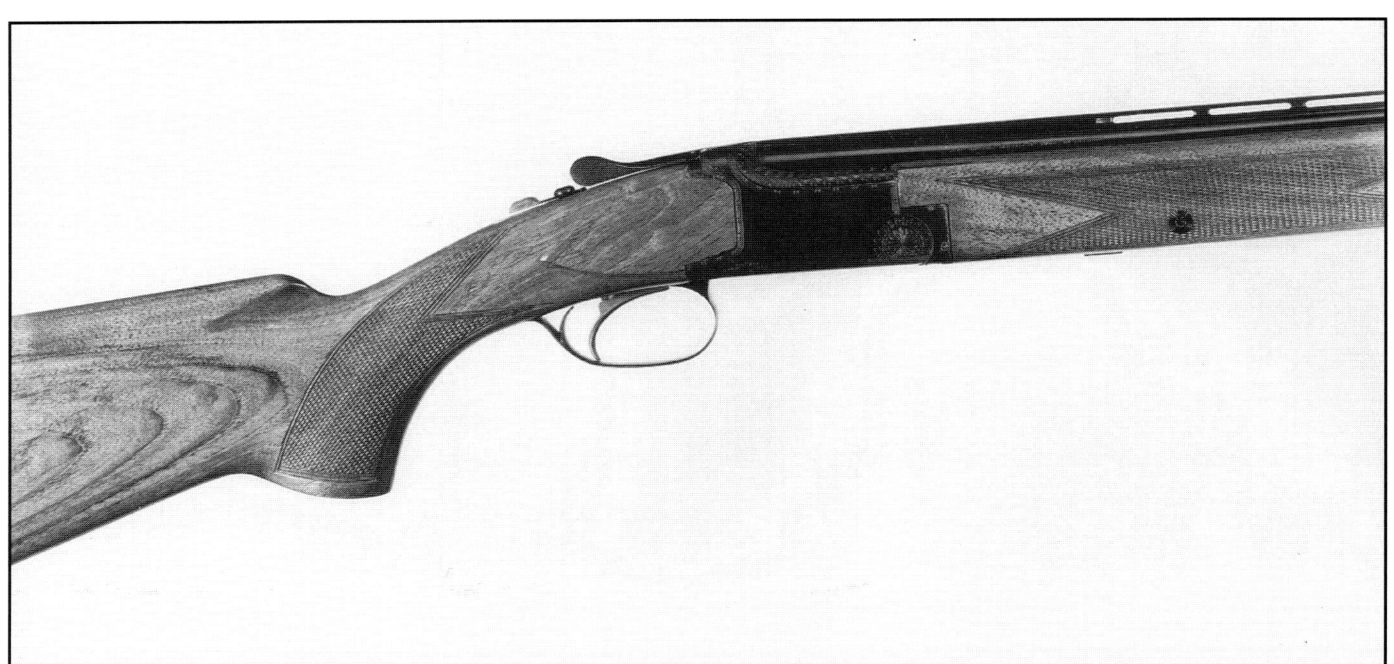

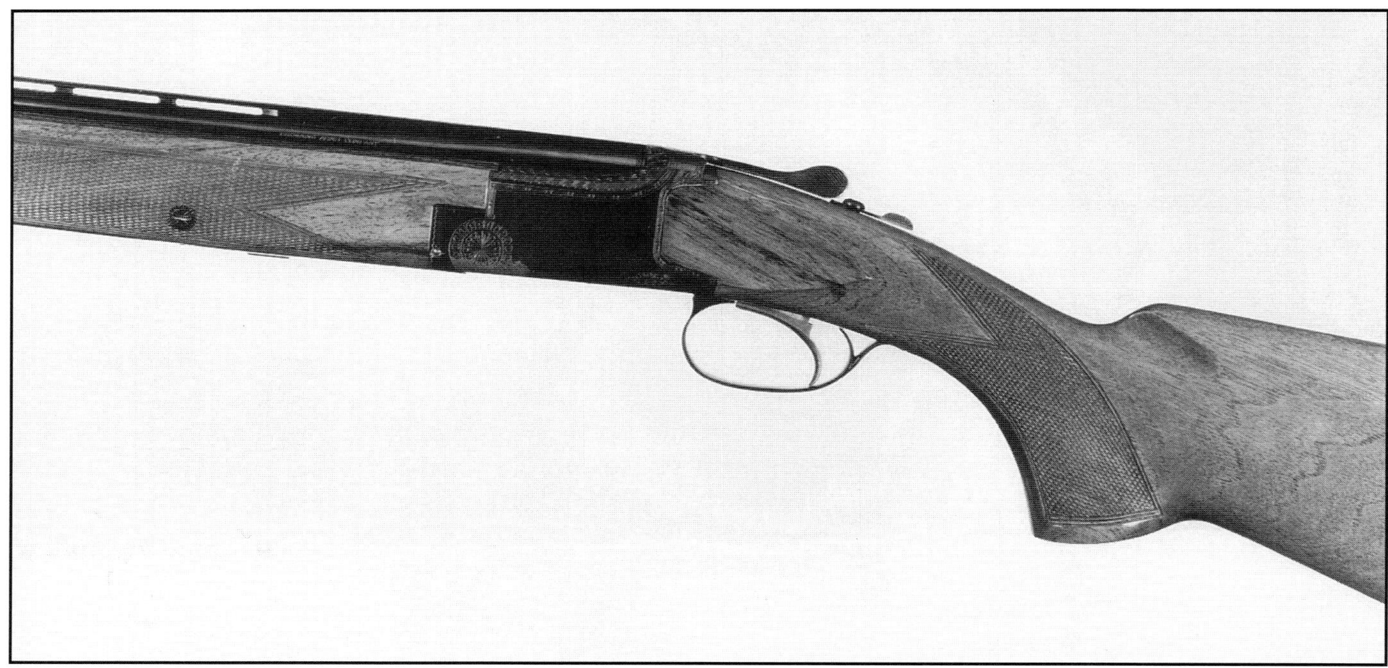

Around 1976 Val Browning directed his most trusted FN manager to build a Superposed .410 bore on a dedicated .410 frame. The whereabouts of this gun is unknown, but we are fortunate to have factory photographs of what Val Browning called, "A perfect jewel of a gun." On the left side of the barrel is stamped "BROWNING ARMS COMPANY" and on the right side is stamped ".410 GAUGE SHELLS 3"-MADE IN BELGIUM." Close examination reveals a different type safety/selector switch. Courtesy Fabrique Nationale Archives.

Liège Model: Introduced in 1973 in an attempt to offer an economy version of the Superposed to offset the constantly rising prices, the Liège was not a great success. Fabrique Nationale maintained the same basic Browning design in the Liège but used more modern manufacturing methods that required some design modifications, such as castings, to reduce cost. FN referred to the Liège as the B-26 to differentiate the design from the Superposed, which the company now referred to as the B-25. The upper and lower tangs together with a crosspiece were forged integrally with one other. The locking mechanism was changed to a "T" bolt design in the Liège. If the gun were to become loose after extensive shooting, instead of replacing the hinge pin as must be done on the Superposed, a small catch fitted to a spring could be adjusted to take up any vertical slack instantly. One could argue that the Liège was a new, more modern Superposed based on the technical and manufacturing advances of the 1970s instead of the production methods of the 1920s. However, the Liège was considered a part of the Browning line for only a short period of time.

Offered in 12 gauge only, the Liège featured a choice of 26-1/2 or 28-inch barrels with 2-3/4-inch chambers, or 30-inch barrels with 3-inch chambers. The single selective trigger was mechanical instead of the inertia type. Automatic ejectors were standard. The buttstock and forearm were carved from French walnut with checkering of twenty-two lines to the inch. A black plastic buttplate was used on guns with barrels shorter than 30 inches while a recoil pad was fitted to the 30-inch model. The rounded field type forearm disassembled completely from the barrels, unlike the Superposed, but could be secured to the barrels for storage when the gun was broken down. The length of pull for the Liège was 14-1/4 inches, drop at the comb was 1-5/8 inches, and the drop at the heel was 2-1/2 inches. The weight of the gun depended on the length of the barrels. Guns with 26-1/2-inch barrels weighed 7 lb. 4 oz., 28-inch barreled guns weighed in at 7 lb. 7 oz., and the 30-inch barreled guns weighed 7 lb. 14 oz.

Bicentennial Model: Introduced in 1976 to commemorate the two hundred year anniversary of America, Browning had FN build fifty-three of these special edition Superposed shotguns. This Bicentennial edition Superposed was not featured in any of the company's catalogues. It carried a retail price of approximately $5,500. The Bicentennial was stocked with Diana Grade American black walnut wood with high luster finish. The checkering pattern closely followed the Diana Grade style. The stock featured a straight grip with Schnabel style forearm. Each gun was chambered for the 12 gauge 2-3/4-inch shell and had 28-inch ventilated rib barrels. The width of the machine matted rib was 5/16 of an inch. All exposed metal surfaces were polished to a mirror finish.

The frame was fitted with sideplates with an engraving motif featuring an American eagle superimposed over the American flag on one side, and a frontier style hunter with wild turkeys on the other side. The scenes were done in gold inlay against a blued background. On the bottom of the frame, in gold inlay, were two olive branches with the dates "1776-1976" engraved in the center. The serial number and state identification corresponded to the order in which the state joined the union. For example, Utah was the forty-fifth state to join the union, hence its serial number UT.1776-45. The fifty-first gun was designated for the District of Columbia. The remaining two Bicentennial guns did not have state markings. One was presented to Fabrique Nationale for display in Liège at the Musee d'Armes, and the other resides at the Smithsonian Institution in Washington, D.C.

Prototype Model: There remains one final variation of the Superposed that was never manufactured, but nevertheless should be mentioned. Around 1976 or 1977, just before Browning sold its interest to Fabrique Nationale, Val Browning undertook to design and build a .410 Superposed on a dedicated .410 size frame. Little is known about the physical characteristics of this diminutive gun, but the first tool room model was built by Mr. Nicolaï at FN. We are fortunate that the photo archives at Fabrique Nationale have preserved a photographic medium of this unique Superposed gun. According to Val Browning it was, "A perfect jewel of a gun."[18]

Superposed Production: 1970-1977

By the end of 1977, when the last of the traditional Browning Superposed guns were built, approximately 255,165 Superposed shotguns in all gauges and configurations had been sold in North America. This figure would be close to the total number of Browning Superposed produced by FN for export into the North American market for the period 1930 to 1977. The total number of Browning Superposed produced and sold elsewhere offers an interesting comparison. For this same time period, 1930 to 1977, it is estimated that FN produced a total of 371,017 Superposed worldwide.[19] Again if we use sales and shipping records as a basis for production, it is possible to estimate the total production numbers for each gauge.

The vast differences between production of various gauges is clearly illustrated by Table 4-4. To better understand the significance of these numbers, keep in mind the total years of production for each gauge from 1930 to 1977. If we subtract the years of German occupation, the 12 gauge Superposed was manufactured for a total of forty-one

[18] Mr. Val Browning, interview with the author, August 15, 1993.

[19] This estimate is based on Fabrique Nationale shipping records and sales records.

TOTAL WORLDWIDE PRODUCTION BY GAUGE, ESTIMATED 1930-1977

Gauge	Browning	FN	Total Production
12 Gauge	186,429	105,271	291,700
20 Gauge	61,513	9,987	71,500
28 Gauge	3,296	263	3,559
.410 bore	3,927	331	4,258
Total	255,165	115,852	371,017

Table 4-4

BROWNING SUPERPOSED ALPHANUMERIC SERIAL NUMBER SYSTEM: 1970-1976

Gauge	1970-1976
Superposed 12 gauge	—S70, S71, S72, etc.
Superposed 20 gauge	—V70, V71, V72, etc.
Superposed 28 gauge	—F70, F71, F72, etc.
Superposed .410 bore	—J70, J71, J72, etc.

Table 4-5

years. The 20 gauge was in production for twenty-nine years. The small bores, the 28 gauge and .410 bore, were produced for only eighteen years.

It is also interesting to note the percentage of different gauges sold to Browning for its markets in the U.S. and Canada, and those sold in FN's markets, specifically the rest of the world. Browning purchased approximately sixty-four percent of FN's production of 12 gauge Superposed. Sales of the 20 gauge Superposed to Browning accounted for eighty-six percent of total FN production of that gauge. Ninety-three percent of FN's 28 gauge production was sold to Browning, and about the same percentage, ninety-two percent, of the .410 bore production went to Browning. This data offers an interesting conclusion: the smaller the gauge, the more likely it was to be sold to Browning for its North American market.

The alphanumeric system put in place around 1962, which added the year of production as a suffix to the serial number, continued through 1976. Thus, serial numbers through 1976 will appear as shown in Table 4-5.

By 1970 more than 200,000 12 gauge Superposed had been built and sold all over the world. By the end of February 1970 approximately 211,700 12 gauge Superposed had been produced, with serial number 11700S70 marking the end of FN's Shipping Journal Number Seven. Shipping Journal Number Eight begins with serial number 11701S70 and ends inexplicably with serial number 41199S75. Shipping Journal Number Nine, written in a different hand, begins with serial number 1S71 on November 1, 1971, and ends with serial number 29500S74 on October 2, 1974. Shipping Journal Number Ten, written in the same hand as Journal Number Nine, begins with serial number 29501S74 and ends in FN's standard serial number scheme in 1978 with serial number 59205S76. Within this last book FN skipped serial numbers 37000 to 41199. No 12 gauge serial numbers are recorded for this range. The gap in serial numbers at this point most likely represents an attempt by FN not to use serial numbers that would conflict with the "Old Series" numbers.

What apparently occurred is that two FN shipping clerks kept two separate journals which paralleled each other from 1971 to 1975. Two sets of similar serial numbers were kept; the only difference is in the alphanumeric code, as the two sep-

SUPERPOSED 12 GAUGE SERIAL NUMBERS, ESTIMATED DATES OF MANUFACTURE 1970-1977

Year	Old Series-1/1/70	New Series-11/1/71
1970	9000S69-14900S70	N/A
1971	14901S70-20801S71	1S71-1640S71
1972	20802S71-26702S72	1641S71-11475S72
1973	26703S72-32603S73	11476S72-21275S73
1974	32604S73-38504S74	21276S73-29500S74
1975	38505S74-41199S75	36999S74-50000S75
1976	N/A	50001S75-55000S76
1977	N/A	55001S76-59500S77

Table 4-6

arate number sequences began in different years. This situation generates considerable confusion for the researcher, but less so for the Superposed owner, who merely sees on his gun a serial number with the date the frame was built. However, it may explain away potential future confusion concerning similar serial numbers on Superposed guns produced and sold between 1971 and 1975. The situation does raise a question: Why did FN continue to use "Old Series" numbers when the changeover occurred to the "New Series?" A plausible explanation could be that the factory had already struck the "Old Series" numbers through 41199 without the alphanumeric date code in anticipation of using the frames at a later date.

A similar situation occurs with the 20 gauge Superposed. Shipping Journal Number Two ends with serial number 61500V70 (the date code "70" is not a misprint) on December 2, 1971. Shipping Journal Number Three begins with serial number 61501V70 on December 13, 1971, and ends with serial number 64301V74 on September 25, 1974. A separate shipping journal, unnumbered, begins with serial number 1V71 on March 6, 1972, and ends with serial number 7627V77 on April 10, 1980. Again, the confusion exists mainly for the researcher, but the reader may want to be aware of the complex and ambiguous FN serial number sequences that may appear on Superposed guns. In the very early 64000 serial number range about one hundred serial numbers are skipped. No entries are recorded for these numbers.

We are less bewildered when studying the small bore Superposed shipping records for the decade of the '70s. Serial number sequences for the 28 gauge and .410 bore Superposed are fairly straightforward with one important exception. From the beginning of production in 1959, the 28 gauge Superposed employed an uninterrupted serial number system until February 21, 1972, when serial number 3307F71 was assembled and shipped to Browning on March 10, 1972. This is the last recorded 28 gauge serial number from the old series. On April 27, 1972, the serial number sequence begins again with serial number 1F71. This 28 gauge Superposed was not shipped until August 31, 1972, also to Browning. FN shipping records refer to this new serial number restart as the "New Series."

After study and interviews with Fabrique Nationale personnel, the significance of these new numbers probably lies in important design modifications made to the Superposed. The changeover to the new mechanical trigger, the new ventilated rib design, the reinstallation of the long trigger guard tangs, and the transition to the internal barrel lug in place of the forearm crossbolt may all have been involved in the decision to begin a new series of serial numbers in order to readily identify those Superposed with the supplementary design additions.

SUPERPOSED 20 GAUGE SERIAL NUMBERS, ESTIMATED DATES OF MANUFACTURE 1970-1977

Year	Old Series-1/1/70	New Series-3/6/72
1970	54700V69-57847V70	N/A
1971	57848V70-61500V71	N/A
1972	61501V71-62621V72	1V71-720V72
1973	62622V72-63742V73	721V72-2500V73
1974	63743V73-64301V74	2501V73-4000V74
1975	N/A	4001V74-5200V75
1976	N/A	5201V75-6400v76
1977	N/A	6401V76-7600V77

Table 4-7

From serial number 9F1 to 3307F71 most, but not all, 28 gauge Superposed were fitted with the old style inertia trigger. From approximately 1F71 to 252F77, mechanical triggers were installed as standard on most of these new series guns. Serial number 252F77 is the last recorded 28 gauge Superposed built using the alphanumeric code.

SUPERPOSED 28 GAUGE SERIAL NUMBERS, ESTIMATED DATES OF MANUFACTURE 1970-1977

Year	Old Series-1/1/70	New Series-4/27/72
1970	2055F69-2500F70	N/A
1971	2501F70-3000F71	N/A
1972	3001F71-3307F71	1F71-50F72
1973	N/A	51F72-100F73
1974	N/A	101F73-150F74
1975	N/A	151F74-196F75
1976	N/A	197F75-227F76
1977	N/A	228F76-252F76*

Table 4-8

* Several additional 28 gauge Superposed were built after serial number 252F76, but they were not consecutively numbered. There were approximately six more 28 gauge guns built in 1977, with the last number recorded being 359F76. In 1984, ten additional 28 gauge guns were special ordered beginning with serial number 3308F84 and ending with 3317F84.

SUPERPOSED .410 BORE SERIAL NUMBERS, ESTIMATED DATES OF MANUFACTURE 1970-1977

Year	Old Series-/1/70	New Series-4/27/72
1970	2891J69-3282J70	N/A
1971	3283J70-3831J71	N/A
1972	3832J71-3868J71	1J72-75J72
1973	N/A	76J72-151J73
1974	N/A	152J73-227J74
1975	N/A	228J74-285J75
1976	N/A	286J75-301J76
1977	N/A	302J76-373J76*

Table 4-9

* This is the last consecutive serial number for the .410 bore Superposed through 1977. The last recorded serial number is 390J76. In 1983 and 1984, two hundred special order .410 bore Superposed were built in consecutive numbers beginning with "New Series" number 415J83.

A similar circumstance occurs with the Superposed .410 bore guns. The "Old Series" of serial numbers ends with 3868J71 on November 29, 1971. This gun was shipped to Browning on December 10, 1971. The "New Series" serial numbers restarted with 1J71 on April 27, 1972, the same day as the 28 gauge restart. Superposed 1J71 was shipped to Browning on July 4, 1972. The FN transition from the inertia trigger to the mechanical trigger and other Superposed modifications affected the .410 bore as well. The final consecutive serial numbered .410 bore Superposed was 373J76, assembled January 28, 1977, and shipped to Browning on May 27, 1977. The last recorded .410 bore Superposed serial number using the alphanumeric code, 390J76, was assembled September 13, 1977, and shipped to Schroeder Brothers in Liège soon after.

Fabrique Nationale stamped its serial numbers on the Browning Superposed in several locations in the same manner as it had done in the decade of the 1960s. The most obvious place is under the top lever on the upper tang. Serial numbers were also stamped under the trigger guard on long tang guns. On the forearm the serial number is stamped on the side of the take-down lever and underside of the cocking lever lifter. FN also stamped the serial number on one or both sides of the barrels just under the ejector extension.

Consolidated Superposed Sales for North America: 1964-1977

In the preceding chapter Superposed sales from 1964 to 1969 were categorized. In this section the cumulative sales for the period 1964 through 1977 will be studied in detail in order to better understand the dynamics of the marketplace. This data will provide the reader with information not only about the kinds of Superposed that Browning was selling in North America, but also the kinds of Superposed Fabrique Nationale was capable of and willing to produce. For the most part, the type of Superposed sold during this consolidated period will generally parallel the data presented for the interval between 1964 and 1969. The final sales numbers will, of course, represent conclusive data about the last fourteen years of traditional Superposed sales in North America. This represents a total of 120,465 Superposed sold, or about forty-seven percent of the approximately 255,165 purchased in the United States and North America between 1930 and 1977.

As stated in the previous chapter, these sales records, while complete, are not comprehensive as to specific types of special order features. For the purposes of this book, all records that listed both Standard and Lightning weights were calculated in the aggregate of both weights and not broken down further. Therefore, for example, any 12 gauge Hunting models available in either Standard or Lightning weight are represented in their combined total. Also, Browning records list Skeet guns by choke and not style. In the early 1960s there was no differentiation between a Skeet model and a Hunting model except choke. This poses no problem until 1968 when the company introduced a dedicated Skeet model, the New Model Skeet. From that point on, any Hunting gun with skeet chokes has been counted as a Skeet gun despite its Hunting configuration. These sales records also do not take into account FN Superposed guns imported into North America outside the Browning corporate sales structure. This includes returning servicemen and individuals who brought their own personal Superposed into the country. These guns will not be reflected in these totals.[20] It is also important to keep in mind that these records reflect sales figures and do not in any way represent FN production totals.

One final note of explanation is in order. Special order sales are guns that have features that are not standard for that particular model or configuration. For example, a recoil pad on a Hunting model that is not a Magnum is considered by Browning to be a special order feature. A recoil pad on a Skeet model is a standard feature and is therefore not considered a special order feature.

If the 1960s were the high water mark for Superposed sales in North America, then the 1970s represent a steady and precipitous decline. Table 4-10 illustrates this point, and clearly shows why in 1977 the traditional Superposed shotgun was discontinued as a production gun. In fact, as early as 1972 Fabrique Nationale no longer manufactured barrels and frames for the Superposed, but used an abundant inventory of these essential components to assemble the dwindling number of new Superposed. Some parts production continued, but for the most part large numbers of principal component parts already on hand were enough to fulfill demand.

BROWNING SUPERPOSED SALES
NORTH AMERICA
1970-1977

Year	Superposed Sales
1970	10,609
1971	10,089
1972	7,444
1973	5,290
1974	3,689
1975	1,276
1976	2,653
1977	1,563

Table 4-10

Table 4-10 distinctly shows the precipitant decline of Superposed sales between 1970 and 1977. From a high of 10,609 Superposed sold in 1970, sales declined steadily through 1977, with the exception of 1976 when there was a slight increase. This increase was probably in anticipation of the final year of production of the traditional Superposed. The declining sales were most likely the result of a sharp increase in retail prices during the period. In 1970 the Grade I Lightning model had a retail price of $455.00. In 1976, the last year the Superposed was carried in Browning's price list, the retail price for the same gun was $1,100.00, an increase of 142 percent. The sharpest price increase of the peroid was one of 107 percent over only four years, 1972 through 1975. This enormous overall price escalation in a comparatively short seven-year period effectively stifled demand and led to the demise of the Superposed as a production line shotgun.

Superposed Sales
By Gauge
See Chart 4-3

Chart 4-3 illustrates what most firearms enthusiasts already know: The 12 gauge Superposed shotgun was the most popular gauge sold in the Superposed line during this period. A total of 76,929 12 gauge Superposed guns in all configurations were sold for this fourteen-year time span, a figure that represents sixty-six percent of total sales during this time. Twenty gauge guns were next in popularity with 34,213 sold, a twenty-eight percent share of overall sales. The number of small bore Superposed guns pur-

[20] For a complete year by year sales analysis see Appendix A.

BROWNING SUPERPOSED SALES, NORTH AMERICA
by Gauge
1964-1977

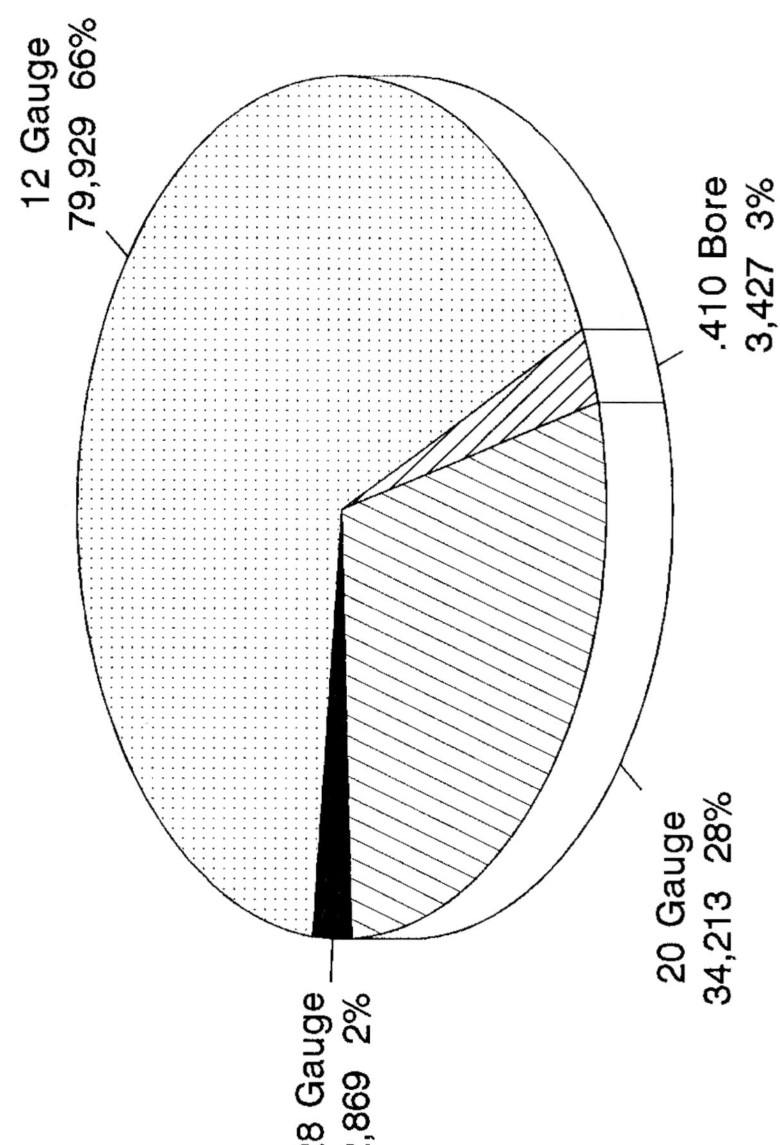

Chart 4-3

chased during this period was small when compared to the 12 and 20 gauge sales. The .410 bore accounted for 3,427 guns, or three percent of overall sales, while the 28 gauge sold 2,896, or about two percent of sales.

12 Gauge Sales
by Type
See Chart 4-4

The composition of 12 gauge Superposed sales will be of interest to the reader because it illustrates the popularity and availability of the different configurations during this period. This information may also prove useful for the shooter or collector in deciding what configuration may be easier or more difficult to locate. Chart 4-4 shows the delineation of 12 gauge Superposed types. The most common 12 gauge configuration is the BROADway Trap with 18,172 guns sold, twenty-three percent of total 12 gauge sales for this period. Following closely behind is the 28-inch Hunting configuration with 16,568 guns sold, or twenty-one percent of sales. The 26-1/2-inch Hunting model was next with 12,166 guns, or fifteen percent of total sales. Together, 26-1/2-inch and 28-inch Hunting models accounted for a total of 28,734 guns sold, thirty-six percent of total 12 gauge sales, which is far greater than the BROADway Trap alone. However, the fourth most popular 12 gauge Superposed was the Lightning Trap model with 8,418 guns sold, or eleven percent of total 12 gauge sales. If we take both Trap models and both Hunting models we will see that the Superposed Trap models accounted for a total of 26,590 guns sold, or thirty-four percent of 12 gauge sales compared to thirty-six percent of sales for both Hunting models. Thus, the Hunting models and Trap models are about equal in distribution of 12 gauge sales.

The remaining 12 gauge sales are divided between the Skeet model with 10,215 guns sold, or thirteen percent of total 12 gauge sales; the 3-inch Magnum with 7,206 guns sold, or nine percent of total sales; the Superlight model with 4,608 guns sold, or six percent of total 12 gauge sales; and special order 12 gauge Superposed sales that accounted for 2,576 guns, or about three percent of sales.

20 Gauge Sales
by Type
See Chart 4-5

The 20 gauge Superposed, the second most popular gauge sold during this period, is analyzed by type sold in Chart 4-5. Clearly the Hunting model with 26-1/2-inch barrels was the best seller with a total of 17,330 guns sold, or fifty-one percent of the 20 gauge total. The Hunting model with 28-inch barrels was a distant second in sales with 9,440 sold, or twenty-eight percent of 20 gauge sales. These two Hunting models taken together account for an impressive seventy-eight percent of total 20 gauge Superposed sales.

The Superposed 20 gauge Skeet model sold 4,749 guns, or fourteen percent of total 20 gauge sales. Special order 20 gauge guns amounted to 1,683 guns sold, or five percent of total 20 gauge sales, and in last place was the Superlight 20 gauge with only 1,011 guns sold, or about three percent of total 20 gauge sales.

28 Gauge Sales
by Type
See Chart 4-6

Sales for the Superposed 28 gauge are represented by Chart 4-6.[21] The Hunting models were obvious favorites among buyers. Barrels of 26-1/2 inches were slightly preferred over the longer 28-inch barrels by twenty-nine percent to twenty-five percent respectively. These Hunting models accounted for almost fifty-four percent of total 28 gauge sales. The 28 gauge Skeet model was the second most purchased type with 1,162 guns sold, or about forty percent of total 28 gauge sales. Special order 28 gauge guns recorded sales of only 178 guns, or six percent of total 28 gauge sales.

.410 Bore Sales
by Type
See Chart 4-7

The .410 bore Superposed sales differed somewhat from the 28 gauge.[22] Sales were almost evenly split between the .410 Skeet model and the Hunting model. Chart 4-7 shows Skeet model sales of 1,687 guns, or forty-nine percent of total .410 bore sales. Hunting models with both 26-1/2-inch and 28-inch barrels also accounted for forty-nine percent of sales with 1,696 guns sold. Special order .410 bore Superposed guns were almost nonexistent,

---

[21] Sales figures for the 28 gauge Superposed contain sales data for 28 gauge Superlight guns as well. Browning did not have an order number for this configuration because it was not shown in the company's catalogues. The number of 28 gauge Superlights sold is not known for certain, although an estimated number is shown later in this section under Superlight sales.

[22] Sales figures for the .410 bore Superposed contain data for .410 bore Superlight guns also. Browning did not have an order number for this configuration because it was not shown in the company's catalogues. The number of .410 bore Superlights sold is not known for certain, although an estimated number is shown later in this section under Superlight sales.

SUPERPOSED 12 GAUGE SALES, NORTH AMERICA
by Type
1964-1977

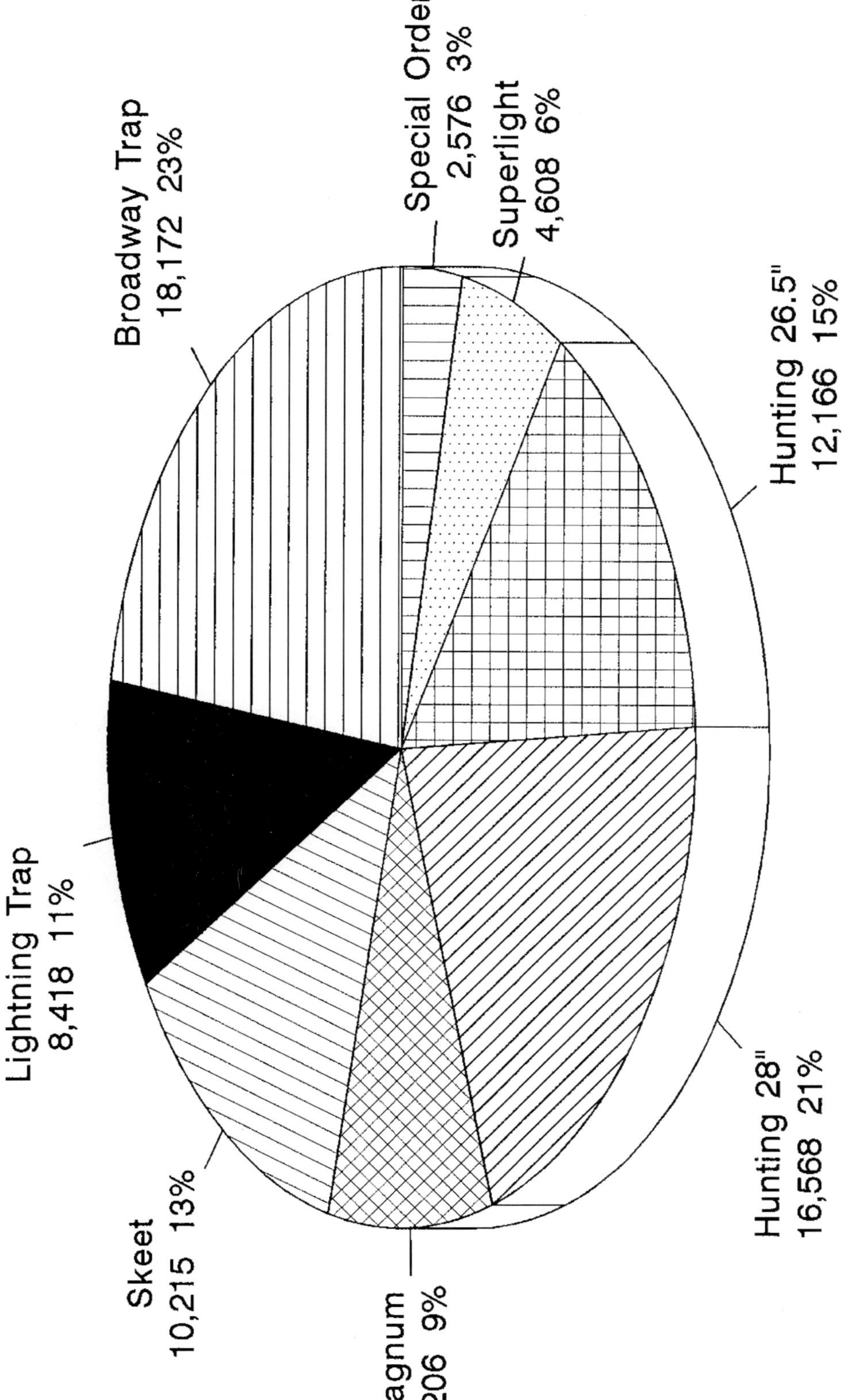

Chart 4-4

SUPERPOSED 20 GAUGE SALES, NORTH AMERICA
by Type
1964-1977

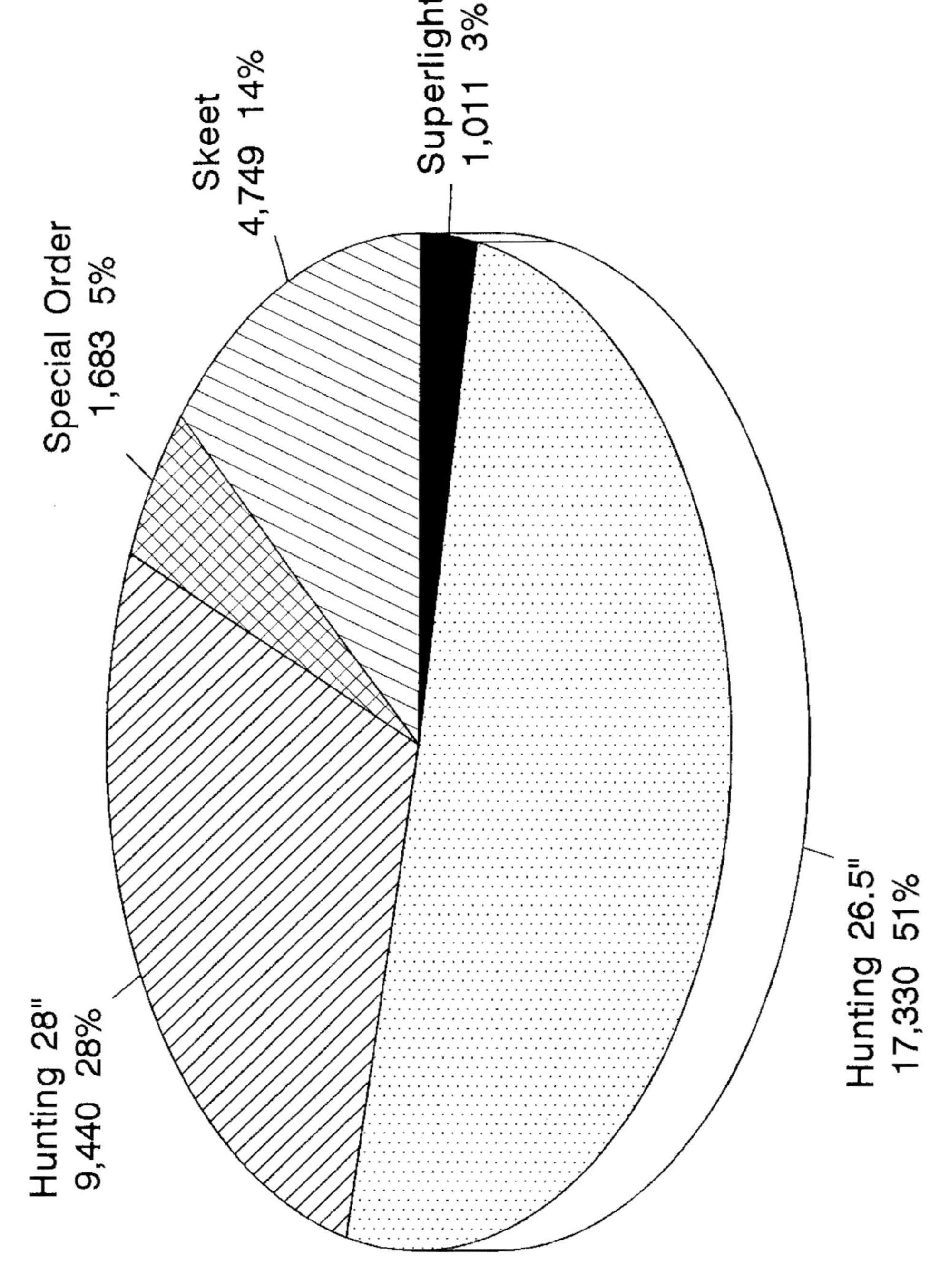

Chart 4-5

SUPERPOSED 28 GAUGE SALES, NORTH AMERICA
by Type
1964-1977

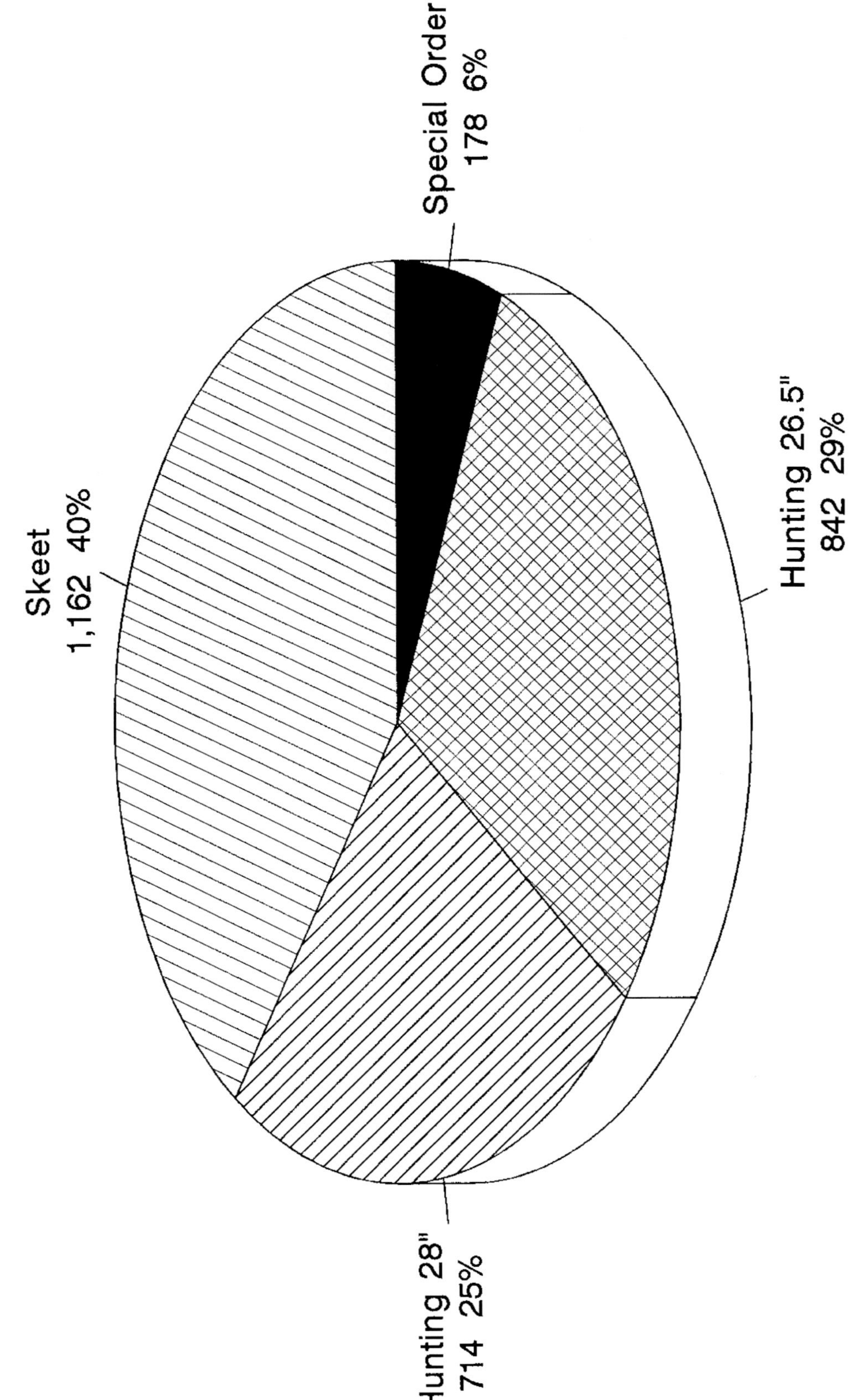

Chart 4-6

SUPERPOSED .410 BORE SALES, NORTH AMERICA
by Type
1964-1977
Skeet
1,687 49%
Special Order
44 1%
Hunting
969 28%
Hunting 28"
727 21%

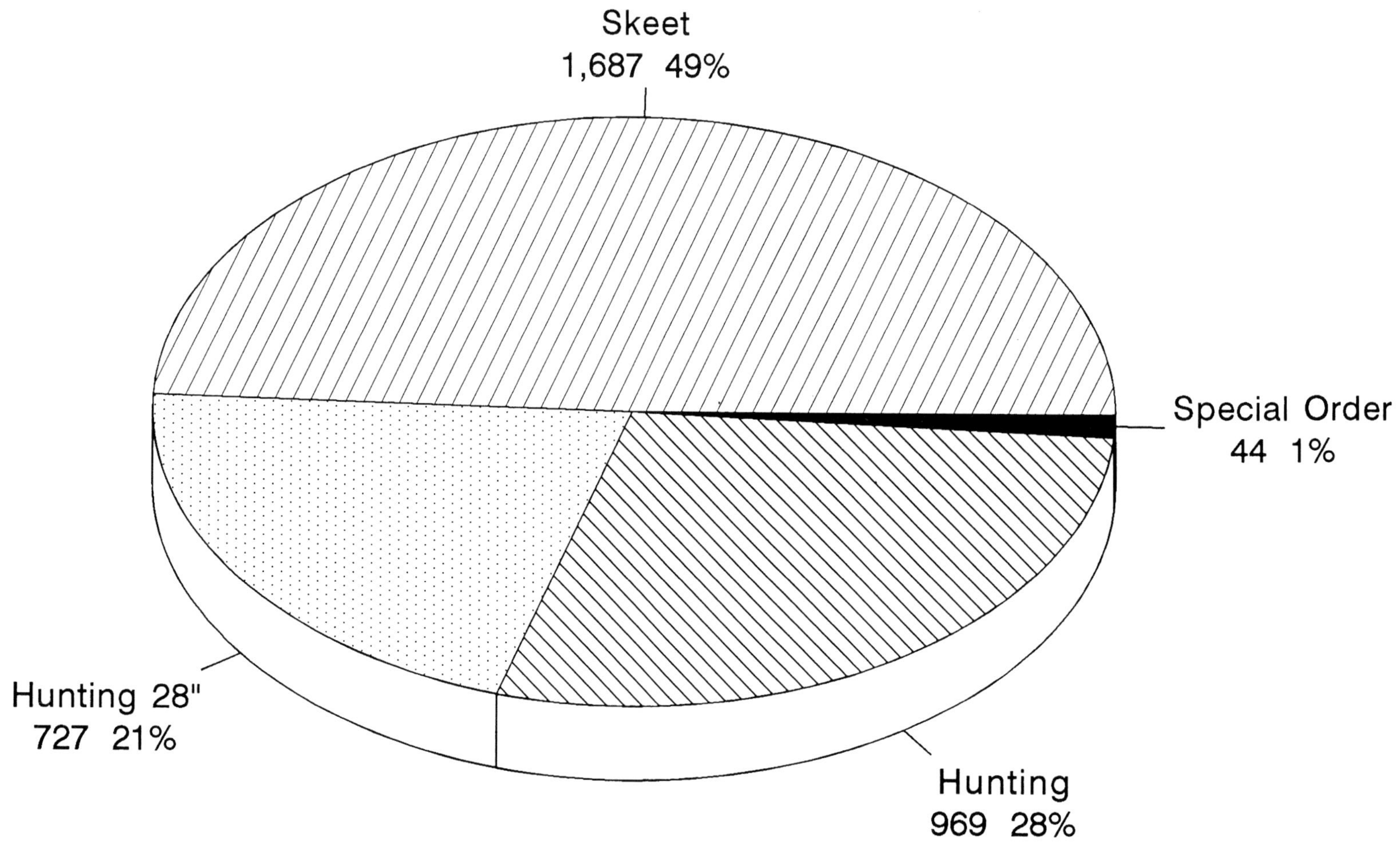

Chart 4-7

with only 44 guns falling into this category, or slightly more than one percent of total .410 bore sales.

28 Gauge & .410 Bore Sales by Model See Chart 4-8

For the small bore shooter and collector, Chart 4-8 gives a comparison of these two small bore Superposed guns. There were about the same number of 28 gauge Hunting models sold in North America as there were .410 Hunting models, but the number of .410 Skeet models outnumber 28 gauge Skeet guns by almost forty-six percent. As far as rarity is concerned, any special order .410 bore or 28 gauge Superposed is unique. Taken as an aggregate, there were only a total of 6,323 of these small bore guns sold in North America between 1964 and 1977. Of those, only 3,252 were 28 gauge and .410 bore Hunting models.

Target vs Hunting Models See Chart 4-9

As a summation to all the Superposed gauges sold in North America, Chart 4-9 gives a valuable comparison to the number of Target guns sold as compared to Hunting models and other categories. If we look at the total number of Target guns sold during this period in 12 gauge, for example, we find that forty-eight percent of all 12 gauge Superposed sold were either Trap or Skeet models, leaving fifty-two percent as Hunting guns in various configurations. This ratio of Target guns to Hunting guns does not hold true for 20 gauge Superposed, however. The vast majority of 20 gauge guns, eighty-five percent, were sold as Hunting models (Superlights are included in this figure), leaving only fifteen percent purchased as Skeet guns. However, the percentage of Skeet models sold in 12 gauge closely approximates those sold in 20 gauge—some fifteen percent. The clear conclusion here is that Browning's Trap models were excellent sellers and accounted for a substantial portion of the 12 gauge Superposed market.

This comparison does not apply to the small bore Superposed sales. Although the 28 gauge Hunting models were a definite favorite, the Skeet models captured a very strong forty-three percent of sales. The .410 bore Superposed were almost evenly split between Hunting and Skeet models with 49.7 percent and 50.3 percent respectively.

Grade I Hunting Models Barrel Length by Gauge See Chart 4-10

One additional piece of data the reader may find interesting is the examination of barrel lengths by gauge of all Hunting models sold in North America between 1964 and 1977. Chart 4-10 illustrates that for Superposed Hunting models in 12 gauge, the most popular barrel length was 28 inches. This represented almost forty-seven percent of sales while 26-1/2-inch barrels were next in popularity with almost thirty-three percent. The longer 30-inch barrels, represented primarily by the 3-inch Magnum model, accounted for nearly twenty-one percent of sales. If we view 12 gauge barrel lengths as a group, then sixty-seven percent of the 12 gauge Hunting models sold during this period were fitted with barrels 28 inches or longer. Almost the opposite is true with the 20 gauge Hunting models, where nearly sixty-five percent were sold with 26-1/2-inch barrels.

With the small bore Hunting models, the ratio is much closer to one to one than it is with the 12 and 20 gauge guns. Both the 28 gauge and the .410 bore Hunting models recorded sales that were slightly more than fifty percent for the 26-1/2-inch barrel lengths. The longer 28-inch barrels for these small bore guns were almost as popular, however.

Superposed Sales by Grade See Chart 4-11

Perhaps the one feature that attracts the most attention to the Superposed is engraving. Both the shooter and collector are very interested in the number of grades sold in various configurations. For the years 1964 through 1977, sales by grade were reported. Chart 4-11 depicts the relationship between the Grade I Superposed and the other high grade Superposed sold during this period for all gauges and models. The left pie chart shows the obvious fact that more Grade I Superposed were sold than high grade guns: eighty-six percent of sales for Grade I guns and only fourteen percent for high grade guns. The right pie chart gives a breakdown of high grade sales. The clear preference is the Pigeon Grade with a total of 8,219 guns sold, or almost fifty percent of total high grade sales for this period. The second most popular engraving pattern was the esteemed Diana Grade, which accounted for 5,129 guns sold, or thirty-one percent of all high grade sales. The prestigious Midas Grade was next in sales with 2,193 guns sold, or thirteen percent of total sales.

SUPERPOSED SALES BY MODEL, NORTH AMERICA
28 Gauge and .410 Bore
1964-1977

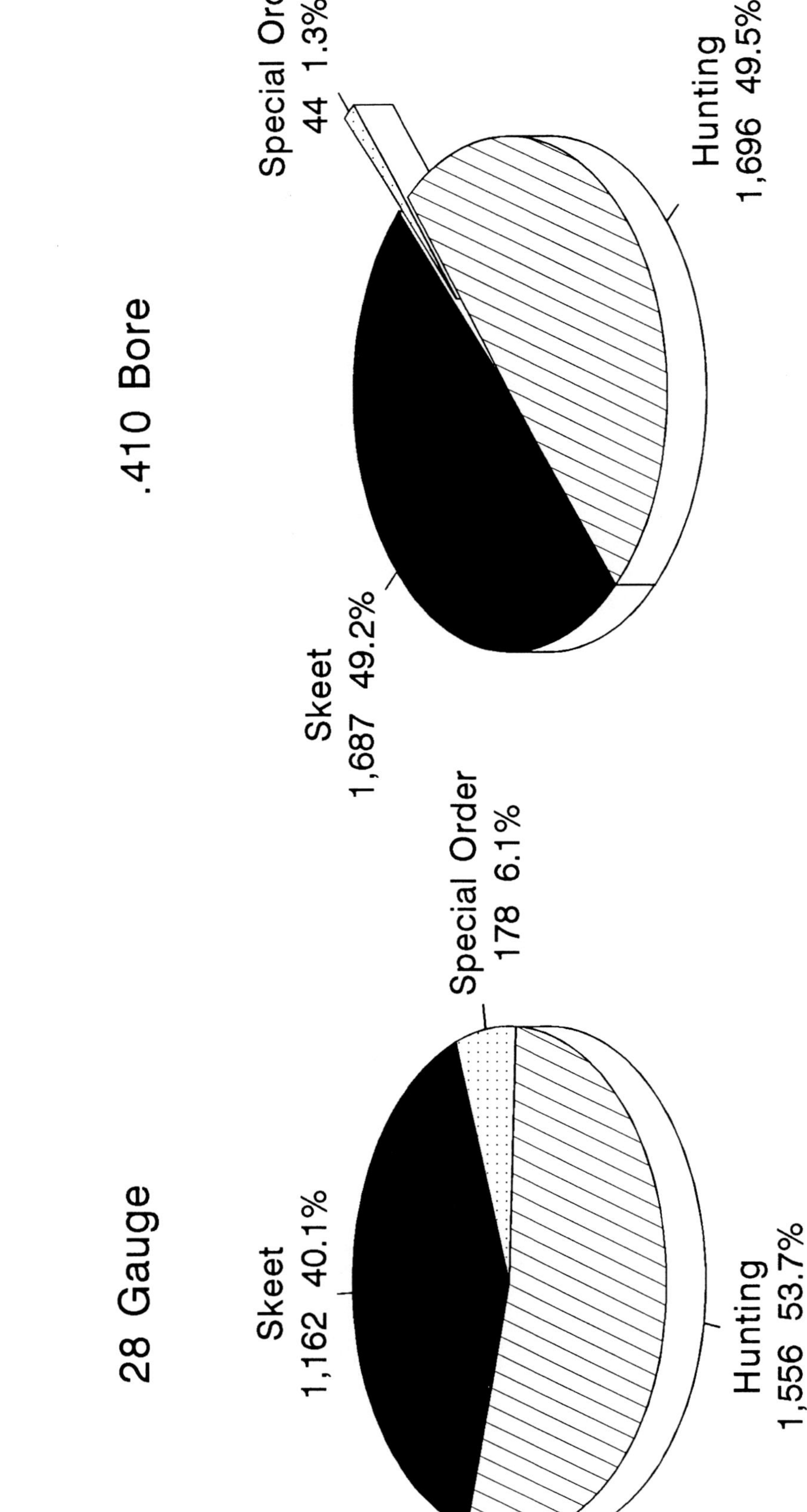

Chart 4-8

TARGET VS HUNTING MODEL SALES, NORTH AMERICA 1964-1977

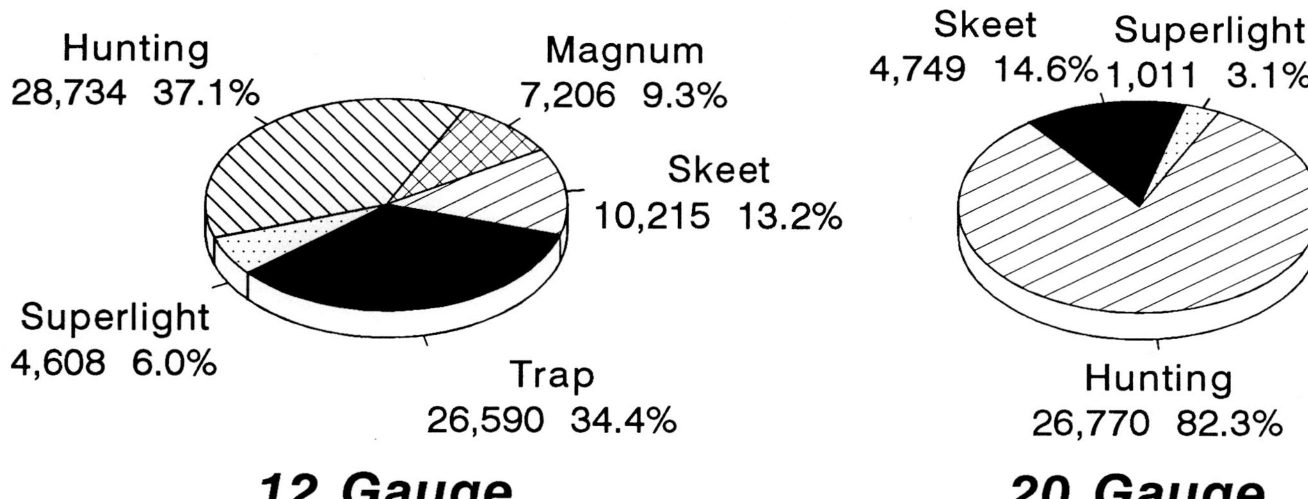

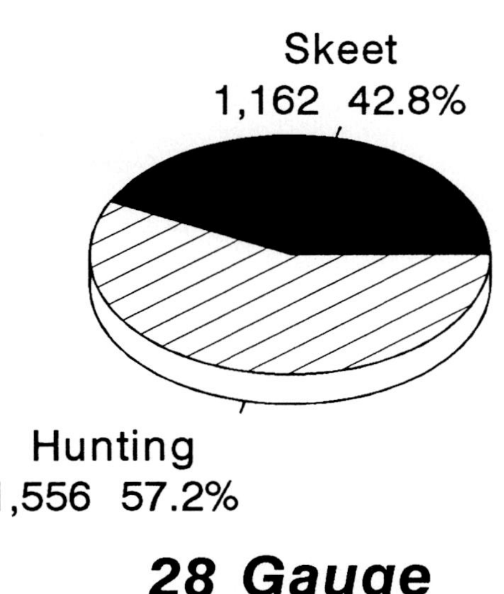

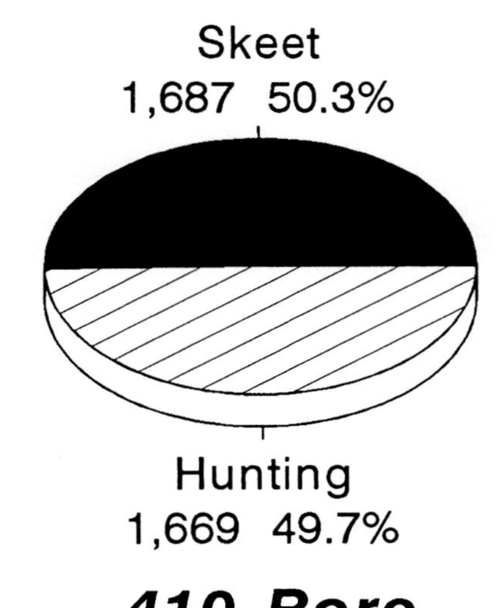

Chart 4-9

SUPERPOSED GRADE I HUNTING MODELS, NORTH AMERICA
Barrel Lengths by Gauge
1964-1977

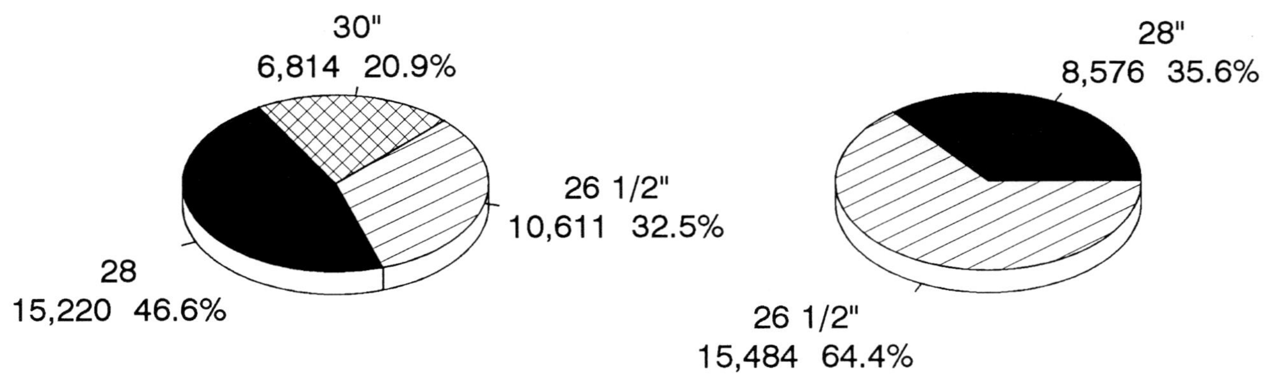

12 Gauge ***20 Gauge***

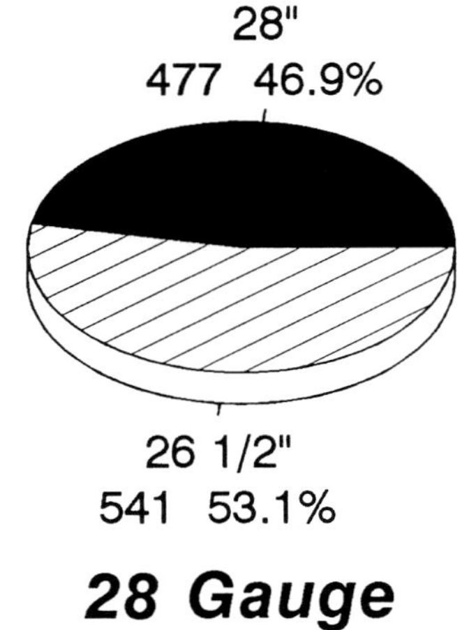

28 Gauge

28"
518 47.3%
26 1/2"
577 52.7%

.410 Bore

Chart 4-10

BROWNING SUPERPOSED SALES, NORTH AMERICA
by Grade
1964-1977
Other Grades
16,670 14%
Grade I
103,795 86%
Diana
5,129 31%
Midas
2,193 13%
Exhibition
400 2%
Pointer
724 4%
Pigeon
8,219 49%

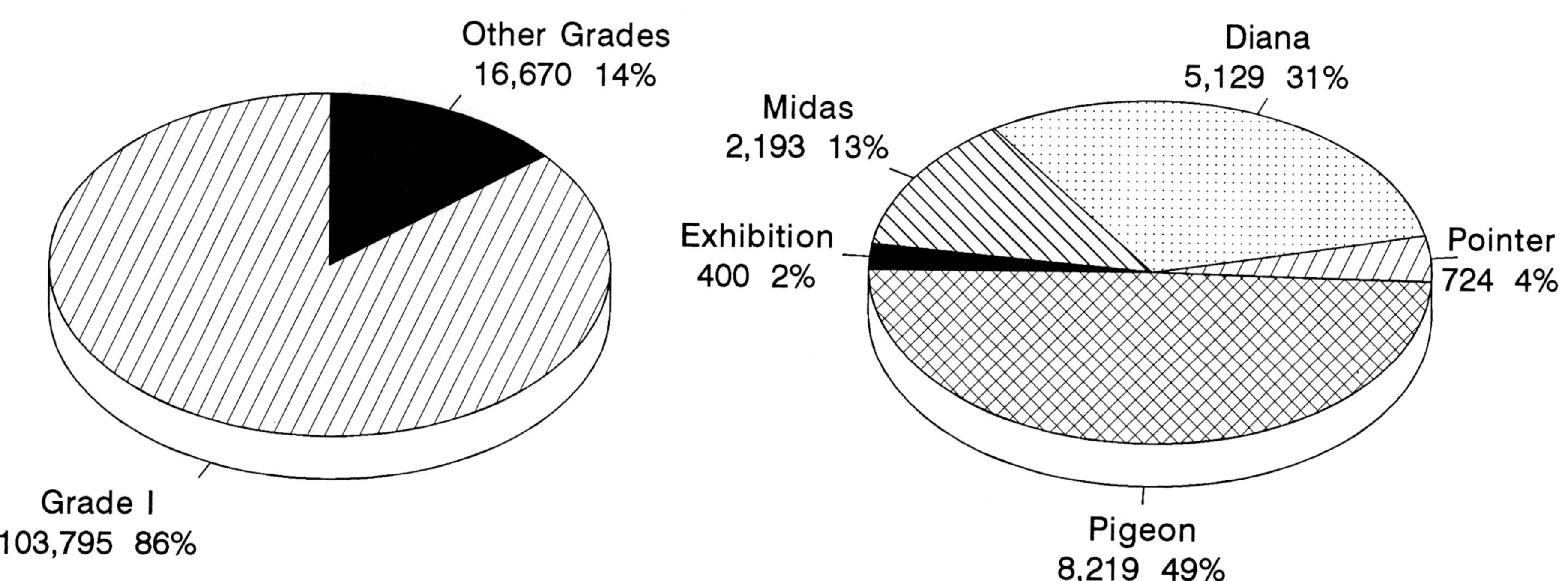

Chart 4-11

The Pointer Grade, discontinued in 1966, accounted for only 724 guns, or a small four percent of sales. The most rare engraving pattern was the Exhibition Grade[23] with only 400 Superposed sold with these unique engraving patterns. This is about two percent of total high grade sales.

12 Gauge Sales
by Grade
See Chart 4-12

The analysis of high grade sales continues with an examination of high grade sales by individual gauge. Chart 4-12 shows the relationship of Grade I 12 gauge sales to high grade sales. The percentage of Grade I sales to high grade sales is about the same as the total given in Chart 4-11: eighty-seven percent of 12 gauge Superposed were sold as Grade I guns compared to thirteen percent sold as high grade guns. The breakdown of high grade 12 gauge sales is also about average, with the Pigeon Grade by far the most popular, followed by the Diana, Midas, Pointer, and Exhibition Grades.

.20 Gauge Sales
by Grade
See Chart 4-13

Grade I sales for the 20 gauge Superposed were also about average. Examination of high grade 20 gauge sales reveals some variances with 12 gauge sales by percentage according to Chart 4-13. The Pigeon Grade sold at the fifty percent level, but the breakdown of the other grades is slightly different. The Diana Grade represents thirty-two percent of high grade 20 gauge sales, up two percent over the 12 gauge. However, the Midas Grade accounted for eleven percent of high grade 20 gauge sales, down from the fourteen percent recorded for the 12 gauge. Pointer Grade percentages were up slightly to five percent over the 12 gauge four percent figure. The percentage of 20 gauge Exhibition Grade sales remained about average at two percent. Of course, there were fewer high grade 20 gauge Superposed sold in North America, but percentage comparisons may prove to be a useful analytical tool.

.28 Gauge Sales
by Grade
See Chart 4-14

Chart 4-14 shows the breakdown of Grade I sales to high grades sales for the 28 gauge Superposed. Notice that the percentage of Grade I sales to high grade guns sold is lower than either the 12 or 20 gauge Superposed by a significant amount. The result is that almost thirty percent of all 28 gauge Superposed sold were engraved guns. Of those engraved guns, forty-five percent were Pigeon, a figure less than average. The second most popular 28 gauge engraving pattern, like the other gauges, was the Diana Grade; but in 28 gauge its percentage of sales was down slightly from the average. The percentage of Midas Grade 28 gauge guns sold was about on par with the average of all Superposed sold, but the percentage of 28 gauge Pointer Grade guns sold was slightly higher at six percent, as was the Exhibition Grade at three percent of sales.

.410 Bore Sales
by Grade
See Chart 4-15

Sales percentages for the .410 bore Superposed are different from the other gauges. While seventy-four percent of all .410 bore Superposed guns sold were Grade I, a figure somewhat similar to the 28 gauge, it was not as high a ratio of engraved guns to Grade I Superposed as the 28 gauge recorded. What is a departure is the breakdown of the .410 bore high grade sales. The Pigeon Grade remained the most purchased high grade .410 bore, but at forty-two percent, it was lower than all other gauges. The percentage of Diana Grades sold was about average for the .410 bore, but the Midas and Pointer Grades were noticeably different. The Midas Grade accounted for sixteen percent of .410 bore sales, the highest of all gauges, and the Pointer Grade represented ten percent of high grade .410 sales, also the highest of all Superposed gauges. The percentage of Exhibition Grades sold was similar to the 28 gauge with three percent of high grade sales.

The above charts offer interesting information with regards to the ratio of Grade I sales to high grade sales for all models and configurations. This information is critical in gaining insight into the nature of high grade sales versus Grade I sales, but one further breakdown may make the sales data even more valuable. This breakdown is an examination into Grade I sales versus high grade sales in relation to Target models and Hunting models. The results of this analysis will add further understanding to sales by grade.

---

23 The Exhibition Grade sales figures include both the "true" Exhibition Grade guns and the "C" Grade Exhibition guns. The exact figures for the "C" Grade Exhibition are 256 guns sold worldwide. Estimated "C" Grade sales for North America are around 231 guns. This would leave approximately 169 "true" Exhibition Grade Superposed sold in North America for this period. Please note that these are estimates only.

SUPERPOSED 12 GAUGE SALES, NORTH AMERICA
by Grade
1964-1977

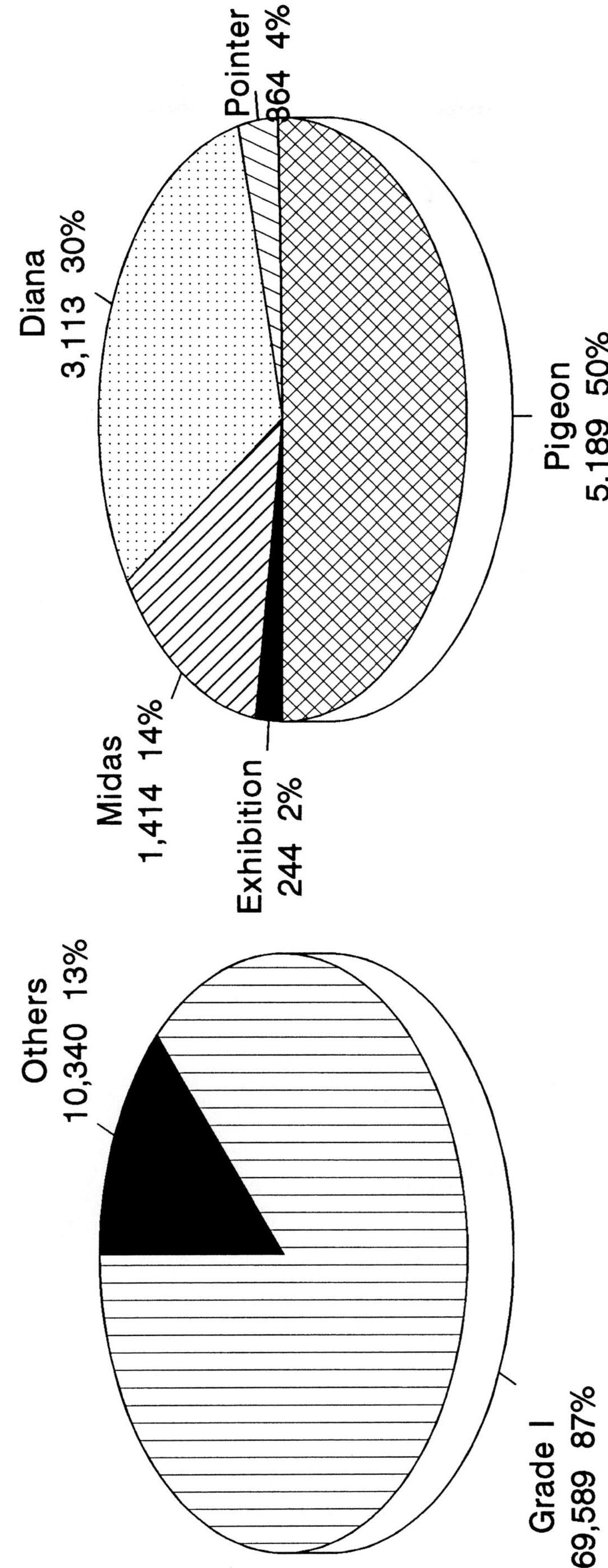

Chart 4-12

SUPERPOSED 20 GAUGE SALES, NORTH AMERICA
by Grade
1964-1977

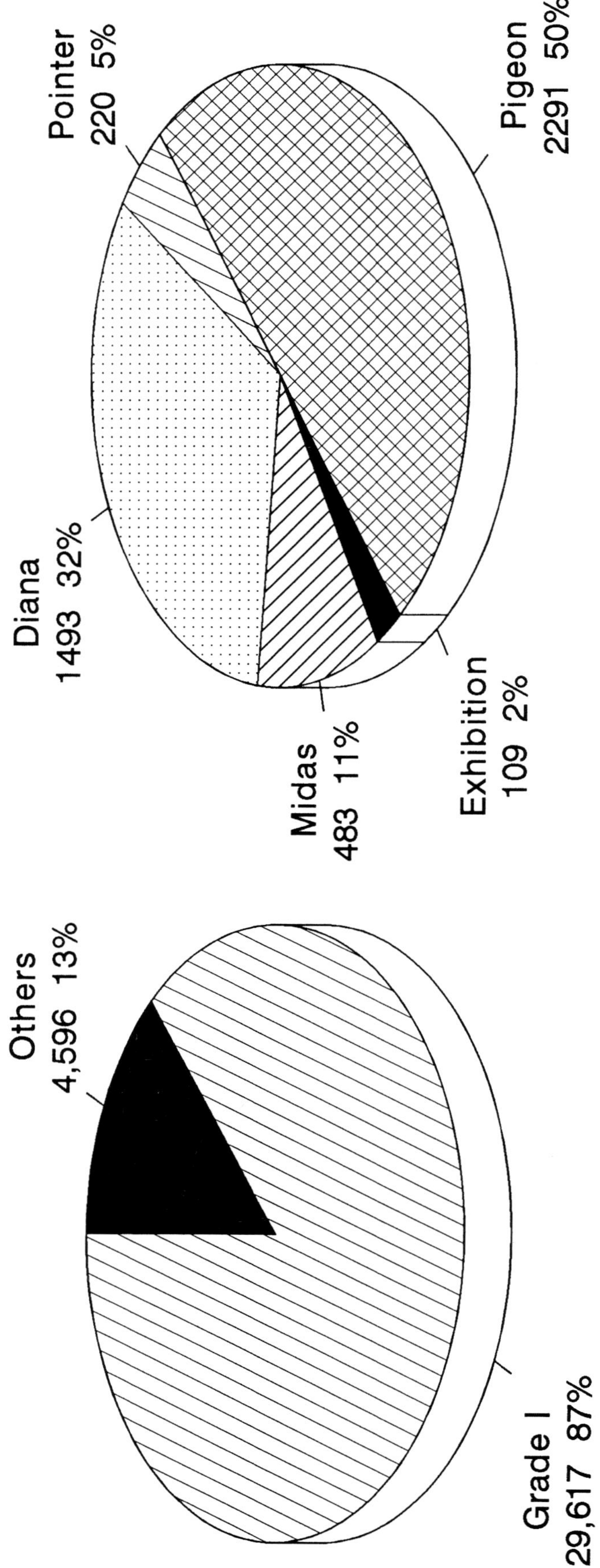

Chart 4-13

SUPERPOSED 28 GAUGE SALES, NORTH AMERICA
by Grade
1964-1977

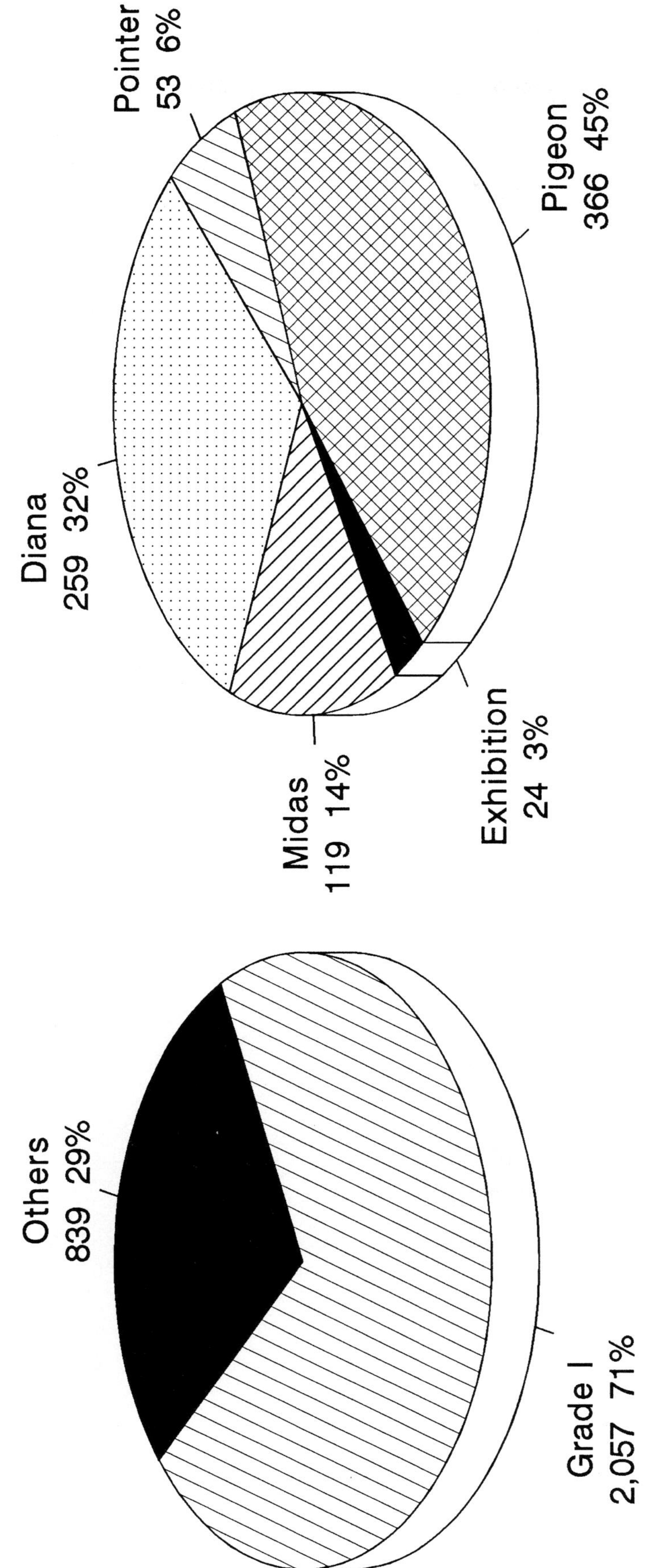

Chart 4-14

SUPERPOSED .410 BORE SALES, NORTH AMERICA by Grade 1964-1977

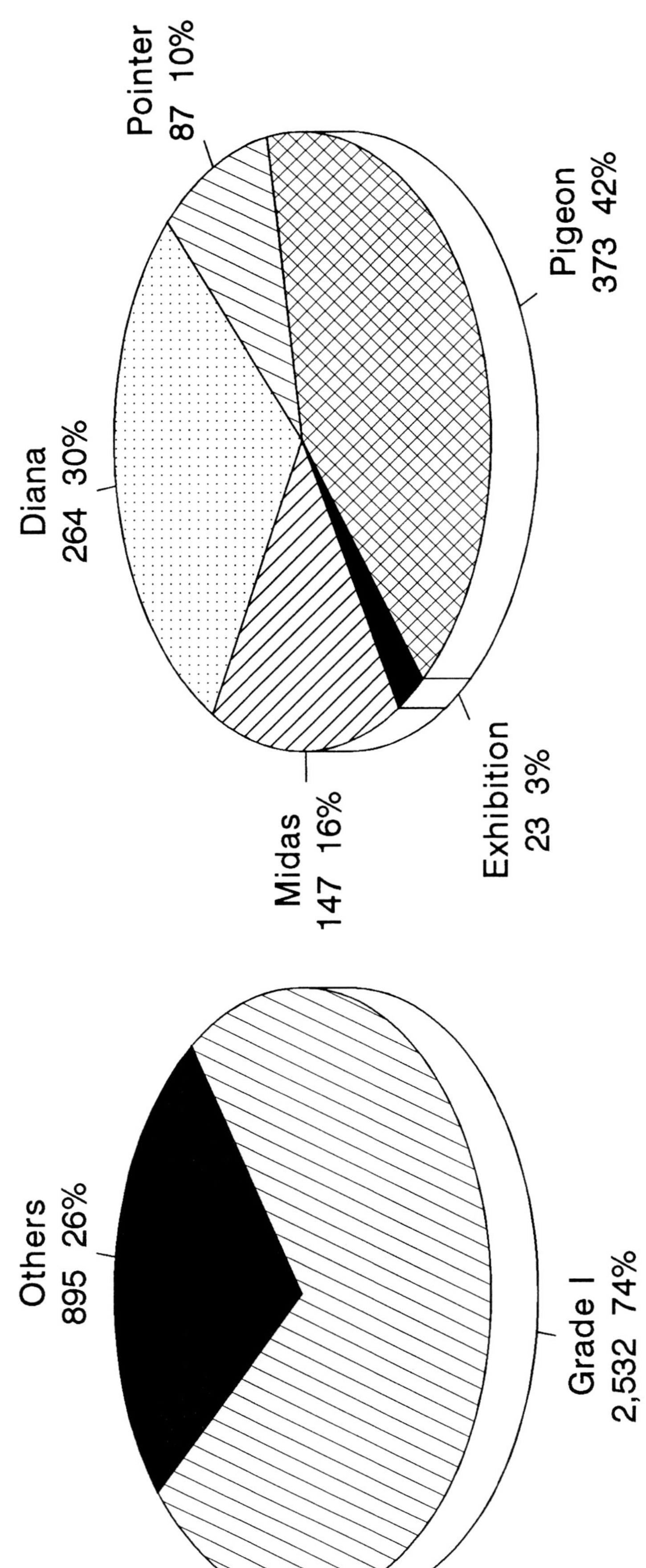

Chart 4-15

SUPERPOSED SALES BY GRADE, NORTH AMERICA
12 and 20 Gauge Target vs Hunting
1964-1977

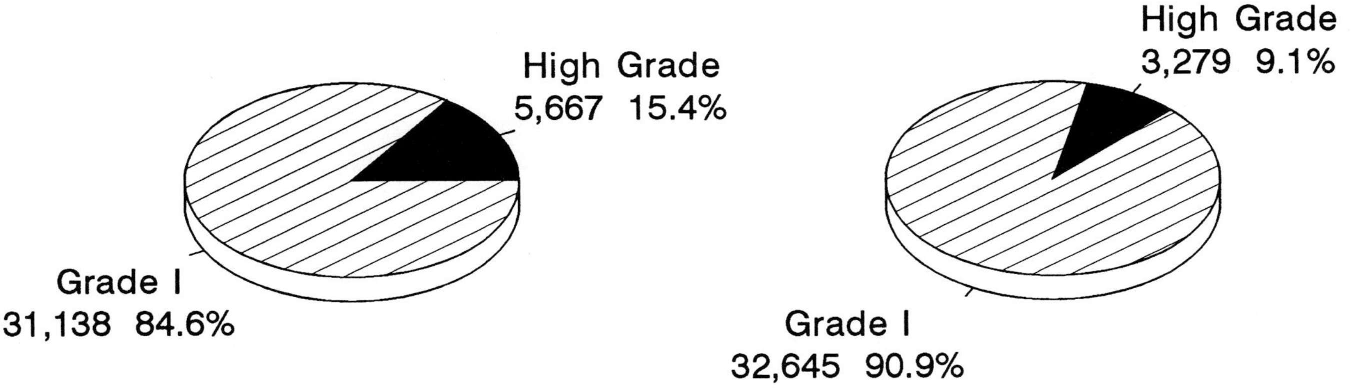

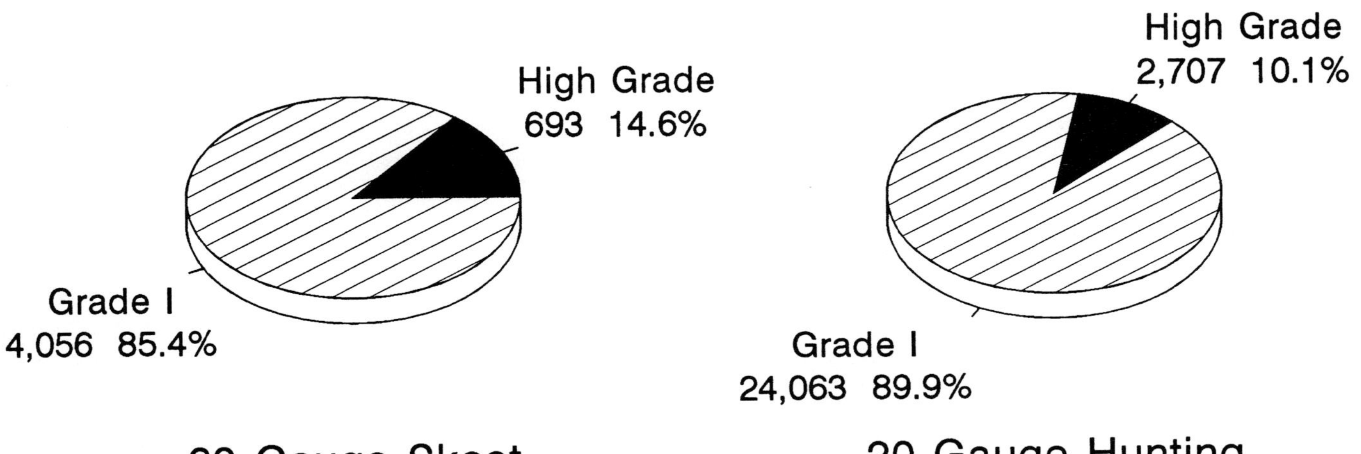

Chart 4-16

Sales by Grade
12 & 20 Gauge
Target vs Hunting
See Chart 4-16

Chart 4-16 illustrates 12 and 20 gauge Superposed as sold by grade with reference to Target and Hunting models between 1964 and 1977. There were more high grade 12 gauge Target guns sold than Hunting guns by a substantial margin. This tells us that 12 gauge Superposed customers who bought Target guns were more likely to buy engraved guns than those who purchased Hunting models.

About the same ratio of Grade I sales to high grade sales exist for the 20 gauge as it did for the 12 gauge. While the actual number of 20 gauge Superposed sold was smaller, the ratio of sales was similar to those of the 12 gauge Target and Hunting models. One statistic that may be of interest is the relatively small number of 20 gauge high grade Target models sold during this period. Only 693 twenty gauge high grade Skeet guns were sold compared to 5,667 twelve gauge Target guns sold.

Sales by Grade
28 Gauge and
.410 Bore
Skeet vs Hunting
See Chart 4-17

This same analysis of high grade Target and Hunting guns was conducted on the small bore Superposed as well. Chart 4-17 shows the ratio of sales for grades with respect to Target and Hunting models for the 28 gauge and .410 bore Superposed. What is interesting about this data are several apparent differences. While there were slightly more high grade 28 gauge Skeet guns sold than the other gauges on a percentage basis, the number of engraved Hunting guns sold was far higher than either the 12 or 20 gauge guns. Grade I .410 bore Skeet guns sales were about average with 15.3 percent of Skeet sales, but noticeably smaller in percentage terms than the 28 gauge Skeet sales. The Hunting model sales were roughly in accordance with the 28 gauge sales ratio of high grade guns to Skeet guns.

The conclusion that may be drawn from this data concerning high grade sales by model would lead one to surmise that a much higher percentage of small bore guns in the Hunting models were engraved than 12 and 20 gauge Superposed in the same configuration. It would also lead one to find that Target guns in all gauges, with the possible exception of the 28 gauge, had about the same ratio of Grade I guns to high grade guns sold regardless of gauge. Another conclusion that may be drawn based on this data is that the larger the gauge, the lower the percentage of engraved guns in Hunting models were sold. Perhaps the most telling numbers are the relatively few high grade Skeet model 28 and .410 bore Superposed sold in North America during this period: a total of only 476 guns. If we look at the total number of high grade 28 gauge and .410 bore Superposed in all configurations sold in North America during this period there are only 1,616 guns, a very small number.

Total Superlight
Sales
1967-1977
See Chart 4-18

The next sales data to come under examination concerns the Superposed Superlight model. Introduced in 1967 in 12 gauge and 1969 in 20 gauge, this model, while filling a small marketing niche, did not experience a large volume of sales. Chart 4-18 shows that the total number of Superlights sold between 1967 and 1977, for both 12 and 20 gauge, was 5,619 guns. The largest sales year was 1968 when 1,024 12 gauge guns were sold. Perhaps the America hunter was not ready to accept the European notion that a straight grip shotgun is easily and quickly mounted and pointed.

Grade I Superlight
Sales
12 & 20 Gauge
See Chart 4-19

Chart 4-19 illustrates the breakdown in Superlight sales for both the 12 and 20 gauge in Grade I. The number of 12 gauge Superlight guns sold was uneven during the years it was offered for sale, but not to the extent of the 20 gauge Superlight. For some unknown reason there was one year where no sales were recorded and one year where only one 20 gauge Superlight was sold. This situation may be explained by the lack of interest in this model and the fact that dealers who could not sell those Superlights they had in inventory did not need to order more. Another possible explanation could be in FN's inability to produce and deliver these guns in a timely manner. The period between 1970 and 1977 was one of great turmoil for the factory, and perhaps the 20 gauge Superlight did not receive the attention needed to adequately fill demand, small as it was.

12 Gauge Superlight
Sales
by Grade
See Chart 4-20

Chart 4-20 compares the sales of Grade I 12 gauge Superlights to high grade guns of the same gauge. The vast majority of 12 gauge Superlights were sold as Grade I guns: an enormous ninety-five percent. Of those high grade 12 gauge guns, of which there were only 209, forty-one percent were

SUPERPOSED SALES BY GRADE, NORTH AMERICA
28 Gauge and .410 Bore Skeet vs Hunting
1964-1977

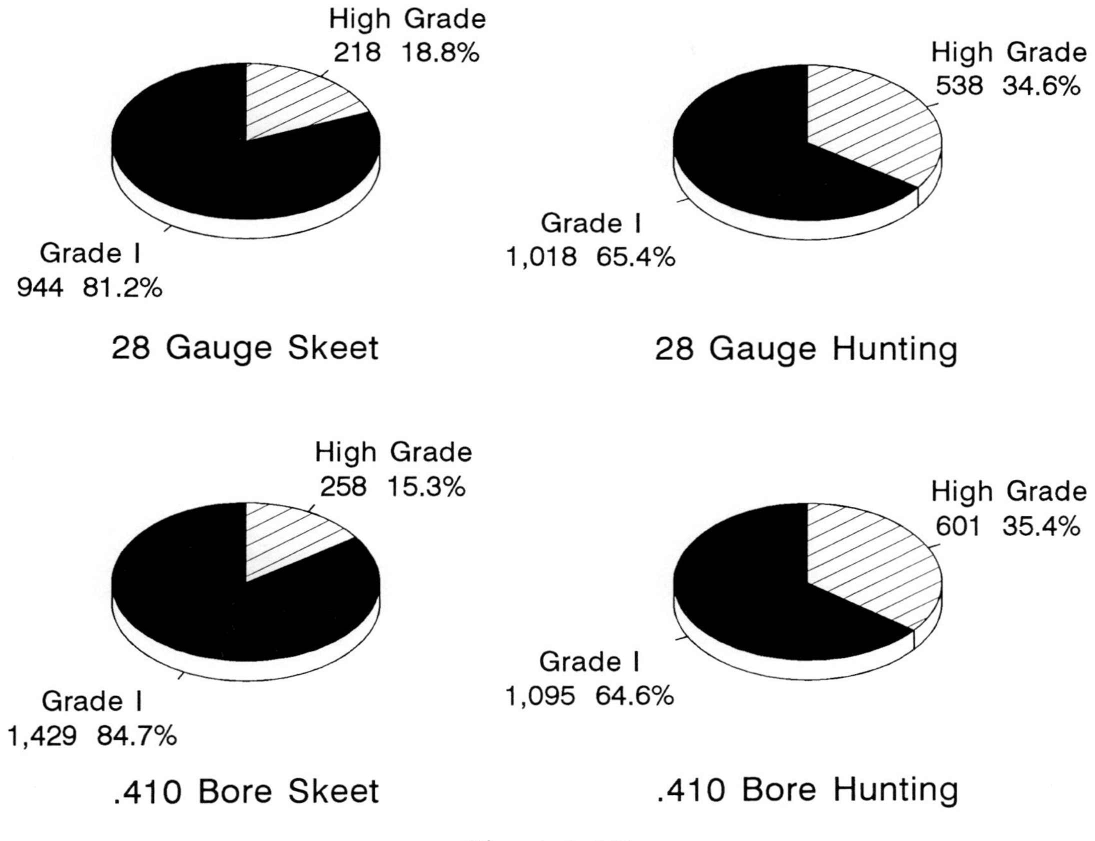

Chart 4-17

Pigeon Grade, thirty-two percent were Diana Grade, sixteen percent were Midas Grade, six percent were Exhibition Grade, and only five percent, or a total of eleven guns, were Pointer Grade. This chart clearly shows that engraved 12 gauge Superlight Superposed were quite rare.

20 Gauge Superlight Sales by Grade See Chart 4-21

The examination of 20 gauge Superlight sales is shown on Chart 4-21. The most obvious difference is in the percentage of Grade I and high grade 20 gauge Superlights sold compared to 12 gauge Superlight sales. The number of engraved 20 gauge Superlights sold is greater than the number of 12 gauge engraved Superlights. High grade 20 gauge sales amounted to twenty-six percent of Superlights sold. The Pigeon Grade 20 gauge Superlight was the engraved gun most sold; the Diana Grade was a close second with thirty percent of sales. The Midas Grade recorded nineteen percent of sales, the Pointer ten percent, and the Exhibition Grade only four percent, or only eleven guns total.

A thorough examination of high grade Superlight sales is illustrated in Table 4-12. One final thought that may be of interest is the conclusion that twenty-six percent of all 20 gauge Superlights were engraved, but only five percent of all 12 gauge Superlights were high grade guns. Moreover, eighty-five percent of all Superlights were 12 gauge, but only fifteen percent were 20 gauge. Table 4-12 gives us a clear indication of the most popular high grade Superlight guns sold in North America and which of these is the most rare. With the exception of the Exhibition Grade, there were fewer engraved 12 gauge Superlights than 20 gauge guns. Again with the exception of the Exhibition Grade, the most rare production Superlight was the 12 gauge Pointer Grade, while the most prevalent high grade Superlight was the 20 gauge Pigeon Grade. In any event, with only 480 total Superlights sold in both 12 and 20 gauge, these are rare and collectable Superposed.

BROWNING CUMULATIVE SUPERLIGHT SALES
North America, Grade I, 12 and 20 Gauge
1967-1977
6,000
5,000
4,000
3,000
2,000
1,000
0
1967 1968 1969 1970 1971 1972 1973 1974 1975 1976 1977
Total Sold
237 1,261 1,696 2,446 3,292 3,917 4,591 4,958 5,116 5,470 5,619

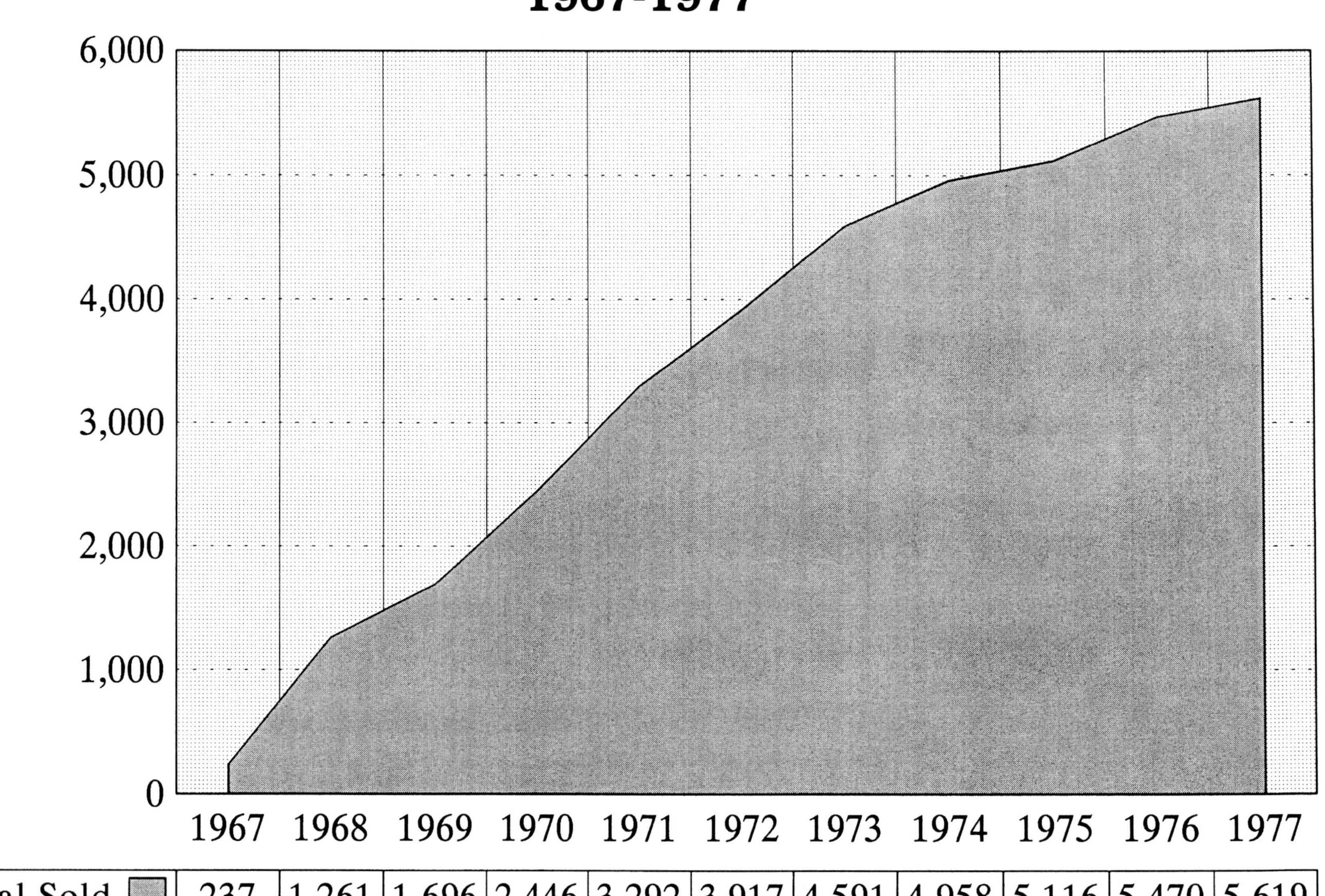

Chart 4-18

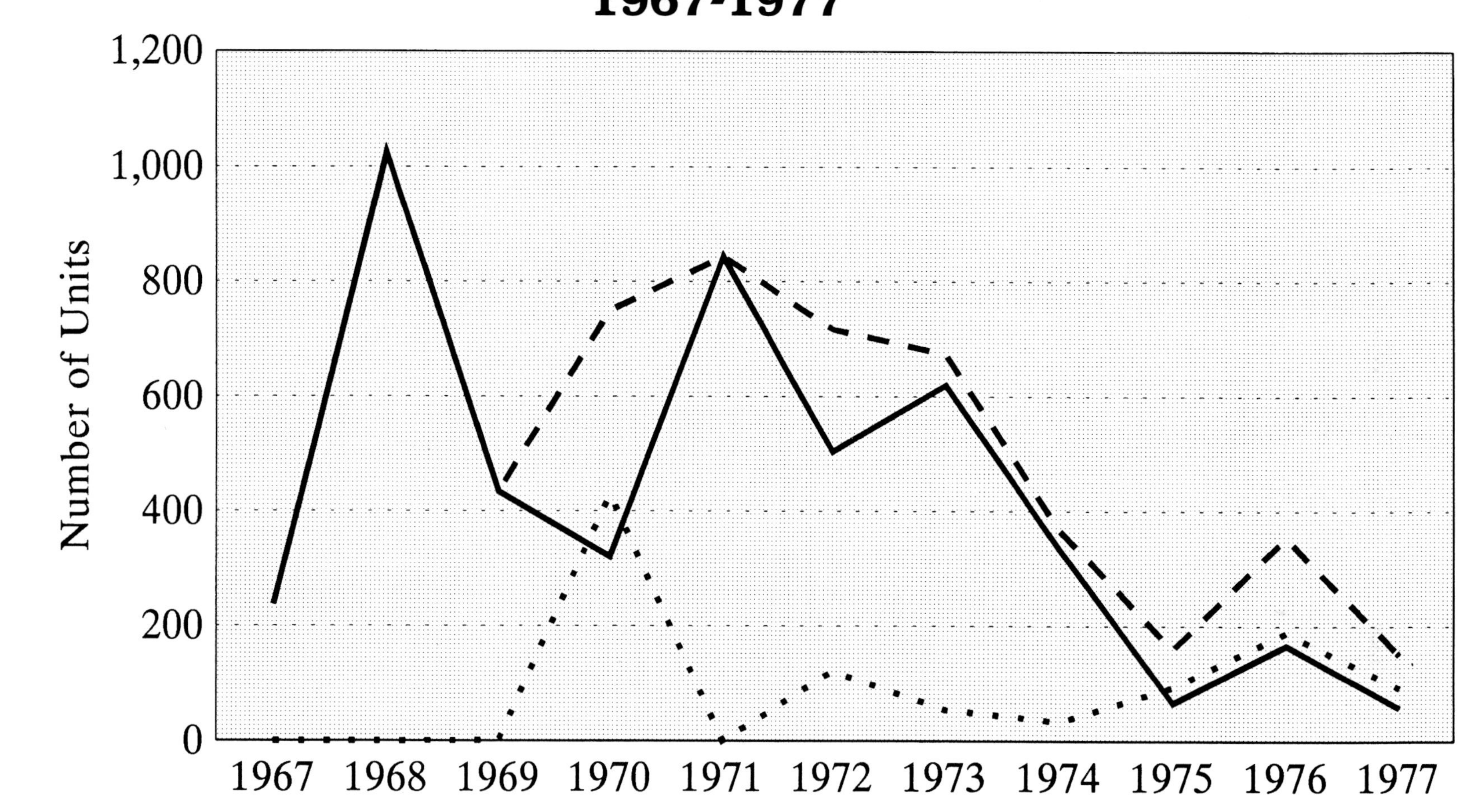

	1967	1968	1969	1970	1971	1972	1973	1974	1975	1976	1977
12 Gauge —	237	1,024	434	321	844	504	620	334	66	166	58
20 Gauge · · ·	0	0	1	429	0	121	54	33	93	188	92
Total Sold - -	237	1,024	435	750	844	717	674	367	159	354	150

Chart 4-19

SUPERPOSED 12 GAUGE SUPERLIGHT SALES
North America, by Grade
1967-1977

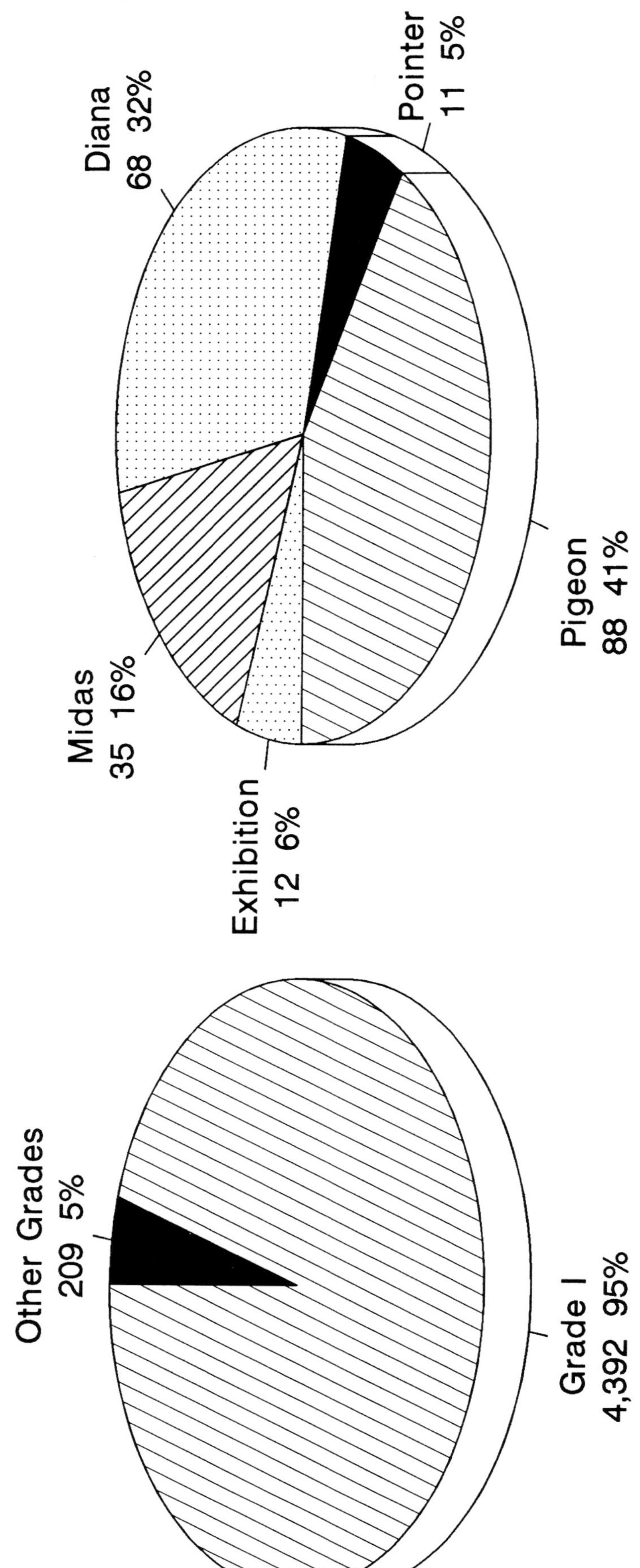

Chart 4-20

SUPERPOSED 20 GAUGE SUPERLIGHT SALES
North America, by Grade
1969-1977

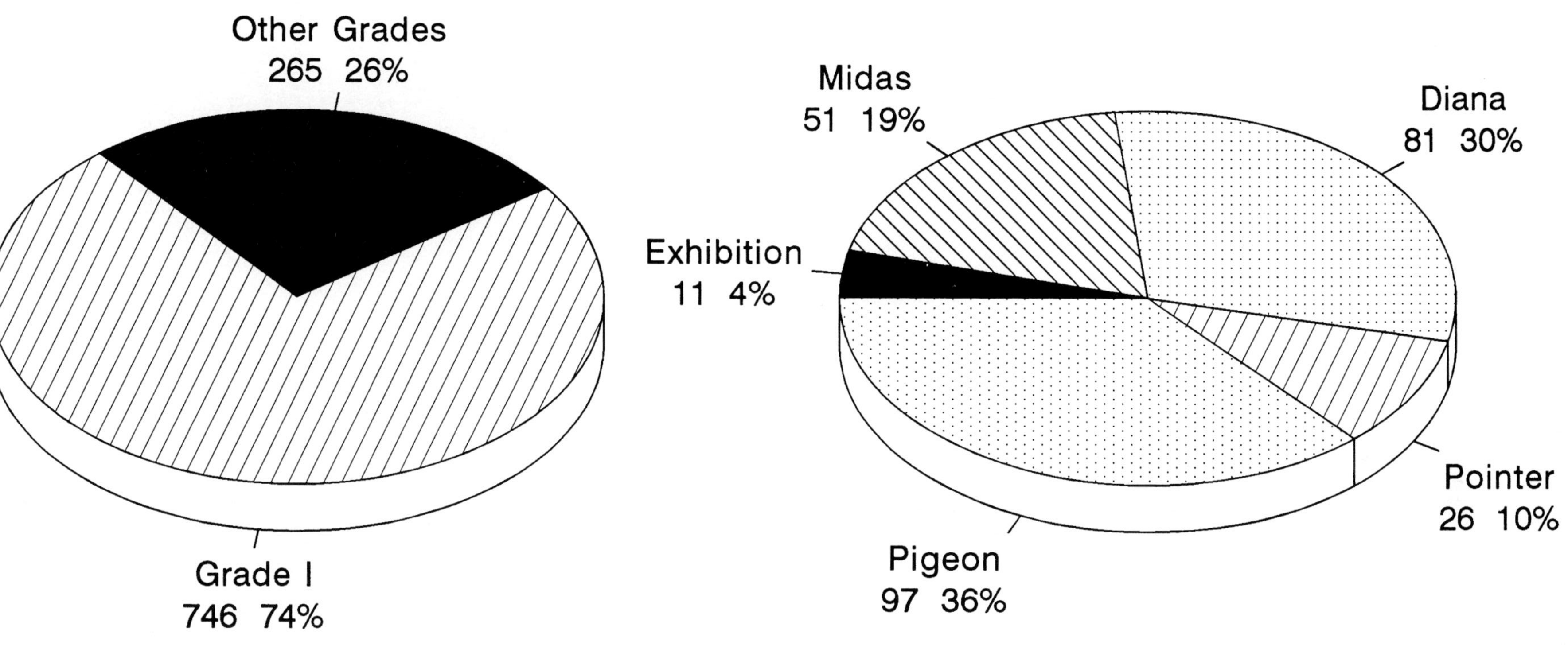

Chart 4-21

BROWNING HIGH GRADE SUPERLIGHT SALES
North America
1971 - 1977

Gauge & Grade	1971	1972	1973	1974	1975	1976	1977	Total	% of Total
12 ga. Pigeon	0	14	23	21	9	13	8	88	18%
20 ga. Pigeon	0	17	35	12	8	19	6	97	20%
Total Pigeon	*0*	*31*	*58*	*33*	*17*	*32*	*14*	*185*	*39%*
12 ga. Pointer	1	2	1	2	4	1	0	11	2%
20 ga. Pointer	0	2	13	6	3	1	1	26	5%
Total Pointer	*1*	*4*	*14*	*8*	*7*	*2*	*1*	*37*	*8%*
12 ga. Diana	0	13	9	18	6	9	13	68	14%
20 ga. Diana	1	14	0	1	23	24	18	81	17%
Total Diana	*1*	*27*	*9*	*19*	*29*	*33*	*31*	*149*	*31%*
12 ga. Midas	0	6	6	0	4	9	10	35	7%
20 ga. Midas	0	7	6	4	8	12	14	51	11%
Total Midas	*0*	*13*	*12*	*4*	*12*	*21*	*24*	*86*	*18%*
12 ga. Exhibition	0	0	0	5	0	7	0	12	3%
20 ga. Exhibition	0	0	0	9	0	2	0	11	2%
Total Exhibition	*0*	*0*	*0*	*14*	*0*	*9*	*0*	*23*	*5%*
Grand Total	2	75	93	78	65	97	70	480	100%

Table 4-12

Between 1967 and 1977, Browning did sell in North America 28 gauge and .410 bore Superlight Superposed on a special order basis. Collectors and Browning dealers estimate that there were somewhere between 50 and 60 28 gauge Superlights sold during this period in Grades I through Midas. They also estimate that there were between 100 and 150 .410 Superlights sold in Grades I through Midas. This information is based only on conjecture and cannot be verified as to specific numbers. In short, it is a conclusion based only on known examples and not substantiated by company sales data. In any event, these Superlights do exist and are considered rare and difficult to locate for the shooter or collector.

Browning Liège Sales 1973-1977 See Chart 4-22

The introduction of the Liège shotgun in 1973 signaled an attempt to turn back the continued upward retail price rise of the Superposed by offering a less expensive alternative. The undertaking failed partly because the gun was priced too high based on the merits of its features. The Liège model managed to generate sales of only 3,013 guns between 1973 and 1977. Chart 4-22 illustrates clearly the initial sales of 2,273 guns in 1973 and the abrupt decline in sales from then on.

This eight-year period in the history of the Superposed and the Browning Company represents a litmus test for the survival of both. There were many distractions during this interval: law suits had to be defended against, company expansion plans had to be closely monitored, difficult challenges regarding inflation and rapidly changing business cycles had to be dealt with, as well as the constant day-to-day demands of running a large dynamic corporation. All of these factors influenced the survival of the Superposed. The decision was made to completely revitalize the Superposed line with the introduction of the Presentation Series. The traditional Superposed was no longer sustainable in its present form. Deliveries could not be met and prices had soared beyond reason. The Presentation Series was the Superposed's final opportunity to survive as a production gun.

BROWNING LIÈGE SALES, NORTH AMERICA
1973-1977
3,500
3,000
2,500
2,000
1,500
1,000
500
0
1973
1974
1975
1976
1977
Total
Total Sales
2,273
658
68
13
1
3,013

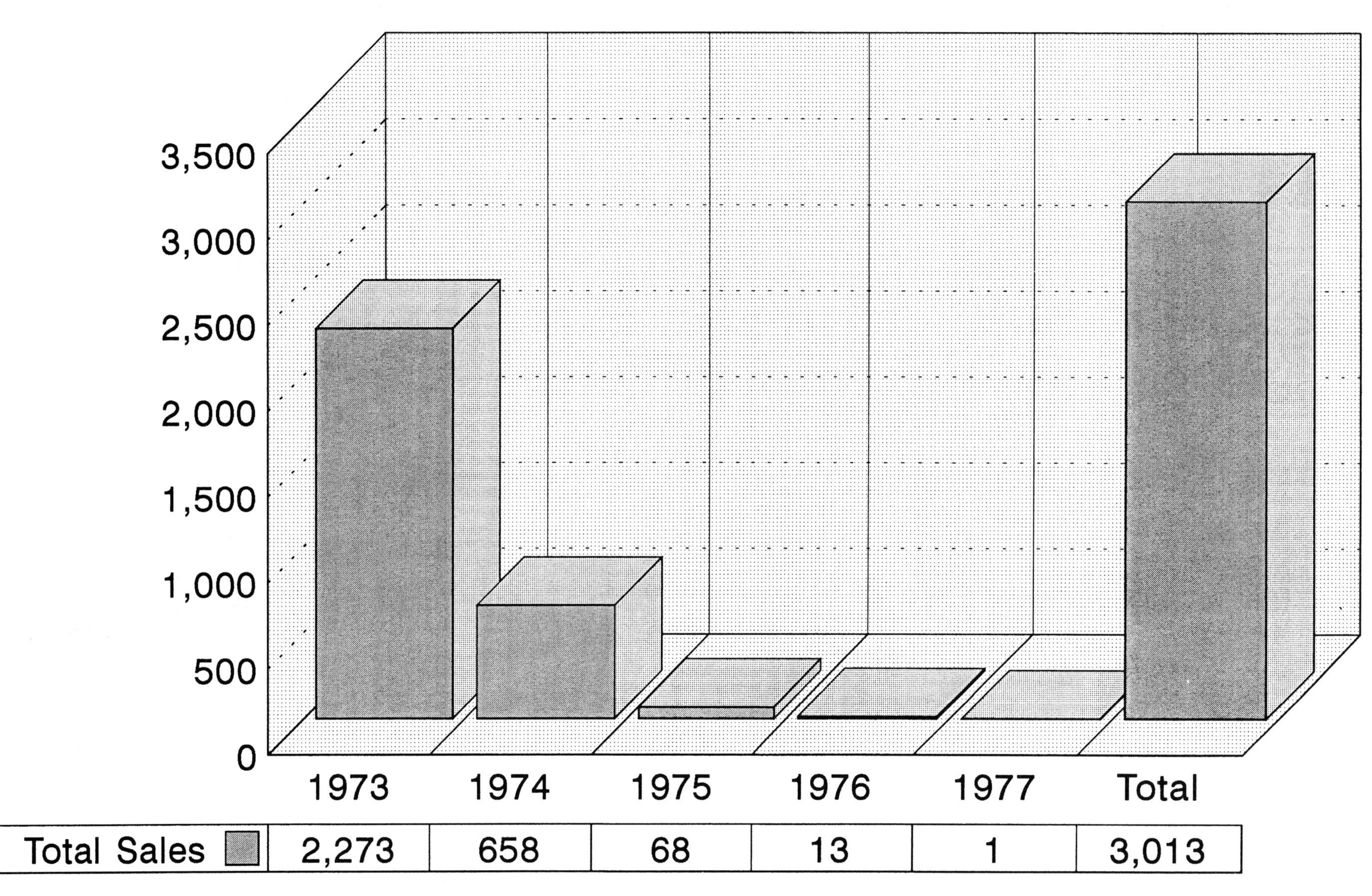

Chart 4-22

BROWNING SUPERPOSED SALES
NORTH AMERICA
1964-1977

Type	Grade I	Pigeon Grade	Pointer Grade	Diana Grade	Midas Grade	Exhibition Grade	Total
12 Gauge							
Broadway	15,247	1594	65	793	409	64	18,172
Trap	7,126	666	32	401	182	11	8,418
Total Trap	***22,373***	***2,260***	***97***	***1,194***	***591***	***75***	***26,590***
12 ga. Skeet	8,397	699	27	383	159	28	9,693
All ga. Skeet Set	368	43	0	59	52	0	522
Total Target	***31,138***	***3,002***	***124***	***1,636***	***802***	***103***	***36,805***
Magnum	6,814	169	12	146	64	1	7,206
12 ga. Hunting 28"	15,220	684	43	400	162	59	16,568
12 ga. Hunting 26.5"	10,611	811	105	450	133	59	12,166
Total Hunting	***25,831***	***1,495***	***148***	***834***	***295***	***118***	***28,734***
12 ga. Superlight 28"	205	0	0	0	1	6	213
12 ga. Superlight 26.5"	4,174	86	11	59	32	6	4,369
12 ga. Superlight Special Order	13	3	0	9	2	0	27
Total 12 ga. Superlight	***4,392***	***89***	***11***	***68***	***35***	***12***	***4,608***
12 ga. Special Order	1,414	434	71	429	218	10	2,576
Total All 12 gauge	**69,589**	**5,189**	**366**	**3,113**	**1,414**	**244**	**79,929**
20 Gauge							
20 ga. Skeet	4,056	370	18	214	74	17	4,749
20 ga. Hunting 28"	8,579	492	23	217	95	34	9,440
20 ga. Hunting 26.5"	15,484	998	94	586	139	28	17,330
Total Hunting	***24,063***	***1,490***	***117***	***803***	***234***	***62***	***26,770***
20 ga. Superlight 26.5"	735	97	25	69	38	11	976
20 ga. Superlight Special Order	11	0	1	11	13	0	35
20 ga. Special Order	752	334	58	396	124	19	1,683
Total All 20 gauge	**29,617**	**2,291**	**219**	**1,493**	**483**	**109**	**34,213**
28 Gauge							
28 ga. Skeet	944	109	5	69	35	0	1,162
28 ga. Hunting 28"*	477	106	9	80	30	10	714
28 ga. Hunting 26.5"*	541	126	30	85	50	10	842
Total 28 ga. Hunting	***1,018***	***232***	***39***	***165***	***80***	***20***	***1,556***
28 ga. Special Order	95	25	7	25	22	4	178
Total All 28 gauge	**2,057**	**366**	**51**	**259**	**119**	**24**	**2,896**
.410 Bore							
.410 Skeet	1,429	119	4	83	52	0	1,687
.410 Hunting 28"*	518	95	8	57	39	10	727
.410 Hunting 26.5" *	577	158	50	122	52	10	969
Total .410 Hunting	***1,095***	***253***	***58***	***179***	***91***	***20***	***1,696***
.410 Special Order	8	1	25	2	4	4	44
Total All .410 bore	**2,532**	**373**	**87**	**264**	**147**	**23**	**3,427**
Grand Total	**103,795**	**8,219**	**723**	**5,129**	**2,163**	**400**	**120,465**

* 28 gauge and .410 bore Hunting models also include Superlight models as well.

Table 4-11

Chapter 5

The Presentation Superposed Era: 1977-1984

This eight-year period in the history of the Superposed and the Browning Company marked a watershed for both. For the first time in its history the company was not owned and controlled by the Browning family. For the first time since 1960 the company was privately held and controlled by foreign interest. Also for the first time, the well-known and admired engraving was chemically etched instead of hand cut.[1] The famous over and under gun was by all outward appearances different from anything that had come before.

The two companies who were so different from each other, and who for so long had such a close association in so many successful Browning designs, were now one. The transition during this union was surprisingly smooth considering that the relationship between the two companies had been turned on its head. Both shared the same basic goals and for the most part Browning USA was allowed to pursue these goals with a relatively free hand. But both companies were still going through transformations with unforeseen consequences. It was during this final period, when the Superposed was still considered a production gun, that the direction and energies of both corporations would finally reach fruition. Understanding this metamorphosis is to understand the demise of the Superposed as a production gun and an end to the ready availability of a high quality, hand built, hand fitted shotgun in the American marketplace.

Browning and FN: The Consolidation Phase

With the acquisition of the Browning Company, Fabrique Nationale was pursuing its goal of diversification which had begun several years earlier. Browning management's keen awareness of FN's growing labor cost and indifferent deliveries were well-known to FN's top management. They realized that because of escalating production costs, the manufacturing of certain sporting arms in its Herstal plant had to be either discontinued or moved elsewhere.

The irony here is hard to ignore because FN finally realized what Browning's management had known for decades: Profitable sporting arms production at Herstal was no longer viable. For this reason FN agreed with and encouraged Browning to expand its Japanese sporting arms line. Fabrique Nationale began to rely more on its assembly plant operations in Portugal. Both companies continued in this direction into the late 1970s and early 1980s, with the B-92 rifle in .44 Magnum introduced in 1979, the B-80 gas operated shotgun introduced in 1980, the Model 81 BLR rifle introduced in 1982, the Citori Grade VI shotgun introduced in 1983, and the BPS Upland Special shotgun first offered in 1984.

After the acquisition of Browning by Fabrique Nationale, the task of managing the company continued to fall on the broad shoulders of Harm Will-

[1] This was not the case for the P-4 Grade, which was entirely hand cut. A further discussion of the Presentation Series follows in the section on engraving in this chapter.

iams. Harm worked closely with George Bya of FN in order to reach realistic goals based on the new ownership. Browning's financial statements and records were no longer made public after the sale to FN, but the company's economic condition did begin to recover in the late 1970s. Partially responsible for this was the sale of various boat-building companies that were not profitable. With these enterprises no longer an impediment on company profits, financial improvement slowly began.

In 1980 Don Gobel was named president of the Browning Company. He was formerly president of Weaver Rifle Scope Company and vice president of firearms at Winchester. Courtesy Browning Company.

Another positive aspect that encouraged improved profits and sales was the value of the dollar to the yen. When the value of the yen was favorable to Browning, profits were easier to manage than when the value of the yen was too high compared to the dollar. The latter reduced the company's ability to show a positive return at the same retail price level. During the late 1970s the value of the yen to the dollar remained in Browning's favor, assisting profits the company made on its Japanese produced sporting guns.[2]

In 1980 Harmon Williams, president of Browning, retired after twenty-eight years with the company. Don Gobel, formerly president of Weaver Rifle Scope and vice president of firearms at Winchester, was named president of Browning USA. In 1981 Grant Goddard, executive vice president, retired after thirty-three years with Browning. The old guard was changing, as were the times, and Browning was beginning a new era under the tireless leadership of Don Gobel. Armed with a carefully choreographed business plan, Browning management moved forward to meet the bold new challenges of becoming the world market leader in hunting, fishing, and outdoor equipment.

If the position of the company's financial condition continued to show improvement during the period of the late 1970s and early 1980s, then it must be pointed out that this was not the case for Browning's Superposed Presentation Series. In 1977, the first year of the Presentation Series, Browning recorded sales of only 151 guns. This amounted to gross sales of less than $400,000. Business improved considerably to 426 guns the next year, but this would mark the high point of sales for the Presentation Series production period.

The declining sales of the Superposed and its offshoots was for the most part counterbalanced by the continued expansion into affiliated products by both Browning and Fabrique Nationale. For its part, Browning consolidated its diversification by making those profitable divisions even more so through continued expansion of product lines and increased market share. Boats, clothing, fishing gear, racquetball, and golf products all helped to move the company's dependence away from what was now a very expensive low volume product line: the Superposed. Fabrique Nationale, through its subsidiary FN Sports, extended these new lines into worldwide markets, even adding a windsurfing board to its sporting goods line in Europe. As FN historian Claude Gaier so aptly states, "With an extensive commercial network at its disposal, as well as various worldwide sources of supply, FN Sports had become a multinational group in its own right, enjoying considerable potential and prestige."[3] In 1982 FN Sports assumed the name of Browning SA and expanded into Africa, Latin America, and Asia.

This period of growth and expansion for Fabrique Nationale was not to endure. The worldwide recession of the early 1980s was to have a serious impact on FN. The recession unmasked severe economic deficiencies, such as a shortage of capital and high labor cost. The efforts and goals of growth and expansion were not sustainable for

[2] Grant F. Goddard, interview with the author, February 22, 1995.

[3] Claude Gaier, *FN 100 Years: The Story of the Great Liège Company, 1889-1989*, p. 142.

The service personnel at Browning's Arnold, Missouri, facility in 1983. In the front row from left to right: Mike O'Brien, Jack Callahan, Larry Brueggemann, Connie Kirkland, Howard Maas, Fred Haunold, Charlie Kelsay, Paul Fuchs, Merrill Helms, and Tommy McGhee. In the back row from left to right: Roy Nobbe, Gene Smugala, Tom Mayer, Earl Womble, Vearl Brown, Dennis Nobbe, John Teague, Dave Schiller, George Hubbard, John Woesthaus, Norman Pyeatt, Dan Warren, Kent Sutton, Rob Semonis, and Mark Burns. Courtesy Browning Company.

FN. By 1984 the company was beginning to consider a totally different objective: consolidation. And so the end of the Superposed as a production gun in the Browning product line also marked the end of economic recovery for Fabrique Nationale. Browning USA did in fact continue to prosper under the steady guidance of Don Gobel, but only because the company had focused on outdoor merchandise that identified with the legacy of the Browning name—a name that was synonymous with high quality and rugged dependability.

Presentation Era Engraving

In 1977 Louis Vrancken, FN's master engraver, left the company to pursue his own independent future. Long recognized as one of the world's leading firearms engravers, Vrancken's talents were in high demand from customers all over the world. He did agree to give Fabrique Nationale one thousand hours a year to its engraving projects, so his strong influence continued on special engraving assignments. Vrancken's influence was seen until his death in December of 1983.[4] His place at FN was taken by José Baerten, André Dierckx, and the inveterate André Watrin. Before his departure from FN, Louis Vrancken was responsible for developing the engraving designs for the Superposed Presentation Series. He was also responsible for the expanded offerings of engraving patterns FN made available on its own Superposed guns offered in its European markets.

Perhaps one of the most gifted engravers ever to work at Fabrique Nationale was José Baerten. Born in Heure-le-Romain, Belgium, on June 29, 1938, José Baerten began as an apprentice at FN under Felix Funken in 1955. In 1977, at the age of 39, he became a master engraver. His principal role was to create designs, but his artistry with a hammer and burin is equal to the world's best engravers. The demand for engraved guns had fallen steadily during the 1970s and work was becoming harder to obtain. FN was having difficulty keeping its engravers fully occupied. Prices for engraving had risen sharply, which in turn affected demand. The decision was made to solve several problems at once. In order to increase the engravers' work, to keep prices from rising, and to revitalize interest in high grade Superposed, FN devised a totally new engraving format.

The redesign of the Superposed engraving patterns fell to Louis Vrancken, a decision that insured renewed interest in engraved Superposed. Unfortunately, the wide choice of patterns and elaborate style and coverage did nothing to hold the line on prices. The notion that acid etching would lower engraving costs was seized upon to solve the problem of cost. Actually, acid etching or photo engraving had been used by Fabrique Nationale since the early 1970s on some models in an

---

[4] Tom Koessl, *Browning Collectors Association Newsletter*, Vol. VII, No. 5, March/April 1986.

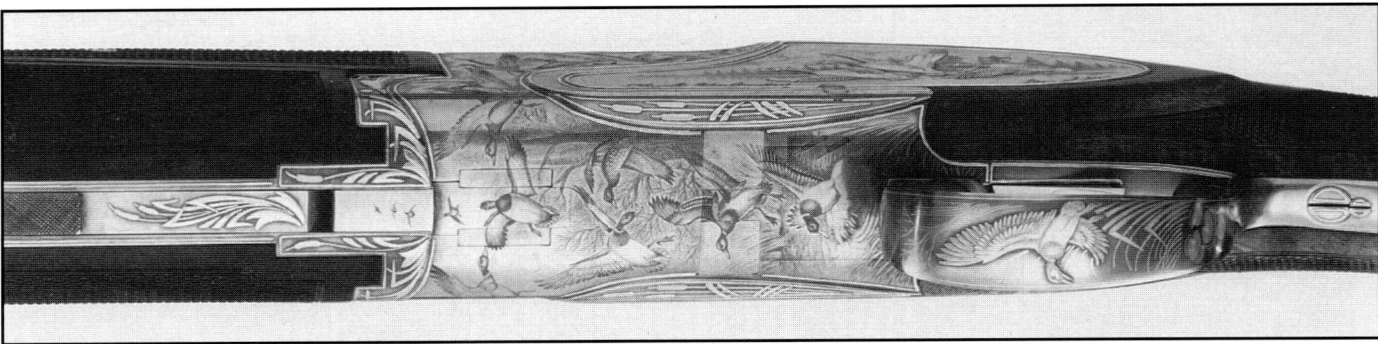

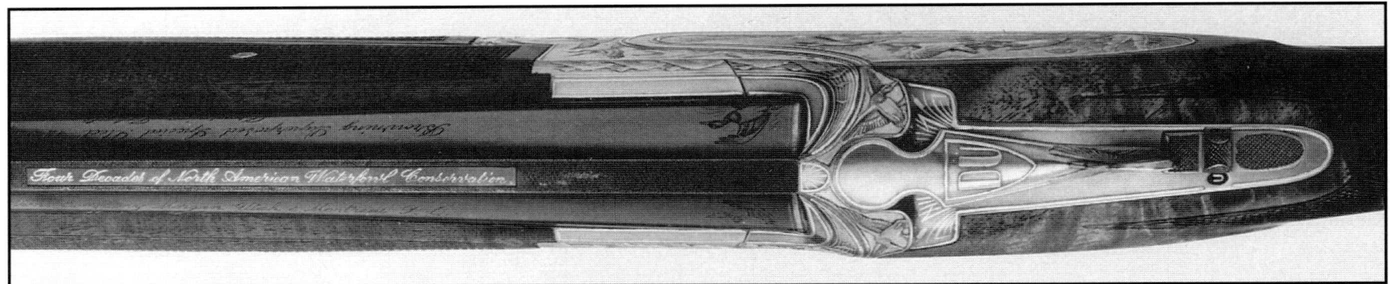

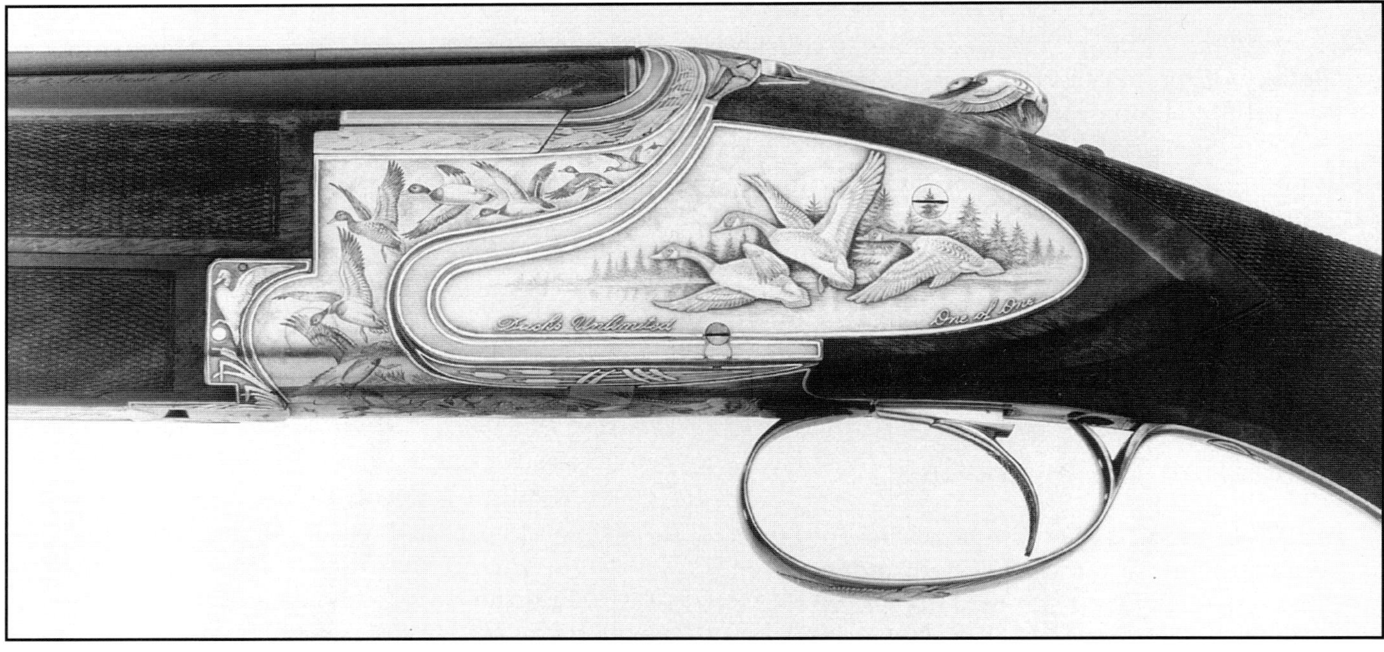

This extraordinary one and only Browning Superposed was built in 1978 to commemorate four decades of North American waterfowl conservation through the efforts of Ducks Unlimited. It was delivered to Browning in December of 1978 and was the focal point of a Ducks Unlimited fundraising effort in 1979. The birds on the sideplate are gold on a gray background; the rest of the ducks, a total of almost one hundred individual birds, are executed in extremely fine detail. Notice the design and shape of the top lever. The beautiful sequence of ducks executed on the bottom of the gun gives a sense of movement and drama. The designer and principal engraver on this remarkable Superposed was Louis Vrancken. Courtesy Fabrique Nationale Archives.

attempt to reduce cost. This process, which produced near perfect results without the need for an engraver, was looked upon by the Custom Shop engravers with contempt. From their perspective the use of this new process was akin to counterfeiting. The engravers refused to sign those Presentation guns that they had partially hand engraved.

This situation led to a strike by the engravers, who considered acid etching an insult to their skill and profession. Cooler heads prevailed, and most of the engravers returned to work but still refused to sign acid etched Superposed. Browning USA had not been informed of the decision to acid etch the P Series Superposed, and management was displeased with the decision but was powerless to stop it. All of this was for naught, for as we have seen, prices of the Presentation Series guns continued to escalate despite these cost cutting measures.

The Creativity of José Baerten

An Engraving Portfolio

José Baerten was a master engraver at the age of thirty-nine. Upon Louis Vrancken's departure in 1977, Baerten assumed leadership of the Custom Shop and became FN's chief engraver. He remained in that capacity until 1987, when all of the engravers left the Custom Shop to establish their own engraving concern. Courtesy Fabrique Nationale Archives.

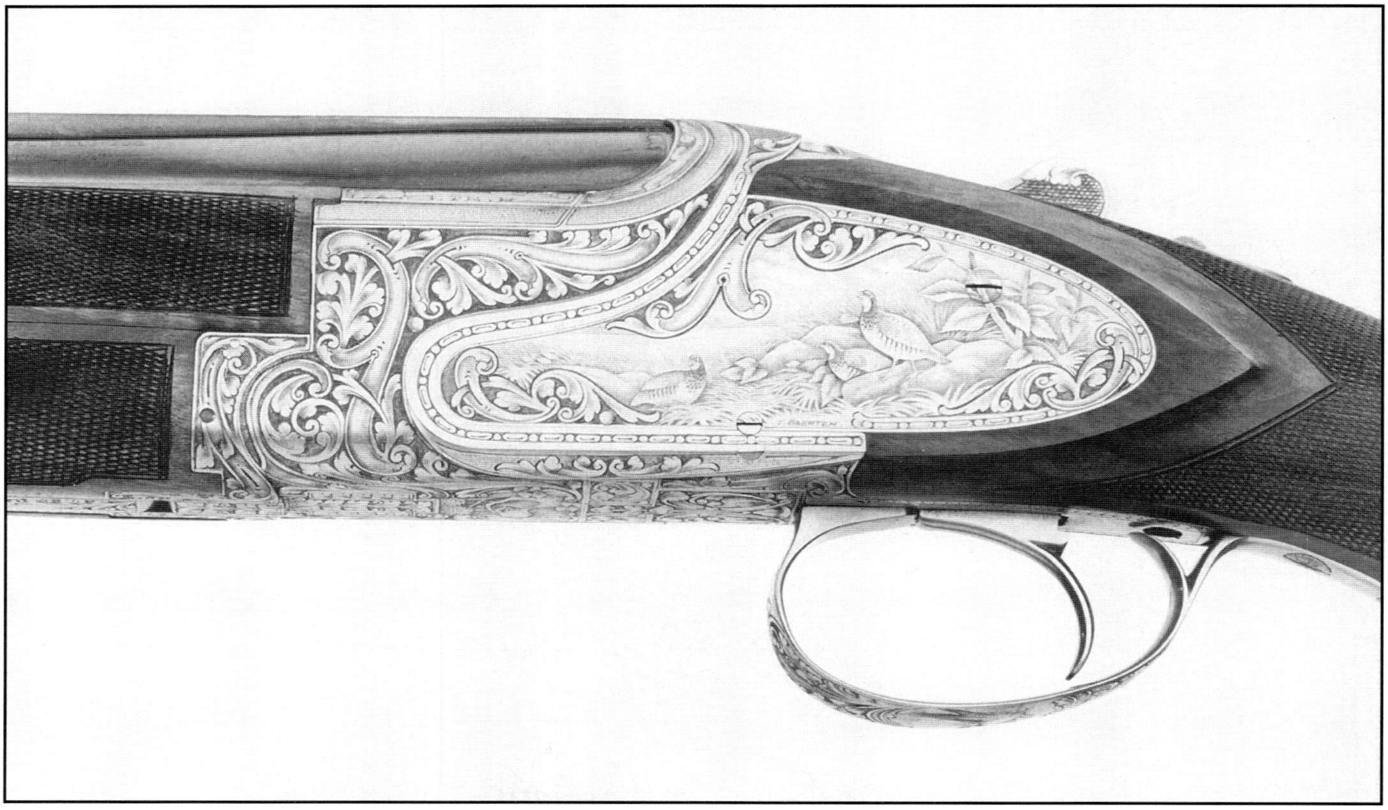

A late 1970s creation by José Baerten. This FN Superposed features sideplates engraved with elegant, finely detailed game scenes. Baerten's placement of his subjects makes them appear realistic and true to nature. Courtesy Fabrique Nationale Archives.

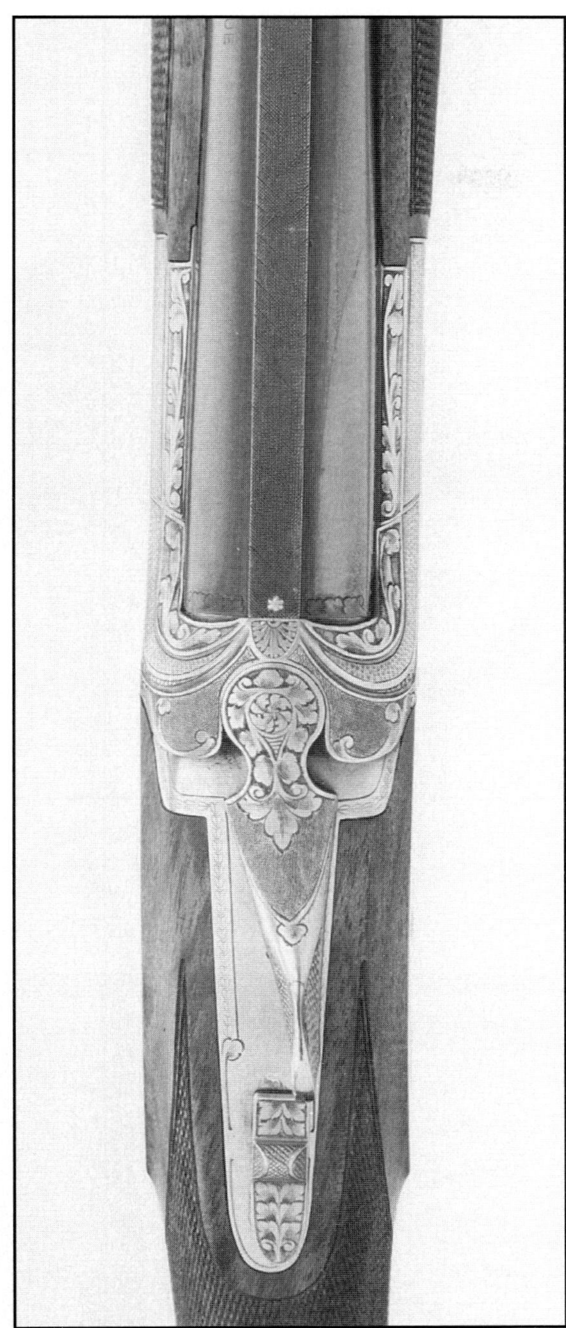

A top and bottom view of Baerten's work. The top was rather sparse, but finely hammered. Notice that the rib was hand matted. The bottom shows one of Baerten's favorite subjects, a retriever's head. The scrollwork treatment gives the bottom of the gun an imposing appearance. Courtesy Fabrique Nationale Archives.

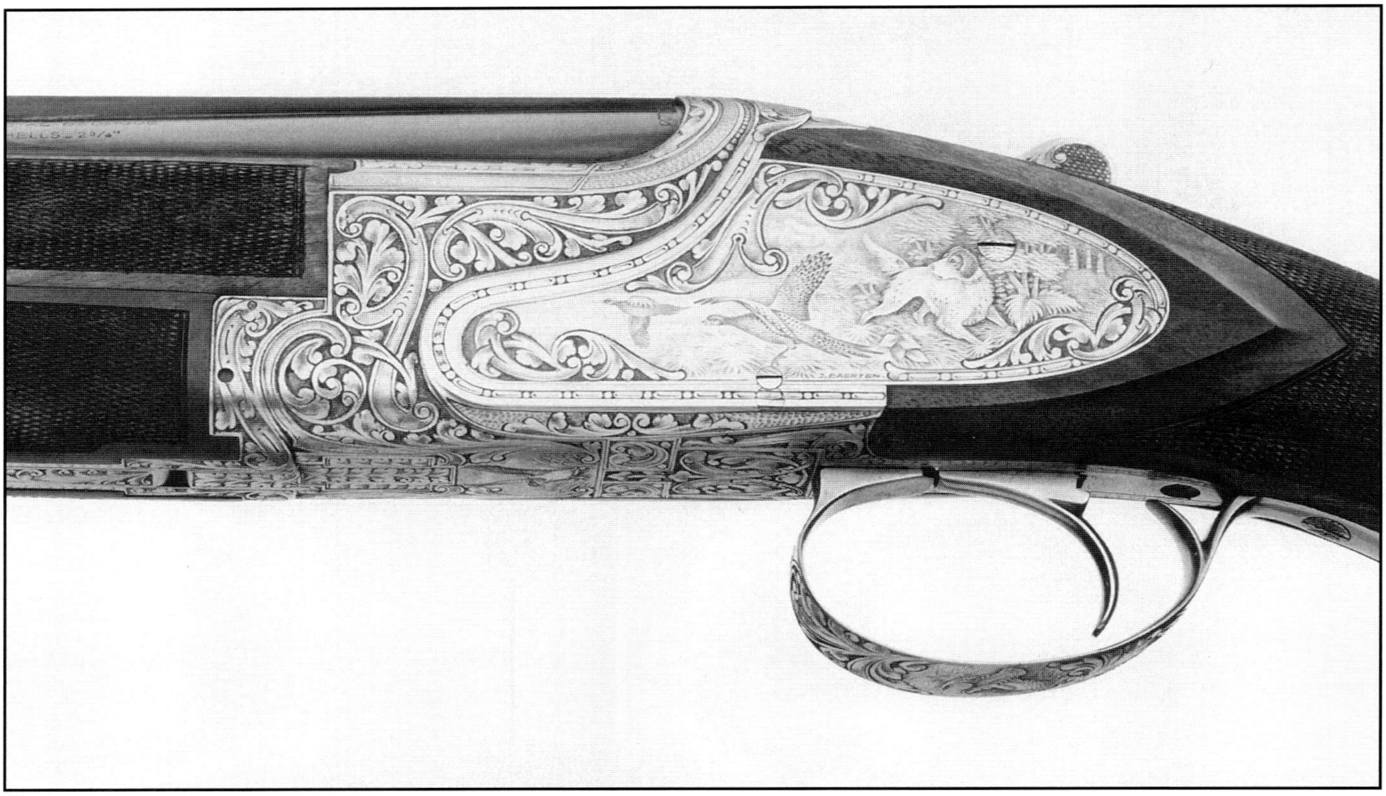

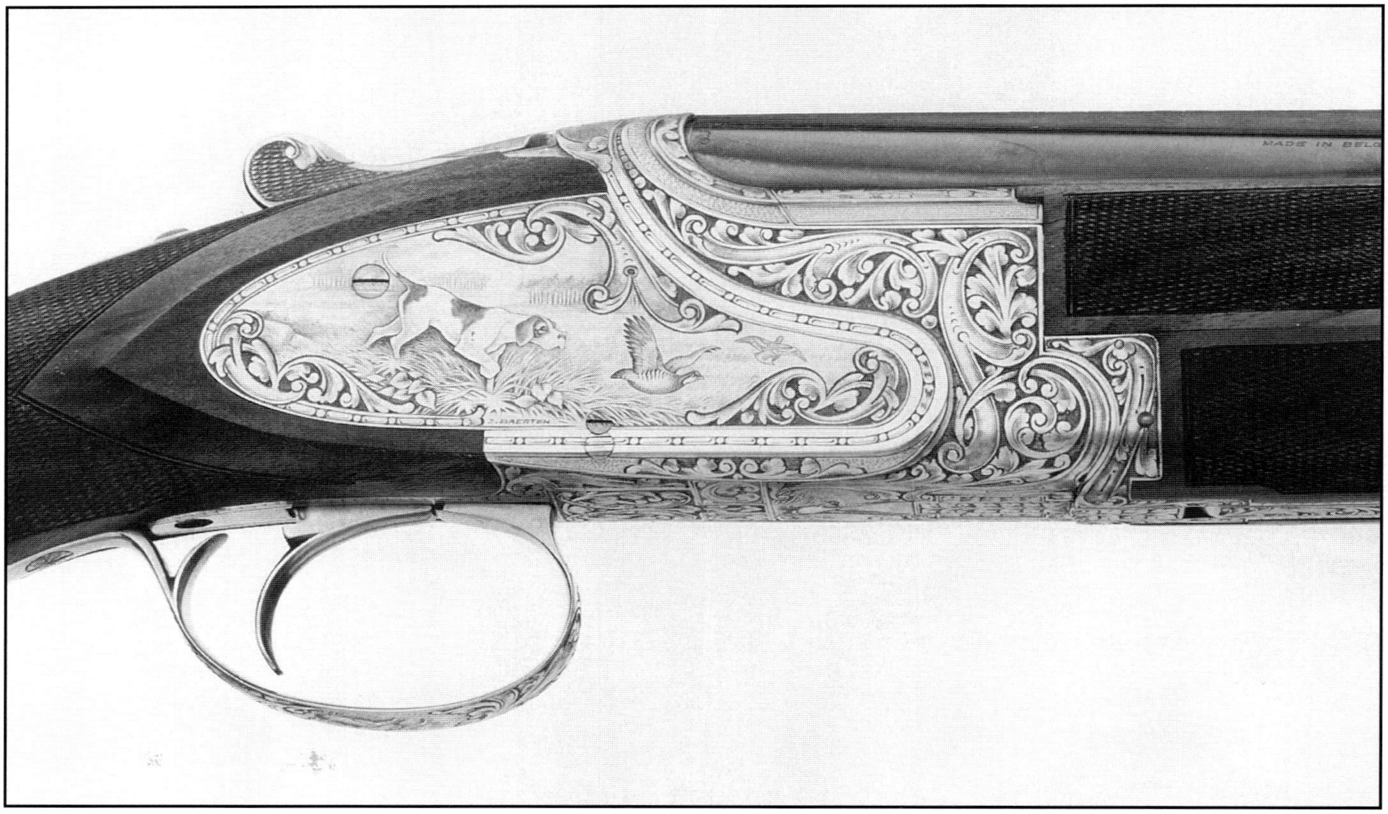

An FN Superposed with sideplates designed and executed by José Baerten. In this example Baerten places dogs and birds in his scenes. On the left side he has given the dog an expression of surprise at the flushing birds. Baerten's realism is perhaps his greatest characteristic and asset as an engraver. Courtesy Fabrique Nationale Archives.

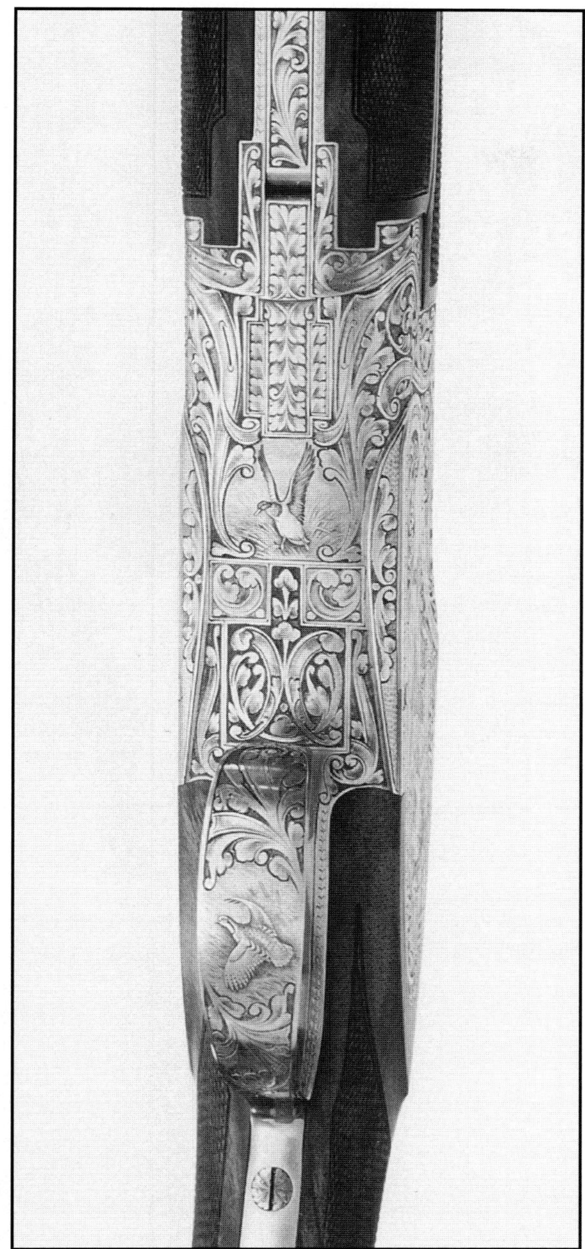

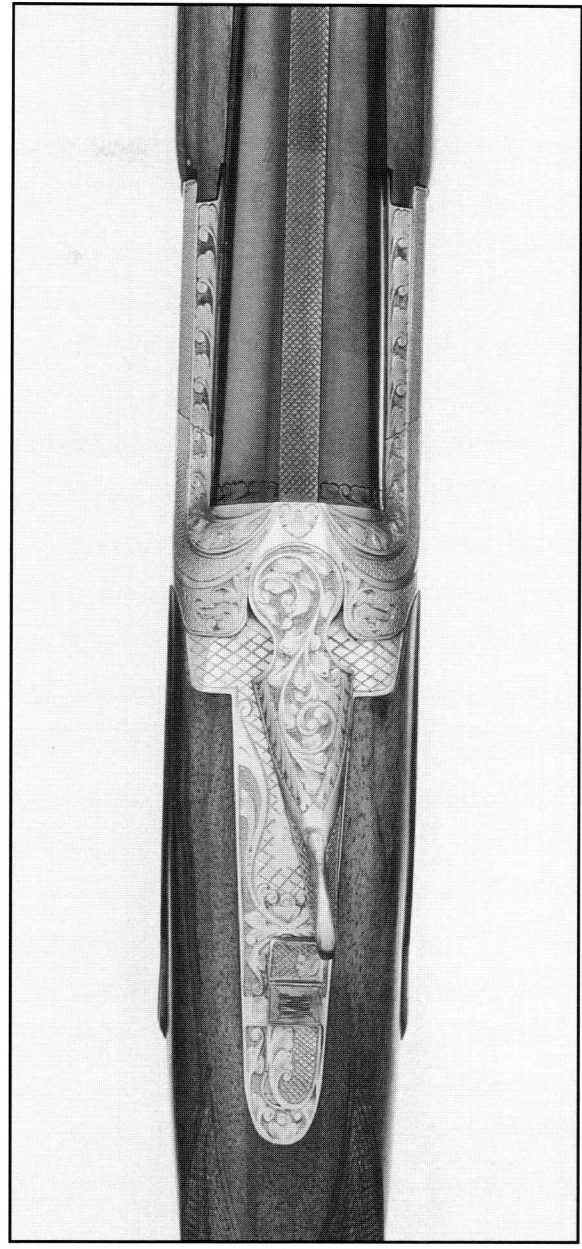

The top view of the Baerten Superposed shows an almost medieval appearance. The bottom of the gun has the usual Baerten look, with impressive scrollwork surrounding elegantly executed birds. Courtesy Fabrique Nationale Archives.

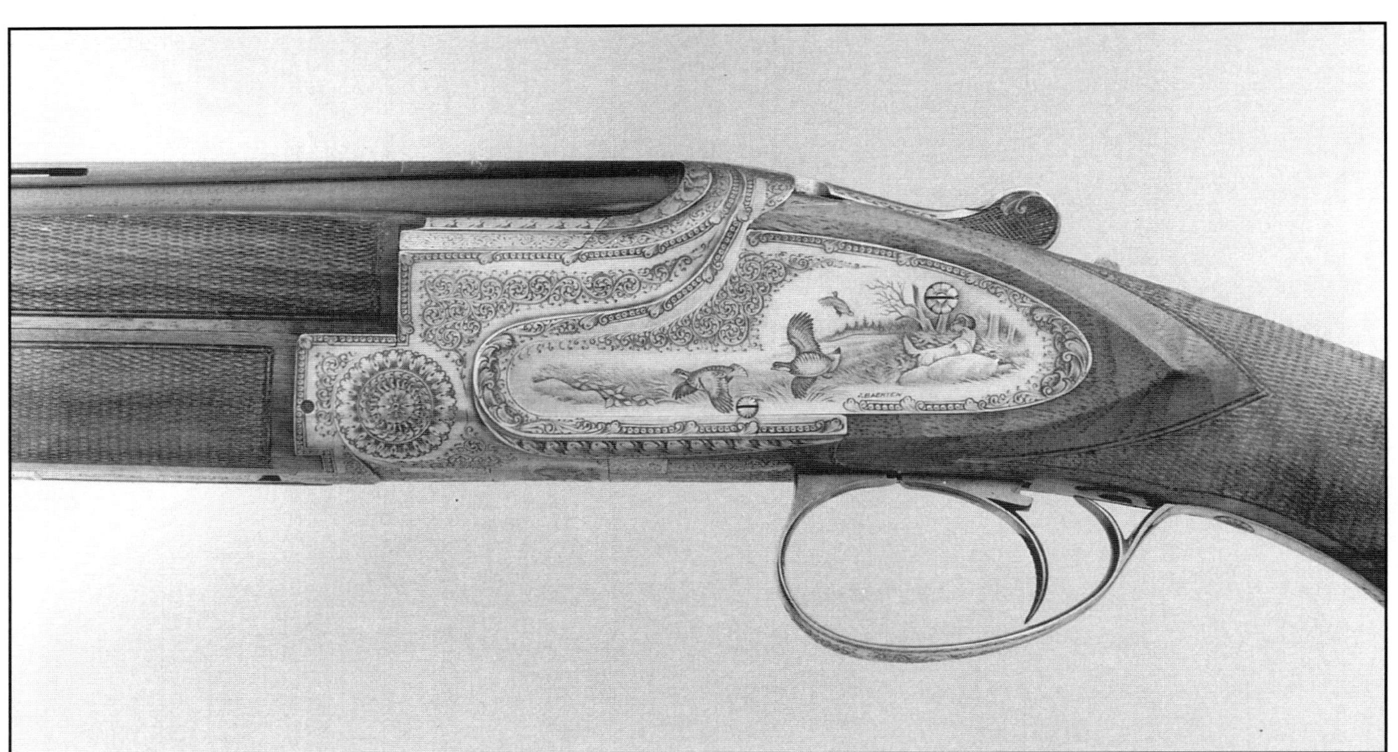

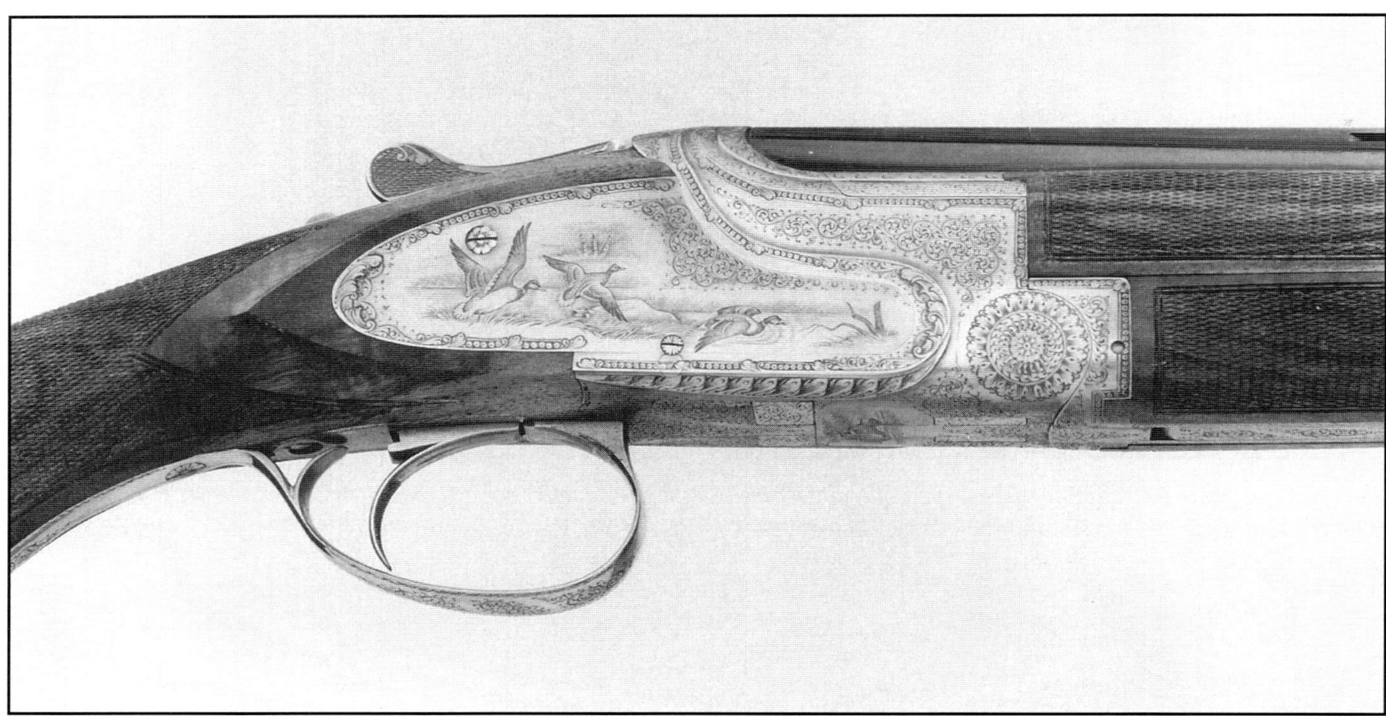

The custom design for this 20 gauge FN Superposed was created by José Baerten in the late 1970s and illustrates very clearly his talent for designing game scenes that seem to come to life because of his expert composition. Baerten utilizes the sideplate area to its foremost potential. Courtesy Fabrique Nationale Archives.

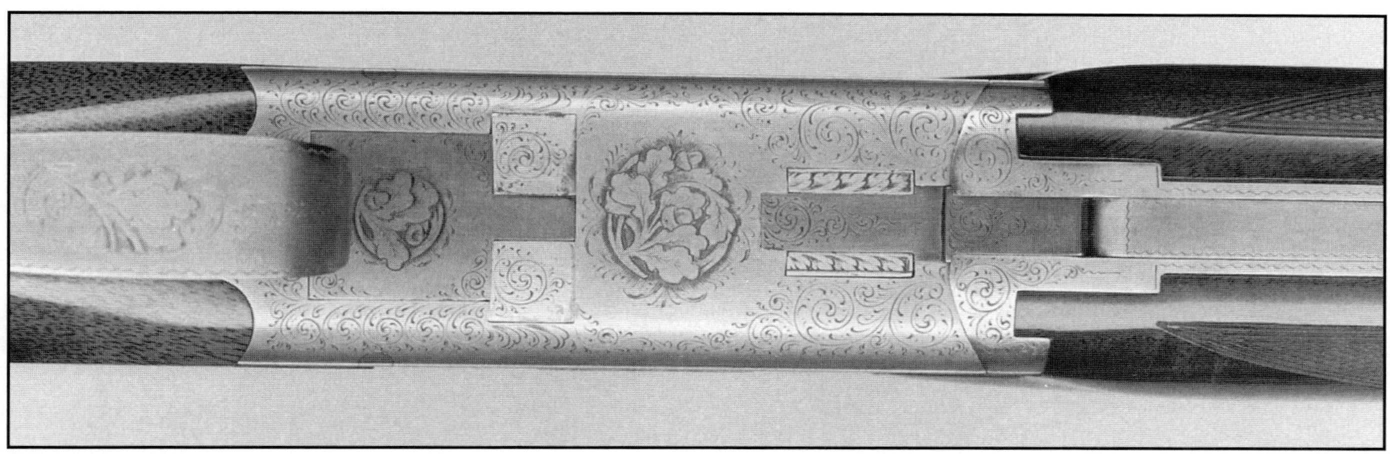

The basic P-1 engraving pattern from the underside of the receiver. Courtesy Browning Company.

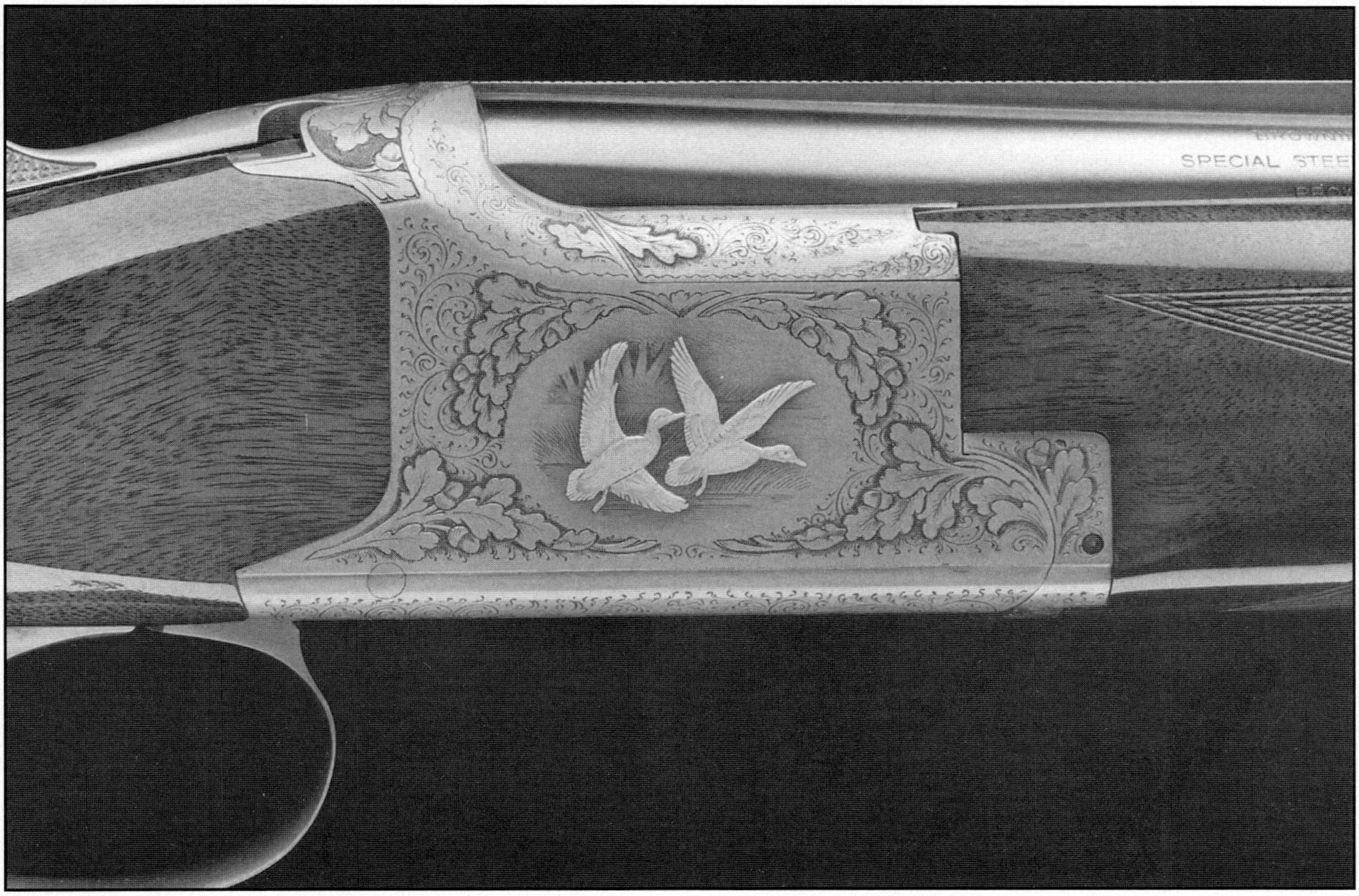

A close-up view of a P-1K with mallard ducks. This particular variation featured gold inlaid game birds. Courtesy Browning Company.

The Superposed Presentation Series offered a broad array of engraving options from which the customer could choose. The Presentation Series was divided into four grades from Presentation One up to Presentation Four. The higher the grade, the more intricate and profuse the ornamentation.

Presentation One (P-1): This was the lowest priced Presentation grade, but it also gave the buyer the most choices. The P-1 had a basic pattern that featured fine scroll on the outer edges of the silver gray frame, with oak leaf clusters near the center and on the bottom of the frame. The customer had a choice of six animal scenes, which were given letter designations, to be engraved on both sides of the frame. The scenes included ringneck pheasants (A), bob-white quail (B), English pointer (C), Labrador retriever with duck (D), mallard ducks (E), and Canada geese (F). All of these

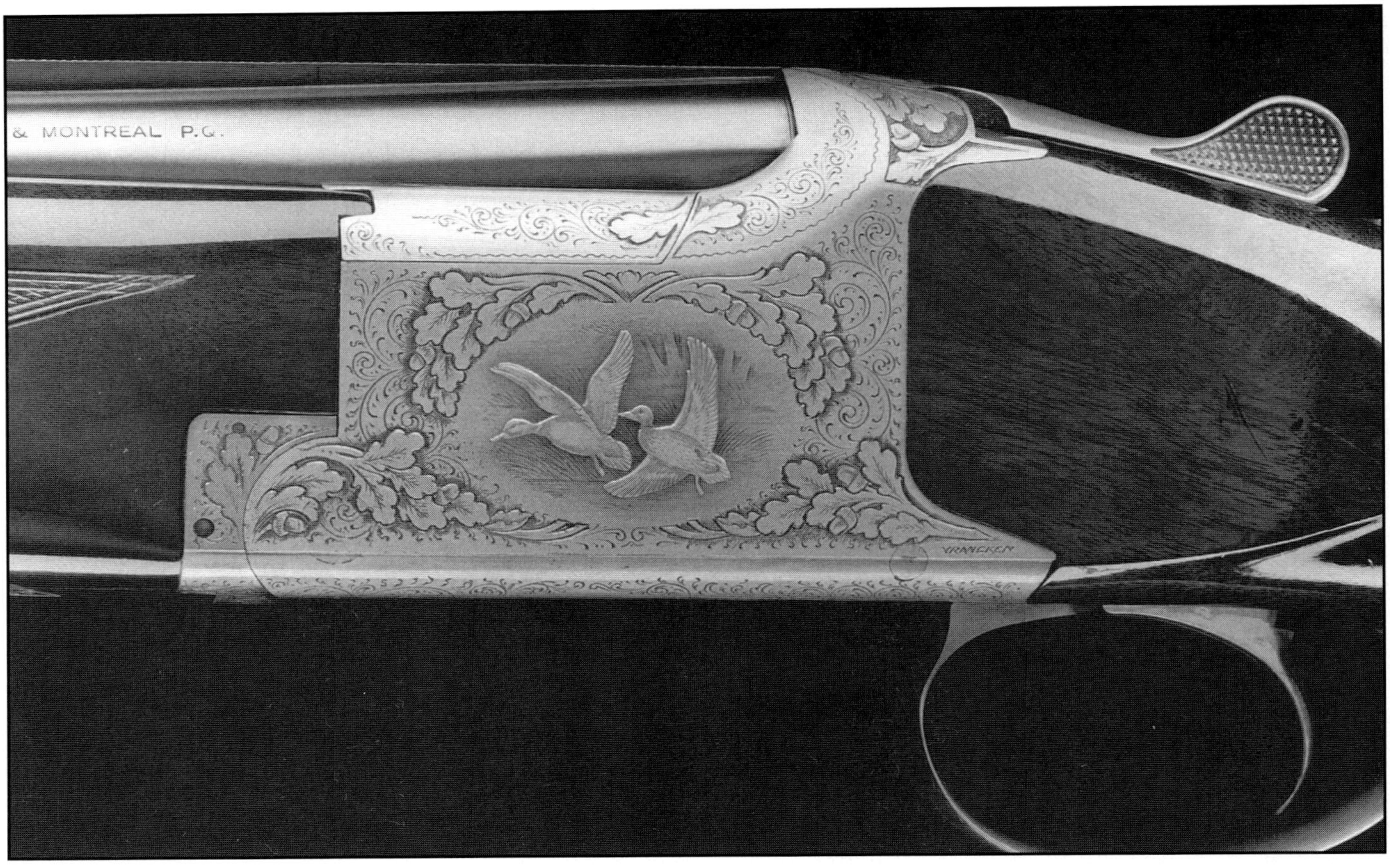

This is one of the very early P-1 Grades in which the game scene was most likely engraved by hand. In this case the gun is signed by Louis Vrancken, who was responsible for the design of the Presentation Series patterns. Most P-1 Grades were acid etched and not signed by the engraver. Courtesy Browning Company.

This is a P-1C Grade with pointer. Notice the rounded frame of this Presentation Series Superposed. Almost all P guns had rounded frames. Courtesy Browning Company.

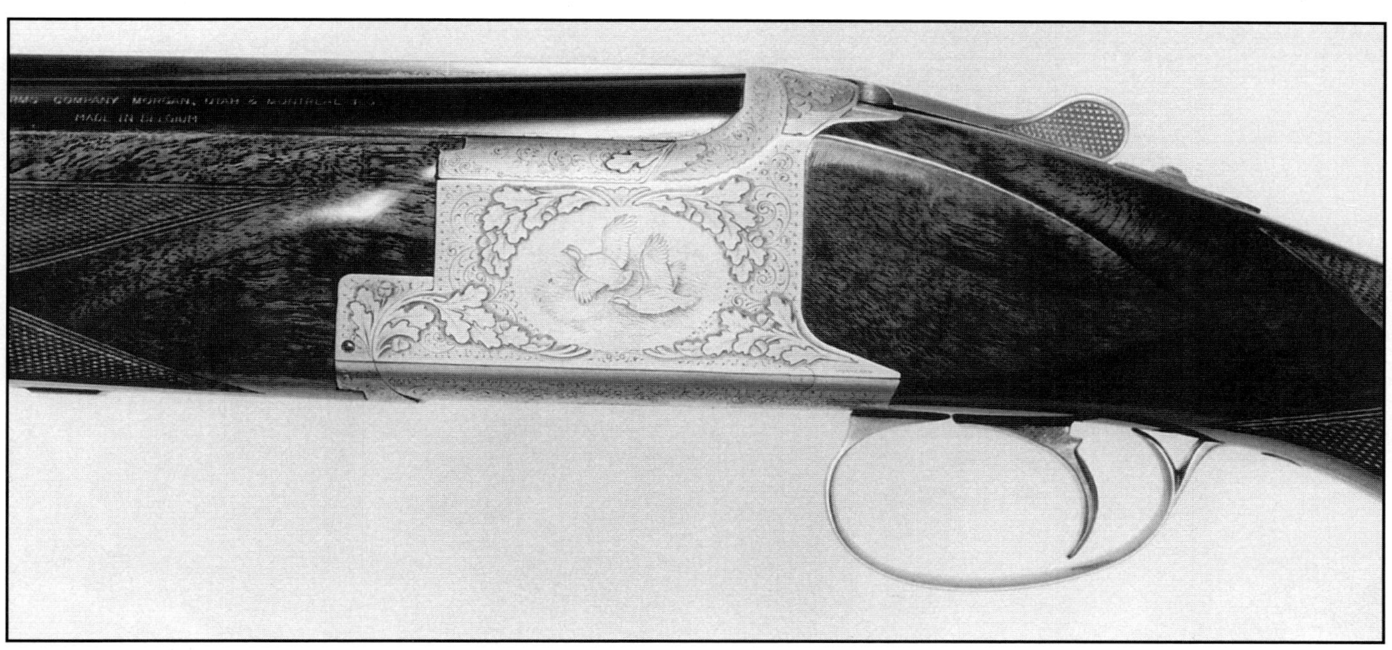

This P-1B Grade is signed by Vrancken, indicating an early gun with hand engraved game scenes. Courtesy Browning Company.

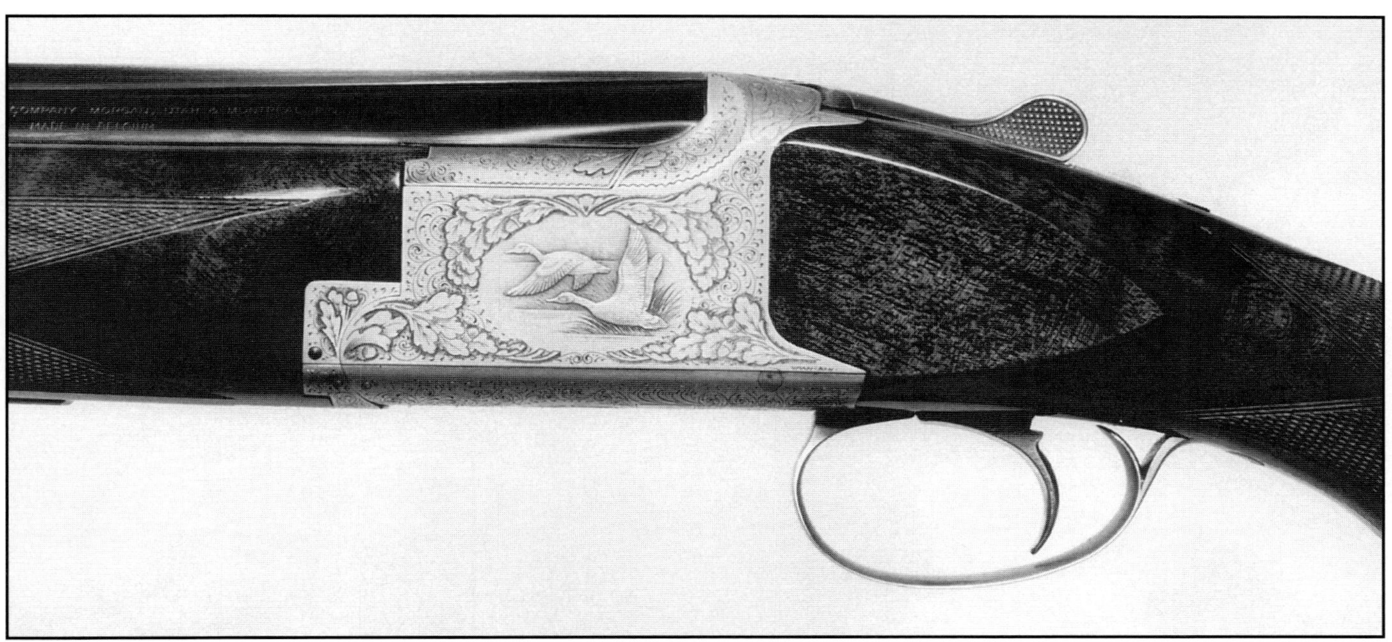

Louis Vrancken signed this early P-1L with gold inlaid Canada geese. Courtesy Browning Company.

scenes were engraved on a grayed frame. In addition to these choices, the P-1 was also available with gold inlaid birds or dogs on a blued or grayed frame. The choices were similar to the engraving patterns above but inlaid with gold. These likewise were given letter designations. The ringneck pheasants (G), bob-white quail (H), English pointer (I), Labrador retriever with duck (J), mallard ducks (K), and Canada geese (L) were all offered with a choice of grayed or blued frame.

The P-1 grade was completely acid etched, which produced a smooth, consistent pattern free from defects. Perhaps only a handful of very early P-1 guns were hand engraved. Most P-1 guns are not signed by the engravers.

Presentation Two (P-2): This is the next highest grade and presents a different look and feel from the P-1. The borders were done in a fleur-de-lis motif with game scenes on both sides of the frame and on the bottom. The customer was given a choice of three distinct motifs on a grayed frame, with each vignette receiving a letter designation. The P-2M featured mallard ducks on the right side with ringneck pheasants on the left. En-

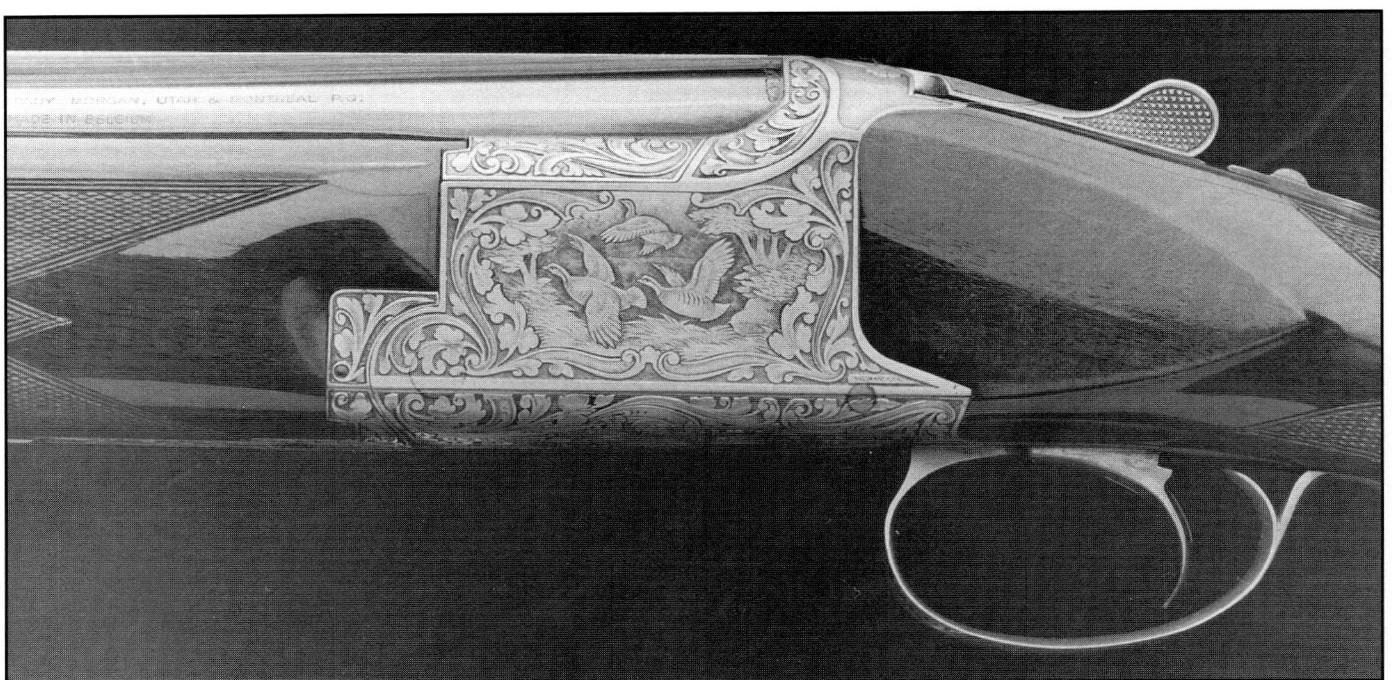

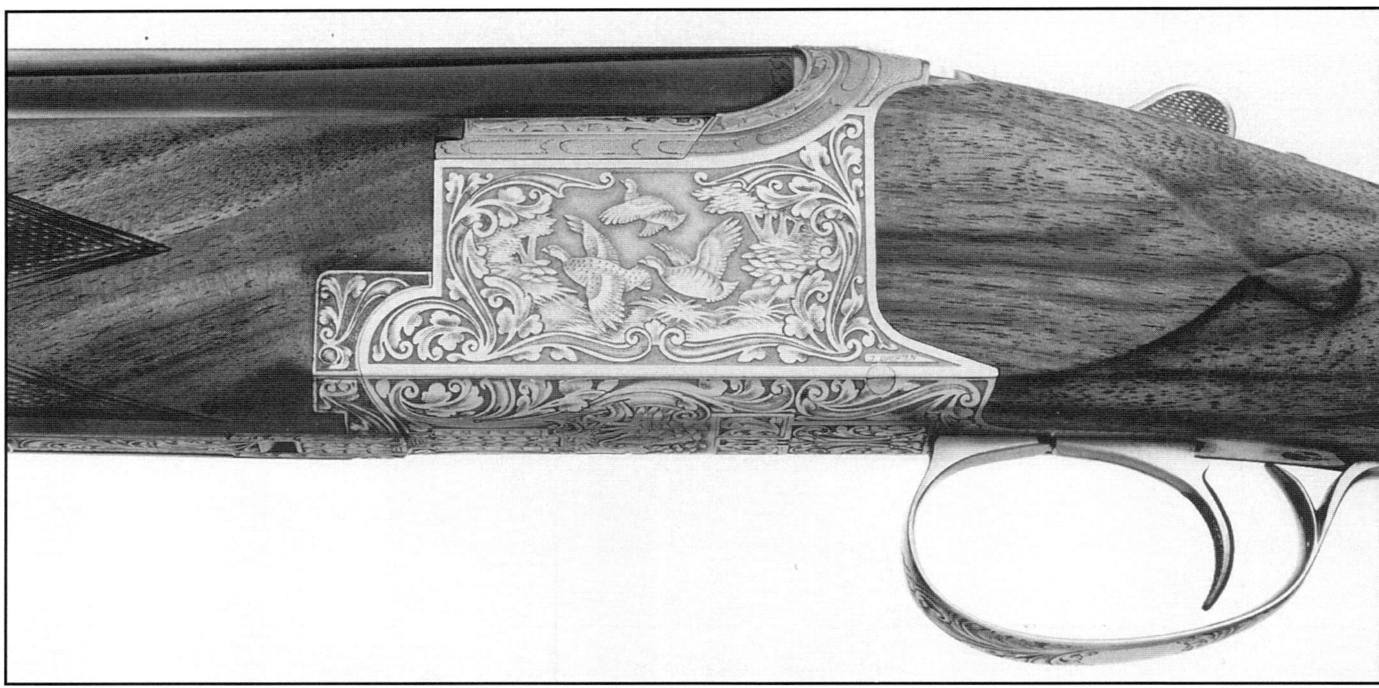

Two P-2O Grades as seen from the left side. On the top is an early gun engraved by Louis Vrancken and on the bottom another early gun engraved by the master José Baerten. Close examination of the two game scenes reveals subtle differences seen only on hand engraved guns. Most P-2 Grade Superposed were acid etched, except for a few very early examples. Courtesy Browning Company.

graved on the bottom of the frame was a bobwhite quail. The P-2N featured a golden retriever on the right side with Canada geese on the left side. A mallard drake was engraved on the bottom. The third scene, P-2O, had mourning doves engraved on the right side, chukar partridges on the left side, and an English setter on the bottom. The P-2 grade also gave the customer the choice of having these scenes done in gold inlay. Grade P-2P featured the mallards, pheasants, and quail; the P-2Q had the retriever, geese, and mallard; the P-2R had the doves, chukar, and setter. These gold inlaid scenes were offered in either blued or grayed finish.

As with the P-1 grade, the P-2 was for the most part a totally acid etched gun, except for a few very early first year guns. Most of the P-2 guns were not signed.

This P-2R Grade is signed by José Baerten and features chukar partridges and mourning doves in gold on a blued receiver. Courtesy Browning Company.

This P-2N Grade is signed by Louis Vrancken, an indication that this is a very early P-2 Superposed. Courtesy Browning Company.

This is a P-2N Grade Superposed signed by José Baerten. Although signed by Baerten, the engraving pattern does not seem to have the depth of detail that other signed P-2 grades possess. This is an excellent example of a P-2 Superposed that is primarily acid etched. Courtesy Browning Company.

Presentation Three (P-3): The P-3 grade was similar in design to the P-2 but with finer details. A choice of three engraving patterns was available, all with gold inlay on a grayed or blued frame. The borders of the P-3 were accented with gold inlay. The P-3S featured pheasants on the right side, partridges on the left side, and quail on the bottom. The P-3T had pintail ducks on the right side, mallards on the left, and a Canada goose on the bottom. The P-3U featured an English setter on the right side of the frame, an English pointer with flushing quail on the left side, and a mourning dove on the bottom.

The P-3 grade vignettes were hand engraved, but the rest of the pattern was acid etched. It is estimated that approximately fifteen P-3 first year guns were completely hand engraved. Many of the P-3 guns were signed by the engraver.

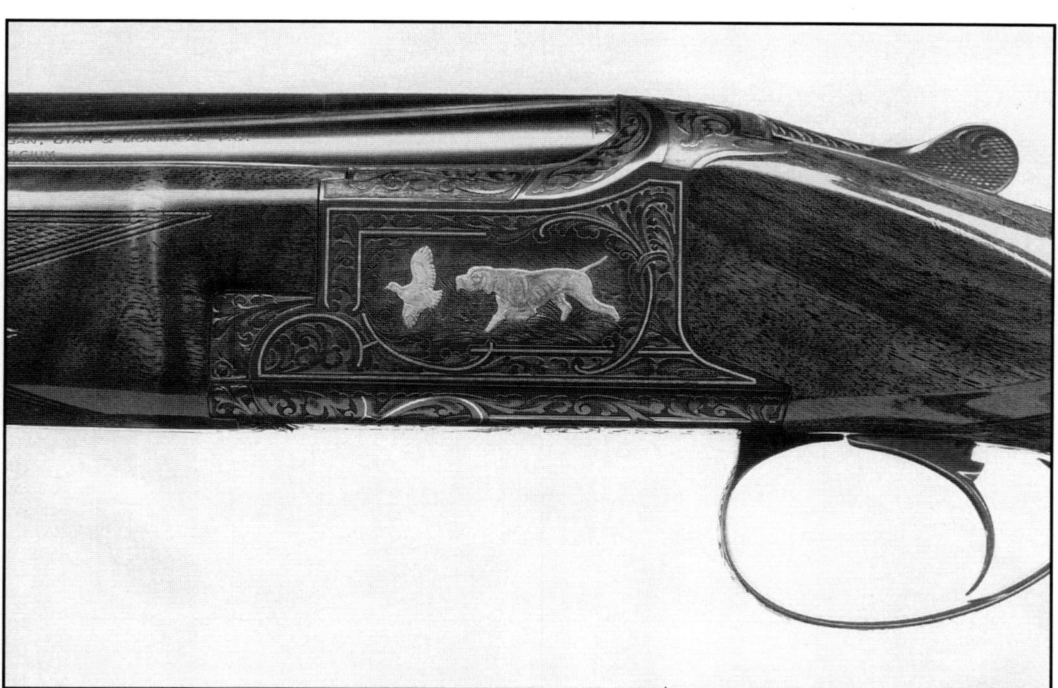

Left, right, and bottom views of a Superposed P-3U Presentation Grade. The scrollwork and borders were acid etched on this grade, while the game scenes were hand engraved. This Superposed is signed on both sides by the master José Baerten. Courtesy Browning Company.

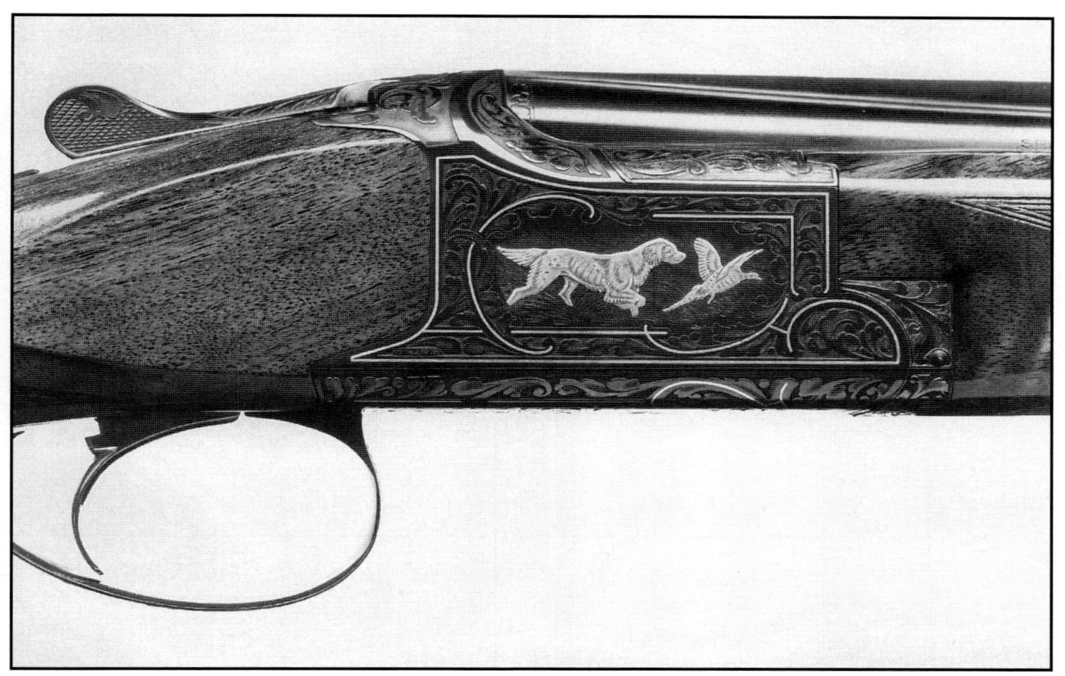

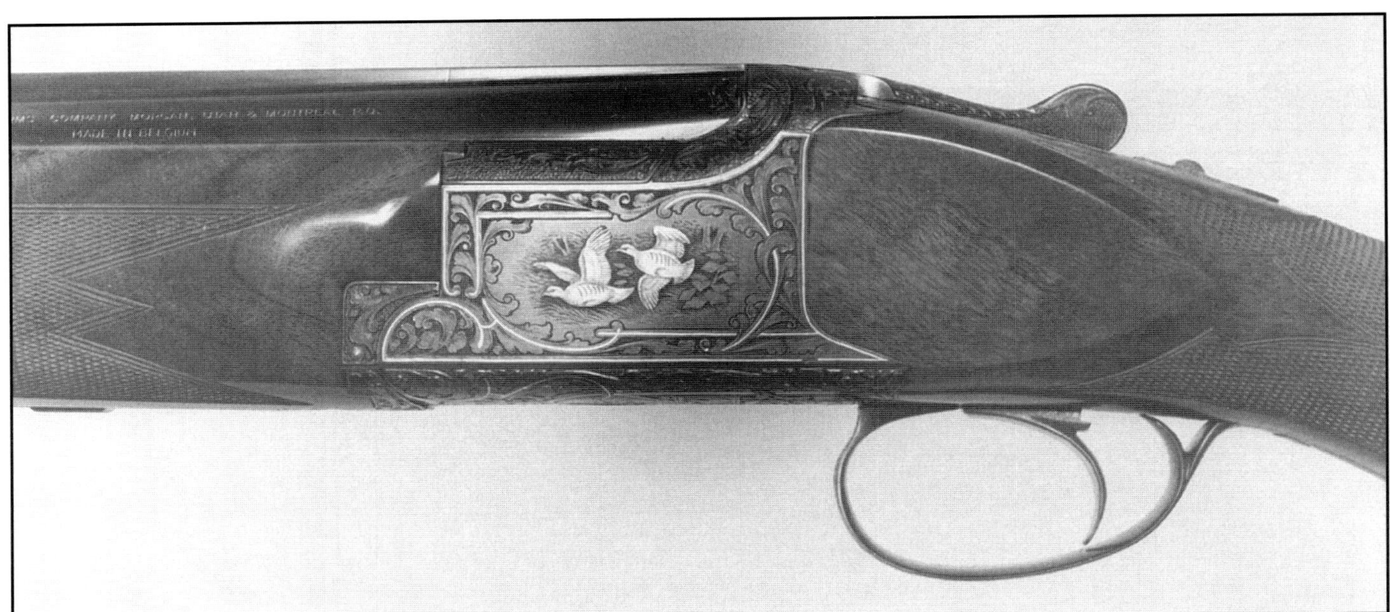

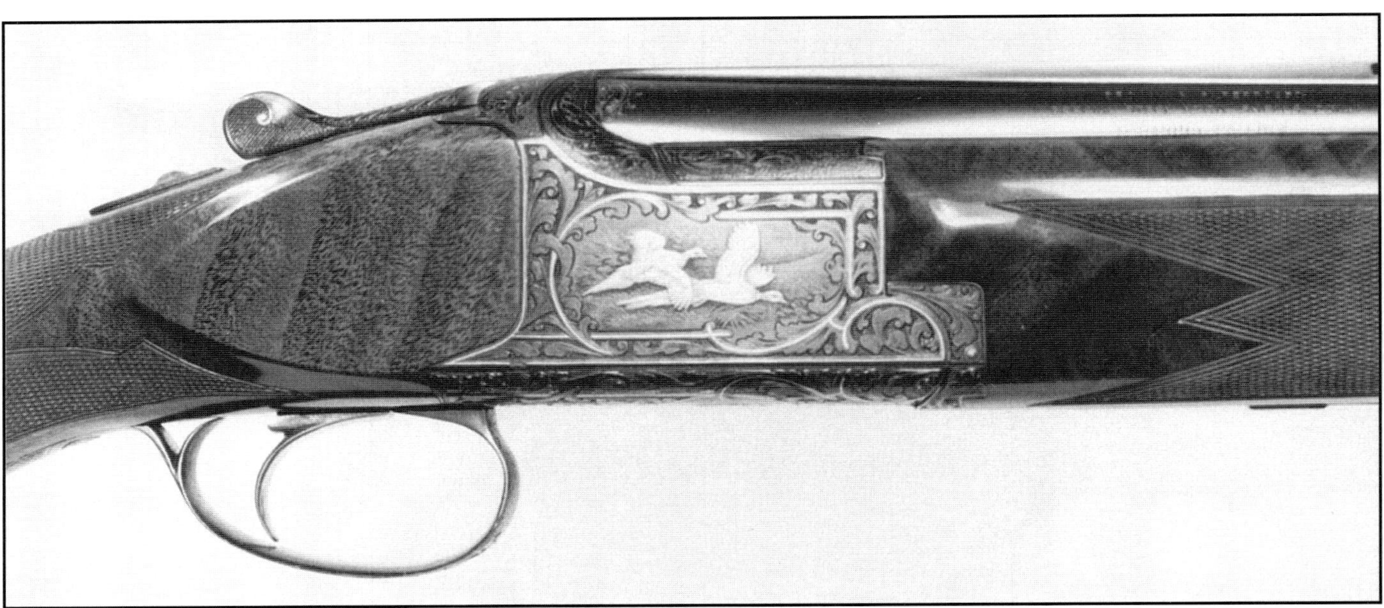

A Superposed P-3S Presentation Grade with gold inlays and deep blue receiver. This gun was signed on the left side by Louis Vrancken. Most P-3 guns were signed by the engraver. Courtesy Browning Company.

Presentation Four (P-4): This grade was the highest quality Presentation Series offered. The hallmark of this grade was its sideplates. The finely done, deeply cut floral engraving covered one hundred percent of the frame except for the game scene itself. Only one game scene was offered: mallard ducks on the right side, ringneck pheasants on the left, and two bob-white quail on the bottom. A retriever's head was engraved on the trigger guard. The P-4V was engraved on a grayed frame, while the P-4W featured the same scene with gold inlays on a grayed frame. All P-4 Superposed guns were entirely hand engraved, and most were signed by the engraver.

Many of the FN engraving patterns were also redesigned. As a result of these new designs, some confusion was created, especially with regard to the FN equivalent "P" grades. Fabrique Nationale incorporated variations of the new Presentation series patterns in its engraving catalogues, but with different numbers and slightly different formats.

The Browning USA P-1 grade featured six basic scenes either engraved or gold inlaid, for a total of twelve P-1 grades. The FN equivalent was referred to as the B5 and was offered in a total of fourteen different scenes in either gold inlay or engraved patterns. The difference was that FN offered its B5 with pigeons while the North American version did not.

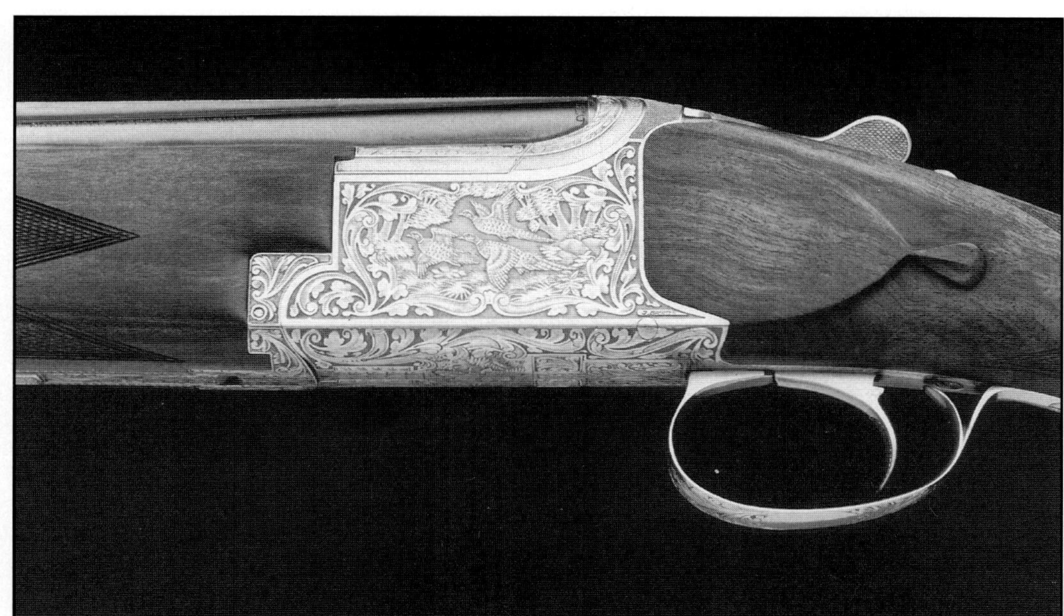

At first glance this Superposed appears to be a Browning P-2M Grade engraved by José Baerten. In fact, this specific Superposed is an FN C4-1 Grade. The teardrop points behind the receiver are an indication, but the Fabrique Nationale barrel address makes the assumption a certainty. Courtesy Fabrique Nationale Archives.

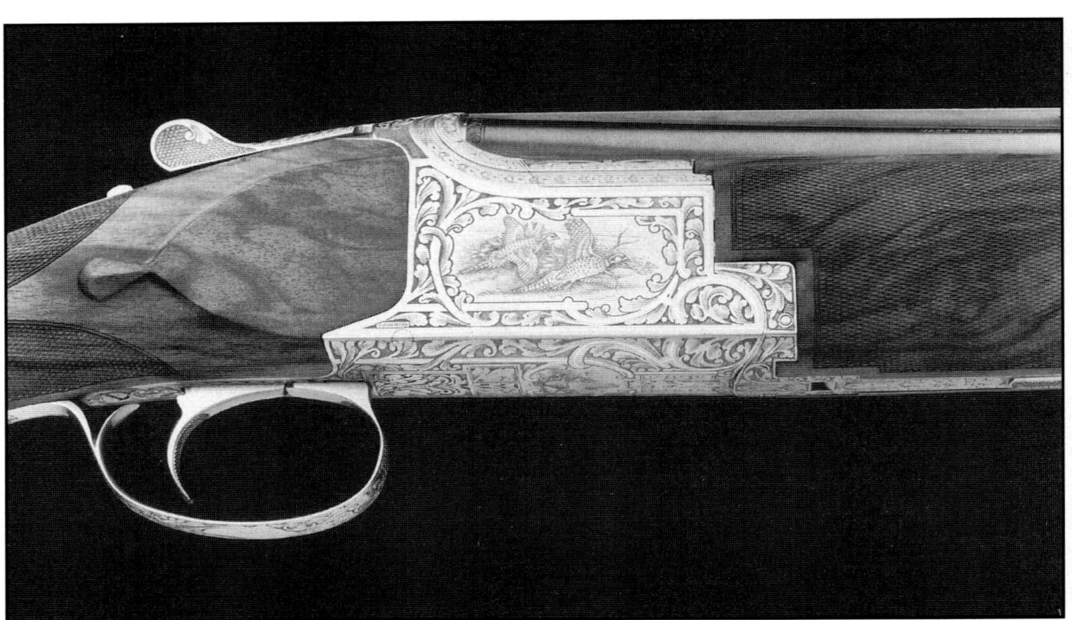

Fabrique Nationale sold through its civilian sporting goods company, FN Sports, a slightly different version of the North American P-3 series Superposed. FN referred to its grade as the D6. It featured scroll and borders much like the P-3 Grade, but the game scenes were executed on a gray receiver with engraved birds rather than gold inlaid. This particular Superposed is a D6-1 Grade engraved by José Baerten. The checkering pattern is different from the P-3 guns as is the standard teardrop feature behind the receiver. Courtesy Fabrique Nationale Archives.

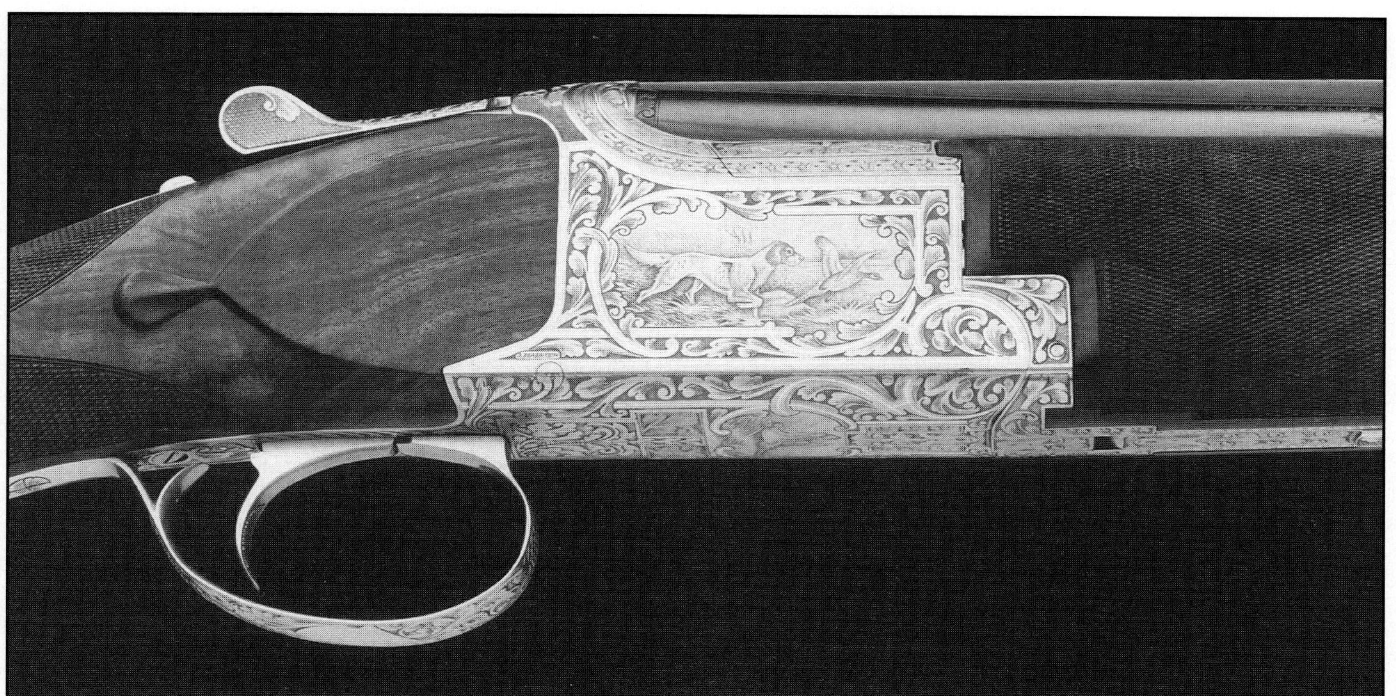

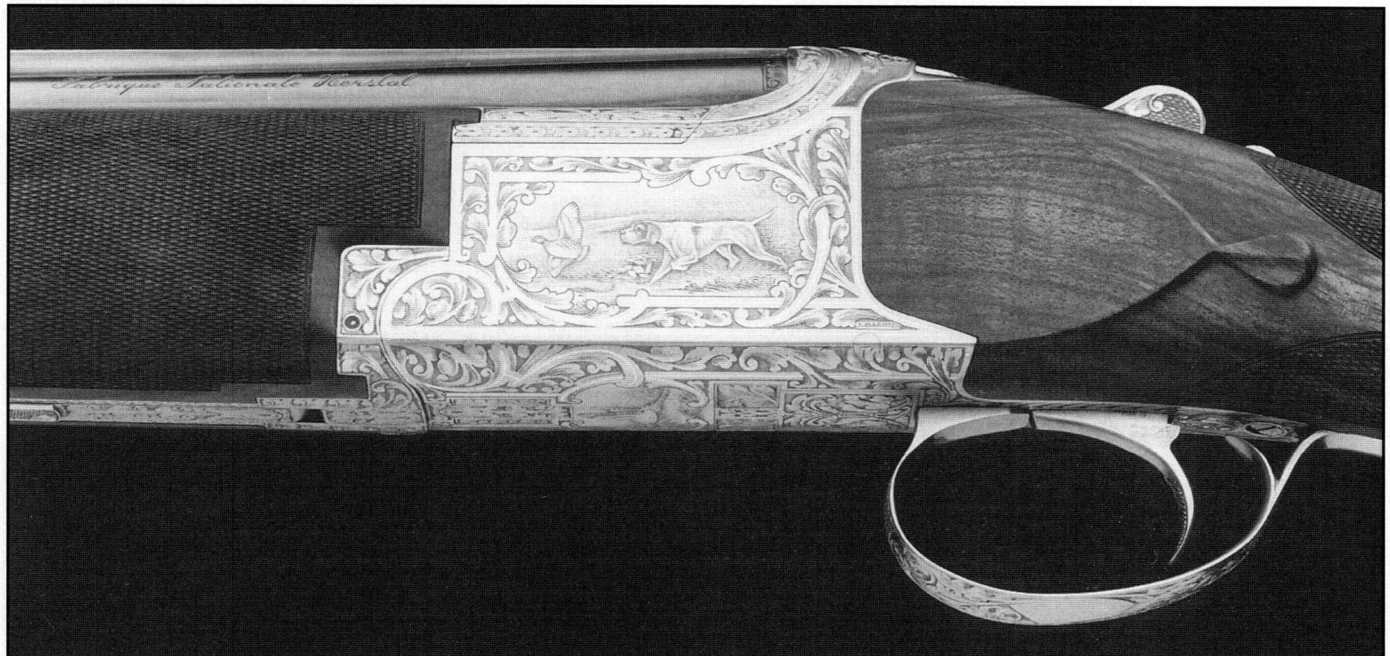

This FN D6-3 Grade is signed on both sides by José Baerten and features the pointer and quail on the left side and the English setter and pheasant on the right side, engraved instead of inlaid as on the North American P-3U Grade. Courtesy Fabrique Nationale Archives.

FN's equivalent P-2 grade was called the C4 and was available in three different scenes similar to the North American Presentation version and with the same choices of gold inlay or engraved scenes. As was the policy of both FN and Browning, custom orders were executed at the customer's request. In one case an FN C4 was executed with the old Diana Grade game scene.

The Presentation Series P-3 Grade was named the D6 for FN's markets. The D6 was offered with either a grayed or blued frame with gold inlays like the USA P-3, or it was available with engraved game scenes, unlike the American version. Again, special orders were performed for customers wanting something unique. One FN D6 was engraved with an English setter on the bottom, similar to the C4 version.

The American P-4 version was also offered on FN Superposed and was referred to as the E1 grade. The E1 was not offered with gold inlays like the North American equivalent. FN considered offering another version of the P-4, and in some early correspondence referred to this grade as the P-4.2. It never appeared in Browning USA catalogues, but it did surface in FN's catalogues renamed as the M2 grade.

These differences between the Browning Presentation Series grades and the FN patterns may help to explain some small but significant distinctions between the two companies' offerings. In all cases, the engraving methods matched each other as to acid etching and handwork despite the differences in grade names.

There was another area of engraving that the reader may find interesting. Beginning in the mid-1960s and accelerating in application throughout the 1970s was FN's burgeoning number of engraving patterns for its Superposed line in Europe. Many of these guns found their way into North America in the mid-1970s with the importation of the "C" Grade Exhibition guns. Beginning in the early 1980s, probably around 1982, Browning was offered another attractive opportunity to acquire a fairly large number of FN engraved B-25 Superposed guns to sell in its North American market. Browning's Rich Bauter, then senior product manager of firearms, recalls making the trip to Herstal to inspect these FN Superposed guns around 1982. All of these guns were built to FN's European specifications with such characteristics as Special Sporting models with 12 gauge 27-1/2-inch barrels and tulip-shaped forearms, or Special Game models in 12 gauge with "swan-neck" buttstocks. Some of these guns were Trap and Skeet models built to European specifications. About three thousand of these FN European Superposed guns were imported through Browning for sale in North America primarily by way of two Browning dealers, Bill Jacqua and Tom Koessl.

Beside their obvious European look, what set these FN Superposed shotguns apart from their North American counterpart was their distinctive engraving patterns. It should be noted that some of these European FN Superposed were modified by dealers to Americanize them prior to their sale. Those guns with "swan-neck" stocks were re-cut, and some with natural matte stock finishes were refinished to a high gloss. The alterations on these guns were done in the U.S. The guns are listed below with their FN European grade names and number equivalents:

Palatinat (A1): This corresponded to Browning's North American Grade I. It featured a very sparse coverage of acanthus leaves on the barrel wings and top of the frame. There was a modest scroll border with rosette engraving on the hinge pin. The frame was blued, the trigger was blued on the Hunting models and gold on the Target models, the wood stock was plain and dark, lacking grain. The wood finish was completed with a satin lacquer. The average retail price, depending on options, was approximately $1,500.

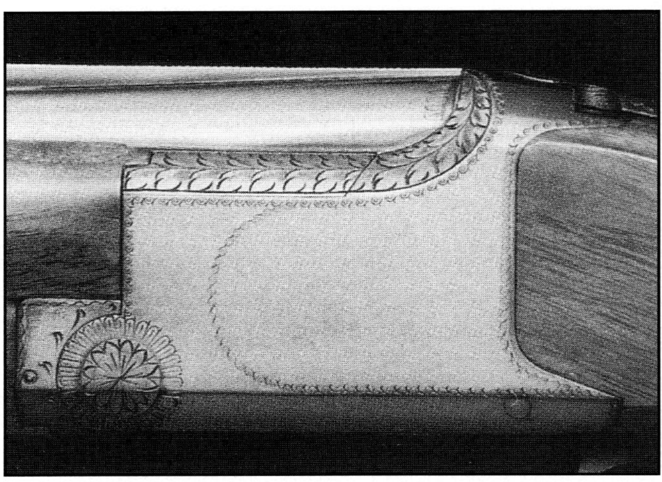

Palatinat (A1)

Palatinat (A2): This was a slightly upgraded version of the A1 model featuring a case hardened frame, plain wood, and somewhat finer scrollwork. The A2 average retail price, depending on options, was also around $1,500.

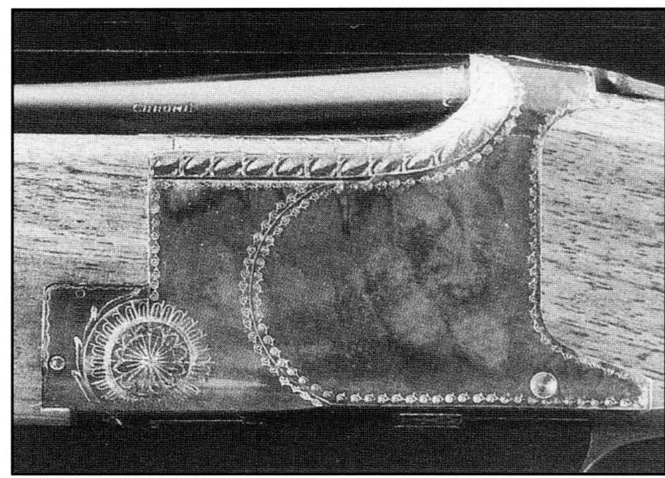

Palatinat (A2)

Lully (B1): This grade had a grayed frame with acanthus leaves engraved on the barrel wings and top of the frame. The border was lightly scrolled with light English style bouquet engraving. The rosettes were finely done. The stock had plain straight grained wood with satin finish. The engraving was acid etched. A recoil pad was sup-

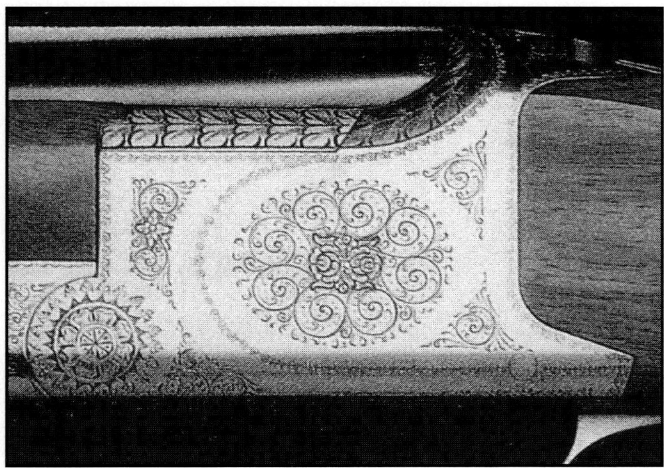

Lully (B1)

plied with the Target models. The average retail price for the B1 was about $2,000, depending on its options and configuration.

Langeais (B2): This grade featured English style engraving with a bead border on the barrel wings and top of the frame. The game scene featured pheasants, grouse, and partridge surrounded by a light English scroll. The frame was grayed. Some of these B2 Superposed were signed by the engraver. The wood was generally very plain. Depending on the options and configuration, the average retail price for the B2 was around $2,200, although some B2 guns were priced as high as $3,000.

Langeais (B2)

Coblence (B2G): The B2G was FN's best selling Superposed grade in Europe. It featured light engraving on the barrel wings with fillets and serpentine border on the fences of the frame. Pheasants or ducks in intaglio engraving are framed with wide scroll and leaves on a gray finished frame. All B2G were signed by the engraver. The stock had French walnut of moderate grain

Coblence (B2G)

with oil finish. The B2G average retail price was approximately $2,200, depending on options and configuration.

Bruges (C 1): The C1 was similar in appearance to the B1 but with more scroll and coverage. The barrel wings were engraved with acanthus leaves with fillets on the fences. The receiver featured light English style bouquet engraving on a gray finish. The wood was a select walnut with carved dopper points and an oil finish. This grade was not signed by the engraver. The average retail price, depending on options, was $2,200.

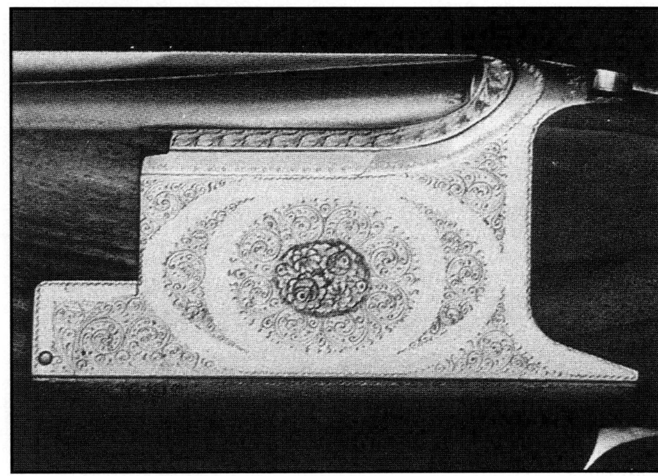

Bruges (C1)

Cheverny (C2): This grade was patterned after FN's classic C2 grade, which had pheasants, grouse, and partridges in light game scene engraving framed by a fine English scroll. The receiver was grayed and the buttstock was carved with dopper points and oil finished. The wood was good to excellent with nice coloring and grain. Most of these C2s were signed by the engraver. The average retail price was $2,500.

Cheverny (C2)

Hanovre (C2G): The C2G had light engraving on the barrel wings. The main body of the receiver was deeply engraved with ducks and partridge framed by a heavy scroll and leaf pattern. The receiver was grayed. The buttstock and forearm were fitted with select walnut with good figure. Dopper points were carved on the buttstock, which was oil finished. Most C2Gs were signed by the engraver. Some C2Gs were priced as high as $3,500, with an average price of $2,500.

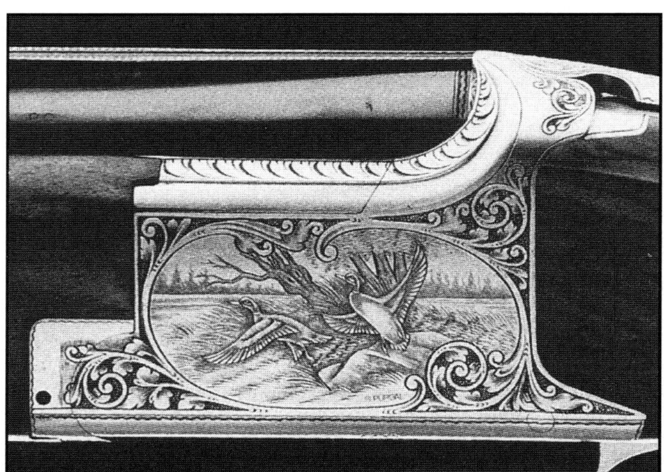

Hanovre (C2G)

Birmingham (C3): A classic European engraving pattern was used on the C3. Fine acanthus leaves were engraved on the barrel wings. The receiver had a gray finish with fine, tight English style lace engraving covering the entire area. Despite the extensive engraving coverage on this grade, it was priced slightly lower than the other C grades with an average retail price of $2,200. A few C3s with few options could be bought for as little as $1,500.

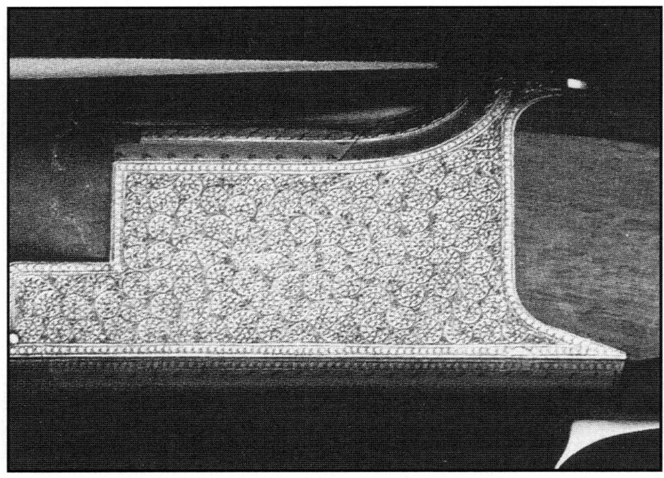

Birmingham (C3)

Clichy (D1): The D1 grade offered a different look. The frame was outlined with a finely festooned border. A very delicate garland of acanthus leaves was engraved on the barrel wings. The frame was deeply blued. Most were not signed by the engraver. The wood was excellent with rich dark figured grain. Some were supplied with three-piece forearms, and most were fitted with checkered butts. The average retail price for the D1 was around $2,200, depending on options and configuration, with certain variations priced as high as $3,000.

Clichy (D1)

Carnaby (D2): A very tastefully done Superposed with beaded pattern borders and scrolls on the barrel wings. The underpart of the frame was outlined with a fine bead border. The frame featured a very fine English bouquet engraving. All of these grades were signed by the engraver. The wood was very dark with heavy figure and was oil finished. Some were supplied with three-piece forearms. The D2 average retail price was also about $2,200.

Carnaby (D2)

Baccara (D3): This grade had a classically executed engraving pattern that featured a very fine decoration of acanthus leaves with English scroll engraving on the barrel wings. The underpart of the frame was outlined by a finely beaded border. The main body of the grayed frame was cut with very fine English scroll of lace bouquets. The engraving coverage on this grade was one hundred percent, and all the guns in this grade were signed by the engraver. The wood was highly figured with a dull natural finish. A Browning recoil pad was factory installed on D3 Target models. The average retail price for the D3 was approximately $2,500, depending on options and configuration.

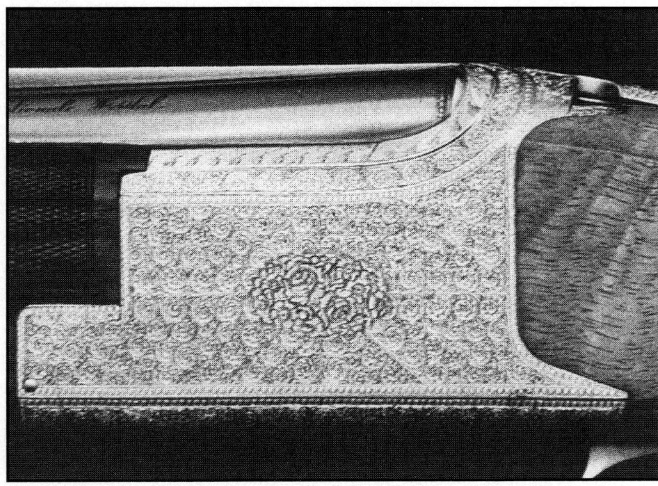

Baccara (D3)

Chenonceau (D4): A classic game scene engraved Superposed similar to the Pointer Grade. It featured a very light garland of acanthus leaves and English style scroll on the barrel wings. Dogs, pheasants, and ducks were lightly engraved framed by very fine English scroll. A woodcock was engraved on the trigger guard. Most were signed by Custom Shop engraver Rene DeWil. The wood was excellent with fine figure. Some were supplied with three-piece forearms and checkered butts. The D4 carried an average retail price of about $2,750, depending on options and configuration. Some D4 guns were priced as high as $3,750.

Chenonceau (D4)

Heidelberg (D4G): This grade featured an engraving design similar to the popular American Diana Grade. The barrel wings were engraved with a very fine pattern of acanthus leaves. The grayed frame was deeply engraved with pheasants and ducks framed by heavy scroll and leaf engraving. All of the D4G Superposed guns were signed by the engraver. The wood had excellent figure with a natural matte finish. The Target models were supplied with a European style hard rubber recoil pad. The D4G had an average retail price of around $3,250, with some guns priced as high as $4,000, depending on options and configuration.

Heidelberg (D4G)

Trianon (D5): This grade featured a very fine Louis XVI engraving style scroll on a grayed frame. The barrel wings were done with a fine pattern of acanthus leaves and flowers. All of the guns in this grade were signed by the engraver. The wood had excellent grain and figure and had a natural matte finish. With an average retail price of $3,000, the D5 was priced slightly less than the D4G, depending on options and configuration.

Trianon (D5)

Louis XVI (D5G): This grade is an outstanding example of the engraver's art. It took over two hundred hours to execute the pattern, which featured a deeply cut Louis XVI style scroll. The wood was highly figured with streaks of colors ranging from medium to dark. Some of these grades were supplied with three-piece forearms. The D5G had a retail price averaging around $3,000, with some guns priced as high as $3,750, depending on options and configuration.

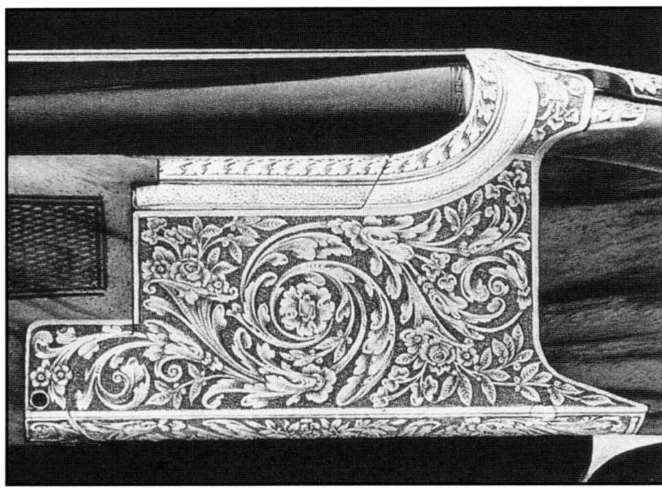

Louis XVI (D5G)

Empire (I1): This Superposed was fitted with sideplates with very fine gold wire work and borders on a recessed frame. The gold inlay was finished in pearls and foliated scrolls on a deep blue background. The wood and checkering was of the highest quality FN had to offer. The Empire grade carried a retail price of $4,000.

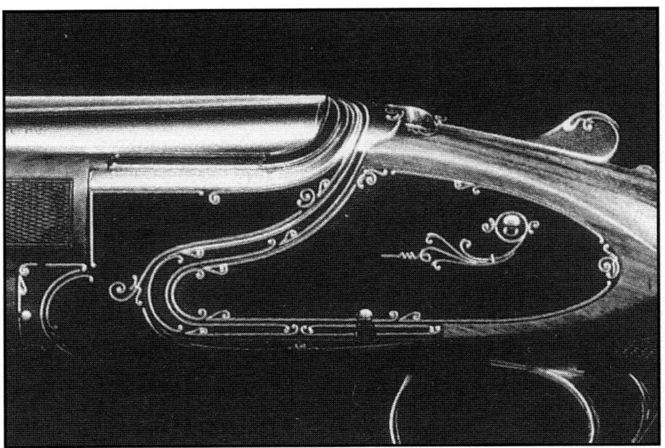

Empire (I1)

Oxford (M1): This grade was also fitted with sideplates on a silver gray frame. A fine English bead engraving formed an ornamental border. The balance of the metal was done in a very fine English scroll with about eighty-five percent coverage. The hinge pin was decorated with a very fine English rosette. The wood and checkering was of the highest FN quality. The Oxford's retail price was approximately $4,000.

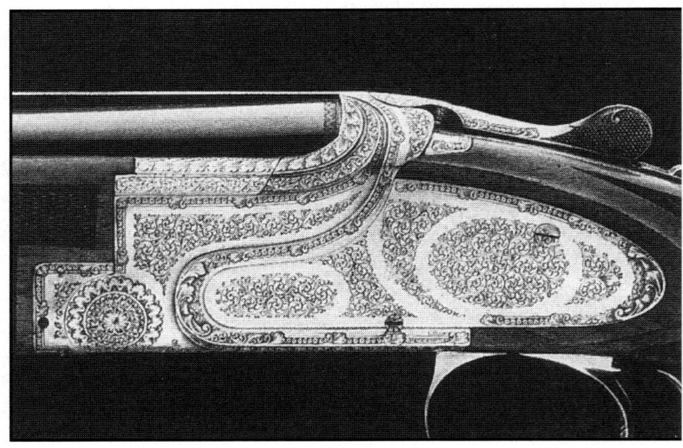

Oxford (M1)

Sherwood (M2): The silver gray frame of this grade was recessed and fitted with sideplates. The border was done in acanthus leaves and fine English style beading. On the sideplates, a medallion featured pheasants and partridges taking flight. The bottom of the frame showed a rabbit framed

The Presentation Era Superposed: 1977-1984

In 1977 the Browning Superposed Presentation Series was first offered in North America. Available in four different grades, each with its own variations, the P Series was by outward appearances a conspicuous departure for both Browning and Fabrique Nationale, but internal characteristics remained the same as previous Superposed models. From top to bottom is the P-1, the P-2, the P-3 with gold inlays, and the P-4 with sideplates. Courtesy Browning Company.

In 1978 Browning offered the Superposed Continental Centennial Edition. This was a limited edition of five hundred guns featuring a two-barrel set. One set of barrels was 26-1/2 inches in 20 gauge and the other was 24 inches and chambered for the 30-06 Springfield cartridge. The receiver was engraved with a design by Louis Vrancken featuring gold inlaid North American game animals. Courtesy Browning Company.

In 1984 Browning introduced its Classic Limited Edition Superposed pictured at the top. This gun was designated by Browning as a B-125 with its barrels and frame built in Japan and engraved and assembled in Belgium. The Gold Classic, shown at the bottom, was not introduced until 1985, but it was an entirely Belgian produced B-25 Superposed. Courtesy Browning Company.

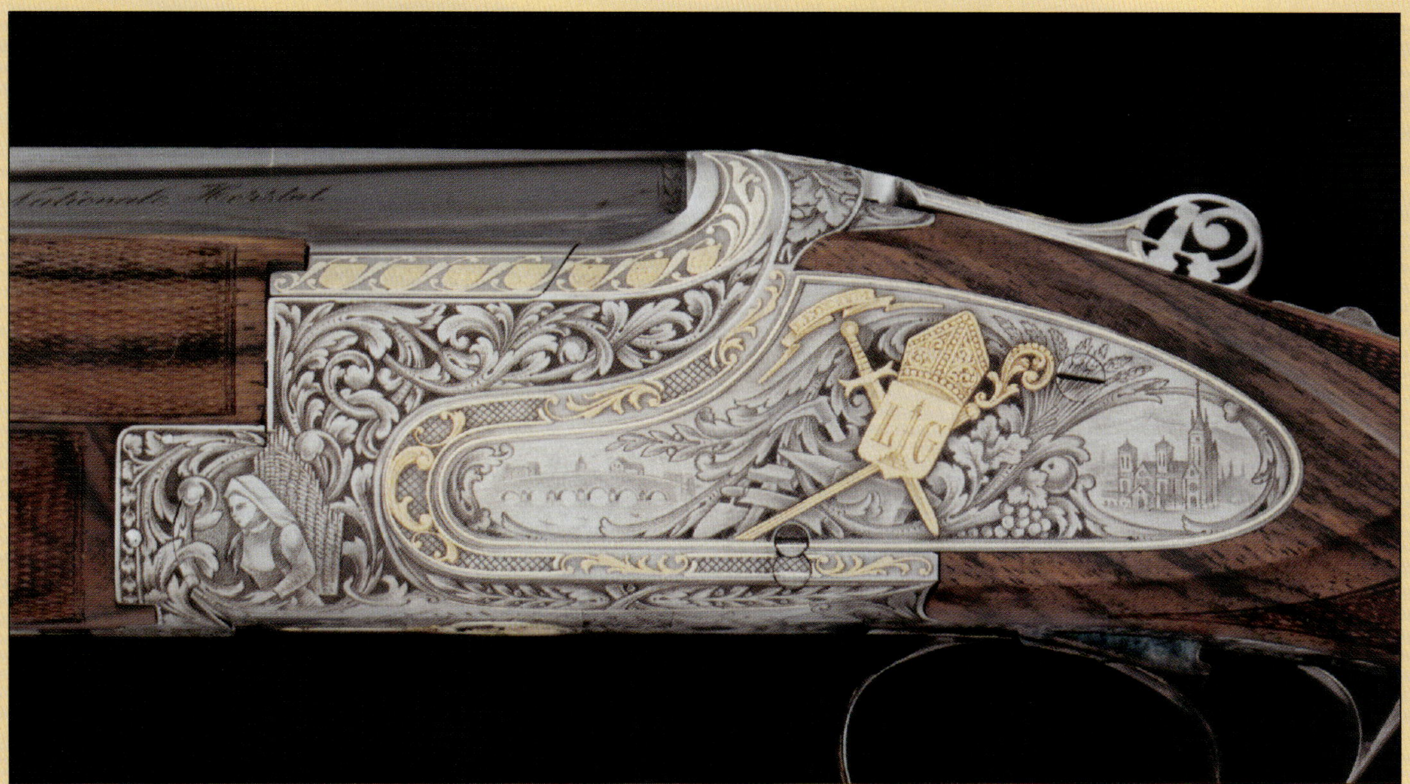

This FN Superposed was built in 1980 to commemorate the millenary of the former principality of Liège. These special Superposed were limited to just ten guns. The design was created and executed by Louis Vrancken. The theme of this design is the countryside and crafts of the Liège region. Courtesy Browning Company.

Right: This pair of P-3U Superposed Superlights, serial numbers P73RR1751 and P73TN1026, are both chambered for the 28 gauge shell and are fitted with checkered butt, oil finish, and three-piece forearm. The P-3U on top has the optional gold inlays with blued receiver. Both guns are fitted with 26-1/2-inch barrels choked improved cylinder and modified, and both guns are unsigned. Bert O'Neill, Jr. Collection. Photo Dennis Degnan.

An impressive display of Presentation Superposed. From top to bottom: a P-4 28 gauge Superlight, serial number P73RN1068, with all options, fitted with 26-1/2-inch barrels choked improved cylinder and modified. The engraving is signed by Claudy Baerten. In the middle is a 28 gauge Superlight P-3U, serial number P73RN1026, with all options, fitted with 26-1/2-inch barrels choked improved cylinder and modified. The engraving is unsigned. There were approximately thirty-six of these P-3 guns sold between 1977 and 1984. At the bottom is a P-2R, serial number P73RN1054, in 28 gauge with 26-1/2-inch barrels choked improved cylinder and modified. The engraving is unsigned. About fifty-seven P-2 Superposed were sold in North America between 1977 and 1984. Bert O'Neill, Jr. Collection. Photo Dennis Degnan.

This P-4W 28 gauge 28-inch Presentation Superposed, serial number P74PM1671, is built in the Superlight configuration and fitted with an extra set of 28-inch .410 bore barrels. The gun is an all option gun with checkered butt, three-piece forearm, and oil finish. The rib is hand filed. Only about twenty P-4 28 gauge Superposed were sold between 1977 and 1984. Very few of these guns were fitted with an extra set of barrels. The engraving was executed by José Baerten. Bert O'Neill, Jr. Collection. Photo Dennis Degnan.

A rare three-barrel P-4W 20 gauge Superposed, serial number P34RP1001, with checkered butt, oil finish, and three-piece forearms. Many collectors refer to this as an "all option" Presentation Series gun. Each barrel has two ivory beads and is numbered with gold Roman numerals. Barrel set I is 26-1/2 inches choked skeet and skeet, barrel set II is 26-1/2 inches choked improved cylinder and modified, barrel set III is 28 inches and is choked modified and full. This rare Presentation Superposed is signed by DeBrus. Bert O'Neill, Jr. Collection. Photo Dennis Degnan.

This group of Presentation Series Superposed are P-2 Grades. The top gun is a P-2R 28 gauge Superlight, serial number P73RN1054, with all options. The bottom gun is also a 28 gauge and is a P-2Q Grade, serial number P74RR1782, signed by José Baerten. This Superposed is also an all option gun and has an extra set of 28-inch barrels choked full and full. It is very rare to see P-2 Superposed with checkered butt, oil finish, and three-piece forearm. These expensive options were usually reserved for the more high priced P-4 Grades. Bert O'Neill, Jr. Collection. Photo Dennis Degnan.

Both sides of a P-4 Grade with gold inlays signed by Jeannine Pirotte. Courtesy Browning Company.

An unsigned P-2R Grade. Courtesy Browning Company.

A P-3U Grade signed by José Baerten. Note the subtle, yet effective, shading employed by Baerten. Courtesy Browning Company.

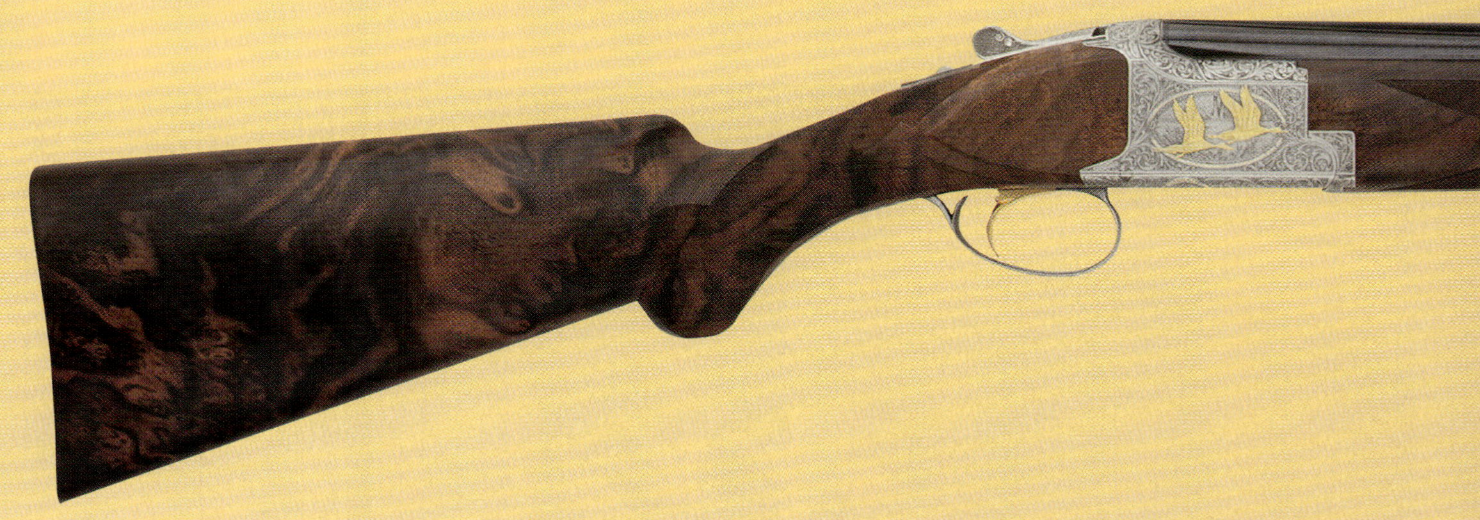

The P-1K Grade Presentation Superposed. Courtesy Browning Company.

The Limited Edition Series Pintail Issue. Courtesy Browning Company.

The right and left sides of the Limited Edition Series Pintail Issue. The left side example is signed by José Baerten; the right side pattern is signed by George Kozlowski. Courtesy Browning Company.

The American Mallard Issue signed by Lucien Ernst. Courtesy Browning Company.

The right side picture of the Black Duck Issue of the Limited Edition Waterfowl Series. This particular pattern was executed by Augusta Pöes. Courtesy Browning Company.

In 1980 Harm Williams, president of the Browning Company, retired. In honor of that retirement he was presented with a custom 20 gauge Superposed Superlight, serial number BL3RN3010, designed and engraved by Louis Vrancken. On the trigger guard tang is the inscription: "Presented by FN to Mr. H. G. Williams in recognition of his 28 years of leadership and service to Browning." Note the outstanding wood grain on both the buttstock and the forearm. Harm Williams Collection. Photo courtesy the Browning Company.

In a letter to Harm Williams dated April 12, 1980, master engraver Louis Vrancken described to Mr. Williams in great detail the engraving features on this unique Superposed. The theme was the state of Utah where Harm lived and worked for so many years. On the left side of the receiver are ducks set in a Utah marsh with Gamble's quail inlaid in gold on the hinge pin. Also on the left side along the barrel and action fences, prehistoric signs are inlaid in gold. The well-known Utah landmark "The Delicate Arch" is depicted also. On the right side of the receiver in gold are a group of flushing pheasants with Gamble's quail on the hinge pin in gold. Harm Williams Collection. Photo courtesy the Browning Company.

A top view of the Harm Williams Superlight shows the ubiquitous seagull, the state bird of Utah. Immediately behind the rib is the Sego Lily, Utah's state flower. On the bottom of the receiver beginning with the forearm iron is the golden spike with golden railroad tracks representing the joining of the Transcontinental railroad in 1869 at Promontory Point, Utah. The large medallion on the bottom of the receiver commemorates the Mormons' settlement of Utah in 1847 and the territory achieving statehood in 1896. On the trigger guard is engraved a tribute to those men led by Brigham Young who realized their dreams when they first saw the Great Salt Lake and declared, "This is the place." There is a total of six colors of gold used on this Superposed. Harm Williams Collection. Photo courtesy the Browning Company.

Both a left and right side view of the B-25 Browning Gold Classic Superposed. The left side is signed by Claudy Baerten, while the right side is signed by his brother, José Baerten. Courtesy Browning Company.

The Legacy Lives On: The Superposed 1985-1995

One of FN's newer engraving patterns for its Superposed is the contemporary Pigeon Special that began to appear in the company's catalogues in the early 1990s. Courtesy Browning Company.

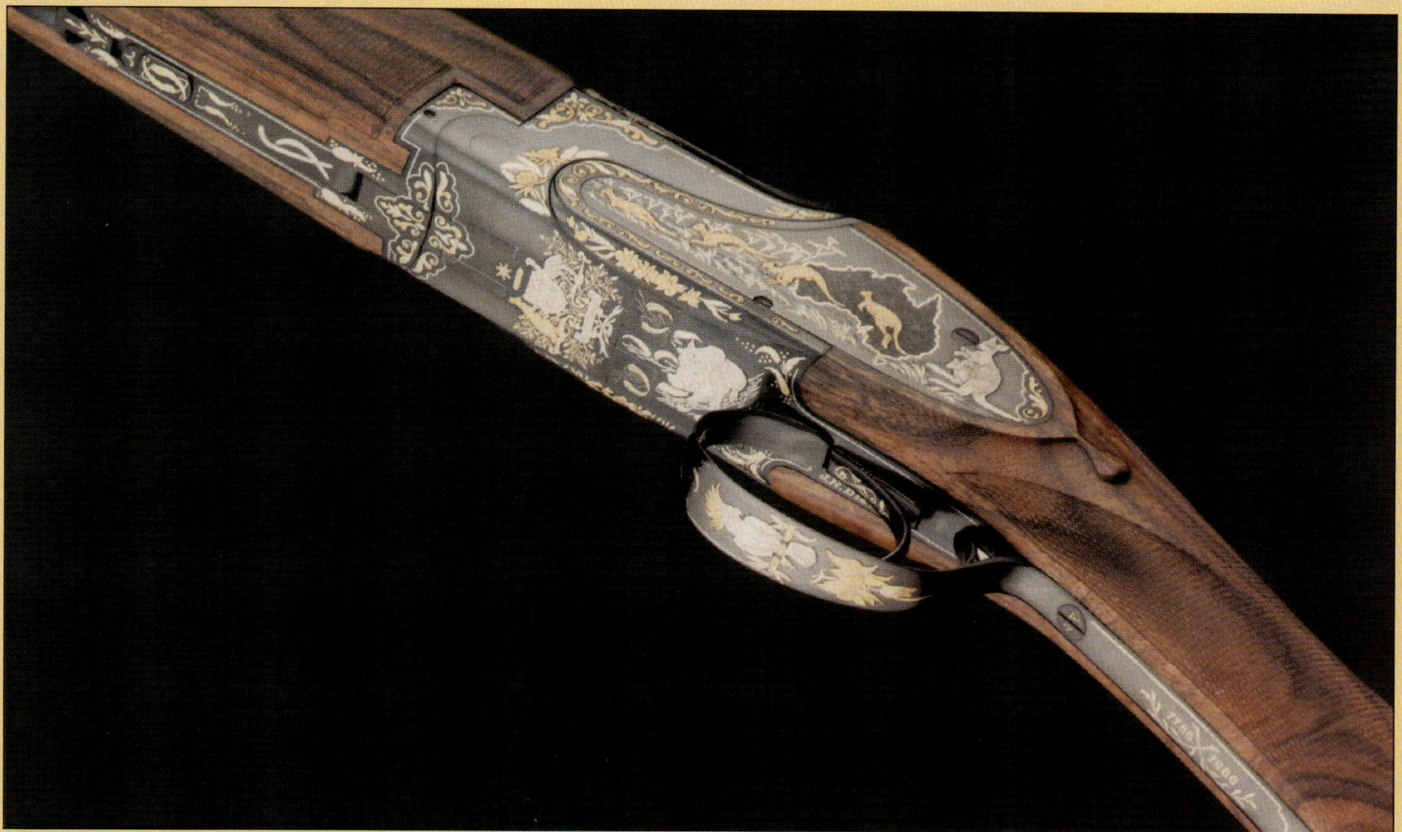

Shortly before the Custom Shop engravers left FN to establish the Engravers Cooperative of Herstal, their own independent engraving firm, FN master engraver Jean Diet completed this outstanding Superposed commemorating the Bicentenary of Australia in 1986. Courtesy Browning Company.

The Centenary FN Superposed built especially for the 1990 SHOT Show. As the background materials suggest, Fabrique Nationale and Browning continue to work closely in developing special projects and building and marketing fine guns. Courtesy Browning Company.

by fine English scroll. The wood and checkering was of the highest quality. The M2 had a retail price of $5,000.

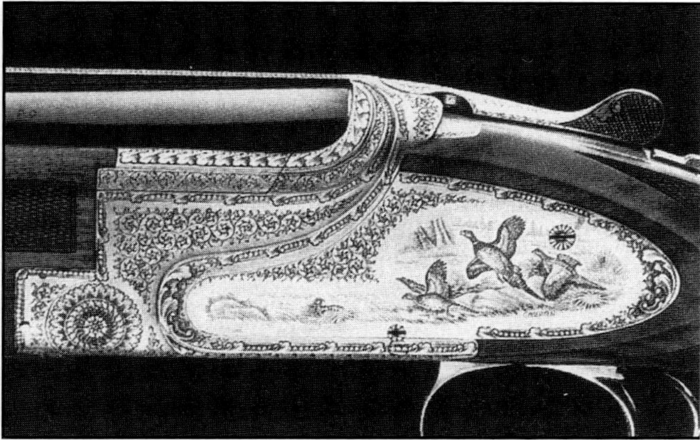

Sherwood (M2)

Chambord (F1): The finest European style engraving pattern FN offered. Referred to as the Royal style, it featured a chain stitched border forming foliated scrolls surrounding a medallion with flushing pheasants and partridges. The bottom of the frame was engraved with flushing ducks. The wood and checkering were of the highest quality FN had to offer. The F1 was priced at $5,500.

FN offered grades other than those listed above, but these represent those FN Superposed imported into North America during the early 1980s, making them the most likely to be seen in this country.

The engraving on Browning Superposed guns, whether for the European market or the North American market, has been and continues to be one of the most attractive aspects of ownership. Some of the finest engravers in the world have adorned the Superposed with patterns that are as recognizable as the guns themselves, or as unique and rare as the world's finest shotguns. Always done with pride and skill, the FN engraved Superposed will perpetually be desired for its grace, beauty, and artistic execution.

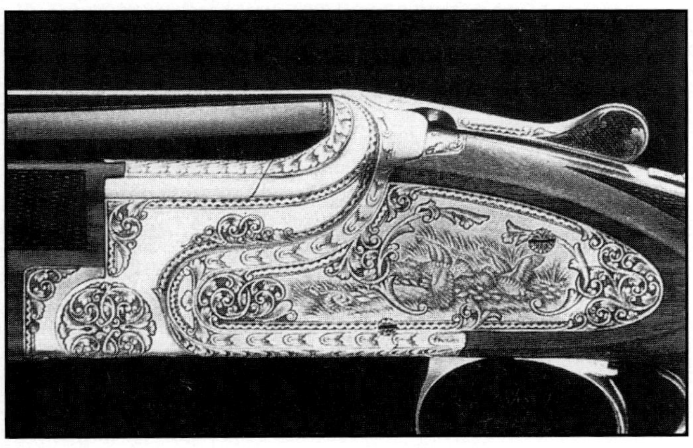

Chambord (F1)

Presentation Era Catalogue Offerings: 1977-1984

The Presentation Series era marked a new direction for the Superposed. Although still a production gun, it was offered with a wide array of extra cost features and new engraving patterns. Browning hoped to lure customers to the Presentation Series Superposed with this wide list of choices and a fairly fast delivery of six months or less according to company claims. Prices were high, but the Presentation Series offered the customer almost an unlimited choice of features and engraving patterns so that each gun built would be a unique creation. This was Browning's attempt to keep the flagship of its sporting firearms, the Superposed, at the forefront of its product line.

1977: The traditional Superposed was still offered in the 1977 catalogue, but only in a limited number of Grade I models. When these were sold only the new Presentation Series Superposed would be available. This year marked the first for the Presentation Series Superposed. The gun was offered in the Lightning, Magnum, Superlight, Trap, and Skeet configurations, much the same as before. The Lightning was offered in 12, 20, and 28 gauge, as well as .410 bore, in 26-1/2 and 28-inch barrel lengths. The 12 gauge 3-inch Magnum model was offered with a choice of 28 or 30-inch barrels. The Superlight was available in 12 and 20 gauge with 26-1/2-inch barrels. The Skeet model was offered in 12 gauge, 20 gauge, 28 gauge, and .410 bore with a choice of 26-1/2 and 28-inch barrels. The All Gauge Skeet Set was also offered with a choice of 26-1/2 or 28-inch barrel lengths. Trap models included the Lightning Trap with 30-inch barrels and the BROADway Trap with a choice of 30 or 32-inch barrels.

The two biggest differences in the Presentation Series as compared to the traditional Superposed was in the choice of options and the style and range of engraving patterns. The Presentation Series was divided into four grades, Presentation One (P-1), Presentation Two (P-2), Presentation Three (P-3), and Presentation Four (P-4). The P-1 was the lowest priced of the four grades and in 1977 carried a retail price of $2,990 for gold inlay on a blued or grayed frame. The most expensive Presentation Series Grade, the P-4, was priced at

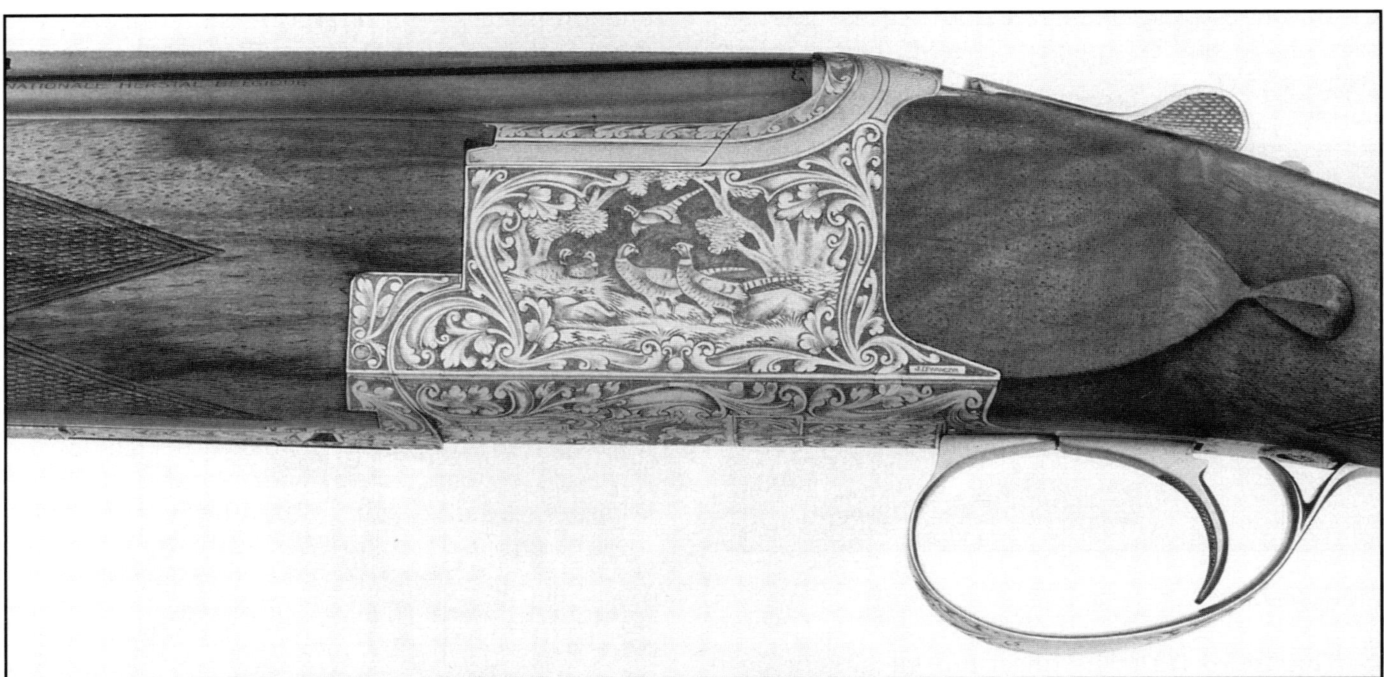

This Diana Grade Superposed, engraved by Jules Lewanczyk in 1977, represents something of an anomaly. The barrel address indicates an FN Superposed destined for sale in Europe. Note the teardrop behind the receiver. Courtesy Fabrique Nationale Archives.

$6,190 for gold inlay on a grayed frame. Each of these grades in turn were divided into a series of different game scenes with or without gold inlays. The available engraving patterns, frame colors, game scenes, and other embellishments were covered in greater detail in the section on Presentation Series engraving earlier in this chapter.

The range of options offered on the Presentation Series gave the customer an opportunity to custom-build his Superposed. The 1977 catalogue gave about twenty-five different extra cost options, but the 1977 price list reduced the number of available options to seventeen. Options ranged from a gold inlaid Roman numeral on the barrel rib for $18.00 to a completely handmade stock priced at $600.00. A few of the options were available at no extra charge, such as front and center ivory sights, and shortening a buttstock up to one inch. Extra sets of barrels were also offered, including same-gauge barrels for the Superlight model in 12 and 20 gauge, or 20 gauge barrels on a 12 gauge Superlight frame.

1978: The Presentation Series offerings continued unchanged for the most part with the exception, of course, of price. The retail price for the gold inlaid P-1 was raised to $3,290, an increase of ten percent. The retail price of the P-4 gold inlaid model was raised from $6,190 to $6,850, also a ten percent increase. Price increases affected the extra cost options as well.

A new addition was made to the Superposed line in 1978: the Superposed Continental Centennial Edition. Designed to commemorate the one hundredth anniversary of the Browning company, the Continental featured two sets of barrels, one set of 26-1/2-inch 20 gauge barrels with 3-inch chambers, and one set of 24-inch barrels that were chambered for the 30-06 Springfield cartridge and had a folding rear leaf sight. The frame was engraved with a Louis Vrancken design featuring gold inlaid North American game animals. The set was furnished with a walnut luggage type case lined with wine red velvet. The retail price for a gun from this limited edition set of five hundred was $6,500.

1979: The Presentation Series Superposed offerings remained unchanged from the previous years except for available options. The completely hand built stock option was discontinued in the catalogue, as were the teardrop points that could be added to this specially built stock. Retail prices were once again increased. The P-1 gold inlaid Lightning model carried a retail price of $3,740, an almost fourteen percent increase over 1978 prices. The P-4 Lightning with gold inlaid game scenes was priced at $7,750, a $900 increase over the preceding year. The Superposed Continental was made available in a Grade I configuration with a retail price of $4,650. The same barrels were offered in both 20 gauge and 30-06, but the frame

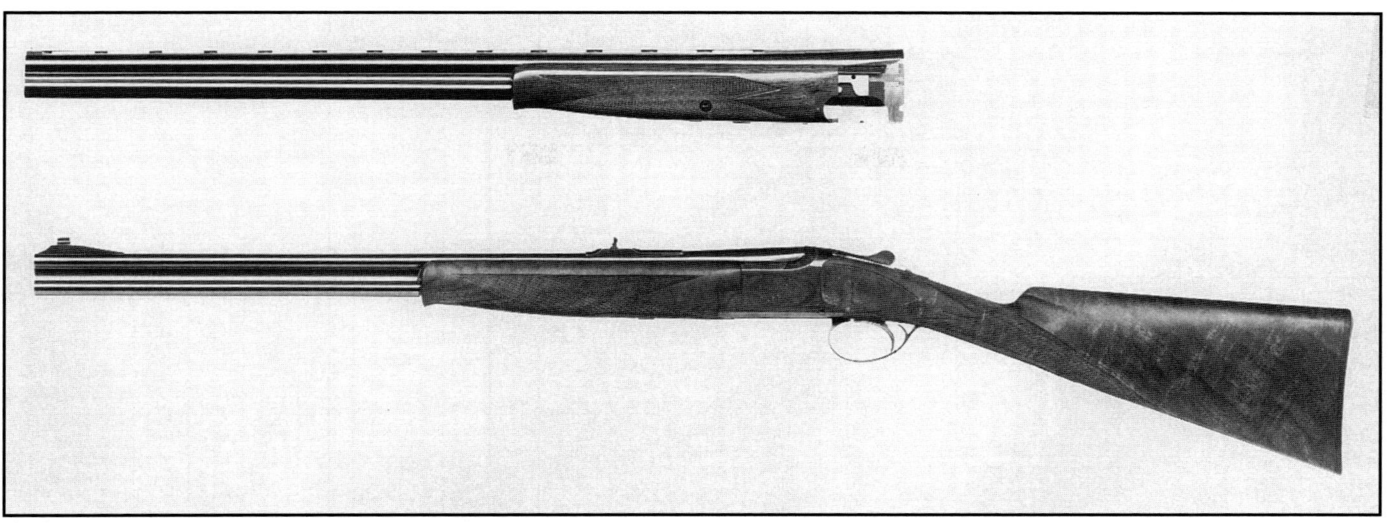

In 1979 the Superposed Continental set was offered in a Grade I configuration with a set of 20 gauge barrels and another set chambered for the 30-06 cartridge. Courtesy Browning Company.

was engraved with the more traditional scroll and rosette design.

1980: Browning catalogue offerings for the Presentation Series remained the same as the previous year. Retail prices were again increased for all grades in the series, with the P-1 gold inlaid Lightning model priced at $4,200, an increase of twelve percent. The gold inlaid P-4 Lightning carried a retail price of $8,600, $850 above the previous year. The Superposed Continental remained in the Superposed line with a retail price of $5,200. Browning did introduce to the Superposed line its new Express rifle, which was essentially a Continental with one set of rifle barrels. The customer had a choice of barrel sets chambered for either the 30-06 Springfield or .270 Winchester caliber. Both rifle barrels were 24 inches in length. The frame was tastefully engraved with scroll and fleur-de-lis designs. The retail price of the Superposed Express rifle was $3,700 for either caliber.

1981: The Presentation Series offerings remained the same, but retail prices were once again increased. The P-1 Lightning model with gold inlaid scenes carried a retail price for 1981 of $4,700, a twelve percent increase. The P-4 Lightning model with gold inlays had a retail price of $9,630, an increase of almost $1,000 over the past year. Both the Superposed Continental and Express rifle continued to be offered in the catalogue for 1981. Again, the company proceeded to present more innovative offshoots based on its Superposed. The Limited Edition Waterfowl Series was introduced with the American Mallard Issue. This issue was limited to five hundred guns in 12 gauge with 28-inch ventilated rib barrels choked modified and full. The frame was engraved with classic scroll and gold inlaid with mallards on both sides, as well as the bottom. The Mallard Issue was cased in a velvet-lined black walnut case with brass latches, and it carried a retail price of $7,000.

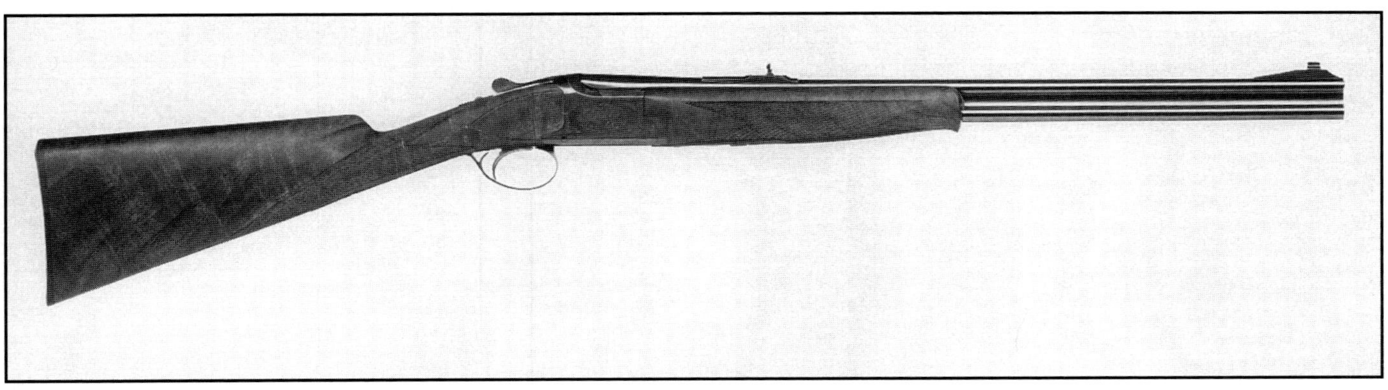

The Browning Superposed Express rifle was introduced in 1980 chambered for the 30-06 or .270 Winchester caliber with 24-inch barrels. Courtesy Browning Company.

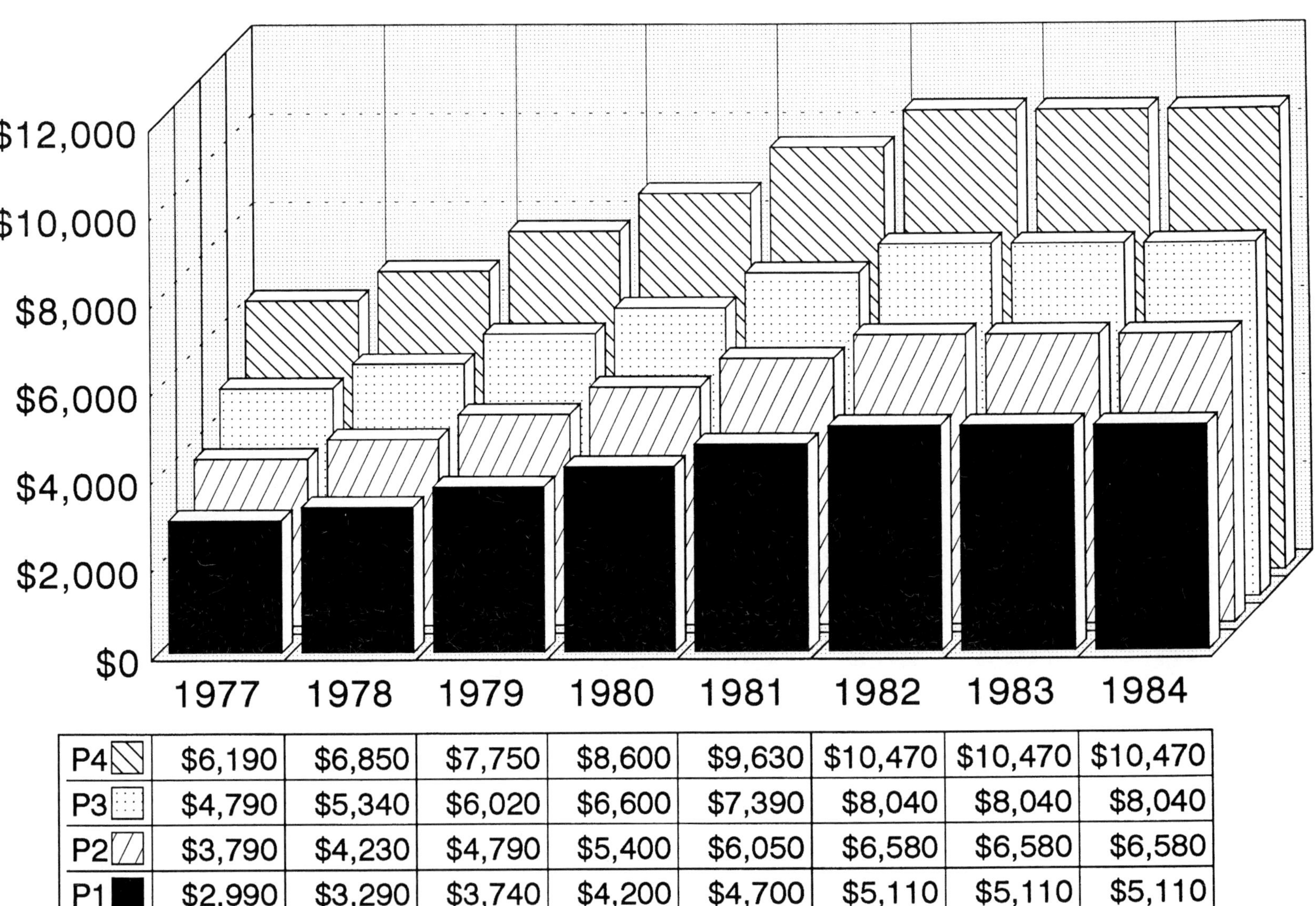

	1977	1978	1979	1980	1981	1982	1983	1984
P4	$6,190	$6,850	$7,750	$8,600	$9,630	$10,470	$10,470	$10,470
P3	$4,790	$5,340	$6,020	$6,600	$7,390	$8,040	$8,040	$8,040
P2	$3,790	$4,230	$4,790	$5,400	$6,050	$6,580	$6,580	$6,580
P1	$2,990	$3,290	$3,740	$4,200	$4,700	$5,110	$5,110	$5,110

Chart 5-1

Beginning in 1981 Browning began a succession of special Limited Edition Waterfowl Series Superposed. The first in the series was the American Mallard Issue. This offering was limited to five hundred guns all in 12 gauge with 28-inch ventilated rib barrels choked modified and full and fitted with a rounded pistol grip stock. Courtesy Browning Company.in

1982: The only change or addition to the Superposed product line for 1982 was the second issue in the Limited Edition Waterfowl Series, the Pintail Issue. This issue was similar in gauge and features to the Mallard Issue of the previous year with the obvious exception of pintail ducks inlaid in place of mallards. This edition was also limited to five hundred guns. Price increases continued their relentless march. The retail price of the Lightning P-1 model with gold inlays was raised to $5,110, a nine percent increase. The P-4 Lightning model with gold inlays was raised to $10,470. The Superposed Continental's retail price increased to $5,720, and the Express rifle's retail price was raised to $4,070. It should be noted that from 1977 to 1982 the retail price for a P-1 Lightning Superposed in 12 or 20 gauge had increased by over seventy percent.

1983: The Presentation Series continued without deletions or additions for 1983 including, for the first time, no price increases. However, the Superposed Continental's retail price was increased to $6,000, and the Express rifle's price was raised to $4,300.

New for 1983 was the addition of the third issue of the Limited Edition Waterfowl Series, the Black Duck Issue. The Black Duck Issue was similar to the two earlier issues, and it too was limited to five hundred guns. The retail price was $8,000.

Perhaps the most interesting development in the Superposed line in 1983 was the return of the traditional Grade I Belgian built Superposed. They were offered only in 12 and 20 gauge in either Lightning or Superlight configuration with choice of 26-1/2 or 28 inch-barrels. The Superlights were offered only with the shorter barrel lengths. The retail price for these traditional Grade I Superposed was $1,995 in either model or gauge.

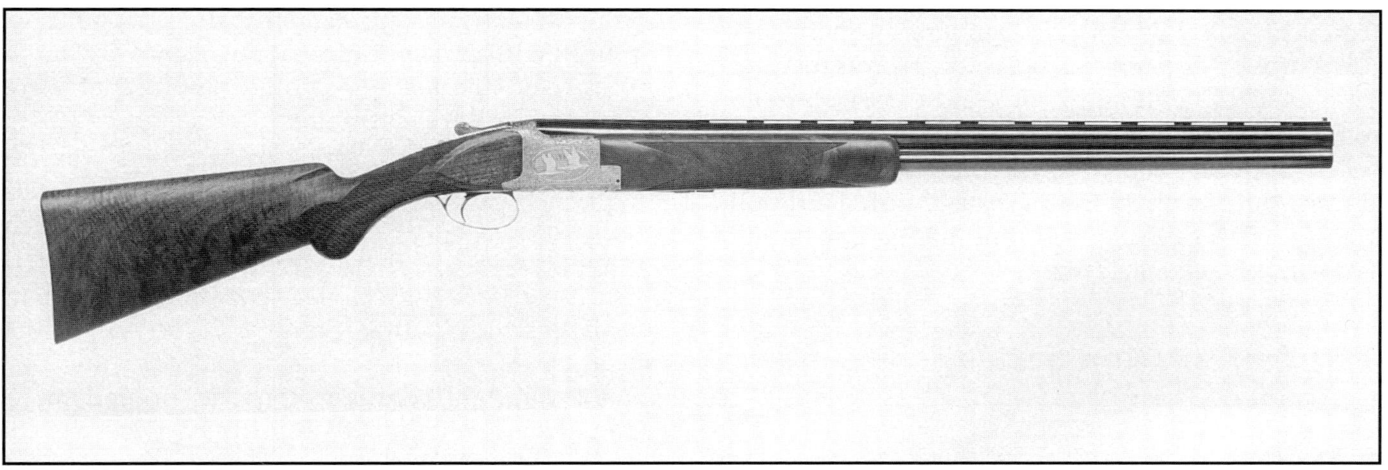

The second in the Limited Edition Waterfowl Series, the Pintail Issue, was introduced in 1982. It, too, was limited to five hundred Superposed in 12 gauge with 28-inch ventilated rib barrels. The gun was fitted with a rounded pistol grip stock. Courtesy Browning Company.

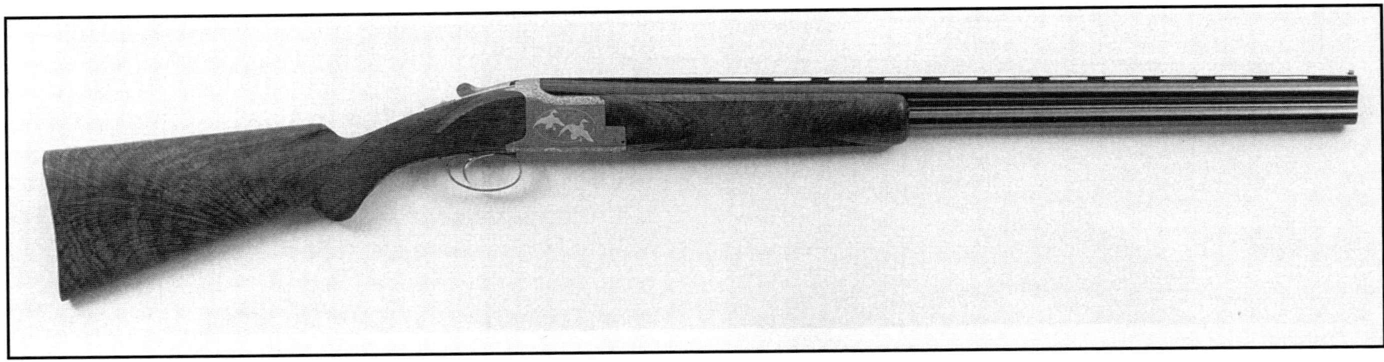

The last of the Limited Edition Waterfowl Series was the Black Duck Issue introduced in 1983. As with the earlier issues it was limited to five hundred 12 gauge guns. Courtesy Browning Company.

1984: This was the last year the Presentation Series was offered for sale in Browning's catalogues. Prices remained stable as did most of the catalogue offerings, with one exception: the discontinuance of the 28 gauge and .410 bore Superposed in the Presentation Series. Availability was limited to inventory on hand.

The Superposed Continental, the Express rifle, and the traditional Grade I Superposed were all offered for sale in the 1984 catalogue. Interestingly enough, prices for the Continental and the Express rifle were reduced. The Superposed Continental set now carried a retail price of $5,600, down from $6,000 the year before. The Express rifle's retail was lowered to $3,925 from $4,300 the preceding year.

Browning introduced its 20 gauge Classic Limited Edition Superposed in 1984. This over and under is not considered by purists to be a true Superposed despite that the barrels were stamped, "MADE IN BELGIUM." The frame and barrels were produced in Japan, the engraving and assembly was done in Belgium at Fabrique Nationale. It was referred to by FN as a B-125. Delivery on these special edition Superposed was not promised until 1986. Its companion gun, the Gold Classic, limited to five hundred guns, was not introduced until the following year. The Gold Classic was a B-25, produced entirely in Belgium. The Limited Edition Waterfowl Series featured only the earlier Pintail Issue and Black Duck Issue.

The Presentation Series Configuration

The Presentation Series Superposed offered essentially the same mechanical design and refinements as the traditional Superposed. The long trigger guard tang with square knob pistol grip was used throughout the Presentation era (except for Superlight guns and special orders), as was the mechanical trigger. Forearm attachment remained the same, as did the innumerable small component parts that made up the whole of the Superposed. Only two real changes occurred. One was the modification of the buttplate from its previous border design to a borderless black plastic style. The other change was that all Presentation Series frames were rounded, a practice found only on Superlights before this period. This rounded frame includes the P-4 grade as well, despite the need to widen the frame slightly to accommodate the fitting of the sideplates. It should be remembered that Superposed in the Presentation years were basically built from parts that were made years earlier. Fabrique Nationale was working off a large supply of inventory, including barrels, frames, forearm irons, ejector mechanisms, and so on. What sets the Presentation Series apart from its traditional Superposed predecessor is its outward appearance, namely engraving patterns and options. Engraving patterns have already been covered in detail in the engraving section of this chapter. This section will concentrate on the relatively large number of options and configurations that were available for the Presentation Series Superposed.

Each Presentation Series Superposed was offered in 12 gauge and 20 gauge Hunting models with 26-1/2 or 28-inch barrels. A 12 gauge 3-inch Magnum model with a choice of 28 or 30-inch barrels was also available. The 12 gauge 3-inch Magnum model was fitted with a factory installed recoil pad.

A Superlight configuration was offered in 12 and 20 gauge with 26-1/2-inch barrels. The 28 gauge and .410 bore were available in a Lightning configuration with either 26-1/2 or 28-inch barrels. There were no catalogued 28 gauge or .410 bore Superlight models offered, although some special order small gauge Superlights were built and sold.

All 12 and 20 gauge Superlights have tapered ribs; the special order small bore Superlights do not.

Trap models were offered in either a Lightning or BROADway configuration with special Trap dimensions, recoil pad, and beavertail forearm. The Lightning Trap was offered with 30-inch barrels, and the BROADway Trap was available with either 30 or 32-inch barrels.

Presentation Skeet models were available in 12 and 20 gauge, as well as 28 gauge and .410 bore. Skeet models were offered with a choice of 26-1/2 or 28-inch barrels. A factory installed recoil pad was standard on Skeet models. All Target models were fitted with ivory front and center sights. An All Gauge Skeet Set was offered with a choice of 26-1/2 or 28-inch barrels. These All Gauge sets were fitted with quarter-inch ventilated ribs.

When the Presentation Series was first introduced in 1977 the number of options was fairly large, but most early first year guns were delivered to the North American market devoid of extras. This lack of optioned Presentation Superposed changed later in 1977 with the influx of P guns fitted with extra cost features. For the balance of the production period most P guns had some options and, generally speaking, the higher the grade the more options the gun was likely to have. However, each grade in the Presentation Series was furnished with certain standard features depending on the specific grade. These standard features are detailed below.

Presentation One (P-1): Each P-1 Superposed was furnished with a ventilated rib with deluxe engine-turned matting on the rib. The chambers were chrome plated, and all P-1 guns were fitted with gold triggers. All exposed metal parts, as well as certain internal parts, were highly polished. The ejectors, cocking lever, and locking bolt were all polished. Each P-1 was fitted with a highly figured American black walnut stock with hand checkering at twenty-five lines to the inch. The buttstock and forearm were finished to a high gloss. Overall the P-1 Superposed was a handsome shotgun with many attractive standard features.

Presentation Two (P-2): The P-2 grade had the same standard features as the P-1 with the addition of a more select higher grade American black walnut stock. The checkering was still a very fine twenty-five lines to the inch. The buttstock and forearm were finished to a high gloss. The most noticeable difference between the P-1 and the P-2 was the style of engraving and the more highly figured stock.

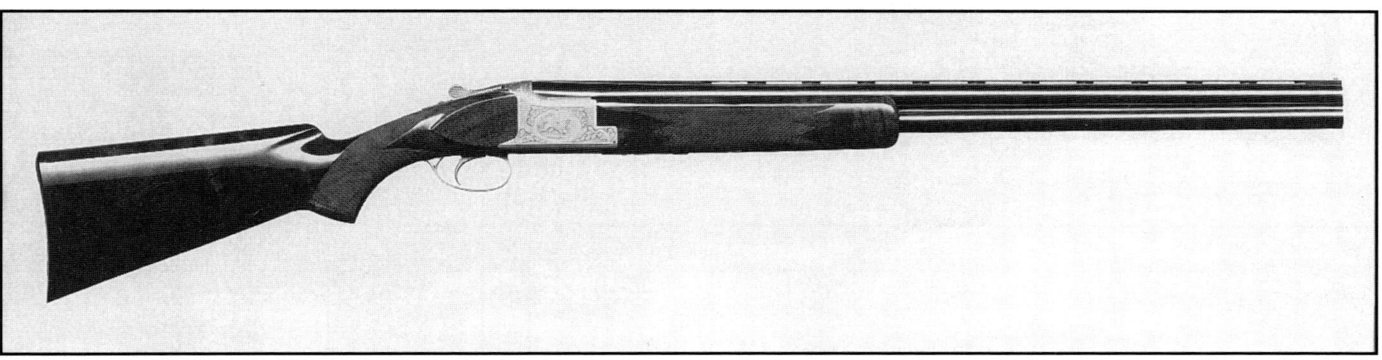

The Presentation One or P-1 Grade. This was the lowest priced presentation grade offered by Browning. The mechanical aspects of the gun were basically the same as the pre-1977 Superposed. Courtesy Browning Company.

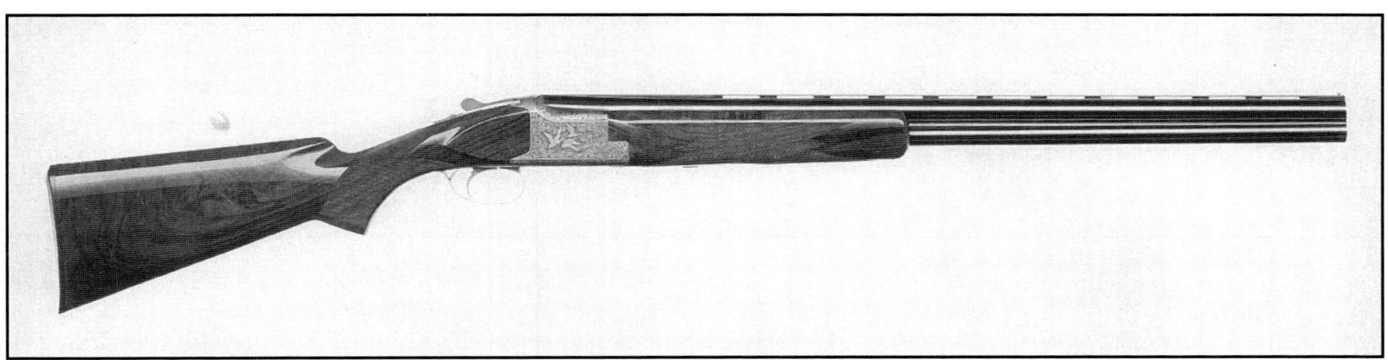

An overall view of the Browning Superposed P-2 Grade. Courtesy Browning Company.

Presentation Three (P-3): The P-3 was furnished with all the amenities of the P-2 with the addition of the finest American walnut Browning offered. The buttstock and forearm were fitted with a beautifully dark, highly figured walnut. The checkering was very fine at twenty-five lines to the inch. Each P-3 was fitted with a sculptured gold plated checkered trigger. The ventilated rib had a very fine engine-turned matting. All metal parts were highly polished, even the breech end of the barrels. The P-3 grade offered some of the finest wood and workmanship available in a production gun regardless of country of origin.

Presentation Four (P-4): The P-4 essentially had all the same features of the P-3 with the addition of sideplates.

Presentation Series Options: Browning offered all of its options on any of its Presentation Series guns, regardless of grade.

1. A straight grip stock alternative was offered on all Presentation Series Superposed.
2. Special stock dimensions were offered for length of pull, drop at the heel, and drop at the comb. If the dimensions requested fell outside Browning's parameters, an extra charge would be made for a completely handmade stock.
3. A Monte Carlo comb was offered on Trap stocks. This is a seldom seen option.
4. Teardrop points on grip. This was an added touch that usually accompanied a completely handmade stock. This option is not often seen.
5. Checkered wooden butt on the sole. This was a popular option and a good looking one as well.
6. Deluxe recoil pad was offered on any Hunting or Superlight model not equipped as standard.
7. Hand rubbed oil finish on buttstock and forearm. A popular option that is often encountered on the higher grade P Series.

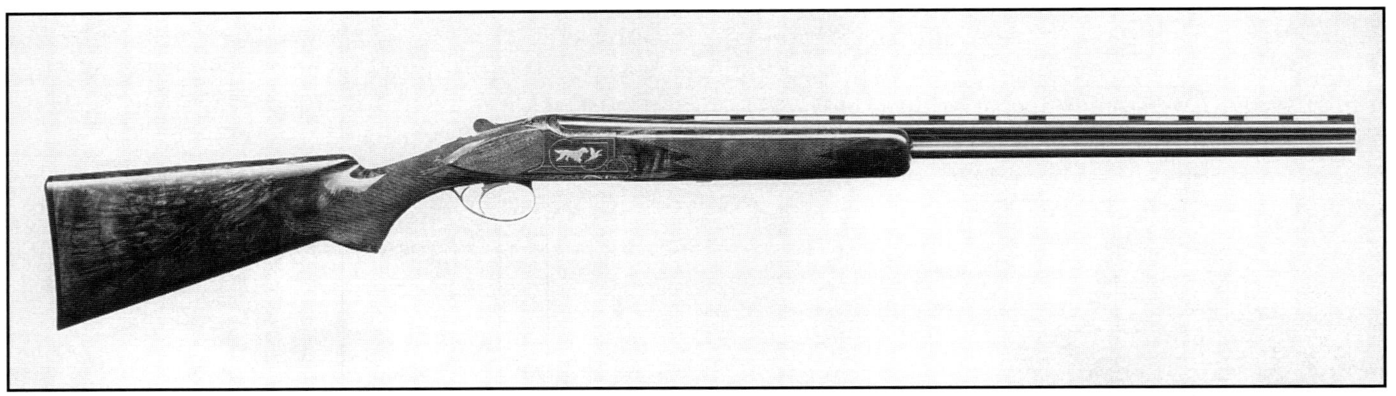

This is a fine example of a P-3 Grade Presentation Superposed. Compared to the P-1 and P-2 Grades, the checkering pattern is elaborate and finely executed. The quality of wood displays more grain and better color. Courtesy Browning Company.

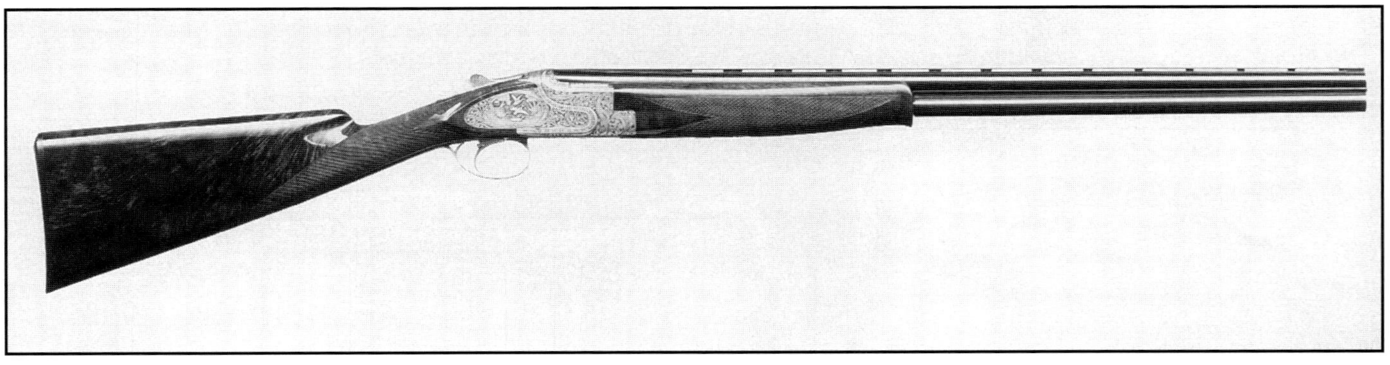

The highest Presentation Grade Browning offered in its catalogues was the P-4 Grade. All Browning P-4 Superposed were fitted with sideplates and stocked with fancy American walnut. The checkering was executed at twenty-five lines to the inch. All interior and exterior metal surfaces were highly polished. The ventilated rib had very fine engine-turned matting. The chambers were chrome plated and the gold plated trigger was sculptured with metal checkering on the forward surface. The P-4 pictured here features a straight grip stock and optional Schnabel forearm. Courtesy Browning Company.

8. Rounded semi-pistol grip (the pre-1968 round knob look). This is a seldom seen option on very early P guns.
9. Schnabel forearm. This is a popular European look that is often seen on straight grip guns.
10. Three-piece forearm. This also gives the Presentation Series guns a very European appearance. More often seen on high grade guns such as P-3 and P-4.
11. A French walnut stock and forearm. An occasionally seen option that results in a stronger stock because of its straight grain.
12. The P-3 and P-4 rib. This option offered a very fine engine-turned matting for P-1 and P-2 guns.
13. Hand matted ventilated rib. An expensive option, $106.00 in 1978, and rarely encountered.
14. Stock oval with initials. Most often this was a gold oval, but silver was offered as well. Frequently encountered in the P-1 and P-2 guns.
15. Engraved or gold inlaid initials on trigger guard.
16. Gold inlay Roman numerals on barrel rib. This option was used for multibarrel sets to designate the barrels by number.
17. Extra barrels consisting of one, two, or three sets, each hand fitted to the gun. Each multibarrel set was sold with a fitted luggage case to accommodate the extra sets of barrels.
18. Browning and FN would build just about any feature the customer desired, provided the customer was willing and able to pay the extra cost. It is possible to encounter almost any imaginable option on a Presentation Series Superposed.

Centennial Continental: Introduced in 1978 to commemorate the one hundredth anniversary of Browning. This set consisted of one set of 20 gauge 26-1/2-inch barrels choked modified and full, chambered for 3-inch shells, and fitted with an engine-turned ventilated rib with German nickel silver front sight bead. The second set of barrels was 24 inches in length and chambered for the 30-06 Springfield rifle cartridge. The rifle barrels were furnished with folding rear leaf sight and a flat-faced gold bead front sight. The trigger was gold plated and was the original inertia type. Selective ejectors and manual safety were also standard. The straight grip buttstock and Schnabel forearm were of select full figured American walnut with twenty-five lines to the inch checkering. An oil finish was used on the stock.

The engraving pattern was designed by master engraver Louis Vrancken and executed by FN engravers. The frame was engraved with a fleur-de-lis pattern with a gold inlaid bob-white quail in flight on one side. On the opposite side a gold inlaid bull elk was featured. The bottom of the frame had a profile of John M. Browning with the dates 1878-1978 engraved among fine line scrollwork. The Centennial Continental was limited to five hundred guns with serial numbers 1878C-0001 through 1878C-0500. The set was shipped in a walnut case fitted with a full-length brass piano hinge and brass corner guards. The inside was lined in red wine velvet.

The length of pull was 14-1/4 inches and drop at the comb was 1-1/2 inches with shotgun barrels installed and 1-11/16 inches with the rifle barrels installed. The drop at the heel was 2-7/32 inches with the shotgun barrels installed and 2-1/2 inches with the rifle barrels in place. The weight of the gun with shotgun barrels in place was 5 lb. 14 oz., and with the rifle barrels installed the weight was 6 lb. 14 oz.

Continental: The Continental was a continuation of the Centennial Continental but without the profuse engraving or fancy walnut stock. The physical dimensions of the gun remained the same. The frame was tastefully engraved with light scroll and rosette designs on the hinge pin. The frame was blued, and the stock was a select walnut with oil finish and twenty-five lines to the inch checkering. The Continental was cased in a fitted luggage type case with silicone impregnated nylon fleece.

Express Rifle: This Superposed rifle was a derivative of the Continental Superposed. It was furnished with a single set of rifle barrels chambered for the 30-06 Springfield or .270 Winchester. The barrels were 24 inches in length, and were fitted with a folding rear leaf sight with a flat-faced gold bead front sight mounted on a matted ramp. The frame was engraved similarly to a Grade I Superposed with scroll and fleur-de-lis designs. The trigger was gold plated. The straight grip, select walnut stock was mated to a Schnabel forearm and both were checkered twenty-five lines to the inch. The rifle was cased in a luggage type case lined with nylon fleece. The rifle weighed approximately 6 lb. 14 oz.

Waterfowl Series: There were three Superposed issues in this series: the Mallard Issue, the Pintail Issue, and the Black Duck Issue. All of these guns were identical except for the engraving, which featured the particular waterfowl of that issue in gold inlay. Each commemorative Superposed was limited to five hundred guns. Each issue featured a 12 gauge set of 28-inch ventilated rib barrels choked modified and full. The buttstock

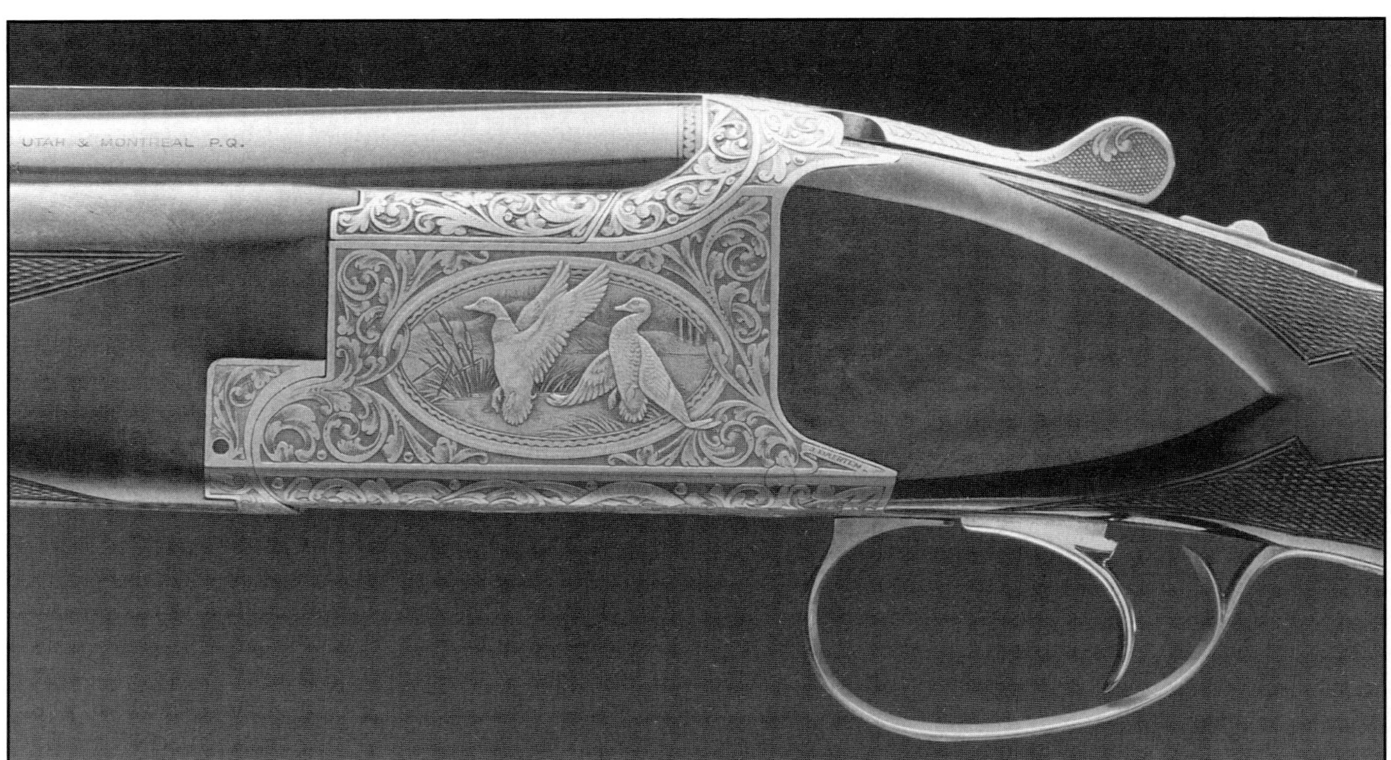

José Baerten engraved both sides of this American Mallard Superposed. The birds were executed in gold on a gray receiver. The result was a very handsome Superposed. Courtesy Browning Company.

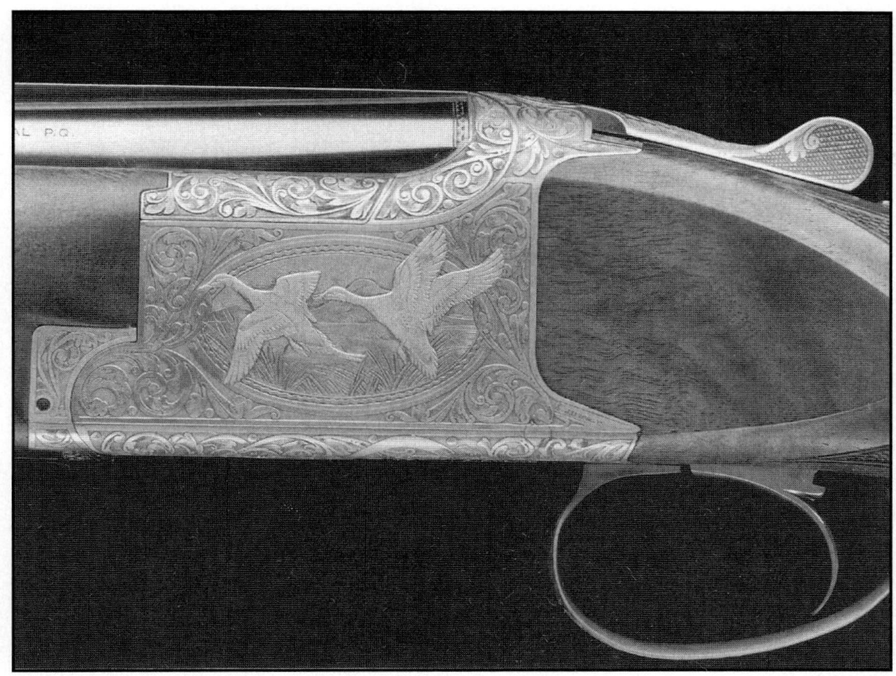

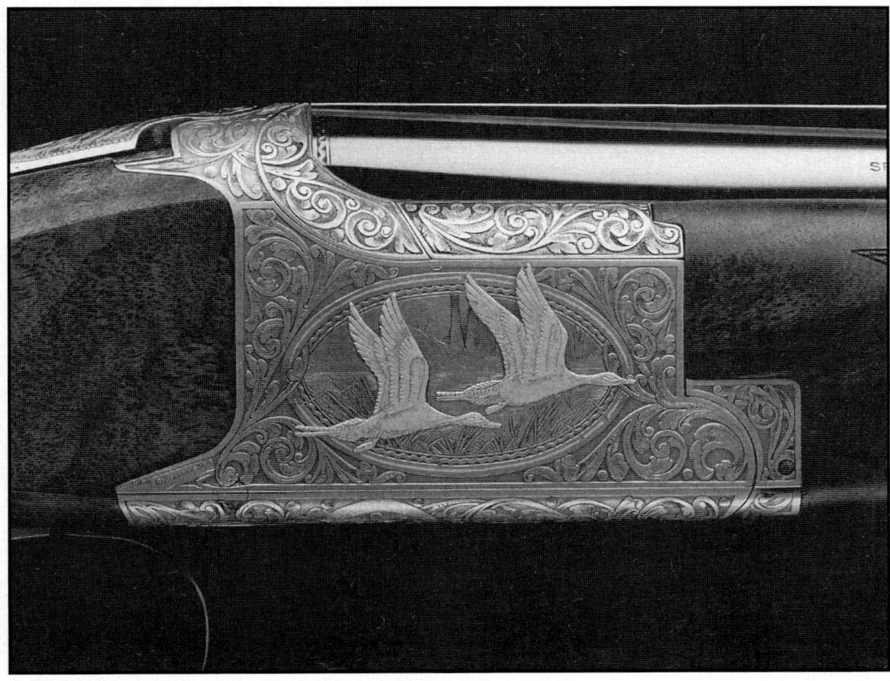

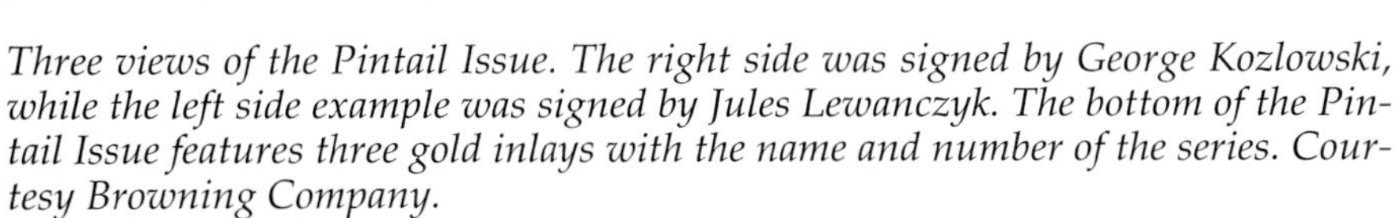

Three views of the Pintail Issue. The right side was signed by George Kozlowski, while the left side example was signed by Jules Lewanczyk. The bottom of the Pintail Issue features three gold inlays with the name and number of the series. Courtesy Browning Company.

featured a rounded pistol grip with twenty-four lines to the inch checkering. The stocks were high grade, darkly figured French walnut with oil finish. These limited edition Superposed were provided with a black walnut case lined with velvet with full-length hinge, brass corner guards, and brass latches.

Presentation Series Production to 1984

Presentation Series production was quite low for this period. Approximately fifteen hundred P guns were built and sold during this eight-year time span. However, what is important to understand during this era is Browning's new serial number system. In a company memorandum dated September 10, 1975, Harm Williams advised his staff that a new serial number system would be initiated during 1976. The reason for this change was stated by Mr. Williams: "Our present system which identifies a product by a letter and its location in the number series is no longer satisfactory since the breath of our models is becoming in excess of the number of the letters usable." Browning incorporated its present coding system into the new serial number by using the first, second, and fourth numbers of the product code. The year of production was also included by using alphabetical letters to designate numbers. The year code was established as illustrated below.

Browning Year Code

Z=1	T=6
Y=2	R=7
X=3	P=8
W=4	N=9
V=5	M=0

The year 1976, for example, is expressed by the letters RT, the year 1977 becomes RR, and so forth. The remainder of the serial number is shown as the production sequence and will start over each year. The beginning serial number will then appear as "1000" followed by 1001, 1002, and so on. This system does not apply to special serial numbers assigned to limited edition Superposed such as the Waterfowl Series. The system was supposed to be in place before the end of 1976 for use on the Superposed, but in reality it did not begin in earnest until 1977. Using prior product codes assigned to the Superposed, the following system was established.

SERIAL NUMBER SYSTEM/SUPERPOSED GRADE I

Grade I Type	Product Code	1976 Serial Number
Magnum 12	1504	153 RT 1000
Lightning 12	2104	213 RT 1000
Lightning 12 Skeet	2B04	2B3 RT 1000
Lightning 12 Trap	2404	243 RT 1000
BROADway Trap	2904	293 RT 1000
Superlight 12	2004	203 RT 1000
Lightning 20	2304	233 RT 1000
Lightning 20 Skeet	2C04	2C3 RT 1000
Superlight 20	2204	223 RT 1000
Lightning 28	1704	173 RT 1000
28 Gauge Skeet	1E04	1E3 RT 1000
Lightning .410	1804	183 RT 1000
Lightning .410 Skeet	1F04	1F3 RT 1000

Table 5-1

SERIAL NUMBER SYSTEM/SUPERPOSED DIANA GRADE

Diana Grade Type	Product Code	1976 Serial Number
Lightning 12	5104	513 RT 1000
Magnum 12	5504	553 RT 1000
Lightning 12 Skeet	5B04	5B3 RT 1000
Lightning 12 Trap	5404	543 RT 1000
BROADway Trap	5904	593 RT 1000
Superlight 12	5004	503 RT 1000
Lightning 20	5304	533 RT 1000
Lightning 20 Skeet	5C04	5C3 RT 1000
Superlight 20	5204	523 RT 1000
Lightning 28	5704	573 RT 1000
28 Gauge Skeet	5E04	5E3 RT 1000
Lightning .410	5804	583 RT 1000
Lightning .410 Skeet	5F04	5F3 RT 1000

Table 5-2

SERIAL NUMBER SYSTEM/SUPERPOSED MIDAS GRADE

Midas Grade Type	Product Code	1976 Serial Number
Lightning 12	6104	613 RT 1000
Magnum 12	6504	653 RT 1000
Lightning 12 Skeet	6B04	6B3 RT 1000
Lightning 12 Trap	6404	643 RT 1000
BROADway Trap	6904	693 RT 1000
Superlight 12	6004	603 RT 1000
Lightning 20	6304	633 RT 1000
Lightning 20 Skeet	6C04	6C3 RT 1000
Superlight 20	6204	623 RT 1000
Lightning 28	6704	673 RT 1000
28 Gauge Skeet	6E04	6E3 RT 1000
Lightning .410	6804	683 RT 1000
Lightning .410 Skeet	6F04	6F3 RT 1000

Table 5-3

SERIAL NUMBER SYSTEM/SUPERPOSED EXHIBITION GRADE

Exhibition Grade Type	Product Code	1976 Serial Number
Lightning 12	7104	713 RT 1000
Magnum 12	7504	753 RT 1000
Lightning 12 Skeet	7B04	7B3 RT 1000
Lightning 12 Trap	7404	743 RT 1000
BROADway Trap	7904	793 RT 1000
Superlight 12	7004	704 RT 1000
Lightning 20	7304	733 RT 1000
Lightning 20 Skeet	7C04	7C3 RT 1000
Superlight 20	7204	723 RT 1000
Lightning 28	7704	773 RT 1000
28 Gauge Skeet	7E04	7E3 RT 1000
Lightning .410	7804	783 RT 1000
Lightning .410 Skeet	7F04	7F3 RT 1000

Table 5-4

SERIAL NUMBER SYSTEM/SUPERPOSED ALL GAUGE SKEET SET

All Gauge Skeet Set	Product Code	1976 Serial Number
Grade I	1A04	1A4 RT 1000
Diana Grade	5A04	5A4 RT 1000
Midas Grade	6A04	6A4 RT 1000

Table 5-5

The data compiled above illustrate in great detail a system that is not likely to be encountered except on rare occasions. The following year, 1977, Browning introduced the Presentation Series Superposed, which for all practical purposes made the new serial number system obsolete. Presentation Series Superposed did, however, share some aspects of the new system. The year code was still part of the serial number as expressed by the letter code; in the case of 1977 the code RR would be used. The production sequence was also utilized in the Presentation Series serial number, beginning with "1000." The most noticeable difference, and to some extent the most confusing aspect to the P gun serial numbers, was the use of the letter "P" as a prefix to the product code in place of the first digit. For example, "P33 RR 1000" indicates that the Superposed in question is a Presentation Series gun produced in 1977 in a 12 gauge Lightning configuration. This new "P" Series code does not disclose the specific grade of the gun or what engraving option was used. In short, the information that is part of the P gun serial number gives different information than what is shown on traditional Superposed pre-1977 guns. The new Presentation Series serial number system will appear as follows:

The serial number codes remained the same throughout the Presentation Series production period, with the only change being in the year code from 1977 to 1984.

The Waterfowl Limited Edition Series also employed a similar serial number code. The product code for the Mallard Series was 8G4, the Pintail was 8H4, and the Black Duck Series was 8J4.

One important note: Browning did not have a product code for a Superlight 28 gauge or .410 bore Superposed. The product code that was used for these guns in the serial number was the same as that used for the Lightning 28 gauge or .410 bore Lightning.

BROWNING SUPERPOSED SERIAL NUMBER SYSTEM PRESENTATION SERIES

Type	1977 Serial Number
Lightning 12	P13 RR 1000
Magnum 12	P53 RR 1000
Lightning 12 Skeet	PB3 RR 1000
Lightning 12 Trap	P43 RR 1000
BROADway Trap	P93 RR 1000
Superlight 12	P03 RR 1000
Lightning 20	P33 RR 1000
Lightning 20 Skeet	PC3 RR 1000
Superlight 20	P23 RR 1000
Lightning 28	P73 RR 1000
28 Gauge Skeet	PE3 RR 1000
Lightning .410	P83 RR 1000
Lightning .410 Skeet	PF3 RR 1000
Skeet – 4 Barrel Set	PA4 RR 1000
Skeet – 2 or 3 Barrel Set	PB4 RR 1000
Lightning/Superlight – 2, 3, 4 Barrel Set	P14 RR 1000
Magnum 12 ga. – 2, 3, 4 Barrel Set	P54 RR 1000

Table 5-6

Presentation Series Era Sales: 1977-1984

Sales data for the Presentation Series Superposed are derived from official Browning Company sales reports. They represent only those Superposed imported into North America by Browning. There were other notable groups of Superposed sold in North America during the period 1977 through 1984. Where sales data for these guns is available, they will be discussed as well. This eight-year period marks the last era of the production built Superposed. The number of Superposed sold through Browning in North America during this interval is relatively small when compared to the decades preceding 1977. It was also a period when a number of FN Superposed guns built for its European market were imported through Browning for sale in North America. The early 1980s were difficult economic times in Europe, and Fabrique Nationale looked to Browning USA as a means of disposing of inventory that was slow to sell in Europe.

Table 5-7 gives a consolidated analysis of Presentation Series sales by gauge, type, and grade. The table provides the reader with an expeditious look at the breakdown of sales, indicating which Presentation guns were the most popular and which were the least popular. It is important to point out that the sales figures for the Lightning 28 gauge and .410 bore include guns sold in the Superlight configuration in those gauges. Browning did not have a catalogue number for small bore Superlights and thus included both 28 gauge and .410 bore Superlight and Lightning guns in the same category. It is therefore not possible to provide a definitive number on these guns.

Presentation Superposed Yearly Sales See Chart 5-2

The most obvious place to start with analysis is in the yearly sales figures for the Presentation Series. Chart 5-2 clearly illustrates the relatively brisk start the P Series had, and the corresponding swift downturn in sales in the years that followed its introduction. The year 1978 represents the high point in Presentation Superposed sales with 426 guns sold. Total Presentation Superposed sold during this production period amounted to only 1,488 guns. Perhaps this chart best explains why the Presentation Series Superposed was dropped from the Browning line as a production gun. Sales simply could not justify its continued production.

Presentation Series Sales by Grade See Chart 5-3

Chart 5-3 shows the Presentation Series sales by grade for the total production period. As expected, the lowest priced P gun, the P-1, was the most popular grade with 584 guns sold, or thirty-nine percent of total P gun sales. That trend continued for each grade, with the P-2 next in sales with 426 guns sold, or twenty-nine percent of sales; the P-3 third with 299 guns sold, or twenty percent of sales; and the most expensive P-4 the least purchased grade with only 179 guns sold, or twelve percent of total sales.

"P" Series Yearly Sales by Grade See Chart 5-4

Chart 5-4 delineates those Presentation Series sales by grade according to year. This analysis gives a more detailed account of sales by grade and clearly shows that in almost every year sales were progressively less from the lower to the higher grades. The most conspicuous exception is 1981 when the P-3 outsold both the P-1 and P-2 grades.

BROWNING P SERIES BY GAUGE, TYPE, AND GRADE
1977-1984

Gauge	Type	P1	P2	P3	P4	Grand Total	% of Total
12	Lightning	117	54	28	20	219	15%
12	Magnum	47	14	7	2	70	5%
12	Superlight	25	23	16	14	78	5%
12	Skeet	18	6	6	0	30	2%
All Gauge	Skeet Set	16	13	10	11	50	3%
12	Trap	14	15	4	0	33	2%
12	Broadway	24	16	9	7	56	4%
Total		**261**	**141**	**80**	**54**	**536**	**36%**
20	Lightning	102	52	30	23	207	14%
20	Superlight	80	93	85	44	302	20%
20	Skeet	16	6	6	0	28	2%
Total		**198**	**151**	**121**	**67**	**537**	**36%**
28	Lightning*	38	57	36	20	151	10%
28	Skeet	5	6	2	0	13	1%
Total		**43**	**63**	**38**	**20**	**164**	**11%**
.410	Lightning*	47	44	37	35	163	11%
.410	Skeet	6	6	3	0	15	1%
Total		**53**	**50**	**40**	**35**	**178**	**12%**
Multi-Barrel Sets #		**29**	**21**	**20**	**3**	**73**	**5%**
Grand Total		**584**	**426**	**299**	**179**	**1488**	**100%**
% of Total		39%	29%	20%	12%	100%	

*The Lightning category for the 28 gauge and .410 bore includes Superlights as well.

Multi-Barrel data for the P4 Grade is incomplete. This is an estimate only.

Table 5-7

PRESENTATION SERIES SUPERPOSED YEARLY SALES
1977-1984
Hundreds
500
400
300
200
100
0
1977
1978
1979
1980
1981
1982
1983
1984
Yearly Sales
151
426
316
143
200
144
35
67

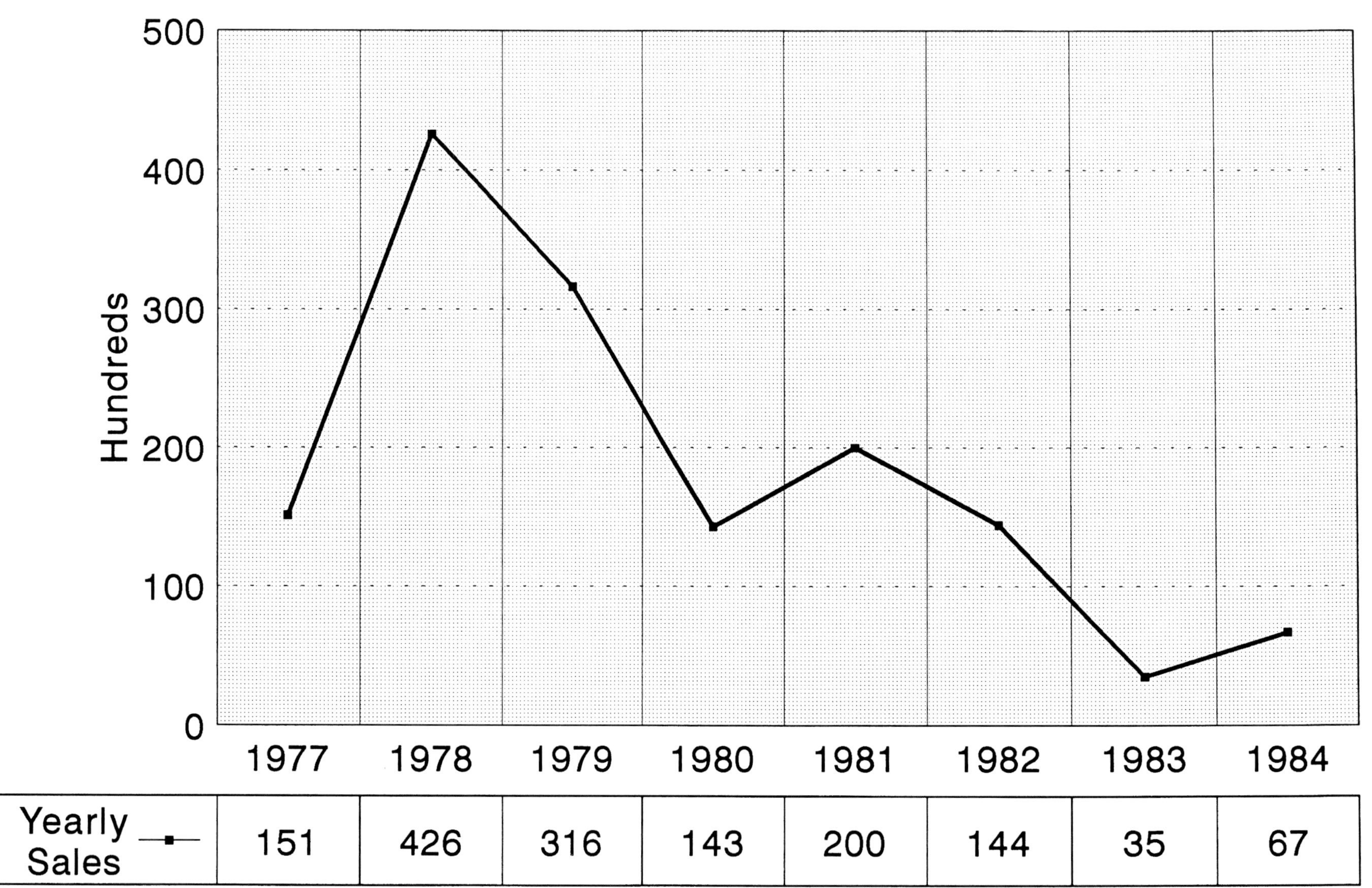

Chart 5-2

BROWNING PRESENTATION SERIES SALES by Grade 1977-1984

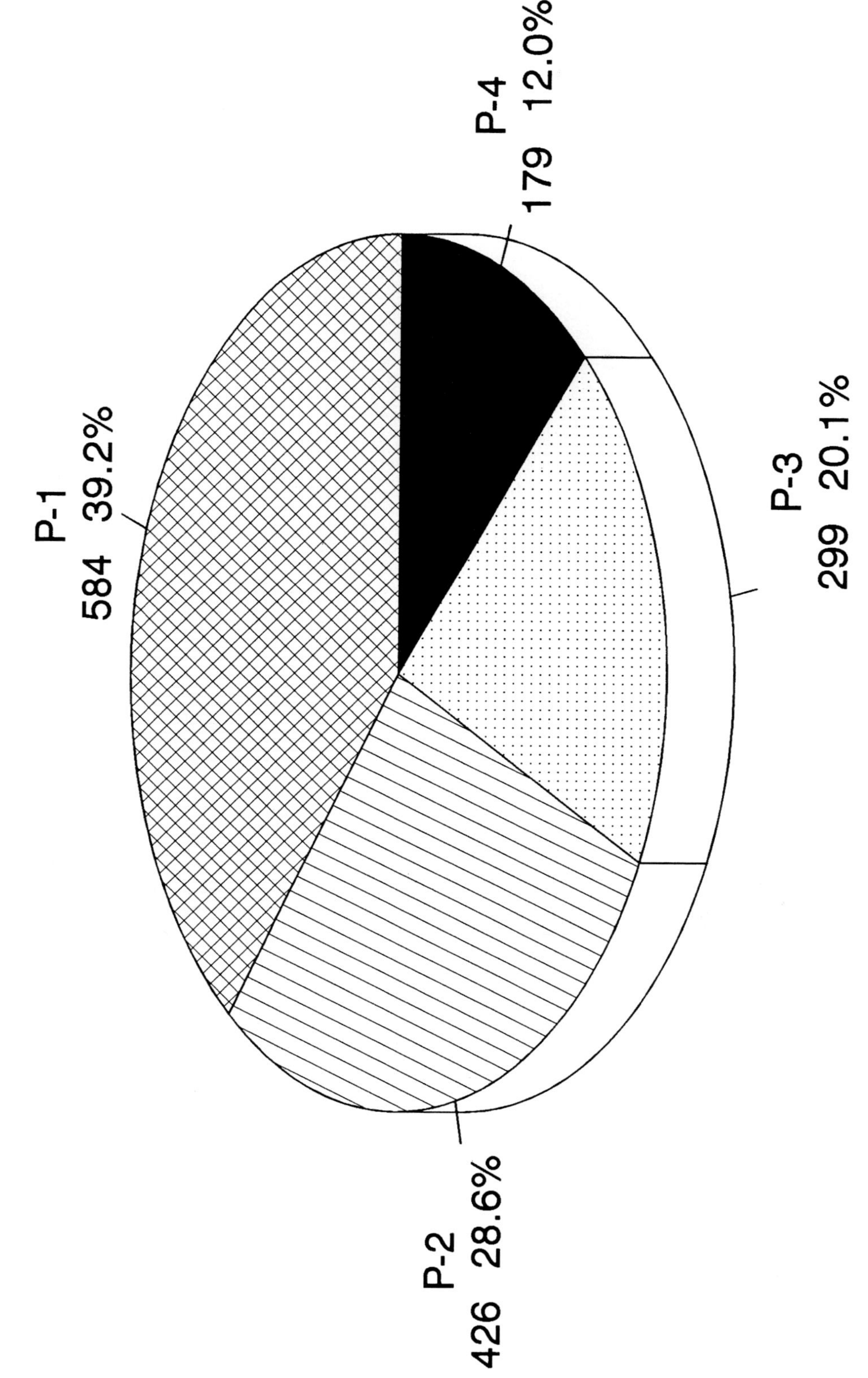

Chart 5-3

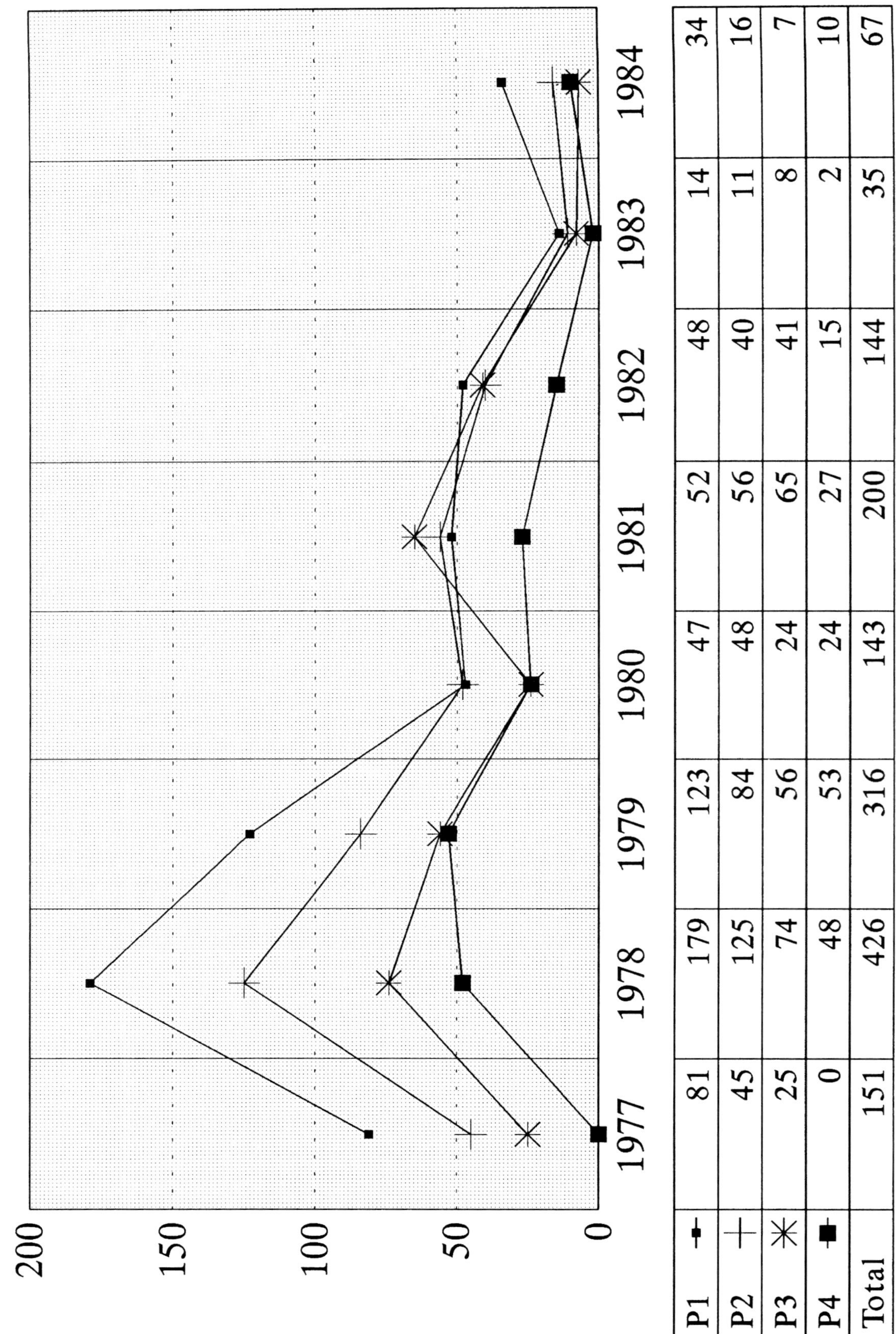

	1977	1978	1979	1980	1981	1982	1983	1984
P1	81	179	123	47	52	48	14	34
P2	45	125	84	48	56	40	11	16
P3	25	74	56	24	65	41	8	7
P4	0	48	53	24	27	15	2	10
Total	151	426	316	143	200	144	35	67

Chart 5-4

Presentation Series Sales by Gauge See Chart 5-5

Sales of the Presentation Series by gauge offer an interesting summary. Presentation sales were almost even for 12 and 20 gauge guns. These two gauges accounted for seventy-six percent of all P gun sales. The 28 gauge sales accounted for twelve percent of sales, and the .410 bore had thirteen percent of total sales. The data shown on Chart 5-5 does not include multibarrel sets, and is therefore based on total sales of 1,415 Presentation Series Superposed.

"P" Series Sales by Gauge & Grade See Chart 5-6

Chart 5-6 shows the breakdown of sales by gauge and grade. This data provides some useful information regarding grades sold in relation to gauge. For example, about ten to twelve percent of P-4s sold were 12, 20, and 28 gauge guns, but almost twenty percent of .410 bore P guns were P-4 grade. When it came to the 20 gauge, 28 gauge, and .410 bore almost twenty-three percent were P-3 grades; the 12 gauge had about fourteen percent sold as P-3 grade. For 12 gauge Presentation Superposed the P-1 was by far the most popular grade; forty-eight percent of all 12 gauge guns were P-1s. The 20 gauge ratio was lower at thirty-seven percent, while the 28 gauge and .410 bore were twenty-nine percent and thirty percent respectively.

During the early 1980s, particularly 1982, Browning imported a large number of FN Superposed built expressly for FN's European markets. Because of a European economic recession, FN offered these Belgian made Superposed to Browning for sale in North America.

Table 5-8 shows the number of guns by grade imported by Browning in 1982. This list does not include FN built European Superposed brought into North America by individuals or by Browning at other times during the period 1977 to 1984.

In 1983 and 1984 a number of special order traditional Superposed were sold by Browning USA in North America. These Superposed were special order guns in Grade I only and came in 12 and 20 gauge in Lightning or Superlight configuration. In 1983 there were approximately 285 of these Superposed sold, and in 1984 there were 578 sold. A breakdown of these special order sales are show in Table 5-9.

Another group of special order Superposed was sold in 1984. These Superposed consisted of 28 gauge and .410 bore Superlights imported by Browning and sold through two Browning dealers, Bill Jacqua and Tom Koessl. These were special order Superposed in every manner, from special serial numbers to tapered ventilated ribs. There were two hundred .410 bore Superlights sold during this period and ten 28 gauge Superlights. Of the two hundred .410 bore, 175 were fitted with 28-inch barrels and 25 were furnished with 26-1/2-inch barrels. Seventy-five of these .410 bore Superlights were produced as sets, so that there were fifteen of each of five grades including Grade I, Pigeon, Pointer, Diana, and Midas. The serial numbers of these sets appear below.

SPECIAL ORDER .410 SUPERLIGHT SETS 1984

421J83-425J83	501J83-505J83
431J83-435J83	511J83-515J83
441J83-445J83	521J83-525J83
451J83-455J83	531J83-535J83
461J83-465J83	541J83-545J83
471J83-475J83	551J83-555J83
481J81-485J83	561J83-565J83
491J83-495J83	

There were an additional twenty-five Grade I Superlights with 28-inch barrels, forty-four Pointer Grades with 28-inch barrels, twenty Diana Grades with 28-inch barrels, thirty-four Midas Grades with 28-inch barrels, and two distinctively engraved Midas Grades by José Baerten.[5] All of these special order .410 bore Superposed serial numbers fall between 415J83 and 614J83. These .410 bore Superlights have an interesting numbering sequence that has Grade I serial numbers ending with 1 or 6, Pigeon Grades with 2, Pointer Grades with 7 or 0, Diana Grades with 4 or 8, and Midas Grades with 5 or 9.

The ten 28 gauge Superlights were sold as follows: two Grade I (serial numbers 3308 and 3313), two Pigeon Grades (serial numbers 3309 and 3314), two Pointer Grades (serial numbers 3310 and 3315), two Diana Grades (serial numbers 3331 and 3316), and two Midas Grades (serial numbers 3312

---

[5] Tom Koessl, *Browning Collectors Association Newsletter*, Vol. XI, No. 6, May/June 1990.

BROWNING PRESENTATION SERIES SALES by Gauge 1977-1984

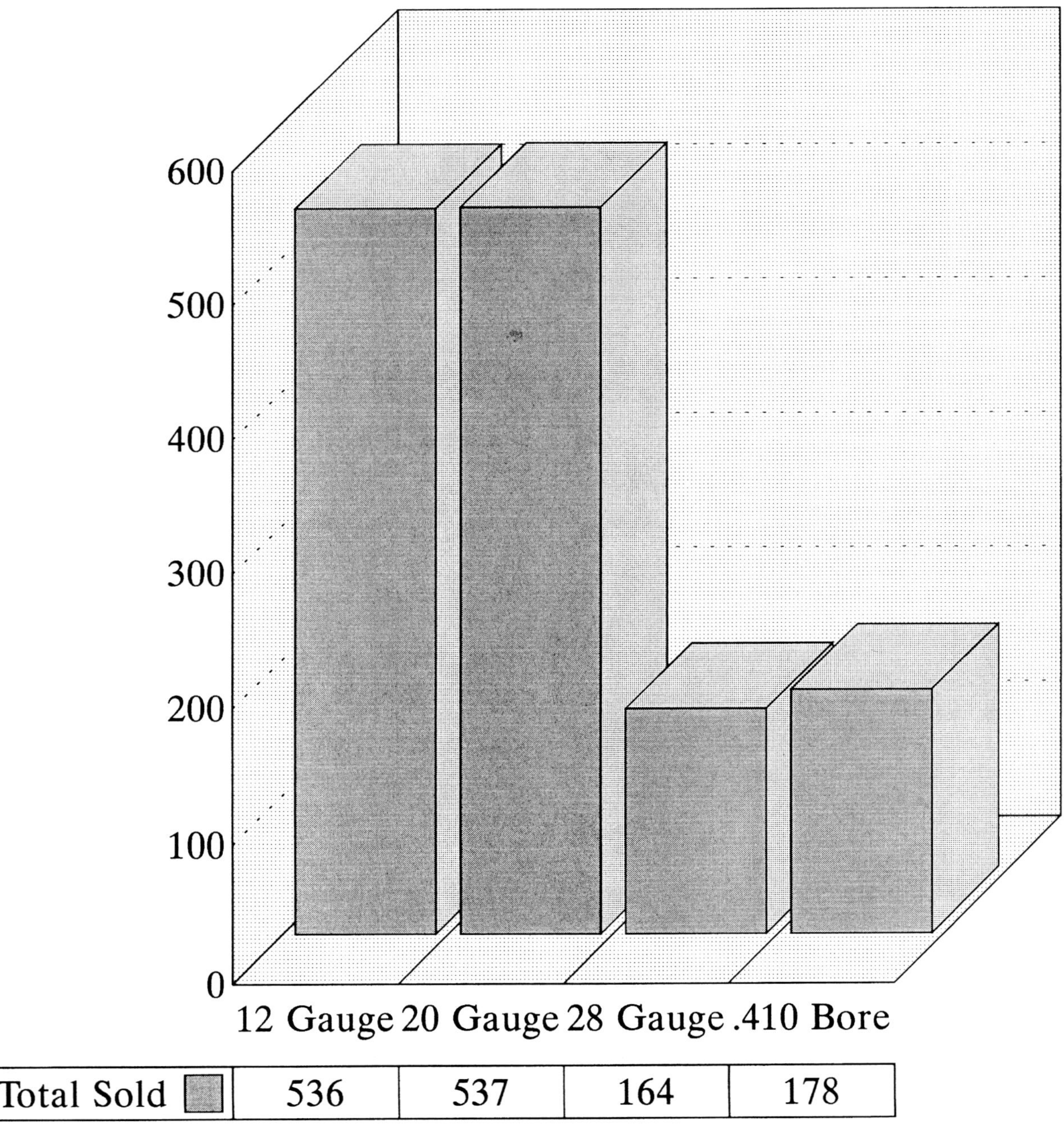

	12 Gauge	20 Gauge	28 Gauge	.410 Bore
Total Sold	536	537	164	178

Chart 5-5

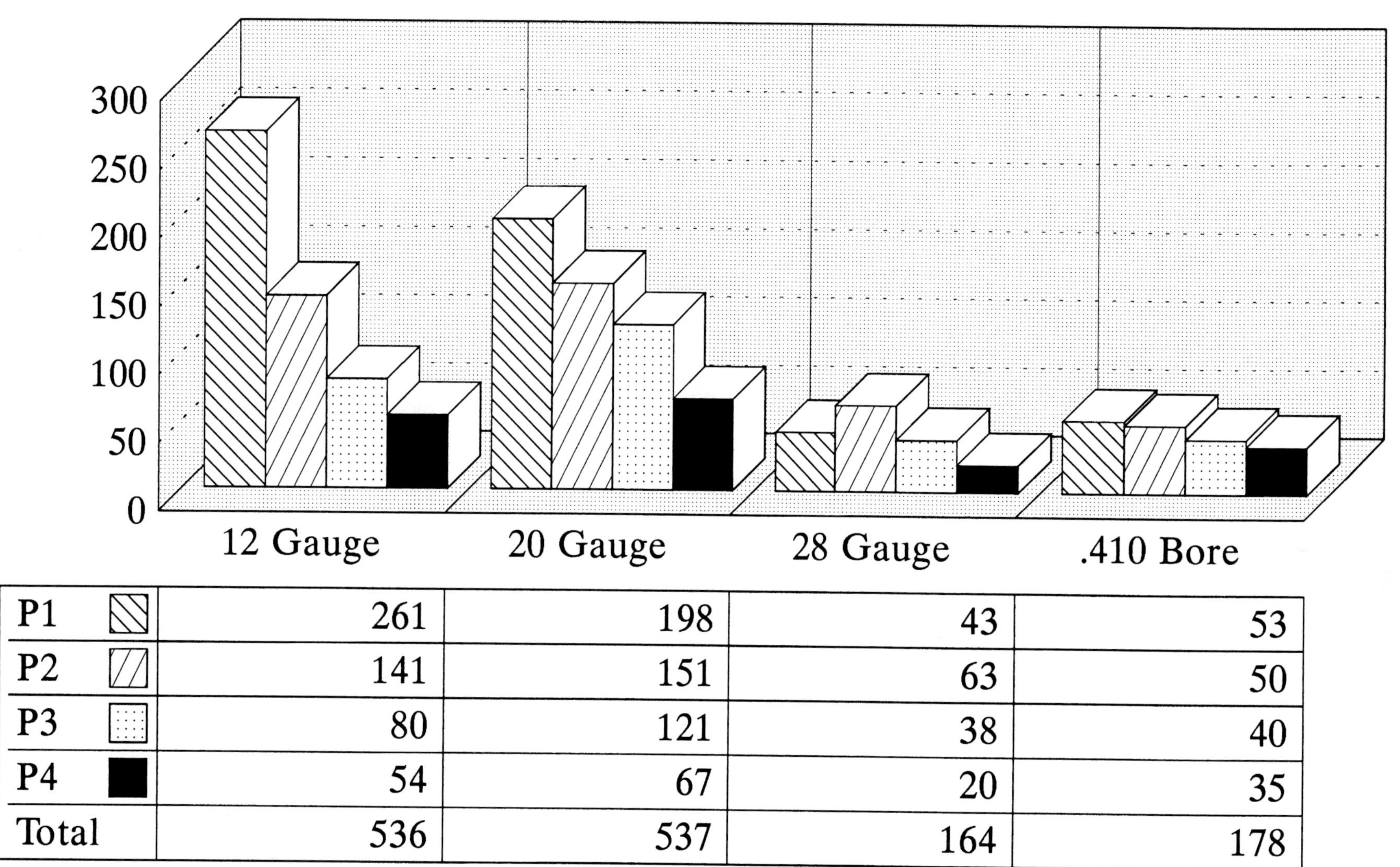

	12 Gauge	20 Gauge	28 Gauge	.410 Bore
P1	261	198	43	53
P2	141	151	63	50
P3	80	121	38	40
P4	54	67	20	35
Total	536	537	164	178

Excludes multibarrel sets
Chart 5-6

BROWNING/FN SUPERPOSED BY GRADE: 1982 SHIPMENT

FN Grade	Quantity Sold	FN Grade	Quantity Sold
A1	1582	D3	59
A2	51	D4	14
B1	370	D4G	13
B2	68	D5	23
B2G	191	D5G	2
C1	120	D7	1
C2	87	I1	1
C2G	107	M1	2
C3	163	M2	2
D1	97	F1	3
D2	19	**Total All Grades**	2,975

Table 5-8

SUPERPOSED SPECIAL ORDER SALES 1983-1984

Gauge	Type	1983	1984
12 ga.	Lightning 28"	55	101
12 ga.	Lightning 26-1/2"	37	94
12 ga.	Superlight 26-1/2"	13	135
20 ga.	Lightning 28"	26	64
20 ga.	Lightning 26-1/2"	45	66
20 ga.	Superlight 26-1/2"	109	118
	Total	285	578

Table 5-9

and 3317). All of these guns were fitted with 28-inch barrels and were delivered in 1986. The serial numbers of these special order 28 gauge Superposed range from 3308F84 to 3317F84.

Between 1978 and 1984 there were a number of limited edition and specialty Superposed produced for specific purposes or promotions. These include the Waterfowl Series, consisting of three issues: the Mallard, the Pintail, and the Black Duck. The Waterfowl Series was scheduled to have two more editions, the Canvasback and the Canada Goose. The Canvasback edition would have been identical to the other Waterfowl Series, but the Canada Goose edition was designed with 3-inch chambers and 30-inch barrels. Neither edition was ever ordered into production due the collapse of the oil markets in the southwest United States.

The Centennial Continental commemorated the one hundredth anniversary of John M. Browning's copious firearms designs, and the Standard Continental and the Express Rifle were attempts to introduce new derivatives of the Superposed. All of the limited editions were restricted to five hundred guns. The Standard Continental and the Express Rifle had no production restrictions and were considered open production guns. All of these Superposed guns sold in roughly the same numbers; limited editions or open production, it seemed to make no difference. The Standard Continental was offered in two choices of caliber: the 30-06 had sales of 239 rifles, and the .270 Winchester recorded sales of 224 rifles. The Gold Classic, a highly engraved B-25, was introduced in 1986, but was offered for sale in the company's catalogue as early as 1984. Table 5-10 illustrates the sales of these Superposed through 1994.

TOTAL SALES OF LIMITED EDITION AND SPECIALTY SUPERPOSED 1978-1994

Type	Total Sales
Mallard Issue	356
Pintail Issue	280
Black Duck Issue	314
Centennial Continental	226
Standard Continental	734
Express Rifle	463

Table 5-10

Throughout the course of the Presentation Series era, Browning imported all manner of FN produced over and under guns. The vast majority of these guns were built on the Superposed design with Belgian labor. A large shipment of Liège guns, referred to as the B-26, were sold in North America during this period, as were other over and under designs. One such shipment consisted of B-27s delivered in 1984. These guns, although over and under shotguns, were assembled in Belgium with component parts from various countries. The gun's forearm was detachable, unlike the Superposed, and its design had been altered to take advantage of the most cost effective manufacturing methods. These over and under guns carried a retail price of about $600 in Grade I and slightly higher prices in Grade II. They were not Browning Superposed B-25s and were never planned to be imported into North America. They were built and sold by FN to celebrate the one thousand year anniversary of the founding of Liège.

And so the production Superposed era comes to a close. Constantly rising prices and inadequate deliveries, coupled with the inevitable falling demand, spelled the end of the production line Superposed. What did not change and would not change, however, was Browning's commitment to keep the Superposed in its product line, albeit as a custom order gun. The Superposed would remain the flagship of the Browning Company, a symbol of John M. Browning's genius and a proud representative of the quality and dependability of all Browning products. To the hunter and shooter, the Superposed represented perhaps the greatest value in a quality built double gun. That quality and value made it the most popular over and under shotgun in North America.

Epilogue

The Legacy Lives On: 1985-1995

The Browning Superposed no longer played the pivotal role in terms of volume or profits that it once had for either the Browning Company or Fabrique Nationale. What the Superposed did retain during this period was its status as the flagship of the Browning Company and an important symbol of pride for Fabrique Nationale. However, both companies were preoccupied with other aspects of their corporate activities. Browning for the most part concentrated on its continued expansion in those areas that had shown great promise, namely hunting and fishing. Most of Browning's firearms line now resided comfortably with Miroku, and the over and under shotgun, once the exclusive domain of the Superposed, was capably represented by the Citori. Fabrique Nationale, in the meantime, turned its energies away from expansion and diversification, and toward survival.

Browning and Fabrique Nationale: A Study in Contrast

Fabrique Nationale began to experience the same economic hardships that had befallen the Browning Company ten years earlier. A severe European recession exacerbated an already fragile corporate structure grown cumbersome by administrative personnel and high business overhead. FN had built expensive plants to handle the expected orders of Belgian military jet engines, but the aircraft industry experienced a severe crisis throughout the world and the great expectations proved somewhat illusory. FN Sports's entry into golfing and tennis was too late to take advantage of the increased demand in those areas. The company was furthermore handicapped by a costly level of debt brought about by this anticipated expansion of business. Fabrique Nationale sought and received vital infusions of much needed capital, but it was not sufficient to satisfy the requirements of the company in its present state of affairs. In 1984 Albert Diehl became a consultant with the task of improving the operations and economic conditions at FN.

The decision was made to revert back to basic operations—those business actions that had brought financial success to the company in the past. From this point forward Fabrique Nationale concentrated on solving the economic crisis that threatened the company. In 1986 Albert Diehl succeeded Michel Vandestrick as managing director, for it was Diehl who was an expert in crisis management. He proceeded to restructure and consolidate the company in an effort to halt the economic deterioration that had already caused so much severe damage. This process was a gradual one, but it marked a steady decline in the number of employees at FN. This was a difficult period for both the company and its workers.

There were some minor successes, but only enough to give temporary respite. The FNC carbine production lasted through the balance of the 1980s, providing much needed factory utilization and profits. The engine division continued to limp along with orders barely enough to cover costs. In 1986 and 1987 the company still showed substantial losses. Continuing high production cost, declining productivity, insufficient resources, and nervous banks were a prescription for disaster.

Albert Diehl called upon the banks and the government to restructure FN's debt or make other arrangements that would allow the company the time to recover from its present emergency. Diehl also reorganized various divisions of the company

FN Sports, later renamed Browning SA, aggressively marketed a wide range of sporting goods products in addition to its Superposed firearms. However, these quality products were introduced too late to take advantage of the increased European demand and they were soon phased out of the company's product line. Courtesy Fabrique Nationale Archives.

by creating subsidiary companies. Excess personnel were laid off and other cuts were made to reduce overhead. This austerity program went on for the balance of the decade and into the early 1990s.

There were some meaningful accomplishments made during Diehl's recovery plan. Losses were lessened, but the company could not cope with its poor position in various markets around the world. In 1988, after a period of complex negotiations, a recapitalization plan for Fabrique Nationale was decided upon. Labor contracts were renegotiated that called for a reduction in the corporate workforce to a level of 5,700 employees. But the situation, while hopeful, did not improve significantly, and by the middle of 1990 the principal owner of Fabrique Nationale, the *Société Générale de Belgique,* decided to seek a buyer for the company. In 1991 the French government-owned company Giat Industries purchased Fabrique Nationale.

The buyout gave the French company, whose predominate products were military tanks and heavy artillery pieces, the opportunity to secure a corporation like Fabrique Nationale with its highly regarded product lines of light infantry weapons and ammunition. FN currently manufactures the MK3, the original Hi-Power semiautomatic pistol, and the BDA9, a double action 9mm pistol. It also builds the 5.7x28mm P90, a fully automatic light submachine gun. The company still manufactures a renowned line of light infantry weapons such as the FNC, the Minimi machine gun, the LAR, the MAG, and the .50 caliber M2HB machine gun. FN fabricates mounted weapons systems for the MAG and .50 M2HB, as well as rifle grenades.

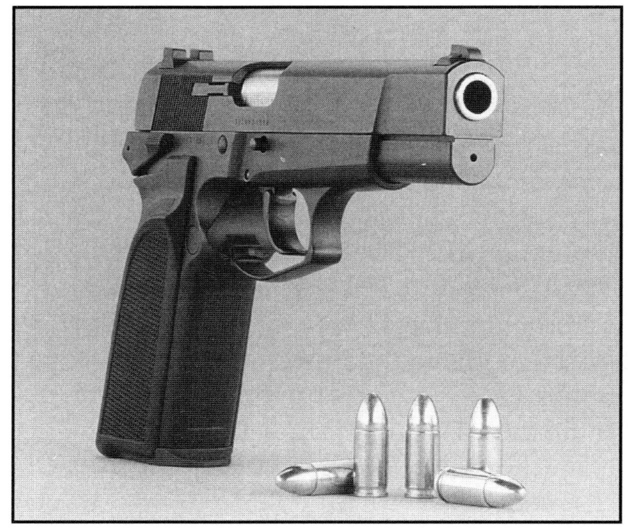

Clockwise from upper left, the family of currently produced FN light infantry weapons: the .50 caliber M2HB machine gun, the 7.62x51mm NATO FRG2 sniper rifle, the 7.62x51mm NATO LAR (FAL) family, the 5.7x28mm P90 personal defense weapon, the 9x19mm NATO MK3 single action pistol, the 9x19MM BDA9 double action pistol, the 5.56x45mm NATO FNC assault rifle, and the 7.62x51mm NATO MAG machine gun. Courtesy Fabrique Nationale Archives.

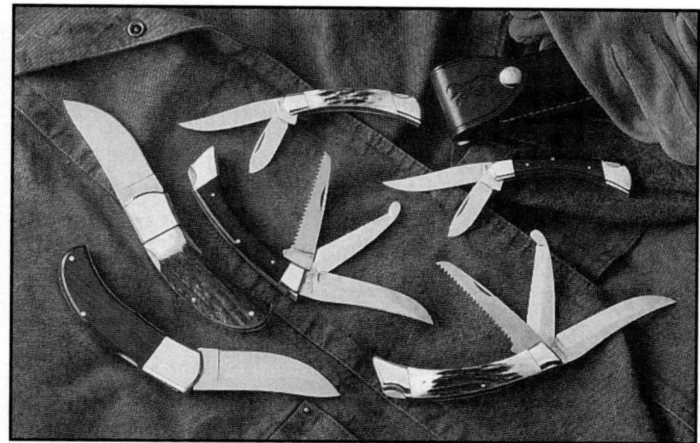

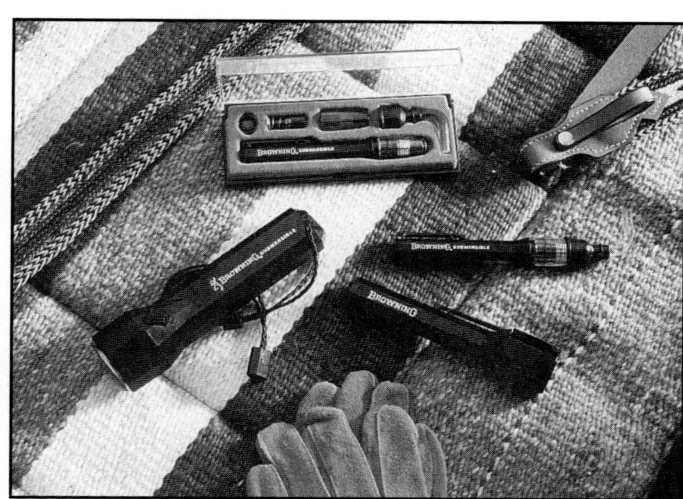

Today the Browning Company offers a wide array of quality outdoor products. Clockwise from upper left: a sample of the company's extensive line of Browning bows, Browning's traditional folding hunter knives, Browning flashlights, an example of its extensive line of outdoor clothing, a sample of its outdoor boots, Browning's line of travel vaults, Browning's cordura and leather rifle slings, and Browning safes. Courtesy Browning Company.

During this period the situation at Browning USA continued to improve. The company dedicated itself to remaining in markets it knew well. With a twenty-year confidence in its Japanese supplier, Miroku, the company expanded its already popular Citori line with the addition of the Grade III Citori. Meanwhile, the A-Bolt .22 was introduced as was the B-80 Upland Special. As the decade progressed, Browning continued to expand its sporting arms line with such additions as the A-500, Grade VI .22 Semi-auto, Buckmark .22 Plus, BT-99 Plus, Model 65, and the Gran Lightning. The service, distribution, and parts center in Arnold, Missouri, continues to provide efficient handling of Browning's comprehensive product line. In the early part of the '90s the service department's twenty-seven gunsmiths repaired more than seventeen thousand Browning firearms, some of which go back to the first year of production of the Superposed in 1930. Original owners of salt wood Browning firearms are still being taken care of with no charge even after almost thirty years.

In 1986 Browning became a subsidiary of Fabrique Nationale and a limited liability company distinct from FN. In 1988 Browning acquired the assets of U.S. Repeating Arms Company, a licensee of the famous Winchester rifles and shotguns. For the first time, two American legends joined forces to create an exclusive worldwide market for these two illustrious brands under the wholly owned parent company Fabrique Nationale. In a sense, after more than one hundred years, the Winchester/Browning partnership is reunited to form one of the most modern and aggressive sporting firearms companies in the world.

Today, Browning USA offers wide-ranging product lines in the hunting field. From shotguns, rifles, and pistols to accessories, knives, flashlights, gun safes, clothing, boots, and archery equipment, the company has worked hard to fill its niche in the outdoor domain. Browning steadily strives to excel in the product areas it knows best.

Giat Industries was founded in 1990 as a wholly owned French state company under the administration of the French Army. In addition to its heavy weapons systems, the company produces portable antitank systems, armored vehicles, ship mounted turrets, and tungsten heavy metal components. With the acquisition of Fabrique Nationale, Winchester, and Browning, Giat Industries acquired three very distinguished brand names that gave it a touch of class and a strong foothold in the small arms business. It also made possible the continuation of business for U.S. Repeating Arms Company and FN, both of whom were in dire financial straits.

GIAT INDUSTRIES

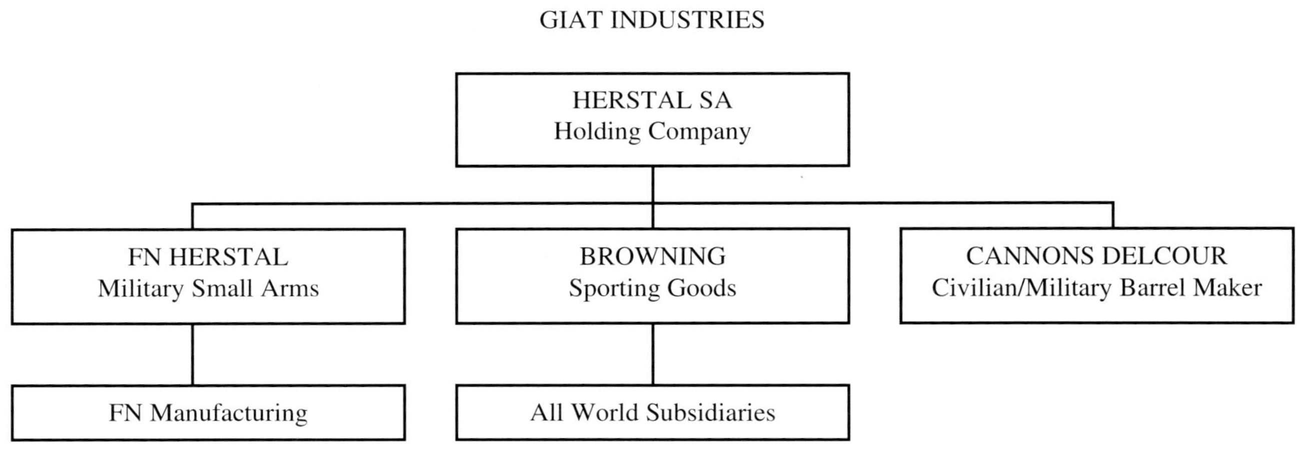

Table E-1

Today Fabrique Nationale, named Herstal Group, employs approximately 3,600 people. Of these, 1,500 work in Belgium, down from the peak years when over 13,000 worked at the factory. Browning SA employs about 180 people in its corporate offices in Hauts-Sarts and the Custom Shop in Herstal. That a French owned company rescued an American company whose legacy is synonymous with the American West, and a Belgian company whose legacy lies at the heart of the Belgian gunmakers tradition is perhaps incongruous. Meanwhile the Browning Company, which had

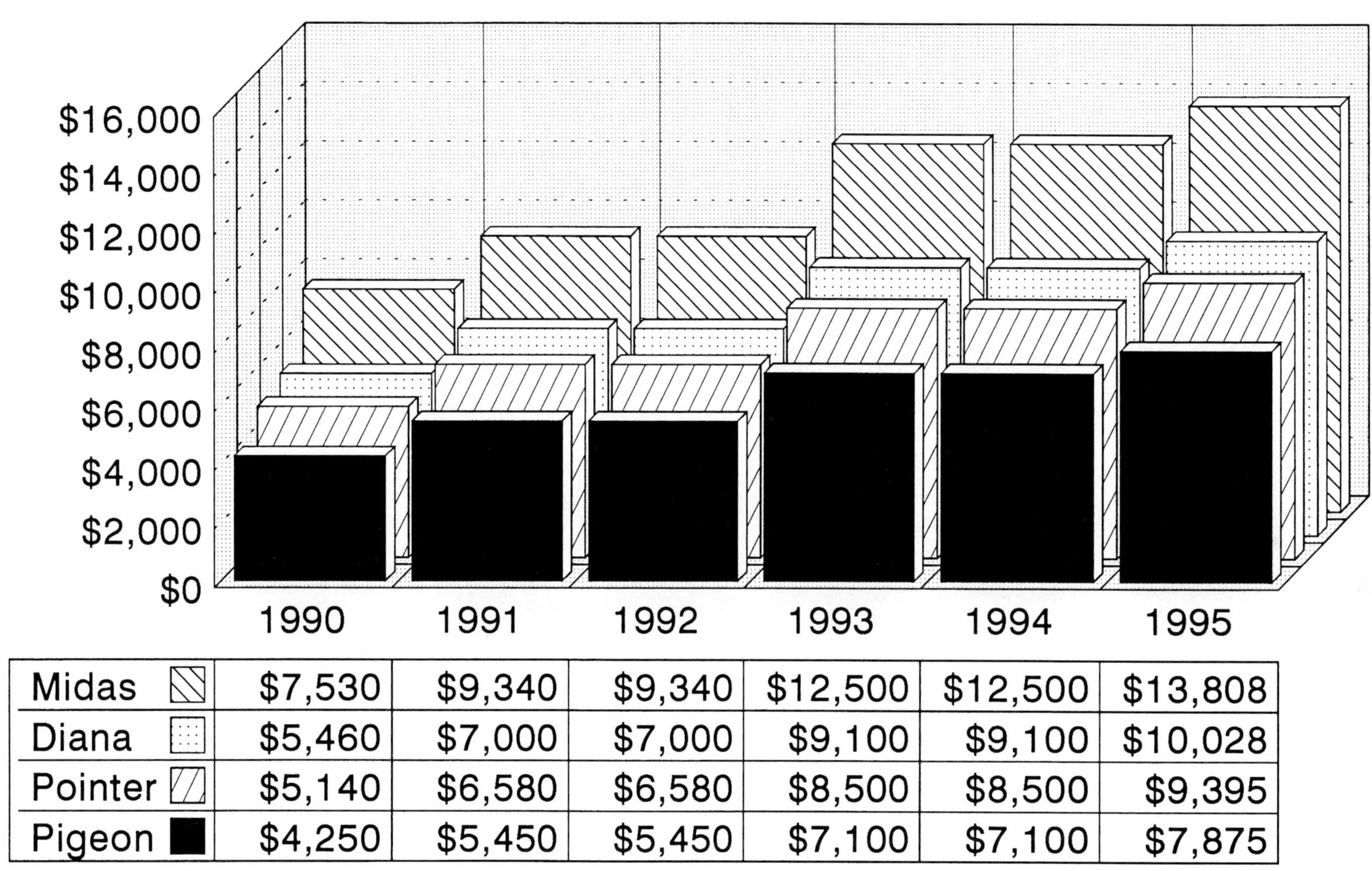

	1990	1991	1992	1993	1994	1995
Midas	$7,530	$9,340	$9,340	$12,500	$12,500	$13,808
Diana	$5,460	$7,000	$7,000	$9,100	$9,100	$10,028
Pointer	$5,140	$6,580	$6,580	$8,500	$8,500	$9,395
Pigeon	$4,250	$5,450	$5,450	$7,100	$7,100	$7,875

Prices are based on Lightning 12 gauge Hunting model with ventilated rib.

Chart E-1

previously been battered by the vagaries and vicissitudes of the business cycle, emerged strong and confident to meet the challenges of the future.[1]

The Restoration of the Superposed

With the failure of the Presentation Series to generate enough volume to justify continued production, Browning discontinued the series in 1985. The company was not about to give up on the Superposed, however. After fifty-five years in Browning's product line, the original Superposed was reintroduced in its original grades as a strictly custom order gun. Offered in Grade I, Pigeon Grade, Pointer Grade, Diana Grade, and Midas Grade, the traditional Superposed had returned to the Browning product line to stay. The Superposed of the '80s was the same as it had been in its original style, from engraving patterns to checkering. It was available in 12 or 20 gauge in Lightning or Superlight configurations with 26-1/2 or 28-inch ventilated rib barrels. Delivery was estimated to be one year, but orders often took much longer. Retail prices for the basic configurations are listed below.

SUPERPOSED 1985 RETAIL PRICES

Grade	Suggested Retail
Grade I	$1,995
Pigeon Grade	$3,200
Pointer Grade	$4,000
Diana Grade	$4,800
Midas Grade	$6,000

Table E-2

The Superposed was also offered with a choice of extra cost options ranging from an oil finish stock to a one-piece Schnabel forearm on the lower grades, and a three-piece forearm and special stock dimensions on sideplate models. Browning was careful to point out that each gun was a special factory order that could not be canceled once it was placed.

In 1986 the Grade I Superposed was dropped from the Custom Shop line for North America, leaving only the high grade Superposed. In 1985 Browning SA, through its Custom Shop still located on Rue Faurieux, devised a new variation of the B-25, the B-125. This derivation of the famed Superposed had all the features of the original over and under, but its component parts were manufactured worldwide in order to take advantage of lower costs. In addition, the engraving designs on the B-125 required less time to execute; thus the B-125 was priced substantially lower than the B-25. In 1990 the B-125 in 12 or 20 gauge Hunting configuration with Style A engraving carried a retail price of $2,505, while a comparable B-25 Pigeon Grade had a suggested retail price of $4,250. During the first half of the 1990s the B-25 Superposed escalated in price much the same way it had during the 1970s and 1980s.

In January of 1987 Browning announced the recall of certain Belgian built Superposed that presented a potential hazard to the operator. As with the salt wood predicament, Browning quickly informed its customers of the potential hazards and offered to correct the problem without charge. The company is still dedicated to maintaining its

[1] This section on the history of Fabrique Nationale relies almost exclusively on the book *FN 100 Years: The Story of the Great Liège Company, 1889-1989*, Auguste Francotte and Claude Gaier, pp. 153-166. For the period following 1989 the author interviewed Mr. Robert Sauvage, Communication Manager for Herstal SA, FN's parent company. Robert Sauvage has personally witnessed many of the events that occurred from 1990 to 1995, and is thoroughly familiar with FN's most recent corporate history.

On May 16, 1995, Val Allen Browning, son of John M. Browning, passed away at the age of 98. He was directly responsible for placing the Superposed in production in 1930 and for the many improvements made to it over the years. He held forty-one U.S. patents, seven Canadian patents, and numerous European patents. He invented the Double Automatic shotgun in 1955. Besides his success as a business executive and inventor, Mr. Browning was a philanthropist with a desire to better his community of Ogden. He was actively involved in funding numerous college and university buildings, high schools, hospitals, and museums. He was a modest man whose achievements were a tribute to his family's sense of community responsibility. Courtesy Browning Company.

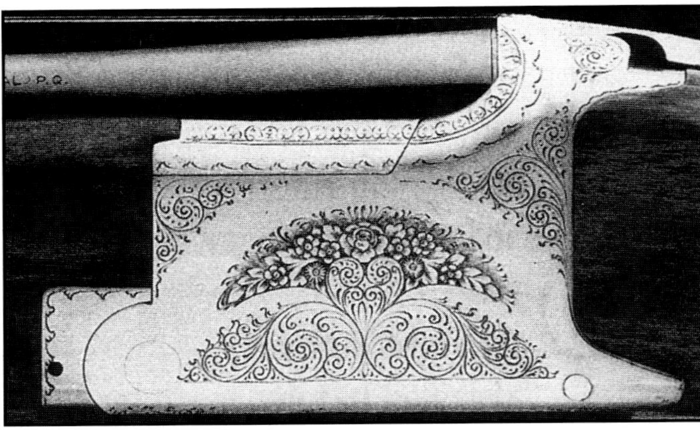

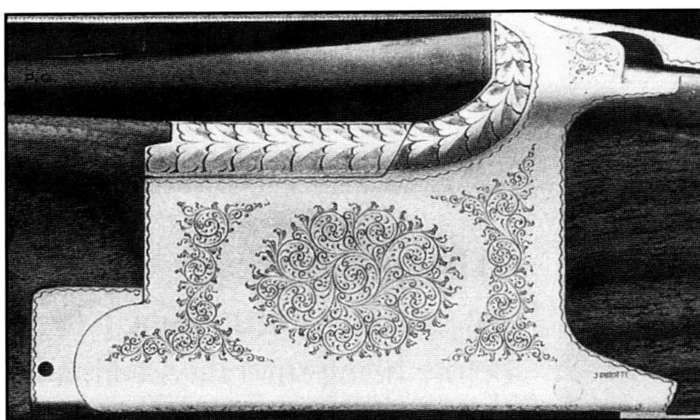

During the mid to late 1980s and into the '90s, FN added several new engraving patterns to its Superposed line. Designed primarily for its European market, these new patterns were an attempt by the company to modernize its Superposed engraving designs. Top to bottom, left to right are some of these newer engraving patterns: the B11, B12, C11, C12, D11, and the D12. Courtesy Browning Company.

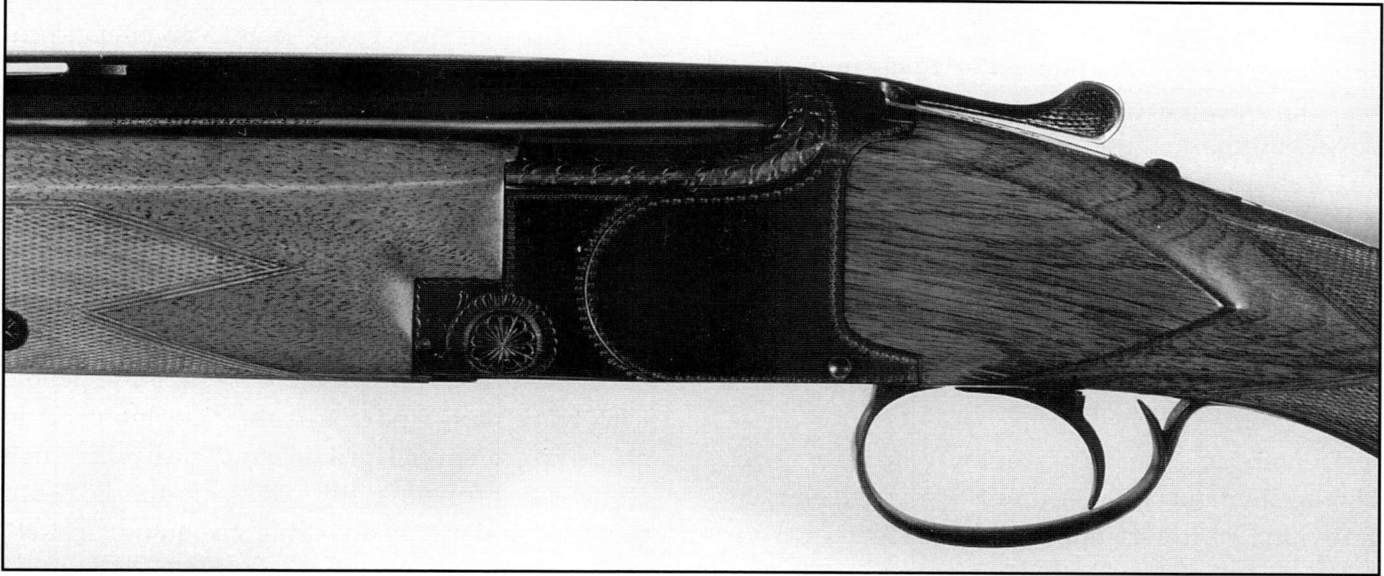

Currently Browning SA inventories the Superposed A1 Grade for its European markets. This is the basic Superposed in 12 or 20 gauge with automatic ejectors, single selective trigger, and vent rib barrels. The A1 Grade has been in the FN Superposed product line since the late 1930s. Courtesy Browning Company.

high level of quality control and honoring its commitment of lifetime service to its customers.[2]

As part of its overall Superposed cost trimming program, FN reduced the number of engraving patterns offered on its B-25 Superposed in its European markets. From as many as twenty different engraving designs in the 1970s, the number was reduced to fourteen by the early 1990s. New grades such as the B11, B12, C11, and C12 were introduced to take the place of some of the older, more obsolete, designs such as the B1 and B2, and the C2 and C3. In addition, there were other add-ons and deletions. Engraving patterns for the B-25 Superposed sideplate styles changed very little, with the only addition being the E1, essentially a P-4 with a grade name change. This consolidation of engraving patterns did little in the way of promoting sales, but it did simplify to some extent the myriad of engraving patterns offered on the European version of the B-25.

The increased prices affected demand, of course, with the result that the B-25 Superposed re-

---

[2] The Browning recall notice stipulated that on certain of its Belgian made Superposed guns the selector-safety, through a series of certain sequences of the safety, while in the off-safe, fire mode, can sometimes cause the gun to accidentally discharge upon opening the breech. The recall notice asked the owner to conduct a self-inspection in order to identify whether or not that over and under may be potentially hazardous. The following is a step by step inspection procedure:
1. Point the muzzle in a safe direction.
2. Open the gun to make certain it is unloaded.
3. Move the selector-safety to one side and then fully forward to the off-safe, (fire) position.
4. With the selector-safety fully forward, attempt to move the selector-safety either straight to the left or to the right.
5. IF YOU CAN SHIFT YOUR SELECTOR-SAFETY TO THE LEFT OR RIGHT, WHILE ON THE OFF-SAFE, FIRE POSITION, you are urged to contact Browning as soon as possible for return instructions.

mained at a relatively low volume of sales throughout the period. Robert Mignon, Browning SA business unit manager for high grade guns, estimates that from 1985 to 1995 only between five hundred and one thousand B-25s were sold each year. Sales were primarily to France, Germany, and England. Despite these low sales levels, Browning SA felt it was necessary to carry the Superposed in inventory for its European market. Just as the Superposed was considered the flagship of the Browning line in North America, so too did Browning SA feel the Superposed was important to its European firearms line. But unlike the North American market, the European trade demanded an off the rack Superposed, with the result that the A1 Superposed, the equivalent to the North American Grade I, is considered a stock Superposed for Browning SA. Sales to Browning USA remained at very low levels during this same interval, with only the North American high grade guns offered on a strictly custom order basis.

Unable to be stay fully employed because of declining demand, the Custom Shop engravers left Browning SA in 1987 and established their own engraving enterprise. With Browning's assistance, and under the direction of Lucien Ernst and Jean Diet, about sixteen former Custom Shop engravers established their own shop called the Engravers Cooperative of Herstal. At the Cooperative the engravers were free to develop their own designs and supervise themselves with the hope of promoting more interest in the fine art of gun engraving. The FN master José Baerten was no longer with the group, having gone on his own, but masters Jean Diet and Lucien Ernst led such well respected engravers as Claudy Baerten, Maire Bodson, Jean Pierre Bailly, Jean Marie Deprez, Jules Lewanczijk, Jeannine Pirotte, Sophie Purgal, and Auguste Pöes. These men and women continued to produce outstanding examples of the gun engraver's art through specially commissioned pieces, catalogued grades, and Exhibition works.

The engravers' move failed to produce the hoped for results. However outstanding and talented they were, the engravers were not promoters, and the venture was not considered a success. Browning could no longer subsidize the undertaking and the Cooperative was abandoned in 1992. From that point on, Browning SA contracted its work to a handful of former Custom Shop artisans on a per piece basis. For the first time in its history the Superposed was not engraved exclusively by company employees but solely by contract engravers. The disruptive nature of this shifting of engravers was not seen in the end product. The grace and beauty of the Liège engraver is still in evidence because these attributes are built on four centuries of pride, experience, and tradition.

The Custom Shop today is still a going concern. It remains under the control of Browning SA and houses the remaining Custom Shop craftsmen, ranging from wood carvers to gunsmiths. Although not as full of activity as it once was, the Custom Shop still produces some remarkable work. Not only is the B-25 built there, but all other special Browning and Winchester models are produced in the Custom Shop as well. It is a place full of confidence and preeminence where the people who work there know that they are involved in producing a special product not easily obtained elsewhere. Browning still considers the B-25 Superposed and the Custom Shop the quality leaders of the company's sporting arms product line. At the present time Browning is taking steps to embark on a new era of product evaluation and growth.

The B-25 Superposed, with its legacy built on quality and reliability, continues to be produced for the most part on a strictly special order basis. The Superposed is more popular in Europe than in North America today, and the people at Browning SA are committed to keeping the gun alive and well. The resolve on the part of the Custom Shop craftsmen to produce outstanding work is just as strong today as it was in Felix Funken's time. The Belgians have a strong sense of national identity developed from a long heritage of craftsmanship built on generations of talent and skill.The Browning Custom Shop is ready, willing, and able to craft some of the finest over and under guns built anywhere in the world. With the rapid disappearance of hand built and hand fitted double guns, the Superposed refuses to vanish. It is the people at Browning and Fabrique Nationale who continue to keep John Moses Browning's last legacy alive and well.

Appendix A

Browning Arms Company Yearly Sales Reports: 1964-1977

BROWNING SUPERPOSED SALES
1964

Type	Grade I	Pigeon Grade	Pointer Grade	Diana Grade	Midas Grade	Exhibition Grade	Total
Broadway	1,740	166	17	25	17	10	1,975
Trap	701	62	8	21	12	0	804
Total Trap	2,441	228	25	46	29	10	2,779
12 ga. Skeet	840	41	9	17	7	0	914
All ga. Skeet	0	0	0	0	0	0	0
Total Target	3,281	269	34	63	36	10	3,693
Magnum	502	11	5	6	1	0	525
12 ga. Hunting 28"	1,842	72	18	27	5	3	1,967
12 ga. Hunting 26.5"	1,128	36	18	17	2	0	1,201
Total 12 ga. Hunting	2,970	108	36	44	7	3	3,168
12 ga. Superlight 28"	0	0	0	0	0	0	0
12 ga. Superlight 26.5"	0	0	0	0	0	0	0
12 ga. Superlight Special Order	0	0	0	0	0	0	0
Total 12 ga. Superlight	0	0	0	0	0	0	0
12 ga. Special Order	205	51	18	14	4	0	292
Total All 12 gauge	**6,958**	**439**	**93**	**127**	**48**	**13**	**7,678**
20 ga. Skeet	363	23	9	5	2	0	402
20 ga. Hunting 28"	832	26	13	14	4	0	889
20 ga. Hunting 26.5"	940	46	22	16	5	2	1,031
Total 20 ga. Hunting	1,772	72	35	30	9	2	1,920
20 ga. Superlight	0	0	0	0	0	0	0
20 ga. Superlight Special Order	0	0	0	0	0	0	0
20 ga. Special Order	111	28	0	0	0	5	144
Total All 20 gauge	**2,246**	**123**	**44**	**35**	**11**	**7**	**2,466**
28 ga. Skeet	61	7	0	2	1	0	71
28 ga. Hunting 28"	23	2	0	3	1	0	29
28 ga. Hunting 26.5"	34	5	2	2	0	0	43
Total 28 ga. Hunting	57	7	2	5	1	0	72
28 ga. Special Order	11	4	0	0	1	0	16
Total All 28 gauge	**129**	**18**	**2**	**7**	**3**	**0**	**159**
.410 Skeet	93	8	0	1	0	0	102
.410 Hunting 28"	19	11	0	2	0	0	32
.410 Hunting 26.5"	28	4	0	1	2	0	35
Total .410 Hunting	47	15	0	3	2	0	67
.410 Special Order	0	0	0	0	0	0	0
Total All .410 bore	**140**	**23**	**0**	**4**	**2**	**0**	**169**
Grand Total	**9,473**	**603**	**139**	**173**	**64**	**20**	**10,472**

BROWNING SUPERPOSED SALES
1965

Type	Grade I	Pigeon Grade	Pointer Grade	Diana Grade	Midas Grade	Exhibition Grade	Total
Broadway	1,360	101	21	42	14	1	1,539
Trap	711	48	11	18	6	0	794
Total Trap	2,071	149	32	60	20	1	2,333
12 ga. Skeet	845	64	18	15	9	0	951
All ga. Skeet	0	0	0	0	0	0	0
Total Target	2,916	213	50	75	29	1	3,284
Magnum	645	5	4	6	1	0	661
12 ga. Hunting 28"	1,678	49	14	18	10	1	1,770
12 ga. Hunting 26.5"	1,057	44	14	19	6	0	1,140
Total 12 ga. Hunting	2,735	93	28	37	16	1	2,910
12 ga. Superlight 28"	0	0	0	0	0	0	0
12 ga. Superlight 26.5"	0	0	0	0	0	0	0
12 ga. Superlight Special Order	0	0	0	0	0	0	0
Total 12 ga. Superlight	0	0	0	0	0	0	0
12 ga. Special Order	181	48	14	29	11	0	283
Total All 12 gauge	**6,477**	**359**	**96**	**147**	**57**	**2**	**7,138**
20 ga. Skeet	423	25	9	9	0	0	466
20 ga. Hunting 28"	943	43	9	0	2	0	997
20 ga. Hunting 26.5"	1,826	61	17	24	0	0	1,928
Total 20 ga. Hunting	2,769	104	26	24	2	0	2,925
20 ga. Superlight	0	0	0	0	0	0	0
20 ga. Superlight Special Order	0	0	0	0	0	0	0
20 ga. Special Order	87	29	5	20	6	0	147
Total All 20 gauge	**3,279**	**158**	**40**	**53**	**8**	**0**	**3,538**
28 ga. Skeet	80	12	5	0	0	0	97
28 ga. Hunting 28"	39	5	3	0	0	0	47
28 ga. Hunting 26.5"	30	6	4	1	1	0	42
Total 28 ga. Hunting	69	11	7	1	1	0	89
28 ga. Special Order	15	0	2	3	2	0	22
Total All 28 gauge	**164**	**23**	**14**	**4**	**3**	**0**	**208**
.410 Skeet	100	4	4	4	0	0	112
.410 Hunting 28"	28	4	4	5	1	0	42
.410 Hunting 26.5"	31	3	3	1	1	0	39
Total .410 Hunting	59	7	7	6	2	0	81
.410 Special Order	0	0	0	0	0	0	0
Total All .410 bore	**159**	**11**	**11**	**10**	**2**	**0**	**193**
Grand Total	**10,079**	**551**	**161**	**214**	**70**	**2**	**11,077**

BROWNING SUPERPOSED SALES
1966

Type	Grade I	Pigeon Grade	Pointer Grade	Diana Grade	Midas Grade	Exhibition Grade	Total
Broadway	1,755	186	13	54	38	2	2,048
Trap	840	90	0	42	17	1	990
Total Trap	2,595	276	13	96	55	3	3,038
12 ga. Skeet	964	95	0	28	5	0	1,092
All ga. Skeet	0	0	0	0	0	0	0
Total Target	3,559	371	13	124	60	3	4,130
Magnum	664	23	2	9	1	0	699
12 ga. Hunting 28"	1,907	64	1	39	5	2	2,018
12 ga. Hunting 26.5"	1,216	83	14	33	0	2	1,348
Total 12 ga. Hunting	3,123	147	15	72	5	4	3,366
12 ga. Superlight 28"	0	0	0	0	0	0	0
12 ga. Superlight 26.5"	0	0	0	0	0	0	0
12 ga. Superlight Special Order	0	0	0	0	0	0	0
Total 12 ga. Superlight	0	0	0	0	0	0	0
12 ga. Special Order	148	76	13	51	22	0	310
Total All 12 gauge	**7,494**	**617**	**43**	**256**	**88**	**7**	**8,505**
20 ga. Skeet	467	70	0	18	0	0	555
20 ga. Hunting 28"	933	42	1	22	6	0	1,004
20 ga. Hunting 26.5"	1,637	122	7	52	15	0	1,833
Total 20 ga. Hunting	2,570	164	8	74	21	0	2,837
20 ga. Superlight	0	0	0	0	0	0	0
20 ga. Superlight Special Order	0	0	0	0	0	0	0
20 ga. Special Order	77	35	14	31	5	0	162
Total All 20 gauge	**3,114**	**269**	**22**	**123**	**26**	**0**	**3,554**
28 ga. Skeet	98	15	0	6	0	0	119
28 ga. Hunting 28"	32	3	0	8	1	0	44
28 ga. Hunting 26.5"	49	9	1	3	3	0	65
Total 28 ga. Hunting	81	12	1	11	4	0	109
28 ga. Special Order	6	3	0	1	0	0	10
Total All 28 gauge	**185**	**30**	**1**	**18**	**4**	**0**	**238**
.410 Skeet	174	23	0	8	0	0	205
.410 Hunting 28"	43	6	4	5	1	0	59
.410 Hunting 26.5"	65	15	2	2	1	0	85
Total .410 Hunting	108	21	6	7	2	0	144
.410 Special Order	0	0	25	0	1	0	26
Total All .410 bore	**282**	**44**	**31**	**15**	**3**	**0**	**375**
Grand Total	**11,075**	**960**	**97**	**412**	**121**	**7**	**12,672**

BROWNING SUPERPOSED SALES
1967

Type	Grade I	Pigeon Grade	Pointer Grade	Diana Grade	Midas Grade	Exhibition Grade	Total
Broadway	1,624	173	3	82	36	1	1,919
Trap	727	78	1	47	14	2	869
Total Trap	2,351	251	4	129	50	3	2,788
12 ga. Skeet	994	109	0	60	22	0	1,185
All ga. Skeet	0	0	0	0	0	0	0
Total Target	3,345	360	4	189	72	3	3,973
Magnum	768	18	0	14	9	0	809
12 ga. Hunting 28"	1,898	74	0	48	21	2	2,043
12 ga. Hunting 26.5"	1,148	66	8	75	16	2	1,315
Total 12 ga. Hunting	3,046	140	8	123	37	4	3,358
12 ga. Superlight 28"	158	0	0	0	0	0	158
12 ga. Superlight 26.5"	79	0	0	0	0	0	79
12 ga. Superlight Special Order	0	0	0	0	0	0	0
Total 12 ga. Superlight	237	0	0	0	0	0	237
12 ga. Special Order	140	51	4	47	35	0	277
Total All 12 gauge	**7,536**	**569**	**16**	**373**	**153**	**7**	**8,654**
20 ga. Skeet	575	78	0	38	1	0	692
20 ga. Hunting 28"	1,096	55	0	26	1	0	1,178
20 ga. Hunting 26.5"	1,834	113	2	60	6	1	2,016
Total 20 ga. Hunting	2,930	168	2	86	7	1	3,194
20 ga. Superlight	0	0	0	0	0	0	0
20 ga. Superlight Special Order	0	0	0	0	0	0	0
20 ga. Special Order	67	48	5	47	8	0	175
Total All 20 gauge	**3,572**	**294**	**7**	**171**	**16**	**1**	**4,061**
28 ga. Skeet	113	22	0	16	2	0	153
28 ga. Hunting 28"	65	10	3	8	1	0	87
28 ga. Hunting 26.5"	60	23	1	6	7	0	97
Total 28 ga. Hunting	125	33	4	14	8	0	184
28 ga. Special Order	14	4	2	4	3	0	27
Total All 28 gauge	**252**	**59**	**6**	**34**	**13**	**0**	**364**
.410 Skeet	219	32	0	18	2	0	271
.410 Hunting 28"	57	12	0	4	5	0	78
.410 Hunting 26.5"	65	9	1	5	3	1	84
Total .410 Hunting	122	21	1	9	8	1	162
.410 Special Order	0	0	0	0	0	0	0
Total All .410 bore	**341**	**53**	**1**	**27**	**10**	**1**	**433**
Grand Total	**11,701**	**975**	**30**	**605**	**192**	**9**	**13,512**

BROWNING SUPERPOSED SALES
1968

Type	Grade I	Pigeon Grade	Pointer Grade	Diana Grade	Midas Grade	Exhibition Grade	Total
Broadway	2,010	222	0	118	75	10	2,435
Trap	937	113	4	62	28	1	1,145
Total Trap	2,947	335	4	180	103	11	3,580
12 ga. Skeet	1,119	62	0	26	12	0	1,219
All ga. Skeet	0	0	0	0	0	0	0
Total Target	4,066	397	4	206	115	11	4,799
Magnum	895	19	0	21	9	0	944
12 ga. Hunting 28"	2,125	98	7	64	20	5	2,319
12 ga. Hunting 26.5"	1,558	268	6	65	17	1	1,915
Total 12 ga. Hunting	3,683	366	13	129	37	6	4,234
12 ga. Superlight 28"	40	0	0	0	0	0	40
12 ga. Superlight 26.5"	984	0	0	0	0	0	984
12 ga. Superlight Special Order	0	0	0	0	0	0	0
Total 12 ga. Superlight	1,024	0	0	0	0	0	1,024
12 ga. Special Order	175	42	0	40	16	0	273
Total All 12 gauge	**9,843**	**824**	**17**	**396**	**177**	**17**	**11,274**
20 ga. Skeet	364	10	0	17	6	0	397
20 ga. Hunting 28"	1,325	95	0	38	21	1	1,480
20 ga. Hunting 26.5"	2,409	173	5	83	28	0	2,698
Total 20 ga. Hunting	3,734	268	5	121	49	1	4,178
20 ga. Superlight	0	0	0	0	0	0	0
20 ga. Superlight Special Order	0	0	0	0	0	0	0
20 ga. Special Order	109	49	2	49	10	0	219
Total All 20 gauge	**4,207**	**327**	**7**	**187**	**65**	**1**	**4,794**
28 ga. Skeet	88	5	0	1	2	0	96
28 ga. Hunting 28"	77	33	3	17	10	0	140
28 ga. Hunting 26.5"	102	28	1	14	3	0	148
Total 28 ga. Hunting	179	61	4	31	13	0	288
28 ga. Special Order	11	9	1	4	1	0	26
Total All 28 gauge	**278**	**75**	**5**	**36**	**16**	**0**	**410**
.410 Skeet	68	1	0	1	1	0	71
.410 Hunting 28"	85	26	0	10	4	0	125
.410 Hunting 26.5"	85	42	3	20	3	0	153
Total .410 Hunting	170	68	3	30	7	0	278
.410 Special Order	0	0	0	0	0	0	0
Total All .410 bore	**238**	**69**	**3**	**31**	**8**	**0**	**349**
Grand Total	**14,566**	**1,295**	**32**	**650**	**266**	**18**	**16,827**

BROWNING SUPERPOSED SALES
1969

Type	Grade I	Pigeon Grade	Pointer Grade	Diana Grade	Midas Grade	Exhibition Grade	Total
Broadway	1,562	197	3	105	40	2	1,909
Trap	893	72	0	43	22	2	1,032
Total Trap	2,455	269	3	148	62	4	2,941
12 ga. Skeet	1,047	84	0	55	25	0	1,211
All ga. Skeet	0	0	0	0	0	0	0
Total Target	3,502	353	3	203	87	4	4,152
Magnum	657	23	0	13	6	0	699
12 ga. Hunting 28"	1,607	86	3	32	25	6	1,759
12 ga. Hunting 26.5"	1,189	84	7	39	18	0	1,337
Total 12 ga. Hunting	2,796	170	10	71	43	6	3,096
12 ga. Superlight 28"	3	0	0	0	0	0	3
12 ga. Superlight 26.5"	427	0	0	0	0	0	427
12 ga. Superlight Special Order	4	0	0	0	0	0	4
Total 12 ga. Superlight	434	0	0	0	0	0	434
12 ga. Special Order	113	33	2	47	26	1	222
Total All 12 gauge	**7,502**	**579**	**15**	**334**	**162**	**11**	**8,603**
20 ga. Skeet	511	44	0	32	12	0	599
20 ga. Hunting 28"	979	57	0	26	14	2	1,078
20 ga. Hunting 26.5"	1,753	138	2	68	21	1	1,983
Total 20 ga. Hunting	2,732	195	2	94	35	3	3,061
20 ga. Superlight	1	0	0	0	0	0	1
20 ga. Superlight Special Order	0	0	0	0	0	0	0
20 ga. Special Order	77	41	8	52	19	2	199
Total All 20 gauge	**3,321**	**280**	**10**	**178**	**66**	**5**	**3,860**
28 ga. Skeet	104	8	0	4	5	0	121
28 ga. Hunting 28"	44	2	2	5	3	0	56
28 ga. Hunting 26.5"	58	15	1	15	8	0	97
Total 28 ga. Hunting	102	17	3	20	11	0	153
28 ga. Special Order	14	1	0	4	6	0	25
Total All 28 gauge	**220**	**26**	**3**	**28**	**22**	**0**	**299**
.410 Skeet	289	10	0	9	9	0	317
.410 Hunting 28"	74	6	0	3	6	0	89
.410 Hunting 26.5"	86	16	1	12	6	0	121
Total .410 Hunting	160	22	1	15	12	0	210
.410 Special Order	2	0	0	0	1	0	3
Total All .410 bore	**451**	**32**	**1**	**24**	**22**	**0**	**530**
Grand Total	**11,494**	**917**	**29**	**564**	**272**	**16**	**13,292**

BROWNING SUPERPOSED SALES
1970

Type	Grade I	Pigeon Grade	Pointer Grade	Diana Grade	Midas Grade	Exhibition Grade	Total
Broadway	1,448	120	0	77	51	2	1,698
Trap	617	52	2	34	2	0	707
Total Trap	2,065	172	2	111	53	2	2,405
12 ga. Skeet	750	30	0	19	6	0	805
All ga. Skeet	0	0	0	0	0	0	0
Total Target	2,815	202	2	130	59	2	3,210
Magnum	625	7	0	13	1	0	646
12 ga. Hunting 28"	1,399	54	0	46	10	1	1,510
12 ga. Hunting 26.5"	1,009	61	4	47	6	2	1,129
Total 12 ga. Hunting	2,408	115	4	93	16	3	2,639
12 ga. Superlight 28"	2	0	0	0	0	0	2
12 ga. Superlight 26.5"	317	0	0	0	0	0	317
12 ga. Superlight Special Order	2	0	0	0	0	0	2
Total 12 ga. Superlight	321	0	0	0	0	0	321
12 ga. Special Order	79	19	1	40	17	1	157
Total All 12 gauge	**6,248**	**343**	**7**	**276**	**93**	**6**	**6,973**
20 ga. Skeet	72	3	0	12	6	0	93
20 ga. Hunting 28"	751	20	0	16	5	0	792
20 ga. Hunting 26.5"	1,578	97	2	61	15	1	1,754
Total 20 ga. Hunting	2,329	117	2	77	20	1	2,546
20 ga. Superlight	428	0	0	0	0	0	428
20 ga. Superlight Special Order	1	0	0	0	0	0	1
20 ga. Special Order	68	3	7	47	12	0	137
Total All 20 gauge	**2,898**	**123**	**9**	**136**	**38**	**1**	**3,205**
28 ga. Skeet	102	10	0	5	5	0	122
28 ga. Hunting 28"	42	2	0	5	3	0	52
28 ga. Hunting 26.5"	48	5	1	5	2	1	62
Total 28 ga. Hunting	90	7	1	10	5	1	114
28 ga. Special Order	5	0	0	3	2	0	10
Total All 28 gauge	**197**	**17**	**1**	**18**	**12**	**1**	**246**
.410 Skeet	58	9	0	3	3	0	73
.410 Hunting 28"	46	1	0	3	3	0	53
.410 Hunting 26.5"	47	6	2	1	2	1	59
Total .410 Hunting	93	7	2	4	5	1	112
.410 Special Order	0	0	0	0	0	0	0
Total All .410 bore	**151**	**16**	**2**	**7**	**8**	**1**	**185**
Grand Total	**9,494**	**499**	**19**	**437**	**151**	**9**	**10,609**

BROWNING SUPERPOSED SALES
1971

Type	Grade I	Pigeon Grade	Pointer Grade	Diana Grade	Midas Grade	Exhibition Grade	Total
Broadway	1,267	138	1	82	35	0	1,523
Trap	638	43	5	33	25	0	744
Total Trap	1,905	181	6	115	60	0	2,267
12 ga. Skeet	544	88	0	52	25	0	709
All ga. Skeet	0	0	0	0	0	0	0
Total Target	2,449	269	6	167	85	0	2,976
Magnum	584	25	0	13	3	0	625
12 ga. Hunting 28"	1,125	58	0	10	24	0	1,217
12 ga. Hunting 26.5"	725	40	7	27	15	2	816
Total 12 ga. Hunting	1,850	98	7	37	39	2	2,033
12 ga. Superlight 28"	0	0	0	0	0	0	0
12 ga. Superlight 26.5"	842	0	1	0	0	0	843
12 ga. Superlight Special Order	1	0	0	0	0	0	1
Total 12 ga. Superlight	843	0	1	0	0	0	844
12 ga. Special Order	128	36	3	43	21	0	231
Total All 12 gauge	**5,854**	**428**	**17**	**260**	**148**	**2**	**6,709**
20 ga. Skeet	610	37	0	29	9	0	685
20 ga. Hunting 28"	539	52	0	22	9	0	622
20 ga. Hunting 26.5"	1,242	95	3	41	8	2	1,391
Total 20 ga. Hunting	1,781	147	3	63	17	2	2,013
20 ga. Superlight	0	0	0	0	0	0	0
20 ga. Superlight Special Order	0	0	0	0	0	0	0
20 ga. Special Order	10	50	10	58	21	2	151
Total All 20 gauge	**2,401**	**234**	**13**	**150**	**47**	**4**	**2,849**
28 ga. Skeet	81	11	0	10	4	0	106
28 ga. Hunting 28"	25	14	0	7	3	1	50
28 ga. Hunting 26.5"	43	8	1	8	5	0	65
Total 28 ga. Hunting	68	22	1	15	8	1	115
28 ga. Special Order	11	0	1	1	2	0	15
Total All 28 gauge	**160**	**33**	**2**	**26**	**14**	**1**	**236**
.410 Skeet	140	6	0	6	6	0	158
.410 Hunting 28"	52	11	0	7	5	0	75
.410 Hunting 26.5"	26	9	3	15	1	0	54
Total .410 Hunting	78	20	3	22	6	0	129
.410 Special Order	5	1	0	1	0	1	8
Total All .410 bore	**223**	**27**	**3**	**29**	**12**	**1**	**295**
Grand Total	**8,638**	**722**	**35**	**465**	**221**	**8**	**10,089**

BROWNING SUPERPOSED SALES
1972

Type	Grade I	Pigeon Grade	Pointer Grade	Diana Grade	Midas Grade	Exhibition Grade	Total
Broadway	964	103	4	74	23	0	1,168
Trap	390	41	1	34	28	0	494
Total Trap	1,354	144	5	108	51	0	1,662
12 ga. Skeet	448	49	0	42	16	0	555
All ga. Skeet	0	0	0	0	0	0	0
Total Target	1,802	193	5	150	67	0	2,217
Magnum	566	10	0	10	7	0	593
12 ga. Hunting 28"	664	29	0	48	19	2	762
12 ga. Hunting 26.5"	661	56	6	60	15	2	800
Total 12 ga. Hunting	1,325	85	6	108	34	4	1,562
12 ga. Superlight 28"	1	0	0	0	0	0	1
12 ga. Superlight 26.5"	468	14	2	12	6	0	502
12 ga. Superlight Special Order	0	0	0	1	0	0	1
Total 12 ga. Superlight	469	14	2	13	6	0	504
12 ga. Special Order	77	33	1	47	14	2	174
Total All 12 gauge	**4,239**	**335**	**14**	**328**	**128**	**6**	**5,050**
20 ga. Skeet	238	33	0	15	13	0	299
20 ga. Hunting 28"	397	37	0	18	13	0	465
20 ga. Hunting 26.5"	899	57	7	70	13	0	1,046
Total 20 ga. Hunting	1,296	94	7	88	26	0	1,511
20 ga. Superlight	80	17	2	14	7	0	120
20 ga. Superlight Special Order	1	0	0	0	0	0	1
20 ga. Special Order	60	20	4	38	10	3	135
Total All 20 gauge	**1,675**	**164**	**13**	**155**	**56**	**3**	**2,066**
28 ga. Skeet	46	3	0	8	7	0	64
28 ga. Hunting 28"	19	4	0	3	0	0	26
28 ga. Hunting 26.5"	38	3	1	4	2	0	48
Total 28 ga. Hunting	57	7	1	7	2	0	74
28 ga. Special Order	3	2	0	2	2	0	9
Total All 28 gauge	**106**	**12**	**1**	**17**	**11**	**0**	**147**
.410 Skeet	58	4	0	7	6	0	75
.410 Hunting 28"	36	5	0	2	2	0	45
.410 Hunting 26.5"	37	10	2	8	1	0	58
Total .410 Hunting	73	15	2	10	3	0	103
.410 Special Order	1	0	0	1	0	1	3
Total All .410 bore	**132**	**19**	**2**	**18**	**9**	**0**	**181**
Grand Total	**6,152**	**530**	**30**	**518**	**204**	**9**	**7,444**

BROWNING SUPERPOSED SALES
1973

Type	Grade I	Pigeon Grade	Pointer Grade	Diana Grade	Midas Grade	Exhibition Grade	Total
Broadway	657	59	0	41	31	4	792
Trap	254	16	0	26	9	0	305
Total Trap	911	75	0	67	40	4	1,097
12 ga. Skeet	371	31	0	28	15	0	445
All ga. Skeet	78	15	0	27	13	0	133
Total Target	1,360	121	0	122	68	4	1,675
Magnum	351	11	0	7	7	0	376
12 ga. Hunting 28"	349	39	0	23	5	3	419
12 ga. Hunting 26.5"	318	26	1	21	8	3	377
Total 12 ga. Hunting	667	65	1	44	13	6	796
12 ga. Superlight 28"	1	0	0	0	0	0	1
12 ga. Superlight 26.5"	579	22	1	9	5	0	616
12 ga. Superlight Special Order	1	1	0	0	1	0	3
Total 12 ga. Superlight	581	23	1	9	6	0	620
12 ga. Special Order	69	16	1	33	18	3	140
Total All 12 gauge	**3,028**	**236**	**3**	**215**	**112**	**13**	**3,607**
20 ga. Skeet	204	18	0	15	9	0	246
20 ga. Hunting 28"	362	25	0	7	5	4	403
20 ga. Hunting 26.5"	525	35	3	29	3	5	600
Total 20 ga. Hunting	887	60	3	36	8	9	1,003
20 ga. Superlight	0	35	13	0	6	0	54
20 ga. Superlight Special Order	0	0	0	0	0	0	0
20 ga. Special Order	35	15	1	29	8	1	89
Total All 20 gauge	**1,126**	**128**	**17**	**80**	**31**	**10**	**1,392**
28 ga. Skeet	42	6	0	6	1	0	55
28 ga. Hunting 28"	21	2	0	10	1	0	34
28 ga. Hunting 26.5"	21	7	0	7	1	0	36
Total 28 ga. Hunting	42	9	0	17	2	0	70
28 ga. Special Order	2	0	1	0	0	0	3
Total All 28 gauge	**86**	**15**	**1**	**23**	**3**	**0**	**128**
.410 Skeet	55	7	0	6	11	0	79
.410 Hunting 28"	25	2	0	3	4	0	34
.410 Hunting 26.5"	33	5	0	8	3	0	49
Total .410 Hunting	58	7	0	11	7	0	83
.410 Special Order	0	0	0	0	0	1	1
Total All .410 bore	**113**	**14**	**0**	**17**	**18**	**1**	**163**
Grand Total	**4,353**	**393**	**21**	**335**	**164**	**24**	**5,290**

BROWNING SUPERPOSED SALES
1974

Type	Grade I	Pigeon Grade	Pointer Grade	Diana Grade	Midas Grade	Exhibition Grade	Total
Broadway	323	83	2	26	15	11	460
Trap	103	32	0	6	2	0	143
Total Trap	426	115	2	32	17	11	603
12 ga. Skeet	231	31	0	12	3	4	281
All ga. Skeet	160	11	0	17	15	0	203
Total Target	817	157	2	61	35	15	1,087
Magnum	258	11	1	1	0	0	271
12 ga. Hunting 28"	340	49	0	5	4	11	409
12 ga. Hunting 26.5"	290	32	5	4	3	6	340
Total 12 ga. Hunting	630	81	5	9	7	17	749
12 ga. Superlight 28"	0	0	0	0	0	2	2
12 ga. Superlight 26.5"	286	20	2	14	0	3	325
12 ga. Superlight Special Order	2	1	0	4	0	0	7
Total 12 ga. Superlight	288	21	2	18	0	5	334
12 ga. Special Order	39	14	0	6	11	1	71
Total All 12 gauge	**2,032**	**284**	**10**	**95**	**53**	**38**	**2,512**
20 ga. Skeet	122	14	0	7	4	0	147
20 ga. Hunting 28"	149	35	0	1	1	11	197
20 ga. Hunting 26.5"	357	38	7	8	7	12	429
Total 20 ga. Hunting	506	73	7	9	8	23	626
20 ga. Superlight	0	12	6	0	3	9	30
20 ga. Superlight Special Order	1	0	0	1	1	0	3
20 ga. Special Order	25	10	0	13	10	2	60
Total All 20 gauge	**654**	**109**	**13**	**30**	**26**	**34**	**866**
28 ga. Skeet	39	6	0	5	1	0	51
28 ga. Hunting 28"	19	25	0	3	3	0	50
28 ga. Hunting 26.5"	15	9	3	2	1	0	30
Total 28 ga. Hunting	34	34	3	5	4	0	80
28 ga. Special Order	2	0	0	3	0	1	6
Total All 28 gauge	**75**	**40**	**3**	**13**	**5**	**1**	**137**
.410 Skeet	42	9	0	7	6	0	64
.410 Hunting 28"	29	10	0	4	1	2	46
.410 Hunting 26.5"	25	16	8	12	2	1	64
Total .410 Hunting	54	26	8	16	3	3	110
.410 Special Order	0	0	0	0	0	0	0
Total All .410 bore	**96**	**35**	**8**	**23**	**9**	**3**	**174**
Grand Total	**2,857**	**468**	**34**	**161**	**93**	**76**	**3,689**

BROWNING SUPERPOSED SALES
1975

Type	Grade I	Pigeon Grade	Pointer Grade	Diana Grade	Midas Grade	Exhibition Grade	Total
Broadway	80	16	1	24	12	8	141
Trap	34	9	0	12	3	0	58
Total Trap	114	25	1	36	15	8	199
12 ga. Skeet	40	2	0	10	3	4	59
All ga. Skeet	27	13	0	13	13	0	66
Total Target	181	40	1	59	31	12	324
Magnum	81	2	0	13	7	0	103
12 ga. Hunting 28"	60	1	0	10	5	9	85
12 ga. Hunting 26.5"	52	5	8	12	17	13	107
Total 12 ga. Hunting	112	6	8	22	22	22	192
12 ga. Superlight 28"	0	0	0	0	0	0	0
12 ga. Superlight 26.5"	41	9	4	4	4	0	62
12 ga. Superlight Special Order	1	1	0	2	0	0	4
Total 12 ga. Superlight	42	10	4	6	4	0	66
12 ga. Special Order	29	12	12	14	13	1	81
Total All 12 gauge	**445**	**70**	**25**	**114**	**77**	**35**	**766**
20 ga. Skeet	39	3	0	7	4	5	58
20 ga. Hunting 28"	44	1	0	11	3	0	59
20 ga. Hunting 26.5"	66	5	12	33	2	3	121
Total 20 ga. Hunting	110	6	12	44	5	3	180
20 ga. Superlight	51	8	3	23	8	0	93
20 ga. Superlight Special Order	0	0	0	0	0	0	0
20 ga. Special Order	13	6	0	4	10	2	35
Total All 20 gauge	**213**	**23**	**15**	**78**	**27**	**10**	**366**
28 ga. Skeet	8	4	0	2	3	0	17
28 ga. Hunting 28"	9	4	0	5	2	3	23
28 ga. Hunting 26.5"	8	1	4	3	3	3	22
Total 28 ga. Hunting	17	5	4	8	5	6	45
28 ga. Special Order	0	1	0	0	0	0	1
Total All 28 gauge	**25**	**10**	**4**	**10**	**8**	**6**	**63**
.410 Skeet	17	3	0	5	0	0	25
.410 Hunting 28"	2	0	0	1	3	3	9
.410 Hunting 26.5"	17	3	9	8	10	0	47
Total .410 Hunting	19	3	9	9	13	3	56
.410 Special Order	0	0	0	0	0	0	0
Total All .410 bore	**36**	**6**	**9**	**14**	**13**	**3**	**81**
Grand Total	**719**	**109**	**53**	**216**	**125**	**54**	**1,276**

BROWNING SUPERPOSED SALES
1976

Type	Grade I	Pigeon Grade	Pointer Grade	Diana Grade	Midas Grade	Exhibition Grade	Total
Broadway	193	11	0	28	21	7	260
Trap	80	6	0	15	9	3	113
Total Trap	273	17	0	43	30	10	373
12 ga. Skeet	111	2	0	9	6	4	132
All ga. Skeet	101	4	0	1	5	0	111
Total Target	485	23	0	53	41	14	616
Magnum	151	3	0	13	9	1	177
12 ga. Hunting 28"	193	2	0	15	9	2	221
12 ga. Hunting 26.5"	203	5	2	23	9	21	263
Total 12 ga. Hunting	396	7	2	38	18	23	484
12 ga. Superlight 28"	0	0	0	0	0	4	4
12 ga. Superlight 26.5"	125	13	1	8	8	3	158
12 ga. Superlight Special Order	2	0	0	1	1	0	4
Total 12 ga. Superlight	127	13	1	9	9	7	166
12 ga. Special Order	26	3	1	7	7	1	45
Total All 12 gauge	**1,185**	**49**	**4**	**120**	**84**	**46**	**1,488**
20 ga. Skeet	46	6	0	9	5	9	75
20 ga. Hunting 28"	117	2	0	12	7	12	150
20 ga. Hunting 26.5"	286	2	3	35	10	0	336
Total 20 ga. Hunting	403	4	3	47	17	12	486
20 ga. Superlight	130	19	1	24	10	2	186
20 ga. Superlight Special Order	0	0	0	0	2	0	2
20 ga. Special Order	9	0	1	5	5	1	21
Total All 20 gauge	**588**	**29**	**5**	**85**	**39**	**24**	**770**
28 ga. Skeet	81	0	0	2	4	0	87
28 ga. Hunting 28"	58	0	0	5	2	5	70
28 ga. Hunting 26.5"	27	3	5	7	9	4	55
Total 28 ga. Hunting	85	3	5	12	11	9	125
28 ga. Special Order	0	1	0	0	3	2	6
Total All 28 gauge	**166**	**4**	**5**	**14**	**0**	**11**	**218**
.410 Skeet	74	3	0	8	7	0	92
.410 Hunting 28"	19	0	0	2	2	5	28
.410 Hunting 26.5"	16	6	8	11	8	6	55
Total .410 Hunting	35	6	8	13	10	11	83
.410 Special Order	0	0	0	0	2	0	2
Total All .410 bore	**109**	**9**	**8**	**21**	**19**	**11**	**177**
Grand Total	**2,048**	**91**	**22**	**240**	**142**	**92**	**2,653**

BROWNING SUPERPOSED SALES 1977

Type	Grade I	Pigeon Grade	Pointer Grade	Diana Grade	Midas Grade	Exhibition Grade	Total
Broadway	264	19	0	15	1	6	305
Trap	201	4	0	8	5	2	220
Total Trap	465	23	0	23	6	8	525
12 ga. Skeet	93	11	0	10	5	16	135
All ga. Skeet	2	0	0	1	6	0	9
Total Target	560	34	0	34	17	24	669
Magnum	67	1	0	7	3	0	78
12 ga. Hunting 28"	33	9	0	15	0	12	69
12 ga. Hunting 26.5"	57	5	5	8	1	5	81
Total 12 ga. Hunting	90	14	5	7	1	17	150
12 ga. Superlight 28"	0	0	0	0	1	0	1
12 ga. Superlight 26.5"	26	8	0	12	9	0	55
12 ga. Superlight Special Order	0	0	0	1	0	0	1
Total 12 ga. Superlight	26	8	0	13	10	0	57
12 ga. Special Order	5	0	1	11	3	0	20
Total All 12 gauge	**748**	**57**	**6**	**72**	**34**	**41**	**974**
20 ga. Skeet	22	6	0	1	3	3	35
20 ga. Hunting 28"	112	2	0	4	4	4	126
20 ga. Hunting 26.5"	132	16	2	6	6	1	163
Total 20 ga. Hunting	244	18	2	10	10	5	289
20 ga. Superlight	45	6	0	8	4	0	63
20 ga. Superlight Special Order	8	0	1	10	10	0	29
20 ga. Special Order	4	0	1	3	0	1	9
Total All 20 gauge	**323**	**30**	**4**	**32**	**27**	**9**	**425**
28 ga. Skeet	1	0	0	2	0	0	3
28 ga. Hunting 28"	4	0	0	1	0	1	6
28 ga. Hunting 26.5"	8	4	3	8	5	2	30
Total 28 ga. Hunting	12	4	3	9	5	3	36
28 ga. Special Order	1	0	0	0	0	1	2
Total All 28 gauge	**14**	**4**	**3**	**11**	**5**	**4**	**41**
.410 Skeet	42	0	0	0	1	0	43
.410 Hunting 28"	3	1	0	6	2	0	12
.410 Hunting 26.5"	16	14	8	18	9	1	66
Total .410 Hunting	19	15	8	24	11	1	78
.410 Special Order	0	0	0	0	0	1	1
Total All .410 bore	**61**	**15**	**8**	**24**	**12**	**2**	**122**
Grand Total	**1,146**	**106**	**21**	**139**	**78**	**56**	**1,562**

Appendix B

Browning Superposed Takedown and Assembly Instructions

REMOVING THE BARRELS

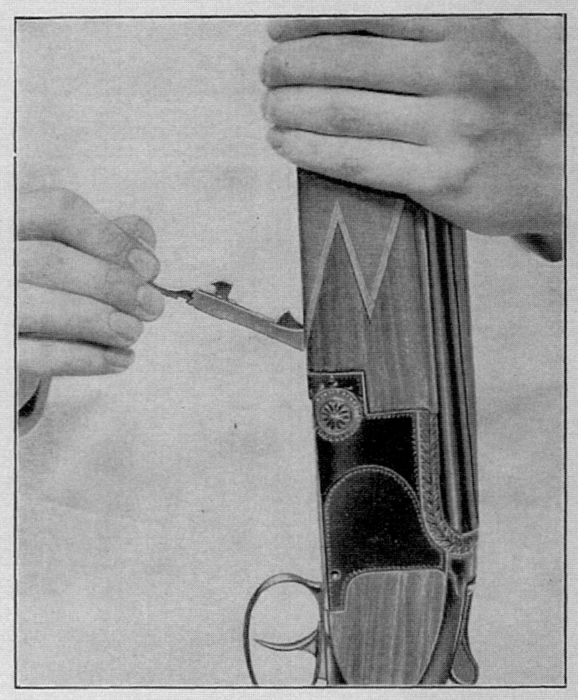

Fig. 1.

Fig. 2.

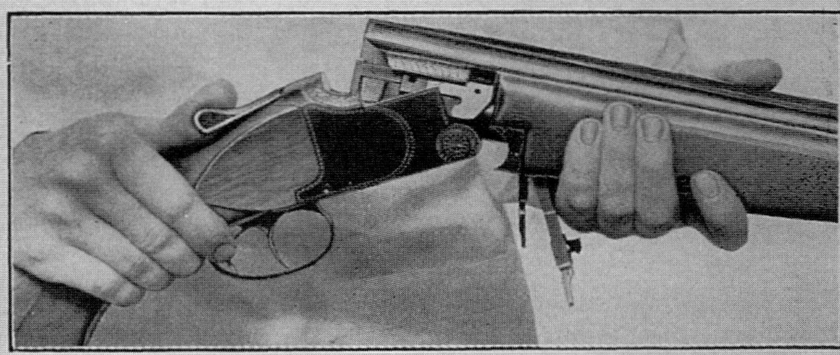

Fig. 3.

1. Press the fore-end lever towards the action and allow this part to hang down. (Fig. 1.)
2. Slide the complete fore-end towards the muzzle so as to disengage the fore-end lock. This will then also hang down. (Fig. 2.)
3. Push the top lever right over, open the gun as normally and lift the barrels clear of the action (Fig. 3.)

REPLACING THE BARRELS

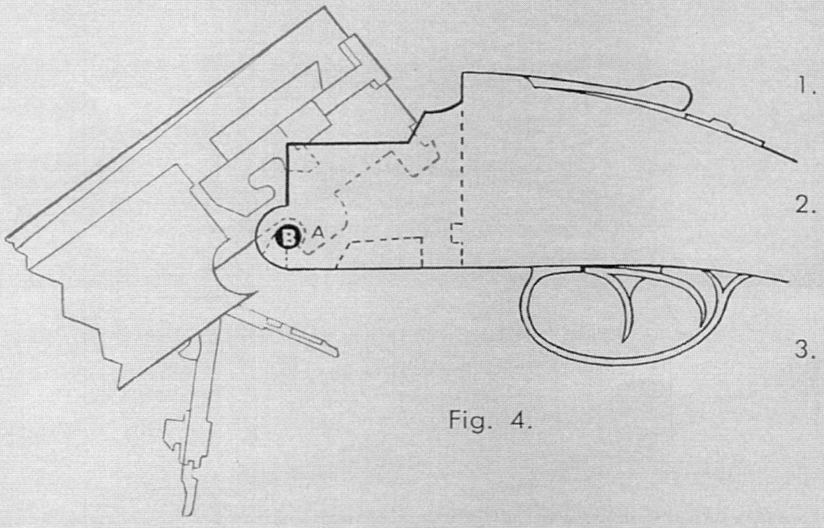

Fig. 4.

1. Place the barrels in the action (Fig. 4) taking care that the hinge pin (B) correctly fits into the barrel hook (A).
2. Hold the top lever right open and close the gun normally, keeping the barrels pressed against the hinge pin during this manœuvre.
3. Raise the fore-end lock and slide the complete fore-end back so as to engage this part and then press into position the fore-end lever.

Appendix C

Superposed Component Parts

For the Years
1931, 1938, 1950, 1961, 1963, 1975

1931

Component Parts Price List

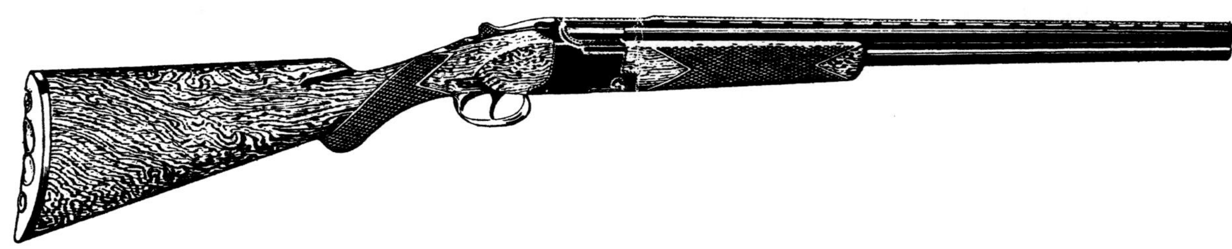

BROWNING SUPERPOSED

12 GAUGE

Headquarters and General Offices

ST. LOUIS, MISSOURI

Browning Superposed Component Parts
Standard Grade—12 Gauge

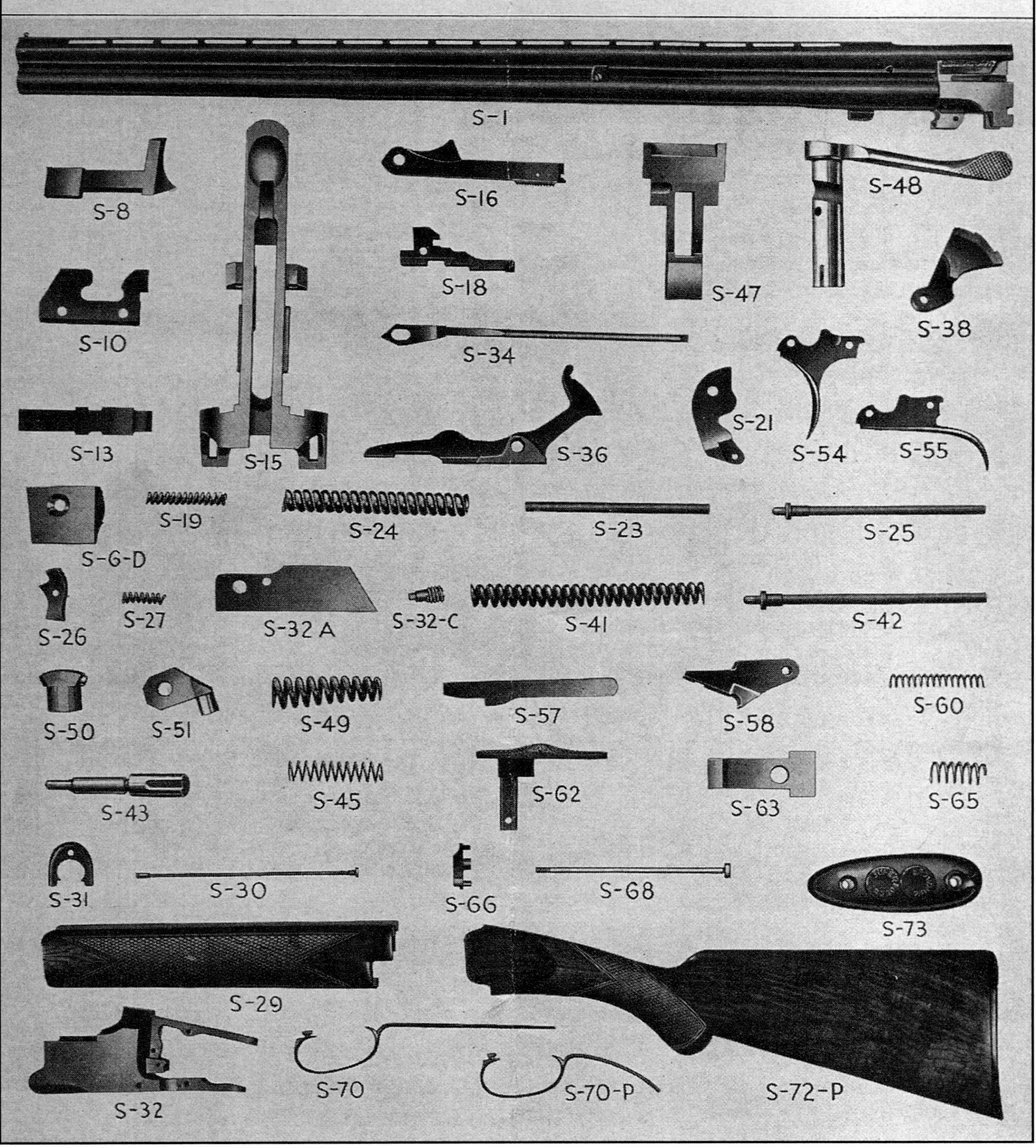

No.	Part		Retail Price
S-1	Barrels with ventilated rib		$73.75
S-1h	Barrels with hollow matted rib		53.75
	(Barrels include parts Nos. S-5, S-6d, S-6g S-7, S-8, S-9, S-10, S-11, S-12, and S-12a and fitting to receiver)*		
S-5	Sight for ribbed barrel		.25
S-6d-6g	Barrel Plates (right and left)	$0.35 each	.70
S-7	Barrel Plate Screws (2)	.10 each	.20
S-8-9	Ejectors (right and left)	1.05 each	2.10
S-10-11	Ejector Extensions (right and left)	1.85 each	3.70
S-12	Ejector Extension Stop Screws (2)	.10 each	.20
S-12a	Ejector Stop Screws (2)	.10 each	.20
S-13	Cocking Lever Lifter		.50
S-14	Cocking Lever Lifter Pin		.10
S-15	Fore-end Bracket		5.55
S-16	Take Down Lever		3.25
S-17	Take Down Lever Pin		.10
S-18	Take Down Lever Latch		1.45
S-19	Take Down Lever Latch Spring		.10
S-20	Take Down Lever Latch Pin		.10
S-21-22	Ejector Hammers (right and left)	1.65 each	3.30
S-23	Ejector Hammer Pin		.10
S-24	Ejector Hammer Springs (2)	.15 each	.30
S-25	Ejector Hammer Spring Guides (2)	.10 each	.20
S-26	Ejector Hammer Catches (2)	.20 each	.40
S-27	Ejector Hammer Catch Springs (2)	.10 each	.20
S-28	Ejector Hammer Catch Pins (2)	.10 each	.20
S-29-29c	Wooden Fore-end (plain and beavertailed)	Pl. Bt.	15.65 35.65
S-30	Fore-end Screw		.80
S-31	Fore-end Cap		2.55
S-32	Receiver		23.15
S-32a	Trigger Separator		.40
S-32b	Trigger Separator Rivet		.10
S-32c	Trigger Separator Screw		.10
S-32d	Trigger Separator Pin		.10
S-33	Joint Pin		.25
S-34-35	Trip (right and left)	1.05 each	2.10

No.	Part		Retail Price
S-36	Cocking Lever		$1.80
S-37	Cocking Lever Pin		.20
S-38-39	Hammer (right and left)	$1.70 each	3.40
S-40	Hammer Pin		.10
S-41u	Main Springs (2)	.15 each	.30
S-42	Main Spring Guides (2)	.10 each	.20
S-43-44	Firing Pins (left and right)	.65 each	1.30
S-45	Firing Pin Springs (2)	.10 each	.20
S-46	Firing Pin Retaining Screws (2)	.10 each	.20
S-47	Locking Bolt		2.30
S-48	Top Lever		2.10
S-49	Top Lever Spring		.10
S-50	Top Lever Spring Retainer		.25
S-51	Top Lever Dog		.65
S-52	Top Lever Dog Pin		.10
S-53	Top Lever Spring Retainer Screw		.10
S-54-55	Triggers (right and left)	2.30 each	4.60
S-56	Trigger Pin		.10
S-57ud-g	Connectors (right and left)	.10 each	.20
S-58u-59u	Sears (right and left)	.75 each	1.50
S-60u-g	Sear Springs (right and left)	.10 each	.20
S-61	Sear Pin		.10
S-62	Safety Platform		2.10
S-63	Safety		.15
S-64	Safety Platform Pin		.10
S-65	Safety Spring		.10
S-66u	Tang Piece		1.50
S-67	Tang Piece Screws (2)	.10 each	.20
S-68u	Stock Bolt		.20
S-69	Stock Bolt Spring Washer		.10
S-70-70p	Trigger Guard (straight and pistol grip)		4.65
S-71	Trigger Guard Screws (2)	.10 each	.20
S-72-72p-72m	Stock (straight or pistol grip or monte carlo)		25.00
S-73	Butt Plate		1.20
S-74	Butt Plate Screws (2)	.10 each	.20

Prices for parts of grades other than our Standard supplied on request

1938

Component Parts Price List

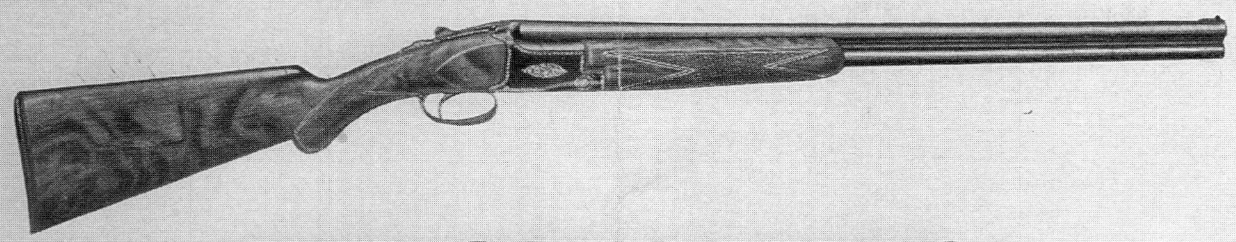

BROWNING
Overunder Shotgun

12 GAUGE

We have authorized service stations conveniently located throughout the United States and the names and addresses will be sent upon request. Our Repair Department is fully equipped to service our guns in every way. Guns shipped to us for repairs should be packed securely and the shipping container plainly marked "Browning Arms Company, Service Department, St. Louis, Missouri." Also mark plainly your name and return address. Write us when making shipment giving full instructions. All shipments should be insured.

We do not buy or exchange used guns or barrels. A charge of $2.50 is made for quoting on repairs when work is not done after receipt of estimate.

On orders for component parts amounting to less than 25 cents a minimum charge of 25 cents will be made to cover the cost of handling. All shipments are F. O. B. St. Louis, Mo. Be sure to include enough for postage in your remittance.

BROWNING ARMS COMPANY

ST. LOUIS, MO.

Our Service is Limited to Browning Guns Only

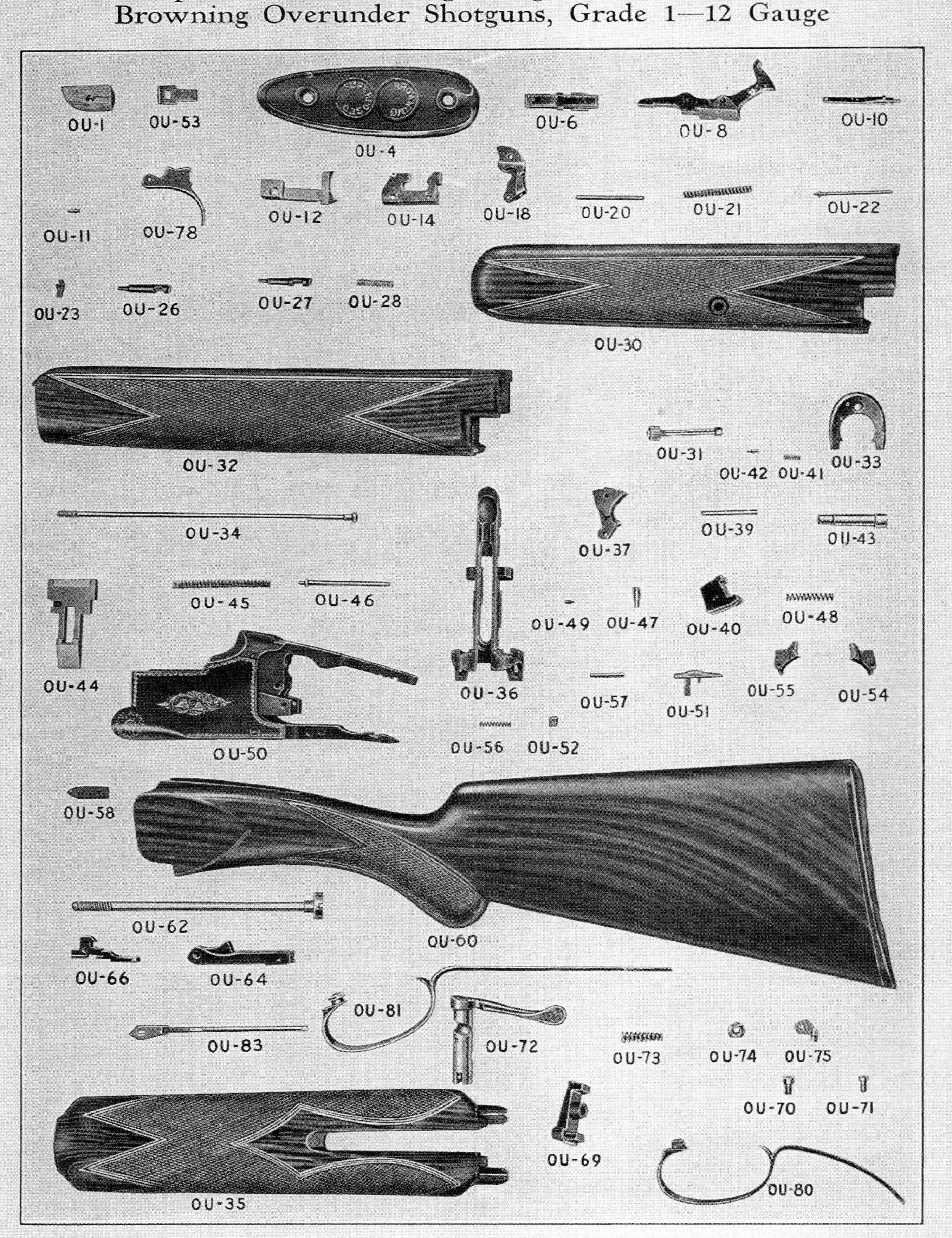
Component Parts for Lightning and Standard Model
Browning Overunder Shotguns, Grade 1—12 Gauge
OU-1
OU-53
OU-4
OU-6
OU-8
OU-10
OU-11
OU-78
OU-12
OU-14
OU-18
OU-20
OU-21
OU-22
OU-23
OU-26
OU-27
OU-28
OU-30
OU-32
OU-31
OU-42
OU-41
OU-33
OU-34
OU-37
OU-39
OU-43
OU-44
OU-45
OU-46
OU-36
OU-49
OU-47
OU-40
OU-48
OU-50
OU-57
OU-51
OU-55
OU-54
OU-56
OU-52
OU-58
OU-62
OU-60
OU-66
OU-64
OU-81
OU-83
OU-72
OU-73
OU-74
OU-75
OU-70
OU-71
OU-69
OU-80
OU-35

KEEP YOUR GUN IN GOOD CONDITION—
Use Browning Gun Oil and Powder Solvent.

No.	Part	Retail Price Each
OU-1	Barrel Plate Wood for Lightning Model (Right)	$0.35
OU-2	Barrel Plate Wood for Lightning Model (Left)	.35
OU-3	Barrel Plate Screws	.15
OU-4	Butt Plate	1.00
OU-5	Butt Plate Screws, each	.15
OU-6	Cocking Lever Lifter	.50
OU-7	Cocking Lever Lifter Pin	.15
OU-8	Cocking Lever	1.75
OU-9	Cocking Lever Pin	.15
OU-10	Connector	.65
OU-11	Connector Stop Pin	.15
OU-12	Ejector (Right)	1.05
OU-13	Ejector (Left)	1.05
OU-14	Ejector Extension (Right)	1.15
OU-15	Ejector Extension (Left)	1.15
OU-16	Ejector Extension Stop Screws, each	.15
OU-17	Ejector Stop Screws, each	.15
OU-18	Ejector Hammer (Right)	1.15
OU-19	Ejector Hammer (Left)	1.15
OU-20	Ejector Hammer Pin	.15
OU-21	Ejector Hammer Springs, each	.15
OU-22	Ejector Hammer Spring Guides, each	.15
OU-23	Ejector Hammer Catches, each	.20
OU-24	Ejector Hammer Catch Springs, each	.15
OU-25	Ejector Hammer Catch Pins, each	.15
OU-26	Firing Pin (Over Barrel)	.45
OU-27	Firing Pin (Under Barrel)	.45
OU-28	Firing Pin Spring for Under Barrel	.15
OU-29	Firing Pin Retaining Pins, each	.15
OU-30	Forearm, Full Grip with Escutcheons for Lightning Model	8.75
OU-31	Forearm Screw for OU-30	.25
OU-32	Forearm, Standard Grip for Standard Model	8.75
OU-33	Forearm Plate for OU-32 and OU-35	1.75
OU-34	Forearm Screw for OU-32 and OU-35	.65
OU-35	Forearm, Beavertail	17.45
OU-36	Forearm Bracket	4.10
OU-37	Hammer (Right)	1.25
OU-38	Hammer (Left)	1.25
OU-39	Hammer Pin	.15
OU-40	Inertia Block	1.25
OU-41	Inertia Block Spring	.15
OU-42	Inertia Block Spring Guide	.15

No.	Part
OU-43	Joint Pin
OU-44	Locking Bolt
OU-45	Mainsprings, each
OU-46	Mainspring Guides, each
OU-47	Piston
OU-48	Piston Spring
OU-49	Piston Pin
OU-50	Receiver
OU-51	Selector
OU-52	Selector Block
OU-53	Selector Spring
OU-54	Sear (Right)
OU-55	Sear (Left)
OU-56	Sear Springs, each
OU-57	Sear Pin
OU-58	Sight Base
OU-59	Sight Bead
OU-60	Stock Type Field, $1\frac{5}{8}$x$2\frac{1}{2}$x$14\frac{1}{8}$, Standard Pistol Grip as illustrated
OU-61	Stock Type Trap, $1\frac{1}{2}$x$1\frac{3}{4}$x$14\frac{3}{8}$, Standard Pistol Grip as illustrated
OU-62	Stock Bolt
OU-63	Stock Bolt Washer
OU-64	Take Down Lever
OU-65	Take Down Lever Pin
OU-66	Take Down Lever Latch
OU-67	Take Down Lever Latch Spring
OU-68	Take Down Lever Latch Pin
OU-69	Tang Piece
OU-70	Tang Piece Screw (Over)
OU-71	Tang Piece Screw (Under)
OU-72	Top Lever
OU-73	Top Lever Spring
OU-74	Top Lever Spring Retainer
OU-75	Top Lever Dog
OU-76	Top Lever Dog Pin
OU-77	Top Lever Spring Retainer Screw
OU-78	Trigger
OU-79	Trigger Pin
OU-80	Trigger Guard Standard Pistol Grip
OU-81	Trigger Guard Straight Grip
OU-82	Trigger Guard Screws, each
OU-83	Trip Rod (Right)
OU-84	Trip Rod (Left)

1950

BROWNING®

PARTS PRICE LIST

for

BELGIAN MADE

Browning Superposed Shotgun

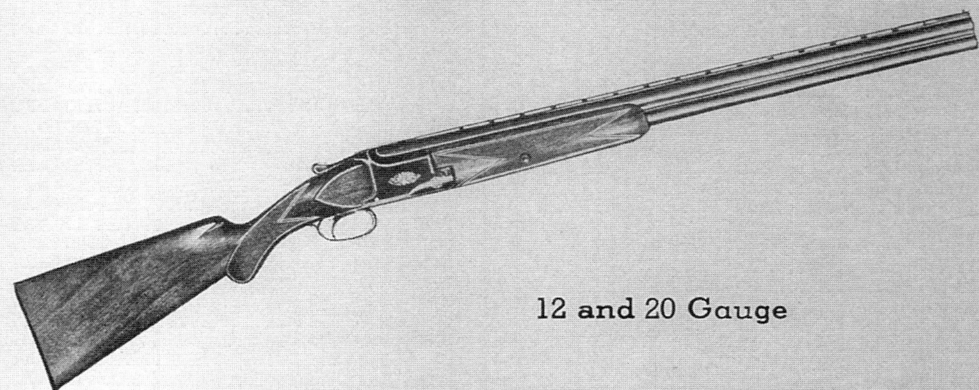

12 and 20 Gauge

Effective December 21, 1950

Deliveries
F. O. B. St. Louis, Mo.

Subject To Change
Without Notice

BROWNING ARMS CO.
St. Louis 3, Mo.

Important: When ordering you *must* specify Part Number and Name, Gauge and Serial Number of Gun.

Series I refers only to 12 gauge Superposed single selective trigger Prewar models with serial numbers below 17,300. Series II refers to Postwar 12 gauge (serial numbers above 17,300) and all 20 gauge single selective trigger models.

*—Asterisk indicates part should be fitted by our St. Louis Service Department.

Where (X)s appear in both columns part is interchangeable.

Part No.	Part Name	Series I	Series II	Retail Price
S1 a	Barrel Plate Wood-Right-For Forearm-S57-S59a . . . 12 Ga. . .	X	X	$ .60
b	Barrel Plate Wood-Right-For Forearm-S59b . . . 20 Ga. . .		X	.60
S2 a	Barrel Plate Wood-Left-For Forearm-S57-S59a . . . 12 Ga. . .	X	X	.60
b	Barrel Plate Wood-Left-For Forearm-S59b . . . 20 Ga. . .		X	.60
S3 a	Barrel Plate Wood-Right-For Forearm-S58 . . . 12 Ga. . .	X		.60
S4 a	Barrel Plate Wood-Left-For Forearm-S58 . . . 12 Ga. . .	X		.60
S7	Barrel Plate Screw . . . 12-20 Ga. . .	X	X	.25
S8 a	Butt Plate . . . 12 Ga. . .	X	X	1.70
b	Butt Plate . . . 20 Ga. . .		X	1.70
S9 a	Butt Plate Screw . . . 12 Ga. . .	X	X	.25
b	Butt Plate Screw . . . 20 Ga. . .		X	.25
S10 a	Cocking Lever-Rough . . . 12 Ga.*.	X	X	2.40
b	Cocking Lever-Rough . . . 20 Ga.*.		X	2.40
S11 a	Cocking Lever Pin . . . 12 Ga. . .	X	X	.30
b	Cocking Lever Pin . . . 20 Ga. . .		X	.30
S13 a	Cocking Lever Lifter-Rough . . . 12 Ga.*.	X	X	.65
b	Cocking Lever Lifter-Rough . . . 20 Ga.*.		X	.65
S14 a	Cocking Lever Lifter Pin . . . 12 Ga. . .	X	X	.25
b	Cocking Lever Lifter Pin . . . 20 Ga. . .		X	.25
S15	Connector . . . 12 Ga. . .	X		1.20
S16 a	Connector . . . 12 Ga. . .		X	1.20
b	Connector . . . 20 Ga. . .		X	1.20
S26	Connector Stop Pin . . . 12-20 Ga. . .	X	X	.25
S29 a	Ejector-Right-Rough . . . 12 Ga.*.	X	X	2.00
b	Ejector-Right-Rough . . . 20 Ga.*.		X	2.00
S30 a	Ejector-Left-Rough . . . 12 Ga.*.	X	X	2.00
b	Ejector-Left-Rough . . . 20 Ga.*.		X	2.00
S31 a	Ejector Stop Screw . . . 12 Ga. . .	X		.25
b	Ejector Stop Screw . . . 12-20 Ga. . .		X	.25
S32 a	Ejector Extension-Right . . . 12 Ga. . .	X	X	2.50
b	Ejector Extension-Right . . . 20 Ga. . .		X	2.50
S33 a	Ejector Extension-Left . . . 12 Ga. . .	X	X	2.50
b	Ejector Extension-Left . . . 20 Ga. . .		X	2.50
S34 a	Ejector Extension Stop Screw . . . 12 Ga. . .	X	X	.25
b	Ejector Extension Stop Screw . . . 20 Ga. . .		X	.25
S35 a	Ejector Hammer-Right . . . 12 Ga. . .	X	X	1.65
b	Ejector Hammer-Right . . . 20 Ga. . .		X	1.65
S36 a	Ejector Hammer-Left . . . 12 Ga. . .	X	X	1.65
b	Ejector Hammer-Left . . . 20 Ga. . .		X	1.65
S37 a	Ejector Hammer Pin . . . 12 Ga. . .	X	X	.25
b	Ejector Hammer Pin . . . 20 Ga. . .		X	.25
S38 a	Ejector Hammer Spring . . . 12 Ga. . .	X	X	.25
b	Ejector Hammer Spring . . . 20 Ga. . .		X	.25
S39	Ejector Hammer Spring Guide . . . 12-20 Ga. . .	X	X	.25
S40	Ejector Hammer Sear . . . 12-20 Ga. . .	X	X	.50
S41	Ejector Hammer Sear Spring . . . 12-20 Ga. . .	X	X	.25
S42	Ejector Hammer Sear Pin . . . 12-20 Ga. . .	X	X	.25
S43 a	Ejector Trip Rod-Right . . . 12 Ga.*.	X	X	1.75
b	Ejector Trip Rod-Right . . . 20 Ga.*.		X	1.75
S44 a	Ejector Trip Rod-Left . . . 12 Ga.*.	X	X	1.75
b	Ejector Trip Rod-Left . . . 20 Ga.*.		X	1.75
S48	Firing Pin-Over . . . 12 Ga. . .	X		.85
S49	Firing Pin-Under . . . 12 Ga. . .	X		.85
S50 a	Firing Pin-Over . . . 12 Ga. . .		X	.85
b	Firing Pin-Over . . . 20 Ga. . .		X	.85
S51 a	Firing Pin-Under . . . 12 Ga. . .		X	.85
b	Firing Pin-Under . . . 20 Ga. . .		X	.85
S53 a	Firing Pin Spring-Under . . . 12 Ga. . .	X	X	.25
b	Firing Pin Spring-Under . . . 20 Ga. . .		X	.25
S54 a	Firing Pin Retaining Pin . . . 12 Ga. . .	X	X	.25
b	Firing Pin Retaining Pin . . . 20 Ga. . .		X	.25
S57	Forearm-For Lightning Model . . . 12 Ga. . .	X		18.60

Part No	Part Name	Series I	Series II	Retail Price
S58	Forearm-(Square End Type) . . . 12 Ga. . .	X		$18.60
S59 a	Forearm-(Round End Type) . . . 12 Ga. . .		X	18.60
b	Forearm . . . 20 Ga. . .		X	18.60
S61 a	Forearm Escutcheon-Right-For Forearm-S57-S59a . . . 12 Ga. . .	X	X	.25
d	Forearm Escutcheon-Right-For Forearm-S59b . . . 20 Ga. . .		X	.25
S62 a	Forearm Escutcheon-Left-For Forearm-S57-S59a . . . 12 Ga. . .	X	X	.25
d	Forearm Escutcheon-Left-For Forearm-S59b . . . 20 Ga. . .		X	.25
S63 a	Forearm Screw-Side Fastening For Forearm-S57-S59a . . . 12 Ga. . .	X	X	.50
d	Forearm Screw-Side Fastening For Forearm-S59b . . . 20 Ga. . .		X	.50
S64 a	Forearm Screw-End Fastening- For Forearm-S58 . . . 12 Ga. . .	X		1.25
S65 a	Forearm End Plate-For Forearm-S58 . 12 Ga. . .	X		2.50
S66	Forearm Bracket-Rough . . . 12 Ga.*.	X		8.00
S67 a	Forearm Bracket-Rough . . . 12 Ga.*.		X	8.00
b	Forearm Bracket-Rough . . . 20 Ga.*.		X	8.00
S68 a	Hammer-Right . . . 12 Ga. . .	X	X	1.85
b	Hammer-Right . . . 20 Ga. . .		X	1.85
S69 a	Hammer-Left . . . 12 Ga. . .	X	X	1.85
b	Hammer-Left . . . 20 Ga. . .		X	1.85
S70 a	Hammer Pin . . . 12 Ga. . .	X	X	.25
b	Hammer Pin . . . 20 Ga. . .		X	.25
S71	Inertia Block . . . 12 Ga. . .	X		1.50
S72 a	Inertia Block . . . 12 Ga. . .		X	1.50
b	Inertia Block . . . 20 Ga. . .		X	1.50
S73	Inertia Block Spring . . . 12-20 Ga. . .	X	X	.25
S74	Inertia Block Spring Guide . . . 12-20 Ga. . .	X	X	.25
S79 a	Locking Bolt . . . 12 Ga.*.	X	X	2.95
b	Locking Bolt . . . 20 Ga.*.		X	2.95
S81	Mainspring . . . 12-20 Ga. . .	X	X	.55
S82	Mainspring Guide . . . 12-20 Ga. . .	X	X	.30
S89	Selector-Safety . . . 12 Ga. . .	X		1.50
S90 a	Selector-Safety . . . 12 Ga. . .		X	1.50
b	Selector-Safety . . . 20 Ga. . .		X	1.50
S91	Selector Block . . . 12 Ga. . .	X		.30
S92	Selector Block . . . 12-20 Ga. . .		X	.30
S93	Selector Spring . . . 12 Ga. . .	X		.25
S94	Selector Spring . . . 12-20 Ga. . .		X	.25
S99 a	Sear-Right . . . 12 Ga. . .	X	X	1.10
b	Sear-Right . . . 20 Ga. . .		X	1.10
S100a	Sear-Left . . . 12 Ga. . .	X	X	1.10
b	Sear-Left . . . 20 Ga. . .		X	1.10
S102a	Sear Spring . . . 12 Ga. . .	X	X	.25
b	Sear Spring . . . 20 Ga. . .		X	.25
S103a	Sear Pin . . . 12 Ga. . .	X	X	.25
b	Sear Pin . . . 20 Ga. . .		X	.25
S104	Sight Base-Plain Barrel . . . 12 Ga. . .	X		1.10
S105	Sight Bead-Large . . . 12-20 Ga. . .	X	X	.25
S106	Sight Bead-Small . . . 12-20 Ga. . .	X	X	.25
S109	Stock-Field Type-1⅝" x 2½" x 14⅛"-Standard Pistol Grip . . . 12 Ga. . .	X		45.00
S110	Stock-Trap Type-1½" x 1¾" x 14⅜"-Standard Pistol Grip . . . 12 Ga. . .	X		45.00
S111a	Stock-Field Type-1⅝" x 2½" x 14¼"-Standard Pistol Grip . . . 12 Ga. . .		X	45.00
b	Stock-Field Type-1⅝" x 2½" x 14¼"-Standard Pistol Grip . . . 20 Ga. . .		X	45.00
S112	Stock-Trap Type-1½" x 1⅞" x 14⅜"-Standard Pistol Grip . . . 12 Ga. . .		X	45.00
S114	Stock Bolt . . . 12-20 Ga. . .	X	X	.50
S116a	Stock Bolt Washer . . . 12 Ga. . .	X	X	.25
b	Stock Bolt Washer . . . 20 Ga. . .		X	.25
S117	Stock Bolt Lock Washer . . . 12-20 Ga. . .	X	X	.25

Part No.	Part Name		Series I	Series II	Retail Price
S118a	Take Down Lever	12 Ga.	X	X	$2.25
b	Take Down Lever	20 Ga.		X	2.25
S119a	Take Down Lever Pin	12 Ga.	X	X	.25
b	Take Down Lever Pin	20 Ga.		X	.25
S120a	Take Down Lever Latch	12 Ga.	X	X	2.00
b	Take Down Lever Latch	20 Ga.		X	2.00
S121a	Take Down Lever Latch Pin	12 Ga.	X	X	.25
b	Take Down Lever Latch Pin	20 Ga.		X	.25
S122a	Take Down Lever Latch Spring	12 Ga.	X	X	.25
b	Take Down Lever Latch Spring	20 Ga.		X	.25
S125a	Tang Piece	12 Ga.	X	X	3.10
b	Tang Piece	20 Ga.		X	3.10
S126	Tang Piece Screw-Top	12-20 Ga.	X	X	.25
S127	Tang Piece Screw-Bottom	12-20 Ga.	X	X	.25
S128a	Top Lever-Rough	12 Ga.*	X	X	3.00
b	Top Lever-Rough	20 Ga.*		X	3.00
S129	Top Lever Spring	12-20 Ga.	X	X	.25
S130a	Top Lever Spring Retainer	12 Ga.	X		.35
b	Top Lever Spring Retainer	12-20 Ga.		X	.35
S131	Top Lever Spring Retainer Screw	12-20 Ga.	X	X	$ .25
S132a	Top Lever Dog	12 Ga.	X	X	.70
b	Top Lever Dog	20 Ga.		X	.70
S134	Top Lever Dog Screw	12-20 Ga.	X	X	.25
S138a	Trigger ¾ Rear	12 Ga.	X	X	2.75
b	Trigger ¾ Rear	20 Ga.		X	2.75
S142a	Trigger Pin	12 Ga.	X	X	.25
b	Trigger Pin	20 Ga.		X	.25
S143	Trigger Piston	12-20 Ga.	X	X	.45
S144	Trigger Piston Pin	12-20 Ga.	X	X	.25
S145a	Trigger Piston Spring	12 Ga.	X	X	.25
b	Trigger Piston Spring	20 Ga.		X	.25
S147a	Trigger Guard-Pistol Grip	12 Ga.	X	X	5.00
b	Trigger Guard-Pistol Grip	20 Ga.		X	5.00
S148	Trigger Guard Screw	12-20 Ga.	X	X	.25
S154a	Trigger Spring	12 Ga.		X	.25
b	Trigger Spring	20 Ga.		X	25

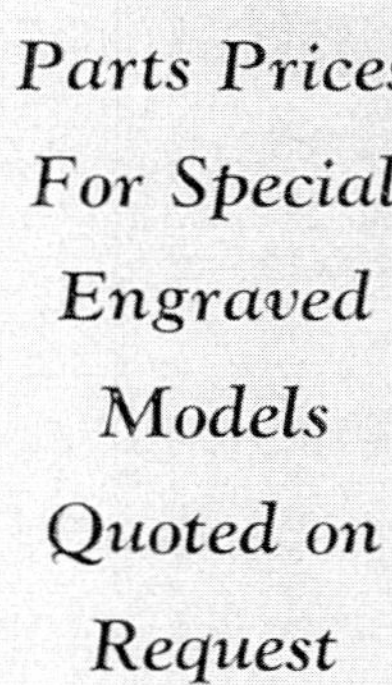

Parts Prices For Special Engraved Models Quoted on Request

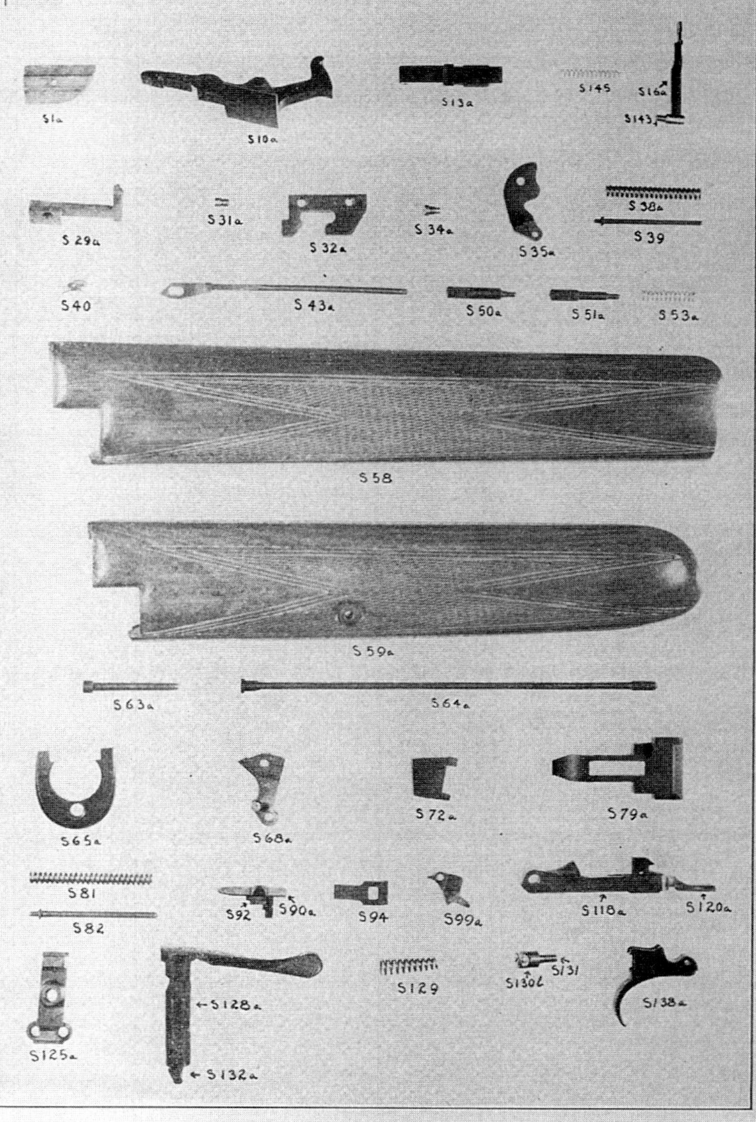

When Possible, Forward Old Parts For Duplication

1961

RUGGED as the Rockies . . .
Smooth as silk
1961
BROWNING
PARTS & SERVICE PRICE LIST
Shotguns . . . Rifles . . . Pistols

BROWNING®

IMPORTANT—When ordering list Code Number, Part Name, Gauge, Model and Serial Number.

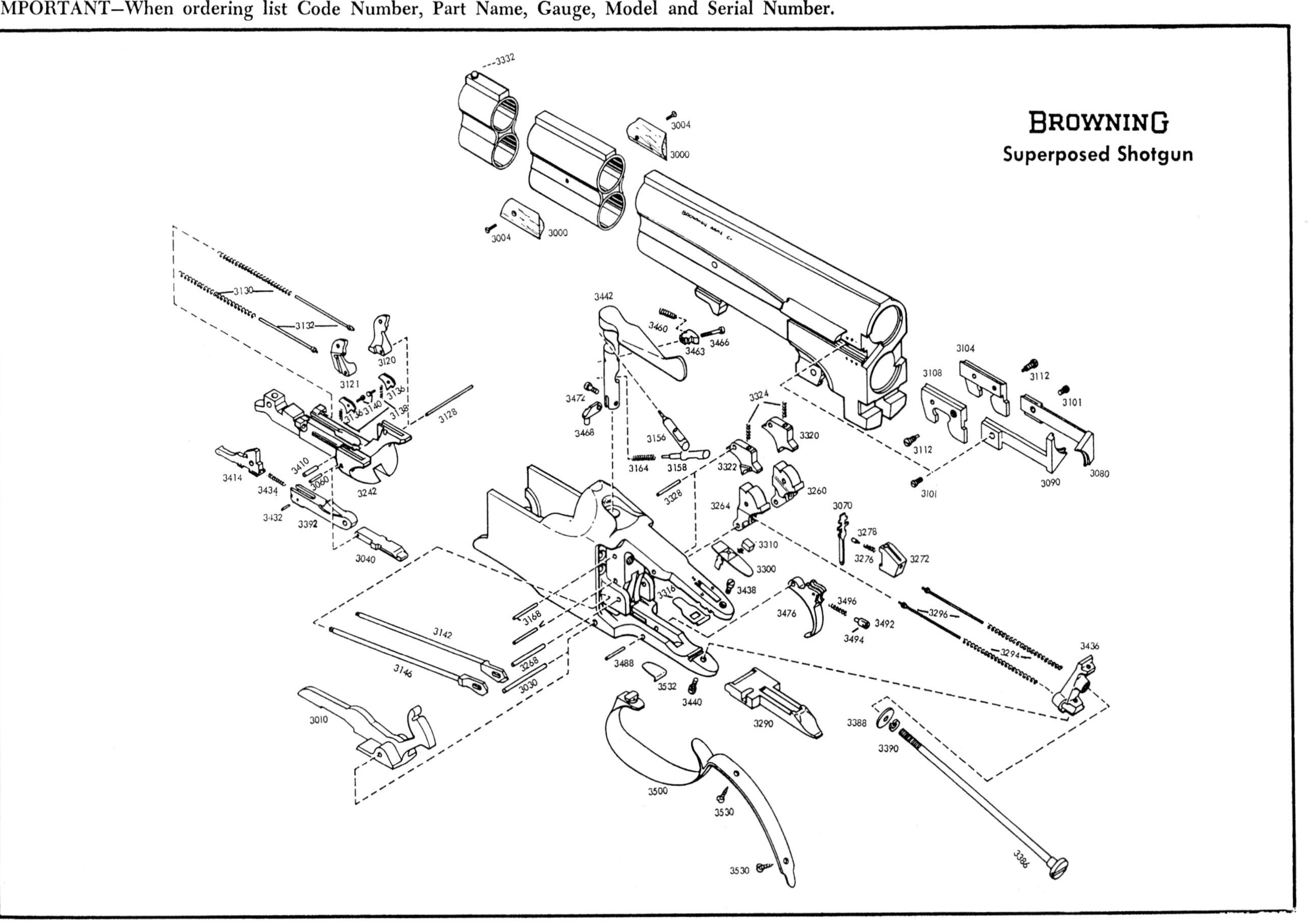

PRICES F.O.B. POINT OF SHIPMENT – SUBJECT TO CHANGE WITHOUT NOTICE

SUPERPOSED SHOTGUN PARTS PRICE LIST

LIGHTNING–STANDARD–MAGNUM MODELS — 12, 20, 28 AND .410 GAUGE

Note—Parts for 28 and .410 Gauge are interchangeable with 20 Gauge, unless otherwise noted.
Please specify grade, parts prices for Pigeon through Midas grades provided on request.

Code No.	Part Name	Retail Price
*3000	Barrel Plate Wood – Right and Left (Rough) 12	$ 1.05
*3001	Barrel Plate Wood – Right and Left (Rough) 20	1.05
3004	Barrel Plate Screws 12-20	.25
3006	Butt Plate 12	2.35
3007	Butt Plate 20	2.35
3008	Butt Plate Screw 12-20	.30
*3010	Cocking Lever (Rough) 12	4.25
*3021	Cocking Lever (Rough) 20	4.25
3030	Cocking Lever Pin 12	.50
3031	Cocking Lever Pin 20	.50
*3040	Cocking Lever Lifter (Rough) 12	1.15
*3051	Cocking Lever Lifter (Rough) 20	1.15
3060	Cocking Lever Lifter Pin 12	.25
3061	Cocking Lever Lifter Pin 20	.25
3070	Connector 12	1.80
3071	Connector 20	1.80
3074	Connector Stop Pin 12-20	.25
*3080	Ejector–Right (Rough) 12	3.00
*3081	Ejector–Right (Rough) 20	3.00
*3085	Ejector–Right (Rough) 28	3.00
*3087	Ejector–Right (Rough) .410	3.00
*3090	Ejector–Left (Rough) 12	3.00
*3091	Ejector–Left (Rough) 20	3.00
*3095	Ejector–Left (Rough) 28	3.00
*3097	Ejector–Left (Rough) .410	3.00
3101	Ejector Stop Screw 12-20	.25
3104	Ejector Extension–Right 12	3.80
3105	Ejector Extension–Right 20	3.80
3108	Ejector Extension–Left 12	3.80
3109	Ejector Extension–Left 20	3.80
3112	Ejector Extension Stop Screw 12	.25
3113	Ejector Extension Stop Screw 20	.25
3120	Ejector Hammer–Right 12	2.20
3121	Ejector Hammer–Right 20	2.20
3124	Ejector Hammer–Left 12	2.20
3125	Ejector Hammer–Left 20	2.20
3128	Ejector Hammer Pin 12	.25
3129	Ejector Hammer Pin 20	.25
3130	Ejector Hammer Spring 12	.25
3131	Ejector Hammer Spring 20	.25
3132	Ejector Hammer Spring Guide 12-20	.25
3136	Ejector Hammer Sear 12-20	.50
3138	Ejector Hammer Sear Spring 12-20	.25
3140	Ejector Hammer Sear Pin 12-20	.25
*3142	Ejector Trip Rod–Right 12	3.00
*3143	Ejector Trip Rod–Right 20	3.00
*3146	Ejector Trip Rod–Left 12	3.00
*3147	Ejector Trip Rod–Left 20	3.00
3148	Firing Pin–Over 12	1.05
3150	Firing Pin–Over 20	1.05
3157	Firing Pin–Under 12	1.05
3159	Firing Pin–Under 20	1.05
3164	Firing Pin Spring–Under 12	.25
3165	Firing Pin Spring–Under 20	$ .25
3168	Firing Pin Retaining Pin 12	.25
3169	Firing Pin Retaining Pin 20	.25
*3171	Forearm–Standard Field–Grade I 20	22.00
*3174	Forearm–Standard Field–Grade I 12	22.00
*3176	Forearm–Standard Trap–Grade I–Semi-Beavertail 12	27.50
*3181	Forearm–Lightning Field–Grade I 20	22.00
*3190	Forearm–Lightning Field–Grade I 12	22.00
*3198	Forearm–Lightning Trap–Grade I–Semi-Beavertail 12	27.50
*3207	Forearm–Standard Field–Grade I 28	22.00
*3209	Forearm–Standard Field–Grade I .410	22.00
3218	Forearm Escutcheon–Threaded 12	.25
3219	Forearm Escutcheon–Threaded 20	.25
3222	Forearm Escutcheon–Unthreaded 12	.25
3225	Forearm Escutcheon–Unthreaded 20	.25
3230	Forearm Screw–for Field Type Forearm 12	.40
3231	Forearm Screw–for Field Type Forearm 20	.40
3234	Forearm Screw–for Semi-Beavertail Fore-arm 12	.40
*3242	Forearm Bracket (Rough) 12	13.00
*3251	Forearm Bracket (Rough) 20	13.00
*3260	Hammer–Right 12	3.00
*3261	Hammer–Right 20	3.00
*3264	Hammer–Left 12	3.00
*3265	Hammer–Left 20	3.00
3268	Hammer Pin 12	.25
3269	Hammer Pin 20	.25
3272	Inertia Block 12	1.70
3273	Inertia Block 20	1.70
3276	Inertia Block Spring 12-20	.25
3278	Inertia Block Spring Guide 12-20	.25
3279	Inertia Block Retaining Pin 20	.25
*3290	Locking Bolt 12	3.90
*3291	Locking Bolt 20	3.90
3294	Mainspring 12-20	.25
3296	Mainspring Guide 12-20	.25
3300	Selector Safety 12-20	2.20
3310	Selector Block 12-20	.35
3312	Selector Spring 12-20	.25
*3320	Sear–Right 12	1.40
*3321	Sear–Right 20	1.40
*3322	Sear–Left 12	1.40
*3323	Sear–Left 20	1.40
3324	Sear Spring 12	.25
3325	Sear Spring 20	.25
3328	Sear Pin 12	.25
3329	Sear Pin 20	.25
3332	Sight Bead 12-20	.25
(1)*3342	Stock-Field Type Standard & Lightning 12	60.00
(2)*3335	Stock–Magnum Type with Recoil Pad–Standard 12	69.00
(1)*3355	Stock–Field Type–Standard & Lightning 20	$60.00
(3)*3374	Stock–Trap Type without Recoil Pad–Standard & Lightning 12	60.00
(3)*3384	Stock–Trap Type with Recoil Pad–Standard & Lightning 12	69.00
3386	Stock Bolt 12-20	.60
3388	Stock Bolt Washer 12	.25
3389	Stock Bolt Washer 20	.25
3390	Stock Bolt Lock Washer 12-20	.25
3392	Take Down Lever 12	3.85
3401	Take Down Lever 20	3.85
3410	Take Down Lever Pin 12	.25
3411	Take Down Lever Pin 20	.25
3414	Take Down Lever Latch 12	3.40
3423	Take Down Lever Latch 20	3.40
3432	Take Down Lever Latch Pin 12	.25
3433	Take Down Lever Latch Pin 20	.25
3434	Take Down Lever Latch Spring 12	.25
3435	Take Down Lever Latch Spring 20	.25
3436	Tang Piece 12	5.00
3437	Tang Piece 20	5.00
3438	Tang Piece Screw Top 12-20	.25
3440	Tang Piece Screw Bottom 12-20	.25
*3442	Top Lever (Rough) 12	5.20
*3449	Top Lever (Rough) 20	5.20
3460	Top Lever Spring 12-20	.25
3463	Top Lever Spring Retainer 12-20	.55
3466	Top Lever Spring Retainer Screw 12-20	.25
3468	Top Lever Dog 12	1.05
3469	Top Lever Dog 20	1.05
3472	Top Lever Dog Screw 12-20	.25
3476	Trigger (Gold Plated) 12	3.90
3481	Trigger (Gold Plated 20	3.90
3488	Trigger Pin 12	.25
3489	Trigger Pin 20	.25
3492	Trigger Piston 12-20	.40
3494	Trigger Piston Pin 12-20	.25
3496	Trigger Piston Spring 12	.25
3498	Trigger Piston Spring 20	.25
3500	Trigger Guard–Pistol Grip–Field Stock 12	7.20
3510	Trigger Guard–Full Pistol Grip–Trap Stock 12	7.20
3521	Trigger Guard–Pistol Grip–Field Stock 20	7.20
3530	Trigger Guard Screws 12-20	.25
3532	Trigger Spring 12-20	.40

(1) Field Stock Dimension: 1⅝" x 2½" x 14¼" without Recoil Pad

(2) Magnum Stock Dimensions: 1⅝" x 2½" x 14" with Recoil Pad

(3) Trap Stock Dimensions: 1⅜" x 1¾" x 14⅜" with or without Recoil Pad

*Indicates that part should be fitted by our Service Department or Qualified Gunsmith.

FABRIQUE NATIONALE LIST OF PARTS FOR SUPERPOSED – 1963

Common to both single and double trigger guns

No.	Qty.	Designation of Parts	No.	Qty.	Designation of Parts
5	1	Foresight	38	1	Right hammer
6ad	1	Right forend cleat	39	1	Left hammer
6ag	1	Left forend cleat	40	1	Hammer pivot
7	2	Screw for ditto	41	2	Hammer spring
8	1	Right ejector	42	2	Hammer spring head
9	1	Left ejector	43	1	Upper firing pin
10	1	Right ejector slide	44	1	Lower firing pin
11	1	Left ejector slide	45	1	Lower firing pin spring
12	2	Stop screw for ejector slide	46	2	Guide spring pin
12a	2	Stop screw for ejector	47	1	Barrel lock
13	1	Cocking lever operator	48	1	Top lever
14	1	Cocking lever operator pin	49	1	Top lever spring
15	1	Forend iron	50	1	Top lever spring head
16	1	Forend lever	51	1	Top lever foot
17	1	Forend lever pivot	53	1	Top lever spring screw
18	1	Forend lock	56	1	Trigger pivot
19	1	Forend lock spring	61	1	Hammer sear pivot
20	1	Forend lock stop pin	66	1	Stock assembly cross piece
21	1	Right ejector kicker	67	2	Screw for ditto
22	1	Left ejector kicker	68	1	Stock assembly bolt
23	1	Ejector kicker pivot	STA 37	1	Grower ring
24	2	Ejector kicker spring	STA 5	1	Assembly screw washer (12 bore)
25	2	Ejector spring head	STA 46	1	Assembly screw washer (20 bore)
26	2	Ejector sear	70	1	Trigger guard
27	2	Ejector sear spring	71	2	Trigger guard screw
28	2	Ejector sear pivot	72	1	Stock
29B	1	Forend wood	73	1	Heel plate
33	1	Barrel hinge pin	STA 28	2	Heel plate screw
34	1	Left ejector operating rod	75t	1	Forend assembly screw
35	1	Right ejector rod	76d	1	Right cup for ditto
36	1	Cocking lever	78	1	Top lever foot screw
37	1	Cocking lever pivot			
No.	**Qty.**	**Single Trigger**	**No.**	**Qty.**	**Double Trigger**
60u	2	Sear operating spring	32a	1	Trigger separator
111	1	Trigger	32b	1	Trigger separator bead
112	1	Sear operating rod base	32c	1	Trigger separator bead screw
113	1	Sear operating rod pivot	32d	1	Trigger separator bead pin
114	1	Sear operating rod pin	54	1	Right trigger
115	1	Sear operating rod spring	55	1	Left trigger
116	1	Right sear	57	1	Sear operating rod
117	1	Left sear	58	1	Right sear
118	1	Sear operating rod	59	2	Left sear
119	1	Block	60	1	Sear spring
120	1	Safety stud	62	1	Safety
121	1	Safety stud spring	63	1	Safety stud
122	1	Safety stud block	63a	1	Safety spring washer
123	1	Block spring	64	1	Safety stud pin
124	1	Block spring head	65	1	Safety spring
125	1	Top tang screw			
126	1	Trigger spring			

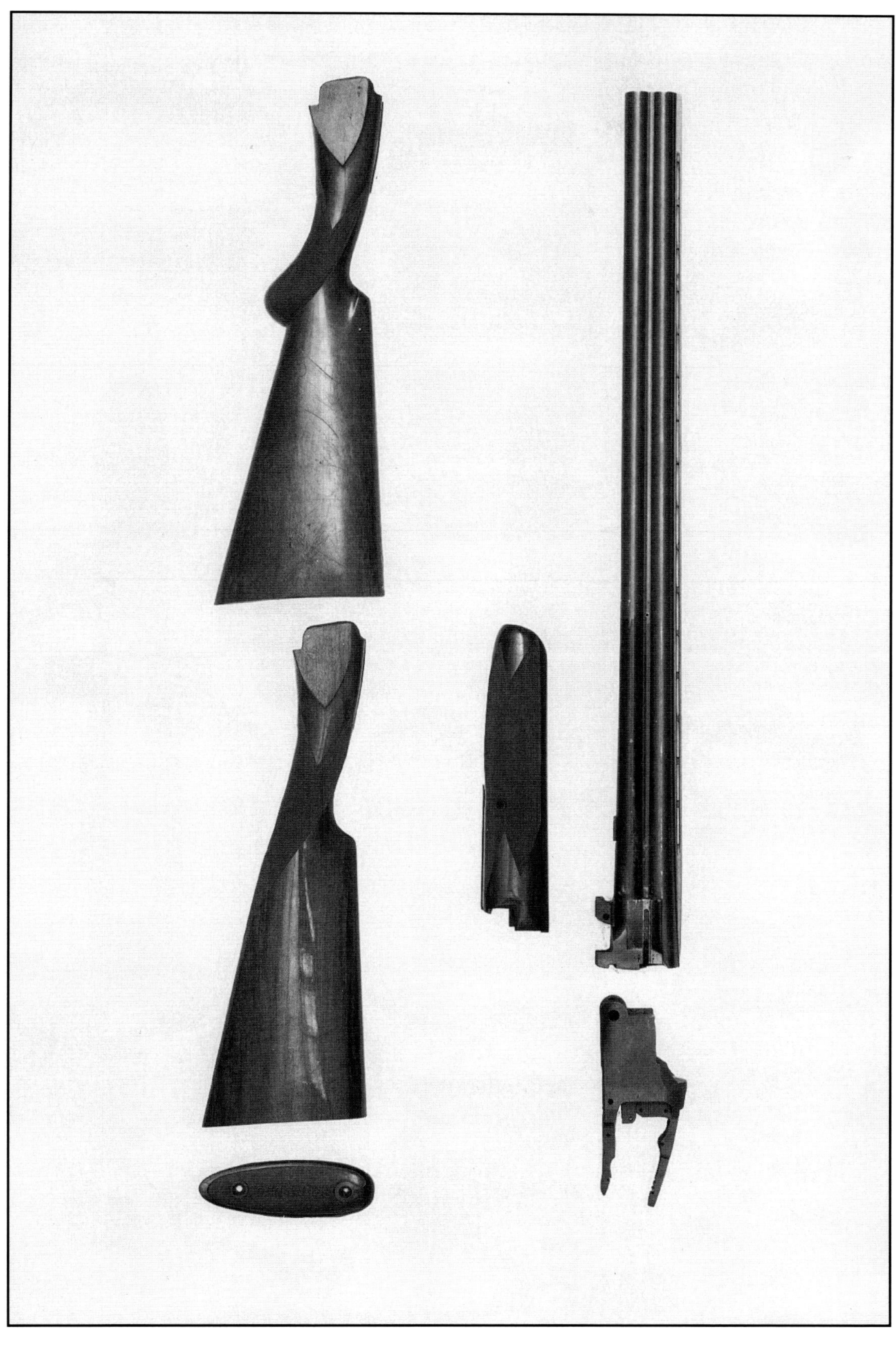

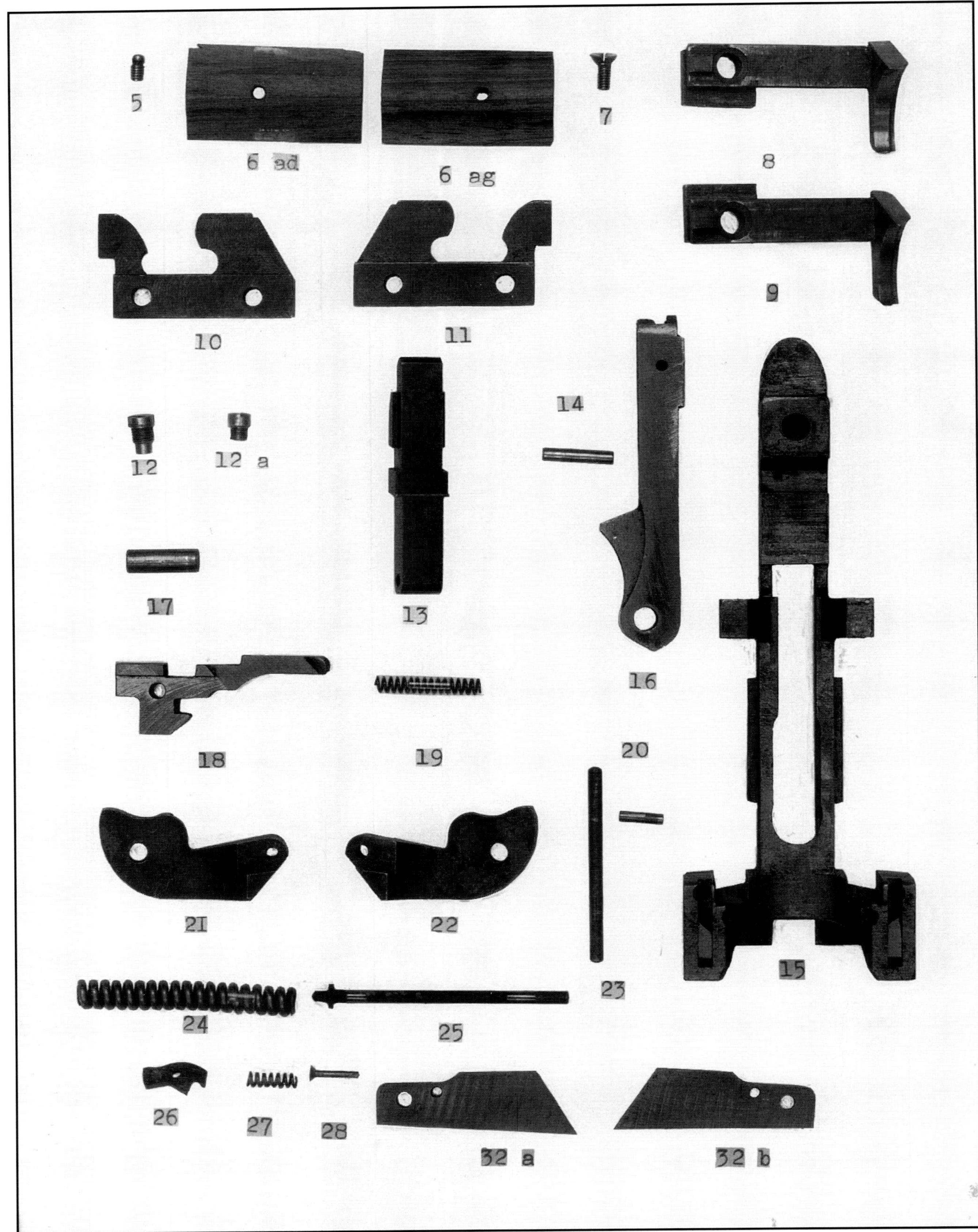
5
6 ad
6 ag
7
8
9
10
11
12
12 a
13
14
15
16
17
18
19
20
21
22
23
24
25
26
27
28
32 a
32 b

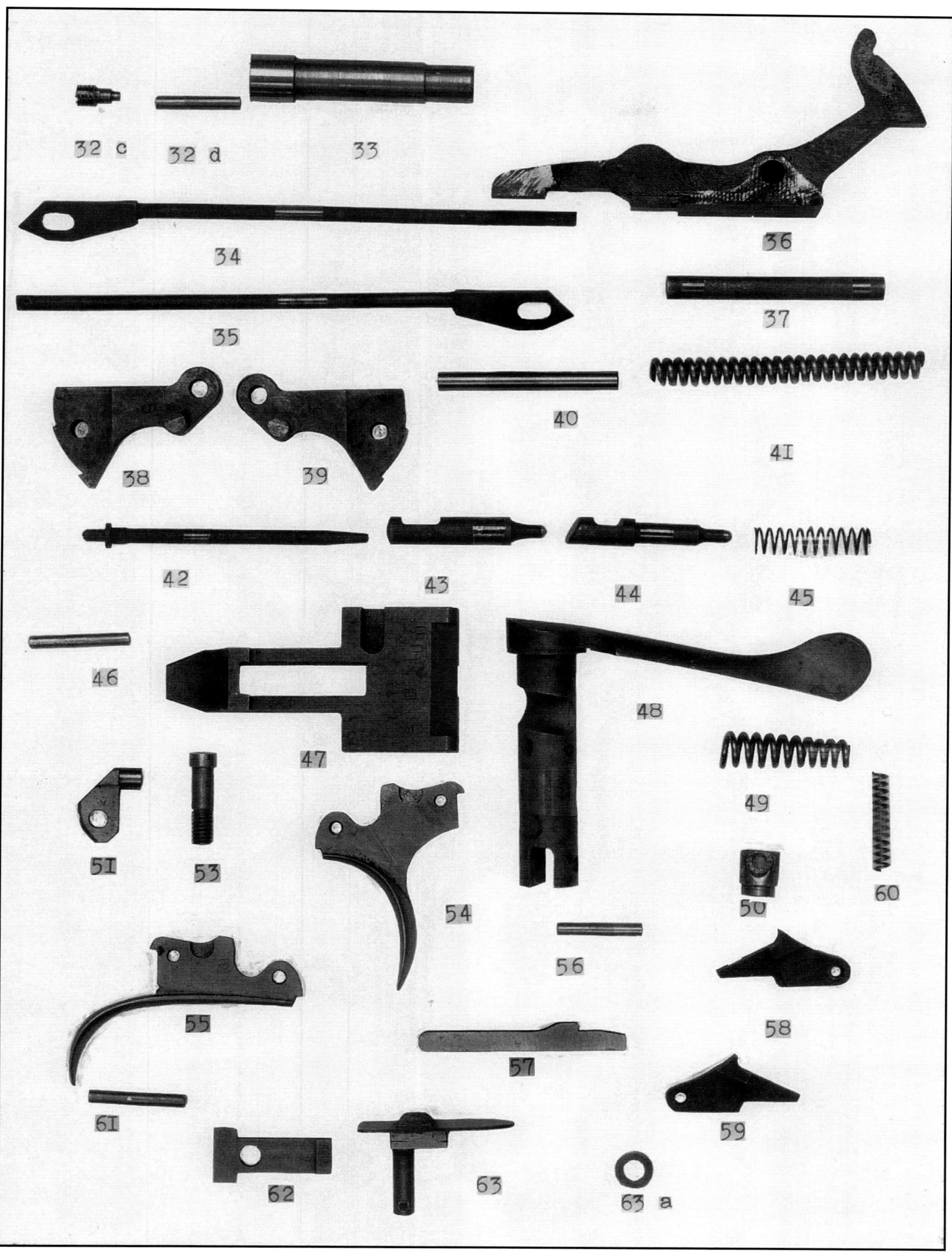
32 c
32 d
33
36
34
35
37
40
41
38
39
42
43
44
45
46
47
48
49
51
53
54
60
50
56
55
58
57
61
59
62
63
63 a

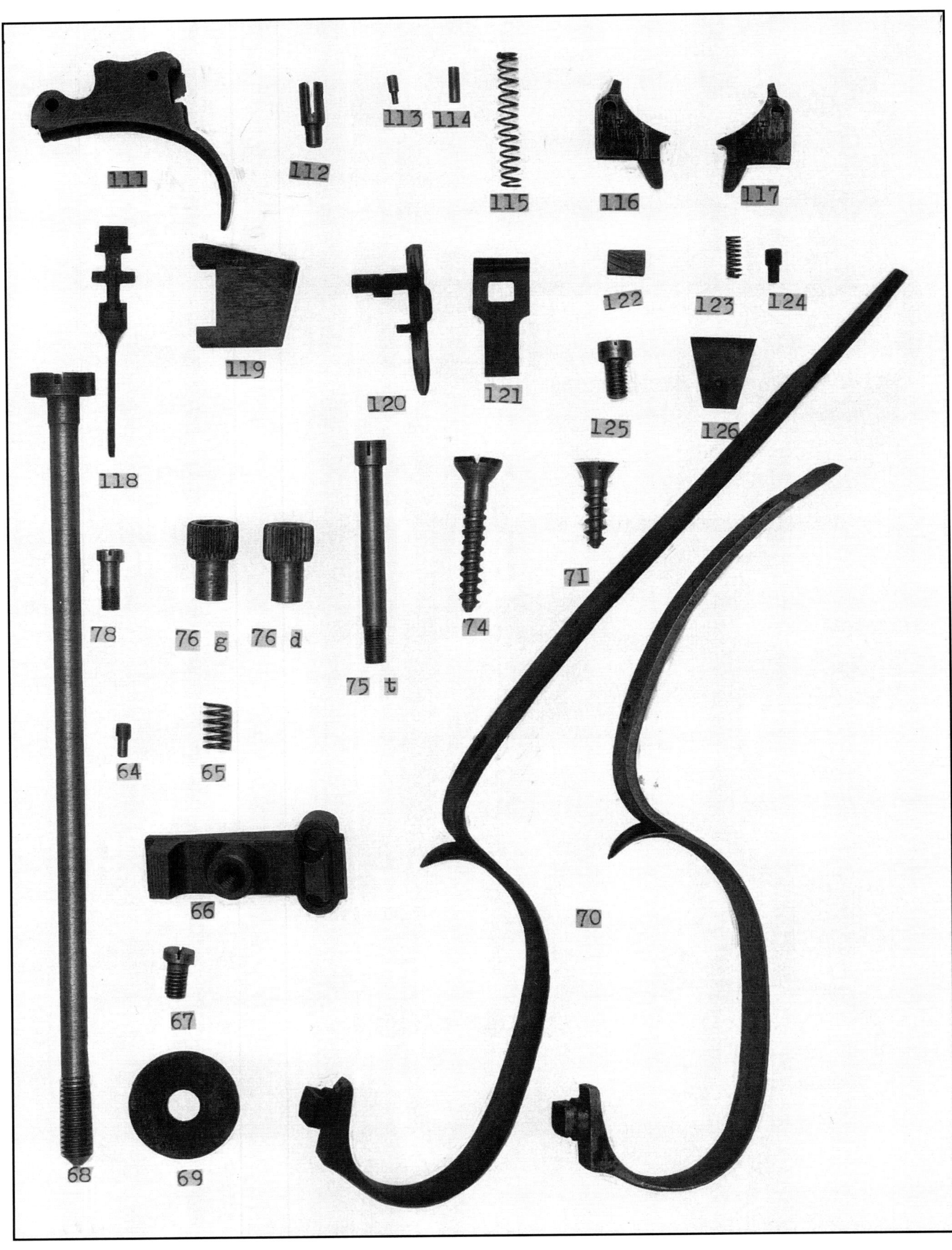
111
112
113
114
115
116
117
118
119
120
121
122
123
124
125
126
78
76 g
76 d
75 t
74
71
64
65
66
67
68
69
70

1975

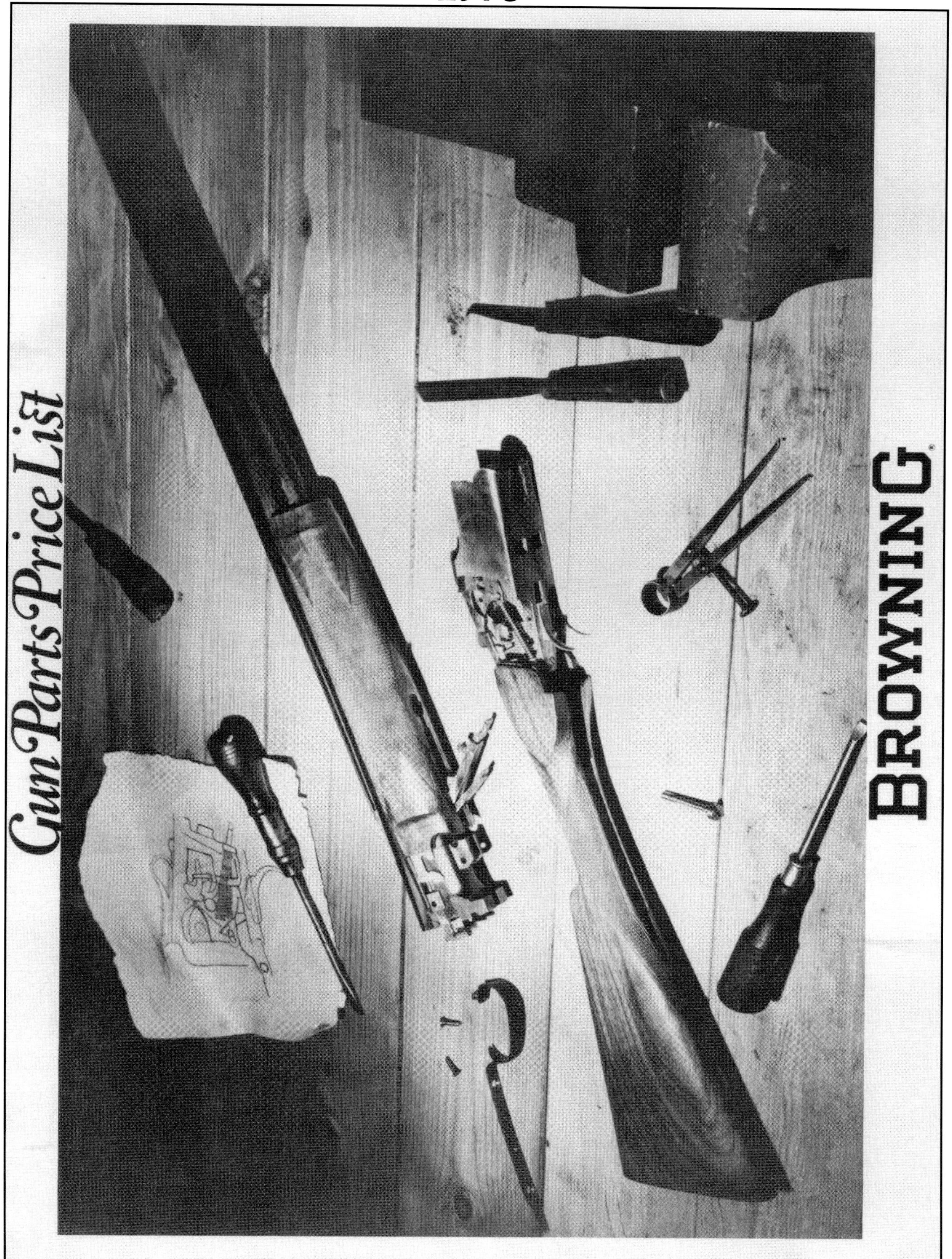

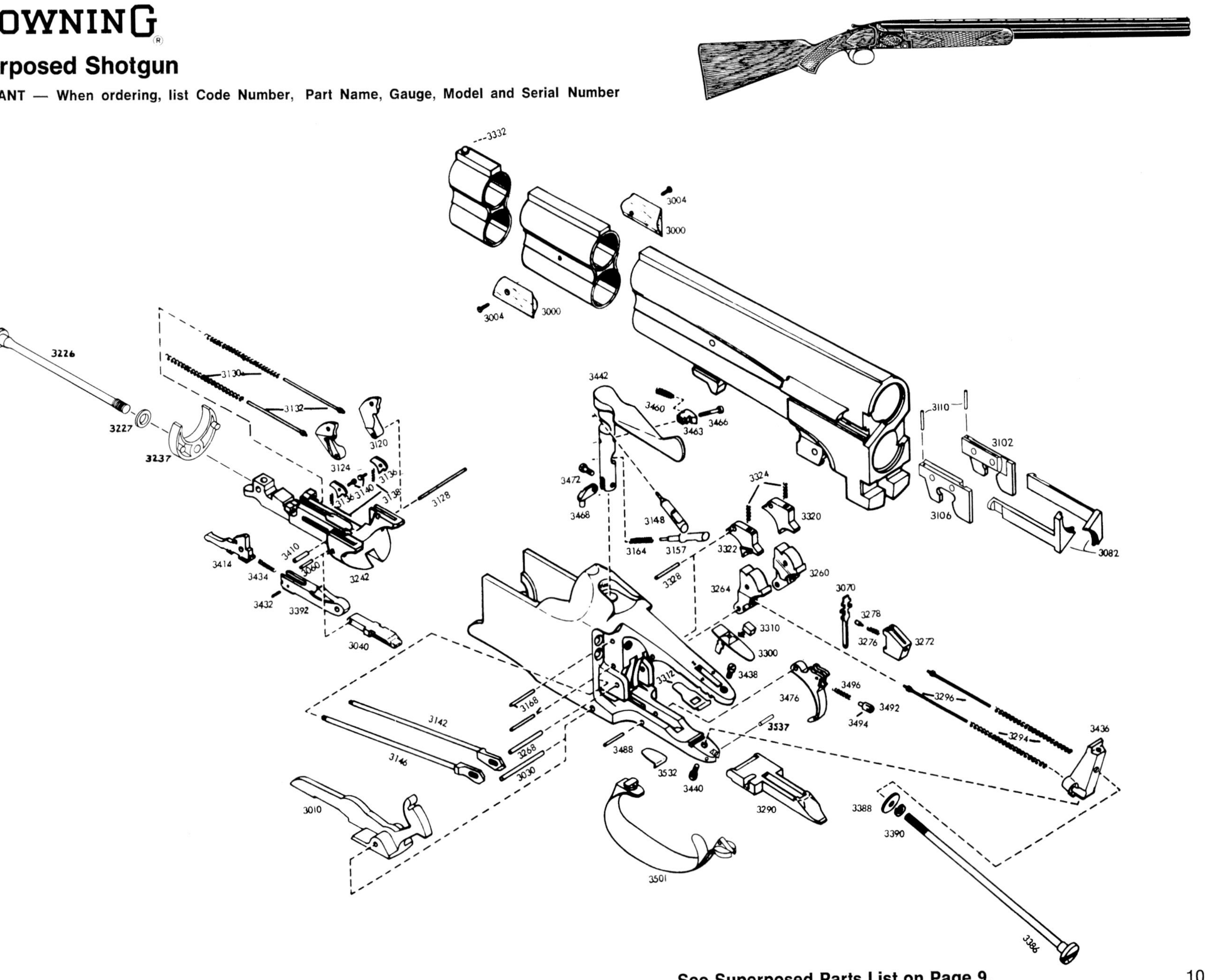
BROWNING®
Superposed Shotgun
IMPORTANT — When ordering, list Code Number, Part Name, Gauge, Model and Serial Number
See Superposed Parts List on Page 9.
10

BROWNING®

Superposed Shotgun Parts Price List

Lightning – Standard – Magnum Models — 12, 20, 28 and .410 Gauge

Please specify grade. Parts prices for Pigeon through Midas grades provided on request
Prices F.O.B. point of shipment — subject to change with notice / minimum billing for parts order $2.00.

*Indicates part must be fitted by our Service Department or Qualified Gunsmith.

Code No.	Part Name	Suggested Retail Price
*3000	Barrel Plate Wood—Right and Left (Rough) 12	$ 1.50
*3001	Barrel Plate Wood—Right and Left (Rough) 20-28-.410	1.50
3004	Barrel Plate Screw 12-20-28-.410	.40
3006	Butt Plate 12	3.50
3007	Butt Plate 20-28-.410	3.50
3008	Butt Plate Screw 12-20-28-.410	.40
*3010	Cocking Lever (Rough) 12	10.75
*3021	Cocking Lever (Rough) 20-28-.410	10.75
3030	Cocking Lever Pin 12	1.25
3031	Cocking Lever Pin 20-28-.410	1.25
3036	Cocking Lever Pin Superlight 12	1.25
3037	Cocking Lever Pin Retaining Screw	.35
3038	Cocking Lever Pin Superlight 20	1.25
*3040	Cocking Lever Lifter (Rough) 12	5.30
*3051	Cocking Lever Lifter (Rough) 20-28-.410	5.30
3060	Cocking Lever Lifter Pin 12	.35
306001	Cocking Lever Lifter Pin 12 Reinforced	.35
3061	Cocking Lever Lifter Pin 20-28-.410	.35
3070	Connector 12	5.90
307030	Connector 12 MT	5.90
3071	Connector 20-28-.410	5.90
307130	Connector 20 MT	5.90
307230	Connector Selector 12-20 MT	.60
3074	Connector Stop Pin 12-20-28-.410	.40
307530	Connector Selector Pin 12-20 MT	.35
*3082	Ejector Right & Left (Rough) 12	10.00
*3083	Ejector Right & Left (Rough) 20	10.00
*3088	Ejector Right & Left (Rough) 28	10.00
*3089	Ejector Right & Left (Rough) .410	10.00
3102	Ejector Extension Right 12	7.80
3103	Ejector Extension Right 20-28-.410	7.80
3106	Ejector Extension—Left 12	7.80
3107	Ejector Extension—Left 20-28-.410	7.80
3110	Ejector Extension Stop Pin 12-20-28-.410	.35
3120	Ejector Hammer—Right 12	7.20
3121	Ejector Hammer—Right 20-28-.410	7.20
3124	Ejector Hammer—Left 12	7.20
3125	Ejector Hammer—Left 20-28-.410	7.20
3128	Ejector Hammer Pin 12	.40
3129	Ejector Hammer Pin 20-28-.410	.40
3130	Ejector Hammer Spring 12	1.25
3131	Ejector Hammer Spring 20-28-.410	1.25
3132	Ejector Hammer Spring Guide 12-20-28-.410	1.45
3136	Ejector Hammer Sear 12-20-28-.410	2.40
3138	Ejector Hammer Sear Spring 12-20-28-.410	.70
3140	Ejector Hammer Sear Pin 12-20-28-.410	.55
*3142	Ejector Trip Rod—Right 12	7.60
*3143	Ejector Trip Rod—Right 20-28-.410	7.60
*3146	Ejector Trip Rod—Left 12	7.60
*3147	Ejector Trip Rod—Left 20-28-.410	7.60
*3148	Firing Pin—Over 12	2.40
*3150	Firing Pin—Over 20-28-.410	2.40
*3157	Firing Pin—Under 12	2.40
*3159	Firing Pin—Under 20-28-.410	2.40
3164	Firing Pin Spring—Under 12	.40
3165	Firing Pin Spring—Under 20-28-.410	.40
3168	Firing Pin Retaining Pin 12	.35
3169	Firing Pin Retaining Pin 20-28-.410	.35
*3171	Forearm—Standard Field—Grade I 20	119.50
*3173	Forearm—Superlight—Grade I 12	119.50
*3174	Forearm—Standard Field—Grade I 12	119.50
*3176	Forearm—Standard Trap—Grade I—Semi-Beavertail 12	119.50
*3181	Forearm—Lightning Field—Grade I 20	119.50
*3182	Forearm—Beavertail—Grade I 20	119.50
*3190	Forearm—Lightning Field—Grade I 12	119.50
*3191	Forearm—Beavertail—Grade I 12	119.50
*3198	Forearm—Lightning Trap—Grade I—Semi-Beavertail 12	119.50
*3207	Forearm—Standard Field—Grade I 28	119.50
*3208	Forearm—Beavertail—Grade I 28	119.50
*3209	Forearm—Standard Field—Grade I .410	119.50
*3210	Forearm—Beavertail—Grade I .410	119.50
3223	Forearm—Superlight—Grade I 20	119.50
3218	Forearm Escutcheon—Threaded 12	.90
3219	Forearm Escutcheon—Threaded 20-28-.410	.90
3222	Forearm Escutcheon—Unthreaded 12	.90
3225	Forearm Escutcheon—Unthreaded 20-28-.410	.90
3226	Forearm Screw—Beavertail Type	2.10
3227	Forearm Screw Washer—Beavertail Type	.35
3228	Forearm Screw—Special Field Type 12 Ga.	2.10
3230	Forearm Screw—for Field Type Forearm 12	1.10
3231	Forearm Screw—for Field Type Forearm 20-28-.410	1.10
3234	Forearm Screw—for Semi-Beavertail Forearm 12	1.10
3237	Forearm End Piece Metal—Beavertail—12	2.10
3239	Forearm End Piece Nylon—Beavertail—20	.50
3240	Forearm End Piece Metal—Beavertail—28	$ 2.10
3241	Forearm End Piece Metal—Beavertail—.410	2.10
*3242	Forearm Bracket (Rough) 12	39.50
324201	Forearm Bracket 12 Reinforced	39.50
324301	Forearm Bracket Stop Block 12	2.90
324501	Stop Block Retaining Screw 12-20	.45
324701	Forearm Retaining Clamp 12	4.60
324901	Forearm Retaining Clamp 20	4.60
*3251	Forearm Bracket (Rough) 20-28-.410	39.50
325201	Forearm Bracket Stop Block 20	2.90
325401	Retaining Clamp Screw 12-20	.35
*3260	Hammer—Right 12	7.40
*326030	Hammer—Right 12 MT	7.40
*3261	Hammer—Right 20-28-.410	7.40
*326130	Hammer—Right 20 MT	7.40
*3264	Hammer—Left 12	7.40
*326430	Hammer—Left 12 MT	7.40
*3265	Hammer—Left 20-28-.410	7.40
*326530	Hammer—Left 20 MT	7.40
3268	Hammer Pin 12	.35
3269	Hammer Pin 20-28-.410	.35
3272	Inertia Block 12	6.30
327230	Inertia Block 12 MT	6.30
3273	Inertia Block 20-28-.410	6.30
327330	Inertia Block 20 MT	6.30
327430	Inertia Block Pin 12-20 MT	.35
3276	Inertia Block Spring 12-20-28-.410	.35
327630	Inertia Block Spring 12-20 MT	.35
3278	Inertia Block Spring Guide 12-20-28-.410	.35
327830	Inertia Block Spring Guide 12-20 MT	.35
3279	Inertia Block Retaining Pin 20-28-.410	.35
*3290	Locking Bolt 12	9.00
*329030	Locking Bolt 12 MT	9.00
*3291	Locking Bolt 20-28-.410	9.00
*329130	Locking Bolt 20 MT	9.00
329330	Mainspring 20 MT	.90
3294	Mainspring 12-20-28-.410	.90
329430	Mainspring 12 MT	.90
3296	Mainspring Guide 12-20-28-.410	1.80
329730	Safety Spring 12-20 MT	.85
329830	Safety Spring Pin 12-20 MT	.35
329930	Safety Spring Screw 12-20 MT	.40
3300	Selector Safety 12-20-28-.410	10.50
330030	Selector Safety 12-20 MT	12.95
3310	Selector Block 12-20-28-.410	2.25
331030	Selector Block 12-20 MT	2.25
3312	Selector Spring 12-20-28-.410	.90
331430	Selector Block Spring 12-20 MT	.40
331530	Selector Biock Spring Follower 12-20 MT	.35
*3320	Sear—Right 12	4.00
*332030	Sear—Right 12 MT	4.00
*3321	Sear—Right 20-28-.410	4.00
*332130	Sear—Right 20 MT	4.00
*3322	Sear—Left 12	4.00
*332230	Sear—Left 12 MT	4.00
*3323	Sear--Left 20-28-.410	4.00
*332330	Sear—Left 20 MT	4.00
3324	Sear Spring 12	.40
3325	Sear Spring 20-28-.410	.40
3328	Sear Pin 12	.40
3329	Sear Pin 20-28-.410	.40
3332	Sight Bead 12-20-28-.410	1.25
*3330	Stock, Field Straight Grip, Superlight, Grade I 20	151.75
*3333	[1]Stock—Skeet Type—Grade I W/Pad, 12	157.75
*3333L	[1]Stock—Skeet Type Long—Grade I W/Pad, 12	157.75
*3334	[1]Stock—Skeet Type—Grade I W/O Pad, 12	151.75
*3334L	[1]Stock—Skeet Type Long—Grade I W/O Pad, 12	151.75
*3335	[8]Stock—Magnum Type with Recoil Pad—Standard 12	157.75
*3342	[2]Stock—Field Type I—Grade I, 12	151.75
*3343	[4]Stock—Field Type II—Grade I, 12	151.75
*3343L	[4]Stock—Field Type II Long—Grade I, 12	151.75
*3352	[1]Stock—Skeet Type—Grade I W/Pad 20-28-.410	157.75
*3352L	[1]Stock—Skeet Type Long—Grade I W/Pad 20-28-.410	157.75
*3353	Stock—Field Straight Grip Superlight	151.75
*3354	[1]Stock—Skeet Type—Grade I W/O Pad 20-28-.410	151.75
*3354L	[1]Stock—Skeet Type Long—Grade I W/O Pad 20-28-.410	151.75
*3355	[3]Stock—Field Type I—Grade I, 20-28-.410	151.75
*3356	[5]Stock—Field Type II—Grade I, 20-28-.410	151.75
*3356L	[5]Stock—Field Type II Long—Grade I, 20-28-.410	151.75
*3369	[7]Stock—Trap Type III—Grade I, W/Pad 12	157.75
*3369L	[7]Stock—Trap Type III Long—Grade I W/Pad 12	157.75
*3374	[6]Stock—Trap Type I—Grade I W/O Pad, 12	151.75
*3379	[7]Stock—Trap Type III—Grade I W/O Pad, 12	$151.75
*3379L	[7]Stock—Trap Type III Long—Grade I W/O Pad, 22	151.75
*3384	[6]Stock—Trap Type I—Grade I W/Pad, 12	157.75
3386	Stock Bolt 12-20-28-.410	3.10
3389	Stock Bolt Washer 12-20-28-.410	.55
3390	Stock Bolt Lock Washer 12-20-28-.410	.35
*3392	Take Down Lever 12	9.00
*3401	Take Down Lever 20-28-.410	9.00
3410	Take Down Lever Pin 12	.35
3411	Take Down Lever Pin 20-28-.410	.35
*3414	Take Down Lever Latch 12	7.90
*3423	Take Down Lever Latch 20-28-.410	7.90
3432	Take Down Lever Latch Pin 12	.35
3433	Take Down Lever Latch Pin 20-28-.410	.35
3434	Take Down Lever Latch Spring 12-20-28-.410	.35
3436	Tang Piece 12	11.75
343630	Tang Piece 12 MT	11.75
3437	Tang Piece 20-28-.410	11.75
343730	Tang Piece 20 MT	11.75
3438	Tang Piece Screw Top 12-20-28-.410	.50
3440	Tang Piece Screw Bottom 12-20-28-.410	.40
*3442	Top Lever (Rough) 12	25.75
*3449	Top Lever (Rough) 20-28-.410	25.75
3460	Top Lever Spring 12-20-28-.410	.55
3463	Top Lever Spring Retainer	1.45
3466	Top Lever Spring Retainer Screw 12-20-28-.410	.40
3468	Top Lever Dog 12	4.25
3469	Top Lever Dog 20-28-.410	4.25
3472	Top Lever Dog Screw 12-20-28-.410	.45
3476	Trigger (Gold Plated) 12	19.25
347630	Trigger (Gold Plated) 12 MT	19.25
3481	Trigger (Gold Plated) 20-28-.410	19.25
348130	Trigger (Gold Plated) 20 MT	19.25
348230	Trigger Spring 12-20 MT	.40
3488	Trigger Pin 12	.35
3489	Trigger Pin 20-28-.410	.35
3492	Trigger Piston 12-20-28-.410	1.60
349230	Trigger Piston 12-20 MT	1.60
3494	Trigger Piston Pin 12-20-28-.410	.35
349430	Trigger Piston Pin 12-20 MT	.35
3496	Trigger Piston Spring 12	.40
349630	Trigger Piston Spring 12-20 MT	.40
3498	Trigger Piston Sprng 20-28-.410	.40
3500	Trigger Guard—Field Type, Long, 12	37.75
3501	Trigger Guard—Short Type, All 12	37.75
350130	Trigger Guard—12 MT	37.75
350130L	Trigger Guard—Long 12 MT	37.75
3510	Trigger Guard—Trap Type, Long 12	37.75
3519	Trigger Guard—Superlight, 12	37.75
3520	Trigger Guard—Superlight, 20	37.75
3521	Trigger Guard—Field Type Long, 20-28-.410	37.75
3522	Trigger Guard—Short Type, All 20-28-.410	37.75
352230	Trigger Guard—20 MT	37.75
352230L	Trigger Guard—Long, 12 MT	37.75
*3530	Trigger Guard Screws, 12-20-28.410	1.00
3532	Trigger Spring, 12-20-28-.410	1.00
3533	Trigger Guard Screw, New Style Front	1.05
3534	Trigger Guard Screw, New Style Rear	1.05
3535	Trigger Guard Screw, Escutcheon	.35
3537	Trigger Guard Pin—Short Type	.35

[1]Skeet Stock Dimensions, 12-20-28-.410 Gauge: 1½"x2"x14⅜"—With or Without Pad, Short or Long Trigger Guard.
[2]Type I, 12 Gauge Field Stock Dimensions: 1⅝"x2½"x14¼"—Without Pad, Long Trigger Guard Only.
[3]Type I, 20-28-.410 Gauge Field Stock Dimen.: 1½"x2⅜"x14¼"—Without Pad, Long Trigger Guard Only.
[4]Type II, 12 Gauge Field Stock Dimensions: 1⅝"x2½"x14¼"—Without Pad, Short or Long Trigger Guard.
[5]Type II, 20-28-.410 Gauge Field Stock Dimen.: 1½"x2⅜"x14¼"—Without Pad, Short or Long Trigger Guard.
[6]Type I, Trap Stock Dimensions: 1 7/16"x1⅝"x14⅞" — with or without Pad, Long Trigger Guard Only. For Pre-1967 Models.
[7]Type III, Trap Stock Dimensions: 1 7/16"x1⅝"x14⅜" — with or without Pad, Short or Long Trigger Guard.
[8]Magnum Trigger Guard Stock Dimensions: 1⅝"x2½"x14" — with Recoil Pad, Short or Long Trigger Guard.
MT=Mechanical Trigger Model.
NOTE: Because of the variety of Superposed Stocks available, the different inlettings, and the types of trigger guards, it is especially important that the serial number and a short description of the gun be sent when ordering stocks.

See Superposed Schematic Illustration on Page 10.

Effective March 1, 1975

BROWNING®

Liege Over/Under Shotgun Parts Price List (12 Gauge)

IMPORTANT — When ordering, list Code Number, Part Name, Gauge, Model and Serial Number

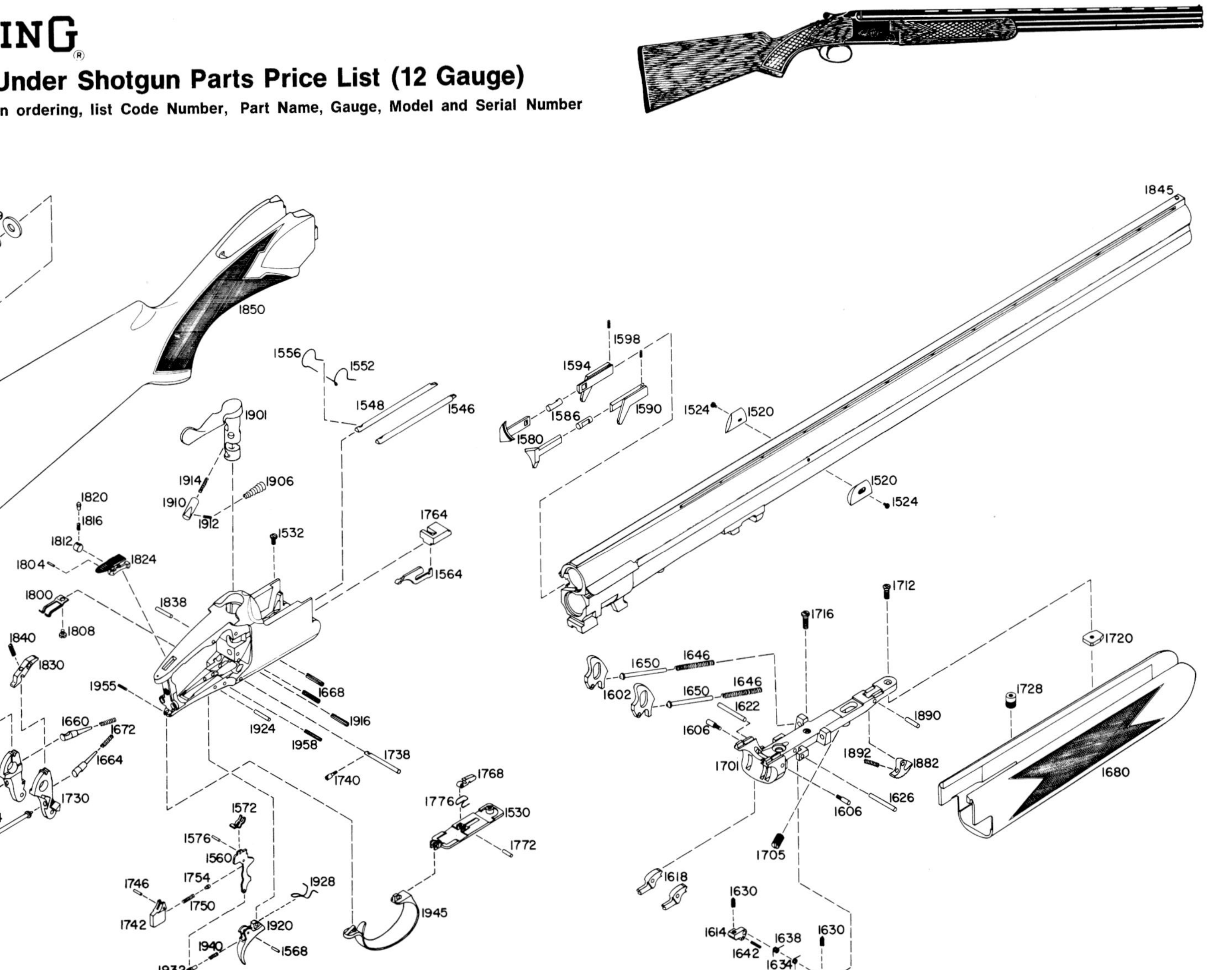

See Liege Parts Price List on Page 11.

BROWNING®

Liege Over/Under Shotgun Parts Price List (12 Gauge)

Prices F.O.B. Point of Shipment — subject to change without notice / minimum billing for parts order $2.00

IMPORTANT — When ordering, list Code Number, Part Name, Gauge, Model and Serial Number

*Indicates part must be fitted by our Service Department or Qualified Gunsmith.

Code No.	Part Name	Suggested Retail Price
*1520	Barrel Side Plate	$ .50
1524	Barrel Side Plate Screw	.70
1530	Bottom Plate	7.55
1532	Bottom Plate Screw	.35
1540	Butt Plate	2.20
1542	Butt Plate Screw	.40
*1546	Cocking Rod Right	2.15
*1548	Cocking Rod Left	2.15
1552	Cocking Rod Spring Right	1.40
1556	Cocking Rod Spring Left	1.40
1560	Connector	1.05
1564	Connector Cam	1.85
1568	Connector Pin	.35
1572	Connector Selector	.55
1576	Connector Selector Pin	.65
*1580	Ejector	6.40
1586	Ejector Connector	.95
1590	Ejector Extension Right	5.25
1594	Ejector Extension Left	5.25
1598	Ejector Extension Stop Pin	.35
1602	Ejector Hammer	4.45
1606	Ejector Hammer Pin	.55
1610	Ejector Hammer Sear Right	3.10
1614	Ejector Hammer Sear Left	3.10
1618	Ejector Hammer Sear Lever	6.40
1622	Ejector Hammer Sear Lever Pin	.35
1626	Ejector Hammer Sear Pin	.35
1630	Ejector Hammer Sear Screw	.40
1634	Ejector Hammer Sear Spring Right	.50
1638	Ejector Hammer Sear Spring Left	.50
1642	Ejector Hammer Sear Spring	.35
1646	Ejector Hammer Spring	.95
1650	Ejector Hammer Spring Guide	1.10
*1660	Firing Pin Upper	1.45
*1664	Firing Pin Lower	1.45
1668	Firing Pin Pin	.40
1672	Firing Pin Spring	.40
*1680	Forearm	55.00
*1701	Forearm Bracket	39.95
1705	Forearm Bracket Adjusting Screw	.35
1712	Forearm Bracket Screw Front	.50
1716	Forearm Bracket Screw Rear	$ .50
1720	Forearm Bracket Screw Plate	1.05
1728	Forearm Insert Escutcheon	.35
*1730	Hammer Right	8.85
*1734	Hammer Left	8.85
1738	Hammer Pin	.35
1740	Hammer Pin Screw	.35
1742	Inertia Block	5.40
1746	Inertia Block Pin	.65
1750	Inertia Block Spring	.35
1754	Inertia Block Spring Guide	.35
*1764	Locking Bolt	8.05
*1768	Lock Open Latch	2.75
1772	Lock Open Latch Pin	.35
1776	Lock Open Latch Spring	.95
1780	Mainspring	.60
1784	Mainspring Guide	1.80
1800	Safety Spring	.35
1804	Safety Spring Pin	.35
1808	Safety Spring Screw	.35
1812	Selector Block	1.65
1816	Selector Block Spring	.35
1820	Selector Block Spring Guide	.35
1824	Selector Safety	8.65
*1830	Sear Right	5.45
*1834	Sear Left	5.45
1838	Sear Pin	.35
1840	Sear Spring	.60
1845	Sight Bead Front	.40
*1850	Stock Field Type	98.95
1875	Stock Bolt	3.05
1877	Stock Bolt Lock Washer	.35
1879	Stock Bolt Washer	.60
*1882	Take-down Latch	1.45
1890	Take-down Latch Pin	.35
1892	Take-down Latch Spring	.35
*1901	Top Lever	20.25
1906	Top Lever Spring	.35
1910	Top Lever Spring Retainer	1.00
1912	Top Lever Spring Retainer Pin	.35
1914	Top Lever Spring Retainer Spring	.35
1916	Top Lever Stop Pin	$ .35
1920	Trigger	8.15
1924	Trigger Pin	.35
1928	Trigger Spring	2.15
1932	Trigger Piston	1.65
1936	Trigger Piston Pin	.35
1940	Trigger Piston Spring	.35
1945	Trigger Guard (short tang)	26.95
1955	Trigger Guard Pin Rear	.35
1958	Trigger Guard Bottom Plate Pin	.35

Effective March 1, 1975

See Liege Schematic Illustration on Page 12.

Appendix D

Browning Superposed Serial Numbers: Estimated Dates of Manufacture

12 Gauge: 1930-1977
20 Gauge: 1948-1977
28 Gauge: 1959-1977
.410 Bore: 1959-1977

Superposed Serial Numbers: A Complex Dilemma

Because of the way FN produced the Superposed, the issue of serial numbers and their meaning becomes quite complex. When the company was manufacturing its Superposed frames in relatively large numbers, the machine operators simply placed the finished frames in a large bin which, when full, was taken to the assembly area—in this case two assembly areas, one for FN Superposed and the other for Browning Superposed—where these frames were put together with other components to make a finished gun. The gunsmiths who did the work were not interested in what the serial number of the Superposed was or when that particular frame was manufactured. They just got their job done and went on to the next gun. When the guns were complete a rack of about twenty was taken to the shipping department where they were recorded in a shipping journal on the date they were received in that department. That date is used as the completion date, assembly date, or date of manufacture for each Superposed. When orders were received, the completed guns were then shipped to the dealer or agent.

A Superposed with the serial number 21500S73 may have been completed on May 19, 1974, or May 19, 1977. The only way to know unequivocally is to look it up in the shipping journal. In my opinion, dates of manufacture are impossible to construct with any degree of certainty based solely on serial numbers. The only alternative is to devise a guide that gives the reader an approximate estimate of when his Superposed may have been assembled. Because of the nature of production procedures at Fabrique Nationale, consecutively produced Superposed (or any other FN built firearm) were a rare occurrence. During the prewar years, as many as four or five years might separate Superposed stamped with sequential serial numbers. During the postwar era this was less likely to occur but it still happened on occasion. This is the dilemma that the research has given to the reader.

One final caution to the reader: Even the alphanumeric date code has its pitfalls. During times of high volume production the date the frame was built was very often within six months to one year from the time the finished gun was assembled. During times of slack production this date could be as much as three to five years behind the actual date of assembly. In other words, the date code merely gives the date the frame was produced, not the date the gun was assembled.

These serial number dates of manufacture estimates are based on FN sales records and FN shipping journals.

Browning Superposed 12 Gauge Serial Numbers Estimated Dates of Manufacture

Year	12 Gauge "Old Series" Serial Numbers
1930	1-1423
1931	1424-3060
1932	3061-4931
1933	4932-5169
1934	5170-5369
1935	5370-7851
1936	7852-10369
1937	10370-14702
1938	14703-16064
1939	16065-16639
1940	16640-17032
1945	17033-17078
1946	17079-17089
1947	17090-17099
1948	17100-17218
1949	17219-18735
1950	18736-20462
1951	20463-24104
1952	24105-30577
1953	30578-34595
1954	34596-39204
1955	39205-44974
1956	44975-49635
1957	49636-52207
1958	52208-57647
1959	57648-70745
1960	70746-79543
1961	79544-89554
1962	89555-99999 1S2-2000S2
1963	2001S2-11960S3
1964	11961S3-24296S4

Year	12 Gauge "Old Series" Serial Numbers	
1965	24297S4-38977S5	
1966	38978S5-52332S6	
1967	52333S6-69252S7	
1968	69253S7-84730S8	
1969	84731S8-99999S69 1S69-4881S69	
1970	4882S69-18900S70	"New Series"*
1971	18901S70-32801S71	1S71-1640S71
1972	32802S71-34702S72	1641S71-11475S72
1973	34703S72-36603S73	11476S72-21275S73
1974	36603S73-38504S74	21276S73-29500S74
1975	38505S74-41199S75	29501S74-50000S75#
1976	N/A	50001S75-55000S76
1977	N/A	55001S76-59500S77

* "New Series" began on November 1, 1971.
# During 1975 serial numbers 37000 through 41199 were skipped in "New Series."

Browning Superposed 20 Gauge Serial Numbers Estimated Dates of Manufacture

Year	20 Gauge "Old Series" Serial Numbers	
1949	1-268	
1950	269-1782	
1951	1783-2775	
1952	2776-4153	
1953	4154-5799	
1954	5800-7618	
1955	7619-8295	
1956	8296-9450	
1957	9451-11154	
1958	11155-13238	
1959	13239-16322	
1960	16323-19340	
1961	19341-22851	
1962	22852-25676V2	
1963	25677V2-29057V3	
1964	29058V3-32054V4	
1965	32055V4-36677V5	
1966	36678V5-40850V6	
1967	40851V6-45064V7	
1968	45065V7-50319V8	
1969	50320V8-54700V69	
1970	54701V69-57847V70	
1971	57848V70-61500V71	"New Series"*
1972	61501V71-62261V72	1V71-720V72
1973	62262V72-63742V73	721V72-2500V73
1974	63743V73-64301V74#	2501V73-4000V74
1975	N/A	40001V74-5200V75
1976	N/A	5201V75-6400V76
1977	N/A	6401V76-7600V76

* "New Series" began on March 6, 1972.
# "Old Series ended on September 25, 1974.

Browning Superposed 28 Gauge Serial Numbers Estimated Dates of Manufacture

Year	28 Gauge "Old Series" Serial Numbers	
1959	9F1-9F49	
1960	9F50-0F281	
1961	0F282-1F319	
1962	1F320-421F2	
1963	422F2-572F3	
1964	573F3-718F4	
1965	719F4-929F5	
1966	930F5-1191F6	
1967	1192F6-1583F7	
1968	1584F7-2053F8	
1969	2054F8-2439F69	
1970	2440F69-2445F70	
1971	2446F70-3000F71	"New Series"*
1972	3001F71-3307F71	1F71-50F72
1973	N/A	51F72-100F73
1974	N/A	101F73-150F74
1975	N/A	151F74-196F75
1976	N/A	197F75-227F76
1977	N/A	228F76-252F76#

* "New Series began April 17, 1972.
# Several additional 28 gauge Superposed were built after serial number 252F76 but they were not consecutively numbered. There were approximately six more 28 gauge guns built in 1977, with the last number recorded being 359F76. In 1984, ten additional 28 gauge guns were special ordered beginning with the "Old Series" serial number 3308F84 and ending with 3317F84.

Browning Superposed .410 Bore Serial Numbers Estimated Dates of Manufacture

Year	.410 Bore "Old Series" Serial Numbers	
1959	9J1-9J50	
1960	9J51-0J282	
1961	0J283-1J340	
1962	1J341-476J2	
1963	477J2-625J3	
1964	626J3-800J4	
1965	801J4-987J5	
1966	988J5-1363J6	
1967	1364J6-1835J7	
1968	1836J7-2261J8	
1969	2262J8-2890J69	
1970	2891J69-3282J70	
1971	3283J70-3868J71	"New Series"*
1972	N/A	1J71-75J72
1973	N/A	76J72-151J73
1974	N/A	152J73-227J74
1975	N/A	228J74-285J75
1976	N/A	286J75-301J76
1977	N/A	302J76-373J76#

* "New Series" began April 17, 1972, with serial number 5J71.
# This is the last consecutive serial number for the .410 bore Superposed through 1977. The last recorded serial number is 390J76. In 1983 and 1984, two hundred special order .410 bore Superposed were built in consecutive numbers beginning with "New Series" serial number 415J83.

Appendix E

B-25 Manufacturing Operations 1995

Operation	Parts
Numbering Preparation of barrel and receiver assembly	Action frame Forend
Hand fitting barrel and receiver assembly	Turning and locking
Hand broaching	Bolt fitting Bolt adjusting Push rod adjusting Parts numbering
Filing	Barrel filing
Mechanical filing	Barrel side wings milling Foresight hole boring and threading Lugs hole boring and threading
Final filing	Complete gun
Preparing wood assembly	Stock checkering Longitudinal barrel side wings Reassembly for wood fitting
Wood assembly	Stock and forend adjusting
Stock/Forend	Refiling
Stock/Forend	Turning and rubbing Blending
Oil finishing	
Checkering	
Barrel first polishing	Small wheel
Company marking	Roll die
Choke	Chambers readjusting Rims making
Preparation for Liège Proofhouse	
Liège Proofhouse	
Return from Proofhouse	Disassembly Preparation for polishing
Complete hand polishing	
Small parts polishing with small wheel	Hammers, trigger rods, forend hole, safety
Preparation for engraving	
Complete hand engraving (Done by outside contractor)	Decoration Scenes Inlaying

Operation	Parts
Return from engraving	Preparation for surface treatment Push rods sent for hardening Slides fitting
Push rod hardening	
Action frame and parts sets finishing	Final corrective actions before going to surface treatment
Parts sets surface treatment	Graying with acid Neutralizing Rubbing
Parts varnishing	
Optional	Case hardening Bluing Grayed finish
Action frame internal parts	Filing and polishing, bottom milling Preparing for lampblack fitting
Barrel top rib	Straightening and centering Checkering and preparing for turning
Barrel head, side wings, and lumps	Polishing
Top rib	Turning
Barrel second polishing	With small wheel Buffing
Barrel bluing with oxidation	Plate bluing Side wings graying
Barrel glossing	Muzzles and chambers polishing Internal parts of barrel glossing
Lampblack fitting	Small parts polishing Final adjustment Complete assembly Adjustment Standards and function checking: impact, ejection, initial weight, etc.
Final wood assembly	Stock and forend fitting on completed gun
Stock and forend	Final corrective action Buttplate cleaning
Final revision	Checking gun conformity to order specifications Checking of functioning and conformity to manufacturing standards
Warehousing	Gun packaging

Annotated Bibliography

This book is based, for the most part, on unpublished sources. A list of individuals who provided historical and technical information is shown in the acknowledgments section at the front of this volume.

Unpublished Sources

Arnold, Missouri

Interviews were conducted with past and present employees of the Browning Service Center. Some of these employees worked at the St. Louis facility. These men provided a wealth of technical information as well as old photographs and valuable personal recollections of their years servicing and repairing the Superposed.

Herstal, Belgium

Official Fabrique Nationale sales figures were also utilized, as were official FN shipping journals from 1930 to 1980. These are presently located at the Browning SA Custom Shop. Official FN drawings for the Superposed were used to verify technical modifications and their approximate dates. These drawings reside at Browning SA in Herstal. The entire FN photographic archives, some estimated forty thousand photos, were also examined. These rare archives span a period from 1906 to about 1984. Some of those photos appear in this book. Personal interviews with FN employees, Custom Shop employees, and Browning SA personnel were conducted. Former employees from these companies were also interviewed.

Liège, Belgium

The *Musee d'Armes de Liège* contains one of the premier arms collections in the world. The director is Claude Gaier. It also houses a comprehensive collection of FN advertisements, pamphlets, and catalogues. A large number of engraver's sketches from the 1950s, as well as some FN sales data, are kept here. Also deposited here is Felix Funken's "Souvenir of My Activities at Fabrique Nationale, 1 June, 1926 to 30 June, 1960." This is an unpublished pictorial diary of the great master during his tenure at FN. It provides an extraordinary insight into Funken's work as well as his personal life while at the factory, all in photos with his personal annotations.

Morgan, Utah

Official Browning Company sales reports were utilized to construct the sales and production data that appear in this book. Browning corporate photos, used by the company for promotional purposes, are used with great frequency as well. Personal interviews with company employees provide much of the historical foundation for the years 1926 to 1995. Interviews with prominent former employees such as John Val Browning, Val Browning, Harm Williams, and Grant Goddard were conducted as well. Important financial information was received from these former managers. The basis for financial figures and operations was found in Browning's Annual Reports to Stockholders from 1961 to 1977.

Published Sources

Books

Browning, John and Curt Gentry. *John M. Browning, American Gunmaker*. Morgan, Utah, Browning, 1964. This volume formed the basis of the introductory chapter to this book. Excellent narrative with a tremendous amount of information on the Browning family and their guns. The book ends with John M. Browning's death in 1926.

Gaier, Claude. *Four Centuries of Liège Gunmaking*. Liège, Belgium, Eugene Wahle, 1985. An excellent history of the entire Liège region. Outstanding photos of Browning guns and many of the people who worked at FN on the Superposed.

Gaier, Claude and Auguste Francotte. *FN 100 Years: The Story of a Great Liège Company, 1889-1989*. Brussels, Belgium, Dider Hatier, 1989. Much of the history of Fabrique Nationale is drawn from this historically accurate and sweeping narrative of the FN company by a man who spent almost thirty years employed there in communications, public relations, and as assistant to management.

Houze, Herb. *To the Dreams of Youth: Winchester .22 Caliber Single Shot Rifle*. Iola, WI, 1993. A well-crafted book based on factual data from various personal and company sources. Excellent company photos as well as Cody Firearms Museum photos.

Articles

Askins, Charles. "The Browning Over and Under." *The American Rifleman*. January 1932.

Betz, Col. W. R. "Felix Funken: Master Engraver of Liège." *The American Rifleman*. April 1983.

McIntosh, Michael. "John Browning's Masterpiece." *Shooting Sportsman*. March/April 1994.

Index

C

D

E

F

G

H

J

L

M

N

O

P

S

U

V

W